PLANET MEDICINE

PLANET MEDICINE

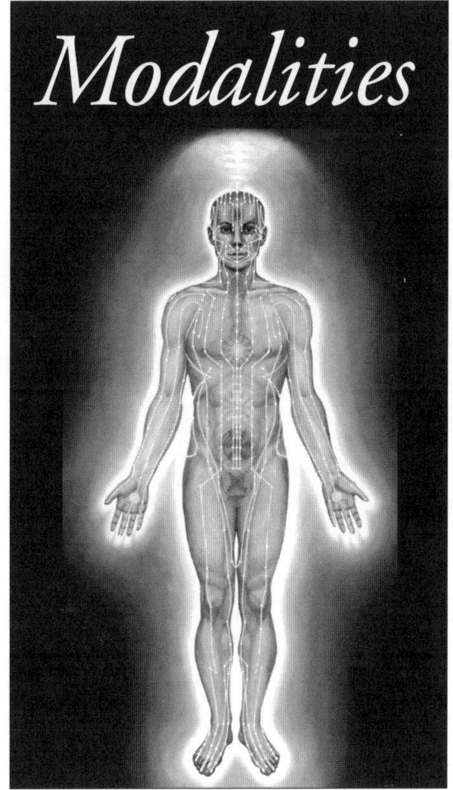

RICHARD GROSSINGER

Planet Medicine

Published by
North Atlantic Books
P.O. Box 12327
Berkeley, California 94712

Cover art by Sergei Ponomarov
Cover and book design by Paula Morrison
Typeset by Catherine E. Campaigne

Printed in the United States of America

Planet Medicine is sponsored by the Society for the Study of Native Arts and Sciences, a nonprofit educational corporation whose goals are to develop an educational and crosscultural perspective linking various scientific, social, and artistic fields; to nurture a holistic view of arts, sciences, humanities, and healing; and to publish and distribute literature on the relationship of mind, body, and nature.

Library of Congress Cataloging-in-Publication Data
Grossinger, Richard. 1944–
Planet medicine / Richard Grossinger.—6th ed.
v. <   >. cm.
Includes major revisions.
Includes bibliographical references and indexes.
Contents: v. 1. Origins— v. 2. Modalities
ISBN 1-55643-179-1 (paper). ISBN 1-55643-214-3 (paper).
1. Holistic medicine. 2. Alternative medicine. I. Title.
R733.G76 1995
610—dc20 95-22428
CIP

1 2 3 4 5 6 7 8 9 / 98 97 96 95

I dedicate this book to those whose vision, compassion, and acts of healing made it possible:

Paul Pitchford

Randy Cherner

Amini Peller

Elizabeth Beringer

Richard Strozzi Heckler

Ron Sieh

Cybèle Tomlinson

ACKNOWLEDGMENTS

THE PEOPLE WHO helped me the most with the material in this book are noted in the dedication and throughout the book. Here I would like to acknowledge those colleagues who contributed directly to the preparation of the text.

I acknowledge and thank Amy Champ for her research on the "Practical Ethnomedicine" chapter of *Origins;* Don Hanlon Johnson for his thorough reading and comments on the entire manuscript; Michael Salveson, Elizabeth Beringer, John Upledger, Bonnie Bainbridge Cohen, Judyth Weaver, Fritz Smith, and Dana Ullman for their reading and comments on particular sections of the text; Kathy Glass for her thoughtful and patient editing; Victoria Baker for her exceptional index; Paula Morrison for her elegant and spirited design; Catherine Campaigne for her technical work in the preparation of the finished book; Janna Israel for her updating of the bibliography; Jay Kinney and Richard Smoley of *Gnosis* for their assistance in finding artwork; and Sergei Ponomarov, Spain, Kathy Park, Alex Grey, and Kathy Maguire for drawing images specifically to fit in the text.

We come from an unknown place and go to an unknown place. These do not concern me. But the trajectory of my life, which I share with this body, does.

I want us all to participate in reconstructing the temple, to heal the planet, which is a masterpiece in danger.

—Jean Louis Barrault (the mime in *Les Enfants de Paradis*)

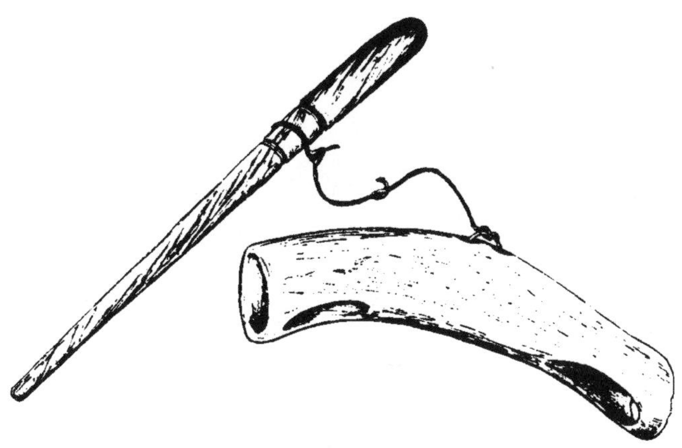

TABLE OF CONTENTS

TABLE OF ILLUSTRATIONS

Many of the illustrations in this book are used in clip-art style from a wide variety of sources. They include rock art, cave paintings, indigenous graffiti, religious woodcuts, amulet insignias, pottery motifs, codex glyphs, illustrations from herbals and old medical books, and traditional totemic designs from the different regions of the Earth. Because some of this material was collected from secondary and tertiary sources, complete citations are not always possible. The artwork in the Introduction is made up of animal motifs used in African decorations (plus an assortment of Australian kangaroo glyphs).

MODALITIES

PREFACE

If we want to arrive at a new understanding, it may be that we need to begin with new assumptions. There is a tale told of a traveling salesman who is lost on a backcountry road in Pennsylvania. He is trying to get to Pittsburgh, but he has lost his way. He sees a farmer walking alongside the road and asks him for directions to Pittsburgh. The farmer walks on in silence. The salesman asks again, and again he is met with stony silence. In a final, pathetic plea the salesman asks yet again for directions to Pittsburgh, to which the farmer replies, "Mister, if I were going to Pittsburgh, I wouldn't start from here."

It is by questioning our assumptions, our "starting place," that we will arrive at different conclusions. This is often what we understand to be creativity.

As a nation, we are actively seeking new solutions to our chronic health problems and in doing so we are—according to the January 28, 1993 issue of the *New England Journal of Medicine*—utilizing "unconventional therapy" in unprecedented proportions. In a "Special Article" entitled "Unconventional Medicine in the United States," the *New England Journal* reports: "Extrapolation to the U.S. population suggests that in 1990 Americans made an estimated 425 million visits to providers of unconventional therapy. This number exceeds the number of visits to all U.S. primary care physicians (388 million). Expenditures associated with use of unconventional therapy in 1990 amounted to approximately $13.7 billion, three quarters of which ($10.3 billion) was paid out of pocket. This figure is comparable to the $12.8 billion spent out of pocket annually for all hospitalizations in the United States."

What is "unconventional" about these therapies and why are we using them with such increasing frequency? And why are we willing to pay for them "out of pocket," without insurance reimbursement?

Something is happening in health care. We are no longer willing to treat ourselves as simply inert, material bodies to be dosed and cut passively. We are now questioning the assumptions that underlie "conventional" medicine as we seek greater participation in the healing of our chronic ills, for it is here that modern, "conventional" medicine fails us most often. We are not abandoning our primary-care physicians, especially when it comes to life-threatening conditions. But we are asking for new approaches to treatment and for a greater variety of therapeutic options.

This is not new. In the nineteenth century the United States supported a very heterogeneous health-care system. Under less restrictive government policies, diverse approaches to therapeutic treatment were permitted. Homeopathy, naturopathy, and osteopathy all had flourishing training schools. With the rise of modern biochemistry and the dominance of materialist science as the only acceptable explanatory metaphor for healing, these established schools of therapeutic knowledge were essentially suppressed for lack of conformity to accepted scientific principles of explanation.

Now, a hundred years later, science looks at the material world differently. We have a renewed interest in the "natural" body and environment (as our technology threatens to displace the natural altogether). These developments make possible a new dialogue about the nature of healing and health.

Planet Medicine is Richard Grossinger's exploration of what the *New England Journal of Medicine* has called "unconventional therapies" but which should perhaps more appropriately be called "natural healing" because, as Grossinger points out, alternative therapies are a natural response to the "ecological and cultural imperatives" that drive the pathology of individuals, social systems, and ecosystems. We have always carried with us a curative and self-curative response to conditions we

find ourselves in. Our diseases are tied to our development. We invent healing modalities appropriate to our circumstances.

It is a central tenet of *Planet Medicine* that the emergence of a vigorous community of practitioners of "unconventional therapies" is merely a contemporary expression of traditional knowledge systems. Indigenous peoples within traditional cultures develop methods of healing that catalyze life-saving responses even if there are no acceptable scientific explanations for their cures. However, the dominant explanatory metaphors of technological cultures leave no room for "healing" that is not orchestrated by technological medicine. Although science itself is part of our attempt to create systems of meaning within which we can heal ourselves, it is not the only such undertaking and certainly not the only possible undertaking. Yet scientific orthodoxy has tended to discredit subjective, inner experience in favor of the objective, the measurable, and the repeatable. Consequently, we undervalue the traditional wisdom of ancient and non-Western cultures and our own pre- and post-scientific wisdom, and we fail to see how we suffer from the absence of such wisdom in our lives. As Grossinger points out, the emergence of alternative forms of healing represents a return of this traditional and "meta-scientific" knowledge in new forms.

Yet what is unexpected about Grossinger's observations on this matter is that, at the same time he notes the importance of traditional wisdom, he propounds the impossibility of returning to or even truly understanding the syntax of indigenous cultures. We are inextricably imbedded in our modern, technological ways. The longing for a return to more "natural" cultures or the adoption of native styles of living is naive and evades the important task of recognizing and cultivating the shaman's instincts in ourselves and using these to articulate appropriate criticisms of our institutions of healing as well as develop totally new modes of healing. Grossinger demonstrates that when we bring the vestiges of ancient practices into the modern world, we reinvent them as what they are now rather than what we idealize them as. Often unconsciously, we reclaim them in a new form as our legitimate

birthright, and we find places for them in modern culture. Without such a process our entire system of professional medicine is static and flawed.

At the heart of *Planet Medicine* is a critique of doctrinaire and over-ideological ways of knowing ourselves and our world along with a passionate plea that we develop cultural forms that will nourish and preserve aspects of our self-knowledge that may not be currently scientifically acceptable but that are ultimately crucial to our ability to heal ourselves. Modern medicine brings gifts, but it also brings dangers, and one of the greatest dangers is its hegemony and intolerance. When these are reflected in public policies that discourage multiple approaches to health care, we risk being disenfranchised from our instinctive abilities of self-healing.

At first glance, *Planet Medicine* looks like an encyclopedia of natural healing. But anyone who has known Grossinger's other writings will recognize in the text a graceful blending of his two modes of expression, the scholarly and the poetic. As he carefully chronicles and critiques the myriad emerging forms of "unconventional therapies" and their cultural lineages, he also invokes and celebrates our vestigial powers of regeneration. He reasons, rants, and chants his way through the metallic, electronic armoring wrapped around the participatory sensitivities of the few surviving cells we have that remember their native powers of self-healing. Grossinger's text is a radical hymn that nourishes those endangered impulses in our bodies and minds that can lead us toward deep healing.

Michael J. Salveson,
Certified Advanced Rolfer
Senior Instructor, Rolf Institute
Former President, Rolf Institute
Berkeley, California
April, 1995

PART I

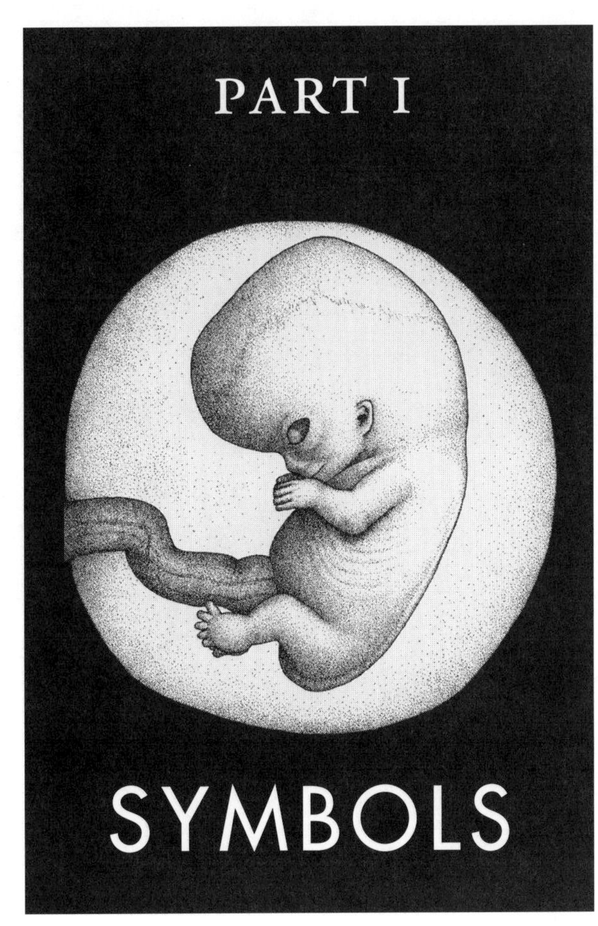

SYMBOLS

Introduction

IN THE FIRST volume of this book I explored the origins of systems of diagnosis and healing. Drawing from ethnographic accounts, historical documents, and the extant versions of ancient therapies, I reconstructed the possible evolution of medicine as both a social institution and a philosophical category. The former has given rise to lineages of doctors and healers, while the latter has spawned diverse epistemologies of disease and cure. Medicine has always been both a therapeutic profession and a reservoir of preconscious symbols.

I showed that the myths arising from our partial recovery of indigenous non-Western medicines inspire two romantic fallacies—one, that modern medical science represents an improvement over aboriginal medicine of almost incalculable dimensions; and, two, that a majority of indigenous medicines continue to be practiced (or have been revived) in their original forms.

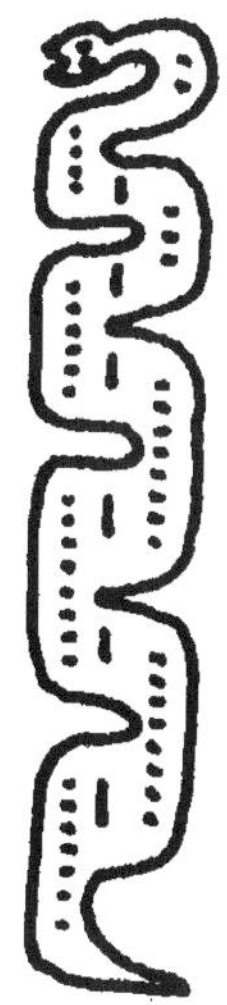

The first fallacy is the common misunderstanding of the priests and sycophants who worship science and progress. It overlooks the fact that scientific medicine is merely the contemporary status of a prehistoric guild of botanists and surgeons, its Rationalist methodology fully established by the time of the Greeks. It also overlooks the distinction between medicine as a branch of natural science (which *is* exponentially removed from aboriginal science) and the art of healing (which does not require medicine and was practiced skillfully aboriginally).

The second fallacy overlooks the fact that all of the ancient and indigenous medicines to which we have access have been reconstrued and reinvented according to contemporary notions of holism, shamanism, and archetypal psychology and no longer exist in their hypothetical pristine forms. This fallacy is the favored inflation of New Age participants who believe that they can claim the gist of any culture simply by declaring their good will and allegiance to global harmony and sharing.

Thus, indigenous systems of healing are closer than we think, for they are woven into the fabric of modern society at both conscious and unconscious levels, and they contribute to a variety of medical and nonmedical institutions. On the other hand, they are further than we think, for, even as we study and reenact their remnants, their original mechanics and phenomenology have been lost, likely forever.

IN THE COURSE of the first volume I proposed six loose categories of medicines:

- simple mechanical, surgical, and herbal techniques that formed the basis of tribal ethnomedicine and led (notably in the Middle East and Asia) to the technological medicines of Neolithic civilization;
- diverse branches of shamanism, embracing psychic healing, symbolic and ritual healing, visualization, divination, sympathetic magic, and primitive psychoanalysis;
- manipulation, originating in the folk traditions of physical adjustment and palpation and giving rise to the outlaw sciences of chiropractic and osteopathy;

- elemental medicine, specifically the pre-atomic and componential cosmologies that incubated therapeutic pantheons in India, Tibet, and China (including Ayurvedic medicine, *Nei Gung*, acupuncture, and related fields);
- symbolic medicine, flowering finally in the formal system of psychoanalysis propounded by Sigmund Freud and transformed by Carl Jung and Wilhelm Reich; and
- reincarnational medicine, proposing a karmic basis for disease and practiced through heterogeneous systems tapping disembodied spirits and energies as curative agents.

In truth, these six categories exist only as a device for defining ancient, non-Western, and holistic medical systems in contemporary terms. In almost every culture their expressions overlap and create one another. It may be said that in any active medical system some of these categories are dormant while others are active. Occasionally one or two of them may have no role at all. In orthodox scientific medicine most of them are suppressed, but that hardly obliterates their influences, which are sustained unconsciously.

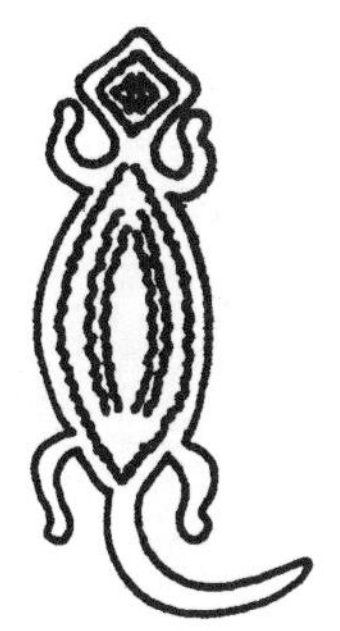

After all, no medicine has ever governed a fixed, concrete methodology. Even more than physics, biology, or astronomy, institutional healing is an antithesis of conflicting symbol chains and levels of concretization. Each medical system struggles with contradictory and paradoxical elements to produce a doctrine that satisfies its clients and the institutions of its milieu. The development of both modern scientific medicine and its holistic alternative has depended on the constant interplay and syntheses of hidden categories.

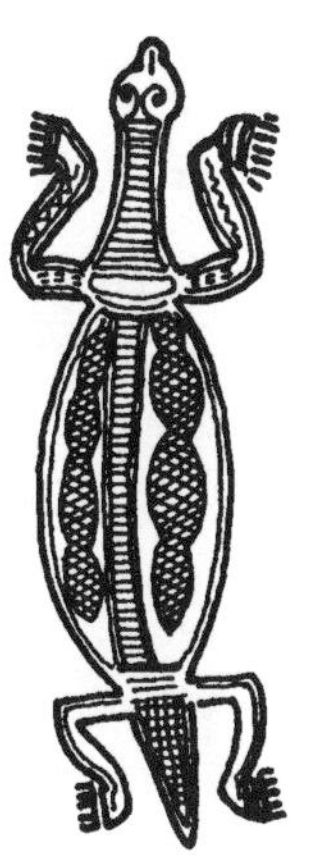

I HAVE ALSO PROPOSED two other major contrarieties of medical thought: Empirical and Rationalist, and Vitalist and Darwinian.

Empirical systems treat patients by trial and error, preserving methods that succeed, regardless of their rationale or likelihood. Most herbal medicines (those using animal and mineral compounds as well) arose

empirically. Without microscopes where else could Stone Age peoples have learned pharmacy except from the ancestors, goddesses, and gods? Divination, symbolic medicines, and healing ceremonies were likely also the outcome of unfoldment by trial and error, differing from herbal medicines in that they treated sick people by totems and "thought objects" rather than by natural substances.

Empirical doctors do not require a scientific or theological explanation in order to prescribe a remedy. They require only that oral tradition or scripture provides a string of happy precedents. Thus, many medical systems (acupuncture, much of Ayurveda, chiropractic, homeopathy, and Navaho sand painting among them) continue to be practiced today not because there is exogenous proof that they work but because (for whatever reasons) they yield satisfactory results. In fact, in most of the above cases, there is scientific "proof" that they *could not work.*

Rationalist systems extrapolate from theory and experiment to application. Models of the body and its functions are used to develop suitable methods of attacking disease processes (which are also modeled mechanically). Treatments are developed according to physical and thermodynamic logic and continue to be applied regardless of side-effects or consequences. Resting on centuries of biological and chemical experiments, modern scientific medicine is the pinnacle of Rationalism. It is sustained by theories of natural law and the continued work of physicists, chemists, biologists, etc. It denounces all cures that cannot be demonstrated according to its orthodox principles of cause and effect.

Vitalism sponsors a multiformity of practices, all of them based on the presumption that either an intrinsic life force or disembodied energy field provides a catalyst for healing. Taoist and Ayurvedic modalities locate their source of energy in the body's *chakra* system, its auras, and its meridians; other canons claim an exogenous medium either in the general cosmic environment (orgone therapy, astrological medicines, and to some degree Polarity) or in material substances (alchemical and homeopathic medicines).

Darwinian science specifically denies the existence of intrinsic or exogenous vital energies and bases its treatments solely on the recognized thermodynamics of living systems.

In the second volume of this work I will explore the variety of modalities that have arisen from different historical traditions and categories of medicine. I will examine them not primarily as intellectual and philosophical constructs but as dynamic forms that are used to treat living beings. Some medicines cure diseases by application of exquisite scientific analyses and sophisticated tools. Some medicines succeed by little more than the touch of a healer's hand or his directed thought. Some medicines operate by language and dialogue, some by lessons and exercises, some by mutual chanting, some by silent internalization, some by interactions between a patient's body/mind and a healer's palpation. All of these are viable. Their success depends on a range of factors linking the healer, the patient, the disease, and the environment. Even discerning the outlines of such factors "through a glass darkly" is a major goal of this book.

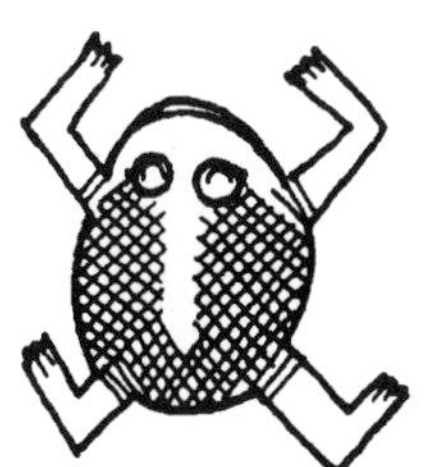

There are medicines that use intentional symbolic matrices. There are medicines that generate symbols spontaneously and unconsciously. There are medicines that try to annihilate symbols. My objective is to discover the principles that underlie all of these variations and to propose ways of accommodating them simultaneously.

I take the conflicts among medical methods to represent the conflicts within and among ourselves. I believe that we suffer ambiguities

of healing because we have lost a sense of who we are. We experience constant shifting identities of bodies, minds, desires, and destinies. As long as we do not not know ourselves, it is difficult to treat our diseases in any substantial or ultimate way. In fact, we are condemned to treating their metaphors, however palpable and concrete such metaphors may seem in Magnetic Resonance Images and lab reports.

I believe also that much of our illness arises from global pathology at an archetypal and psychospiritual level and that we must employ a new model of healing to begin to restore our human balance and the environment of this planet, though it will take many generations of slow self-discovery and accretion to accomplish this. My "planet medicine" proposes an immediate revision of therapeutic philosophy and institutions so that a more inclusive paradigm of healing can guide our species through the intricacies and impasses of its present crisis.

In the medical environment of late twentieth-century Western civilization, one type of modality predominates. A patient expects a doctor to externalize the genealogy of his or her malaise and to apply a rational cure based on scientific premises. The patient thinks of his disease as a natural event, arising circumstantially, and treatable most efficaciously by an objectification of both his body and the operant medicine. Invariably he is unaware of the cultural prejudices he brings to the doctor's office or the role that those prejudices play in his either improving or failing to improve from the remedy given. The dance of symbols about him truly eludes him.

It would be astonishing to most people to consider that they could be healed more effectively by a Bear shaman or Zen priest. Some might acknowledge this as a poetic fancy or an unattainable ideal, but few are able to take it seriously and act on it.

It would be even more astonishing to most people to learn that on a symbolic level their body/minds already impose the equivalents of Bear shamans and Zen priests in an attempt to mediate and effectuate the sterile cures of science. On a clandestine and syntactic level alchemists and academic physicians still trade robes and empower each other. The

true cure is at once more available and more elusive than the average person imagines.

It is particularly difficult for people to conceive alternatives once they are sick. They tend to externalize the disease event and hunt for a sanctioned modality to make them better. Even when they patronize the alternative medical kingdom, they select natural cures that are the seeming equivalents of pharmaceutical and surgical ones—a bottle of herbal pills rather than a bottle of antibiotics. Perhaps they decide to improve their overall health by a regimen of exercise or a more conscious diet. What is more difficult for them is to address the persona of the disease in themselves and to turn inward for the cure. If they were capable of this, any medicine they chose would be more effective. In fact, at this level the most divergent treatments are not all that different from each other.

The primary functional distinction is not between orthodox scientific medicine and the array of holistic therapies and modalities of faith healing. It is between understanding disease as a process in oneself and regarding disease as an outsider. As long as diseases are reified as outsiders, they can never be totally cured. Their most painful and explicit symptoms may be alleviated in the name of cure, but their core will give rise to endless new manifestations.

By presenting so many discrete modalities in such detail, I hope to give readers a full understanding of the alternatives available, both of practical therapies and meanings. By going into depth on each modality and comparing them at their most essential levels, I mean to provide readers with a key to the different aspects of themselves represented by each of these medicines. Thus, they will begin to regain their native ability to travel among the meanings of modalities and to redefine themselves in terms of unlimited possibilities rather than familiar orthodoxies and radical substitutes.

There are no right or wrong medicines *per se;* there is only an alternative between rigidity of thought and freedom of action. Limitation inevitably means fear of disease and one's body/mind as a commodity

to be auctioned in the medical marketplace. Freedom may still entail fear of disease, but the body/mind is one's own, and one can follow whatever path enhances depth of experience and personal growth. In either realm, healing may represent anything from a quick fix to a diagnosis of incurability to a miraculous remission. The path of healing not the endgame of cure is the true aspiration of medicine.

"If I want a life that lasts a thousand years," Korean Zen Master Seung Sahn told his students, "it's not possible. Before one thousand years, already you are dead. So, if you understand what human beings are—what this world is really like—then you understand that you cannot decide anything. You have only this moment. If this moment is clear, then your whole life is clear."[1]

Each act of cure is a moment becoming clear—no more, no less.

THIS VOLUME WILL BEGIN with a discussion of the most mysterious of all medical systems—those that treat patients without an anatomical model, without drugs, and often without even a palpable connection between the physician and the patient. Faith healing illuminates the frontier of the possible. From there we can travel only backwards to more encumbered, less supersonic methods. Faith healing gives us a touchstone. As long as we account for the fact that healing seems to occur spontaneously and to be transmitted without any theories or implements, we can accept the intricacies and paradoxes of more embodied therapies.

I do not propose faith healing as the ultimate method. Our incarnation in a physical world requires real material transformation. Faith healing proves that mountains can be moved in the blink of an eyelid, but it does not change the fact that armies trample through vineyards daily, machine-gunning the inhabitants and burning their homes. When an act of faith is not available to stop a rampant plague, we must encounter the nitty-gritty of infection and worldstuff. The often bizarre treatments and visualizations that occur in actual systems may be little more than methods of conducting pure healing energy through the

labyrinths and distortions of mind/body anatomy. Each nuance, each discrete system may be not so much a departure from natural healing as an avenue for engaging a healing dynamism with a mode of psychosomatic resistance. Finally, even the most subtle internalizing processes require arduous physical and mental practices in order to engage our very substantial flesh.

I will move from psychic healing to somatic healing and examine the wide range of modalities that have developed under the rubrics of movement therapy, bodywork, osteopathy, manipulation, and adjustment. I will then explore a great diversity of healing modalities (including martial arts, sexual therapies, meditational practices, prayer, esoteric medicines, sensory medicines, dietary and herbal medicines) as well as the aspects of healing that lie beyond category or modality and are indistinguishable from art, sports, war, politics, economics, and crime. After all, if we are to heal ourselves and this world, there can be no exceptions. We must heal guns, money, factories, armies, governments, laws, prisons, schools, and medical institutions, or at least their representations in ourselves. Insofar as these are the projections and externalizations of unresolved pathologies, they too must be treated by a real "planet medicine."

Notes

1. Zen Master Seung Sahn, in a talk at the Cambridge, Massachusetts, Zen Center, May 7, 1993.

CHAPTER ONE

Spirit Healing

Miraculous and Charismatic Healing

SHAMANIC AND FAITH healing have a dynamic all their own. They defy any science which turns out doctors by a standard procedure from its medical schools, for they propose to accomplish the same cures without any of the tools. That is, they intend the manufacture and transmission (or channeling) of cures on the basis of thought alone or from a reservoir of elixir naturally abundant throughout the universe in pure energetic forms. They assume that sickness is likewise conducted by "thought" patternings of matter. "Disease will never be cured or eradicated by present materialistic methods," warned Edward Bach, the originator of flower-petal remedies, "for the simple reason that disease in its origin is not material. What we know as disease is ... the end product of deep and long-acting forces."[1] Spirit healing purports to engage those deep and long-acting forces by entering their own invisible and immaterial arena.

Although a spirit healer may sometimes be skilled in medical mechanics and knowledgeable about physiology, he or she practices—in whole or in part—by drawing on energy fields beyond ordinary views of mind and matter. Successful healers have cured people long-distance merely by laying hands on their letters or by sending positive thoughts in their direction: Edgar Cayce's treatments by mail are legendary. He is widely known to have successfully projected cures from the United States to "patients" on the other side of the world with only one known error (when he mistakenly "got" the twin of the person in France for whom he intended his remedy). The general rationale is: ". . . [D]istance is not important, for there is no time or space in spiritual reality."[2] The question then would be: how does a healer shift the exchange between himself and his client from the realm of time and space to the realm of spirit?

Disciples of the Japanese healing art Reiki practice a rigorous protocol of long-distance healing, with both parties scheduling an appointment at which neither is *physically* present. According to one Reiki healer, "The results of absentee treatment are in no way inferior to those attained by the direct method, although patients will usually feel the effects of the latter more distinctly. In both cases, the energy will be the same. Many practitioners can feel the flow of Reiki energy in the various parts of the patient's body when they are treating with the absentee method. . . ."[3]

A training manual instructs:

> . . . [M]iniaturize the client, while holding him between your hands. You encapsulate the individual in *Christed Golden White Light.* The *Christed Golden White Light* looks like a glorious illuminated halo of vibrant crystalline shimmers of liquid white "mother of pearl" with sparks of gold floating through the depths and on the surface of the light. . . . When contact is established a fullness between the hands is felt. You are holding a ball of energy, a part of the etheric fabric of the healee's spiritual essence. You will physically sense the inability to close your hands, palm to palm, as long as energy is being received by the healee. . . . Keep in mind that subtle energies registering *from the Etheric Bodies* may not be known or obvious to the client.[4] (italics are the author's)

Is the image actually a replica of the client, like a holographic voodoo doll, or is it a symbolic device through which the healer sprays his intention into the vast paraphysical unknown? In the latter case, do

his "effects" bounce off many etheric "mirrors" like a pinball before connecting with some projected target? We will come back to such questions many times throughout the chapter.

As in sorcery, belief and even willing participation of the target do not appear to be prerequisites to a successful session. Many faith healers recall "successfully" praying over "atheists" with life-threatening diseases at the request of worried family members.[5] Certainly projectors of voodoo and other curses do not seek their subjects' consent.

The pony-tailed, part-American-Indian healer taking the name Drunvalo Melchizedek is unequivocal about the accuracy of teleported energy:

> It doesn't matter *at all* if [the] person is physically in front of you or if they are on the Moon. They could be anywhere at all. Physical location means nothing for transfer of *prana* and thoughts. If they are physically there, then they're physically there, but if they're not there, then what I do is: I either visualize or bring in their essence (if I don't know exactly what they look like).[6]

In some instances, homeopaths have achieved the precise expected effects of a remedy just by intending to prescribe it, without ever actually dispensing a pill (which would have lacked substance anyway!).[7]

This is not party games or dabbling in Ouija boards. It is not simple visualization either. It is practical long-distance medicine. The sick person is supposed to finish the session, even if he or she is unaware that it occurred, cured or improved in some concrete way. The treatment is literally miniaturized and transported with no regard for limitations imposed by the laws of thermodynamics or the recognized topology of time and space.

No one would propose that spirit healing is the stuff of science; however, if the patient is cured, need it matter? In healing, there can be no promises and no outlaws. If a psychosurgeon or Reiki master succeeds where a trained physician fails, this does not cheapen the cure. The cure, in fact, cannot be cheapened. As noted in our discussion of

vitalism in Volume One, the explanation, even the need for an explanation, is a residual issue for our intellect to resolve. People do not seek spirit healers for physics or philosophy.

Spiritual healing is remarkably impenetrable to judgment or evaluation of any sort. How can one know if an invisible or even "nonexistent" energy lands accurately or arises at all? How can we distinguish its purported effects from those of other spontaneous or random changes? What traits, if any, distinguish the work of one healer or sorcerer from another? These questions are further compounded by the behavior that commonly follows attempts at immaterial medicine.

If a patient is unaffected by a treatment, the healer can always claim transcendental interference. On the other hand, if a patient derogates a particular modality being applied to him, he can attribute any subsequent improvement to natural causes, notably the fact that most conditions are self-limiting and eventually improve. No matter how exhaustive an unsuccessful trail of M.D.s might have been (sometimes over years), no matter how dramatic, instantaneous, and complete a miracle cure for the same condition, it always seems to the skeptic that nothing happened. "Oh," a rejected doctor might say after hearing his patient had unexpectedly improved, "it was probably only psychological in the first place." It probably was, but at a whole different level than he means.

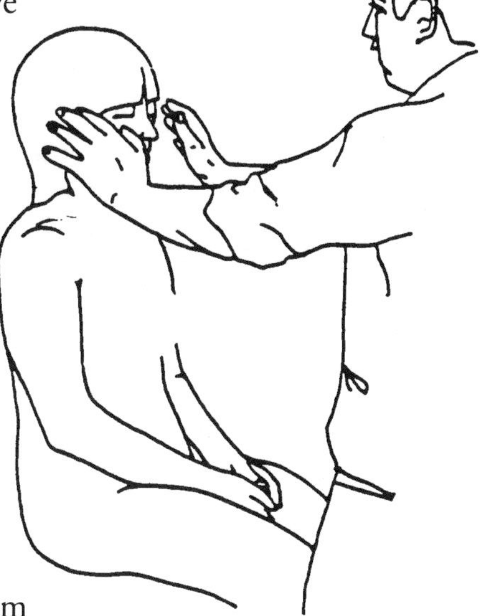

One homeopath told me his favorite story of a sister who, suffering from acute stomach pains for ten years, had visited a number of doctors without any cause being found. A trenchant disbeliever in homeopathy, she saw no harm in taking pills from her brother. When he didn't hear from her for several months, he assumed that his medicine had done nothing. But eventually he got a chance to ask her about her condition.

"Oh," she said. "The pains just went away."

"Was it when you took my medicine?" he asked.

She thought about it, then agreed it was curiously right after putting the little white balls under her tongue. She hastened to add that she considered it a coincidence.

After recounting this sequence of events, the homeopath mused, "That's the way it always is. The cure is so profound that the disease just slips away. The person forgets that he was ever sick. The body knows something has happened to it; it changes. But the person doesn't remember anything in his mind."[8]

All medicine that works inexplicable cures runs into the same dilemma: there is no way of establishing a relationship between the medicine and the cure.

If a patient treated by acupuncture or homeopathy improves, what can the improvement be attributed to? How can needles inserted in the arm correct a stomach ulcer? How can pills with no drug in them have any effect on very physical diarrhea? How can an adjustment of the spine affect a kidney ailment? Many of the practitioners of medicines proposing such cures have theoretical explanations based on energy transfer and vital properties of substance. This is their post-scientific bias, even as the shaman's certainty of spirits and supernatural forces represents a pre-scientific bias. But any cure could equally well be explained by the ubiquitous placebo effect, by the curative benefit of plain old attention, by the telepathic intercession of the doctor's unconscious, or a poltergeist—no matter the operant technique.

In *The Alchemy of Healing,* Edward Whitmont recounts a case from the 1950s in which a placebo functioned as a long-sought miracle cure for cancer. The story concerns a Mr. Wright who had a far-advanced lymphosarcoma. When a supposed miracle drug ("Krebiozen") was dispensed at his hospital during a clinical trial, Mr. Wright was not even selected to receive it because of the advanced state of his illness. However, the enthusiasm of the patient and his persistent begging finally persuaded the doctor to slip him this medicine against the rules. Not only did Mr. Wright come back from the verge of death, but his

"tumor masses had melted like snowballs on a hot stove, and in only [a] few days they were half of their original size."[9] Ten days after being a terminal patient with an oxygen mask, he flew home.

Two months later the results of Krebiozen trials from many different clinics were released, and it was found to be not only ineffective but inert. Upon hearing this, Mr. Wright had an immediate relapse. He returned to life support.

With the patient's death all but certain again, the doctor decided to play a trick. He told Mr. Wright that the reason for his relapse was the rapid deterioration of Krebiozen over time. He offered him "a new super-refined, double-strength product"[10] which was actually just fresh water. Not only did the patient improve again, but this time the results were even more dramatic. Mr. Wright became quite healthy as he continued to receive water injections. Two months later, though, he read in the newspaper that the AMA had concluded that Krebiozen was useless in the treatment of cancer. In a few days he returned to the hospital in a terminal state and died less than forty-eight hours later.

Whatever else we might conclude about this unsettling course of events, it is clear that the dominant research protocol of our time, while searching relentlessly for one kind of explicit medicine (and spending billions of dollars in the process), is ignoring a whole other medicinal event that might have exponentially more value than any new line of wonder drugs. The success of "nothing" is neither a fluke nor an outrage. It is the key to a science of transmutation.

Medical educator Dana Ullman has observed that, "Homeopathy is either the most sophisticated way of stimulating placebo response, or it is a highly refined though mysterious way of stimulating powerful healing responses."[11]

What if this dichotomy is never resolved? If a placebo response is consistently this effective, why deprecate it? Perhaps a whole new ontology of disease is needed to understand the mechanism of placebos. Far from indicating naiveté or fraud, placebo "cure" may be an opportune opening into an unexplored, unknown realm of medical possibilities.[12]

Faith Healing

FAITH HEALING, the religious wing of spiritual medicine, is practiced in markedly divergent ways. It can operate within the boundaries of traditional and evangelical Protestantism, as it has with Phineas Quimby, Mary Baker Eddy, Oral Roberts, and various Appalachian Fundamentalists, some of whom use radio shows to reach their patients, and others of whom dance with snakes draped around their bodies (according to their interpretation of Biblical injunction). Religious medicine has arisen independently within Hinduism, Buddhism, Sufism, Shintoism, Christianity, etc. It has been practiced by yogi Paramahansa Yogananda, Sufi musician Hazrat Inayat Khan, Reiki founder Mikao Usui, various Tibetan lamas, Persian Sufis, and countless others. It has also been "channeled" by "ancestors," or disincarnate beings—a newly popular revival in the United States during the latter part of the twentieth century.

When the training of a healer or an actual healing is channeled, the "doctor"—remember—is "on the other side." This makes good sense. As we discussed in the section on "Esoteric Sources of Healing Paradigms" in the previous volume, reincarnation is the most stunning possible triumph over illness—a literal transcendence of its direst effects through metamorphosis into an entirely new body. Hence, those who are already dead (and still petitionable) might well be the most powerful teachers and purveyors of healing available. Theirs is power not over disease *per se* but over the passage between dimensions.

The signature of Jesus of Nazareth was his ability to cure major illness. He restored sight to the blind by the touch of a hand and summoned Lazarus back from death. Jesus' method was basic: he said you were healed, and you *were* healed. The particular disease or its origin hardly mattered. To a large degree, the *New Testament* is the singular inspiration and injunction for faith healing in the West. Practitioners need only claim a lineage from Jesus (or faith in him) to be able to heal under his aegis. The chapters and numbers of verses from the Bible are

often draped from walls at sporting events or held aloft on signs; these are amulets and numerological totems, reminders of "the faith."

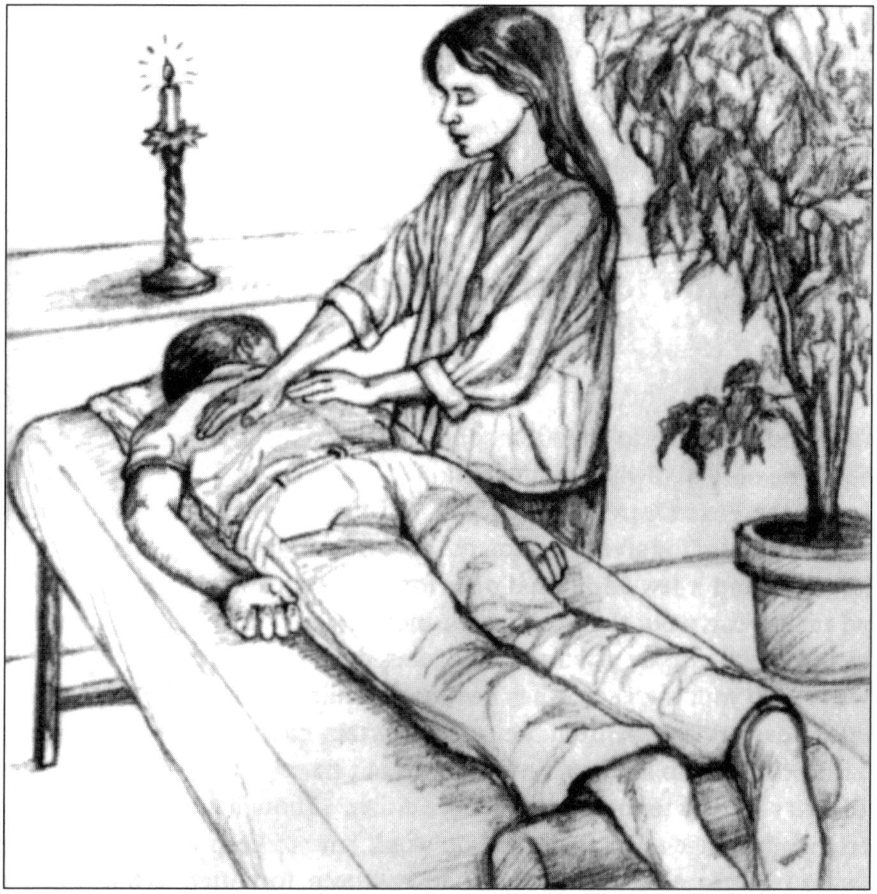

As the Son of God and the Holy Ghost, Jesus' power is so great that not only do time and distance melt, but hack preachers in his name become spiritual "doctors" of the first magnitude. This is not an unusual outcome. Faith healing in other cultures also derives from ancestors, spirits, and legendary beings.

The premise of faith healing is that all disease is spiritual in its root causes. The healer is merely a messenger between cosmic forces and the patient's body/mind. The context of channeling is necessarily cultural.

Christian patients shake at the invocation of Jesus just as Haida patients shake upon the entry of the "killer whale." Biologically, it is the same shaking.

Energy Fields

Most "faith healing" is not omnipotent and requires either therapeutic props or intermediary fields. Secular healers propose (quasi-scientifically) to be able to read energy patternings around the body—that is, to "see" wavelengths invisible to the average human eye. These fields may be associated with the aura, the electrical and magnetic pulses of the vital force, the astral body, the Hindu *chakra* system, the Egyptian *ka* "double," the Pali Eckankar, or perhaps all of them to some degree. Those who cure by diagnosis of energy fields "read" a disturbance in the field, usually as a pattern or color—bright chartreuse or yellow, a blob, sparkle, or loop of light. They sometimes explain their work as "restoring the natural wavelength" or "conducting pure energy." The healer's life force transmits a vector from itself through the sheaths of the patient's various "bodies" to a depth at which it can be received and distributed like blood or breath. The change then becomes visible in the energy field of the patient.

Demonstrations of such events have not been left to mere assertion of believers. Kirlian photography, developed by Simeon and Valentina Kirlian just after World War II in the Soviet Union, is the most renowned in a lineage of electrical image-recordings on the fringes of science. When a proximate high-frequency spark generator (putting out 75,000 to 200,000 electrical pulses per second) is activated in the vicinity of a life-form—for instance, a finger or flower—in contact with a photographic plate, the processed image reveals a radiant field or corona. This proposed "bioplasmic" energy, according to one parapsychologist, Thelma Moss, "shows no correlation with the usual physiological parameters such as Galvanic Skin Response, peripheral vascular dilation, temperature, or sweat."[13]

Kirlian-derived images seem to reveal that a healer in the act of healing generates "radiation" of some sort. Before the act, her field is bounded. At the moment of projection, radiation emits from her fingertips not unlike light from a bulb. Moss calls this "a form of energy which emanates from people and interacts with other people or with objects. Of course," she continues, "if you put your hands on somebody, it's not supposed to do a bloody thing to them. . . . But we've done controlled experiments and obtained sometimes dramatic changes both in the person doing the healing and the one being healed—even if the healer's hands are held at a distance. It's not contact which produces the effect. It's an interaction of fields."[14]

If "medicine" can be projected from auras or activated directly from a healer's hands, then all other therapeutic modalities become mere artifice or affectation. Scientific demonstration and standardization of this process would certainly give rise to a whole new institution of medicine.

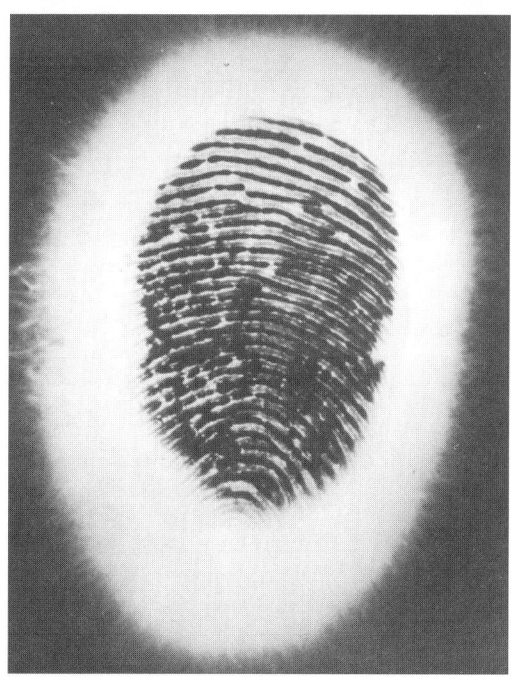

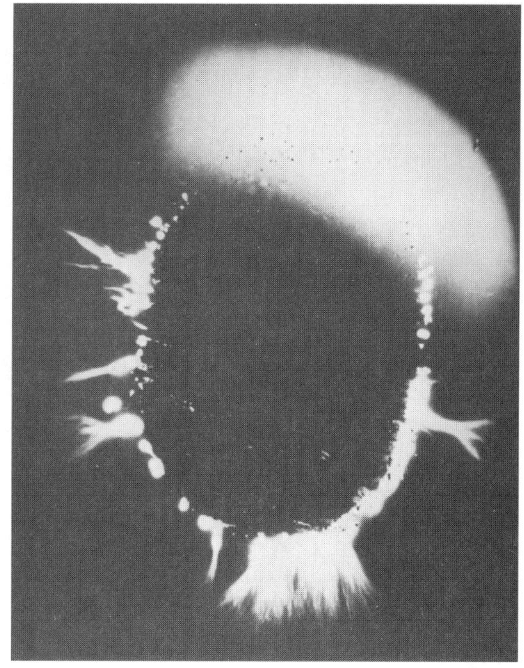

The Training of a Spiritual Healer

ORTHODOX MEDICINE TRAINS chemists and doctors, not healers. This oft-repeated homily is worth repeating again here. Healers gain their power and skill from *not* going to medical school: either they are "born" with it (however one explains that), or they develop it through personal discipline, prayer, vision quest, and/or initiation. The ability often transcends any individual system. A healer is able to use a particular coda in which he or she is trained, or, in some cases, works the universe without portfolio. Remember Quesalid, the Kwakiutl shaman who became proficient in the very system he was about to expose as a fraud! (See "Practical Shamanism and Psychoanalysis" in Volume One, Chapter Five.) Not only faith healers, but many of our professional doctors—without realizing it—came upon their preferred modalities just as mysteriously.

A notable percentage of successful healers were average individuals who discovered their talent spontaneously, becoming "curative" almost like becoming infectious. Herbert Barker, the early twentieth-century British bone-setter, was prevailed upon to treat the dislocated elbow of a fellow passenger on a sea voyage to Canada. He was surprised by his own success. He had had no training at all at the time, but a cousin later taught him rudimentary medical methods. He then proceeded to realign bones, joints, and ligaments on the spot with such success that the British War Office employed him *sub rosa* during World War I.

Barker could not defend himself against the onslaught of medical criticism, and he was unable to explain his own method. He said he was not even sure how he did it. Unable to train successors, he left no system behind.[15]

Oral Roberts, the American TV evangelist, though widely suspected of fraud, convinced enough people of his gift that he built an empire upon it and even ended up underwriting branches of the medical establishment and national sports teams! He describes hearing an inner voice

when he was young that told him simply to "be like Jesus." Several months earlier he had been healed by a preacher laying hands on him (he had tuberculosis). His own first success occurred during a public test he set up for himself before twelve hundred people. During his sermon, an old woman's withered hand seemed to come alive. With that sign, he began healing others in the room.[16]

Thomas Johanson, a contemporary British healer, was "chosen" by a Roman Catholic monk in a trance as a man with healing ability. He was placed, against his own protests, in a Catholic clinic where he figured he might as well put his hands on patients and pray. Although he felt nothing, the people he treated reported a heat emanating from his touch. A decade later he was healing between eight hundred and a thousand people a year. Presently he is the head of the Spiritualist Association of Great Britain (SAGB), which (by request) has overseen the addition of a spiritual-healing section to more than 2,000 clinics.[17]

Harry Edwards, another contemporary British spiritualist, began his career (like Quesalid) as a skeptic. He had been told by several mediums, independently of one another, that he had a gift of healing. Curious, he began to try out his reputed magic on people who were seriously ill. The first time he touched a sick person, he felt a strong charge passing along his fingers, as though the cure were percolating through him. Years later, in an interview, Edwards summarized his position:

> Spiritual healing is a *science*. . . . It indicates that an intelligence superior to man's is operating. Therefore, it also implies that the spirit intelligence who carries out the healing has a knowledge far superior

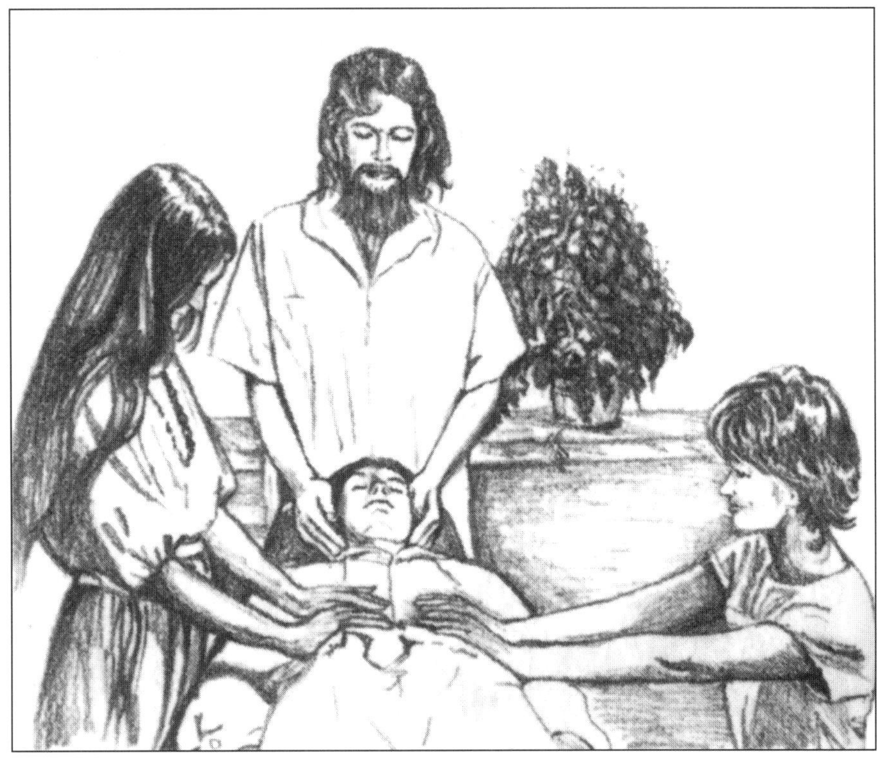

> to human science. It also means that it has a much more extensive knowledge of the laws that govern physical science, energies, and things like that.[18]

This would certainly cover the intercessions of paraphysical entities like Seth, Ramtha, Thoth, Babaji, and others by whom successful healers have claimed to be guided in their practices.

John Lee Baughman, a contemporary American healer, graphically describes four spiritualists and a doctor praying together to rid the doctor's wife of cancer:

> We saw these cells under the influence of God, and the action stemming from the subconscious to the cells, wherever they were, and they were being fed their proper direction again, and their form, and their movement.[19]

When healers suggest that they communicate directly with the etheric and astral levels and that these messages are then enacted on a physical plane through the genesis of new cells in the patient, we understand only that this is what *must* happen—likewise, when a patient actualizes his own spontaneous cure. That is, whether it happens or not, it *seems* to happen. It is a cover story for an appearance.

Symbols

We might like to believe, with the optimistic homeopath, that matter can be spiritualized and then communicated to the Intelligence of the soma. But that is mainly still our apologia. Notions like these are like science-fiction stories of transcendent powers among aliens from other worlds. Until we mingle with these visitors in everyday life or develop such powers ourselves, the models are projections of our own isolation relative to such a condition.

The facts, on the other hand, merge back into the streets with the anonymous masses. The world goes on oblivious, preferring to trade futures in abstractions of otherwise very material substances like pork bellies and gold. In that sense, placebos prove everything and nothing. Each act of cure is discrete and, as advertised, without reference to time and space.

Psychic Surgery

HEALERS COME FROM all over the Earth and use a diversity of techniques, some of which, like the bloody down (see Volume One, Chapter Five), may be solely props, while others, like praying together or laying on hands, may be direct and straightforward. Few methods are as idiosyncratic and inexplicable as the psychic surgery of Tony Agpaoa of the Philippines and José Arigo and Thomaz Morais Coutinho of Brazil. These "doctors" cut open flesh with a small penknife or a motion of their hands, quickly touch the tissue (or seem to), and then close the wound without a scar. At least this is what is reported by thousands of visitors and what has been recorded on film. Of course, psychic surgeons have been accused of fraud, sleight of hand, etc., and

Spirit Healing

quackbusters have routinely dismissed the concept as ridiculous to the point of not even meriting rebuttal. However, other scientific observers have found no evidence of trickery and expressed wonderment at what they observed (see also the discussion under "Practical Shamanism and Psychoanalysis" in Volume One, Chapter Five). John G. Fuller's description of Arigo includes an account of the first time Andrija Puharich, an American physician, and his friend Henry Belk observed the Brazilian's surgery:

> Puharich and Belk watched incredulously as the people moved up in line to the table, rich and poor, of all ages. Arigo would barely glance at them. For most, his hand began almost automatically scribbling a prescription at incredible speed, as if his pen were slipping across a sheet of ice. Occasionally he would rise, place a patient against the wall, wipe the paring knife on his shirt again, drive it brutally into a tumor or cyst or another eye or ear, and remove whatever the offending tissue was, in a matter of seconds.
>
> There was no anesthesia, no hypnotic suggestion, no antisepsis—and practically no bleeding beyond a trickle.[20]

Bloody down or real disease object?

At one point Arigo asked Puharich to perform the operation himself on a patient's eye. Puharich was terrified even to hold the knife, certain he would slash the eyeball. He hesitated but Arigo said, "Do it like a man!" so he plunged the blade against the eye.[21] He expected the worst, but instead experienced a repelling force coming back from the tissue. He never actually penetrated or harmed it.

Mechanically, physiologically, it makes no sense. But what about the Navaho patient who leaves the sand painting cured? What about the revival meeting where the lame throw down their crutches and walk away? Is this all placebo? Is it all sleight of hand and fraud?

The only thing that stands *for* these events is that they happen. They vanish like snowflakes in spring. They cannot be replicated and no science can be fashioned from them. The idea itself of a faith healer is too hypothetical, too subjective, and too eccentric for the establishment to

approach. It is even an uncomfortable prospect in many holistic-health circles, where the general belief is that specific unorthodox techniques (like the palpation of bones or the potency of herbs) are themselves the proximate causes of cure. Yet faith healing not only persists in a scientific era, in its manifold forms it may be the most popular medicine on the planet.

Symbols

The man restored by magicians or voodoo-masters takes his health home with him. His immediate associates and family perhaps explain it by his faith or good luck (whatever these might be). The local doctor may of course question whether he was sick in the first place, or whether perhaps more comprehensive tests will reveal the disease still present. The usual verdict is: "outright fraud" or "entertaining stage magic."

In at least a few instances where some attempt at medical documentation was undertaken, the proclaimed cure does *seem* to have been authentic. Psychic surgeons have handed over gallstones extracted from patients who clearly had gallstones before their surgery and did not afterwards. The surgeons did not appear to carry in gallstones that could then be substituted by sleight of hand; they presented their extractions immediately, and the stones were later chemically analyzed.[22] Of course any qualified stage magician will attest to the range of tricks that can dupe well-meaning but innocent observers.

X-rays and diagnostic exams of people treated by psychic surgeons often show tumors, cataracts, tuberculosis, etc., before the operation, then no evidence of these conditions afterwards. This occurred even in one case (witnessed by a Brazilian neurosurgeon whose patient was being treated) in which the healer was eating dinner one mile away at the ostensible moment of surgery![23] But what occurred? Teleportation of cure? Placebo effect? Spontaneous healing? Clever sleight of hand? Duplicity or sincerity?

Spirit Healing

"You are doing what you are charged with, are you not?"[24] an exasperated judge asked Arigo at a trial in Congonhas, Brazil.

"I must say I don't even know myself whether I practice illegal medicine or not," replied the healer. "I am not the one who is doing this. I am just an intermediary between a spirit and the people.... All I know is that whenever anybody comes to me for material or spiritual help, I must try to help them. I will not turn them away."[25]

Reiki

Mikao Usui, a Japanese theologian, founded the Reiki lineage in the mid-nineteenth century. In search of the lost healing modality of Christ, he traveled from a Christian seminary in Kyoto (of which he was the principal), to the University of Chicago (where he earned his doctorate in theology, yet without finding the secret), to Northern India on pilgrimage, then back to a monastery in Kyoto. On the twenty-first day of meditation and chanting *sutras* on the Holy Mountain, he finally received the transmission of energy he called Reiki.

> He saw a shining light moving towards him with great speed. It became bigger and bigger and finally hit him in the middle of the forehead. Dr. Usui thought he was going to die when he suddenly saw millions of little bubbles in blue, lilac, pink, and all the colors of the rainbow. A great white light appeared, and he saw the well-known Sanskrit symbols in front of him glowing in the shining gold and he said, "Yes, I remember."[26]

From then on he seemed to be the conduit for a universal healing energy. This constituted not just the reservoir of his own body/mind but the limitless energy of the divine and cosmic realm. In Reiki it automatically streams through the healer and penetrates the area of the sick person's body most in need of treatment.

In its basic form (first degree of training), Reiki is primarily a system of nondiagnostic touch—the gentle laying of hands with fingers together on various parts of the patient's body. Each position is held

from three to five minutes but sometimes (in problem areas) for as long as half an hour. Treatments are given four times a day for four days, although the regimen may vary. Reiki practitioners also treat animals, plants, stones, and bodies of water. One European healer regularly transmits to butterflies.

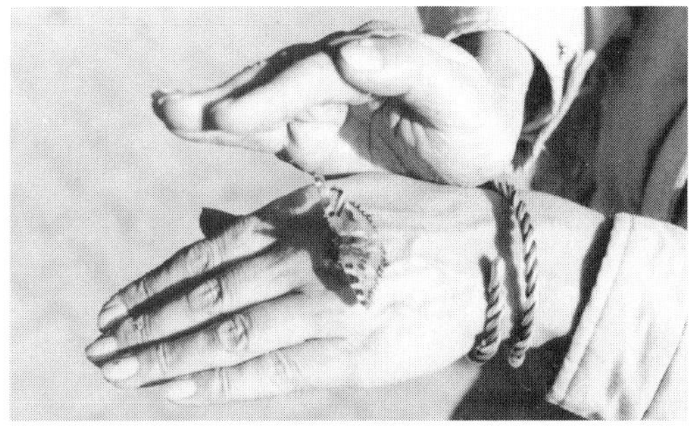

On the surface, this resembles bodywork or radionic healing (which is how many view Reiki); in actuality, it is a ritualized form of faith healing or contemporary shamanism. The practitioner can serve as the conduit for this universal life energy only because she has been initiated into its lineage of transcendental channels.

In practice, Reiki is often integrated with dietary and psychological counseling, Chinese herbs or homeopathic medicines, and psychospiritual jargon and dialogue with the goal of learning the esoteric cause behind a disease condition (i.e., whether it is emotional suppression, withdrawal, separation of spirit and body, etc.). At its best,

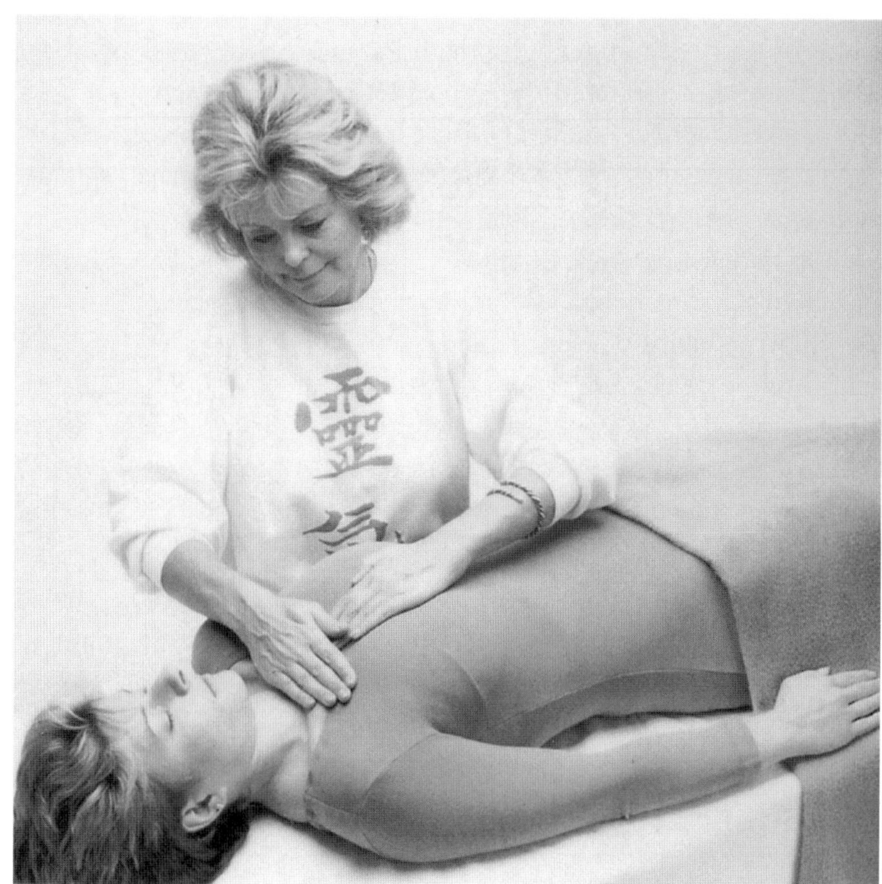

this is psychic mediumship and anatomical astrology. At its worst, it is manipulative New Age psychobabble.

In theory, anyone can touch another person and attempt to transmit a healing force. Reiki formalizes and institutionalizes that process. Combining Christian mystical authority, the Hindu *prana* system, the theosophy of the etheric field, and the heightened awareness of Zen (with New Age marketing techniques), present-day Reiki projects an ambition to become global spiritual medicine. While offering a catchall disincarnate energy source for practitioners of all persuasions, it sets a standard for corporate faith healing.

After all, Reiki is also a church that charges substantial fees for initiating new practitioners while regarding a monetary arrangement as part of the symbolic union of healer and healee (Reiki doctrine firmly states that there can be no healing without some prior exchange between the two parties). It justifies the expense in terms of an occult doctrine which regards money as a symbol requiring constant mutation and interchange. Money is simply another form of energy, a powerful catalyst in and of itself.

THE POTENTIAL HEALER first cleanses herself (physically of toxins and spiritually of doubts) and then, in a ritual of transubstantiation, a person from the Reiki lineage marks her to channel the divine force. The training provides the precise positions in which to place her hands and the method of visualization for transmission:

> From your hand chakras and your 3rd eye you send a beam of Second Degree energy. The location is normally a specific part of the healee's anatomy. You activate the laser beam by visualizing the *Empowerment Symbol* directed from each hand and 3rd eye into the anatomical part and complete the *intoning* of the *sacred words.* . . . If you are knowledgeable in gross anatomy, have specific diagnostic information about a client's health challenges, and are capable of detailed visualization, you can work within the physical structure of an organ, gland, vascular or lymphatic duct, muscle, ligament or bone. . . .[27]

It is common for systems of spiritual healing to value a knowledge of physiology, if only as a way to tune and address the transfer of energy. Physiology also provides a way to "name" results. A Reiki manual portrays the dialogue between healer and organs in peerless New Age rhetoric:

> . . . [A]ll of a sudden you hear the *Adrenals* holler out, "I am really depleted, please laser in on me and recharge my batteries." When they are balanced, the *Liver* might speak up and say, "The body has overloaded me with toxins, how about a little additional Reiki to clear me out?" Then, when the *Liver* is happy, the *Spleen* might light

> up and say, "This stress has tired me down and the immune system needs strengthening before the body loses its ability to resist the emotional onslaught of a viral thought floating through its tired consciousness."[28] (italics are the author's)

In the higher degrees the Reiki healer attunes herself to deep-seated fear responses, psycho-emotional imbalances, and what is referred to as "the collective unconscious soul memory for this incarnation."[29] The goal of treatment becomes much more than healing diseases and injuries; it is nothing less than opening the person to the truth of their existence and the simultaneity of all things.

In this context, healing in absentia takes on a deeper meaning, for it is not merely the ability to project energy over a great distance; it is access to the higher levels of creation and karma. It is a fusion of religion and medicine in the Indo-European avatar lineage encompassing both Christ and Babaji:

> *Absentia* is a direct contact through the mystical powers of the *Sacred Words* and *Symbols* from the healer to the Christ consciousness of the healee. We are making contact with the 5th Etheric Body, the Body of the 7th Chakra.... If the energy does not flow from your hands when you attune to the energy of *Absentia,* the healee's Christ Self is speaking to you saying, "The lower desire consciousness will not utilize the energy for his highest good and is not ready to change his present consciousness, perception and vibrational energy level...." It is his free will choice to continue as he is now. If you become emotionally involved or angered at his resistance, simply bless both you and him and surround each of you with unconditional love, forgiveness and light. When the time is right (Divine time), his free will shall desire to reunite with his "I Am Christ Consciousness," and no longer have the desire to be lonely and separate from God's promise to humankind: to be One with the Father.[30]

There is no way to lose here. The options are evolve now or postpone evolution until one is ready.

Rebirthing

As taught by Leonard Orr and his disciples, rebirthing and its offshoot vivation are presently the most popular set of psychospiritual breathing exercises. The legend of rebirthing places its origins in an unlikely episode. Feeling strong anxiety upon remaining too long in a bathtub, Orr decided to override his urgency to get out and experimented instead with breathing sequences. As the rhythm of his breathing changed, he began to undergo profound emotional releases, including what seemed to be birth memories.

Rebirthing therapy is no longer limited to the reliving of one's own birth and its associated traumas. It is meant to elicit a breath-based repetition of all moments not fully integrated at the time they were first experienced. The presumption is that the lack of integration was either amplified or locked into a repetitive pattern by a concomitant inhibition of breath. A fuller breath allows the reexperience of the trauma to be relaxed and even joyous; thus the attendant block is released. "Breathing is the basic healer," Orr acclaims. "We can clean ourselves inside and out with spiritual breathing. Our natural divine Breath of Life can become inhibited at birth and throughout the School of Hard Knocks. Conscious breathing is a delight. It is more satisfying than fine food."[31]

As a technique, therapeutic rebirthing teaches a strong, rhythmic breathing cycle guided by a positive imagery that may seem naively optimistic from outside the context of the therapy. As the patient breathes in and out, she gradually propagates a connected flow of breaths (the bathtub has become unnecessary, and dry rebirthing is now much more common).

Initially one's forced breathing is erratic and painful, and it is difficult to establish any rhythm. One may feel as though she is drowning in air. When a smooth cycle is established, one floats—the body through the passage of breaths, the mind through a wonderland of images. In optimum circumstances, the journey takes on the ecstatic quality Orr described. The breaths come as waves. There is little sense

of time passing. Stuck places are experienced as bumps, or choppy surf, some of them barely more than blips, others as breakers and often quite frightening. If a smooth breathing cycle is maintained, one passes through this surf not only unharmed but in some sense unburdened of the source traumas that are energizing it. Rebirther Bob Frissell explains:

> . . . [T]his is not a regressive process to take you back to birth, early childhood and so on, even though memories of these experiences may come up for you in a session. What alone matters about these incompletions from the past is what you are currently carrying with you in a way that continues to manifest in present time. . . . What you are carrying with you in the form of stuck energy definitely feels like something, and you can access it in that way. . . . The process then is about breathing, relaxing, and tuning into feelings and shifting the way in which you have been habitually holding them in avoidance, resistance, and making wrong.[32]

One might add that in this regard feelings serve as markers for diseases. Obstructions are not just emotional; they germinate into colds, flus, allergies, asthma, and other more serious disorders. They are the seeds of potential tumors. The flood of breath literally melts these knots in their earliest stage as thoughts or barely materialized intentions. If they are already materialized, it begins softening and dissipating them. One races through the knots as mere energy. Rebirthing is thus a process of cultivating one's own natural healing breath.

The exhale is forcibly shortened and swept up immediately in a new inhale (a process of *prana* circulation sometimes denigrated as hyperventilation). In a simultaneous exercise of affirmation, one transforms this breath into a spiritual energetic act. At the deepest possible level we acknowledge our basic situation and embody it. Because our lesser mind is preoccupied with its egoistic concerns, it is up to the Higher Self to "remember" who we are. We affirm from this Self that our experiences and sensations (however frightening or painful) are positive, that the most sublime forces in the universe are trying to heal

us, that we are meant to be healthy, and that even a threatening event is exactly what we chose for ourselves right now.

As Higher Self, we invented this universe and willed it into being. Now that it is happening, we can't pretend to be its innocent victim.

We not only tell ourselves this in a series of resolutions or a parable. We open all the pores and energy gates of our bodies to its rightness. We want not simply to affirm or believe it but to *become* it. We want to feel as we would if we were this confident of our own birthright and the universe's good intentions. Then every event in the world and every experience inside ourselves becomes curative. (As an experiment, the reader might try a simple version of this practice the next time he or she feels a recurrent stress pattern or a knot of anxiety, or awakes in the middle of the night and is unable to go back to sleep. Simply breathe and affirm every feeling, including discomfort, and, if that doesn't change things, breathe more consciously with a shorter exhale and make the affirmations more real and less merely "going along with the game." Believe them *literally*.) Affirmation is what turns mere breath into *prana*.

The rebirther's cadence is not the jogger's engine of inhale/exhale; it is an overall kinesthetic, mind/body integration of sensations and feelings as they arise. Affirming is not just a matter of making adversity okay, as in the familiar Western process of toughing things out, running the last mile with gritted teeth. That won't accomplish anything in rebirthing. It is more a matter of: "This experience is perfect. If it does not feel perfect, I will make it so simply by declaring it. My word is unnecessary because the universe is saying the same thing. But my word is enough." Frissell adds:

> Fundamental to expanding your ability to relax into and feel the bodily sensations is the context in which you are holding your experiences. At the very least you need to be willing for sensations to be the way they are, even if you don't like them. This *will* work. Even more useful, however, is the willingness to hold everything you are feeling as a healing in process. By relaxing into and allowing your feelings on the deepest level you will create your own healing.[33]

One is never deemed deficient for having been sick or blocked in the first place. Guided by our Higher Self, each of us is simply involved in a protracted learning process which at this very moment has come to its perfect fruition. That is why we are consciously breathing. Familiar affirmations in rebirthing are:

> Pretend that you personally ordered whatever you are making wrong to be exactly the way it is. . . . See that whatever you are making wrong is part of being alive right now, and it is exactly the way it is. It is a miracle that whatever you are making wrong even exists and that it happened at exactly the right time for you, didn't it?[34]

These could sound like instances of the most sentimental and myopic New Age tripe, but they could also be taken seriously precisely as stated. We can put our attention on the stubborn facts of misery and disease and dismiss energy and affirmation as wishful thinking, but then our problems become self-fulfilling prophecies. Cynicism, after all, affects the person who holds it (and has internalized it) more deeply than the person toward whom it is directed in contempt or machismo. On the other hand, we can naively accept the sensations of connected breaths and breathe ourselves into another place.

As expanded breathing heightens awareness, one automatically returns to those past unintegrated experiences and begins to reprocess them in a healthy fashion. This includes physical diseases, chronic conditions, and even acute maladies. Although one must be a skilled rebirther to heal visceral organs, in principle it is possible. Frissell describes it as house cleaning. "Who would want to live in a house that hasn't been cleaned for forty years?" he asks. "But," he says, "many of us live in exactly such dwellings." The rebirthing breath blows through the house with the searing luminosity of *prana,* dislodging malignancies, traumas, nausea propensities, indigestion, etc., in a single lucidifying wave. All of these are swept away as cobwebs of shallow breathing.

The longer the breathing goes on, the more traumas and debilities are reclaimed—usually the deeper and older ones last. For those who hold a past-life belief system, the breathing cycle not only "rebirths" the most recent painful birth (and everything thereafter) but unfinished moments from other lifetimes.

The role of the practitioner is that of a guide and protector. She may occasionally give instructions to remind the breather to stay conscious of the breath cycle and to continue to allow experiences to arise and then to affirm them. Just by breathing fully in concert with her client, she reminds him of the journey they are on together. It is as though the pair were traveling through parallel internal landscapes. Skilled rebirthers learn to share (perhaps telepathically) the actual crises of their clients on the precise breaths in which they are undergoing them and thus to supply their own breathing as part of the greater healing and repatterning cycle. They realign themselves and the stuck person with one universal flow of energy.

Yet rebirthing is not bodywork. The rebirther does not aid the client by massage or even light touch. The system's guidelines emphasize that any person has the ability to rebirth naturally and will do so if physically unaided. Were a rebirther to assist the process (and here the birth metaphor prevails), she would be reinvoking the intrusive obstetrician who (in most instances) made birth a traumatic experience the first time.

Leonard Orr gradually came to view his guided breathing as much more than just a process of aerobicizing and healing with meditation and positive thinking. He suspected he was on the verge of a science of immortality, and he began training the breath as an agency of total bodily transmutation. If creatures naturally cycle *prana* as well as air, they should be capable of incredible feats of cellular mutation. They should be able in fact to renew their basic anabolic energy. The adverse is also true: unless they expand to permit *prana* flow into their systems, its nourishment is dissipated and lost—or worse—transformed into an adversary which turns against them as fear and rigidity. Cut off from their natural healing energy and confronting it as an enemy, they become sicker and their life-span is shortened.

By extension of this logic, traumatic experiences and ailing sites do not just come to awareness randomly during rebirthing cycles. They return literally because *prana* is so powerful and pure that anything which is less pure is drawn immediately to the surface to be addressed. This is why the process of affirmation must be continuous and conscious and the breathing ever more precisely delegated. Unless the momentum of the breath is facilitated by the widest possible systemic assimilation, it begins to shrivel back into lower breathing. There is no middle ground: one is either expanding or contracting.

With rebirthing, we are reclaiming the *pranic* base of ourselves, running our dark and impeded energy through a cosmic cleansing. If we do not constantly remind ourselves that this is not only perfect but precisely perfect, the process might trigger terror and retreat. In fact, it often does initially arouse terror, but by our immediately embracing it, the sensations behind that terror become joyful and link us to the larger cosmos. Orr ultimately came to promote his system as a rediscovery of a lost Vedic science:

> Rebirthing is an American form of prana yoga that is closest to Kriya Yoga. It may be called scientific breathing rhythm or spiritual breathing. Simply described, it is a relaxed, intuitive, connected breathing rhythm, in which the inhale is connected to the exhale, and the inner breath is merged with the outer breath. This merging of pure life energy with air sends vibrations through the nervous system and circulatory system, cleaning the body, the human aura, and nourishing and balancing the human mind and body.[35]

As his original persistence in the bathtub proved, Orr was not one to take halfway measures. During a trip to India he purportedly met the immortal saint Babaji in an embodied form and received his permission to transmit the esoteric yoga of healing and immortality to the West. Orr describes Babaji and their relationship:

> For Jesus to go through physical death or for us to do it is a big deal, but Babaji is the total master of life and death. For Him physical death is a plaything which He uses to raise the consciousness of his Devotees.
>
> He appears to me [now] almost daily as a bird, bug or as a human. At a certain point in your relationship [to him] you can tell the difference and, at another point, there is no difference. Babaji is all over. He is a particular historical person and also omnipresent.... He is mortal and immortal at the same time.[36]

So whereas rebirthing may have begun as a lay therapy for transforming a painful delivery from the womb, it grew into an occult science and a theosophical religion. At an exoteric level it still functions as a breath journey for assimilating and transforming all negative emotions; at an esoteric level it is a system fusing breath and mind to alter cell activity and assemble a new conscious body. From this standpoint, every human being is potentially Babaji, can master the physical realm, and thus can continuously heal, refresh, and rebuild his or her body at the organic base, even as Yogananda was reported to have done. Orr's destiny became a doctrine of immortality for the masses:

> The belief that death is inevitable will kill you if nothing else does. But the truth is that your spirit is already eternal, you only have to move your mind and body into harmony with your eternal spirit.... Unless your parents are already immortal, you have probably inherited a death wish.... You kill it by unraveling your negative thoughts and feelings about death one at a time [like the waves experienced in rebirthing]. Death has no power except what you give to it in your own mind. Nobody can kill you but you. No one can kill you without your consent. Life is stronger than death.[37]

As religious metaphor this is neither unique nor new. But Orr didn't mean it as metaphor. He proposed immortality as an accessible technique on the level of learning to drive a car, arguing that the only reason this hasn't achieved universal recognition yet is a profound species-wide death wish—that is, death is the most deep-seated and

stubborn habit of the human race. People die because they assume they will die and are taught this from the beginning of life and because they refuse to change their minds and assimilate the pure energy that is available. Living forever is a natural skill to be cultivated:

> The physiology of Physical Immortality is based on personal inner awareness of our energy body. It is learning how to clean and balance our energy body on a daily basis with earth, air, water and fire.[38]

Whatever judgment one may have about this notion as science (or hubris), one should not overlook the implications of the mind-sets it trains. I accept Orr's good faith and take him at his word. I also think he is going to die. But by stating the incredible so matter-of-factly he presages a more credible possibility: one can transform the habit of neurosis and presumption of misery through a breathing technique and make oneself into a healer. After all, if death is a mirage, what is lack of self-esteem or physical disease?

The esoteric level of rebirthing trains a new attitude toward the relationship between body and spirit—an attitude expressed simultaneously in breathing and thought patterns. Immortality is the password for that relationship; it is not meant to be a guarantee of everlasting life.

Ideas about transfusion of body into spirit (matter into energy) are not in themselves shocking. They are part of everyday Christianity. They permeate science, holography, telecommunications, and cybernetics. But we do not usually take such ideas personally. Not only do we not live them, we do not know how to live them. In fact, most people believe that we cannot live them. They are meant for the general universe, not for us as individuals. "Think again" is, in essence, what Orr says.

A more conventional and watered-down version of his thesis might be: We are assemblages of elemental substances based in energy fields. Our minds are also energy fields. If we cleanse and renew these fields in the manner taught by ancient yogis and avatars, then we can travel at will between matter and energy, body and spirit. We can redirect negative thought patterns and deter their replication in the flesh. We might also be able to change the basic catabolic "thought pattern" that leads to our dying. After all, if mind and body are both energy, then if we become absolutely skillful we should be able to prescribe any pattern for them we want, including new bodies (like the Kriya master Bhartriji who "can have two bodies if he wishes [and] . . . can adjust the age of his body as easily as we adjust the dial on our TV").[39]

But Orr is not saying it is easy to become that skillful. I do not even think he is saying that it is possible, though he would surely dispute me on this point. Trickster that he is, Orr states everything with the same casual certainty, so it is not possible to know what he truly believes. I am not sure it is even important. The real issue is: does rebirthing work? Does it heal neurosis and physical disease?

If rebirthing works, then the rhetoric is merely another affirmation, a means of invoking the correct mind state for personal growth.

We have no idea what might be possible eventually through human consciousness. Of course I know that, despite the legends of Babaji and Bhartriji and Orr's confident assertions, average people cannot simply turn immortal. However, I wonder what *can* they accomplish by simply breathing and taking responsibility for healing themselves *as if they might live forever?* And what might be possible after many centuries or even millennia of such practices? How would an Earth populated by many such beings change? If we don't ask such questions and entertain such possibilities as real, we will never unlock the potential of humanity. Even beginning this process may be generations away from us, but that is no excuse for not taking the first step and finding out what it does.

"Not your average American lifestyle,"[40] Orr wistfully concludes.

Faith Healing and Karma

WITH SO MUCH potential in laying on of hands, channeling discarnate spirits, shooting energy out of palms, and breathing immortal bodies, why then do people get sick and die? Why is spirit healing at best sporadic? Why can results not be replicated? Drunvalo Melchizedek offers one explanation:

> We live in a school, and so diseases actually do serve a function. There is a learning process in it. A lot of times when I ask permission of someone if I can heal them—not me, but if I can be involved in that process—their Higher Self will come in and say, "No, uh-uh, get away." And I have to back away from it. In fact, I find this about fifty percent of the time because that person's learning something. They're learning compassion; they're learning patience; they're learning humility.... On the other hand, sometimes the person has learned the lesson but has become attached to the pain or the situation and doesn't know how to break that—in which case the Higher Self will usually say, "Yeah, if you can do something, go ahead." I had to learn a hard lesson on that one time when I had a very good friend who was almost dying in the hospital—she had a baby who had died in her and been dead about a month, and the infection went through her whole body. And they didn't think that she would live for another two or three days. My inclination was, "I want to help you." And when I went to her Higher Self, it said, "No, stay away!" In fact it was very energetic about it. It really did not even want me to get near her. I backed away and said, "Okay." But I felt in myself that she would probably die—which is okay too. I mean there's nothing wrong with dying; it's part of life. But what happened was—and I saw the wisdom in the whole thing afterwards—she healed herself all by herself, and in the process became a much stronger and better person.... My interference could have really harmed her.[41]

We have touched on this theme before in our discussions of Reiki and the extraction of the disease object in psychic surgery. Spiritual healing proposes to embrace every kind of medicine, drug, and technique but only in the context of the sick person's karma and place on the path of life and death. Potentially the spirit healer can do anything, but if he did, then there would be no need for the complexity of life experience. Everyone would become healthy and complete and behave

only in behalf of universal compassion. We barely have a healer on the planet capable of this, so we can hardly hope to cure the whole populace. Instead, we are being asked—and this is explicit in the global situation—to heal ourselves.

Agency

THIS SECTION OF the book is a shot in the dark. It picks up on the medley of wild speculation from the first edition and carries it through to the mid-1990s.

In keeping with my discussion of faith healing and Immortality Yoga, I propose the following series of scenarios as the way we must think about ourselves in order to swim toward who we are. None of the scenarios could be true; yet each one expresses a splinter of the greater truth. They are meant to intimate the vastness of the backdrop against which we are searching for our small answers. Sometimes I imagine that the fabric of reality is cohesive enough that we can trace cause and effect in cures; other times I believe we are fooling ourselves with a make-believe coverlet that is coming unravelled at every possible margin, and we merely pretend to explain the simplest thing. The cosmos is likely far murkier than we ever allow, and what we call truth may be better characterized as the "truth mystery."

The interpretations of mythology and magic that underlie all of the upcoming scenarios may be profound and radical on one level but they are utterly naive and nonsensical on another. For most educated people, such speculation is outrageous to the point of being beyond the dignity of a simple hearing. My goal is not to take the side of readers who jump ship here or those who feel I am finally getting to the heart of everything. The "stories" I am about to tell reflect a verity we cannot intuit any other way. In fact, it may be that our most significant truths are hidden so far beneath the surface of appearances that they can be plumbed only by extraordinary statements of myth and hyperbole.

Such accounts—both hermetic and extraterrestrial—are rich and detailed along a parameter that encourages and privileges our dreams and intimations of something remote and invisible. They are also impoverished to the point of absurdity along any parameter of structural depth or acknowledgment of sublimation, distortion, and concealed text. Their basic rule of thumb goes something like: this was written in stone in the Sumerian tablets; this was reexperienced under hypnotic regression; this was communicated during an abduction; I channeled this from Ramtha and Seth; this is what the Huichol elders say; this appears identically in Tibetan and Egyptian sacred art; this crashed at Roswell, New Mexico, and was *not* a spy balloon; the dimensions of the Great Pyramid repeat the orbital relationships of the Earth, Moon, and Sun; the structures on Mars describe a star tetrahedron; hence, this is all divine law . . . and this was left by extraterrestrials.

Sigmund Freud, Jacques Derrida, Claude Lévi-Strauss, and others provide structural models for the human mind and for our institutions and myths. People are presumed not to have received cosmic messages from outsiders, totem beings, or ancestors but to tell such a story because there is no other way to explain our amazing situation or arrive at meaning (see "The Origin of Social Categories" in Volume One, Chapter Three).

Human beings hide things endlessly in other things: words and categories within other words and categories merely by happenstance and random semantic play, fantasies in myths and myths in fantasies, small gestures in barely larger gestures that eventually encompass themselves and each other in a jungle of symbols. Most of this activity is carried out with exquisite subtlety but not even mundane let alone cosmic significance.

The sacred-geometry, faith-healing scions project *only* cosmic significance onto every myth, temple grid, and coincidental reference. The structuralists find only the invention of culture (raw and virgin) in the "savage mind."

One side (psychoanalytic) locates the depth of our consciousness

in its sheer labyrinth of mostly neurotic and incomplete thoughts (which nonetheless contain significant power to heal pathologies of psyche and even tissue); the other side (sacred) presumes the depth of our consciousness in the fact that we remain clandestinely in touch with a cosmic network of which we are part. From their standpoint, all our fables represent attempts of a higher and more cohesive (not a lower and more disjunctive) intelligence to contact us. Both sides believe that healing arises from our fragments and unconscious awareness; yet each side is unequipped to respond to the richness and complexity of the other. I can hardly picture an intelligent dialogue between José Arigo and Claude Lévi-Strauss, though I could be wrong. I *know* that there can be no intelligent dialogue between Jacques Derrida and Leonard Orr.

My sense is that both sides reflect the truth mystery of our human situation, but they are visions arising from entirely different temperaments, intellects, and sensibilities.

Scenario One: Spirits in Other Dimensions

The universe is not as we perceive it. Although scientists propose to characterize all events, they like the rest of us are operating with five senses that record a meager portion of the *known* spectrum of radiation (and they are relying as well on only a few aspects of those five senses). Data—or the claim of data—received internally and subjectively must remain a separate kingdom with its own precedents, ethics, and rules, but that kingdom occupies a large space within the folk traditions and street wisdom of the Earth.

Many people "experience" poltergeists and/or other spirits. In her book *The Unquiet Dead* (the title of which speaks for itself), Edith Fiore describes how, with clients under hypnosis, she is able to address the distinct personalities of a virtual legion of spirits, all with their own motivations and agendas, who attach themselves to anything with a body.[42] The original realms of these spirits are not perceptible to us in a routine way. Psychics who dissent in the particulars of their descriptions of these other realms all agree that our dimensional level on the

Earth is but one possible zone in which to be alive and aware, and (the bulk of them assert) it is not a particularly elevated one.

Scenario Two: Aliens, or Aliens and Spirits Confused

Our purported involvement with spirits is not quite the same as our embattled relationship to extraterrestrials. After all, extraterrestrials are presumably the outcome of molecular chemistry and natural selection on their own planets and have had to travel here over vast distances in ships, whereas spirits, whatever planet was their origin, are not presently embodied on this plane at all. If they "traveled" here, it was through a nonmaterial dimension. However, the two sets of outsiders tend to overlap in our interpretations of them. As long as contactees do not know the source of an encountered humanoid or leprechaun (and these visitors either do not tell them or give every indication of lying), we could assign any such beings either to the unknown realms of other dimensions or merely across vast physical distance to other solar systems. Even this distinction may not be a durable one. After all, the supertechnologies of more advanced planets may allow multidimensional travel.

The general failure to make a distinction has come under greater scrutiny late in the twentieth century when people—almost randomly with respect to regions of the world, educational levels, and walks of life—report intimate contact with intelligent creatures who are seemingly not human and claim that they come from other planets. These beings, not unlike those from exotic races portrayed in the "Star Trek" TV series, invariably have developed remarkable techniques for psychokinetic healing and/or machinery that allows microsurgery and genetic engineering far beyond our level of expertise. One popular rumor is that the ancestors of one of these races cloned our species hundreds of thousands of years ago from their own tissues and the tissues of native terrestrial primates like Pithecanthropus. They presently cut flesh out of cattle and steal dead birds for continuing biotechnological research.

Scenario Three: Exile and Repatriation

The Earth ostensibly has been a stronghold of the Lucifer Rebellion for the past 10,000 years. Thus, our whole technology is a kind of rinky-dink imitation of the real internal science most of the higher races of the cosmos have mastered. We have cars and planes and computers and use rockets pathetically to penetrate the most meager spans of the universe. We treat our diseases from without. Meanwhile, the real science of most of the beings in the universe is the science of healing (and creating) through mind and breath. The whole of spiritual and faith healing is an attempt to get back in touch with a cosmic order of physicians.

Yet as long we build and rely on machines, we will lose in ourselves the precise equivalents of each power those machines tender. We cannot cross galaxies because we have restricted ourselves to mere spatial travel. We cannot heal directly, except sporadically, because we have created artifacts to work in our stead. The cosmic order of physicians is willing, but our hearts are closed.

In a millennial prophecy that seems to arise as much among American Indian secret societies as among UFO contactees, the spirits and/or visitors now claim that the whole Earth is about to pass into a new dimensional manifestation (the usual deadline is the second decade of the twenty-first century), into a realm variously iconicized as the Fourth World, the fourth dimension, or one of the lower overtones of the fourth tier of vibration. Hopi and other native American and Western esoteric versions differ here, for the Indian versions are totemic and based on ancestral lore. On one thing, all variants agree: Everything which represents material reality will dissolve and either disappear or (in the postmodern version) deteriorate environmentally to the point that, in three dimensions, Earth will resemble Venus—a terminal greenhouse ravaged by sulphuric rain. "There won't even be a bug left," cautions Drunvalo.[43] But by then, he adds, we will safely be inhabitants of a utopian, Garden-of-Eden Fourth World—all of us, even those who have died. Leonard Orr could not have made a more outrageous promise.

A planet transforming itself collectively at the Earth's stage of development is so rare—probably unprecedented in the history of this universe—that concerned and curious spectators have come from all over to view the spectacle, not only from within the Milky Way Galaxy, which represents some fairly hefty distances, but from other galaxies as well. To remain unobserved, as is required by higher law, their spaceships arrive in the fourth overtone, but this latitude is apparently so swamped it has come to resemble a shopping-mall parking lot the week before Christmas. All newcomers in 1992 and thereafter have had to park in the fifth overtone!

Scenario Four: Love

How do the aliens travel so far so swiftly?

Drunvalo proposes a very ancient split in the universe between those who partook in the so-called Lucifer Rebellion and thus have attempted to build substitute external *merkabas,* without love or spirit, and those who use pure love to move among starfields.

Merkabas (sometimes translated from the Semitic as "chariots") are vehicles. In a primitive form, they can be simply cars or planes. In a more sophisticated context, they are devices used for passage between star systems and galaxies, time travel, and transdimensional relocation.

To create an internal *merkaba* one must activate the relationships among the numerical properties of shapes by a process of breathing and affirmation. Pyramids, star tetrahedrons, isocahedrons, duodecahedrons, pure spheres, etc., are the underlying matrices of the very cosmogenesis that brought stars, time and space, worlds and their life forms, and our own mode of consciousness into being. *Merkabas* can be constructed microcosmically if we weave them from a beacon of light, breath by breath, into an astral cloak.

Such an internal *merkaba* is literally a spaceship created by a spiraling sequence of sixteen or seventeen breaths, each fused with (and thus ostensibly energized by) a feeling of love and an image based on three star tetrahedrons. Self-respecting transit across the cosmos has *absolutely nothing* to do with metal ships and jet propulsion but leapfrogs in *merkaba* vehicles from one whole region of the universe to another through the centers of stars. Entry into Sirius, for instance—a foolhardy act which would occasion instantaneous incineration in our primitive form of spacecraft—in an appropriate vehicle sets one on a swift issuance out through our Sun. These vehicles are composed of feelings as well as matter; their propellant (and the medicines and life-support systems of their occupants) is the full-blown transmission of pure love![44]

Pure love is not romantic love or anything resembling a Valentine's Day conceit. It is molecular-telepathic love, divine love as an actual

force, like gravity, which Christ consciousness once drew on in its Divine Incarnation on Earth but which we are now having difficulty manifesting even in trifles because of our obsession with machines. It is the purest and most resonant energy in the universe and the only one that propels mind and matter at speeds faster than light. This force is the major factor in the cohesion of substance and gives rise to romantic love and all creatures born from syzygy. It is the basic universal medicine. (Reich's cosmic superimposition arrived at stellar orgone and galactic medicine from a diametrically opposite point of reference.)

In summary, so-called UFOs can be fashioned in two different ways: they are either built of metal and fuelled by chemicals or fabricated out of sacred images and fuelled by feelings.

Scenario Five: Scenario Two Revisited

"Love" is only one possible answer. Once we admit a plethora of outside entities and divine forces, there is no end to what is possible. All manner of disincarnate intelligences and transdimensional energies—for cursing or for curing—can be summoned by a magician or healer. Each suggests a medicinal or disease system. More materialistic and scientifically advanced beings from other worlds and dimensions can contribute psychotronic tools and technologies still removed from us by billions and billions of years, machines that resemble the artistry of pure love and seem as powerful (from our primitive vantage) but are actually its diametric opposite. By such a time, argue some enthusiasts, anything will be possible, including intervention in our world across time.

So we are confronted with the contradiction of aliens or spirits who either wound and hypnotize or heal and empower and who resemble or masquerade as each other. Any of these extraterrestrial creatures might behave identically to the postulated hidden intelligences of cells and coronas of the body, so their hypothetical presence becomes another way of explaining the same things. We can blame our misfortunes or credit our healings to extraterrestrials and humanoid intelligences much

in the way aboriginal peoples assigned agency to pagan spirits and ancestors. By this argument the agency of faith healing is always spirit guide or trickster. He, she, or it needn't even visit our planet or dimension (read on).

Scenario Six: No Extraterrestrial Visitors or Spirits but Messages and Implants

Let us take this investigation further into fringe science and science-fiction myth: Electronics engineer L. George Lawrence, in experiments conducted in 1971 in the middle of the Mojave Desert (in Southern California) with cacti, wild oak, yucca, electrodes, and a telescope pointed at the heavens seemed to pick up messages from planets in Ursa Major, or rather he claimed to pick them up in the living vegetal tissue of terrestrial plants! At least the parameters of shielding and directionality he applied suggested that interpretation to him. Thus, there are no ETs in this scenario but merely a holographic movie of them projected so powerfully onto the Earth that it can be tracked in every flower, the cells of every wasp, and in the lattices of our collective unconscious minds.[45] We imagine their presence—and even their activities and accoutrements—only because they are transmitting a subliminal mandala of their world into our minds, holding us collectively in a psychotronic trance. Those who are most sensitive to this transmission report "close encounters" of various kinds; others repress the images and do not even know they exist.

Scenario Seven: Cosmic Conspiracy

Robert K. G. Temple, a British astronomer, proposed in a book published in 1976 that the mythologies of Africa and Egypt contain such exact and accurate references to the double star Sirius (including the existence and rotational period of the companion star, unknown until the late twentieth century) that the Earth might have been visited by beings from one of the planets in this system around 4500 B.C. He suggests (with dubious modesty) that his own account may be the "cosmic

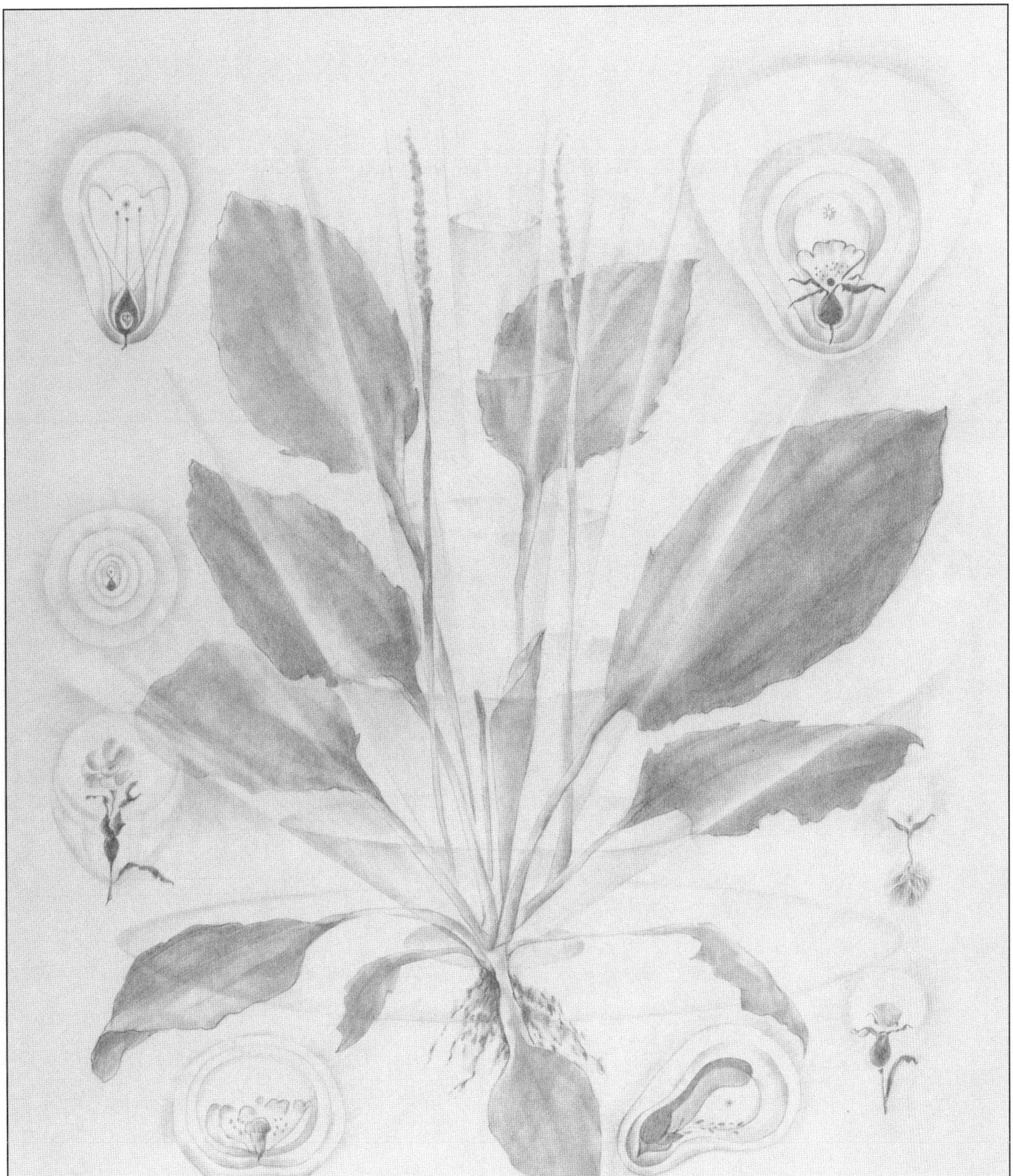

trigger" signaling these beings, who are still monitoring the Earth, that our planet is now ready for direct communication.[46] From this book, Robert Anton Wilson took the title *Cosmic Trigger* for a book propounding his own galactic epic, which links these events and interplanetary botanical communication with the prison martyrdoms of both Wilhelm Reich and Timothy Leary and with the discovery of the psychocosmic potential of LSD 25 by Leary—a conspiracy so vast and over-arching as to encompass all of history and to include the assassinations of John F. and Robert F. Kennedy and Martin Luther King, Jr.[47]

The plot begins with the proposition that our human DNA originates in the planetary system of Sirius and continues to receive or (perhaps) activate messages from there. Political assassinations become intergalactically instigated murders connected to a Secret Government which hopes to horde immortality for themselves, kill the rest of us, and squelch the democratic colonization of space. Wilson suggests that the development of an immortality medicine is our best potential solution to the present terrestrial crisis. Only by a longer life-span can man and woman hope to transit space and complete their galactic mission by traveling in bodies back to Sirius, though this

would hardly be necessary if one could create a UFO of sacred geometry and love and transcend time and space (obviously Wilson prefers the more materialistic route). He also proposes that Leary's LSD is the sole forerunner of such immortality and thus is the biochemical basis of our future. Leary himself is quoted as saying that he fully expects to be alive when our Sun bursts into a supernova and burns to an icy core. Reiki and psychic surgery seem tame beside such manipulations of time, space, and matter.

Scenario Eight: Scenario Two Again, with Ancient Astronauts Masquerading as Spirits

We are trapped in a mechanical-spiritual paradox. We do not know whether we should blast out of here by rockets, lasers, virtual realities, LSD, and their offspring or melt inward and travel from the heart.

We also continue to have a Halloween problem worthy of a Steven Spielberg/Paramahansa Yogananda collaboration. Who is to say the "astronauts" are not leprechauns or spirits or that the archangels and elves of ancient times were not back then, conversely, extraworldly visitors? The pyramids of Egypt are assigned equivalently to Earth-based (if transdimensional) hermetic cults and to advanced races from elsewhere. Remember: even if proposed extraterrestrials could not visit the Earth (too far or too inconvenient!), they could hypothetically communicate the same energy to us telepathically across galaxies (like Reiki masters), intrabiologically through plants, or even as messages in nucleic acid from which they seed the Earth (or once did). This primal substance would then have spawned not only our bodies but our collective unconscious minds. At such a point, the occult rituals of the Egyptians, enacted by Aleister Crowley in the cult of the Golden Dawn, become etiologically synonymous with the wisdom of the Hathor race on the fourth overtone of Venus or ocean-dwellers on the planet system of Sirius.

Scenario Nine: Sacred Geometry in the Hands of Aliens, Ancient Astronauts, or Spirits, or Implanted by Higher Intelligence

This universe is seen as a grand experiment in geometry, a play of forms in which we are the original mathematicians who have located ourselves experientially in an event we continue to improvise. Here on the cutting edge we make reality as we go. And we are alone. Or we are "them." All power extends from the internalization of numerical ratios and primes of numerology (34/21, 46 mitoses to generate the cells in the human body, universal constants such as pi, etc.) in the context of simultaneously opening our heart *chakras*. This is how love in the universe is translated into energy and vehicles of transit, originally by compassion (as in Buddhism) and by direct *prana* breathing (rebirthing), then by a combination of these while building *merkabas* in our *chakras* through a progression of ratios and primes.

In this scenario, the interplay between the binary sequence and the Fibonacci Series is more than just a mathematical equation; it is a source of energy immeasurably greater than nuclear fission, inexhaustible, healing, and nonpolluting.[48] This would then be the hidden source (agency) of all spontaneous healing.

I WILL LEAVE these scenarios and their arguments in turmoil because they go on forever. I went this far with them because I did not want to end the discussion of faith healing with only vague references to cosmic energies and disincarnate intelligences and wild claims about immortality. The hypothetical healing agency is always going to be more complicated than that once you get into the nitty-gritty. Even the most reliable spirits and energies are intermittent, and there is a serious question about their "motives," no matter whether these spirits and energies dwell outside us or are projections of our own *prana* and intelligence. Unfortunately, the idea (and hope) of translating mind or matter consistently into spirit is not the same as the concrete fact of it.

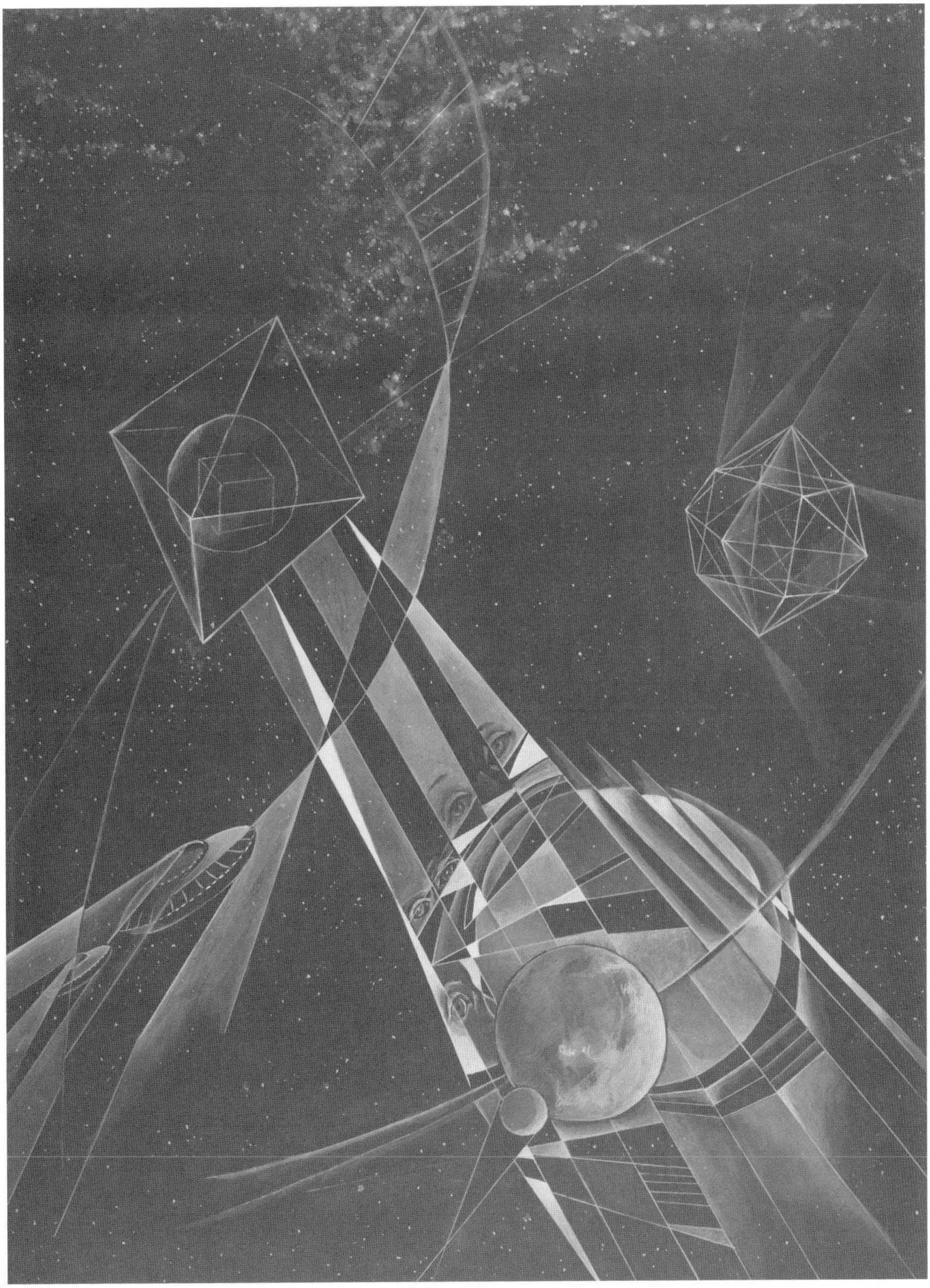

Finally, our relationship to natural healing power is compromised by all our belief systems, whether those systems be ones of utter skepticism or naive acceptance. Any time we assert that "this is what spirit healing and vital energy are" and "this is where they originate," there is someone else with a different allegiance and just as good a story. So, in the end, we are doomed (and destined) to practice and cultivate something which is ineffable and unknown in the context of a greater unknown.

Notes

1. Edward Bach, *Heal Thyself* (London: C. W. Daniel, 1931).

2. David G. Jarrell, *Reiki Plus: Professional Practitioner's Manual for Second Degree* (Celina, Tennessee: Hibernia West, 1992), p. 11.

3. Bodo J. Baginski and Shalila Sharamon, *Reiki: Universal Life Energy. A Holistic Method of Treatment for the Professional Practice/Absentee Healing and Self-Treatment of Mind, Body and Soul* (Mendocino, California: Life Rhythm, 1988), p. 67.

4. Jarrell, *Reiki Plus,* pp. 12–14.

5. Paris Flammonde, *The Mystic Healers* (New York: Stein & Day, 1974).

6. Drunvalo Melchizedek, "Flower of Life Workshop," Dallas, Texas, February 14–17, 1992 (video recording).

7. Edward Whitmont, personal communication, 1986.

8. Anonymous (by request), personal communication, 1987.

9. Edward Whitmont, *The Alchemy of Healing: Psyche and Soma* (Berkeley, California: North Atlantic Books, 1993), p. 66.

10. Ibid., p. 67.

11. Dana Ullman in the preface to Richard Grossinger, *Homeopathy: An Introduction for Skeptics and Beginners* (Berkeley, California: North Atlantic Books, 1993), p. ix.

12. See also Norman Cousins, "The Mysterious Placebo," *Saturday Review,* October 1977.

13. Thelma Moss, "Kirlian Photograph and the Aura," interview with Roy L. Walford, in *Io #19, Mind Memory Psyche,* Plainfield, Vermont, 1974, pp. 173–74.

14. Ibid., p. 174.

15. Brian Inglis, *The Case for Unorthodox Medicine* (New York: Putnam, 1965), pp. 109–112.

16. Paris Flammonde, *The Mystic Healers,* p. 71.

17. Ibid., pp. 165–66.

18. Ibid., pp. 153–54.

19. Ibid., pp. 143–44.

20. John G. Fuller, *Arigo: Surgeon of the Rusty Knife* (New York: Crowell, 1974); reprinted by Pocket Books, New York, 1975, p. 20.

21. Ibid., p. 234.

22. Ibid., pp. 196–200 et seq.

23. Lee Pujols and Gary Richman, *Miracles & Other Realities* (San Francisco: Omega Press, 1990), pp. 169–70, 215.

24. Fuller, *Arigo,* p. 121.

25. Ibid., pp. 119–21 (quotes rearranged for emphasis).

26. Baginski and Sharamon, *Reiki: Universal Life Energy,* pp. 22–23.

27. Jarrell, *Reiki Plus,* pp. 14–15.

28. Ibid., p. 15.

29. Ibid.

30. Ibid., p. 11.

31. Leonard Orr, *Bhartriji: Immortal Yogi of 2000 Years* (Chico, California: Inspiration University, 1992), p. 22.

32. Bob Frissell, *Nothing in This Book Is True, But It's Exactly How Things Are* (Berkeley, California: Frog, Ltd., 1994), pp. 178–79.

33. Ibid., p. 176.

34. Ibid., pp. 203–204.

35. Leonard Orr, *Physical Immortality: The Science of Everlasting Life* (Sierraville, California: Inspiration University, 1980), p. 11.

36. Orr, *Bhartriji,* p. 18.

37. Orr, *Physical Immortality,* p. 9.

38. Orr, *Bhartriji,* p. 22.

39. Ibid., p. 25.

40. Ibid., p. 29.

41. Melchizedek, "Flower of Life Workshop."

42. Edith Fiore, *The Unquiet Dead* (New York: Ballantine Books, 1988).

43. Melchizedek, "Flower of Life Workshop."

44. Ibid.

45. Peter Tompkins and Christopher Bird, *The Secret Life of Plants* (New York: Harper & Row, 1973), pp. 46–49.

46. Robert K. G. Temple, *The Sirius Mystery* (New York: St. Martin's Press, 1976).

47. Robert Anton Wilson, *Cosmic Trigger* (Berkeley, California: And/Or Press, 1977).

48. Melchizedek, "Flower of Life Workshop."

CHAPTER TWO

Healing, Language, and Sexuality

The Healing Dialogue

No matter how much power (and in what physical or spiritual form) is transmitted from a healing source, nothing will improve unless the sick person can receive and assimilate the message. The receptivity of the patient is ultimately more activating than the power of the physician. Somehow, through the nervous system and viscera, the various energy fields hypothesized around the body, and/or the "Intelligence" associated with the cells themselves, a meaning called "cure" is transposed from a medicine or healer into flesh. However little we know about its ontology, the cure must not only communicate to the essential nature of the organism but communicate convincingly *one tiny thing*. An acupuncture needle, a microdose of arsenic, or a surgical excision are equally subject to this law. All healing rests on the potentiation of a curative message.

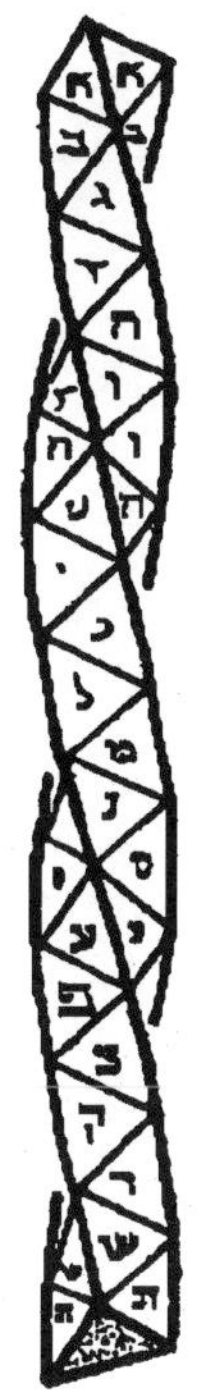

Even conventional medicine awakens the dragon. As much as faith healing it begets a subtextual "dialogue" that conveys personal meanings. The actual curative message may travel not only apart from but *despite* the express methodology of the healer. The best surgeons may be the ones who communicate an *essence* of healing while, at the same time, making appropriate physiological repairs.

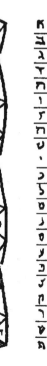

The "worst" doctors are the ones who simply cannot be "spoken to" and—despite their words—say nothing. They continue to talk in the deceptively neutral language of technology and business. They prefer to abstract the patient and to be abstracted. They may be "nice" to a fault, but that niceness is mostly affect—an unintentional parody of the concerned healer. Their expressions of concern mask a lack of real concern. They cannot help but transfuse the persona of the uncaring robot they aloofly mime.

LAYERS OF CODES denominate the various obscurities of our world. Behind every known language is an unconscious language—not only associative codes of the psyche, but buried girders of lost forms and unremembered memories. The archetypal stone axes and hunting paths of ancient tribes are as seminal in this regard as the blueprints for cities and tabloid news. Margaret MacKenzie reports that shamans in the Cook Islands lapse into ancient languages only they and the sick person understand, and then only during actual treatment.[1]

In reality, it is all "language," from cell formation to texts of mathematics describing those cells. We are located in bottomless subtexts of chromosomes, tissue fields, common laws, belief systems, jurisdictions, "technologemes," etc. Even our claims to location in time and space (individually and collectively) are more diagnostic than historical. "Past" and "present," "mind" and "symptom," are conventions. The writing of the world on its own body approaches us as intimately as any disease, so each disease and each cure writes us again as a text.

Some investigators in the early 1990s (most notable among them, Stan Tenen of the Meru Foundation) purported to have discovered a universal series of shapes behind all alphabets and languaging code systems, so that a sacred morphology (representable in its most basic form as a series of two-dimensional projections of a torus inscribed in a three-dimensional tetrahedron) can give rise to all Hebrew, Greek, Arabic, and perhaps even Roman, Chinese, and Cyrillic letters. An alphabet that speaks in the rudiments of creationary geometry and Divine Intelligence is telling us, no matter what we say otherwise, that we are constructed—body and mind as well as speech—from a sacred binary

sequence. Hence, while the text of Genesis narrates the myth of the Creation in one voice, it lays out the precise mathematics of it like an anagram in the assemblage of its Hebrew letters. In this interpretation, there would *always* be two simultaneous writings: one in contemporary vernacular code and the other in the esoteric code of the root iconography. Curative power might thus come from the potentization of a latent alphabet that translates the seed forms of sounds into sequences which are potentiated in the objective psyche and soma. The Qabbala purports to depict the genesis of all matter and shape from the alphabet of Yahweh's speech.[2]

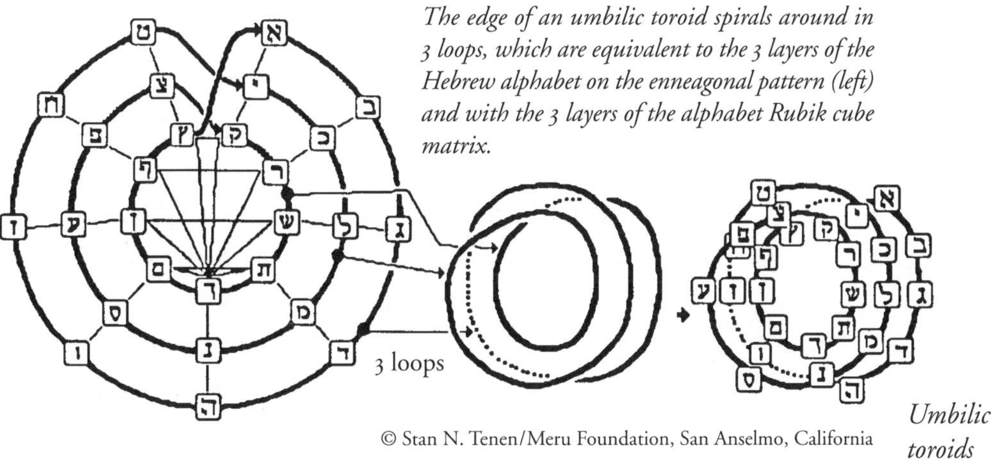

The edge of an umbilic toroid spirals around in 3 loops, which are equivalent to the 3 layers of the Hebrew alphabet on the enneagonal pattern (left) and with the 3 layers of the alphabet Rubik cube matrix.

Umbilic toroids

According to chiropractic theory, "signaling errors" are transmitted from the articulations of the bones, from the nervous system, and within the viscera and settle in both the skeleton and personality. Curative encroachment into this pattern means to tap or arouse signaling mechanisms that are either repetitively tracking or numbed and to break their involuntary nullities. In the simplest, most mechanical sense, the adjustment of the subluxated vertebra merely eliminates the impingement. But, by contemporary definition the chiropractic adjustment is a kind of skeletal "primal scream," releasing energy in a discrete burst. Feldenkrais and Alexander Technique alter

patterning more by "reinstructing" stress cycles. Continuum Therapy arouses subtle motile gestures. Craniosacral unwinding is an indirect seduction of an organism through the intrinsic "desire" for unimpeded function expressed in its cerebrospinal fluid. All of these are language systems, not in the polite or diplomatic sense but insofar as they transmit one form of structured code into another.

Faith healers likewise cure by *addressing* disease, making words and chants into instruments of power and summoning in "divine" rather than "social" voices. Shock of inner recognition is far more effective than mere insight into events. Oral Roberts can stay in Oklahoma; he doesn't have to attend school (if a school is needed, he can start his own). His so-called Christian bias is after the fact. The patients he treats are also Sooners in some fundamental way. He touches the objective part of them, which can recognize him as their medicine.

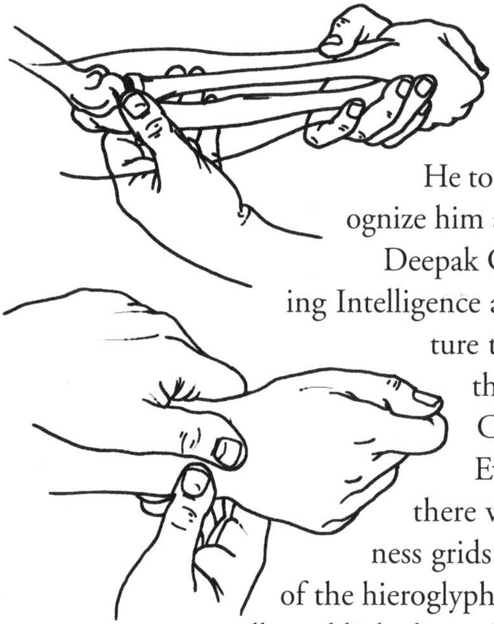

Deepak Chopra posits a field in nature woven of vibrating Intelligence and permeated by waves of cosmic sound (picture these as you will). The billions upon billions of threads that represent the *sutras* of Vedic science, Chopra says, are the "superstrings" of physics. Even as subatomic particles assemble reality where there was nothing, symbolic "messages" can alter illness grids at their core. Cure thus resides in the potency of the hieroglyphs, symbols, or sound units themselves, individually and linked together in sequences. For that reason, he proposes a link compressing "mind, body, DNA, and bliss into one undivided whole,"[3] adding:

> Ayurveda would say that many diseases begin where there is . . . a break—bliss slips out of its groove, so to speak, throwing off the cell's intelligence. To repair the break, a specific signal needs to be inserted back into the circle—a primordial sound. In this way, a vibration is used to cure a vibration. . . .[4]

But it is not always possible:

> Both cancer and AIDS seem to be cases where the proper sequence of *sutras* must be unraveling at the deepest level. In other words, they are failures of intelligence, like "black holes" where bliss gets distorted out of its normal pattern. What makes both diseases so intractable is that the distortion runs so deep—it is locked inside the DNA's own structure. This causes the cell's self-repair mechanism either to break down or turn against itself.[5]

Such may be the case in immune diseases such as lupus and multiple sclerosis, as well as neurological disorders such as strokes and epilepsies. The sickness mimics signaling errors in ways that suggest a reversed replica of embryological code—a cellular speaking in tongues that, rephrased in bliss or some equivalent, might restore the *sutra* of the failed biological transmission.

"Consciousness would be curing people today," Chopra is convinced, "except that we diagnose disease too late, after years of stress have hardened the physiology and made it difficult for bliss to penetrate. But the gate is always open, even if only by a crack."[6]

Holism and Coherence

Holistic practitioners go from whole picture to whole picture. Healers and shamans share this modality of seeking to grasp the coherence of a person, his or her *essential nature,* even when they know little of a disease process. They seek the missing "signal," the primordial sound.

In orthodox medicine, on the other hand, symptoms are separated into quantitative events and set in narrative time-space. Doctors attempt to cure diseases in the ways they have named them. They follow Ariadne's thread through labyrinths of diagnosis: they can stop at any point, effect a partial adjustment, pick up, and follow their thread on, to further partial adjustments—each one a known category.

A holistic healer has established that he will not be working by abstraction or in parts, so he does not need different remedies for different aspects of diseases or ever stronger pharmaceuticals to penetrate the stubborn mass of the body. If a thing is a one, it can be altered by altering, even to an infinitesimal degree, any facet of that one.

Legend has it that Babaji was pestered repeatedly by a yogi who said he could not practice because of a pain in his knee. Finally, the master said, "I will fix your sick knee." He spat on his hand and flung his spit toward the knee. Suddenly it no longer hurt.

I believe the issue here is not the holiness of the spit but the gesture of disinterest, "spoken" so precisely it cut into the obscurity of the other's life. It addressed the deeper distortion, of which the knee was only a warning. Zen koans lead to sudden transformations of being in much the same fashion.

For someone reading this book whose main orientation is allopathic, the objection will arise at some point—if it hasn't already—that "real" medicine treats diseases whereas these various modalities and treatment styles are only self-improvement techniques, placebos, or pseudo-psychotherapies. Whatever one chooses to believe, it is important to remember that holistic treatments are directed toward individuals, not diseases. They are *all of the above:* self-improvement, auto-suggestion, psychoanalytic transference, etc. But they are predominantly medicines. The presumption is that treatment along holistic parameters will influence the *entire* organism and that the transmission of a "meaning" (or, in the previous chapter, an "energy") will be assimilated at all its physical and psychological levels, including those where infections, viruses, tumors, and the like are located. Thus, the holistic disciplines *are* real, though for reasons of an entirely different order from the rationales of scientific medicine.

Where holistic practitioners fail, by their own definition, is when they miss the whole, or when the patient cannot receive or assimilate it. It is one thing to *seek* to grasp essence; it is another to grasp it actually. No partial virtuoso solution can correct this; a healer is committed to the

whole. If he goes to the wrong whole, he has missed the case. But his errors become a path toward future interpretations: he may well arrive at the whole by successive instructive mistakes, as long as he doesn't capitulate to palliating individual symptoms. Homeopaths do this as a matter of course; a wrong remedy can throw everything into perspective and show why something masquerading convincingly as pathology is not the operant disease. Then a new remedy is given, not for the dominant symptom but for the next whole picture. A stomach inflammation may be less deep-seated than a speech impediment or a lameness, especially if these go back further historically and attach more tightly to systemic roots. The body unerringly directs attention to its strain lines: a limp or stutter might deflect the organism many degrees from center, with flaring up in the stomach one highly affected symptom of this tilt.

Healing is finally a dynamic interaction between the character of the disease and the character of the medicine (broadly defined), no matter how these are framed.

Addressing the Practice of Self-Cure

On the level of disease and cure the organism probably goes through a process of unconscious training and reeducation similar to that of a beginner at martial arts. Students of *t'ai chi ch'uan* often remark how their form changes over the years even though they were ostensibly always doing "the form." One practitioner told me he was startled to realize only after some five hundred classes "That's what the teacher means by 'move from the center.' He doesn't mean, 'Get an image of the center and sort of shift that way.' He means—there really is a center to the body."

Likewise, the master instructs the student to "sink." But how? Peter Ralston, a proficient martial artist, recalled that for many years he tried to lower his body in every imaginable mechanical and mental way, using different exercises and images, and suddenly one day he let go

of an unexamined image on which he was relying without realizing it; then his entire being sank as though on its own.

For instance, Ralston continued his tale with another story: "You know you're there when a car whips around the corner and there's no time to think. Instead of jumping up, which is perhaps the first instinct, you go right to the ground and stride past low down. It's faster than thought. You don't think, 'Oh car! I better do what my teacher says and sink!' You find yourself having sunk because you know it at the deepest level."[7]

THE SELF ACTS only on the basis of what it knows for certain. The unconscious, unarticulated animal never visits the physician, or at least never declares itself when the social persona brings it there. The most intransigent diseases lurk in its shadow, but also the most miraculous cures. They exist on the primordial level of a crocodile or wild mouse, which do not even address their existence ontologically, let alone their ailments and dying.

The intellect, no matter how placating and convincing, cannot sell the animal self anything that threatens it. In fact, as Freud recognized, the self already knows the tricks the intellect has for convincing it, so it cannot be convinced. That is the role of the healer. He or she must contact the animal inside the person, the creature on whose needs the fate of everything rests and who can die and take the body with it, without the mind ever suspecting the disease originated in internal conflict and symbolic distortion rather than in germs.

So tricky is the personality that it will take any lesson it learns from the self and exaggerate it in order not to have to learn any more. The success of realignment depends on *not* replacing one inflated gesture with another—that is, it depends on curing cleanly with the stroke of a sword rather than slapping aside a disease like a punching bag only to have it come swinging back later with more force.

One physician writes of the alliance that must be negotiated with "the patient's *practice of self-cure,* which is rigidly established by the time

he reaches us. To treat this *practice of self-cure* merely as resistance is to fail to acknowledge its true value for the person of the patient. It is my belief from my clinical practice that very few illnesses in a person are difficult to handle and cure. What, however, is most difficult to resolve and cure is the patient's practice of self-cure."[8] (italics are the author's)

"When I was very young," Manocher Movlai, the founder of Breema bodywork, told a practitioner, "they brought somebody who had a back problem to my great-grandfather. My great-grandfather asked me, 'Manocher, what do you say about this person?' I said, 'He is sick, he has a back problem.' Then my great-grandfather said, 'That's what you don't understand about Breema! This man is a complete man, a healthy man, nothing wrong with him, and he's playing being sick, he's playing having a back problem!' "[9]

In other words, a patient's practice of self-cure has probably been successful for him *until* this present disease. If he is resisting treatment, it is not because he wants to be sick but because he is trying to participate in a "cure" in the one way he knows how. The physician must convince him to abandon his over-collaboration at the level at which it interferes—that is, abandon its negative aspects without abandoning its characterological energy. Once again, it is not a matter of literal dialogue between doctor and patient, but one of the doctor seducing the patient's latent resistance to aid rather than hamper a cure. This can be in the form of a needle at the correct point on the correct meridian, an herbal formula, an allopathic pill, an insight, or calling attention to a butterfly suddenly in the room.

Medicine will remain obscure to the degree that our lives are obscure. A system of healing must finally reach within and touch real imperatives, as the Yellow Emperor reached within the lives of his "subjects." It simply doesn't work to give up all to science and technology and to the verdict of Western history and ask them to solve it—and then only when it is manifested as disease and discomfort. We are more in the battle than this.

Character

EMPIRICAL INDIGENOUS MEDICINES are invariably based on reading character. Each system develops its own method of "character," both of people and illnesses, and sometimes also of medicines. In psychiatry, character is defined in terms of personality, but in most medicines on the Earth it is defined mythologically and converted as such into healing modalities. It may disclose itself as a shaman mask, a toad or killer whale, a sand-iconograph of clouds, or the visage of a spirit. For this reason, native bodywork may incorporate invocation of demons or acting out of supernatural beings. Chants may embody not only the breath and throat muscles but the whole objective psyche/soma: heart, intestines, limbs, emotions, and totems. Within the unity of Spirit/Intelligence a mandrake cry radiates throughout the anatomy, partly in the breath, partly along the integrative network of meridians, and partly in the long-term relationship between the voice and the frame of meaning in a society. Character is a replica of energy—both energy expressed and energy denied. It literally takes its "character" from the person's whole energetic state. Psychoanalyst John P. Conger defines this in contemporary language:

> Character provides a meeting place for psyche and soma. Character as a defense structure gathers us when we are scattered and organizes us into an identifiable pattern of rigidity and energetic withdrawal, binding our anxiety, rage, sadness and longing. Character is what keeps us separate, exempt and special, and what holds us back from surrender to our energetic nature. Character represents a practice of self-cure, an ongoing, hasty, rigid solution imposed over our instability to maintain an intact sense of self. Daily our anxiety persuades us not to relinquish our protections.
>
> Typically, when character establishes itself in a growing organism, it disrupts and inhibits the scheduled somatic function, so that muscle remains flaccid and unresponsive. With our diaphragm contracted and the ribs gripped with

> fear, we may never establish a pattern of full breathing. We may never develop coordinated movement between the left and right side. We may never stand up and walk in a natural easy way. Character is the shell that energy leaves behind, and as such it provides a house; but the shell, as we grow, becomes too small.[10]

African, native American, and Aboriginal Australian character exists always with respect to gods, supernatural forces, and systems of totemism, even as our character manifests in respect to our own social system. A poor doctor in any culture fails to grasp the relationship of the levels on which psyche and soma reconstellate and thus drives the patient around in a superficial mythological, symbolic, and, hence, behavioral circle.

Wilhelm Reich's *Character Analysis* is a basic Western text for reading disease. It would serve equally for an acupuncturist, a homeopath, or a psychiatrist. Freud declared the first rule in reading character: Pay attention to *exactly* what the patient tells you. Reich took it a notch further: It is not what he tells you but how he tells it—his mode of description, his breathing and movement and disposition of energy while he talks, the eye contact he makes or fails to make, his precise choice of words and rhythm of speech, the general sense he has of who is doing the talking. This character knows far more than either the doctor or patient about the ailment. It may be part man, part god; part woman, part ancestor; part human, part beast, part hungry ghost. That is why the Yellow Emperor puts forth what to us looks like a massive diversion constituting a whole system and why the Zen master, from the other side of the coin, continues to ask the student *who,* who is doing the talking.

In ancient Africa, Amerindia, and Australia, although they are not documented as such in the ethnographic literature, we can find thousands of cases of mind-body ceremonies which obviously have a character-emotional import. Consider the following two from Australia and Bali, respectively. We do not know the inside of them, but it is

clear they have equally profound physiological and emotional impacts. Even their mythologies, i.e., their inner voices and drama, have subtle physiological effects transcending our conventional notions of mind and body.

The first case continues the physician initiation in Australia from Volume One, Chapter Five:

> ... a very old doctor threw some of his crystalline stones and killed the novice. Some of the stones went through the latter's head from ear to ear. He then cut out all his insides, intestines, lungs, liver, heart, in fact, everything, and left him till next morning, when he placed more of these stones in his body, arms and legs, and covered his face with leaves. After "singing" over him until the body was swollen up, he put more stones in him. He then patted him on the head, causing him to "jump up alive," and made him drink water and eat meat containing magic stones. When he awoke, he had forgotten who he was, and all the past.[11]

The second case describes the finale of a healing ceremony in Bali:

> By the spell, the krisses in the hands of the men turned against them, but the magic of the Barong hardened their flesh so that, although they pushed the sharp points of the daggers with all their might against their naked chests, they were not even hurt.... Some leaped wildly or rolled in the dust, pressing the krisses against their breasts and crying like children, tears streaming from their eyes. Most showed dark marks where the point of the dagger bruised the skin without cutting it, but blood began to flow from the breast of one, the signal for the watchmen to disarm him by force.[12]

With intimations of acupuncture, bioenergetics, and *Chi Gung,* these ceremonies leave little doubt about the trans-signification of self and other.

I cannot emphasize how subtle and inextricable character is and how central to accessing the core of personality, disease, and health. In the words of Paul Radin, Maori character "is very complex and unusually profound. According to them, man and every sentient being ...

consists of an eternal element, an Ego which disappears after death, a ghost-shadow, and a body."[13]

The eternal element is called *toiora.* It is a spark of the vast divine force materializing mortally. The pure Ego comprises three elements. Its *mauri* arises as its active life principle and also as the symbol for that principle. A material *mauri* might be a tree planted at the birth of the child and an immaterial *mauri* might be the totem of that tree. The Ego also includes the life-essence *(hau)* and the physiological manifestation *(manawa ora).* No standard Freudian (or even Reichian) character analysis will work in a Maori context without addressing these elements of psyche and soma. It may well be that a specific tree (or the symbol of that tree) must be treated at the same time as the person.

> In the ghost shadow, the *wairua,* we are dealing with the soul, strictly speaking. It is partially visible but does not properly possess a material form until it appears in the underworld. *Wairua* is the ingredient which mediates us to the external world; we would be lifeless and decay without it. We might possess the life principle and form but we could not be seen. In the same way it is the *wairua* that enables us to give form to things, to actually accomplish them. A Maori remarked to [Elsdon] Best, "My *wairua* is very intent on this work that it may be well done." It is well to remember this, to realize that it is not simply with our senses that we see and touch and think. "Be of good cheer," a woman was told, "although we are afar off, yet our *wairua* are ever with you." And it is in the same strain that an old Maori wrote to Best, "We have long been parted and may not meet again in the world of life. We can no longer see each other with our eyes, only our *wairua* see each other, as also our friendship."[14]

Healing in a Maori context must incorporate, even as an unstated assumption, the role and condition of the *wairua.* Whether it is "real" or not in a concrete, scientific sense, it is absolutely real in a "character" sense. It is the glue of Maori life.

> Although the *wairua* could not be destroyed, a person could be killed through his *wairua.* It was easily affected by magical spells. It was the *wairua* also that was affected when a man found himself afflicted with fear of becoming evil, with a dream of impending danger, or if he had polluted his *tapu.*[15]

The Maori recognize the physiological body of stomach, intestines, and liver, but it is fully integrated with the *toiora, wairua, mauri,* and *manawa ora.* Elements of personality reside simultaneously in organs (feelings and desires in the heart and stomach, the seat of thought and the mind in the viscera, memory in the stomach, etc.) and in the immaterial aspects of the self.

> Looked upon as a material entity [the body] may have an immaterial form, and regarded as an immaterial entity it may possess a material form. In other words, it possesses, as an integrated unit, both form and substance. The first the Maori call *ahua* and the second, *aria.* . . . Best quotes a Maori as follows: "I saw clearly his bodily form *(ahua);* it is not the case that I saw distinctly *(aria).*"[16]

Yet to heal, one must first see.

When the shaman calls out the illness, he *is,* in that moment, the illness externalized. "I am the crocodile," he chants. "I am lightning. I am a lion. I am a shooting star." Of course, he can externalize the illness only to the degree that his supplicant can internalize him. When his performance resonates along the vector of power and pathology in native vernacular, he merges with the disease and becomes the force which can heal. "My psychic power is strong enough to cause others to believe in themselves,"[17] explained an Australian indigenous healer. All medicine men and doctors address the precise coda in which

character is written in their cultures. The Yellow Emperor likely spoke as the psychoanalyst of his time:

> Beginning and creation come from the East. Fish and salt are the products of water and ocean and of the shores near the water. The people of the regions of the East eat fish and crave salt; their living is tranquil and their food delicious. Fish causes people to burn within (thirst), and the eating of salt injures (defeats) the blood. Therefore the people of these regions are all of dark complexion and careless and lax in their principles. Their diseases are ulcers, which are most properly treated with acupuncture by means of a needle of flint. . . .
>
> Precious metals and jade come from the regions of the West. The dwellings in the West are built of pebbles and sandstone. Nature (Heaven and Earth) exerts itself to bring a good harvest. The people of these regions live on hills, and, because of the great amount of wind, water, and soil, become robust and energetic. The people of these regions wear no clothes other than those of coarse woolen stuff or coarse matting. They eat good and variegated food and therefore they are flourishing and fertile. Hence evil cannot injure their external bodies, and if they get diseases they strike at the inner body. These diseases are most successfully cured with poison medicines. . . .
>
> In the North is the region of storing and laying by. The country is hilly and mountainous, there are biting cold winds, frost and ice. The people of these regions find pleasure in living in this wilderness, and they live on milk products. The extreme cold causes many diseases. . . .[18]

This means precisely what it says and, on the other hand, is so generalized and anonymous it means nothing. It bears a relationship to reality not unlike that of a dream. Its text is literal, but only when we have penetrated its other, surface literality. It substantiates a closed system of diagnosis and health maintenance—a complex which works prior to any application of needles or ingestion of herbs. Its unknown originators have not chosen their images because they are picturesque and suggest Oriental painting. They have chosen them because they were already imbedded in the world, hence in personalities.

The homeopathic materia medica is a compendium of character statements posing as symptom complexes. The doctor must routinely match the image of an individual whole with the image of a disease and a medicine; it is not sufficient simply to add up a majority of parallel symptoms in both. For instance, *Nux vomica,* the poison-nut remedy, is used for a diverse range of ailments, but always on the basis of underlying traits of the medicine, not of symptoms. The *Nux* person is husky, strong, ambitious, hard-driving, even over-ambitious to the point of working all night. He is self-destructively competitive, fastidious, and lacks perspective, preferring to drive himself. This symptom complex is also prone to stimulants and compulsive sex. We must emphasize that these character traits lie beneath any visible pathology yet sustain even life-threatening malignancies. In homeopathy they are "derived" from potentized substances in provings (that is, from the characterological effects that these substances have on healthy people), and medicines made from them are prescribed only on the basis of the Law of Similars. This is homeopathic singularity: the Simillimum in the minimum dose is the single message that potentiates character rigidity into vital energy.

Acupuncture would seem to rest primarily on the subcutaneous transmission of energy from the insertion of a needle, opening internal channels for the circulation of *chi* energy. The acupuncturist, however, starts by taking the patient's pulse. Each wrist has three pulses, and any pulse can be diagnosed at two different levels; in these twelve pulses there are twenty-eight common readings, every one a distinct persona. The pulse may be empty, disappearing on pressure. It may be too urgent, too sunken; it can float on the surface of the skin from the Wind Evil. It may slip and slide; it may overflow from Fire floating and Water dried up. It may bounce like a fiddle string; it may be inflating but leathery from the cold; it may be blurred; it may be shaped like an onion skin, hollow from great loss of blood. It may be overquick and halting or soft and fine; it may be shaped like a bean from fright.

According to *The Yellow Emperor:*

> The feeling of the pulse should be done according to method: for when it is slow and quiet it acts as protector and guardian. In the days of Spring the pulse is superficial, like wood floating on water or like a fish that glides through the waves. In Summer days the pulse within the skin is drifting and light, and everywhere there is an excess of creation. In Fall days the torpid insects underneath the skin are about to come out. In Winter the torpid insects are all around the bone, quiet and delicate like the nobleman residing in his mansion.[19]

We couldn't ask for a more sensitive rendering in layers of character and disease.

Of course, any self-respecting allopath explores beneath the surface, too. His training is to investigate beyond the description and to pay attention to actual physical occurrences *in* the patient rather than to what the patient says. He has access to radiation images and computer analyses; he can utilize surgery and antibiotics, which are directed toward identifiable results. Yet, to be successful, he has to read the patient absolutely at simultaneous levels of nuance and viscera. He cannot fall back on gross diagnosis as an excuse to single out those things that are heavily stated; he cannot rely solely on his tests and X-rays. Otherwise he may cure a layer which is inflamed or psychosomaticized but not truly sick, and not only leave the disease to fester but cut off one of its avenues of expression and dissipation. The surgeon has to first "see" the disease too—the characterological aspects of lab tests and radiation images.

Codes

An obscure healing system which accentuates the symbolic components of cure is "Curative Eurhythmy," a treatment arising from Rudolf Steiner's anthroposophy. Eurhythmy is simultaneously a paralinguistic code of indeterminate depth and a literal rhythmic symbology. Each medicine is "taught" to the patient as a motion-sequence made up of the letters of a "word" the therapist has chosen as a cure.

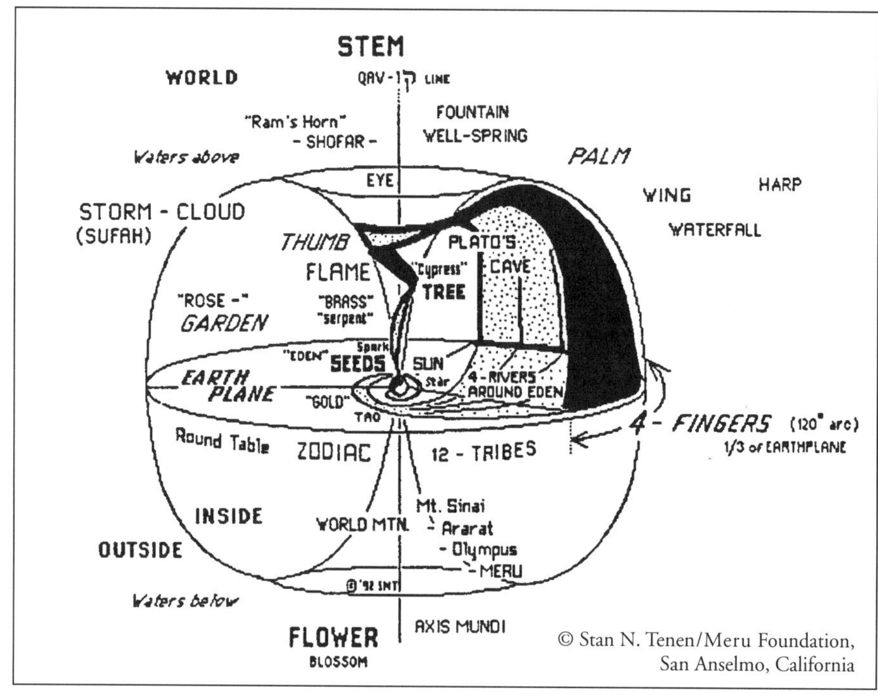

© Stan N. Tenen/Meru Foundation,
San Anselmo, California

He demonstrates the word over and over, and the patient imitates him until he picks it up. The stages of correction *are* the healing process. Each successively less imperfect spelling communicates a layer of compensation to the character—the faulty template of self-cure—but, as the spelling becomes truer and truer, a cure is transmitted.[20] We see elements of this method also in Buddhist mantra healing and Reiki. Eurhythmy summons, as it were, through a glass darkly, the sacred morphology of Tenen's alphabets mentioned earlier in this chapter.

While the seeds of Eurhythmy are basic units of human language, those of *t'ai chi ch'uan* are movements of animals—snakes, birds, fish, monkeys. In Eurhythmy, the body is addressed in letters on the assumption that the etiology of disease and the etiology of language-making share a chrysalis deep in some biological or archetypal code. But *t'ai chi* regards cognitive language as a hindrance to internalization. Men and women must imitate not their own artificial modes of speech but

those natural movements animals make because animals purely exist in the expression of their bodies, *as* language (i.e., signatures) prior to language. There is no strategy or hedging in the escape of the fish or deer, no considered persona behind the attack of the rhinoceros or tiger. They extend objective expressions of their total beings, and it is objective being that we learn from them. We will develop this issue in the next section.

The Steiner "alphabet" is made up of Germanic calligraphy acted out as body postures and movements. Each letter has a gesture, the enactment of which can occur on a number of different planes or scales. A "U" for instance can be written close to the ground or high in the air. It can be suspended vertically or extended horizontally. It can be made with the toes or fingers or with the whole body. The underlying goal is to communicate medicinal essence.[21]

Although vowels and consonants seem to be semi-arbitrary graphemic units of sound, Steiner considered their representations a fixed aspect of their meanings. While a semantic "meaning" is communicated to the conscious self, the inner self receives the discrete primacy of a sound or shape. The relationship of semaphors to actual words is considered true on some level. The sound "M," where it occurs, from "mother" to "hum" to "rhythm," is a Eurhythmic seed, empowered by its relationship to other seeds in a cluster. "S" in "sun" and "sleep" and "asthma" is the same "S," so a remedy with many "S's" might be given to someone with asthma, or those "S's" might be mixed with other seeds in making up different medicines. A person with heart disease might well be given "H's" and "R's" to enact, but only to the degree that they matched his disease. He might also be fed "L's," which would not be surprising, since "L" is "love" and "light" and "life."

A prose song (abridged below) was composed by a lupus patient working eurhythmically with the internal "L" which represented her own name Laura as well as the name of her disease:

> To summon inside—The brave shining warrior, glittering hero of the skies, with flaming sword, astride a horse so white you *know* you

> are ready, to meet and overpower the dreadful. I've got my firm together now, my word drawn up, to hold and to swing into warning. Big "L's" begin lifting, for lightness and levity, raising the sediments Up in the body. L is for *lucia,* I said with my slipper, for all of the liquid that rises and falls into falls to further the flowing to keep us in motion. . . . The globe itself hovers there before you. Yes, you can touch it, give it a little "L."[22]

It may be idealistic to think that we can cure the crab of cancer with microdoses of poison nut or drive out the wolf of lupus by acting letters, but it *is* apparently possible in some manner to confront and tame diseases as characters and masks even as Haitian voodoo actors and Kwakiutl totem dancers do. There is a long tradition on the Earth of chanting and making icons to banish diseases. For people to engage in complexity, rhythm, and art is transformative in some primal sense. These modalities may well persist in medicines because the deepest codes respond to them.

Martial Medicines

IN A CULTURE in which words and symbols make up the trap, discussion and diagnosis are not the best way out of that trap. While Wilhelm Reich certainly nailed that precaution onto psychoanalysis, the characterological base extends, by interpretations of homeopathy, shamanism, chiropractic, Eurhythmy, etc., to biological and archetypal levels. The practice of the somatic—not exercise or affect but the actual practice of the somatic—is a deep-acting medicine.

Many of the current male and female initiation rites (notably the empowered males drumming and dancing to confront the symbols of their weak but tyrannical fathers—and their counterparts, the newly shamanized females of the once and future matriarchy) are *ideas* masquerading as acts. Playing at being shamans and warriors shows how we overendow image and product, how we are incorrigible spiritual materialists.

It is healthier finally to get instruction from a master of *chi.* By engaging with a tradition going back generations one at least is not naively trying to reinvent all of ontological practice. Psychoanalysis and psychological ritual often make this very mistake.

Martial practice allows one's self to bottom out in the expression of one's body. The so-called "soft" martial arts are silent, but recruits must fight their way out of fears and stuck points. Where the self bottoms out, the shadow is no longer the *idea* of a nightmare, a memory of damage done or a fear of danger colored by past trauma; it is a present and actual inability to strike and defend oneself. An opponent, even in a practice situation, is a shadow representation of one's disease tendencies, hence his attack provides ceaseless opportunities to practice movements which are simultaneously martial strikes and feints and medicinal seeds. As the opponent is repelled, the medicinal meaning is communicated inwardly (Eurhythmy). But even if the opponent is not repelled, the body/mind receives a blow or jolt that breaks its apathy (chiropractic).

How one engages an *external* opponent is translated into a healing process through an internalization of combative movements, and vice versa. Whereas psychotherapy proposes to locate trauma in a primal event and then to expiate it through cathexis, *t'ai chi ch'uan* and *aikido* provide sets of affectless moves—aggressions and their neutralizations, punches and their feints, uproots and their evasions, all in the present. These forms integrate *Chi Gung* breathing modes, subtle responses to pressure, sensation of fields around the body and beneath the feet, and fundamental principles of mobility and energy. The activities learned through practicing sets (martial alphabets) are then integrated into sequences of blending with opponents.

In Lomi workshops, traditional martial moves provide modes of character interaction. Students engage their fears by standing in the path of actual strikes and

stepping aside at the last moment. In Wendy Palmer's groups, students train in intuition and blending under the title "Aikido as a Clairsentient Practice." She explains:

> In body-oriented situations like aikido or sports, we do not have time to ask a mental question. By the time we have asked the question, it is too late. In fact, we want to keep the intellect out of it altogether and allow our energy field to respond automatically. In order to suspend thinking, we occupy our attention with basic practice. We concentrate on the movement of our breath, the balance and perimeter of our field, and gravity and our receptivity to the earth. When we focus in this way, our system responds automatically, sometimes brilliantly.[23]

Peter Ralston's "Mind" course is a combination vision quest/psychosynthesis in which participants learn the subtle mental components of all relationships, including those of combat. Unknowing pedestrians on Telegraph Avenue in Oakland often do a double-take upon spotting the sign proclaiming Ralston's School of Martial Arts and Ontology. Yet who could question that dealing with other creatures through conflict is a fundamental mode defining existence. "'I am here and you are there' is a profound statement,"[24] Ralston reminds his students. It is a premise equally of healer and warrior. In case they listen without really hearing, he repeats it, often more than twice: "I am here and you are there."

THE IMPORTANCE OF being present (as concretized by combat and blending) cannot be underestimated. There suddenly is no retaining wall of symbolic traumas—the so-called trauma is re-energized again and again as a rigidified state of body/mind *and* the attack of the opponent. One must blend each time anew, and, despite exhaustion or distraction, summon up resources

to engage this "other." The roots of impediments are discovered autonomously. In fact, one discovers not only one's obvious armoring but limitations one did not know existed, discovers them simply by breaking through (via a rollback, cartwheel, throw, or synchronized retreat) into unrestricted territory beyond. Without the attack, there is no impetus to do such things. Without the crisis of the external opponent, the inner necessity is unregarded and unclaimed.

It is possible that some aspects of this therapy could be accomplished by pure exercise—and no doubt are—but the internal martial arts provide techniques and their execution in a concrete system of self-discovery and initiation; they also enforce clear discrimination between pretenses of effectiveness on the one hand and true actions on the other. Speed and power in isolation are ineffective; brawn and agility *per se* are like "drunken mind" prior to meditation. A praxis of groundedness, attention, and timing is required, which means going ever deeper in oneself. Thus, an actual "alphabet" is trained.

The martial arts practitioner must stay "real" because he or she must respond to and accommodate an actual opponent rather than a fictional or symbolic one. She must neutralize not only the imagined threat of "bad guys" but a liturgy of misleading psychobabble and empty reassurances. After all, potential victims of violence in the street are as much the prey of their own minds as the plague of crime and weapons. In a model training, the linear confrontation of foes (or predator and prey) is replaced by two people in a sealed energy bubble, each—whether they know it or not—trying to fill every hole in the field between them as it arises. The battle becomes their collaboration, their healing. They are each other's doctor. Palmer writes:

> In aikido the blend is what dissolves the conflict. When we blend we go *with* the energy or direction of the attack. From a mental standpoint, the head

> center, we "see the world from the attacker's point of view." The heart center tends to feel what our partner is feeling. The *hara,* or belly, knows how and where the body will move. When all three centers make contact with those of our partner, we have the sense that we have disappeared. We become so like the person who has attacked us that there is no one to attack.[25]

In the flow of filling holes and the impersonal strikes and neutralizations of an opponent, primal events are re-enacted and transformed (though the practitioners may not experience this consciously). They intuit a growing capacity for subtle feeling in their bodies, which is heightened by a procession of deep images from within (much as during rebirthing). If a student respects these levels of feeling—along with sensations from the energy field of his opponent, the "signaling errors" of his own tension, and the constant of gravity—these forces combine in a somatic transformation. Traumas and energetic blocks are reexperienced, cathected, and overcome. Whereas in psychotherapy such a process is mediated by words and symbols, in martial play it is evoked through energetic interaction with partners.

Disease is a most subtle and grievous opponent, but—as we have noted throughout this book—at what point do you distinguish armed teenagers in a neurotic society from the pathogens of industry in the same society? The boundary of internal and external effects finds only the self, seeing both ways that the ultimate enemy is one's own imbalance and tension.

As Juan Matus taught Carlos Castaneda, one is a potential victim of spirit forces that can take any form—thug, vandal, wild beast, or disease. If a person moves in balance, her internal organs are in balance and resist disease. Likewise, her outer body is resilient enough that an attacker has a more difficult time targeting, injuring, or killing her (and may even harm himself trying to do so).

An opponent (even a real attacker) is an imbalance, like a disease; he provides too much energy before one is ready for it. If one were ready, one would deflect the attack and thereby heal the attacker. Paul

Pitchford recounts returning from seeing an herbalist in San Francisco's Chinatown in 1975:

> Suddenly these two men came up to me. They wanted to give me energy. I tried to tell them that that was quite generous of them, but it was more than I needed. I told them I couldn't use so much energy. But they were real insistent on giving it. So I had no choice but to return it to them.

This is a charming tale of a street skirmish, but things have since deteriorated beyond the possibility of such deeds. One is rarely ready these days, and the diseases of urban civilization, intensified by domestic abuse, drugs and guns, are hardly curable by anything less than a legion of Taoist masters. In the imaginary cities of some utopian world, such street samurai might be the police, healing many "criminals" on the spot by converting their energy of rage to medicines.

When a proficient martial artist learns massage therapy, he or she can utilize the attributes of *chi,* blending, and sensitivity to function directly as a healer. Forms of *shiatsu* and osteopathy which effect deep cures from seeming surface manipulations draw on the reciprocal relationships among muscles, nerves, skeleton, and organs. Palpation includes an engagement of internal organs, leading to myofascial distribution of subtle impulses. In principle, the two-person sets of *t'ai chi ch'uan* done with a different emphasis become equivalents of these therapeutic massages. Japanese *shiatsu,* for one, requires the practitioner's firm contact along the meridians. *Nuad bo-rarn,* traditional Thai massage, employs slow full-body stretches and joint releases with conscious breath. There is both a superficial and profound parallel between these and various *san shou* and *ta lu* sets in *t'ai chi ch'uan.* The vulnerable zones of the opponent's body, with a revision in attitude, become the energetic points of the patient's body. The martial artist conducting force at their precise vectors also transmits *chi* and startles the viscera into activity.

Kumar Frantzis explains this practice in depth:

> All of the Ba Gua techniques and movements as well as the techniques of Taoist meditation have a direct cognition of the way in which you move your energy for healing. These techniques also have direct applications for healing. The hands-on healing technologies of Tai Chi, Hsing I, and Ba Gua are all derived from Chi Gung. They are collectively called Tui Na, or more specifically, Chi Gung Tui Na. Chi Gung can be considered a healing method that uses

> your energy to heal your body. Once you become proficient in Chi Gung it is a logical progression to apply your sensitivity and energy to heal someone else's body using Chi Gung Tui Na. . . .
>
> Chi Gung Tui Na has hundreds of basic hand techniques that include tissue work like massage, deep tissue work with the fascia, muscles, tendons, and ligaments, and balancing the energies of the body by working with the energies of the internal organs. These last methods are typically used on people suffering with extreme diseases. Other techniques include joint manipulation, bone-setting, working specific points of the body as in Shiatsu, and shooting your energy through the energy lines of the patient, including work with the spinal and cerebrospinal systems and glands.
>
> More sophisticated techniques include raising the vibratory levels within a person's body. The Ba Gua system has a particular method of using vibratory sounds to effect the energies of eight energy bodies. . . .
>
> The author's experience of working for more than ten years as a Chi Gung Tui Na doctor in clinics and hospitals in China is that while the three systems of Hsing I, Tai Chi, and Ba Gua share many techniques, each has its own particular specialty areas of medical bodywork. Hsing I people are well known for their bone-setting skills and deep tissue work. They are also skilled at repairing heavy traumatic damage to the body, called Die Da in Chinese. Tai Chi people are very sophisticated in working with the yin aspects of Chi and are particularly skilled at treating diseases of the internal organs and cancers. Ba Gua people are proficient in all of these areas, with very specialized skills in working with the central nervous system and nerve damage.[26]

The world is a much more complex place than one in which attackers do only bad and healers do only good. In the *dojo, nage* and *uke* become doctor and patient, each in their respective roles, trading potential blows. Too much energy harms, maims, or kills; less energy more discretely applied stimulates and heals (Ayurvedic charts of kill points on an elephant are also guides to treating sick elephants with acupuncture). Adhering movements done even more softly and with erotic intent become seductive. "Shoot Tiger," a *t'ai chi* move for immobilizing an opponent by twisting his arm upward and back and delivering a blow to his shoulder blade, may also be enacted with gradual pressure to heal tensions at that same point as well as diseases forming along its meridian.

Sexuality and Medicine

Any contact between humans is potentially therapeutic. Healing occurs from touch and because intimate contact is processed through personality. For a moment of passion, healer and healing agency are identified with each other and understood as one. The series from martial to curative to sexual clarifies an important aspect of healing in general. Healing is not so much a generic category as a focus and an intention.

The affinity between the healer and the lover is commonplace. In our American vernacular, we speak of physical love as a "medicine." Popular music is filled with such references: "You heal me," "I was sick until you came along," "I'll die without you," and so on. *Witch Doctor* and *The Voodoo Man* are love songs.

Yet these songs also disguise in their comic riffs the vulnerability of our situation as lovers and healers. The real healing implications of lovemaking remain unacknowledged. Men and women prefer sex to be cool, in all meanings of the word. Even the heat of passion is stylized as "chic." The playboy/playgirl version insinuates itself through the culture as a declaration of artifice and conquest. Lovemaking becomes a game of power, and power can manifest in any number of ways. But these are just words—sound bites—and none of them actually contradicts the healing function; in fact, play, seduction, and power are significant components of shamanic healing, too.

Lovemaking *is* medicine, an equation Reich institutionalized in his insistence on the medical value of sexual intercourse, prescribing it for a variety of diseases, few of them explicitly emotional. Reich is hardly

the first scion of sexual medicine. Tantric yoga for millennia has taught a *prana*-based form of sexual activity resembling *Chi Gung,* in which charge is generated between partners, channeled through their body/minds, and converted into systemic energy—orgasm without discharge. Tantric stances are not only sexual but more profoundly so than most so-called erotic activities, combining difficult yoga positions with genital *chakra* activation. Here both lovemaking and healing are mature and committed, and partners, while opening the meridians of their own bodies, provide each other with vital energy.

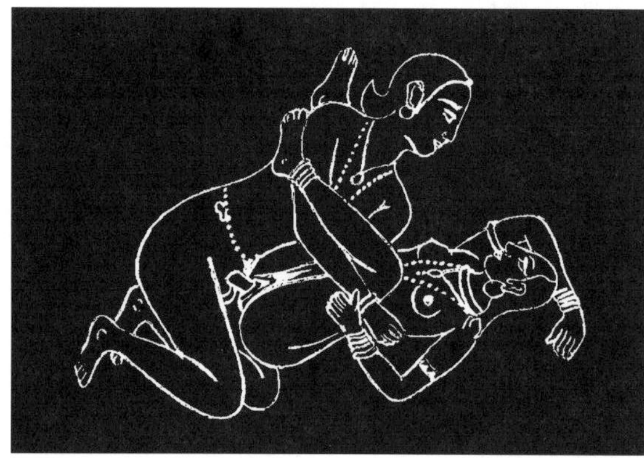

The main impediment to erotic healing is perhaps even less a shallow view of sexuality than an epidemic denial of healing itself. This denial is neither simple nor singular. For instance, those holding conventional sexual roles and unexamined views of "fun" may reject healing partly because self-awareness is not an issue for them in *any* part of their lives. They are armored against it. However, even among "New Age" men and women who honor healing rhetorically, there is often a failure to understand the depth and danger of acts of sexuality. Just as there is no healing machine, there is no lovemaking machine. Attraction between people is not obligatory and, despite excessive merchandizing, sexual healing is no more universally accessible than any other kind of medicine. Lovemaking becomes healing only when the shadow is integrated and actual contact is extended between partners.

Our society has defined such an enormous repertoire of ostensibly seductive behavior (and misbehavior) that we have virtually no repertoire at all for other forms of touch or exchanges of energy, especially between the sexes. While we wildly overestimate both our appetite and capacity for genital activity, we virtually ignore our hunger for sheer contact. As the former becomes more virulent in the frustrations and abuses it generates, the latter becomes depleted, and the combined effect is a neurosis of touch and human contact that gives rise to exotic pathologies in both somatic and psychological realms. If the line between massage and seduction is blurred, it is no wonder that the line between healing and loving is blurred. And, somehow transcendent of all this, remains the ritualized motto that healing *is* love. How do we find this again as an innocent and accessible thing?

In an oddity of our present civilization, sex has been isolated in a category all its own (a null set containing only itself and paraded everywhere in lights). As sociologists, psychologists, philosophers, and political historians began to deconstruct this glitzy cipher in the 1990s, it became evident that people were carrying out an exotic variety of activities under the pretense of having sex (or fantasizing about sex), only a portion of which were sexual. Some of our most obsessive acts of sexuality are in fact projections of healing (and love). Others, of course, are projections of alienation, depersonalization, and rage.

Moshe Feldenkrais describes "how many mistake the longing for affection or the need for social power for sexual tension, and proceed with the sexual act to satisfy these cravings.... [P]eople who proceed with sexual action when there is [only] the tension of habitual extraneous motivations that were mixed up with sex ... rarely relieve that tension. They just mitigate it and they find themselves changing one partner after another in the hope of finding one who will do the trick for them."[27] Many, he adds, supplement actual sex with aphrodisiacs and vitamins in search of a lost potency.

Behind each of our catchwords ("erotic," "seductive," "love") lies such a host of cultural habits and prejudices that we hardly know what they each mean in any absolute sense. When does mere contact become erotic? Must the sexual intent be shared? Does true "eroticism" always lead toward genitalization? Can there be erotic touch that does not have genitalization as a goal?

One practitioner offers a partial clarification:

> The healing potential of shiatsu might well originate in creative or sexual energy. At its very best shiatsu contact is very nurturing, loving and a great turn-on. As Reuho [Yamada] professes, "Human energy is sexual in essence, but in shiatsu that energy melts into a more general ecstatic feeling. Ooooo, feels good. That's all. Sometimes I call my shiatsu Tantric Zen."[28]

Yet this is also shifting ground. At a gut level we suspect that if an interaction begins as therapeutic touch and changes into seduction, there has been a violation of boundaries and ethics. But how do we distinguish sexual energy from other forms of healing energy? Do we have any real notion of the role eros plays in the energetics of therapeutic touch? Could suppression of eros (in either party) hinder healing? Might not all healing touch require some erotic component?

If any of these questions get answered in the positive, then the successful somatic therapist must learn to mutate feelings of attraction rather than hide or deny them. This is a difficult task, for Western culture is particularly depleted in providing stages one goes through to transmute energies. Many powerful forms of healing touch die in their first impulse because that impulse seems to arouse inappropriate erotic feelings. The heart within healing is stifled as it passes through the lower *chakras.* If the practitioner could contain and blend with its feeling rather than either act rashly upon it or suppress it, then he or she might find energetic attraction suddenly converted into an effective therapeutic tingling resembling the flow of *tantra.* This would be an initial step toward a condition in which all healing is a form of love.

That portends a long journey for those who are not even clear on the difference between the overly eroticized imagery churned out by the desire mill of media and their actual sexuality. How could they tolerate the complex feelings that arise from attraction or contact in any form? Muddles on this point lead us to misidentify some of the more intimate forms of healing touch with seduction because we have had

so much human contact interpreted only in terms of its potential flirtatious nuances.

This is not just a Western problem. After all, in some cultures women must hood their faces to avoid even the scintilla of attraction. In other societies, clitorises are castrated in primitive surgeries. The potential wounds being protected against must be fearsome indeed to require as prophylaxis such brutal disfigurements. In many tribes the fear of menstruation is so great as to lead shamans to disavow and disclaim the healing power of blood.

Breema bodywork, which includes embraces, belly-to-belly contact, and holding partners in cradle-like positions, is so frequently misinterpreted that its primary American practitioner, Manocher Movlai, has stated on a number of occasions he believes vigilance about sex corrupts our ability to make physical contact with each other to such a degree that it threatens the existence of the species. In reaction to one student's complaint that some of his postures were exploitative of women, this giant Kurdish man paced the room making astonishing and fearsome funny faces while pronouncing that he was a bear, then prancing as a horse. "The bear is so cute," he growled. "The horsey we think is cute. But people, no! What? If I want to make love, I don't need this [imitates the posture in question]. I can make love to a single hair on her head."[29]

Sexual and Healing Massage

It is not entirely happenstance that the term "massage" has become a euphemism in our own culture not only for a hedonistic, hands-on treatment but for prostitution itself. So-called massage parlors are businesses where sexual pleasure is marketed under the guise of muscle relaxation, or, in some cases, not even under a guise at all, except as a zoning cover. This has two implications: that sex is more merchandisable than healing, and that pleasure and sex are unconsciously confused with each other.

But the body does not make intellectual or semantic discriminations; it responds. Men visiting massage parlors are (in terms of their latent hungers) going to the "doctor." Though few of the prostitutes are intentionally involved in healing, as long as there is seductive touch (or even a charade of making a client feel good), the archetype is inescapable. They are unskilled nurse-physicians practicing a rough medicine the body recognizes without the mind. That doesn't mean that the experience is always positive, but it does place its dyad within a therapeutic context.

Women are natural healers insofar as they bring life into the world and nurture it. Even women who never give birth develop aspects of their being receptive to healing. Men may seek sex more ardently partly because they lack (i.e., have not developed) their own healing functions. They are dependent on others to supply these aspects because their biology and their sanctioned personae and roles combine to prevent them from developing it in themselves. In another culture, males might cultivate what to us would be feminine or receptive aspects but are mere gender roles and not solely biologically based.

Sex within a setting of prostitution may convey the benefits of therapeutic treatments for precisely those elements of it which are considered most exploitative. In a culture that eroticizes to the point of idol worship and floods its media with images of sexuality as nirvana, the prime category of curative contact a person is conditioned to seek or becomes somatically receptive to is genital. Sex becomes its own existential solution—a reason for living and for seeking at all. Even a symptomatic relief of this fever metaphorically translates through the body as a real medicine. It is an archetypal potion, with all the dangers attendant.

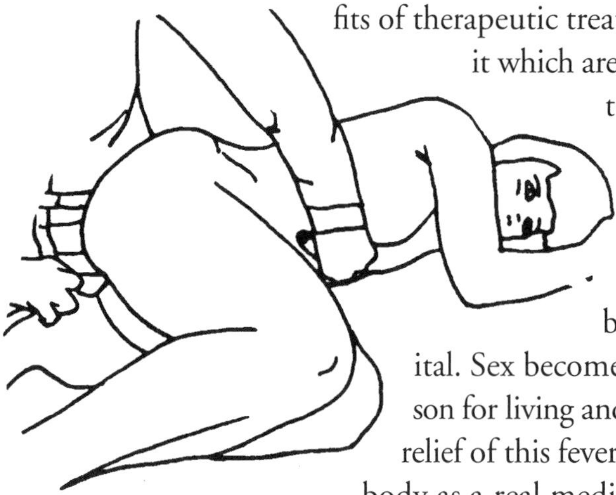

A deep craniosacral treatment or a skilled *shiatsu* massage can be effective treatments for someone with capacity for sensual expression and translation of it to their organs. A person without those capacities may be seeking an approximation of the same sensations through genitalization. The paradox is that, although it is often not sex which people seek in sex, only sexual contact will get it for them. The lust so overrides natural hunger that satiation, while symptomatic, becomes the only means of breaking the obsession and allowing the mind, if it is receptive, to reclaim the body's actual need.

In this context sex surrogates function as doctors, initially on the level of healing specific sexual dysfunctions but secondarily on the level of literally transmitting therapeutic erotic energy. This is particularly the case where these therapists are hired by physically disabled people or others considered so unattractive by society that sexual contact otherwise is a virtual impossibility.

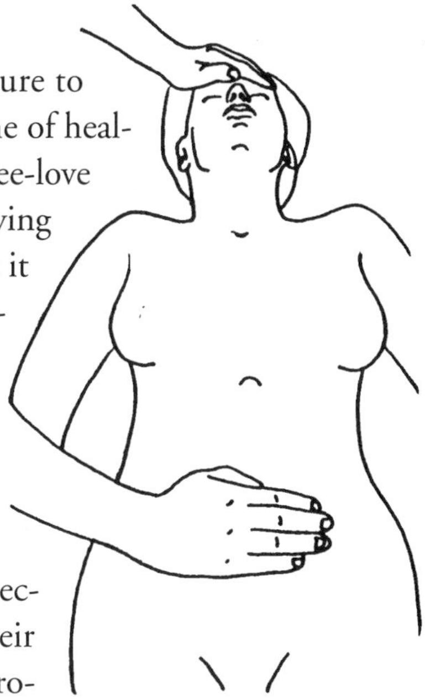

It is difficult enough for most people in our culture to accept the relationship of lovers as fundamentally one of healers. But once that is established (as it sometimes is in free-love circles), it becomes difficult (anew) to explain why, if loving is healing, often sex is pathological and destructive. Yet it should be no surprise if, during impassioned and emotionally charged episodes of physical contact, a person's compulsions around sexuality are often reinforced instead of its healing aspects. A seductively forced opening can lead to a deeper closing later. Incest is a taboo for psychological as well as sociological reasons.

For instance, both a therapist and patient may, respectively, confuse sexual attraction with intimations of their inner beings. Such attraction in a healing dyad sparks profound underlying feelings with which both are most likely out of touch. It is important to realize that beneath the surface of desire is often a more fundamental holding back. If the therapist is lucid and clear on his or her own feelings, the patient experiences the fantasy without seduction and moves through it. So does the therapist (and, as we saw earlier, the massage practitioner thereby deepens his or her touch). Always beneath titillation and fantasy is a deeper sexuality that is slow and serious and has no compulsive quality; it is the fundamental arrangement the self makes with its male or female personality, and from it alone authentic sexual feelings emerge.

This distinction is significant in light of the evidence that psychiatrists (and, likely, other doctors) have been having sexual intercourse with patients at an alarming rate, a phenomenon discussed as an ethics issue as early as the 1976 meeting of the American Psychiatric Association.[30] Although most speakers tried to blame this event on the failings of specific doctors, it speaks to a breakdown in the therapeutic model. The desperation is not only the inability of the psychiatrists to produce positive change in their patients but the lack of self-esteem and clarity on both sides that results from that failure. There *are* therapies of sexual relations, but they do not arise improvisationally from insight analysis.

Just as an assailant is more dangerous than a training partner for degrees of energetic output, so love-making may release (for either partner) more energy than can be handled (or energy into the wrong channels). For instance, by letting too much charge flow into one plexus of the body (one *chakra*), sexual activity may somaticize biases and blocks which are ultimately quite degenerative. It may also reinforce habits of somatic rigidity. No matter how pleasurable the experience may seem, people do not open themselves until they are ready at the deepest level. Thus, energy has no place to go.

Exploitation of sexuality often generates inability to tolerate it at all, so people go from promiscuity to abstinence. Where erotic contact is totally corrupted or inaccessible, something else, such as dancing, sports, or gang rituals, may take on the archetypal healing function.

Non-Reichian Orgastic Systems

A NEW DISTINCTION between gender and sex in the 1990s has begun to unravel some of our heterosexual biases. Between any two people—*any* two people—there is a quality, whether it gets their attention or not. It can be anger, repulsion, attraction, or warmth. It is the basis for the common arrangements people have, including marriage, sporting events, governments, communities.

Clearly "male" and "female" are social categories at the same time as they are biological distinctions. In each society biological domains are set at birth (with the exception of transsexual operations), but what is manly or womanly ("macho" or "feminine") is an outcome of intricate layers of cultural history and modes of social development which define gender roles. There is a whole class of people defined as "intersexuals" in our society. These are individuals born with at least the rudiments of both male and female genitals, one set of which is surgically excised at birth according to the recommendation of an endocrinologist. The usually arbitrarily selected "ambiguous" genitalia is removed not for health reasons, but because gender is considered an absolute in Western civilization. You are not allowed to be both male and female. Yet as adults, many intersexuals experience a sense of having been robbed of their complete sexual identity. Perhaps intersexuals have unique healing abilities, which are also excised with their ostensibly superfluous genitalia. Behavioral sex is yet another realm and does not require any of the above distinctions (there is auto-erotic sex, gay/lesbian sex, *tantra,* and there are also acts of rage and frustration that deviate into sexual modes).

In recent years the requirement of male-female genital embrace for orgone exchange and health has been openly challenged by the rediscovery of same-sex sexuality in the West. Gay men have developed whole systems of *tantra* based on males working together in exciting charge and withholding sperm. Thus, there may be many other *tantras* and myriad diverse genres of orgone embrace, including auto-erotic ones.

More University, a commune based in Lafayette, California (with branches in a number of large cities), offers a series of courses on Enhanced Sexual Performance (ESP in their terminology) in which individuals increase their capacity for orgasm as an intrinsic ability. Women (in particular) learn to expand their orgasms—to lengths ranging from an hour to fourteen hours and even longer. Although heterosexual contact may be involved (and usually is), orgasm through genital intercourse is considered an overrated, acrobatic feat. Instead, sequential mutual masturbation is taught, with an emphasis on each partner aiding the other in enhanced sensation (sequences and rhythms are taught to prolong tumescence and extend the experience). Sexual contact is viewed mainly as an aid—it is more "pleasurable" (hence, more orgasmic) to be acted upon than to act upon oneself. Intercourse is viewed as detumescent—a coming down from the heights of pure orgasm.

The goal of this activity is cultivation of one's own pleasure. In the overall More philosophy, full orgasm is a prerequisite to the expression of natural human generosity and consequently to community harmony. It would be heresy among the practitioners to state it this way, but in the terms of our present discussion, we could infer that individual capacity for feeling and erotic pleasure is viewed at More as medicinal. In fact, in More parlance, the degree to which one is "getting off" is the best indicator of their state of health.

Although denigrated in the press as a "sex commune" and belittled in both holistic-health and left-wing circles, More has survived since 1968 with its orgastic credo and produced the kind of socially cohesive and responsible community at which most traditional spiritual and political egalitarian groups have failed. While many Buddhist, Catholic, Maoist, and other guru-led communities are torn apart by abuses of power and sexual exploitation or denial (and also have difficulty finding time for more than sporadic or rote charity), More seems almost an epitome of the mature expression of compassion. The main occupations of their various communities are teaching courses on sensuality and man-woman relations and feeding the poor. In fact, quite anonymously, they run one of the largest charities in the United States.

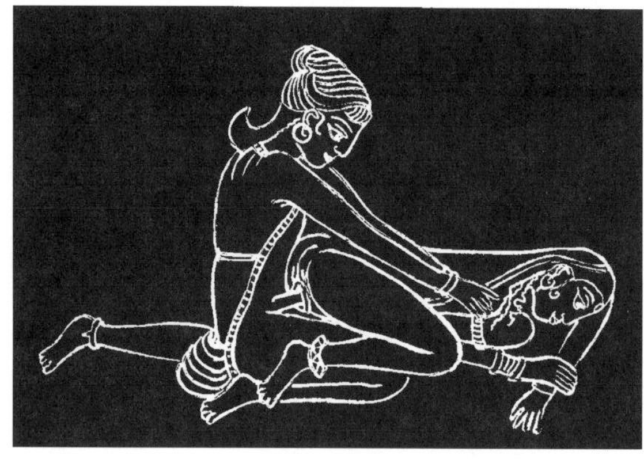

Every member of every More house (and many of their outside students) participates throughout the year collecting groceries and other surplus goods and distributing them in hardcore inner cities at personal risk. More has mastered logistics for how to give away subsistence goods in places where poverty, drugs, and guns abound. They also provide a large portion of their commune for the homeless to camp. They feed and provide shelter for these "guests" and fight a daily battle with zoning agencies to continue and expand this activity.

This is not altruistic or strategic generosity; it is not a protocol of social action or piety. It is the biological generosity of an open and committed body/mind.

Generosity is more than just a More credo. It is a functional basis of sexual identity, community, and charity. Men and women give to one another not because they think it is right or expect something in return but because gifts open to them their own unlimited bounty and the profoundest reaches of their hearts.

This philosophy is the diametric opposite of the ritual victimhood practiced not only by therapy groups but as a political tactic throughout American society. All too many people seek to be victims because they plan to exact a legal or emotional claim on someone else or on a social institution. Also, victimization legitimizes their sorrow and failures.

More treats such avid martyrdom as the abnegation of personal power. To indulge in wretchedness is what makes us wretched. To be bounteous liberates our own richness to ourselves. One More member told me, "Our philosophy is, when you wake in the morning, ask yourself, 'What is it today which I have to give?' If it is nothing but grief, then ask, 'To whom may I make a gift of my grief?'"

Under such course titles as "Money, Sex, and Jealousy," "Estrology," "Basic Hexing," and "Love for Sale," More confronts our sexual customs and politics as directly as any current institution. From years of study at the commune, the members have come to believe in distinct human estrus cycles in which females unconsciously arouse males and control male sexual behavior. Hence, they hone in on both male and female denial of the actual mechanics of seduction. Their courses and evening community sessions (called Mark Groups) reassign responsibility in ways that require a new balance between the sexes. While More teachers seek to expose women's estrological seduction of men, they place even more weight on showing men's abuse of their power. Men, they argue, dominate the sexual act with their own more limited capacities, devaluing the exponentially greater range of female orgasm and creating the entire social and professional pecking order by their own unconscious (or at best semi-conscious) act of rating women according to desirability—a rating they make little sexual use of except to fulfill their own minimal needs. "All women are judged by all men according to their fuckability," the More legacy proclaims. "No matter how men deny it; no matter whether these women are their mothers, daughters, or sisters; no matter their age, from children to great-grandmothers; no matter how feminist and socially conscious the male—women are rated and given status by how fuckable men consider them, and are denied status on the same basis. All women. Equal-rights laws notwithstanding." One

More teacher warns, "Watch out especially for those men who claim they are above this or don't do it, for these are the ones who do it most covertly and cover their tracks most skillfully. In fact, they use their claims of being advocates of women to disguise their more devious and desperate appropriations of them."[31]

The More goal is to make men and women aware of these habits (women denying unconscious seduction and feigning innocence of how men get turned on, men denying the role of sexism in how they treat women and kidding themselves that their attraction for *some* women gives them the moral authority and impartiality to assign social domains to *all* women). Only then can each begin to be real with the other.

No doubt there are abuses of authority and sexuality at More too (some apostates have made very specific claims), but the relative success of the practice of sensual joy for social well-being and sanity is a sign that planetary justice and health are based on physical contact and recognition of sexual danger to a greater degree than allowed in our belief systems and religious practices. In the absence of contact and recognition, we exist in a melee of unacknowledged desires and projections of lust, frustrated violations of each other's boundaries and misappropriations of freedom, and dysfunctionalizing sexual taboos that seem to hide actual sexual expression in a host of bizarre sex-image customs and rigid erotic rituals. It is no wonder that such abuses of core energy lead to serious sexual pathologies, including pedophilia, necrophilia, and necrophagia. In truth, the forerunners of these exist everywhere while erupting full-blown only in a few individuals.

The Pathogenic Healer

IN THE WEST there is the illusion that methods are what cure disease. As Jung observed, we honor "... the 'right' method irrespective of the man who applies it." But this, he pointed out, overlooks an ancient Taoist law: "'... if the wrong man uses the right means, right means work in the wrong way.' "[32] By this measure, it is not the method but the physician who determines the success of the remedy.

What binds preachers, oncologists, shamans, homeopaths, psychologists, massage therapists, and surgeons is that, in reading the "character" of their patients according to the systems in which they work, they stand as mirrors in which sick persons see themselves. The mirrors are there before any medicine is administered. The mirrors are the medium through which the medicine is administered (much like the water that mirrors turn into in Jean Cocteau's *Orphée* when special gloves are worn). In seeming to discover psychoanalysis as medicine, Freud may have actually discovered the gloves and mask behind which all medicine men and women hide.

That is, it might well be that transference, perhaps inculcated by the adventure of mutual discovery, is what cures people in psychotherapy. In the discussion of a dream, for instance, it may not matter what symbolic referrents the doctor and patient establish as long as in the process they experience a curative dialogue between themselves, as long as their collaboration seeds new elements in the psyche. After all, cultures survive not because their beliefs and ideologies are rational or accountable but because people respond to one another in satisfying ways. No laws can enforce this; yet a functional community, from its feelings of connection alone, can arrive at appropriate institutions. More prisons cannot protect a community nor can harsher laws restrict criminal activity. One might as well argue with diseases. This is the street basis of health.

To the degree that a doctor is comfortable with his or her own life and role as a physician, he or she will practice medicine at an appropriate level without projecting disease complications. Yet, any confusion the doctor has, conscious or unconscious (but particularly unconscious) will be transfused onto the patient along with the cure. Projection is inevitable as long as there are two breathing animals. This is most obvious in therapies like shamanic healing and psychoanalysis, but it is *always* the case. Sometimes projections may get minimized

or deflected, but, despite all attempts at a neutral clinical environment, they roam unimpeded. They are the great howling silence in every hospital and medical office in the West—the unacknowledged and uncompensated-for madness behind the act of antiseptic, spiritless cure. The more technological healing facilities become, the darker the shadows they will cast, the more heinous the monsters that will arise from those shadows to dominate the very furniture of waiting rooms and officious facial expressions of those involved. The doctors are mere secretaries for steel-silicon giants girded with artificial intelligence. *Their* motives are projections of something unknown and unprobed in us (what about those science-fiction tales in which machines develop personalities and become restless creatures or "terminators"?).

For all we *see* in a hospital, the absolute reality staring us in the face is virtually invisible. In fact, we are hypnotized not to see what is happening.

Set aside the vast ritual of institutional health care and disposal of bodies for a moment. Edward Whitmont points out that, on even the simplest level, the field between doctor and patient routinely includes not only "the patient's wounds and complexes, his or her pain, anger and yearning for healing . . ." but the doctor's "empathically tuned resonance that arises from his own wounds and his more or less consciously realized anger at the limitations of the human situation as it affects himself as well as the patient, as well as his urge to assert his capacities for helpful intervention. . . . [These are] mobilized when the pathogenic impasse is activated in the encounter."[33] The implication here is not so much that there are neurotic doctors but that the very profession of objective medicine, its epistemological shallowness and disregard of the shadow, is generative of neurosis and archetypal physical disease.

"Most—yes, *most*—physicians are suffering from Post-Traumatic Stress Disorder," writes Bernie Siegel, the renowned M.D. author. "They have a classical exposure to traumatic events and no place to appropriately express them. Many are ashamed to show their pain, and cry in hidden places."[34] The effect of this emotional suppression is a

disquieting projection through the doctor's professional persona. Sorrow and pain unexpressed become an alarming mask, its smile and good will pasted on. A patient instinctively fears such a persona but can find no rational justification for her unease. Suppression also leads to a more mechanistic practice of all aspects of medicine. If one is trying to conceal feelings, they manifest continually both as ghosts and rigidities.

Whitmont again:

> A great healer once remarked that "a physician never enters the sick room alone, but is always accompanied by a host of angels or demons." Whether the healer comes with angels or demons will be determined by the degree of the healer's conscious awareness of his own wounds and impulses toward wounding and by his ability to process them, to potentize them to their symbolic essence and hence not to be carried away by them nor to project (and projectively induce) them in his patients.[35]

The illusion that the doctor can be an efficient machine—or that he can feign neutrality successfully—overlooks the fact that his or her own "illness potential" is activated by not only the patient's symptomatic pathology but the particular complexes in the patient's personality that resonate with that potential: "When the healer unconsciously acts out those complexes, they operate like poison and add to the patient's disturbance."[36]

Later, Whitmont adds:

> The surgeon scrubs to free himself of infectious material he might introduce into the patient. Yet "infection" is not merely a physical, bacterial or viral phenomenon. It is a field dynamic that occurs in every human interaction and deserves special attention in the healing dyad because of its potential to confuse the process and even inject iatrogenic pathology.[37]

Perhaps the most dangerous aspect of the healer is his very adoption of medical authority. This mantle is conferred on him by his role

and stature within the community and reinforced by his warrior stance confronting the disease. Whitmont insists that it is no accident who become our doctors, for "... to the degree that [a] doctor's unconscious obsession and fear of death, the urge to control illness and death for his or her own preservation, happen to motivate the choice of profession, he or she will fight illness and death as such."[38] Again, I emphasize, this is true on an unconscious level no matter what talents the physician manifests outwardly and no matter how neutral and technologically proficient his manner of healing. Often the more technically skilled a doctor the more virulently he activates a patient's difficulties with parental authority. Those attitudes determine how the patient receives and assimilates the medicine. Thus, the role of doctor(-shaman) always contains within it the seeds of its opposite: potentiator of pathology. The pathogenizing healer must unwittingly again and again subordinate his patients to demonstrations of the power he has achieved over their diseases (demonstrations to himself as well as to them). This sacrifice once required the trappings of voodoo, but no longer; it is enacted in surgery and internal medicine every day with various degrees of consequence:

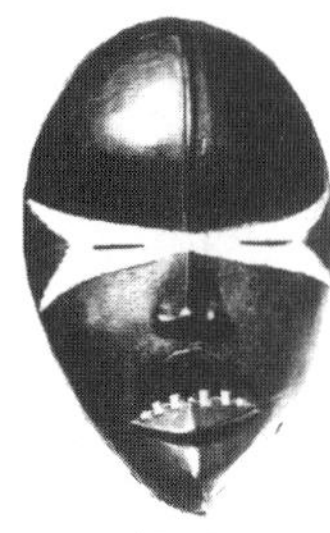

- The patient is reduced to an object.
- The empathy the doctor attempts to project rings false, so an intuition of deceit replaces that of presumed good will.
- The doctor aggressively takes on himself the role of dispelling the illness and deprives the patient of his or her own healing power (in fact, the doctor may unconsciously resent any healing that cannot be attributed to him).
- Identifying with his own falsely inflated role thereby erodes the doctor's real skill in whatever modality he practices.
- The patient, depersonalized—perhaps even infantilized—becomes so passive (again, usually unconsciously—there may be collateral assertions of activity and participation in getting well) that he or

she does not draw on natural healing powers or fails to perceive the profound level on which change is needed in order to be cured (the patient may have considerably more resistance to deep transformation than to merely being a good citizen, following regimens, etc.).

- The doctor may also get carried away with his image of what the disease is and practice outside the realm of his competence, attempting to heal something that isn't present or subtly transforming the actual disease into his imagined disease.
- He may diagnose on the basis of superficial signs because he is unconsciously always seeking the same adversaries (this explains the tendency of certain doctors to find the identical conditions over and over in patients bearing entirely different etiologies).
- He also may literally transpose his misrepresentation or (sometimes) exaggeration of pathology onto the patient, who will unconsciously pick it up and become sicker (thus the doctor will become not the specialist diagnosing a complex but, transpersonally, the source of disease).[39]

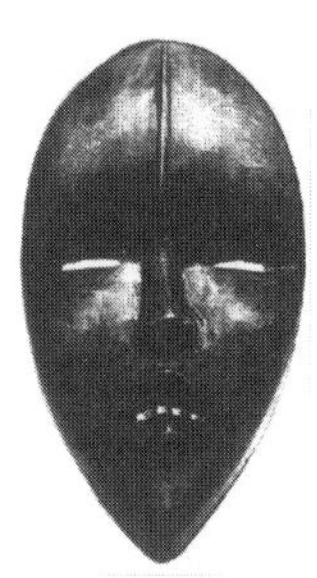

All the while, on the surface, the doctor may be carrying out his role as hero-physician to a tee and the patient may be enacting the model recipient. Underneath, though, they are evoking a darker mythology in which the patient actively resists the doctor's authority and becomes sicker in order to confound it, while the doctor uses the patient as a field into which to project the unresolved conflicts of his own life. As latent complexes in doctor and patient select one another, both attract the shadows that give them the greatest difficulty and thus present the most compelling challenges. The patient's disease and doctor's training invent an arena in which the unlived lives of both parties play themselves out. Thus, there is always the possibility that the professional relationship in the service of cure may have as its subterranean goal a resolution of quite separate affairs. When the doctor views himself as a

hero and the disease as his adversary, it is not far from there to the patient becoming the adversary, especially if he or she does not respond appropriately.

Because we are neophytes in understanding the role of mind in transmuting matter, we do not know the degree to which a doctor's projections can cause neuroses, attachments to already-existent diseases, and resistance to self-cure in patients. Maybe such transmutations occur purely on the psychological level and become somaticized only over long periods of time and only when other negative co-factors also exist—thus, they do not constitute a major iatrogenic factor in the causation of tumors *et al.* Maybe, on the other hand, patients can walk into a doctor's office with relatively minor diseases and leave with far more dangerous ones inculcated spontaneously during the examination. What happens is that the physician actually projects a malaise he later diagnoses as present.

This is the terrifying and imponderable question every society faces when it looks squarely in the eye of voodoo and sorcery. Bad will causes accidents and transmits infection as surely as it fires guns. I am not suggesting that doctors unwittingly fling diseases into patients like pins into voodoo dolls. I am merely indicating that as long we do not know all the parameters of either negative or positive projection, we should be careful about whom we choose to treat us.

All of the above is of course not just limited to doctors and patients; it is the dynamics of life, seen even more dramatically in the relationships of spouses and secondarily in boss-worker, teacher-student, pilot-passenger dyads of all kinds. In the doctor-patient realms it immediately contacts pathology and thus becomes entangled in the language of disease and cure.

It is worth resummarizing this plot: Doctors may not intentionally abuse their roles or the power bequeathed them, but underlying confusions about that power will *always* lead to the projection of pathologizing distortions. It is not possible for human beings not to abuse power. Whitmont notes, "It is a pathological aspect of ego functioning

and cannot be dealt with in a simple way by ego-will and good intentions. An attempt by the ego to renounce power is as unhelpful as ego hubris and the misuse of power for self-gratification. Both extremes equally arouse the wrath of the transpersonal elements."[40] That is, both ring false in a situation where authenticity is crucial, an authenticity required by the literality of the disease and the existential trial it sets forth. This is why medicine is so difficult to practice and why it does not finally work as mere technological formulas. A doctor attempting to get around the power issue by neutralizing it and asserting his all-abiding good-will actually invokes it in the arrogance of his very attempt. Thus, in pretending to be more a doctor he becomes less a doctor.

In a conclusion to the tale from the last chapter, Drunvalo Melchizedek offers another view of the ego dynamic in faith healing:

> You've got to get your ego out of the way and not [presume] that just because you think someone should be healed they really should be. . . .
>
> Healing someone else means taking on the responsibility for that person. It might not just be a five-minute little thing or something you do. It might mean you have to spend a year with them. If you're not willing to totally stay with that until it's done, maybe you should go fix cars or something.[41]

CHANGING THE WHOLE medical system is impossible. The archdiocese confronting William Clinton in 1995 is more deep-seated than the Vatican, and it functions as a giant megacorporate psychoanalytic mirror of the materialization of bodies, minds, and spirits. Who we think we are stares back at us in X-ray and other radiation images as little more than a puppet-activated corpse. Yet, in individual cases (where alone healing is manageable), therapeutic impasses and negative projection cycles are broken magically at the levels at which they occur. The doctor subconsciously undergoes the transmutation of a shaman (who himself experiences an illness, at least in symbolic form, in order to serve as the vehicle of its cure). Whitmont explains:

"The fact that the healer's propensity to his own illness is activated in a mutually containing field with the patient makes it possible to have his own 'illness' become the 'simillimum' that is offered for the healing process."[42] The same illness potentials, "when 'potentized' into symbolic awareness by the healer ... help the healing process."[43] A transpersonal event paralleling the mysterious alchemization of homeopathic microdoses from toxic substances transforms pathogenic attitudes into beneficent transference. The debilitating factor in the physician is itself potentiated into the cure. Likewise, an unacknowledged "microdose" can originate either metachemically or cognitively even within the framework of allopathy. As shamanism enters each medicine in a set of its own archetypes, the doctor's personality becomes the vehicle of the cure rather than its impediment:

> Often this activation of the simillimum is brought about as the result of the pain of having to renounce one's desire for intimate personal relationship with the patient and the acceptance of the ensuing loneliness, should this be the case. It also may be the effect of the doctor's training or personal experience in which he passed experientially through the illness-healing process himself.... It helps him or her to partner the patient's individuality on an inner quest, by feeling, perceiving and resonating with him or her, and hence also perceiving the nature of the ailment and its appropriate therapeutic modality and curative similarity ... such as a proper potentized substance, the meridians or points to be activated, and even his or her own relational influence.[44]

He can still be heroic and a warrior:

> The archetypal function of the healer includes the function of the sacrificial *pharmakos,* the scapegoat who offers himself and his sensitivities and ability to suffer pain as a sacrifice. He chooses to carry and metabolize his patient's ills, and shares his patient's imprisonment in the incubatory container....
>
> He allows himself to know that he is meant to carry and suffer the "evil," the pathology of others. Hence, in order to avoid "infecting"

> others (his own infection he cannot avoid), he . . . undergo[es] a constant "purification," that is, [he] must maintain a perpetual scrutiny of the nature and appropriateness of his reactions (and/or overreactions) that may be similar to the patient's state.[45]

When the physician steps back and adopts his or her role as the true healer, then the patient gains access to the archetypal healer, as mediated by the physician, and a mutation takes place that transcends and transforms both of them.

The Archetypal Healer

THE ACTUAL HEALER is the same, oft-mentioned hologram of independent cells orchestrated as tissues and organs that formed embryogenically from the seeds of the zygote and continues to restore its template. Transit across a lifetime is itself a passage into the innermost chambers of a genome—and this process is unique and inscrutable in each person. It cannot be generalized or socialized according to formulas of demography or even genetics, and it cannot be dealt out in mass medicine. It can only be catalyzed or impeded by doctors.

If all disease is etiologically karmic and psychospiritual, then the truest guise of a healer is his or her ability to activate archetypal and cosmic factors. The practice of a particular modality, with its skills and paraphernalia (which may comprise synthesized drugs, complex movements, sophisticated surgeries, or years of physical or psychological therapy), may also involve an unconscious training of a doctor to pass through his own resistance to healing greater than any actual mechanical act of medicine. By this definition all healing is, to a certain degree, shamanic ritual, and all feats of medicine are sleights of hand. The techniques are temporally functional but do not themselves effect embryogenic transformations. They initiate healer and patient to the wonders of this diverse world. They deepen experience. Thus, the greatest variety of healing systems is necessary not because of the variety of diseases

but the variety of routes of access to individuals and the discrete languages in which these are mythologized.

The successful healer presents an "other" in the form of either a concrete medicine or his (or her) own presence that enables the "sick" person to "perceive" his own health. And this perception may be conscious or unconscious, biochemical or psychospiritual, highly cathected and painful, or silent and brief as a breeze over a field of clover. The same mystery that marks autonomous self-healing lies in the twaining of healer and patient.

Healing is a direct result of resonance between the doctor and the patient on whatever plane we choose to reify it. A message is sent to the wholeness of the body, either emotionally, vitally, by meridians, by muscles and nerves, structurally, or by language and other linguistic codes. The integrity of the system interprets the message and organizes around it anew.

Healing has an amplitude and a periodicity. Components may change, but a wave asserts itself. Even a healing experience which is a shock or jolt expresses itself finally as a wave. The cure may originate as a crack or a ping, but the ripples from it are perfect wholes.

Healing occurs at a frequency present in the patient and tuned to the physician. As long as the physician makes a good choice, what happens subsequently may not matter—even a lapse in the relationship. After all, changing the frequency or the stimulus does the same thing to a cure that it does to a wave; it changes its quantity without changing its quality. Its shape may be different, but its congruence remains.

The patient also experiences the wave before the treatment, *is* the wave, but in a fragmentary sense or without sufficient energy to mobilize it. He does not feel his life as a unity. Thoughts are scattered; purposes are at cross-purposes; physical movement is uncoordinated; organs are restricted; responsiveness is uncommitted and interrupted. The wave of life is broken, or experienced intermittently.

The signal is uniform, but the body does not perceive it singly or take its own existence seriously. "Tired of livin' an' skeered of dyin'"

was the lament of the black dockworker Joe in "Ol' Man River." When the resiliency of biological existence is not there, one also shuns the final singleness imposed by death. If an organism cannot express its whole nature, it seems to need all of time in which to accumulate and express its partial natures, so it is greedy. Living and dying are both somehow violations of its hoard of fragments.

A good healer does not do too many things or too much. He tries to do the one necessary thing. The person who is being healed cannot judge the experience from the standpoint of symptomatic relief. It is up to both to assert the wave and not become distracted, to end the patient's outgrown practice of self-cure.

Bone cracking is "silly," but the bones that are cracked do not laugh. Their pulse rides into the body like a horse throwing back its head in midflight, the *hsing-i* horse which delivers a powerful blow. Spasms may interrupt unity, but eventually the wave completes itself because it is already there. Disease also has a singleness of expression, and it will reimpose itself if there is no wave to sustain the insight of its release.

A WHOLENESS COMES ON GRADUALLY. A person first feels better, has fewer chronic symptoms, is less depressed. Then she experiences more coordination. Relapses may be resting periods before greater freedom. Later on, the person feels springy and responsive. She mocks herself less in interactions with people. If she laughs, that is also coordinated and part of her expression as a living creature. Eventually the wave will express itself in social situations; she will make better decisions, have more coherent thoughts, experience more poignant and cohesive ideas. Unity becomes irresistible.

Her death is now a single thing too, and she must face it, as part of the wave, with deep feeling that is no longer restless nostalgia or fantasy. If the life is made up too much of nostalgia, and feeling is always in the past as sweetness of memory or in the future as daydream, then the experience of the wave will be, temporarily at least, as remote as the intimations of a daydream.

The process called "bodywork" gets that name not because it is physical rather than mental, but because it honors our psychic incarnation in a physical universe as an irrevocable condition of therapeutics. It little matters whether we believe that spirit has arisen in matter or matter itself is possessed of remarkable attributes: the cure requires that we have manifested in bodies alone. We cannot out-think or spiritualize our anatomical destiny; we must think *in* it, find mind through it. In this sense, bodywork (and healing in general) is a restatement of the condition of birth. We come into being through the body of another who came into being likewise, back to the beginning of a universe. The doctor must replicate, in some manner, the act of birth. It is not that she has to be a maternal force, but her cure cannot evade the literality of biology and genetic continuity. She must impose herself into the biological message with the same seriousness with which the mother *is* the biological message.

Christ's dying for our sins archetypally empowers healers to "save" sick persons through their own bodies. Psychoanalytic transference reenacts the Crucifixion symbolically, not because the doctor is sacrificed but because the Western patient accepts the intercession of a shamanic being in his own cure. The Crucifixion and transference are different faces of the same latent belief system.

When doctor and patient begin to work together, a breathing together is established, and everything in both individuals is represented in that breathing somewhere. The two bodies reclaim the ancient message—or, as Johnny Cash sings: "Flesh and blood needs flesh and blood, and you are what I need."

He means loving not healing, but the meaning could not be clearer.

Notes

1. Margaret MacKenzie, personal communication, 1978.

2. Stan Tenen, *The Matrix of Meaning for Sacred Alphabets* (San Anselmo, California: Meru Foundation, 1991), VHS videocassette.

3. Deepak Chopra, *Quantum Healing: Exploring the Frontiers of Mind/Body Medicine* (New York: Banatm Books, 1989), p. 247.

4. Ibid., pp. 248–49.

5. Ibid., p. 250.

6. Ibid., pp. 251–52.

7. Peter Ralston, dialogue during a class, Oakland, California, 1990.

8. M. Masud R. Khan, "Toward an Epistemology of Cure," quoted in John P. Conger, *The Body in Recovery: Somatic Psychotherapy and the Self* (Berkeley, California: Frog, Ltd., 1994), p. 95.

9. Cybèle Tomlinson, "Breema Bodywork," *Yoga Journal,* November/December, 1994, p. 94.

10. Conger, *The Body in Recovery,* pp. 95–96.

11. A. P. Elkin, *Aboriginal Men of High Degree* (Sydney: Australasian Publishing, 1944), p. 125.

12. Miguel Covarrubias, *Island of Bali* (New York: Alfred A. Knopf, 1938), p. 334.

13. Paul Radin, *The World of Primitive Man* (New York: Grove Press, 1953; Revised Edition, 1960), p. 58.

14. Ibid., pp. 58-59.

15. Ibid., p. 59.

16. Ibid., p. 60.

17. Robert Lawlor, *Voices of the First Day: Awakening in the Aboriginal Dreamtime* (Rochester, Vermont: Inner Traditions, 1971), p. 370.

18. *Huang Ti Nei Ching Su Wên,* trans. by Ilza Veith as *The Yellow Emperor's Classic of Internal Medicine* (Berkeley, California: University of California Press, 1966), pp. 147–48.

19. Ibid., p. 163.

20. A. Veronica Reif, "Eurhythmy and Curative Eurhythmy," Berkeley Anthroposophical Society, 1978.

21. Ibid.

22. Laura Chester, "In a Motion," unpublished manuscript, 1978.

23. Wendy Palmer, *The Intuitive Body: Aikido as a Clairsentient Practice* (Berkeley, California: North Atlantic Books, 1994), p. 72.

24. Peter Ralston, statement during a class, Oakland, California, 1991.

25. Palmer, *The Intuitive Body*, p. 94.

26. Kumar Frantzis, *The Tao in Action: The Personal Practice of the I Ching and Taoism in Daily Life*, unpublished manuscript at the time of publication (Berkeley, California: North Atlantic Books, 1996).

27. Moshe Feldenkrais, *The Potent Self: A Guide to Spontaneity* (New York: Harper & Row, 1985), p. 26.

28. Barbara L. Schultz, "New Age Shiatsu" in Berkeley Holistic Health Center, *The Holistic Health Handbook* (Berkeley, California: And/Or Press, 1978), p. 195.

29. Manocher Movlai, in a class at the Breema Institute, Oakland, California, 1991.

30. "Sex Between Therapist and Patient," transcript of a meeting of the APA, June 21, 1976, *Psychiatry*, Vol. 5, No. 22.

31. These quotations are informally recalled from a lecture entitled "Love for Sale" at More University in 1993.

32. C. G. Jung, *Psychological Reflections*, edited by Jolande Jacobi (New York: Harper & Row, 1953), p. 71.

33. Edward C. Whitmont, *The Alchemy of Healing: Psyche and Soma* (Berkeley, California: North Atlantic Books, 1993), p. 188.

34. Bernie Siegel, "Letter to the Editor," *Common Boundary* (September/October, 1994), p. 9.

35. Whitmont, *The Alchemy of Healing*, p. 200.

36. Ibid., p. 189.

37. Ibid., p. 198.

38. Ibid., p. 208.

39. More complete descriptions of some of these may be found in Chapter Nine, "The Healer," in Whitmont's *The Alchemy of Healing*, pp. 187–212.

40. Whitmont, *The Alchemy of Healing*, p. 203.

41. Drunvalo Melchizedek, "Flower of Life Workshop," Dallas, Texas, February 14–17, 1992 (video recording).

42. Whitmont, *The Alchemy of Healing*, p. 197.

43. Ibid., p. 189.

44. Ibid., p. 198.

45. Ibid., pp. 208–209.

PART II

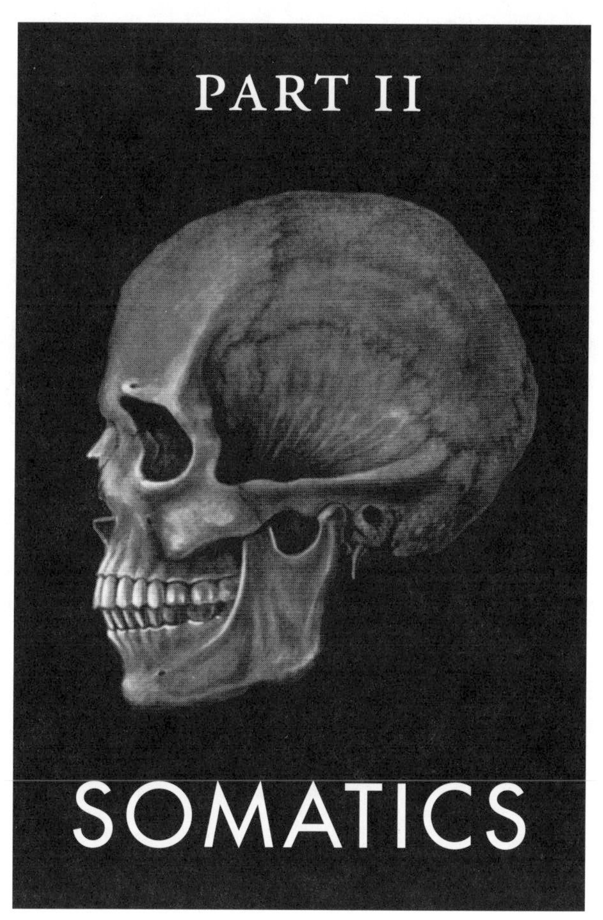

SOMATICS

CHAPTER THREE

Osteopathy and Chiropractic

Bone

The skeletal frame of the body is made of the same material as its blood, retina, and heart. Cells within bone share an immediate, direct ancestry with cells of muscles and organs. Of course, all cells in a body originate from the single sperm and egg, and those that become skeletal must past through more visceral phases before hardening at the core. They do this by packing more closely together, not by altering their animate nature.

Bone is living, changing tissue—fluid and even sensual. It is biochemically active and participates in metabolism and immunity. To engage bone therapeutically is to work not at a superficial level but in depth and at the core.

Systems of therapeutics based on the handling of bones are core therapies. They are often more essential than the most powerful drugs and radiation. The impression that they are simplistic and mechanical is an unexamined offshoot of the notion that bone is fixed and inert—a stony rack for the critical functions of brain, blood, and kidneys. Though not all osteopathic professions acknowledge skeletal vitality directly, all are based on the fluidity of bone and its faculty of transmitting medicine into the entirety of body/mind. This medicine may be an actual biological substance, an electrical signal or message (as discussed in the previous chapter), or an energetic change that spreads globally. However categorized, it is a foundation medicine, a vehicle for the embryogenic power of *prana*.

An adjustment of bone is an adjustment of self. The failure of psychoanalysis to recognize this has forestalled a possible healing discipline of great effectiveness combining cranial osteopathy and Freudian transference.

Cells are truly alchemical in their transmutation not only of extrinsic substance but their own intrinsic nature. They go from sex cells to raw undifferentiated tissue to layers of flesh moving in unison to banks of cones focusing light. I have said (at many points in both volumes of this text) that the prime—in fact, the only—capacity medicine has is to hitch itself to this embryogenic process. If a single cell contains the whole plan of an organism and the mechanism for enacting it, how can a physician rival this? He can assist it, catalyze its sluggishness, and attempt to remove the more blatant impediments in its way, but he cannot sculpt or brew anything resembling a raw lump of protoplasm let alone a breathing, conscious, philosophizing organism. Thus, medicine aboriginally is meant to awaken the goddesses and totems that lie at the heart of development, to encourage the miracle to go on happening in this strange and compelling world of color and sound. For such a reason alone, Bear Shamans and osteopaths can be as effective as—or often more effective than—surgeons and internists.

In skeletal therapies, bone is used to simplify confused tendencies, ground their crossed motivations in prior unity, and transmute their essentiality (see "Zero Balancing" in Chapter Four). Anthroposophically, bone is considered the hardened state of the first wave of spirit to encounter the realm of matter. Raw soul, entering the force field created by the embryo, is whorled deeper and deeper into the physical dimension until it resembles stone—a fascial cave of dripping lime. In this singular deed of grounding, it remains spirit; it also becomes newly crystalline and electromagnetic, a sacred quartz or voodoo doll at the heart of the body's manifestation. This doll develops unique characteristics, even as hydrogen and nitrogen manifest new qualities when

liquified or frozen. In the case of bone it is a psychospiritual, somatic liquifying and freezing, and the effect is medicinal.

Bones serve as pathways to the neuromusculature, immune system, and psyche in a number of ways (that are probably different versions of one way). They build up and store the tension of displacement from environmental and internal bumps and twists. They impinge upon and restrict viscera and nerves. They communicate a sense of wholeness or fragmentation. In another interpretation each individual bone (atlas, sphenoid, sacrum, pelvis, etc.) is a puzzle piece within the wholeness of the organism. This means each individual bone in terms of its gross shape but also each individual bone in terms of the subtle variations of angle, density, and rounding that separate one person from another and one species from another.

A comparison of mammalian bones (see illustrations) reveals a precision and specificity of variation leading to the evolutionary functions of particular creatures—the way in which each uses its shape to engage the world and express its identity. Each human atlas, sacrum, and pelvis likewise holds secrets which are transmitted through dreams, dances, diseases, desires, and personae. It is precisely the subtle and discrete equivalents of anatomical differences that occur at the level of species discrimination that the osteopathic therapist attempts to contact and transmute at a psychosomatic (or psychospiritual) level within individuals. Each animal can be interpreted as a dream or a "disease"—a totem (as American Indian doctors implicitly understood). The map of mammalian bone variations is a map of character and (metaphorically) a chart of both successful and unsuccessful styles of self-healing (survival). Each totem contains within it a charge powerful enough to make the difference between a bobcat and a squirrel and the domains they master in nature. Clearly then it has the power to restore local pathologized tissue to a healthy state.

PELVIS

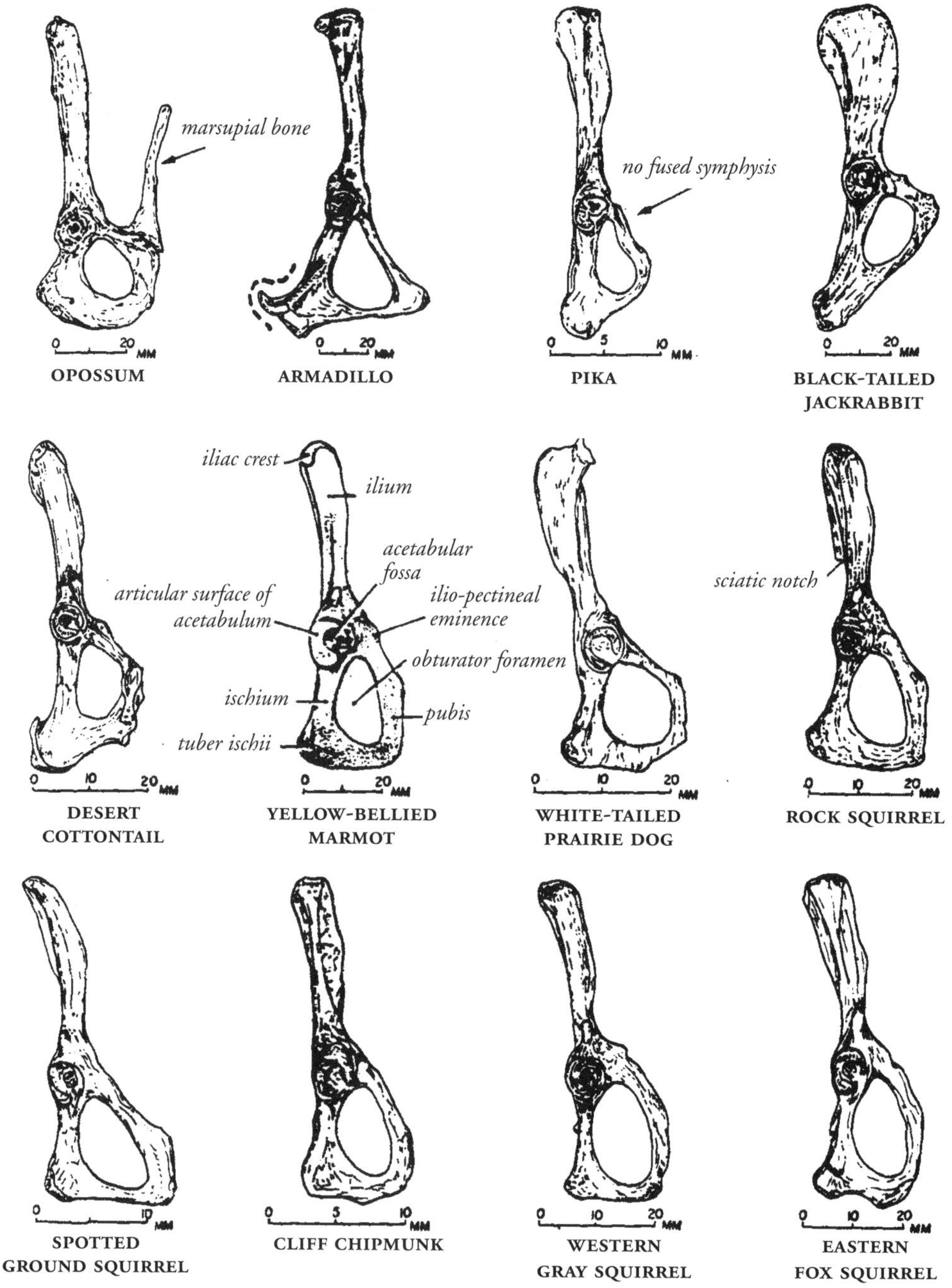

marsupial bone

0 20 MM

OPOSSUM

0 20 MM

ARMADILLO

no fused symphysis

0 5 10 MM

PIKA

0 20 MM

BLACK-TAILED JACKRABBIT

0 10 20 MM

DESERT COTTONTAIL

iliac crest

ilium

acetabular fossa

articular surface of acetabulum

ilio-pectineal eminence

obturator foramen

ischium

pubis

tuber ischii

0 20 MM

YELLOW-BELLIED MARMOT

0 10 20 MM

WHITE-TAILED PRAIRIE DOG

sciatic notch

0 10 20 MM

ROCK SQUIRREL

0 10 MM

SPOTTED GROUND SQUIRREL

0 5 10 MM

CLIFF CHIPMUNK

0 10 20 MM

WESTERN GRAY SQUIRREL

0 10 20 MM

EASTERN FOX SQUIRREL

SACRUM

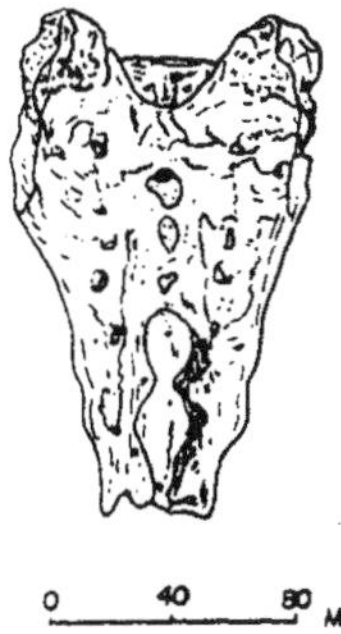

0 40 80 MM

BLACK BEAR

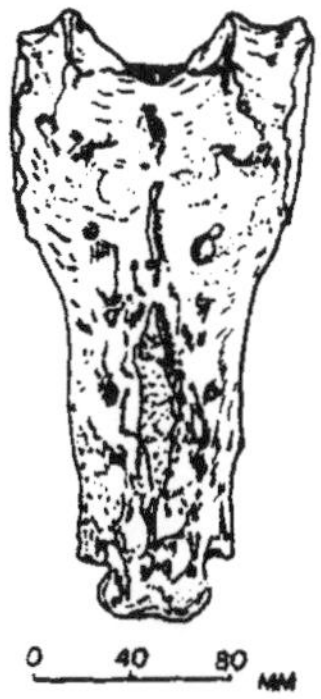

0 40 80 MM

GRIZZLY BEAR

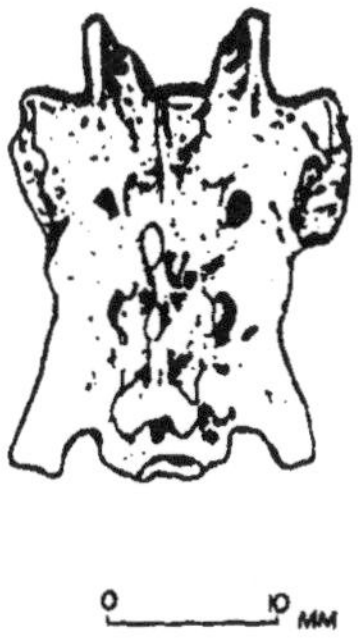

0 10 MM

CACOMISTLE

0 10 20 MM

RACCOON

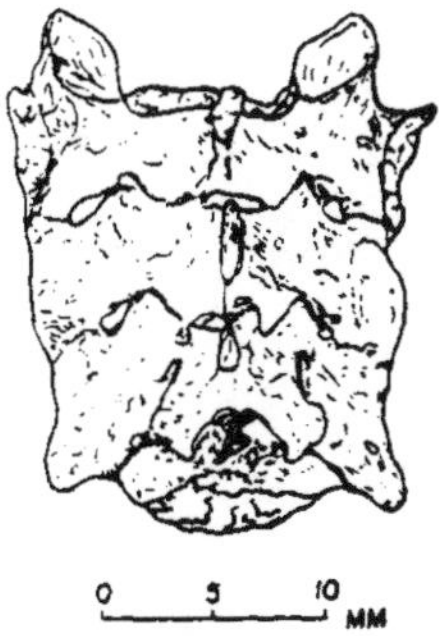

0 5 10 MM

COATI

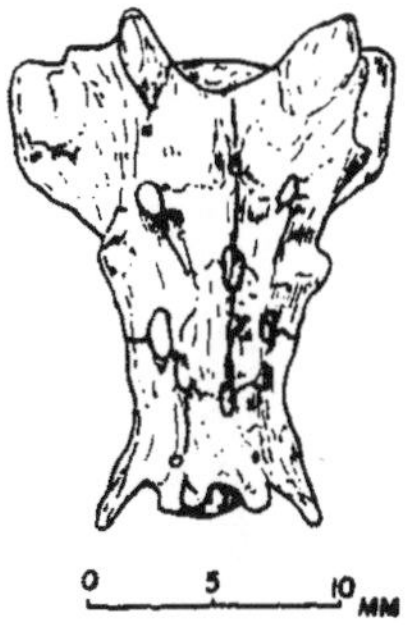

0 5 10 MM

MARTEN

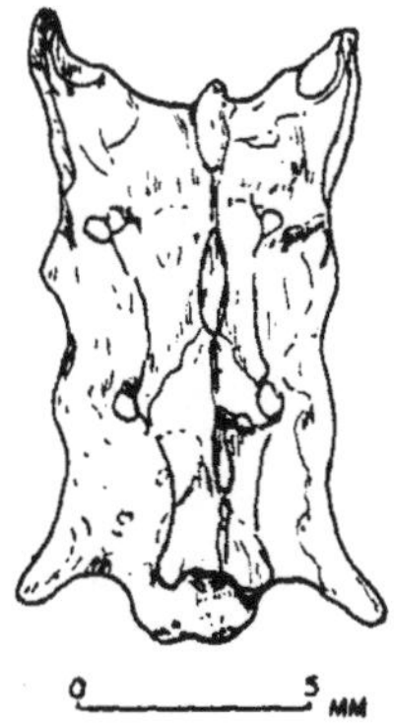

0 5 MM

LONG-TAILED WEASEL

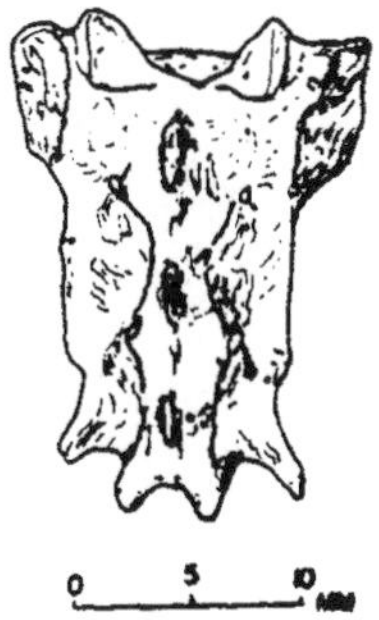

0 5 10 MM

MINK

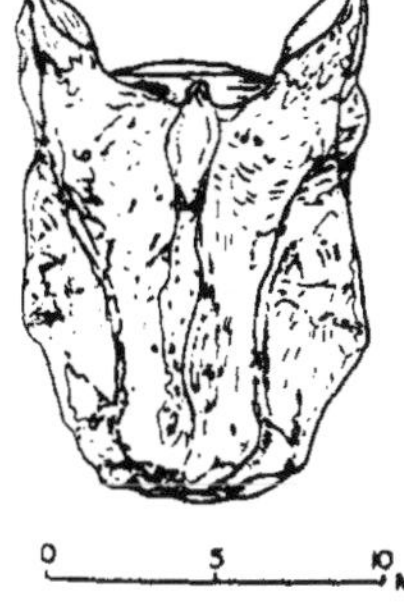

nearly square and blocklike

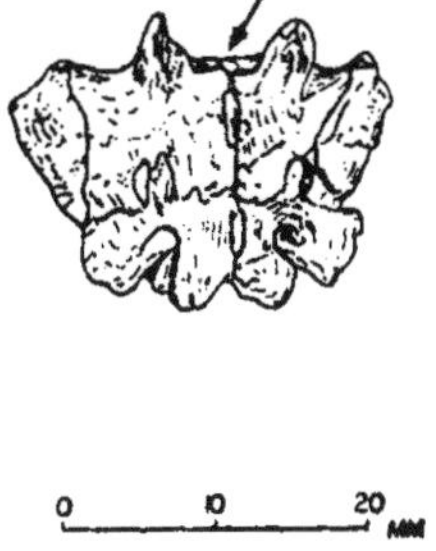

0 5 10 MM

BLACK-FOOTED FERRET

0 10 20 MM

BADGER

0 10 20 MM

STRIPED SKUNK

0 10 20 MM

HOG-NOSED SKUNK

ATLAS

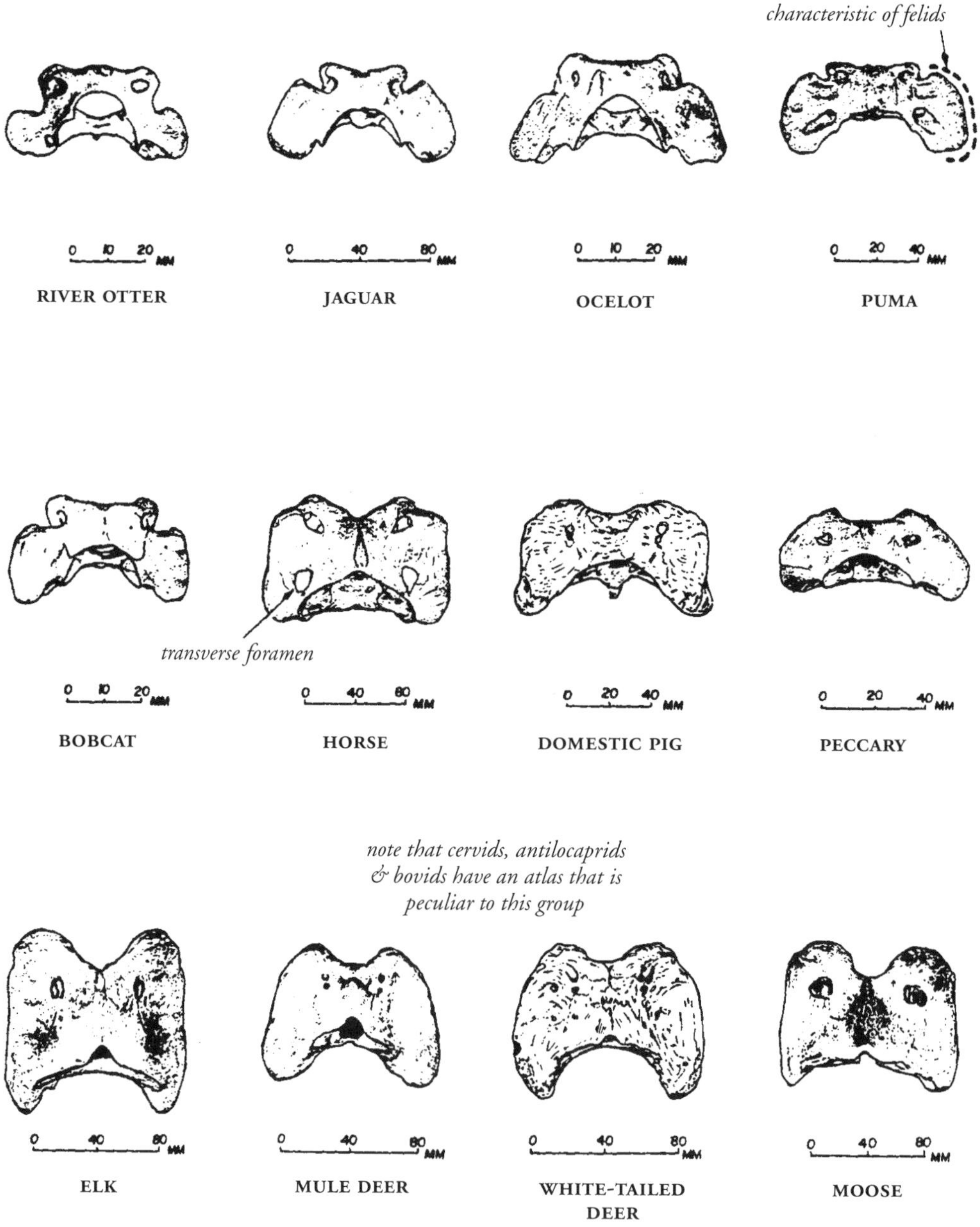

characteristic of felids

0 10 20 MM

RIVER OTTER

0 40 80 MM

JAGUAR

0 10 20 MM

OCELOT

0 20 40 MM

PUMA

transverse foramen

0 10 20 MM

BOBCAT

0 40 80 MM

HORSE

0 20 40 MM

DOMESTIC PIG

0 20 40 MM

PECCARY

note that cervids, antilocaprids & bovids have an atlas that is peculiar to this group

0 40 80 MM

ELK

0 40 80 MM

MULE DEER

0 40 80 MM

WHITE-TAILED DEER

0 40 80 MM

MOOSE

Osteopathy

OSTEOPATHY PROVIDES AN intact model for the role of traditional hands-on therapy in the development of alternative medicines. Historically, osteopathy contributed to other major somatic disciplines, including Polarity Therapy, Rolfing, and Zero Balancing. Both Randolph Stone and John Upledger could be considered osteopaths operating at different cutting edges of a vast medical paradigm. Even in its most adulterated mechanistic forms, osteopathy has preserved a direct experience of the body and kept the physician a hands-on practitioner; in its present holistic mode, it has contributed energetic techniques directly to other alternative medicines, including modes of visceral massage, craniosacral application of stillpoints, subtle palpations, light touch for activation, and energetic balancing.

Osteopathy embraces a profound contradiction. The theorems of spinal-visceral connections that underlie its development could not be true in their most literal sense. Thus, it would appear that A. T. Still, while proposing rather simple and Solidist medical precepts, inadvertently discovered another system and, without realizing it, enlarged his original model by radically different paradigms of therapeutic activity. Like Samuel Hahnemann, who stumbled upon microdoses because he did not have the "knowledge" that they were pharmaceutically inert, Still entered a realm of visceral energy because he did not understand that his mechanical model was incidental to his results. The paradox was that, while using a mechanical crutch, he tricked himself into inventing a system of energetics. Osteopathy began as a surgery-like treatment and spawned a method as vitalistic as Reiki or homeopathy.

On the surface, the osteopathic perspective is Solidist and Rationalist, viewing the body as a dense geometric grid endowed with nerves and permeated with channels flushed by systolic and diastolic motion. But its treatments were predominantly empirical and vital. First Still and later, osteopaths such as William Sutherland and John Upledger continued to arrive at innovative modes of working with the interrelationships of bones, nerves, viscera, blood flow, cranial pulse, and psyche. This continuity of invention and institutionalization of its own techniques set osteopathy apart from all other manipulative medicines, prehistoric and modern. It eventually made osteopathy a quasi-academic medicine with specialized branches of research and application, much like allopathy.

AT THE TURN of the twentieth century, most physiological therapies were sectarian and segregated by their modality. They did not influence mainstream therapeutics and were isolated from one another. Some were breathing-oriented or exercise regimes associated with spas. Some were offshoots of vitalistic schools employing theories of magnetism and life-force stimulation. Others involved linear applications of manipulation or calisthenics to skeletal and muscular frailties, or they undertook corrections of culturally defined defects of the body. Amateur surgeries in the context of phrenology and other metaphysical systems of diagnostic anatomy also informed osteopathy and chiropractic.

Underlying all of these was an ancient guild of doctors who treated the body directly, maintaining a rigorous integrity of techniques and using all available tools and insights. They did not ignore scientific medicine; anything that contributed to cures they adopted. They had no single rational model for the nature of disease or the properties of health. Members of the original medical sodality, these medicine men and women shared a blue-collar identity and work-ethic with carpenters, boat-builders, food preparers, nurses, and hunters through the evolution of society. They did not ultimately join the elitist guilds of philosophers and scientists. They

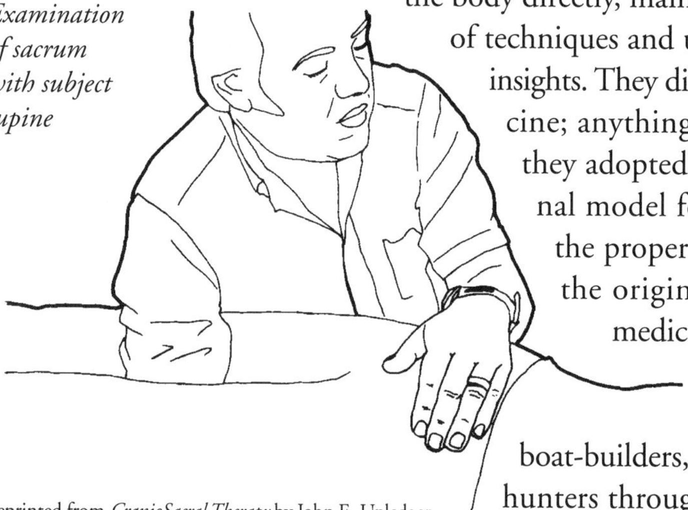

Examination of sacrum with subject supine

Reprinted from *CranioSacral Therapy* by John E. Upledger and Jon D. Vredevoogd with permission of the publisher, Eastland Press, Inc., P.O. Box 12689, Seattle, WA 98111.

may have participated at some level in the Hippocratic synthesis, but they were back on their own by the time of Galen. Paracelsus did not forget to consult them one by one *in situ.*

Folk traditions of trampling in the fields, "weighing salt," and "the shepherd's hug" existed worldwide and hearken back to Neolithic and probably Palaeolithic times (see "Mechanical Ethnomedicine" in Volume One, Chapter Five). Sailors at all ports still find remarkable native manipulators and bone-setters practicing on the streets. They heal organic diseases as well as skeletal ones, but have no written tradition, no formal school, no medical theory, and no contact with one another from Tahiti to Mexico to India to Madagascar. Still's invention and Palmer's variation were initially limited American cults, sharing more with religion and carpentry than with these ancient indigenous medical guilds. Yet they revived the manipulative template and provided a mainstream arena for the fusion of all modalities of therapeutic adjustment and palpation. By now, both osteopathy and chiropractic have been enlarged and transformed to incorporate a great variety of native and Oriental hands-on techniques.

Weighing salt

Osteopathy was initially a unique offshoot of the bone-setting tradition, a way of looking at anatomy and disease that was modernized and formalized in the nineteenth century by A. T. Still and subsequently developed its own distinct lineage. Trained primarily as an engineer, Still could not help but view the organism as a dynamic system that occasionally developed congestions or blocks. He made corrections based on his intuition of mechanical relationships among

its parts (i.e., bones, fascia, circulations of fluids). As the son of a doctor, he had originally attempted allopathy:

> I was born and raised to respect and confide in the remedial power of drugs, but after many years of practice in close conformity to the dictation of the very best medical authors and in consultation with representatives of the various schools, I failed to get from drugs the results hoped for and I was face to face with the evidence that medicine was not only untrustworthy but dangerous.
>
> The mechanical principles on which osteopathy is based are as old as the universe. I discovered them while I was in Kansas. You can call this discovery accidental or purely philosophical. I was in the practice of medicine and had been for several years. I treated my patients as other doctors did. A part of them got well and a part of them died. Others both old and young got sick and got well without the assistance of the medical doctor.
>
> As I was an educated engineer of five years' schooling I began to look at the human framework as a machine and examine all its parts to see if I could find any variation from the truly normal among its journals, belts, pulleys, and escape pipes. I began to experiment with man's body as a master mechanic would when he had in his charge any machinery which needed to be kept perfectly adjusted and in line in order to get perfect work. There are many ways by which a machine may be adjusted. An osteopathic operator is not expected to depend on any one method or manipulation for the adjustment of a bone.[1]

Still did not. He developed modes of treatment based on ever more subtle analyses of anatomical relationships. "We, as engineers, have but one question to ask," he asserted: "What has the body failed to do?"[2]

The kinetic junctions among bones, muscles, and nerves are more or less obvious, so there is no reason to question the potential effectiveness of osteopathy in the treatment of injuries, strains, sciatica, or even constipation. In this context osteopathy is an expanded version of massage and even maternal care-giving. But Still used his method to treat pneumonia, diabetes, mumps, hysteria, alcoholism, mental disease, and the like. Even though he also employed pharmacy, diet,

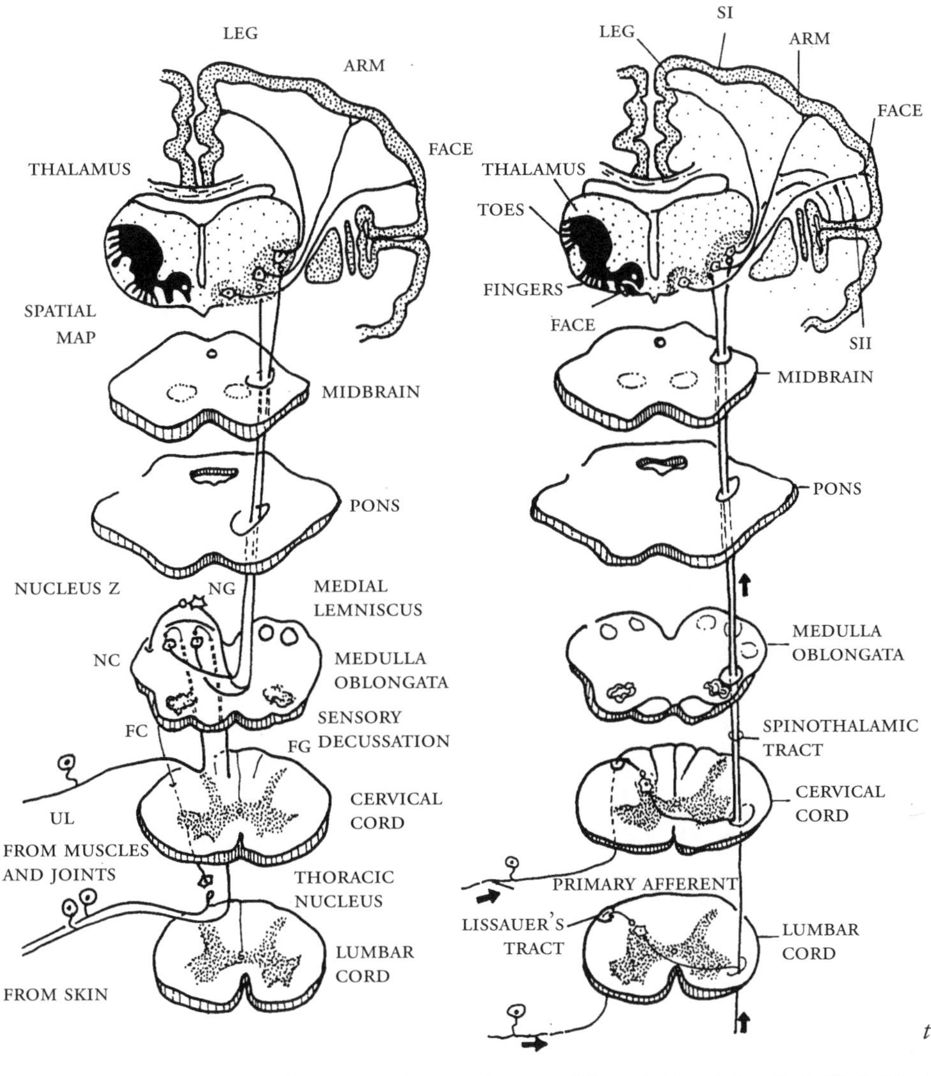

Dorsal column—lemniscal pathway (left)

Spinothalamic tract (right)

Reprinted from *An Introduction to Craniosacral Therapy* by Don Cohen, D.C., North Atlantic Books, 1995.

hygiene, surgery, and verbal therapy (he meant osteopathy to be a complete system of medicine), his emphasis was primarily on understanding anatomy, not only in the gross sense but as ever more subtle levels of hormonal and fascial microanatomy.

Although there was no precisely replicatable formula to Still's techniques, he did generally seek to restore blood supply and nerve respon-

siveness in afflicted areas, from the perspective that natural flow would lead to the organs' reestablishing themselves harmonically. He did not intend to antidote every germ and flush out every toxin because a kinetic system regaining its efficiency would accomplish all that without interference.

Still endowed that kinetic system with almost magical properties. He perceived that the circulation of fluids, energies, and substances through the body was highly complex and occurred on many levels simultaneously, including not only arterial, venous, nervous, lymphatic, and cerebrospinal components but also others foreshadowing axoplasmic flow. What he could not explicitly assign to a level of circulation, he assigned to the collective circulatory mechanism of the organism. In this sense, he likely came upon some of the same ostensibly vital reactions that *Chi Gung* therapists and Hippocratic doctors attributed to other causes specified by their own paradigms. While Still's treatments activated ever more discrete and discriminative layers within the body, with results almost magical in scope, he stuck patriotically to his mechanical epistemology:

> To the osteopath who understands the human body as the engineer does his engine, all the mysteries disappear.... He squares, plumbs and levels all foundations, journals and boxings. He examines all pulleys to know that they are in place and position. He examines the belt to see if one side is longer than the other. He corrects and goes on.... With the square and plumb he adjusts the drive wheels, pulleys and journals, then he inspects all pipes conducting water to his boiler and all pipes conducting steam to the chest.[3]

Still emphasized diseased conditions originating in the head, neck, thorax, abdomen, and pelvis, with particular concern for encumbrances in the pelvic zone, all of which ultimately engaged organs like the kidneys, spleen, lungs, and heart. His mechanical treatments are models of ingenuity, and they were responsible for much of osteopathy's success. For instance, he explained pneumonia as a constriction of the thoracic/pulmonary system leading to stagnation of the venous system and

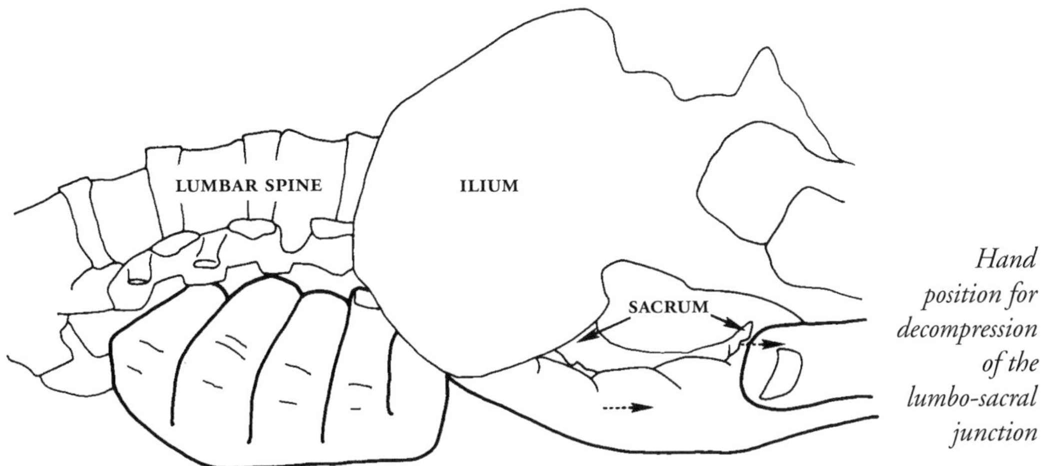

Hand position for decompression of the lumbo-sacral junction

Reprinted from *CranioSacral Therapy* by John E. Upledger and Jon D. Vredevoogd with permission of the publisher, Eastland Press, Inc., P.O. Box 12689, Seattle, WA 98111.

impure blood curable through sequential adjustments of different bones. In the case of a cataract of the eye, he advises:

> Adjust the bones of the upper spine, ribs and neck and re-establish normal nerve and blood supply. Then make a gentle tapping of the eye to loosen the crystalline lens a little. With one finger give a few flips or gentle taps on the back of another finger the soft part of which is held against the side of the eye. This tapping should be just strong enough to make the eye ache a little. Without any surgical interference whatever I have been rewarded in a majority of cases by the disappearance of that white substance in the eye called a cataract.[4]

For constipation:

> . . . [W]hen the pelvis is crowded and impacted with bowel, uterus, bladder, fecal matter or any foreign growths he [the osteopath] must get a free return of the venous blood with a normal action of the lymphatics, in order that they may throw off the water fluids to supply the intestines. He can expect normal action of the bowel to appear very soon after the drawing up of the viscera from out of its impacted condition in the pelvic cavity.[5]

For drunkenness:

> I found the ribs in the region of his left shoulder pushed upward. I threw his arm up putting the ribs on a strain and placed them back into position, and then said to him, "Now go into the saloon and come back, and if you do not want to turn sick at the smell of liquor I will pay for the whiskey."[6]

Osteopathy still rests more upon a working set of intuitions and empirical discoveries than upon a formal theory of disease causation and cure. Still himself was forced to revise even his own primary axiom. According to medical historians:

> ... [W]hen it was made clear to him that any spinal dislocation large enough to block the artery would give rise to a complete paraplegia, if not instant death from rupture of aorta, he changed this "Rule of the Artery" to pressure on a nerve, disease now resulting from the cessation of vital force transmitted to an organ along the nerve-trunk. This idea has scarcely been modified since....[7]

That is not true. The "meaning" of osteopathic adjustment is certainly not linear or unidimensional. It has been modified from decade to decade and is now fully in the service of a psychosomatic and holistic archetype, casting its lot with other so-called "quantum medicines." The nerves have become merely a concrete metaphor for the transfer and transmutation of a substance far more resembling *chi* than chains of axons and dendrons. The uncritical reference to nerves among osteopaths is also a subtext that "feeling" (or its negation) in some fashion lies at the basis of most pathology.

Osteopathy is, in another sense, generic Hippocratic medicine carried out with faith in touch, dexterity, and according to the anatomical guesses of the doctor rather than by disease classes and through biochemical or surgical remediation. It features the physician as acrobat and martial artist rather than as laboratory technician and taxonomist. The initial prejudice is to think that osteopathy cannot be the same as medicine because it lacks sophisticated tools and intellectual

categories and utilizes mere mechanical and skeletal adjustment or visceral massage—as though to stroke the intestinal region could cure a cancer as effectively as to cut into the very tissue could. But if we view the osteopathic principles from a different perspective, we can see that osteopathy is also a complex and complete medicine. It proposes treatments based as much on mechanical cause and effect as allopathy, though it translates the burden of mechanical correction to the already-functioning organism, which is viewed as perfect. It doesn't need heavy equipment because, like other "homeopathic" treatments, it relies on the viscera to respond self-curatively to a quantum of energy directed appropriately in the right spot.

Allopathy, with its more entropic view of the universe, takes account of the grand array of parasites, germs, viruses, bacteria, toxins, and "bad" genes and assumes constant remedial work is needed for each of us even to survive. In a sense, modern medicine boggles itself with the complexity of the universe to such a degree that diagnosing and curing defects become substitutes for ordinary living. Osteopathy, by contrast, assumes that almost any pathology can be reversed by mechanical stimulation or manipulation. It assumes that the body is already working well enough to solve most of its problems but will respond to a firm and artistic mechanical adjustment. Like a skilled dancer catching the beat of music, the organism picks up the curative vector. If the latter example is a case of gross medical oversimplification, the former is a fallacy of hygienic obsession.

Yet many of the techniques which are common in allopathy also occur in osteopathy in somewhat disguised forms—almost always simpler, and less intellectual and academic—because osteopathy assumes that we exist primarily and functionally at the level of bones, fluids, and viscera. It considers most of the highly refined chemical, radiational, and surgical modalities dangerously invasive, for they literally undermine an ontologically prior level of function and self-healing homeostasis to penetrate, on a simply conceptual and idealized level, the molecular realm where disease products are said to originate and spread.

By the allopathic line of reasoning, atomic and subatomic medicines may one day become our mainstays in tracking the origin of diseases. But what if none of this is necessary? What if the molecular and atomic realms are not the functional dimension in which to seek? What if these contain mere synergistic effects of events originating elsewhere, inalterable there? What if creatures have all the requirements for health holistically integrated at a far grosser level?

From Still's standpoint, osteopathy is not only directly medical but more medical than surgery. Far from being superficial, osteopathic touch is scientific, and the physician works his way into the patient's system by following sensations to their exact source. What could be more empirical? What is surgery that should make it any more scientific and profound than such guided manipulation? Who set the rule that you should have to touch and incise actual disease products in order to heal tissues?

> The philosophy of manipulations is based upon an absolute knowledge of the form and function of all bones belonging to the bony framework of the human body.... Simply to know that our heads are situated upon the atlas and the atlas on the axis, that we have

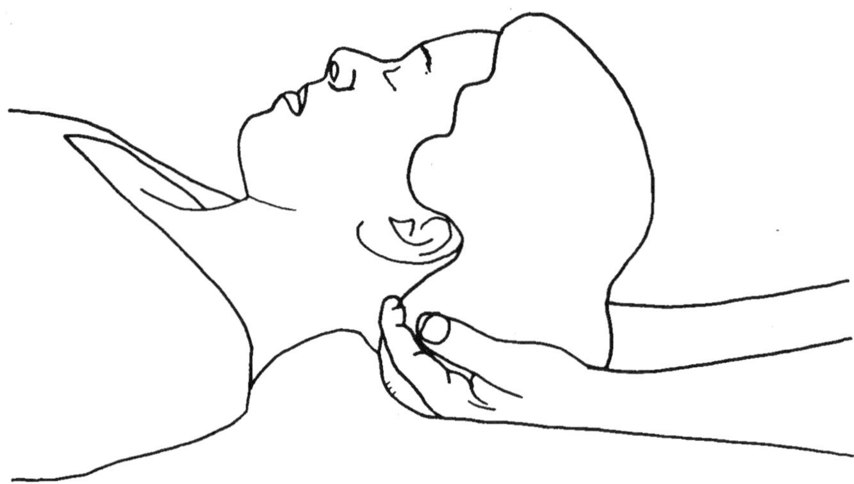

Occipital decompression

Reprinted from *An Introduction to Craniosacral Therapy* by Don Cohen, D.C., North Atlantic Books, 1995.

> seven bones in the neck, twelve in the dorsal region and five in the lumbar is of little use. We must have a perfect image of the normal articulations of the bone or bones that we wish to adjust. We must be critically certain that we know all articulations of the bones in the whole system. We must know how blood is supplied and when that arterial blood has done its work we must know how it returns and what would be an obstruction to prevent its return.... Nature is a living critic and the answer must be yes or no....[8]

By these standards, surgery is not a technological advance but a retreat from pure science—a refuge only for the allopath who does not want to consider the whole system and its interrelationships as much as he wants to find shortcuts to produce temporary but dramatic results. His access to a machinery of overkill and his allegiance to the lineage of that machinery leads to his removing structures which may have future use:

> I am proud of osteopathic surgery which never uses a knife for the removal of tumors of the breast, abdomen or any other part of the body, until the arterial supply and venous drainage have failed to restore vitality and reduce the system and its organs to their normal functioning. Through the arterial supply and the venous drainage a large percent of tumors of the abdomen and breast will vanish in the hands of a trustworthy and philosophical osteopathic doctor.[9]

So Still, though obliquely mechanical to the end in his world-view, opened the way to a direct naturopathic treatment of the body. His osteopathy may have been a new system, but it was also a post-scientific rebirth of an original mechanical medicine practiced no doubt idiosyncratically and with a million variants from the tribes of Africa and the rain-forest bands of South America to the island peoples of the Pacific and the folk doctors of Europe and the New World. A man who began as an ardent materialist ended up describing the lungs as "'organs, beings or personalities of life.' Similarly, he saw the bowels, kidneys, skin, and fascia as excretory structures. In the case of the fascia, he clearly was experiencing something different than most other investigators of

the human body. Elsewhere he notes that the functions of the heart include imparting life and knowledge to the blood."[10]

Still was the founder of osteopathy as a system, but the later branches of cranial osteopathy and craniosacral therapy owe their development to an insight of William G. Sutherland. A student at Still's College of Osteopathy in Kirksville, Missouri, Sutherland was familiar with the school's famous mounted disarticulated skull—that is, a skull in which the individual cranial bones were pulled apart and wired into positions true to their original structure yet revealing the complexity of their sutures. In 1899, "glancing at the Beauchene skull, he became transfixed by the squamosal suture of the temporal bones, the rolling-overlap joint between temporals and parietals. The words 'Bevelled like the gills of a fish, and indicating articular mobility for a respiratory mechanism' flashed into his mind."[11] At the time, even in the osteopathic world, the cranium was presumed beyond a doubt to be a deeply and intricately interlocked dome (to this day there is no clear recognition of the pliability of the bones of the skull in most American medical texts).

It was not until his fifth year of practice in Minnesota that Sutherland actually got to explore his intuition. He purchased a football helmet, small pieces of India rubber, leather, straps, shoemaker's buckles, and sewing materials and turned the helmet into a laboratory for restricting the individual bones of skull and thus testing their ranges of motion. That is, he immobilized his own supposedly immobile bones and, to the distress of his wife, induced an astonishing array of neuroses and internal ailments. Their naturally occurring counterparts, of course, would lend themselves to cure through cranial manipulation.

As he experienced the subtle and sinuous cycles of motility among the often-tiny articulated bones, he painstakingly remapped the skeletal cranium itself as dynamic tissue. Then he developed means of manipulating and balancing its individual zones, always with great precision because of the subtle properties of such miniscule fields of articulation.

He soon built a practice based on treating a variety of emotional and physical disorders, including migraines and various mysterious cranial maladies.

Sutherland's next level of experimentation came from a curiosity to find out what happened when he tied down all the straps at once. In this profoundly uncomfortable headlock (which, all the same, should have been entirely static from the standpoint of almost all medical theories) he was astonished to feel his sacrum begin to oscillate rhythmically while becoming warmer. He had located what was to become the "core link" of cranial osteopathy, the energetic and mechanical conjugation between the occiput and the sacrum through the supple spinal dura. "Indicating articular mobility for a respiratory mechanism" indeed!

Ram's horns

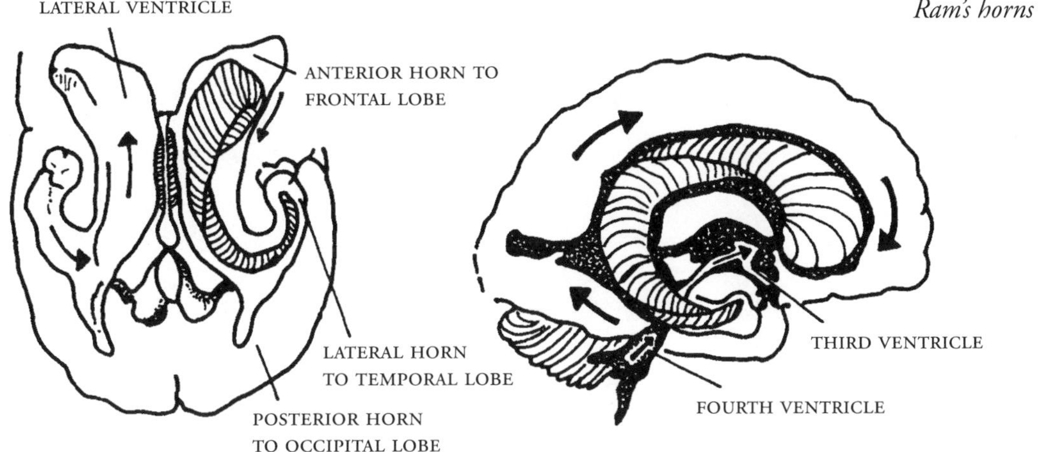

Reprinted from *An Introduction to Craniosacral Therapy* by Don Cohen, D.C., North Atlantic Books, 1995.

The design of the temporal bones provided the original inspiration for William G. Sutherland's concept of cranial bone motion. He noticed that the temporal sutures are "bevelled like the gills of a fish" and the bones swivel around a rotatory horizontal axis in a spiraling fashion that in flexion flares the anterior aspects laterally, like gills, and approximates the mastoids. The motion of the temporals reflects the "ram's horn" configuration of the lateral ventricles.

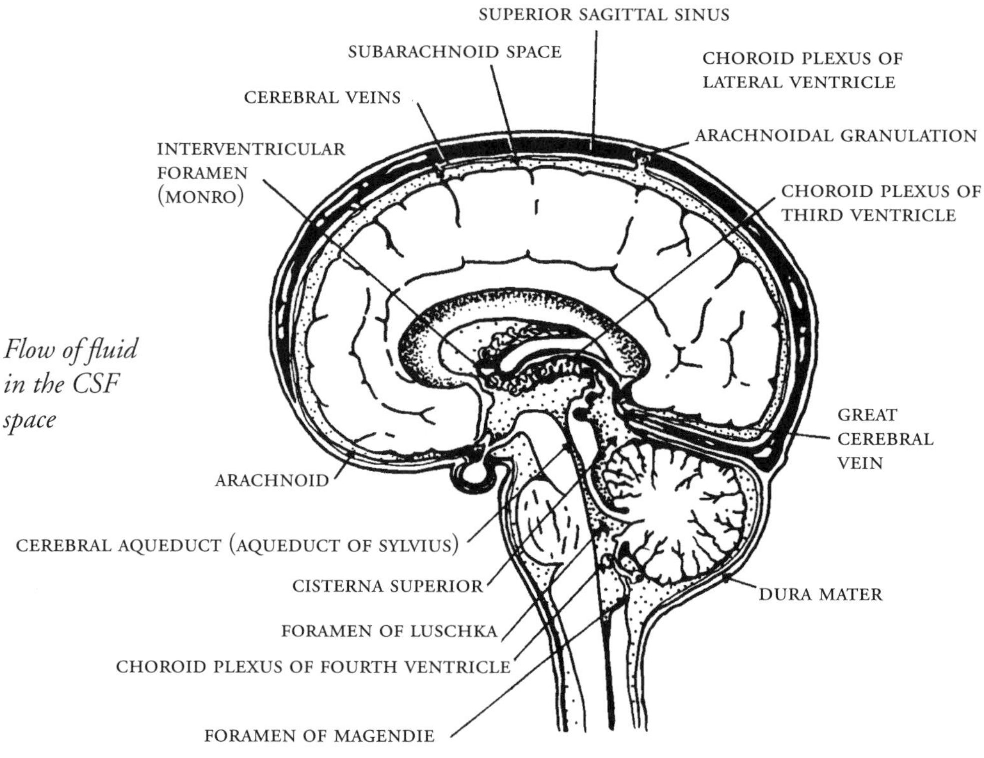

Flow of fluid in the CSF space

Reprinted from *An Introduction to Craniosacral Therapy* by Don Cohen, D.C., North Atlantic Books, 1995.

> [Sutherland] would describe his experiments upon himself to his wife:
>
> He told of lying down, his head in the V-shape head rest; of imposing compression by gradual tension of buckle and strap. He described the sensations he had experienced as he approached near-unconsciousness. And that although weakened, he had succeeded in releasing the leverage strap. "A sensation of warmth followed," he explained. "And also a remarkable movement of fluid up and down the spinal column, throughout the ventricles.... Fantastic!"[12]

He later described the experience of listening to the cerebrospinal fluid—Still's "great river of life"—irrigating the central nervous system "like water going under ice." He eventually ascribed the onset of most diseases to the "inactivity of the cerebrospinal fluid, lymph, and blood."[13]

Ultimately Sutherland came to rediscover the body as a subtle, fluid entity, combining respiratory, circulatory, skeletal, emotional and other properties in a series of interrelated functions. The flow of cerebrospinal fluid was a crucial player in this symphony:

> In [my] experiments of controlling or directing cranial respiratory movement, it was found that the diaphragmatic respiratory mechanism changed its rhythm to that of the cranial. Hence the conclusion that the diaphragmatic respiratory system is secondary to the cranial....
>
> This hypothesis views the lateral ventricles as dilating during the period of inhalation; the convolution of the hemispheres in the meantime expanding. During this same period the third ventricle dilates in a V-form manner, the fourth ventricle in a lozenge form, while the spinal cord is drawn upward; and the CSF fluctuates within the sub-arachnoid spaces and the ventricles. During the period of exhalation, the convolutions relax, the ventricles contract, the spinal cord drops downwards, and the CSF again fluctuates within the sub-arachnoid spaces and ventricles.[14]

This is vintage osteopathy, dancing between phenomenological anatomy and scientific observation.

The medicine of sensitivity and vitality Still initiated is not fully realized even today. There is a general illusion that osteopathy was accepted and incorporated into mainstream medicine decades ago. After all, osteopaths have their own sanctioned medical schools and practice in allopathic hospitals. This outcome, however, speaks not to the success of Still's and Sutherland's science but to the effectiveness of the AMA in frightening its actual practitioners into submission. Osteopaths who were loyal to their tradition either went into hiding or practiced like thieves. I have heard accounts of old-school doctors who had to know a person really well before they would treat him with their full repertoire or even show him their writings. Otherwise, they practiced a superficial version of osteopathy, always in fear of inspectors. Many

refused to sell their published books and destroyed their unpublished writings at death.

A great number, however, totally abandoned the aspect of their trade that made them real osteopaths and became allopaths with an accent, an incidental specialty. In that form, yes, osteopathy made it into the mainstream, but as cranial osteopathy and energetic medicine—and as a lay medicine that could be practiced by those without a medical degree—it all but disappeared.

The inherent contradiction of osteopathy—that its techniques were far more sophisticated than its formulaic paradigm—inevitably lured practitioners to seek the chimera of official recognition and sanction. After all, they had many successful cures and happy patients in their resumé. Yet, like homeopathy, osteopathy presents a medical impossibility (at least by allopathic standards). It cures the sick but cannot say precisely why or how. As a team of orthopedic historians smugly recounts, the early British attempts at legitimization were a disaster:

> Curiously enough, the osteopaths ... tried to establish themselves legally, as practicing an alternative system of medicine, by an application to the House of Lords in 1935, but their answers to the medical questions put to them at the hearing brought them into a number of impossible situations. In the end, their position became untenable. Small wonder; for they denied standard tenets built up during centuries of research by doctors all over the world, without putting forward a shred of disproof, and affirmed an alternative creed without offering any evidence in its favour. They claimed to practise a complete and revolutionary alternative system of medicine, but when the Lords asked on what grounds these remarkable assertions rested, none was put forward. This ventilation was an advantage; for the osteopaths were shown in their true light, not only to doctors and the public, but also to themselves. As a result, few even of the most bigoted now claim to cure *all* diseases by manipulating the spine....[15]

But in truth the claim that all diseases can be cured by manipulating the spine is merely the historical launching point for osteopathy—

at best, a ritual superstition to which only the most poorly trained osteopathic hacks still cling. It is no wonder these would prefer to petition entry to the mainstream of medicine because their osteopathy is merely a superficial imitation of Still's methods without the guided intelligence of his touch. It is not intuitive enough to be an art and not rationalist enough to sustain a modern scientific practice. However, as we shall see, while maybe only the most bigoted sought to join allopathy, many of the rest indeed continued to treat a wide array of diseases by manipulating not only the spine but the viscera, fascial tissue, and other bones.

Yet one can certainly understand the mainstream outrage at publicized osteopathic claims insofar as the more pedantic osteopaths and chiropractors do little more than adjust bones from a world-view that simple subluxations restrict all healthy life-flow. These are the same practitioners who produce exploitative X-rays and feign improvements of these by adjustments they do not actually succeed at (and which, if they did, would accomplish little or nothing). They are neither intuitive grass-roots bone-setters in a folk tradition nor skilled vitalistic physicians in a contemporary energetic paradigm. They are trapped between these poles in a middle ground made up of the worst of primitive medicine (crude linear manipulation) and the worst of technological medicine (X-ray simplification of disease etiology). They are osteopaths who want to be doctors without taking the necessary courses. Perhaps they are also amateur doctors who want to be osteopaths but without any ability at diagnostic touch. When I propose a future osteopathic medicine, I mean the ancient skills and genius of the native cranial osteopath combined with the medical skills of the contemporary manipulative physician.

Although the above-cited orthopedic critics would have little sympathy for such a profession, they do note the separate realms of manipulative physiotherapist and M.D. and cite the need for well-trained auxiliaries to standard physicians:

> The family doctor would no longer be forced either to manipulate himself, perhaps hurriedly with unskilled assistance, or covertly to advise recourse to some layman. He would send the patient for manipulative physiotherapy; this would be faithfully carried out as a matter of course by an auxiliary fully trained in these methods and accustomed to working side by side with the medical profession. The arrangement has already been established in Norway, where a special register of those skilled in manipulation is available to doctors.[16]

From my viewpoint, this is a halfway measure that, while recognizing the importance of manipulation, attempts to limit it to a subset of exactly the linear and Solidist viewpoints that doomed osteopathy never to become a full medical system. It is an attempt to claim the most trivial aspects of manipulation for the medical hierarchy (those aspects that cannot threaten it) and discard the innovative system that arose from them.

It was primarily a successful medical osteopath, John Upledger, who had the credibility and ingenuity to revive cranial osteopathy in the late 1970s, develop it, and demedicalize its model of practice. His "coming out of the closet" horrified not only orthodox doctors but the osteopathic establishment, and he was informally ostracized from the profession. However, on his appointment to the National Institutes of Health Office of Alternative Medicine panel in 1993, the osteopathic journals reclaimed him as one of their own. Reinventing osteopathy was crucial, for it took it out of a domain in which it could not grow or attain legitimacy, and more crucially, it freed it to become what it was by developing its techniques in concordance with massage, spirit healing, shamanism, movement arts, and somatic psychotherapy. The Upledger Institute, with its research center in West Palm Beach, Florida, now offers a diverse and radically innovative curriculum taught in hotels and meeting rooms in cities around the world. It has become both the current locus of the realization of osteopathy and the nucleus of a new, unexplored medicine arising from osteopathy (see the Resource Guide).

IT IS NOT UNUSUAL for systems to gravitate toward their opposite pole. Psychoanalysis began as language and linguistic therapy and inevitably drifted toward the "body as shadow" in Reich and also drug therapies. Homeopathy began as vitalistic characterology and swung toward statistical materialism. Allopathy began as hygiene and care-giving and evolved as vivisection and microanalysis. After all, a system does not necessarily continue to address the world on the level it initially proposes. Its subtexts take on their own life.

Still was an engineer. He construed the organism as a divine machine of flesh and bones. His strategies for repairing that machine originated in familiar technological metaphors. He was confident that the Architect of the machine was of Christian and progressive persuasion and welcomed the improvements of science as a celebration of his own design. Yet once Still (and his followers) began grabbing bones and fascia by their protrusions and draining tissue like a sponge, they entered into the mysterious realm of the body's reciprocities and homeostases and the impregnation of the mind in organs. They were dealing with a machine perhaps, but it was a cybernetic, holographic machine of an order that had not yet been imagined.

Osteopathy opened a whole realm of hands-on medicine embracing manipulation but also moving beyond it into realms of innovative quantum healing. The first osteopaths unwittingly invented a model for palpation itself as a healing technique; then they set a priority of subtlety. It is the original internalized projection of osteopathy that keeps providing bodywork with a medical paradigm even as it is external research in a laboratory that makes allopathy scientific.

It is possible that all of the functions of the living body are reducible to fulcra, levers, pulleys, and pumps, but if that is so, it occurs as extremely complex gradations of kinetic energy between the gross and the subtle, with motion constantly flowing downwards from the skeletal to the cellular and upwards from the molecular to the organic. Cells and molecules also have fulcra, pulleys, pumps, etc. The overall machinery of the body is multidimensional and kinesthetic and, within the

domain of mind, fluctuates as surely as photons between waves and particles.

Still set a machine in motion, and the resonance he kindled between his fingertips continues (through the present osteopathic disciplines) to be distributed down to the subtlest levels of flesh and to return from there. Yet, no matter how the operator behaves, the machine can never be run as a simple assembly-line robot. Soft and sentient in every aspect, it takes vectors imposed onto it and transposes them into other vectors which generate yet others. What Still did not fully perceive was that the force he directed into the body from the premise of a machinery was received by that machinery as nonlinear impulses and stimulation of protoplasmic currents. The same was true for Sutherland; his (albeit delicate) clockwork of cranial osteopathy was also a transfusion of imagery and energy of an indeterminate nature. Thus, osteopathic palpation reinvented itself in its own living medium. The original machine of Still has not been discarded; it continues to translate simple into complex energy. It is the kind of machine that, once it perceives a conductor, leads him silently into its own plan.

Today osteopathy is both a manipulative medicine (in fact, *the* pure manipulative medicine) seeking legitimacy under the blanket of professional health care and supporting medical trainings that mirror conventional ones, and an innovative science tracking ever subtler currents in the living machine. It has also become, for some, a mode of placing hands on bones and viscera and touching the soul.

Chiropractic

In developing chiropractic, D. D. Palmer proposed that three factors influenced the chronic subluxation patterns in patients. They were deep-seated traumas, poisons (including autotoxicities), and autosuggestions (or self-hypnosis). All of these generate self-replicating cycles through which the organism loses its inherent "cure" capacity; they literally deplete the potential to transmit healing oscillations and signals.

The resulting facilitated segment, as defined by the chiropractor, is a level of spinal cord that has become hyperactive or hair-triggered from postural and emotional stress and, while perpetuating itself, numbs potentially therapeutic impulses en route to surrounding muscles and skin, which consequently become restricted and amorphous. That is, a vertebra becomes subluxated; in this condition it impinges upon nerves, blood vessels and lymphatics traveling through the intervertebral foramen; the conduction of autonomic neural pulses is impaired; and parts of the organism subject to that vertebra's nervous tonus become predisposed to disease. The facilitated segment comes to represent essentially a dynamic, dysfunctional interaction between the somatic system, the viscera, and the autonomic nervous system on the one hand and the mind on the other.

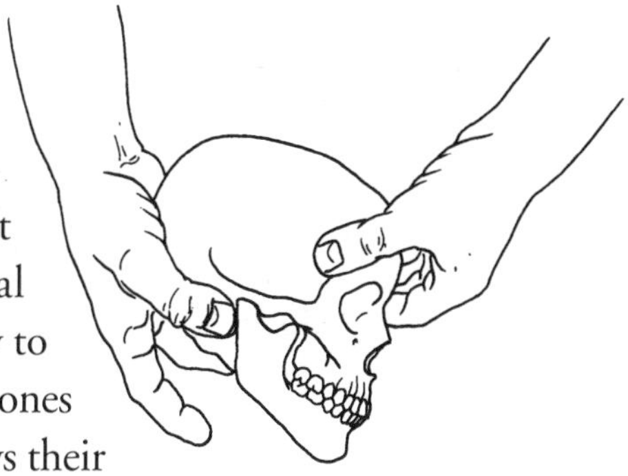

The chiropractic formula for adjusting such subluxations is: the minimum force, in the correct direction, at the maximum speed. Each movement is enacted confidently and with an elegant jolt that transcends its gross mechanics. The cranial osteopath likewise uses the least pressure necessary to induce a reaction, but then, instead of forcing the bones and viscera into a presumed normal path, he follows their intrinsic movement. Both systems emphasize intention over pressure, though traditional chiropractic tends to prefer (often to the exclusion of directly palpating the viscera) dramatic skeletal jolts with immediate energetic outcome.

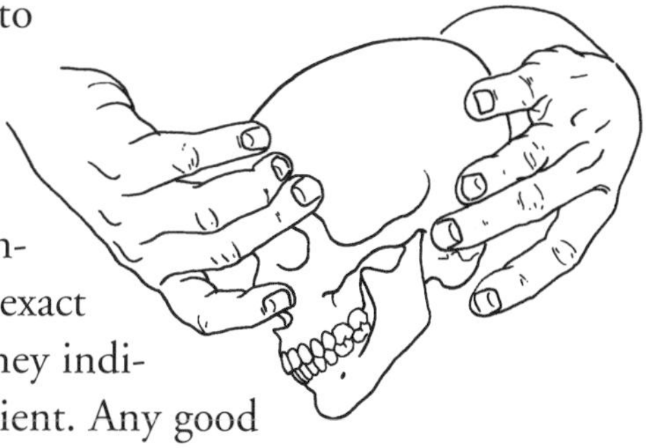

For the modern chiropractor, disease is not simply a matter of bones out of alignment, but the exact vectors of such tilts and restrictions and what they indicate about the life and responsiveness of the patient. Any good physician must interpret the signaling errors from a holistic point of view, not jumping to conclusions that the body's awkwardness or asymmetry *per se* are functional statements of illnesses. He may adjust skeletal tissue to restore health, but, remember, the original tilt was carried out by a disease or injury which set the biomechanical charge for such realignment. Chiropractic is to that extent "homeopathic," since its remedies reenact aspects of diseases. They go toward the direction of the block and then release back. They do not try to budge anatomy into the right position. Even allopathic surgery is unintentionally "chiropractic" insofar as it attempts to "outdo" a disease on its own plane, imposing its precise disfigurement and adding its didactic "wound" to the pathology.

That so many chiropractically defined lesions and osteopathic restrictions and energy cysts are imperceptible to orthopedic surgeons may scream unabashed fraud to the medical establishment, but this might also indicate the layers of subtlety in the body itself. Chiropractors and osteopaths might see "diseases" that slip through even the most rigorous allopathic exams.

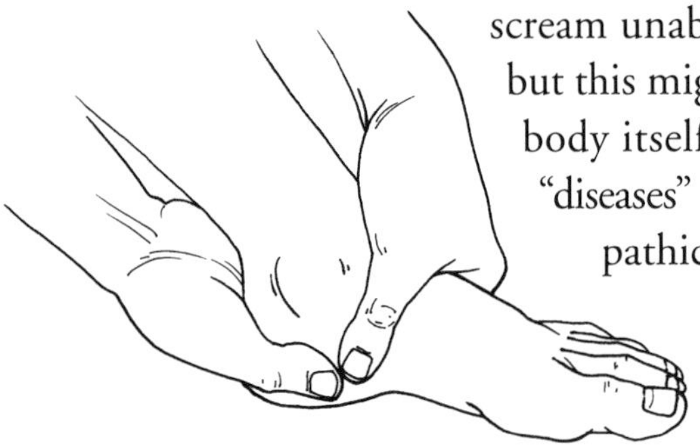

Sometimes when a surgeon fails to recognize anything pathological on an MRI and finds no clinical basis for dysfunction, and when anti-inflammatories and other mechanical treatments (such as orthotics) have no remedial effect, yet the patient is in such pain he cannot walk, the reason is that the condition exists only on multiple psychosomatic levels, expressing its dysfunctional cohesiveness and power to restrict on no one level completely enough to be diagnosed there. The pathology is dynamic, holistic, and single. The conventional doctor cannot locate it because its visceral or skeletal symptoms by themselves are not sufficiently impacted to leave telltale scars, and the psychiatrist cannot track a deep-seated emotional cathexis in the fascia and neuromusculature. Thus, no one is able to give a name to the condition—or to help.

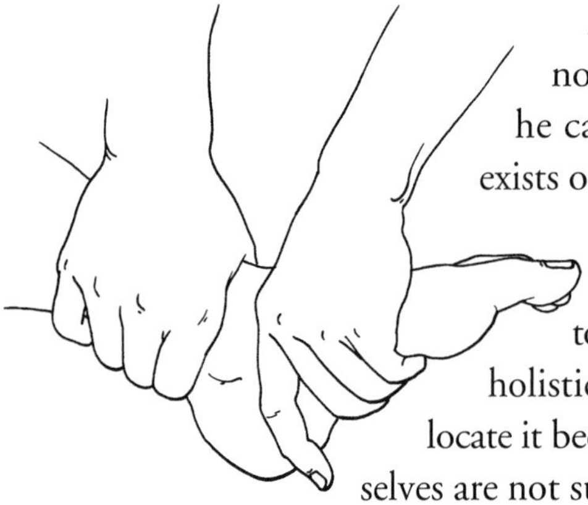

This is why osteopathy and chiropractic have found their niche in medicine between surgery and psychiatry. People are often in pain for "no reason" allopathically. What the chiropractor feels with his hands (allowing him to venture a treatment), as concrete as it seems and as acceptable the results of his subsequent adjustment to the patient, cannot be located or named either before or after in allopathic terms. Even if there is an allopathic disease, it is by definition a different energetic complex. The prescribed regimen likewise may vary so much as to require, for instance, immobilization allopathically and induction of movement chiropractically. It is like the difference between moving vertically and horizontally or between compressing and diffusing.

The same contradiction exists on the axis between psychoanalysis and chiropractic. A headache with weeping would seem psychiatrically to have its origin in a personal event, whereas a chiropractor might find its agitation at the fifth vertebra, making the psychological origin incidental to his quick and efficient cure. Ten years of psychoanalysis would accomplish nothing, at least vis-à-vis that ailment, though it might accomplish other therapeutic things. Sometimes the psychosomatic penetration of character shares more finally with the chiropractor and acupuncturist than with the psychiatrist.

Bone adjustment can be like standing on a very high mountain, looking at everything far away. That's how bones are. They create the sense of space the body encloses. If a bone is damaged or shifted out of place, even infinitesimally, the disorientation is vast; identity becomes shapeless. At the moment the adjustment takes place—the famous bone cracking—there is not so much pain as immense surprise. The spacing within shifts and the muscles momentarily hang on nothing. Energy releases electrically through the system and toxins flush out. The viscera respond instantaneously. The stomach expands and fills its own hollowness and sensations of sadness. The lungs and chest

surge with air as if it were magnetically drawn into them. They expand and contract easily and fully; the breath rushes into them as into deep, sucking cavities.

Such fundamental reorientation may activate new fear, but a very faraway fear, as a shape seen from a mountain. That separation from panic at the same time it is experienced is crucial. At the moment when the bones crack and right afterward, the sensation is as though the person is standing above a river, a river which rushes between his legs, limitless in both directions. Suddenly he is lifted above the river and dropped on both sides of it at once. He struggles to his feet, but he is on both sides, he is on opposite sides, he is on the wrong side from himself and must somehow cross over in order to get back together, but as each half tries to cross, so does the other half. There is the momentary amnesia that he has ended up on the wrong side and he can never get back to the right one. Then the effects settle, and the new side becomes the right side. In fact, it is familiar as the right side from long ago, before the loss of function.

In acupuncture, by contrast, the needles go directly into the body's mind. They feel like bee-stings, but their actual locations are redistributed by the field they create. It is not so much the pain of the needles that is uncomfortable but the overall sense of being out of alignment, of being torn between two selves. Even thought hurts, for the same thoughts can no longer travel in the old way.

One makes a new grid for the river of his or her own being. After the treatment the river will gradually shift toward its familiar bed, but it will have been slightly redirected. Over time, through recurrent needle treatments, herbs, *t'ai chi,* Feldenkrais work, or other remedies, the river may forge a fresh channel. Whatever this river is made of—nerves, blood, *chi,* mind, or some synergistic fluidity—it carries the organs with it, for they are elementally subsequent. At every juncture of experience an alteration of current is felt because the entire field of the meridians is being realigned.

In the end, it does not matter what side of the river one is on or what happens when the tingling stops. Life continues from there, as whatever life is.

Applied Kinesiology[17]

In 1964 Dr. George Goodheart, a chiropractor in Detroit, Michigan, was working with a patient on a muscle that manually tested weak. That is, he came upon a weakness while contracting the person's muscles in precisely controlled vectors, continuously varying his intensity of counterforce and mobilizing a response. Weakness was experienced as collapse, flaccidity, and lack of opposition. Through experiment Goodheart found that the weak muscle could be strengthened by his stimulating its point of origin and insertion. Inspired by this simple but profound demonstration of functional improvement, Goodheart continued to test variations of relationships leading to changes in muscle function. He eventually correlated each muscle on a map with acupuncture meridians and organs, as well as with specific reflex points, including most notably those from the lymphatic reflex work of Frank Chapman, an osteopath, and the neurovascular research of T. J. Bennett, a chiropractor. (Bennett developed his concept of vascular reflexes in the late 1950s by holding certain reflex points while observing the vascular engorgement of the organs under fluoroscopy. Unfortunately, he and several of his patients died of leukemia as a likely result of their exposure to X-ray.)

Adapting the methods of standard orthopedic muscle examination with an understanding of the direct relationship between structure and function, Applied Kinesiology utilizes binary responses of muscles to evaluate functional systems of the body based on what Goodheart calls

"the five factors of the intervertebral foramen": nerve, blood vessel, lymphatic vessel, acupuncture meridian, and cerebrospinal fluid.[18]

The trademark of Applied Kinesiology is the concept that the organism can be "communicated with" directly, utilizing its own inherent responses to various stimuli in an attempt to uncover the dysfunction that underlies each symptom. In the most comprehensive and systematic attempt at establishing dialogue with the autonomic system that has ever been documented, Goodheart and his associates have spent thirty years exploring and mapping such diverse territories as:

- the relationships of muscles and organs, and the interpretation of body language;
- the relationships of musculoskeletal dysfunction, organ and lymphatic function, nutritional requirements, and emotional stress overload;
- the nature of allergies;
- right and left brain function;
- endocrine function;
- nutritional function;
- the lymphatic system;
- headaches;
- immune function;
- environmental sensitivities and syndromes of maladaptation;
- chronic fatigue syndrome;
- the multiple functions of the liver;
- the function of the heart in facilitating corpuscular valence;
- herpes simplex;
- arthritis, bursitis, and tendinitis;
- the cellular function of RNA;
- hypertension;

and a multitude of other physiological functions.

Applied Kinesiology interprets muscle responses in two primary investigative formats: Challenge and Therapy Localization. In Challenge, the practitioner introduces a question in the form of a stimulus, for example by pushing a joint together or pulling it apart, and then watches the response of the muscle. In Therapy Localization, the subject (patient) touches his own body and the practitioner observes a similar response. For example, upon touching the lymphatic reflex for the liver with his hand, a patient's pectoral muscle might change from weak to strong (or vice versa), indicating a possible organismic response to a deficiency in this system. The meaning of the response to any test rests with the practitioner, and herein lies the flaw of Applied Kinesiology. There have been a multitude of unreliable conclusions drawn by various practitioners on the basis of seeming change in an "indicator muscle." Alarmed patients have been told that their kidneys, heart, and liver are weak, or that they are allergic to spaghetti, based on a superficially conducted muscle test. Goodheart himself has vehemently and publicly condemned such hasty applications of muscle testing, insisting that muscle response is but one indicator of a possible need for further investigation, and preferring to correlate his findings with objective tests and indicators of all kinds. Much to Goodheart's chagrin, his warnings have often gone unheeded and Applied Kinesiology has been discredited by various claimants who might make their living by, for instance, determining that a subject demonstrates a need for megadoses of Vitamin E by placing a bottle of the substance on her belly and testing the deltoid muscle.[19] Applied Kinesiology, in this version, generates many a cartoon satirizing the New Age.

When used in the context of other systems, Applied Kinesiology opens an original realm of somatic investigation, contributing to holistic allergology, environmental medicine, visceral manipulation, and Western applications of Ayurvedic taste theory, all of which it has merged with at one time or another to form hybrids of muscle testing with herbal or somatic remediation. Applied Kinesiology also provides a physical basis for diagnosis within purely vitalistic and psychic modalities

like homeopathy, Bach Flower Remedies, and radionics. It is basically a subtle form of chiropractic focusing on muscles and neuromuscular activity directly and treating "signaling errors" as a literal biological means of noting systemic reactions to substances in the world at large. When combined with Applied Kinesiology, chiropractic itself takes on more of the features of internal medicine and becomes less dependent on skeletal adjustment alone.

Visceral Manipulation

As refinements of traditional osteopathy, visceral manipulation and craniosacral therapy differ from chiropractic in many aspects, including their interpretations of functional anatomy, the relative directness or indirectness of intention in their modes of manipulation, and the degree of weight or force behind their touch. That is, most chiropractic tends to be more direct and heavier. However, in practice, individuals may (and do) combine elements of chiropractic and osteopathy under the names of either (and from training in either). So particular practitioners blend chiropractic and osteopathic modalities or propose unique syntheses of them.

Another generalization that does not apply to either all chiropractors or all bodyworkers practicing visceral manipulation and craniosacral therapy is that chiropractic tends to deal directly with the electrical basis of the body and to release energies through skeletoneuromuscular shocks, while osteopathic therapists tend to deal with the watery basis of the body and to activate ripples and eddies from light palpation. Thus, chiropractic is more akin to elemental fire—igniting dormant potentials and charging inert spaces. Conversely, visceral manipulation and craniosacral therapy presume that the watery predominance of the body will carry even the tiniest motions along currents inward to the core.

Since the late 1980s one of the major events among alternative therapies has been the development and spread of systems of *nonverbal*

dialogue (at the relative expense of more familiar neo-Freudian systems based on verbal or semantic components). Therapies prioritizing insight, neuromuscular mobility, and the cause-effect realm of the central nervous system (ranging from classical psychotherapy with its gestalt and bioenergetic branches to a diversity of visualization techniques and the myriad schools of massage and bodywork) are still more accessible and more dramatically characterized in the popular imagination than those emphasizing the subtleties of the autonomic nervous system, visceral motility, and the hydrodynamics of bodily fluids (muscle-testing, *katsugen undo,* the school of visceral manipulation identified with French osteopaths Jean-Pierre Barral and Pierre Mercier, craniosacral therapy, and the like). Yet therapists of many persuasions are gradually incorporating dialogues between internal somatic rhythms on the one hand and skeletal, muscular, emotional, and spiritual aspects on the other. I do not mean to imply here that such therapies were invented during the 1980s, only that their stature has increased, the practice of them has become more sophisticated (in terms of their relationship of both anatomical and psychological components), and they are providing quite unexpected paradigms for the mystery of disease and cure. The methods themselves—remember—are either very old or have their origin in systems that are very old.

Probably the most significant single factor in the advance of autonomic therapies has been the shift of focus within certain schools of osteopathy, following Sutherland's graphic self-experiment, from musculoskeletal systems to visceral and craniosacral systems. The therapies this revolution has launched have dwarfed traditional osteopathy within the alternative community.

VISCERAL MANIPULATION PROPOSES, classically enough, that insofar as the organs of the body are made of the same material as the muscles, their healthy functioning is based on their unrestricted movement. At all times, while providing nutrition, oxygen, elimination of wastes and proprioception, the viscera are also making slight adjustments,

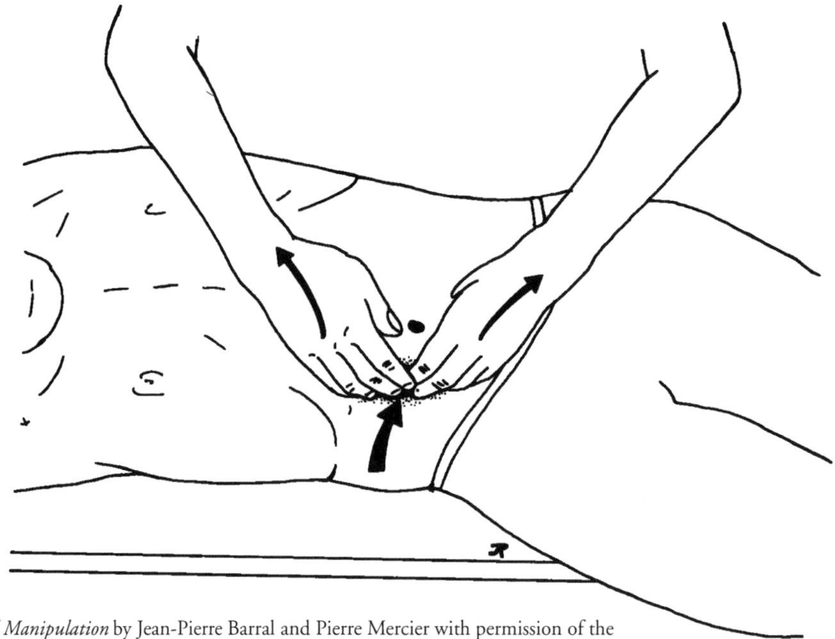

Direct manipulation of the duodenum

Reprinted from *Visceral Manipulation* by Jean-Pierre Barral and Pierre Mercier with permission of the publisher, Eastland Press, Inc., P.O. Box 12689, Seattle, WA 98111.

reorienting themselves along subtly diverging vectors and axes. Thus, health does not lie entirely in their functional output and contribution to the machinery of the body but in their facility to shift continuously in involuntary search for an equilibrium the requirements of which also change from moment to moment. These organic movements are both cyclical (following a diurnal-nocturnal shift of energy circulation) and situational (based on a variety of extrinsic factors). This is in many ways a restatement of the Yellow Emperor's precepts—the hourly progression of organ activity and the relationship between, on the one hand, emotional range and flexibility and, on the other, liver or kidney function.

The processing of air and food and distribution of their by-products, for which the body is rightly famous, simultaneously have the potential to irritate and restrict viscera (much as incidental activity can knock, bump, and dislocate segments of the skeleton). Likewise, emotional

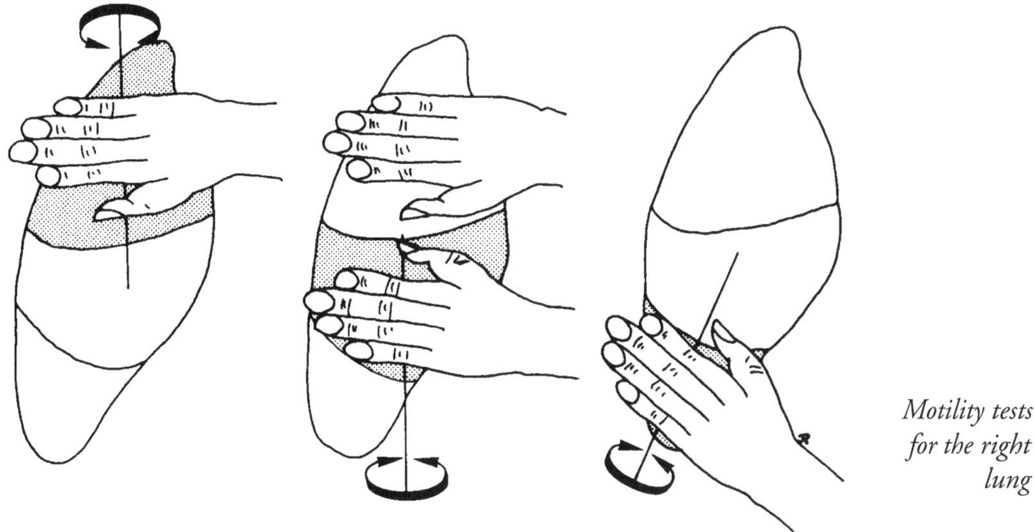

Motility tests for the right lung

Reprinted from *Visceral Manipulation* by Jean-Pierre Barral and Pierre Mercier with permission of the publisher, Eastland Press, Inc., P.O. Box 12689, Seattle, WA 98111.

changes, with their endocrinological and chemical constituents, directly impinge on visceral motility. Barral and Mercier write:

> A visceral restriction occurs when an organ loses part or all of its ability to move.... [V]isceral articulations are made up of sliding surfaces and means of connection. A restriction may arise either at the level of these structures or on the walls of the actual organ, and can usually be assigned to one of three categories ...: articular, ligamentous or muscular.
>
> One can also distinguish functional from positional restrictions. With *functional restrictions,* only the function of the related organs is affected; their positional relationships are not changed. With *positional restrictions,* the anatomical relationships of the organs are changed and their articulations are modified. For example, with a right renal ptosis, the kidney loses all contact with the liver—a veritable visceral subluxation.[20] (italics theirs)

In formal visceral treatment, various modes of touch and palpation are used to ascertain an organ's tonicity, position, size, freedom of cir-

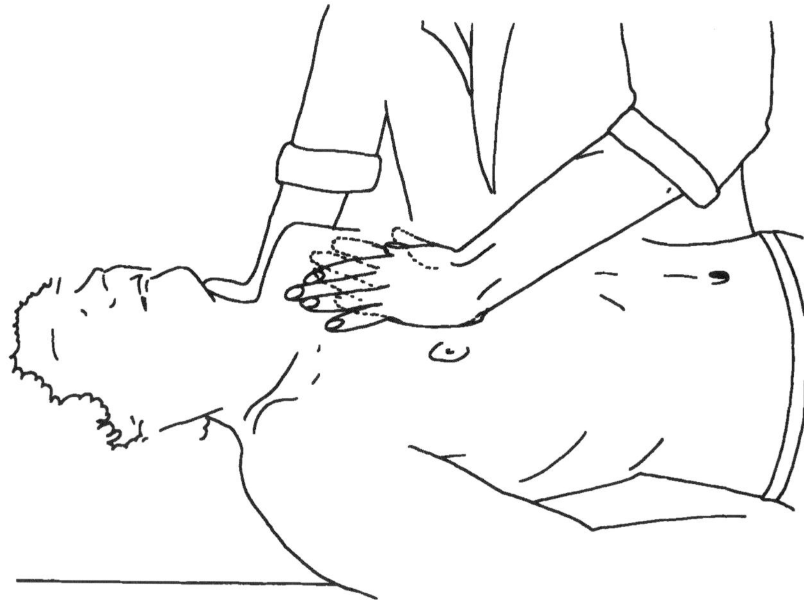

Motility test for the sternum

culating fluids, rhythm, angle of orientation vis-à-vis other organs and their orientations, and degree of restriction. Gentle and precise, these techniques of hands-on listening blend into a type of manipulation that follows each organ's tendencies and elicits its natural rhythms. According to Barral and Mercier, "Visceral manipulation is a method of restarting the mobility or motility of an organ utilizing specific, gentle forces.... We manipulate to the point where the body can take over in order to achieve self-correction, not to force a correction on the body."[21] Thus, the physician's relationship to internal organ dysfunction is not one of a surgeon or even a classical bodyworker—mechanical alteration toward a goal of what constitutes "normal" shape and function. It is more the art of a musician, at once feeling for a hidden cadence and seriality and imparting just the right stimulus in the right direction to evoke it naturally.

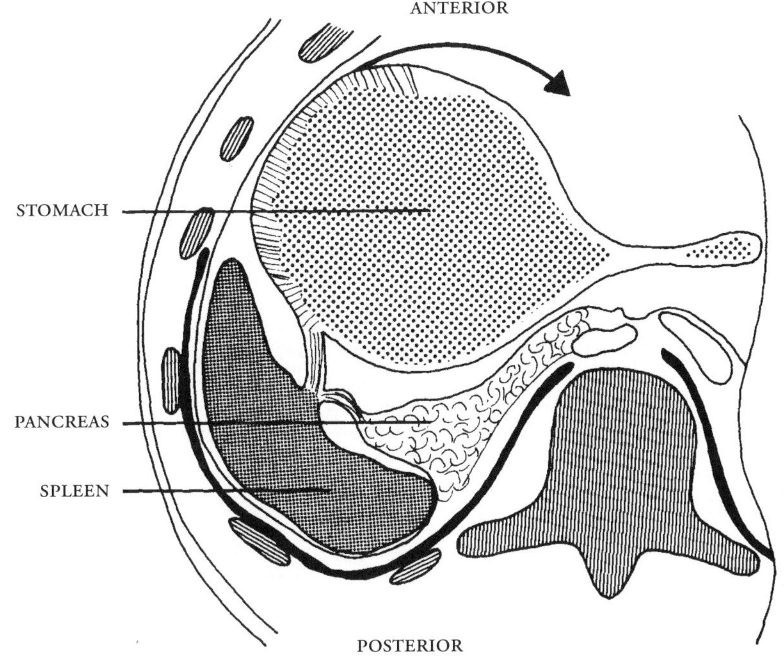

Mobility and motility of the stomach—transverse plane

To the patient the sensation may be extremely subtle, like the separation of layers within oneself that were stuck together in a background. Manipulation of the liver or colon is not painful like a "minor surgery." It is more like remembering something internally that was always there but unnoticed because it had become kinesthetically numbed. Parts of the background excoriating gently feel like layers of extremely familiar unlived or abandoned lives. It is a powerful, trance-inducing state.

> To perform induction, you must know the proper and precise directions of motility for each organ.... In listening, the hand passively follows the pendulum-like motion of the organ. During induction the same hand will slightly accentuate or encourage the larger motion

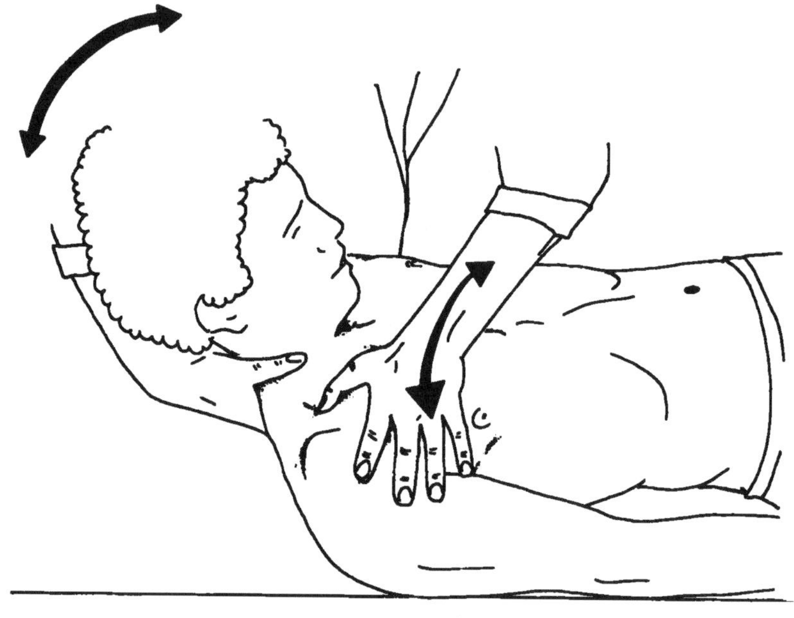

Combined manipulation of the pleural dome

> which is that in the direction of greater excursion. Continue this process until the induced motion coincides with normal motility of the organ in terms of direction, amplitude and axes. . . .[22]

This is a standard osteopathic mode of correction: encouraging a segment of viscera (or neuromusculature) to "go" in the direction it "wants" rather than in the normalizing direction. The assumption is that it can "find" its own correct orientation through enhancement of its tendency, whereas it may never stay in a position into which it is just placed. (Osteopaths tend to support and reinforce rhythm, even when they encounter highly erratic motions and hard blocks.)

In this sense, visceral manipulation both imitates surgery and opposes it. It in fact *is* surgery insofar as it has a surgical goal, which it accomplishes by gradual inducement (without incision) over one or more

extended treatments. Needless to say, it challenges surgery by achieving that goal indirectly and by a combination of intrinsic visceral movement and palpation.

> For each case, you must tune into the patient and feel the rhythm, vitality and resistance of the tissue you are working with. Problems arise from insufficient understanding of the osteopathic concept. One of the big mistakes beginners make is trying to "push" the organ too quickly; the organ cannot adapt to the unnatural speed of change and the treatment is ineffective. If, after treatment, the organ goes through about ten normal cycles, you may consider the treatment to have been effective.[23]

There should also be no misunderstanding about the intended scope of this treatment. Visceral manipulation is decidedly not massage relaxation; it is meant to diagnose and treat a full range of clinical pathologies originating in the organs of the human body. It is a whole medical science in the Hippocratic and empirical lineage.

Craniosacral Therapy

There is no inherent reason why the work of Still and Sutherland should not have led directly to a fully holistic, psychological medicine long before the Human Potential Movement of the 1960s and '70s. After Sutherland discovered the movements of the cranial and sacral bones, he developed a system for their subtle manipulation. As a Swedenborgian mystic, he believed that he was close to touching the roots of the soul in the body and that his manipulations were sending waves directly into spiritual consciousness. He laid the groundwork for osteopathic psychotherapy.

But, as noted, this trend within osteopathy ceased abruptly in the 1920s, as osteopaths, hounded by the AMA, could no longer practice the system they had trained in. Subsequent generations became more concerned with their acceptance into the allopathic establishment, and they emphasized the mechanical, quasi-surgical aspects of their treatments

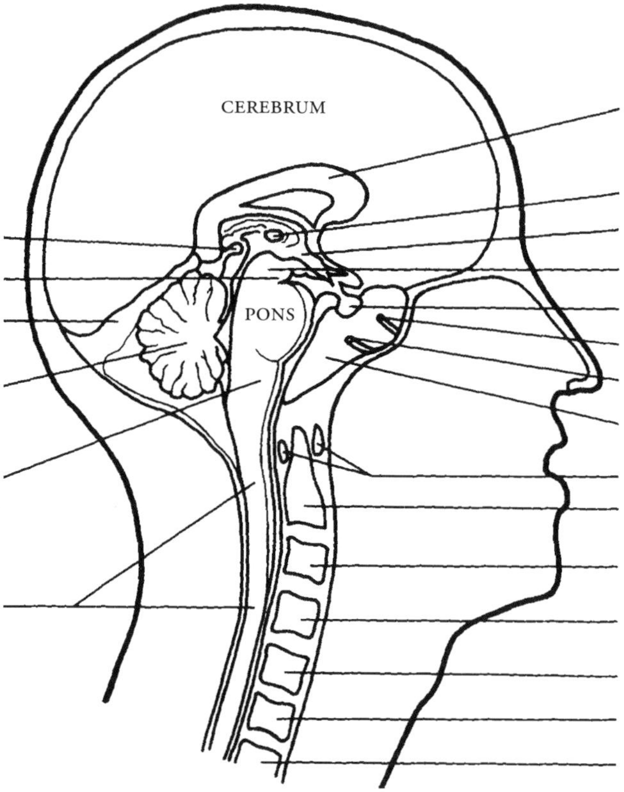

CEREBRUM
CORPUS CALLOSUM
THALAMUS
PINEAL BODY
HYPOTHALAMUS
MIDBRAIN
TEGMENTUM
STRAIGHT VENOUS SINUS
PONS
PITUITARY GLAND
OPTIC N.
CEREBELLUM
OLFACTORY N.
SPHENOID
MEDULLA OBLONGATA
C1
C2
C3
SPINAL CORD
C4
C5
C6
C7

Midsagittal view of midbrain and brainstem

(and even practiced standard pharmacy) to the point that cranial osteopathy almost disappeared from the field. However, in the 1980s, through a whole new paradigm of treatment, it was not only reborn but itself gave birth to an entire modality of healing.

The trademarked system of craniosacral therapy and somatoemotional release was developed by osteopathic physician John Upledger and his associates at Michigan State University in the mid-1970s. Prior to this time, cranial osteopathy was maintained by its last dying practitioners as a kind of cult. These loyal disciples of Sutherland would only teach their methods to the one group least interested in learning them—AMA-sanctioned doctors. Cranial osteopathy both fled the scrutiny of allopathy and courted its approbation. In fact, cranial osteopaths privately published their own books and would not sell them to the general public. It took lawsuits based on the First Amendment simply to make the writings available in the 1960s.[24]

Upledger not only liberated cranial osteopathy from its sectarian church and revived the cranial-fluid model with its visceral palpations and stillpoints, but, as noted, he thoroughly demedicalized it, both in terms of what it proposed and in reaction against the false legitimacy it sought (and which limited its range to precisely the meager territory its opponents would permit it). In defiance of both the medical and osteopathic establishments he taught a widening spectrum of techniques to large numbers of lay people in seminars in hopes of increasing the base of qualified healers and practitioners in the world (something that surely would not have happened had he relied on either just osteopaths or osteopaths and M.D.s).

As one recent example of the fruits of this training, in late 1994, with the support of the Bosnian Government and the World Health Organization, the Upledger Institute dispatched a team of its own craniosacral therapists (few of them medical professionals) to treat Post-Traumatic Stress Disorder in the former Yugoslavia. Cadres practicing lay volunteer healing in crisis zones clearly should be one goal of a humane "planet medicine" as we approach the year 2000.

In Upledger's classic mode of treatment, healer and patient engage in a complex rhythmic interchange much like that of visceral manipulation but rooted in the requirements and manifestations of the craniosacral system. This relatively unfamiliar realm (intuited by Sutherland) constitutes a subtle bodywide hydraulic network driven by the pressure of the cerebrospinal fluid (as more of it is produced by the choroid plexuses within the ventricular system of the brain than is reabsorbed by the arachnoid bodies). The craniosacral modality is named for the cranium and sacrum through which it is most easily accessed.

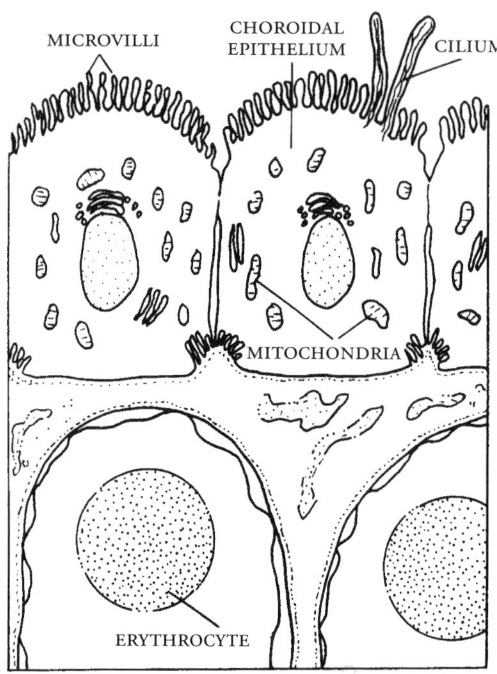

Choroid plexus tight junctions

Reprinted from *An Introduction to Craniosacral Therapy* by Don Cohen, D.C., North Atlantic Books, 1995.

Craniosacral methods form a larger coherent healing system with the techniques of visceral manipulation insofar as both therapies involve probing zones of restricted motion and stimulating their release. The bones, membranes, myofascia, fluids, and nervous system interact to form a coherent, intelligent, self-correcting hydraulic neural network that underlies psychic and somatic life. Through layers of this system, the personality and character defined by psychotherapists can also be addressed directly. These are functional postulates underlying a diverse repertoire of techniques.

Craniosacral rhythm is a fundamental pulse like breath and heartbeat, though quieter and less hunger-driven than the rush of either blood or air. It was substantially known to Sutherland, but Upledger observed its regularity, intensity, and centrality during surgery (he was trying to hold the dural membrane still for plaque removal by using two sets of forceps, but its pulsing movement prevailed). He verified his findings clinically and in extensive autopsies. Subsequently, he based much of his therapy upon accessing far-ranging domains through this previously little-understood force.

The motion extending down the dural tube to the viscera is likely generated because the dura-mater membrane is almost completely impermeable to the cerebrospinal fluid. Within this membrane, a homeostasis develops, regulating and rebalancing forces that build and release pressure. Insofar as the craniosacral system includes at its core the brain, spinal cord, and pituitary and pineal glands (hence the endocrine system and its hormones as well as corresponding functions of the mind-body interface), it is highly sensitive to emotional influences. The goal of the therapist is to find an access into these homeostases through palpation, to locate zones of dysfunction and restricted function within them, and to disencumber these areas through (mostly) indirect techniques, that is, by stimulation of intrinsic rhythms or even exaggeration and support of a dysfunctional pattern until it swings so far to its favored side that it returns normally to the other (restoration by going *with* rather than fighting a distortion is familiar from visceral manipulation described above).

In working with either viscera themselves or the craniosacral rhythm, the therapist encloses a part of the body with both hands, perhaps one on the lower back, one on the belly. He then adds pressure with the top hand until he feels the tissues start to move. The motion is followed with both hands until it stops. This is one form of basic release. However, if the motion keeps returning where it came from or repeating a cycle, the therapist can gently convert (in successive rounds) the path most insisted upon by the tissue to one of release *from* this direction. Variations of the process can be adapted to almost any part of the body.

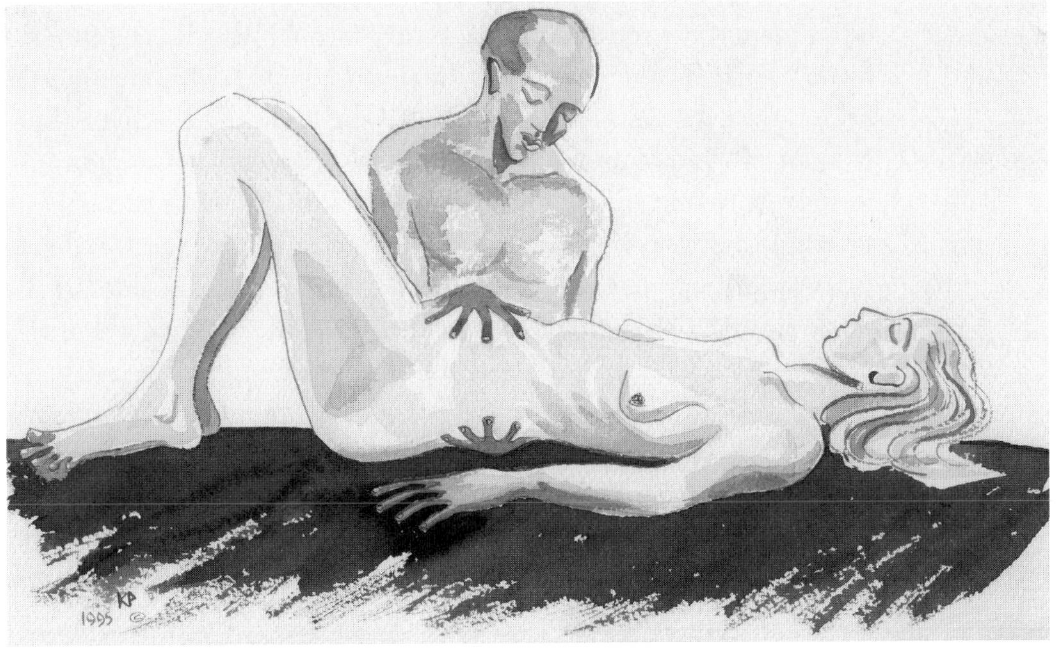

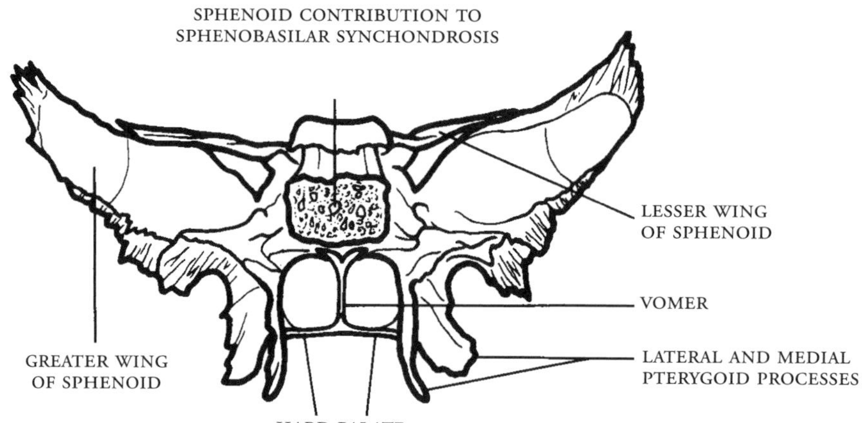

Posterior view of the sphenoid, vomer, and hard palate

The bones of the cranium are particularly important because of their proximity to the reigning functions of the nervous system and their tendency to translate distortion downhill (along the spine and its dural membrane secondarily, and then through the fascia and ligaments). Cranial components like the sphenoid bone (which lies mostly behind the eyes and nose), the falxes cerebri and cerebelli, the occipital, parietal, and temporal bones, etc., are the levers, valves, and pistons of the system. They must be palpated from outside precisely in terms of their shapes, positions, and dynamic components—this is (once again) not massage or chiropractic. The sphenoid—butterfly in shape and possibly homologous to the pelvis at the other end of the spine—is accessible to palpation only at the outer tips of the eye sockets and is adjusted by light compression, decompression, twisting, and sliding. The temporal bones can be set in traction by a pliant tug of fingers grasping the external ear. Other cogs in the system may be accessed only from inside the mouth through the teeth or hard palate or from a remote stimulation of the dural membrane itself (relying on motion transmitted inward).

Don Cohen, a chiropractor who practices a diversity of systems, provides a more subjective description of this work:

> . . . [L]istening to the neurologic rhythms and refraining from stimulating the patient with your perceptions and remedial advice (treatment) can be a powerful therapeutic mode. The recognition of intelligence in neurologic tissue is not pathetic fallacy (in which human traits are attributed to inanimate objects). It is apparent that the nervous system is no dummy and knows when it is being listened to, and appreciates that quiet and accepting forum. I have had the experience at times of working with a patient intently, trying with all my effort to effect a real change by various means, adjusting, myofascial work, etc., and suddenly becoming aware of the tension in my own body and in the situation, and relaxing, softening my grip, and sitting down to listen to the neural rhythm. The body comes alive, pulsating, processing, revealing a mind of its own. . . . That this autonomic response is deliberate will be obvious to anyone who experiences it. This is the power of communication, for which all nervous systems and all people hunger.[25]

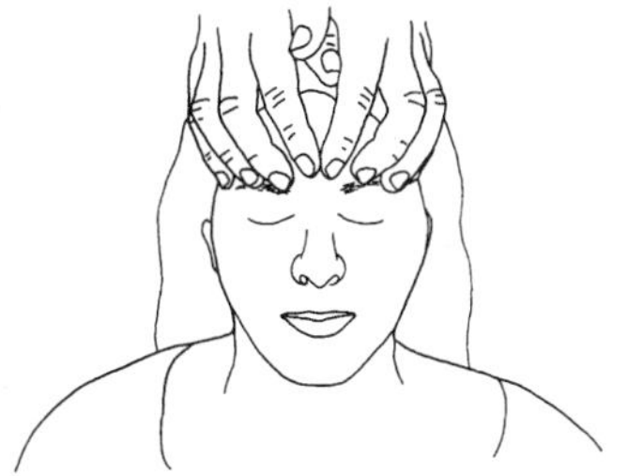

Frontal lift

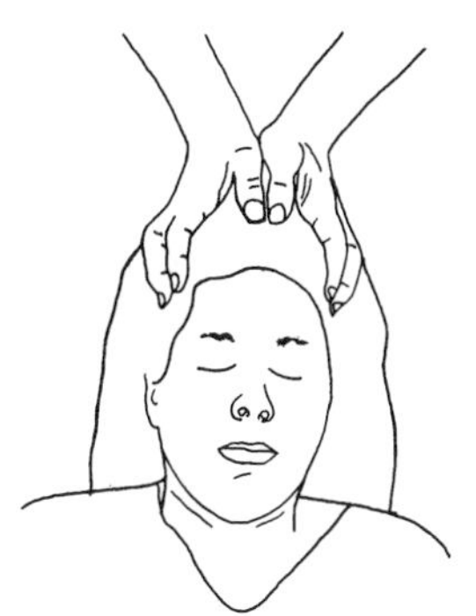

Parietal lift

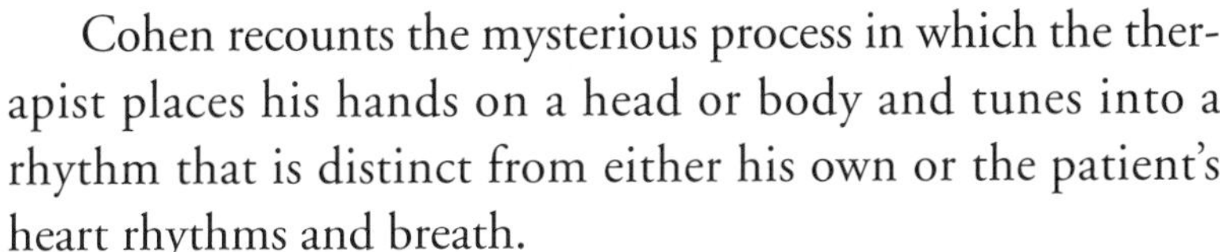

Cohen recounts the mysterious process in which the therapist places his hands on a head or body and tunes into a rhythm that is distinct from either his own or the patient's heart rhythms and breath.

> . . . [L]et your attention float up and down the dural tube and through the body. It's easy to imagine. Can you feel subluxations through the tube? With passive proprioception, feel tension and pressure gradients and their influence on the cranial rhythm. Trust your impression. Then tug very gently, almost imperceptibly, on the tissues to gain a further impression of where the tissue is hung up. Again focus your attention down the body. Ask yourself: where would I place a push pin or a piece of tape to create this same pattern of resistance?[26]

This is likely the location of a trauma.

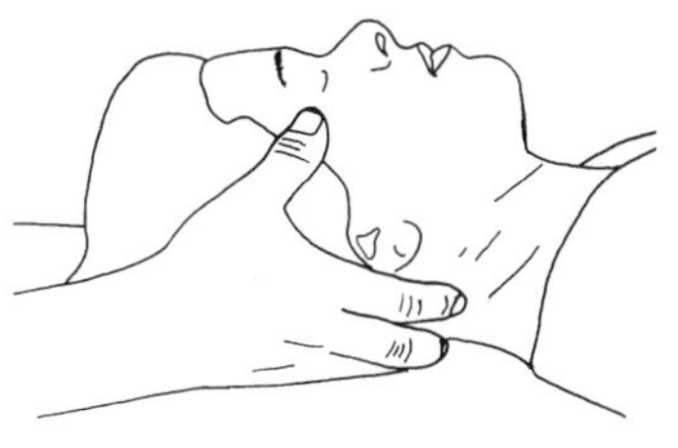

Sphenoid lift

Reprinted from *An Introduction to Craniosacral Therapy* by Don Cohen, D.C., North Atlantic Books, 1995.

If the therapist is skilled enough to track the rhythm to traumatized sites ("energy cysts" in Upledger's terminology), then the traumatic physical forces stored at those sites may be, one by one, released. The therapist does not release such energy in a predetermined fashion; instead the patient unwinds herself in response to a sympathetic palpation which guides her to her own native rhythm and movement as it responds to the healing intention behind the touch.

Once the touch becomes too heavy (generally more than five grams), then the organism begins to respond less on the level of craniosacral or visceral sensitivity and more in terms of neuromuscular tension and stress patterns. This is not like going from good to bad; it is just switching therapeutic modes (and is rarely successful). Too light a touch activates only auras or external energy fields; too heavy a touch engages muscles. Craniosacral traction falls precisely between.

The presumption (in craniosacral language this time) is that at an instant of traumatization a negative energy matrix was injected into the patient's system and somaticized—the stronger the force or deeper the trauma, the more extensive and intransigent the cyst. The person holds onto the site emotionally through fear and panic, guilt, shame, and grief. In principle, it doesn't matter if the originating force was a gunshot wound from a carjacker, years of junk food, or the humiliations of a narcissistic parent. The environment ceaselessly transmits immobilizing pathologies on all levels (mind, body, spirit). One of Upledger's earliest insights, reinforcing our characterization of the pathogenic physician (see Chapter Two), is that surgeons transfer their attitudes directly through their scalpels into the tissue layers of their patients—that their anger and disdain and, conversely, their generosity and caring are codified in visceral memory patterns. Even the tone of the surgeon's voice while speaking idly to his assistants lodges in an anesthetized patient's tissues. Upledger found that patients could recount tales of surgical encounters with extraordinary accuracy even though they were unconscious at the time. More significantly, their bodies had

somaticized the emotional tenor of the experience. "If molecularly simple recording tape has such a memory," he asks, "why not cells?"[27]

These seemingly extraneous factors determine not only the speed with which surgical wounds heal but the success of the very surgery. In fact, Upledger has decided (in 1994) after engaging for many years in inaugural research in diverse branches of alternative healing that the only medical event he is still interested in proving scientifically is the fact that *electrically measurable energies* are transmitted directly from a physician to a patient—through hands, surgical and dental tools, and attitudes—and that these energies affect the degree and rate of healing in an explicit, quantifiable way.

By the same principle, the less trauma (physical and emotional) there is augmenting the formation of a cyst, the less subsequent dysfunction will arise from that cyst. As one therapist remarked, "The football player who catches the game-winning pass while injuring himself does not have the deep-seated trauma of one who gets the same injury and misses the pass." Hence, physical problems originating from relatively nontraumatizing causes yield to treatment more readily because they are not as deeply imbedded in cysts by emotional charge.

When a trauma is kept from releasing, the body has to continue to function around its area of entropy. It takes energy to wall off and contain a trauma and also energy to continue to function in its context. The organism twists and oscillates and builds those twists and oscillations inward. Not only that, but in the sudden formation of a wound or distortion, the body is responding instantaneously to an external force while moving viscerally and internally, deflecting the vectors of entry so that a linear blow from an assailant, vehicle, or stationary object bumped into imbeds itself in the system at many different angles over even mere milliseconds of time, much like a barbed hook fashioned to catch and hold a fish. Emotional traumas have even more complex courses of entry through the neuromusculature.

The therapist, by tracking and unwinding somatic vectors as they lead to their source, ultimately locates the afflicted site and directs his

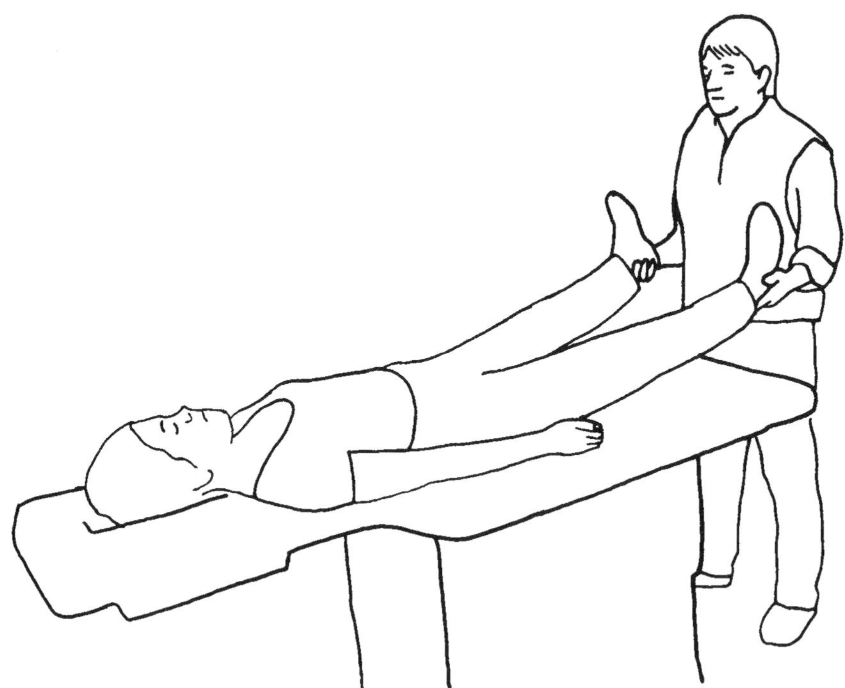

Unwinding

Reprinted from *An Introduction to Craniosacral Therapy* by Don Cohen, D.C., North Atlantic Books, 1995.

or her palpations into it at matching angles. Many ailments have multiple causes and form in layers, thus must be located in layers and cured layer by layer—the tractions always joining at the point where the various energetic sources of a condition meet.

In reality, there is no straightforward map either to the diagnosis of cysts or the release of them. The therapist must use a combination of insight and perception. Some practitioners clearly see a patient's energetic and functional breaks by looking at the body. Others don't "see" it until they close their eyes and stare at the after-image. Many scan it at slightly deflected angles. Some who can't see such patterns at all can feel them in their hands as they pass them above a patient's body. A fair number of people have to touch the body directly to track the flows in it. The process of using the differential ripples emitting through a fluidic, visceral organism to situate the spot of a splash is known as arcing—divining as by a rod the nucleus of many deflected arcs.

Energy cysts and somatoemotional traumas represent different levels of the same phenomena. The Upledger system distinguishes between a mechanical process of therapeutically releasing cysts and a more extensive procedure of full somatoemotional release. Cysts are treated first by arcing to their source (a process which in itself stimulates energetic release) and then dissolving them, usually through indirect osteopathic techniques. Sometimes just holding and supporting the body at the precisely correct point and angle (and then at each successively revealed point and angle) is sufficient to allow the viscera to release themselves. The organism knows what it needs and will often not only lead the therapist to the appropriate sites but cue him in his techniques by seeming to pull his hands in like suction or a magnet on iron filings. Following sensation is (as usual) the key to treatment. One must avoid any prejudgment about what is functionally required for cure. In fact, the most direct techniques, regarded as more invasive by the system, may sometimes stimulate deepening of the cyst. "Don't make the patient have to defend against you," Upledger warns, "which is not the problem he came in with."[28] If the therapist makes himself the problem through overzealous activity and unconscious projections, then instead of release, a new layer is added to the pathology.

Hand position for release of spheno-maxillary impaction

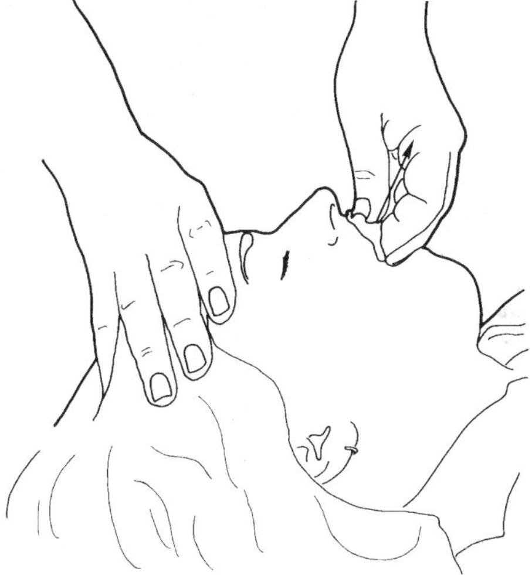

Reprinted from *CranioSacral Therapy* by John E. Upledger and Jon D. Vredevoogd with permission of the publisher, Eastland Press, Inc., P.O. Box 12689, Seattle, WA 98111. Copyright 1983. All rights reserved.

Full somatoemotional cure combines physical, verbal, and emotional elements. The therapist not only diagnoses and releases cysts but guides the patient with questions about images and feelings and then follows intrinsic movements generated by the body

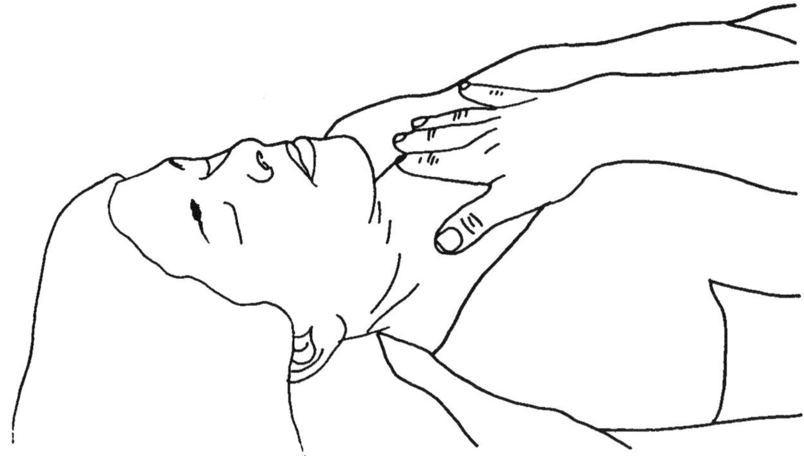

Thoracic inlet release

Reprinted from *An Introduction to Craniosacral Therapy* by Don Cohen, D.C., North Atlantic Books, 1995.

wherever they go (even to entirely different energy complexes). All the time, the therapist is encouraging expression, following patterns, and interpolating the craniosacral rhythm as a guide.

Traditionally the process of somatoemotional release begins with freeing the "avenue of expression": the full thoracic inlet and throat *chakra,* the first and second ribs, the clavicle, all the hyoid muscles (around the Adam's apple) and their related fascia and bony attachments, the hard palate (and through it, the vomer and palatines), and then the tongue, gums, and teeth. Each of these areas may contain impediments or imbedded rhythms from events and circumstances in the person's life, and these deter full expression up from the gut out through the mouth. The teeth, for instance, have often been deeply traumatized by dental drilling and orthodontics, with these strictures passing inward into the vomer, sphenoid, maxilla, and affecting the heart of the craniosacral flow itself. Each tooth can be guided and "unwound" in the same way other parts of the body are (by following the yarn of its intrinsic motion with a single finger or between a finger and thumb). Such a process apparently not only releases the tooth

but helps with periodontal problems by stimulating bone and gum restoration.

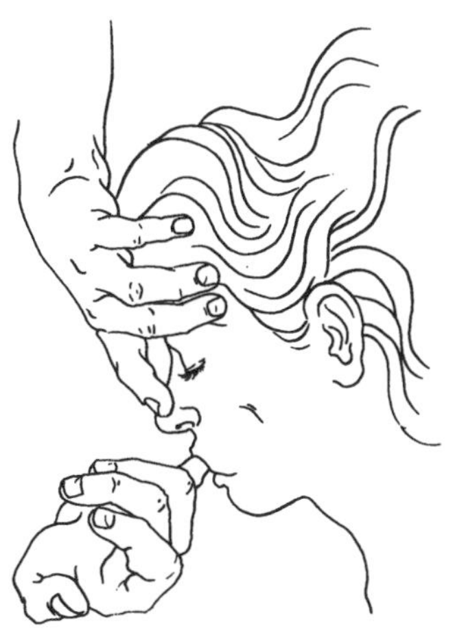

The pretzel of immobilization may be so complex in its visceral, skeletal, and emotionally cathected components that it may take as many as five or six assistants helping the therapist support the body and following its unwindings simultaneously. Like handlers of a giant snake, they follow the body off the table and hold it in midair allowing it to "unwrithe" its traumas with as few restrictions as possible. Many ailments are actually a knot of such giant snakes locked in different dimensions and symbolic systems. "I felt myself come flying off the table," an acquaintance told me in recounting his first astonishment at how craniosacral therapy actually works. "Suddenly I was spinning in midair and bouncing off walls."

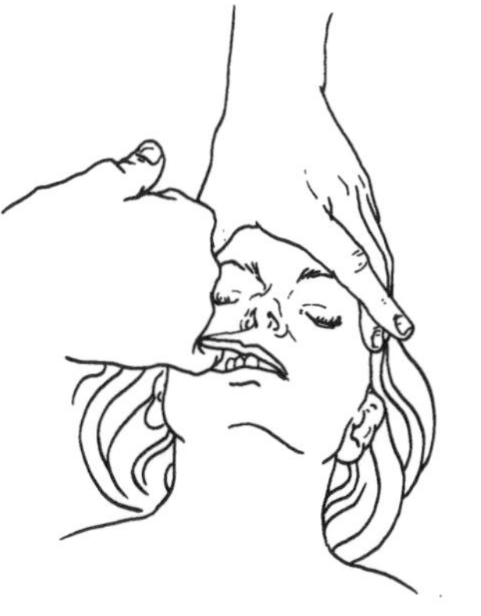

(This is reminiscent of at least one other system of involuntary movement. Studied by both Moshe Feldenkrais and Bonnie Bainbridge Cohen, it was taught by a Japanese healer named Dr. Haruchika Noguchi, who married a cousin of the Emperor. In one description of a mass training that conjures up images somewhere between a riot and a giant worm, Noguchi instructed an entire stadium: "The people got up from their seats and went down to the center of the stadium—waves of people, all exercising in the stadium floor. They did what he called *katsu-gen-undo,* a vitalizing movement wherein people move in any way that the body makes them move. It is supposed to become an unconscious way of moving, and it gains a certain momentum.... [People] would begin to move, and their body movements would get bigger and bigger. Some would continue moving in this way. Others would be jumping up and down, crawling, sitting, standing—whatever they wanted to do."[29])

As the craniosacral therapist steers into blocks, the patient responds by transferring motility ever deeper. The innermost

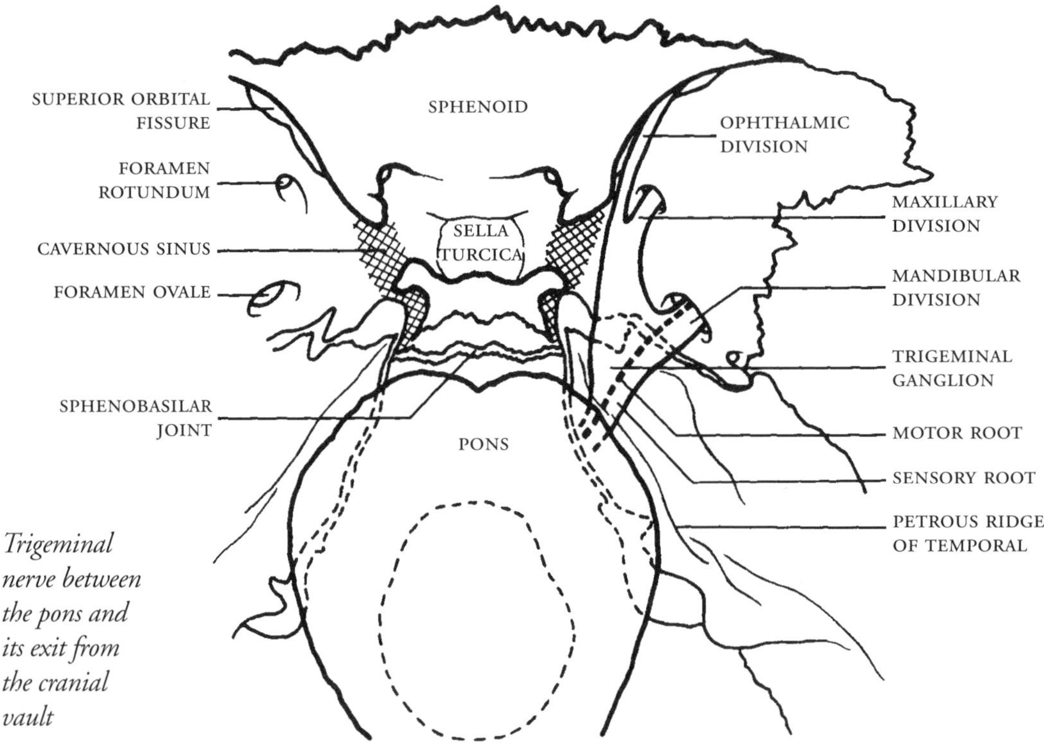

Trigeminal nerve between the pons and its exit from the cranial vault

zones are less familiar and often astonishingly powerful. Just having his or her rhythm located and touched imparts a curative momentum both emotionally and physically. For the deepest reaches of the body, it is like "being seen" for the first time. After all the years of functioning not only in darkness but total nullity, suddenly these movement patterns feel themselves connect to the conscious mind, the numinous "self." At the moment of becoming conscious, they "exist." As they exist, they communicate how dense and vast they actually are. They are not just the momentary static of internal exercises; they are part of the seemingly cosmic background of existence. As they differentiate from the background, they envelop the person in an awareness of who

he or she actually is and they gravitate toward whom he or she might yet be. They literally change identity.

There is no traditional explanation for the power and range of the cerebrospinal force. That is just the way we are put together embryonically. The mechanism no doubt has been experienced kinesthetically and medically in some fashion or other since the Stone Age, but it was not clearly identified as a separate cerebrospinal pulse until cranial osteopathy (though Ayurvedic and Taoist practitioners might object to this characterization, as I shall discuss in Chapter Five). There is also no theoretical reason why treatment of the body and psyche through interaction with and induction of the craniosacral rhythm should have such substantial psychological and psychospiritual components. This was pure empirical, improvisational medicine, initiated by Sutherland and practiced by countless others since. One finds cures in the act of practicing them.

A common mistake is to assume that because Upledger focused on the craniosacral rhythm and used the name "craniosacral therapy" to describe his work that the process has primarily to do with conditions of the cranial, spinal and sacral skeleton and the movements of those bones. Anyone who has read to this point must know by now that craniosacral work is global. The rhythm is a guide to events within the whole organism—viscera, psyche, and etheric fields. Though one may guess at the evolutionary reasons, the fact is that the craniosacral pulse and its visceral adjuncts are the branches of a pathway to the core. We evolved that way, and we form that way anew each time in the embryo. A dialogue with the craniosacral rhythm, conducted physically, psychically, and psychologically, is a dialogue with one of the deepest accessible levels of an organism's existence.

Upledger's intent was never to prioritize craniosacral functions or to develop a new specialty within general osteopathy. It was to find the most direct path into the extraordinarily complex system of cell and tissue layers and symbol referrents that make up a human being. Because the craniosacral rhythm appears to be the closest representative of such

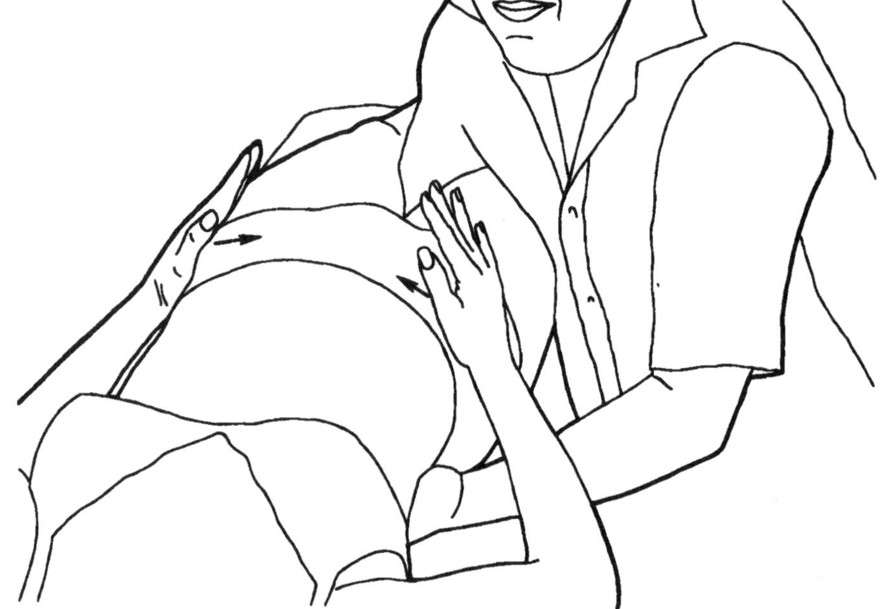

Patient assistance in the disengagement of the sacrum from the ilia

a locus, it is studied, befriended, and hitched upon in an often wild and bumpy passage through the range of phenomena within an organism. Subsequently it provides its own meanings.

Using techniques developed from this basic therapy, Upledger has ministered to Vietnam veterans with Post-Traumatic Stress Syndrome, autistic children, children with Down's Syndrome, paralyzed victims of accidents, amputees, etc., with remarkable and often inexplicable results. For instance, when he treated a person who had part of his clavicle removed after a motorcycle accident, Upledger put an emphasis on encouraging the bone to grow back. He saw no physical reason why bone might not be able to crystallize again, but he also had no rationale for why the method combining imaging and craniosacral therapy he was using should have that effect. In fact, a large portion of the patient's clavicle grew back and his mobile functions were restored, allowing him to steer his motorcycle again.[30] It is never a matter of simple visualization but of visualization in the context of craniosacral "following" and somatoemotional release, often requiring many treatments over a period of time. In cases of cancer, Upledger has prescribed imaging a golden layer of cells radiating light and, whether for this reason or another, dissipation of a tumor often followed. (See also Appendix, Volume One.)

Upledger chooses always to consider the cure the responsiveness of the organism, the role of the doctor being that of a blue-collar helper simply following the guidance of the patient's own expert "inner physician." The entire epistemology of craniosacral therapy is that the body provides its own methods—as mysterious as the music of Bach or a Hopi kachina dance and as implacable as the deeds of an executioner or an epileptic fit.

ONE OF THE MOST effective techniques is the classic "stillpoint" of Sutherland, which is little more than a temporarily imposed cessation of the craniosacral rhythm. This state can be elicited in a prone patient by the slightest outward pressure placed on the inside of his feet. A hand keeping the base of the patient's spine either in flexion (when the craniosacral system is at an extreme of filling with fluid) or extension (when it is emptying or emptied) also stops the rhythm. The most common method, however, is by the therapist encouraging the base of the patient's occiput to rest under its own pressure between his hands.

Hand position for stillpoint induction

Reprinted from *An Introduction to Craniosacral Therapy* by Don Cohen, D.C., North Atlantic Books, 1995.

Inducing a stillpoint enhances fluid flow, allows forces to gather momentum and redirect themselves, releases minor restrictions throughout the membranes, and relaxes the sympathetic nervous system. This in itself can be a powerful healing state, like a brief dream which disperses itself through the membranes, cleansing and clearing.

Although he was not referring to the stillpoint of the craniosacral pulse, in "Burnt Norton," the first of the "Four

Quartets," T. S. Eliot evokes an archetypal "still point" that includes the cerebrospinal one:

> At this still point of the turning world. Neither flesh nor fleshless;
> Neither from nor towards; at the still point, there the dance is,
> But neither arrest nor movement. And do not call it fixity,
> Where past and future are gathered. Neither movement from nor towards,
> Neither ascent nor decline. Except for the point, the still point,
> There would be no dance, and there is only the dance. . . .
> The inner freedom from the practical desire,
>
> The release from action and suffering, release from the inner
> And the outer compulsion, yet surrounded
> By a grace of sense, a white light still and moving,
> *Erhebung* without motion, concentration
> Without elimination, both a new world
> And the old made explicit, understood
> In the completion of its partial ecstasy,
> The resolution of its partial horror.[31]

The feeling, to the patient, of being treated craniosacrally is much like a kind of waking dream in which internal landscapes blossom and flit by almost magically; the mind and body go together on a journey into familiar but forgotten zones of being. Compared to other trances, this state is emptier and less imagistic, more resembling contentless dreams which are instantly forgotten anyway. But unlike noctural dreams, they have no narrative or angst and there is no sense of loss from their terminus. They are like the dreams of organs which have no agenda (in language anyway) but seek participation and recognition in the waking drama of the organism. Through this process, without necessarily any specific hand-to-pathology blueprint, the craniosacral rhythm unwinds deeper and deeper in the sense that it contacts more and more basic coherences within the organism and ultimately transmits a resolution.

Whereas artificial stoppages of the craniosacral rhythm (stillpoints) may be imposed therapeutically, the abrupt cessation of the craniosacral rhythm while "following" is always regarded as a deepening. Because the craniosacral system is a core system, it operates at a profound level with substantial import. It pulls the physician and patient inevitably to the right place (often marked by such a screeching halt in the rhythm). At these spots, the system simply does not know where to go. It puts out confusion, rightly intentioned but wasted energy. The therapist supports this place and waits for a change. Responsiveness does not require cognitive knowledge of the cause of the trauma; palpation simply provides it a protected way to radiate back out. It is of little use for traditional physicians and therapists to attempt to tap the meanings of such a process through conversation and directional massage.

However, if the patient is verbally responsive at the time, the rhythm can be consulted, almost like a lie detector, to determine when he is telling the truth. A full stoppage usually means, "Yes!" Likewise, if the patient is simultaneously experiencing an image or feeling, these are considered authentic reenactments of their traumatic source. Even if an image seems irrelevant at that moment to the therapist, he must override his prejudice and trust the craniosacral rhythm whenever it says, "Stop here and wait."

Often craniosacral cessation coincides with "memories" of either being in the womb, coming out the birth canal, or in the midst of what seems to be another lifetime. During one workshop a woman I was treating suddenly changed her name from Deborah to Jonathan, deepened her voice, took on an accent, began laughing uproariously, and became an elderly man committing suicide by leaping from a cliff and attempting to glide over the ocean. The moment of elation in flight was followed by intense "pain" which led her to writhe upward off the table and to reenact the jump with three of us guiding her in midair.

Whatever these images and sensations truly represent, they were crucial to the organism in exactly the form in which it chose to express them. Some people may select past-life images, others scenes from early childhood; some may choose episodes of racial, ethnic, or archetypal significance. There is no attempt to assign priority to one world-view or another. It is what happens energetically that is important.

Conversely, if the patient experiences graphic and revealing images, perhaps of being murdered in another lifetime, perhaps of painful sexual abuse in childhood, but the craniosacral rhythm continues unimpeded, the images are relatively discounted. They are not denied but are regarded as likely to be transitional, perhaps a form of melodrama guarding the true painful events, or perhaps the portals into a larger experience.

Craniosacral therapy is *like* psychoanalysis in its induction of an ongoing, deepening dialogue between doctor and patient. What is astonishing is that the ostensibly mute act of osteopathic "following" replicates, as it were, psychotherapeutic discourse and transference at the level of the membranes and viscera. Notwithstanding his own restaging of the analytic exchange in a physical arena, Reich likely would have been contemptuous of claims of subtle inertial palpations generating curative energy. After all, he invented a mode of somatic psychology that found its way "in" solely through neuromuscular armor and explicit character traits.

Yet the mere engagement of the craniosacral therapist with an autonomic and seemingly noncathected rhythm appears to approach the somatic underpinnings where emotions fix traumas. It speaks to the trauma in the language of its cathexes and engages it along avenues of direct charge. Whereas once a louder voice (letting out "the primal scream," pounding a bed with a tennis racquet, etc.) was deemed requisite to awaken demons below, now a quiet voice is preferred for seducing those same demons. There is no imperative of orgasm or deep-tissue work because of their seemingly greater energy quantum always to take

precedence. The whisper alone is what awakens Sleeping Beauty or, like the princess's kiss, turns the frog into the prince.

Some have objected quite vociferously in public forums that craniosacral work is psychodynamically and spiritually naive—that it doesn't resolve transference and that it tends to infantilize patients and build up inviolable dependencies on therapists unequipped to deal with projections.[32] The danger is in their overlooking the complexity of sublimation, projection, and transference and thus considering a case solved by one manipulation (or even worse, addicting the patient to the treatment without actually curing the ailment).

I have not observed these particular abuses, but I certainly appreciate their potential. What I *have* seen, on occasion, are gullible practitioners making broad assumptions about traumatic memories and encouraging a patient in oversimplified reenactments of, for instance, childhood abuse by a parent. These become mere séances supplemented with rudimentary craniosacral touch in place of a candle and Ouija board ("Oh, that must have been painful! Do you remember if she struck you?" And so on.) I have tended to discount them as unrepresentative of the system. In any case, it has become just as important these days for somatic therapists to honor transference as it has become for psychologists to deal with the energetic rather than just the semantic components of neurosis.

I have also watched trained therapists practice a brilliant amalgam of Freudian and craniosacral work. In one instance, I was present at a session in which a psychoanalyst unwound a patient from a deep embryonic curl through an elaborate series of back-and-forth, direct and indirect maneuvers as the woman gradually recalled, image by image, sexual abuse by her father. Three assistants had to intervene to accommodate each of the vectors chosen by the woman's limbs and torso. Toward the end, the therapist encouraged the woman to find a way to "spit" (pelvicly) the intruding genital out of herself. At this point she began to improvise her own exercises and verbal injunctions and to unwind her body in spasms and shudders. Finally she stood like a giant, radiant and in

full possession of her autonomy as she fired quite stunning curses toward her attacker. It was hard to recall her from the beginning of the session—tiny and self-effacing, violated by even the request to become a demonstration subject.

What impressed me then was not that craniosacral work is immune to oversimplifications (it has brought its share of New Age psychobabble into the world) but that it opens avenues of inner recognition and release not available in psychotherapy as it is currently practiced. In so doing, it has transposed the healing dialogue to a visceral and fascial level without ever degrading its essentially semantic and syntactic character. Hypnotism at times seems to have a similar capacity but, despite its occasionally remarkable demonstrations, the field seems stuck in feats and metaphysical riddles, to say nothing of its own outrageous abuses of transference. Craniosacral therapy is neither a cosmic trial nor stagecraft; it is a pure therapeutic tool.

In contradiction of the above (and supporting the psychoanalytic critique) is a general and persistent fallacy in all somatics, not just craniosacral therapy—that of energetic literalism. Body therapists come to assume that their attention to extremely subtle, infinitesimal quanta permits them to make links between physiological events and core meanings. Yet tracking traumas and dysfunctions somatically is subject to the same dynamics of projection, distortion, and interference as tracking them psychologically. Often the best somatic treatment still leaves the patient's body/mind not knowing how to locate itself. While astute and well-intentioned, the therapist introduces psychosomatic dysfunction by overlooking the inertial symbolic levels at which the patient receives meanings. Energetic sincerity often fails to address character. Content is cured while pathology is introduced into context.

Language is critical. When bodyworkers speak of contacting the liver or the heart *chakra*, we might question whether this is an actual direct intercession between touch and cells, energetic or mechanical, or whether language itself, which names organs and treatments (and gives unconscious meanings to acts of touch), does not play an equally active and intercessionary role such that the "spleen" or "kidney" may be affected symbolically as well as physically, with the symbolic treatment being the active one. (See also page 323.)

The concreteness of somatic systems lies finally not in their anatomic immediacy but in the powerful metaphors they generate while creating and transmuting myths of accessible anatomy.

Craniosacral and visceral palpations are based on projecting intention while trusting that the slightest tendency can be more powerful (and closer to Intelligence) than directed force. One learns to detect the bare glimmers of mind and motion and to track those glimmers within grosser anatomy. There is an irony in the history of this system that points to a realm where vitalistic and surgical medicines may yet meet. Because John Upledger is one of the great independent anatomists of his time, his insights on the essential, the mysterious, and the unquantifiable have the credibility of the concrete. His claims are not those of the usual psychic healer. The craniosacral system of therapeutics originated from discoveries made during surgery and confirmed and expanded in autopsies. It is based on highly precise anatomical grids, with reference points and vector analyses more exact than most anatomical loci used in allopathy. At the same time, it is a system that relies on the transmission of extremely fine energies even to beneath the level at which they can be perceived. For instance, Upledger has independently explored acupuncture, the *chakra* system, Kirlian photography, psychic energy, pyramid power, and channeled spirits, and even teaches a V-spread technique in which intention is projected through a focal trough aimed by two fingers into a patient's body toward a parallel "backboard" formed by the palm of the other hand held on the opposite side of the recipient's body! Hence, telekinesis and psychic (or *chi*) energy are fully integrated into the domain of multidimensional anatomy and functional analysis. As time passes, this may become the nucleus for a whole new system as extensive as either

allopathy or osteopathy. In fact, it seems to foreshadow a twenty-first-century medicine as permutable and "information"-based as holography and as paradoxically componential as quantum theory.

In the field of energy medicine one of the most difficult feats is to remain relevant and present in the way that a patient is. The eliciting and transmission of rainbows, lightning, buzzes, miracle remissions, and the like are popular demonstrations of a healer's virtuosity. Many alternative therapists who engage simultaneously in *chakras,* meridians, subluxations, cysts, and language develop elaborate and ornate styles plus a kind of New Age summoning of spirits and energies. Such treatments always seem somewhat idealized and extrinsic. They arrive from outside the patient and put on a show using the ailment as a prop.

Perhaps the most notable thing about Upledger's practice is its utter simplicity and directness. He manages to find a patient's wavelength and meet it. He never seems self-consciously spiritual or energetic. He gives the impression he can feel primacy, whatever others choose to name it. He never adds more in an overpowering way. The moment he locates core, he goes solely where it leads him. He lets the patient determine the path and pattern of healing because only the patient can lead the way through the ellipses and labyrinths of his own condition. During this process it may occur to Upledger that one thing is the *chakra* system, another is the meridians, another is the craniosacral system, but the interpretation is incidental because he is *following* what he feels.

Upledger is also a former professional jazz pianist (in his youth in Detroit during the 1950s before he attended osteopathic college). His personal version of craniosacral treatment has in it obvious rhythm and riffs with long stretches of brilliant improvisation. When Upledger does hands-on work, it is as though an artist with the genius of a Charlie Parker or Miles Davis had taken as his instrument the human body. Watching Upledger perform is watching a great jazz musician play. His whole body follows the music. Even his language is brash and jive—it is blues and street talk, which the organism probably respects more than the effete verbiage of a physician. He might address the heart

chakra with, "You're a hardhearted woman!" or proclaim, "Coming down into San Anton'!" as he picks up and follows a resurgence of the craniosacral rhythm. Lightness and humor are also considered critical elements of treatment and cure. For one, they keep things simple and do not allow the illusion of psychospiritual complexity to cloud the concrete fact of physical existence. "Somehow," Upledger muses, "anyone who can laugh at their condition is closer to healing than another person who takes it overseriously."[33]

Upledger tells the story of a patient repeatedly sodomized as a child by both his father and uncle. He worked through 160 painful episodes of sexual abuse before he finally broke out laughing and declared, "Doesn't Uncle Charlie look ridiculous coming into the bathroom after me with his fly open and that stupid grin on his face."[34] It is not that the seriousness of the wound was diminished or its traumatic nature trivialized. It is that the charge associated with it, emotionally trapping the barbs of the physical aspects of the cyst, was released. All that was left was the somatic wound, which could be dissolved without complication.

It is precisely this separating of layers and treating of each distinct trajectory that grounds craniosacral work in the classically osteopathic precision of its forebears. Still's solid pulleys and levers have transmuted as if through a black hole into holographic ghosts now the quanta of a holistic psychotherapy as seminal as Freud's dreamwork.

Notes

1. A. T. Still, *Osteopathy: Research & Practice* (Seattle: Eastland Press, 1992) (originally published in 1910), p. xxii.
2. Ibid., p. 19.
3. Ibid., pp. 23–24.
4. Ibid., p. 40.
5. Ibid., p. 113.
6. Ibid., p. 223.
7. Eiler H. Schiötz and James Cyriax, *Manipulation Past and Present* (London: William Heinemann Medical Books, Ltd., 1975), p. 144.
8. Still, *Osteopathy: Research & Practice*, p. 21.

9. Ibid., p. 7.

10. Ibid., page xvi (foreword by Harold Goodman).

11. Hugh Milne, *The Heart of Listening: A Visionary Approach to Craniosacral Work,* unpublished manuscript at the time of publication (Berkeley, California: North Atlantic Books, 1995).

12. Ibid.

13. Ibid.

14. Ibid.

15. Schiötz and Cyriax, *Manipulation Past and Present,* p. 123.

16. Ibid., p. 95.

17. Insofar as I have no direct experience of Applied Kinesiology, I have relied entirely on material provided by Don Cohen, whom I gratefully acknowledge.

18. Quoted by Don Cohen, *An Introduction to Craniosacral Therapy,* unpublished manuscript at the time of publication (Berkeley, California: North Atlantic Books, 1995).

19. Cohen, *An Introduction to Craniosacral Therapy.*

20. Jean-Pierre Barral and Pierre Mercier, *Visceral Manipulation* (Seattle: Eastland Press, 1989), p. 17.

21. Ibid., p. 21.

22. Ibid., p. 23.

23. Ibid., p. 25.

24. Michael Salveson, personal communication, Berkeley, California, 1994.

25. Cohen, *An Introduction to Craniosacral Therapy.*

26. Ibid.

27. John Upledger, verbal communication, seminar, San Francisco, January 1994.

28. Ibid.

29. Mia Segal, Interview in *Somatics* (Autumn/Winter 1985–86), p. 16.

30. Upledger, verbal communication, seminar, San Francisco, January 1994.

31. T. S. Eliot, *The Complete Poems and Plays* (New York: Harcourt, Brace and Company, Inc., 1930), p. 119.

32. Don Hanlon Johnson, personal communication, 1994.

33. Upledger, verbal communication, seminar, San Francisco, January 1994.

34. Ibid.

CHAPTER FOUR

Overview and Ground Systems

Body

Nothing more centrally expresses the body's creative power than the fact of its physical existence. One of the underlying themes of this book is that the development of a full being from an embryo requires coherence and complexity far more resembling metaphors of mind than of body. Our organisms continue to sustain themselves and grow from cell division through a lifetime, even as they retain the ability to cast their seed into other living systems, theoretically to the ends of time itself. This process contains mysteries, mysteries that do not have to be solved for us to embody them, and, by embodying them, to think them without thinking them, to express them in our analysis of everything else, every moment we live. Beside this deeper mind, the mind of psychology and philosophy is a brief flash in an abyss.

Those who deal professionally with the body—doctors, athletic coaches, and physical therapists included—tend to see a functioning unity of organs and systems, of which one, the nervous system, connects mind to the overall network. By this formula, dance is assigned to body and choreography to mind, but a description of physical mechanics hardly covers the range and multiformity of the former; likewise, body can be intuitive and imaginative with resources of creativity rivaling mind at its most translucent.

Can we speak of coordination separate from a mind? Can music exist without a body? Is telekinesis only the brain pulling? How does the mind even know it exists in order to pull? Is the heart only a pump or was the mediaeval notion of it as the seat of emotions and spirit somehow appropriate to our human situation? Is meditation the work of mind or of body? And healing—is it mindwork or bodywork? For the traditional Apache of the Western Hemisphere and the Aborigine of Australia these questions do not exist. Their science intersects the living entities that make up the world, human and otherwise, in a different plane.

Things which are neither and both are things not in our system. Yet the Jívaro boy and Pomo bear shaman (see Volume One) both stake their life on a fact that is both mind and body and neither mind nor body, assignable to neither, even by component, as we might assign the impulse behind a dance step to mind and the breathing of meditation to body. The somatic definition of "body" is such that it means just about everything the familiar use of the word "body" contradicts.

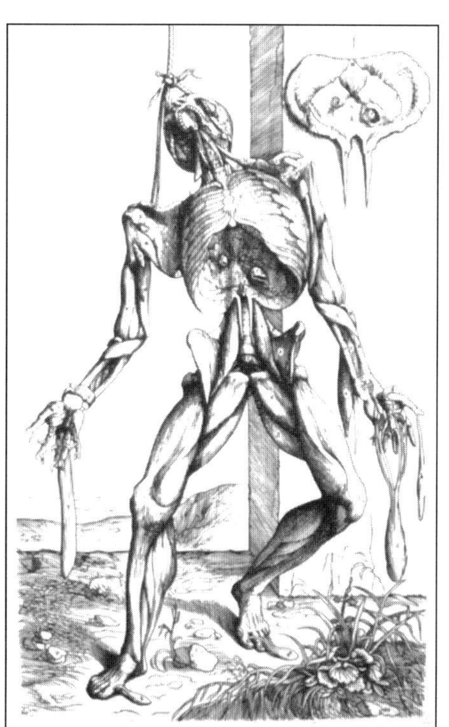

THE SO-CALLED mind-body split that we work holistically to unify is probably better described as a split between the mind of the body and the mind of the mind. It is not mind-body as such because, as long as we are incarnate, we are separated from the vast unconscious archetypal body. The problem is that we are often pathologically separated from the mind of the body as well. Meditation, various forms of bodywork, some schools of psychoanalysis, and, even occasionally, more "physical" therapies like chiropractic and herbs clearly address the mind as body (or the body as mind), that is, open a channel through

our moment-to-moment proprioception into the patterns of energy and substance in our organs. If the process is successful, physical and mental change are simultaneous.

This dynamic might be made clearer by our distinguishing between the intellectual mind, which objectifies itself from the phenomena it experiences (in one of its most sophisticated forms, it is the scientific mind), and the mind of the body, which uses its subjective experiences to develop an internal language of feelings and functional connections. When we speak abstractly of the heart in relation to love for instance, we are not attributing characteristics to the physical aorta; we are identifying the charge we feel from the pumping of blood and the deep oxygenation of the organs *and* our capacity to contain and integrate that charge, to translate it into feelings about another person and acts of emotional exchange. The *aikido* master identifies the same "love" with the harmony of spirals between *uke* and *nage.* When one puts his or her heart into an act, the projection is far more complex than either the semantic metaphor or the life-giving actions of the circulatory system.

Certainly a major failing of Western culture, and industrial civilization in general, is that it cuts off everyone—capitalists as well as workers—from the mind of the heart, i.e., cuts them off not only from the healing but the acts of compassion that arise from there.

Breath

CONSCIOUS BREATH—nothing more than the act of aware breathing—is a crucial modality in holistic medicine. It is a major active element in meditation, *Chi Gung,* and various breathing therapies, including the famous nineteenth-century German breathing schools of which the last remaining *in situ* is Ilse Middendorf's "perceptible breath" (still taught by the founder herself in Berlin in 1994). Breath (integrated with movement and internalization) underlies yoga, *Chi Gung,* and the Taoist martial arts. In all somatic therapies, including Reichian work, Feldenkrais, Rolfing, Lomi, chiropractic, craniosacral

touch, and standard osteopathy, the breath of both practitioner and patient form an integral and indispensable axis. The differences between these somatic systems and so-called direct "breath" forms like rebirthing (see Chapter One) are merely ones of emphasis. The universal goal is to achieve deeper breathing, usually breathing which can be distributed from the lungs and belly to the organs and limbs. A more subtle point is that the breathing of the practitioner is no less critical than that of the patient; in fact, the practitioner's fullness (or shallowness) of breath is communicated to the patient, thus can unconsciously cue his or her breathing (or rigidity). This is as true for the M.D. as the bodyworker.

Horizontal breathing—forming a center

Where a specific breathing technique is not taught, it is often encouraged—sometimes by explicit exhortation, sometimes through exercises, sometimes by the energetic exchange of the treatment itself. The shock of bones being adjusted, the uncomfortable burning of the acupuncture needles, and the tissue-shaping of Rolfing automatically all summon deeper and fuller breathing which then energizes the whole mind/body.

Let the middle area gyrate

Lomi breathing work, rebirthing, and many massage-breath forms usually have a moment in them where one feels one simply cannot go on breathing fully. This is exactly the point at which one must go on, for it is fear, not physical pressure, that holds one back, though there is a weariness and a sense of not being able to push any further or maintain concentration. Once one travels past this point, breathing begins to be freer. The body is transformed by a previously disguised unity of muscles, emotions, organs, and breath (for which breath is the catalyst and agent). Instead of continuing to resist, the flesh tingles right down to the viscera; concentration becomes more suspended; attention hangs in an alert but relaxed state.

Lower area with rising breath

In Ilse Middendorf's classes, students learn the minute differences between cadences and levels of breath, how to perceive these ever more subtly, and to deepen them by following their paths and

expanding their range. One places his hands successively on different parts of his own body and takes time to allow each natural breath and its sensation to arise and take shape there. This may be as subtle as touching the outside of the nose and feeling the nostrils saturate with air or chanting a vowel and sensing the shape it transmits through the viscera. The breath, once aroused, grows in unexpected ways, becomes embodied at deepening levels. It trickles, glides, chants, dilates, rebounds, pirouettes, excites, and expands. As the breath—or the projection of the breath's metaphors through mind—contacts the periphery of the body, it vitalizes digestion, circulation, immunity, and makes the spinal column more flexible. Repetition of these exercises increases the range of the perceptible breath.

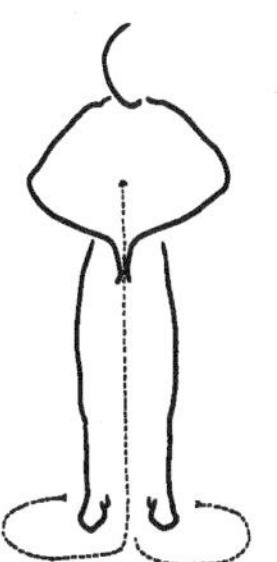

Straightening up with rising breath

Middendorf's assumption is that if "natural" breath comes into resonance throughout the whole body and subsumes more isolated, artificial breaths, health will naturally follow. The center will gather strength and disperse it to the periphery. She writes:

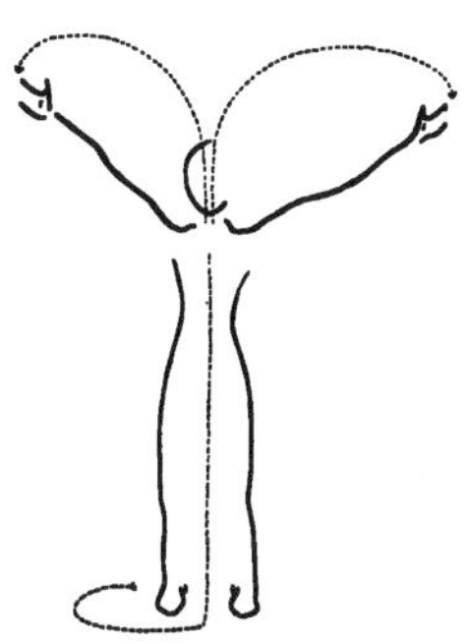

Inhalation in the upper area

> The breathing coming out of your own conscious and unconscious meanings, freed from the control of your ego, shows itself to you through the movement you allow yourself, resulting in a pleasant feeling of release, and directs itself to your creative forces which, once released, express themselves full of joy. . . .
>
> The perceptible breath always needs patience, especially as every new start of the movement growing out of breathing extracts material from one's depths, new, and unknown. . . .
>
> In such work, you become aware of where you really stand. . . .[1]

Bodywork Psychotherapy

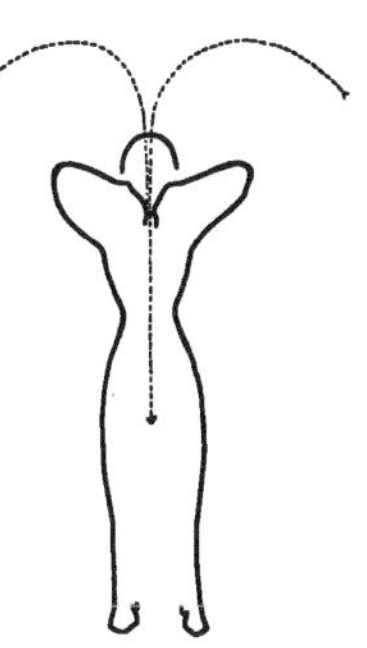

Bending down again as you exhale

SPEECH OCCURS ON two levels—one as words, shaped by the mind into meaning; the other as sound, shaped by the breath and muscles into expression. Chanting and conscious breathing are clearly somatic, but so is mere chatter. How a person talks is part of how she also moves and breathes, how her body talks to her and how she talks to her body.

Interpretation of the psychosomatic basis of language has given rise to many of the so-called "direct" and "gestalt" psychotherapies that use a combination of speech, action, gesture, tonation, etc., as collective inroads to character. In Gestalt therapy, for instance, language is used not for a verbal recovery of information nor purely energetically in the Reichian mode, but as the compass in a psychodramatic reenactment of a present or historical conflict. The therapist does not deny the existence of traumatizing incidents, but she wants to encounter their contemporary form, and this cannot be a gamble of truth-telling or the day's mood. She must elicit an engaged interaction in the context of transference. In bioenergetic therapy this interaction is even more physical.

The laws of holism demand that everything be present at every moment in some form. So even the most verbal holistic therapies emphasize the physiology of character. In fact, a modality that is at once herbal, somatic, and psychospiritual (like Polarity or Still's osteopathy) is vintage "alternative medicine," for holism is precisely the *nondistinction* between treating with an herbal remedy, with palpation, and with words or prayers. In many cases a Tibetan turquoise pill can be the functional equivalent of a *kum nye* exercise or a chiropractic adjustment.

Full health is dependent upon breath, skeletal harmony, and free metabolic rhythm. Without the skeletal, massage, and visceral traditions—many of them originating from decidedly unholistic therapies—there would be no holistic health as we understand it. There would be no emotional, energetic link between pure physical exercise on the one hand and vitalistic pharmacies and shamanic rituals on the other. Most people cannot just jump into meditation and *Chi Gung* without help. The body has learned its habits too well to "think" its way out of them. Bodywork provides support for unaccustomed uses of breath and neuromusculature. Likewise, potentized pharmaceuticals, organic vegetables, and vision quests in and of themselves cannot restore deep physical health for most people. The viscera need "osteo-

pathic instruction," Rolfing, or even, in some instances, allopathic drugs or surgery before they are strong enough to sustain a different lifestyle. One of the weaknesses of many of the "New Age" adaptations of traditional herbal and homeopathic medicines is that they overlook the multi-layered energetic basis of anatomy and character in their enthusiasm for the energetic components of their pills and potions. Bodywork fills that gap.

VIOLATIONS IN THE bodily coherence of an organism include shallow breath, nervous speech rhythm, uncoordinated posture, and tight control of diction; these are symptoms not just of emotional disturbances (as is most commonly assumed) but also of skeletal, muscular, and visceral diseases. They can be viewed as psychosomatic waves locked in fixed patterns. After all, the heart and the liver have no other way to express themselves. Language emerges from the body and speaks its mind, and, as the bioenergetic therapist Stanley Keleman tells us in the title of one of his books, the "body [also] speaks *its* mind." The teaching of the mind may pass as philosophy, but the teaching of the body is not athletics. It is the body's version of philosophy and is just as intricate, subtle, and multilevelled. The kidneys and lungs have their own distinct personalities, but we are rarely aware of them.

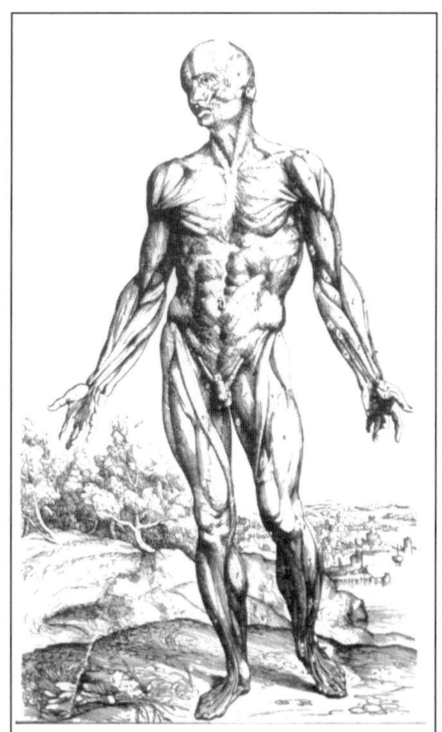

In holistic medicine, definitions of health are based upon the organs' subtle relationships to one another. If personal behavior or organic function are aberrant, then the organs must also be out of position. It does not matter which came first, which initiated the drift; it is "neither and both" and functionally the same. The chiropractor believes that by adjusting bones he reorients muscles; by

reorienting muscles, he changes tissue qualities. The changing tissue qualities cause the body to reorganize itself and, as the body reorganizes, the intellect begins to recognize its neuroses and deepen the expression of its life.

Gestalt and bioenergetic therapies are transmitted as movement and voice exercises. Not all of them are strenuous. Some are as simple as tightening and loosening the throat or trying to experience breath in a certain organ. For most people, as *t'ai chi* master Benjamin Lo recounted, simply to stand symmetrically at their natural height is a major undertaking (see "Chinese Medicine" in Volume One, Chapter Nine). The strain from this task is not because it is punishing—or even necessarily because of physical frailty; it is because the person is organized away from normal functions, usually out of fear and protection. He is avoiding the feelings that go with past failure and discomfort or that represent these in the economy of the psyche.

As feelings rush up during a session or exercise, a deep rhythm from the system tries to impose itself and, since the rhythm is more fluent, more coherent than the personality, it will run into blocks posing as attitudes. The person will tighten and resist, and this will be felt both as pain and the wish not to continue the exercise. Although the discomfort is immediate, it is also historical. It hurts now because something else hurt back then, and the body numbed itself away from that in protection or hardened against it in defense. The present resistance is what hurts, not the actual mechanics of the task.

Feldenkrais exercises in particular are used to engender gradual sensual pathways toward restoring function. The person learns by replacing awkward or painful mechanics with new movements that support passage through the same somatic territory. The movements are not feats. They must be learned in tiny increments, like restoring sensation to the movement of the pelvis or ankles.

Since safeguarded feelings are perceived as pain, there may be an apprehension that to persist in such exercises will cause injury or disease.

The irony is that a disease feared, such as back strain or even heart failure, is more likely to be caused by the *absence* of the exercise than by following it through—by the decades of stiffness, shallow breathing, and withholding. Fear of disease, in this case, is fear of self; and from fear of self, malignancy arises. Reich left little doubt that he considered cancer and heart disease literally diseases of the personality, the heart, and the genitals. If such is the case, character exercises keep the body from somaticizing emotions into pathologies.

The complaint that Lo's exercises were merely difficult calisthenics was more a confirmation than a dismissal. In a sense, prior to *chi*, they *are* merely calisthenics, but not calisthenics in which one pushes oneself past the point of feeling or numbs oneself to pain in order to achieve some victory. They are calisthenics in which one tries to regain a natural, pre-armored structure and mobility, a sense of ease with simply standing in gravity in the world and breathing air. This process itself causes feelings to bubble up and surge, sensations which were suppressed or ignored. An athlete may sometimes be able to use these to spur performance; other times he must override them as inspiring distractions.

In somatic disciplines (unlike sports), one *must* accept and integrate the feelings aroused by the use of the body exactly as they come up and in the way in which they come up—first in the exercise, subsequently in life itself. There is no extraneous meaning, no goal; the meaning is simply: this is what's happening; this is who I am.

We can see this more graphically in the example of an exercise from Keleman:

> ... [K]icking can ... help us understand, experientially, the notion of self-forming. Kicking encourages the use of the voice as well as moving the whole body into action, either as protest or an expression of joy. Kids kick with glee. Tickle a child, and watch its legs start bouncing around. When a child is angry, he screams and his legs want to move. Then finally, it ends with jumping for joy, or stomping in a tantrum and walking away.

> Lie down on your back with your shoes off. Make sure you can move and breathe easily. Now begin to kick the bed. Start with raising your legs to right angles to your body so that they go straight up in the air toward the ceiling. Then bring them straight down, hitting the bed with your heels. Keep kicking, always lifting your legs at right angles to your body. Begin to feel what the emotional experience is as well as the action.[2]

Deep into a bioenergetic exercise, a patient may become the animal she is, wailing in creature sounds, doing creature movements. The inner being is brought into alignment with the surface personality and shares a moment of coherence with it. This coherence is so sweet and medicinal that its superficially unattractive traits are prices worth paying.

In experiencing these things, the personality understands that there is another life it has not been living. It comes to a point, past exhaustion and past the driven expression of emotion, where the self begins to express its own being only. This pours through the flesh as an elixir, but also as an ancient familiarity, a recognition. Suddenly anger or passion no longer needs a situation; it is one of the core things in the body. The voice now speaks for the "It" also.

A physiological change takes place—muscles are stretched, the skin changes color and temperature, liquids and breath move through the flesh—all in the context of feeling. Molecular changes may also take place; after all, oxygen is molecular in its activity.

Fake psychodrama perhaps, but then no one protests that a pill or an operation isn't real because one is prescribed in language, the other performed in a clinical setting. As mind and body flow together and achieve their nondifference, tension momentarily lightens. The sky outside the window becomes as luminescently blue as Reich, in his vision of orgone bliss, would have had us believe it is. The blossoms on the trees hang as globes of fuzzy light, expanding eternally without weight and made of tenderness more than of matter. Memories that seemed to have been lost forever flood back in delicate sensings. Life becomes so large and expanded in their return that it is itself sufficient and ample;

there is enough to drink forever, but there is not so much that one would drown. One's size changes, the sense of being cramped in a body softens. The torso expands to hold a figure which is at once more muscular and firm and more angelic and graceful. For the duration of the feeling, lost functions are intuited and sometimes even recovered.

A single such experience may not dissolve deep internal illness. It is the accretion of such moments and their chains of perceptions that ultimately penetrate rigidity or immobility at the base.

Background to Somatics

No topic so much characterizes *Planet Medicine* as the definitions and meanings of different bodywork systems. They are the lynchpin of any epistemology of healing. However, the "Bodywork" chapter from my original edition presented not only a very limited selection but viewed all systems in a Reichian hierarchy popular in 1976 and now quite dated. For that reason, I have dispersed most of its contents among other sections of the text and the opening three sections of this chapter and created four otherwise new chapters on "Somatics."

My recent education in the area of healing has been primarily in somatics. Between 1975 and 1979 I was a client of Ian Grand at The Center for Energetic Studies in Berkeley and of Polly Gamble at Lomi School. During the mid-1980s I worked with Lomi co-founder Richard Heckler. More recently I have had at least some experience with craniosacral therapy, Polarity Therapy, Feldenkrais Method, Zero Balancing, Rolfing, Alexander Technique, *Chi Gung*, and rebirthing.

I have also been trained as a somaticist. From 1990 through 1993 I was a member of Randy Cherner's weekly professional seminar in Corte Madera, California (see Epilogue). During the same period I attended one year of classes at the Breema Institute, studied for two years at Peter Ralston's Cheng Hsin School of Martial Arts and Ontology (and three years after that with Ralston's former students Ron Sieh and David Tircuit), and took weekend workshops on Body-Mind Centering with

Bonnie Bainbridge Cohen and *Chi Gung* with Kumar Frantzis. Between 1992 and 1994 I completed four-day seminars comprising the first three levels of craniosacral training administered by the Upledger Institute ("Craniosacral Therapy I" and "II" and "SomatoEmotional Release I").

My orientation within somatics is heavily influenced by the teachers with whom I have had direct experience. This should not be misunderstood as an attempt to portray these as the sole sources of such material or the most noteworthy innovators. Perhaps what distinguishes somatics in the late twentieth century is the degree to which, throughout North America and Europe, and to a lesser degree the world as a whole, innovation has eclipsed the authority of traditional systems. Somatics has become a medicinal and professional version of poetics and jazz, extending the generosity and personal energy that once characterized a community of writers and musicians.

The real somaticists are not the ones who are most public with their work but those hidden away in nooks and crannies, improvising on their own or as small clusters in collaborative training groups.

People experimenting with somatics are inventing variants out of every imaginable component—meditation, guerrilla training, theater, puppetry, tennis, wildlife management, Gurdjieffian exercises, African drumming, basic sensuality, sailing, skiing, sweat-lodge rituals, dancing to rock music, movement improvisation, hallucinogenic plants—or like F. Matthias Alexander, they stand in front of a mirror and ask how (and where) the human mind/body begins to move.

Defining somatics in the context of medicine is at once deceptively easy and extraordinarily complicated. The easy part is simply to note (again) that, throughout the habitation of our species on Earth, body therapists have restored or enhanced health by massage, adjustment, hands-on energetic changes, and (more recently) guided exercises. The osteopath reinvented the jack-of-all-trades Pleistocene doctor. In this regard, somatics *is* medicine. If we had to choose one modality whereby to treat everything, its ontology would be somatic:

surgery would be its acute branch and pharmacy would provide an alternate method of penetrating and altering viscera.

The complicated part is that somatics now deals with not only well-being but meaning. It addresses physical existence directly and holistically. It locates healing energy in the flesh and its immediate field and does not seek exogenous sources. Its methods arise from the epistemology and phenomenology of a body and reach beyond the body itself to a body image, an inner body realm, social communication, and space itself. Thus, somatics has more to do with the body experienced from within than the body manipulated from without.

> [Somatics] dates back to the mid- and late nineteenth century Gymnastik movement in Northern Europe and the Eastern United States. At a time when physicians were still engaged in the crudest forms of surgery and medication, and when psychotherapy was just beginning, the practitioners of various branches of Gymnastik were already doing sophisticated healing work using expressive movement, sensory awareness, sound, music and touch.[3]

The founders of this movement included Frederick Matthias Alexander in Australia, Leo Kofler in New York, and Gerda Alexander, Ilse Middendorf, and Elsa Gindler in Germany. They did very little writing and transmitted their systems mainly to participants in workshops, so their innovations went undocumented.

> World War I broke up the early interdisciplinary Somatics community, leaving individual schools intact but isolated and fragmented.

> World War II further dispersed the pioneers, forcing many of them to put aside the more visionary aspects of their work, and to eke out a living as refugees, marketing their work under the more acceptable forms of physical rehabilitation or psychotherapy.[4]

This certainly describes the journey of Gindler disciple Marion Rosen who, upon escaping Hitler's Germany in the 1930s, came to the United States and, not finding any public receptivity for somatics *per se,* began doing rehabilitative therapy. Out of this practice she eventually developed her own Rosen system of movement awareness.

IN DESCRIBING HER modality years later, somatic elder Gerda Alexander wrote:

> In touching we do not reach beyond the surface. In eutonic "contact" we move consciously beyond the visible boundaries of the body. Through this "contact" we can include also the surrounding space in our awareness. Thus, without touching, we are able to make real contact with other human beings, animals, plants and objects, passing through external boundaries.
>
> This conscious "contact" has greater influence than "touch" with regard to changes in the tonus and the circulation.[5]

A definition of somatics originates in a distinction between straightforward modes of touch and exercise and inner perception of embodiment and experience. The new model can never be just massage or palpation, no matter how skilled or inventive. It evokes layers that simply don't exist in physical therapy. One can be a resourceful and talented cranial worker, Rolfer, Feldenkrais practitioner, etc., simply by carrying out diagrammatic postures and manipulations. What distinguishes radical somatotherapy is a conversion to viewing the body—in particular, one's own body—as a medium of inquiry at the heart of existence. Thus, a dedicated student of *t'ai chi ch'uan* can be a more authentic somaticist than a veteran bioenergetic therapist.

Perhaps more than any other present field of investigation, somat-

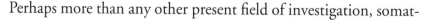

ics points to the emergence of a kinesthetic paradigm of reality, one that shares aspects with chaos theory, models of the brain, holography, structuralism, deconstruction, and quantum physics. In fact, somatics throws open the question (in daily life) of who is the observer, who is the subject.

At times, of course, somatics seems to be less medicine than a blend of pop philosophy and positive thinking. Its techniques and trainings suggest psychological exercises and mind-bending more than real cures for concrete diseases. Thus the mainstream of medicine feels smug in ignoring them.

But the mainstream of medicine is also somatic to the extreme—doggedly and literally so—without any phenomenology or philosophy beyond rationalism. Right from the beginning, alternative somatic philosophies do not treat the body as a concordance of independently functioning viscera or as a separate entity in dialogue with a mind. As we have noted repeatedly, somaticists address not the body *per se* but the mind in the body and the neural, corporeal aspect of the epiphenomenal mind. This is what defines the profession.

Practitioners working with postural and functional integration have come to understand that body stances (including systemic pathologies) reflect customs of etiquette and professional or militaristic discipline more than underlying somatic requirements. Emotional traumas and lesions get built into static poses. Thus people *become* their personal histories, their niches in society, their jobs, rather than their humanity or flowingness. Such rigidities lead to psychological as well as structural diseases. Somatic therapies treat the full complexity of this situation. Eutony, Alexander Technique, Feldenkrais Method, and Rolfing are all forms of realignment and body balancing that are intended to affect simultaneously the personality and dynamic physiological state of the organism. They address (almost exclusively among medicines) the dysfunctional habits of poor "self-cure."

We should make clear, though, that somatics is not directly related to a host of other processes defining themselves by superficially similar

terminologies. The EST of Werner Erhard is not somatics, nor are other "positive thinking" and empowerment practices and seminars. These are secular religious rites not dissimilar from corporate sales meetings. Guided visualization, affirmation processes (as in rebirthing), hypnotherapies, psychotherapeutic insight, and instructional change by imperative from biofeedback machines are also not somatics in the sense I am defining here. These are all systems of behavioral modification. They impose an external authority inculcating a particular pattern of behavior or lifestyle. By contrast, somatics teaches people how simply to listen to themselves and awaken their own inner life impulses. It does not mask ideological agendas.

True somatic therapies are also spiritual processes. The cranial osteopath follows her touch inward to a fluttering that seems to lie at the very "soul" of the organs. Ilse Middendorf's breathwork not only enhances physical health, it leads a person into the meanings of her own untouched profundity. Eutony cultivates feelings through rhythm. Polarity massage is guided to karmic levels within the self where feelings of the most personal sort are protected and where the destiny of the organism lies. Just as indigenous peoples entered their sweat lodges with a prayer to have their spirits soar like an eagle, so somaticists bring the parameters of the sweat lodge with them and impose the functional equivalent of such heat on their clients. They are the unconscious "other" who acts upon the "self."

IN A LETTER to the somatics community dated April 12, 1993, Bonnie Bainbridge Cohen, founder of Body-Mind Centering, challenged the limited public and professional perception of a somatic branch of medicine. She pointed out that, although Bill Moyers, in his just-completed television series "Healing and the Mind," had presented the topic in a "heartful and sensitive" manner, he went all the way to China to demonstrate hands-on bodywork and movement.[6]

"Was/is Bill Moyers unaware," Cohen asked, "of the sophisticated approaches here in the West?"[7]

She then cited examples of the modalities listed in the National Institutes of Health Guide, that is, sanctioned categories in which to apply for grant money that Congress made available for alternative medical approaches.

These include: diet, nutrition, lifestyle changes (macrobiotics, megavitamins, diets); mind/body control (art therapy/relaxation, biofeedback, counselling, guided imagery, hypnotherapy, and sound/music therapy); traditional medicine and ethnomedicine (acupuncture, Ayurveda, herbal medicine, homeopathic medicine, Native American medicine, natural products, and traditional Oriental medicine); structural manipulations and energetic therapies (acupressure, chiropractic medicine, massage, reflexology, Rolfing, therapeutic touch, *Chi Gung*); pharmacology and biological treatments (anti-oxidants, cell treatment, chelation therapy, metabolic therapy, and oxidizing agents); and bioelectromagnetic applications (transcranial electrostimulation, neuromagnetic stimulation, electroacupuncture).[8]

Individual somatic therapies are included in as many as four of these categories (depending on one's definitions), but the field of somatics is not clearly recognized as a profession. After reviewing this list Cohen asks:

> Why in Mind/body control are dance and movement therapies not mentioned (e.g., Dance/movement Therapy, Movement Therapy, Continuum, Authentic Movement, Laban Movement Analysis, Kestenberg Movement Profile)?
>
> Why in Structural manipulations and energetic therapies are the body therapies that include both hands-on manipulations and movement (e.g., Alexander, Feldenkrais, Body-Mind Centering, Aston Patterning, Trager) not mentioned?[9]

The explanation would seem to be that the purest and most methodologically experimental somatic modalities are still confused with traditionally nonmedical activities and that their direct, systemic challenge to allopathy in its own domains is not yet recognized. At the same time, somatic modalities that can be viewed as more limited specialties and

distinct adjuncts to other forms of medicine are listed, in essence, as mechanical or energetic subsystems. Cohen emphasizes that the distinguishing features of the field of somatics (as defined at a 1992 San Francisco conference) are "focus on body image, anatomy, sensory and kinesthetic education, and nonverbal language."[10] I take this to mean the *simultaneous* priority of all five domains.

IN OUR CROWDED CIVILIZATION, we have become dislocated from a sense of mutuality and contact with one another. In earlier times physical contact melded a richer and more diverse set of experiences, both spontaneous and ritualized. The pure kinesthesia of love and hate was somaticized instead of being sublimated and commoditized in the way it is today. Although this included acts we presently define as abuse and torture, the overall framework of human contact was tactile and embodied.

The rebirth of "touch" has come about, at one pole, from disciplines of physical and psychological therapy and medicine seeking another avenue of therapeutic access and, on the other, from a suppressed and depreciated function of mutuality seeking new and acceptable modes of expression. It has emerged simultaneously from the arts, including dance and experimental theater, and the previously underestimated realm of the exercise class (of course, now we know that true "exercise" includes yoga and *Chi Gung*). These represent varieties of our conscious and unconscious imperatives to somatic practices, and they fuse seamlessly where our hungers and our objective analyses cover each other's tracks. Our modern situation has become so desperate that we must turn to professional guides for how to love, how to express anger, how to begin and end relationships, rather than to our own intrinsic, instinctual nature. Bioenergetic therapist Stanley Keleman writes:

> The deprivation of actual physical contact is so enormous in our culture that anything that touches us has such an enormous impact, and anyone practicing touch becomes a guru.[11]

Fields of Somatics

SOMATICS AS A recognized field of research may presently be in a disordered state, but fortunately the result is creativity rather than confusion. However, because of the profusion of systems, it is impossible to deal adequately with even the majority of them in this book. In order to map the variety and complexity, I have approached the various disciplines in terms of their shared lineages and themes, comparable (and noncomparable) techniques, and fusions and divergences. Where possible, I have submitted earlier drafts of this book to either the founders of fields or contemporary practitioners, and I have integrated their comments in the text.

AS WE HAVE SEEN in Volume One, the various somatic subfields have for the most part developed independently of one another. The combining of elements of unique disciplines is very much a post-holistic phenomenon. An underlying question remains: are the specific techniques that define any one subfield more functional as components of a larger and as-yet-only-partially-realized somatic synthesis, or are they most productive in the contexts of their own systems? That is, when a Rolfer stops his tissue integration to respond to the craniosacral pulse, does that enhance or detract from the cohesiveness of the integration, and is the craniosacral work as productive as it would be in the context of its own hierarchy? Are the various therapies coalescing into a single system (or a repertoire of related techniques that might be taught in different courses within the same program), or will they remain substantially separate fields unintegratable by future practitioners?

This composite question can be approached in a number of ways, none of them definitive. For instance, it is quite possible that neither Rolfing nor craniosacral techniques are as effective in hybrid treatments as either would be in its own context, but that the combination of modalities adds contextual (and perhaps critical) elements to single

treatments. For a combination to be explicitly counterproductive, it would have to induce confusion and inculcate loss of cohesion in the organism of the person receiving it.

Since everything can't be done, the selection of what *is* done is paramount. Any technique is at the expense, potentially, of another. A skilled practitioner, trained in more than one system, can cross boundaries as long as she is aware of her patient's changing capacity to respond to what she is doing. The danger of switching from one set of techniques to another is that the organism being worked on will be divided (or overloaded) and respond to neither. The possible gain from switching systems is to provide somatic information and adjustments not available in any one unadulterated system. Thus, the success of a hybridization of techniques would depend upon the skill and sensitivity of the practitioner rather than any explicit universal synthesis or priority of purism.

We might also take the point of view that each set of techniques is uniquely valuable in its own right. Our dilemma then would be less one of synthesis versus purity than how we preserve the rich variety of different methods. How does each individual practitioner develop his or her skill (sense of touch) apart from formal systemic considerations? This transfers emphasis to the artistry of therapists from the reputation of their modalities. It may be, as we suggested in Chapter Two, that some people are just successful, no matter what means they employ.

A historical question still remains as to whether the somatic fields are headed toward a synthesis resembling a whole new medical field theory or whether they are primarily each perfecting their individual systems. On the basis of my observations, I would say that both are happening. In areas where techniques are similar, parallel, or even, in some cases, provide different paths to the same structure (including formerly related techniques that have diverged from one another), synthesis is occurring and practitioners are learning one another's methods. Some of the newer forms (such as Zero Balancing and Body-Mind Centering) and many traditional disciplines (notably chiropractic, *Nei*

Gung, and cranial osteopathy) are practiced both as tight formal systems and as general somatics, so, in some cases—certainly not a majority—a client will discover that his therapist is totally eclectic and improvisational as to what modality she chooses at any one session.

Body-Mind Centering, for instance, teaches its own independent method of following energy and strain patterns, resembling, to some degree, traditional osteopathic techniques but having a separate origin. Thus, a "bilingual" practitioner can alter the intention of her touch to convey subtle differences between the two modes, following and holding a bit more in the craniosacral pattern and leading and developing spirals in the Body-Mind Centering pattern. If also trained in *Chi Gung*, the practitioner could interpose Taoist methods of transmitting vital energy.

Zero Balancing offers a variation in which the single bones are held at points of tension. Strain/Counterstrain provides another variant positional procedure and method of palpation. Likewise, a chiropractor, if so educated, can select moments at which to apply visceral work instead of adjustments in order to realign specific organs, or she may even choose to lead the patient in a series of Feldenkrais or Alexander exercises.

Randy Cherner recalls that in the early days of his practice he relied heavily on a straightforward use of "chiropractic-like" palpations. Patients would come in; he'd look them over, spot their distortions, and correct them with swift, direct motions. The patients would feel relief, thank him (often profusely), and he thought, "This sure is easy work."[12]

His first warning that it wasn't going to be so easy occurred when patients began coming to their next appointments not only with their ailments recurrent but often more severe versions. Gradually he came to realize that it wasn't enough just to adjust their shapes; one had to engender a sustaining attitude beneath the shape, to address the forms of being in the personality/organism from which the shapes were originating, and to give the person a means of experiencing his or her own process on an ongoing basis.

As his practice developed, Cherner began searching less for effective modes of immediate correction and more for an elegance of function. He prioritized overall coordination and a freedom to move (especially in the presence of formidable mental impediments—what he called "scoliosis of the brain"). In classic osteopathic fashion, he began emphasizing indirect work, always *away* from the area of the problem. Instead of grappling with the jaw of the lion, he would find an arm or a leg and begin working it inward, reaching the jaw only at the end of the session or in a subsequent session. The goal was to educate the patient in how she was the source of her own condition and thus its most competent remediator. This was best accomplished by giving her the broadest field of proprioceptive evidence. The transmission was mostly somatic, with only a few carefully chosen words.

The truth of somatics, at the most subtle and sophisticated level, is that the intrinsic strength of a deep-seated function, especially once it is somaticized, overwhelms the relatively linear and simple effect of an adjustment. Bodywork itself—and medicine in general as a technological refinement of bodywork—cannot establish lasting change unless it engages the one thing more powerful than the mechanics of a dysfunction, and that is the prior cohesiveness and elegance of natural function. This is true even in the case of people born with disabilities. Life itself is an elegant solution to entropy. The bodyworker who palpates and adjusts merely mechanically is like someone trying to affect the ripple pattern in a lake by stirring the surface of ripples. Whereas a lake cannot be altered at the appropriate level, at least by nonheroic means, an organism has a mind, a consciousness, which directs levels of intention and reconsiders posture and alignment down to the subtlest fascial—and perhaps even cellular—integer. Thus, the right combination of touch, energy, intention, and sometimes language, can create a whole new moiré proceeding out of the source. It must be wooed, not wrenched, though that does not exclude some very powerful direct techniques. After all, those sitting zazen welcome the refreshing strike of the master's stick.

Ida Rolf set as one of her prerequisites for understanding structural alignment an ability to work with reciprocal relationships of organs and neuromusculature. If there was a "problem" someplace, that was never the source but the place where the organism was holding out in order to protect a deeper dysfunction or sense of incapacity and emptiness, which invariably manifested many other places as well and was rooted in some core structural dilemma. Working on a problem directly did not solve the problem; it merely gave the organism a new problem—to find another place to hold out. Working on reciprocal sites (for instance, the hamstrings instead of the muscles of the neck to deal with restriction at the neck) allowed the organism to experience its whole and adjust accordingly across a great breadth. It restored to the organism the capacity to fill in its own space.

In this manner, prior to any complete field theory, the different somatic systems can be used to balance one another in terms of education, passivity versus activity, and depth of change inculcated. For someone with heavily bound musculature, Rolfing may provide a necessary first step for reorganizing structure to reduce strain, but then, without Feldenkrais or Alexander work to reeducate the "uses of self," the person may deviously resculpt many of the strain patterns. On the other hand, someone else may be trenchantly resistant to Rolfing, so Feldenkrais education may suitably come first, with Rolfing never used or broached only much later after the sense of "body" has deepened. Or chiropractic may be utilized in place of Rolfing—bones and junctures emphasized instead of muscles and support (of course, Rolfing also works on bones and chiropractic on muscles). Some people respond better to less mechanical and less behaviorally directive techniques and are far more able to assimilate and enact change merely suggested by craniosacral or Breema touch. Such change might be induced in a fashion much more obscure to the individual practitioner introducing it than their own treatments are to the anatomically astute Rolfer, chiropractor, or Feldenkrais practitioner, but that doesn't prevent it from leading toward a similar, even more sustainable integration.

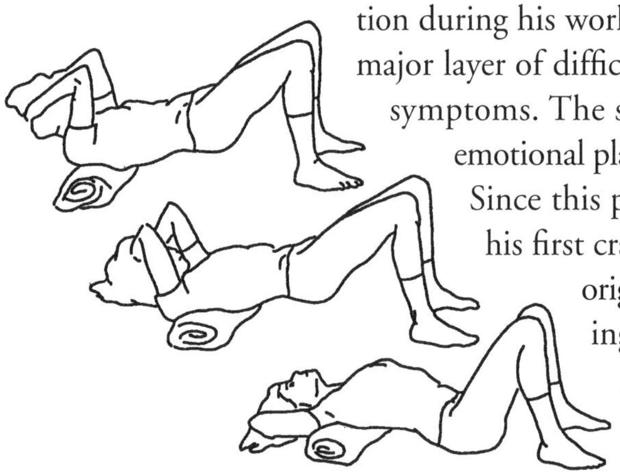

Functional transitions between somatic systems may also be less polar and more incremental. I know of one instance in which a person with a stress pattern encompassing diverse physiological symptoms was first treated craniosacrally through his mandible and the temporal bones of his skull. This relieved an outer layer of discomfort and dysfunction. A year later (more through fortuity than design) the person did a series of lessons with a Feldenkrais practitioner. She led him through sequences of head, eye, and pelvic movements while his upper torso was twisted at different angles respectively in relation to his sacral torso and legs. This subtle investigation of habitual and nonhabitual movement reified another layer of obstruction so that it was gradually "taken off" in daily life. Success made the person receptive to educational somatics and, during an equally chance encounter with an Alexander practitioner two months after that, he was inspired to ask for an example of how Alexander work differed from the Feldenkrais Method. In his office the Alexander practitioner taught the person how to inhibit a habitual series of gestures that always arose prior to his undertaking certain incidental activities that nonetheless seemed to exacerbate the remaining layers of the syndrome. Practicing that change of orientation during his work life, he experienced the dissolution of a major layer of difficulty along with some of its more painful symptoms. The syndrome was now situated more on an emotional plane with less purely physical outcroppings. Since this person had done Lomi work years before his first craniosacral treatment, he went back to his original body therapist with his insights. During a Lomi session a month later the practitioner asked him if he could locate and amplify the neuromuscular pattern at the base of his effective inhibition. Since the signal to inhibit was initiated at such a subtle level, the client could not initially discriminate it and did so only after a number of exercises conducted in front of a mirror. However, once he "found" his point of activation in certain tiny facial movements he was able to make these more palpable and express the minute rivulets trailing from their impulses. He tapped into a whole network of emotional blocks and unexpressed feelings going back to early childhood. These became his next layer of work. After that he was able to approach the purely visual aspects of the condition by the Bates Method.

I have oversimplified the patterns involved here, but what I mean to emphasize is that symptoms themselves and their roots are biological and psychospiritual while somatic systems are syntactic and paradigmatic. The match of any system to any condition is temporal and approximate. The above sequence might have equally gone from Body-Mind Centering to Eutony to Continuum to Hellerwork. There are limitless modes and progressions of access to a core. Where one system may accomplish a quicker, deeper, or more lasting cure, that does not disqualify any system from working at its own level toward a resolution. If it is the "wrong" system (i.e., if there is a more essential, less peripheral approach), the "wrong" system may prepare the client for the transition to another modality. It may also accomplish similar goals but over a longer period of time. Or it may never get to the core by itself or even redirect the client. The person not fully treated still lives a rich and satisfying life. In that sense none of us is ever "fully treated." We live from missed opportunity to fortuity to ever new possibility. Between formal treatments (if they even occur) we treat ourselves naturally and are "adjusted" by the environment. There is no programmatic outcome to any of these sequences. In somatics more than in general medicine, existential and mechanical issues overlap and are entangled.

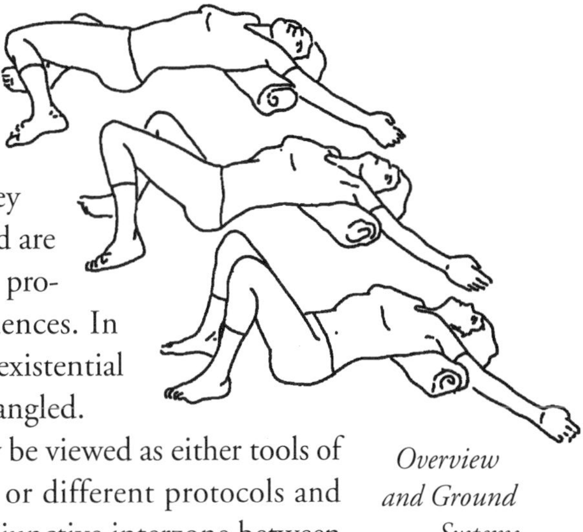

The individual somatic modalities may be viewed as either tools of different sizes, shapes, and fulcral points or different protocols and ontologies to deal with the ragged and disjunctive interzone between

semantics and tissue (language and embodiment). Usually practitioners of the separate modalities acknowledge the virtues of others and recognize clients whose conditions or temperaments predispose them elsewhere. However, to the more ideological adherents of any one system, theirs is the premier and purest therapy. Reich, Alexander, Rolf, Feldenkrais, Movlai, Upledger, etc., are revered as saints and gurus by their loyal followers. Worshippers and xenophobes will always deny that the work of their system is improved by the techniques of another, or that some people are better served by a different somatic practice. They strive to keep their own systems growing holistically rather than to develop a diverse network of somatics. But the purists are important to us, for the logic and cohesiveness of each given system may be lost in too great an ease of switching between systems. Problems may never be solved when the context is always changing and a condition is constantly being redefined.

If this argument seems to be going in circles, it is because there are nothing but circles here. They are the circles which exist everywhere today in the somatic field. They support the traditional trainings and disciplines, and they work toward producing idiosyncratic and syncretic systems. If any syncretic mode becomes individual enough (like aforementioned Zero Balancing or Trager Approach), then new subfields within somatics are born. When sectarian techniques are redistributed among fields, then they change their meanings and uses. If, over time, a technique becomes more universal than sectarian, its whole original field may disappear, as has happened with naturopathy (now a catchall for "natural medicine"). Allopathy (conversely) is a deceptively unified set of principles and activities made up actually of quite independent fields of inquiry and contradicting principles of diagnosis and treatment.

I WILL MAKE ONE other general point here: the adherents of most systems have at one time or another defined their own field as either energetic or something else (mechanical, skeletal, integrative, cognitive,

or neuromuscular). Craniosacral therapists, Breema practitioners, Polarity therapists, *Chi Gung* masters, and Zero Balancers usually (but not always) refer to their methods as energy based. Although they do not deny mechanical components, they usually interpret those components as secondary to the movement of energy (and, as must be clear by now, energy can be defined in a range of ways, from the passage of feeling, to *chi*-flow, to the intercession of paraphysical fields). Likewise, Rolfers, chiropractors, instructors of the Alexander Technique, and a diverse range of other hands-on therapists view their work as mechanical and structural to one degree or another (even when they purport to move something they call "energy"). An individual structural practitioner might emphasize the energetic component of his or her work, but the system rests on its anatomical logic.

I believe, however, that despite any rhetoric to the contrary, all systems are energy based. I don't accept that there is such a thing as pure mechanical alteration. The reason Rolfing and Feldenkrais yield results is that energy is moved and continues to build on itself after the treatment is concluded (call the manifestation of that energy—like the energy itself—whatever you will).

Likewise, I believe that all systems have a material logic even if the practitioner of them is not aware of that logic (sometimes the hands are more intelligent than the brain). I would argue that except in those rare instances that approach faith healing, practitioners are better off with a sound knowledge of anatomy, even if their system does not make direct use of that knowledge. Anatomy provides the precise path to energy. It also offers an equation of relative degrees of fluidity and congestion at any given moment. The anatomy of the body is an energetic outcome and expression, and the energy of the body is transmitted from its anatomic grid.

Even as I make this point, I must add that the distinction itself is gradually becoming obsolete, as somaticists are seeking new language to describe their work. Energy-versus-mechanics may remain an issue in the popular lexicon of healing, but it is clearly limited and simplis-

tic as a criterion of description. No one can define precisely what "energy" means in a biological context; hence, "energy medicine" becomes little more than a jargon by which some systems claim superiority over others (which are "merely mechanical"). In that sense, "energy" is subtext for the claim to "psychospiritual" medicine. But what healer or somatic educator would not presume to embody psychospiritual dimensions?

Nowadays purely somatic practitioners prefer to avoid the word "energy" altogether and to seek some other terminology to describe the functional aspect of their systems. Feldenkrais teachers, Rolfers, and Alexander practitioners speak instead of educating and transforming whole human beings (as the complex creatures they are). Moshe Feldenkrais routinely deconstructed "energy" when people used it in the context of his work. Citing his own background in physics, he would remind them that there is a quite precise thermodynamic definition of energy by comparison to which loose jargon is totally uninstructive. He would not have validated the language describing many of the energetic systems in Chapter Five, except insofar as he agreed that a quite different experience was evoked by Oriental methods.

I present this issue now, at the outset of my discussion of individual systems, because, although I would like to maintain a yardstick of clarity from system to system, there is no way I can describe these systems without using the discriminations of energy and structure they adduce in defining themselves. I urge the reader to keep in mind that despite the repetition of certain terminology to describe types of processes, the processes are in many cases mysterious and undetermined, and the terminology is merely a device by which to instruct initiates or provide a usage for outsiders.

Alexander Technique

Alexander Technique is the honorary godfather of twentieth-century independent somatics. It was the first to fashion its own

unique set of heuristic exercises out of empirical experimentation. It had no lineal predecessors, and most of the later systems owe it a debt, either directly or indirectly.

The originator was F. Matthias Alexander (1869–1955), a Tasmanian-born Shakespearian actor, recitalist, and tea-taster who was humiliated by the loss of his voice during plays. He had suffered from asthma and other respiratory diseases during childhood, but his health had generally improved except for a debilitating hoarseness that increased only during performances. Standard medicine offered either "Stop talking and your voice will come back" or gargling with ineffective throat sprays, so, in desperation, Alexander took up his own line of research.[13]

Because his throat was "normal" early in performances and also during general conversation, he presumed that something he began to do only *while* speaking somehow caused the malady. Observing himself in the mirror while he recited *The Merchant of Venice*, Alexander noticed (only after many tries) that before he ever uttered a word, his intention to speak initiated an exquisitely complex series of events. First, he slightly pulled back his head. The slumping of his head compressed his larynx. Then he began to suck his breath through his mouth in a gasping way. The stress pattern had two ingredients: "(1) a postural one which involved the needless tightening of networks of muscles, and (2) a thought component of repetitive ideas about performing in front of an audience, which identified the network of stress as 'right.'"[14]

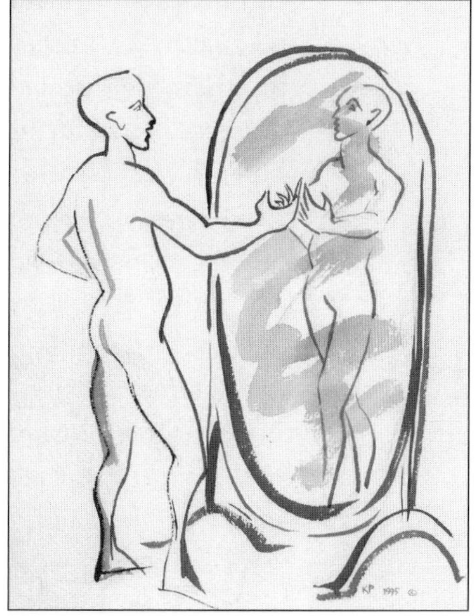

Although Alexander could not prevent the compression of his larynx or gasping breath by any direct action, he found that letting his head move not just forward but also upward from his body allowed the larynx to release. When he finally succeeded in inducing his head to move in this manner from his body, the vocal aspect of the malady was dramatically ameliorated.[15] By freeing his neck and releasing his head forward and up, he was able to get his back to lengthen and widen. Subsequently he dubbed the head-neck-back relationship the "Primary Control," because it served as the fulcrum for the entire organization of bodily movement.[16] The head-neck-back relationship is not necessarily more important because of any undue emphasis on the cranial and spinal regions but because released patterns in that nexus invariably transfuse outward (and inward) to the rest of the body.

For the next six years Alexander went on to examine total posture: the dynamic interactions among the head, neck, and torso, and the relationship of these to the way the limbs were deployed, the pelvis held, and the feet kept in contact with the ground. Working with his brother Albert Redden Alexander, he developed a network of lessons and instructions which became the basis of the Technique. Together the Alexander brothers spent six years in Sydney and Melbourne teaching their method to others. They were so successful that Matthias decided to transplant his practice to the arena of Europe; he left for London in 1904 and set up an office upon his arrival. During World War I he moved to the United States and taught the Alexander Technique successfully there. Subsequently he alternated between continents until establishing a school for children in London in 1925. His practice and training remained in England for the next thirty years.[17]

The Alexander system was communicated in four books published sequentially approximately a decade apart beginning with *Man's Supreme Inheritance* in 1910, followed by *The Use of the Self, Constructive Conscious Control,* and *The Universal Constant in Living.*

Alexander's method implemented the belief that a body moving in balance with minimal effort established natural breathing habits and fluid circulation and relieved pressure on its vertebrae. He claimed not that any particular postures were responsible for people's organizational difficulties, but that all repeated postures reinforced rigidifying patterns.

> Shaped by years of faulty even abusive teachings about what [Alexander] calls "the use of the self," the adult is not in a situation where he or she can trust judgments and decisions based on unclarified feelings. Everyday sensations of how to sit without back pain, how to keep one's eyes on a golf ball, how to form words without stuttering, even how to make love, are distorted by learned usage within a skewed social world.[18]

Children, for instance, suffer long hours of sitting in chairs in school, which indoctrinate inflexible attitudes. The very attempt to conform to etiquette and sit still leads to muscle tension and a host of emotional compensations. Among adults, lack of exercise, goal orientation (Alexander's "end-gaining"), shallow breathing, apprehension of social embarrassment, and mentally leaving the present to dwell on past or future all contribute to put muscles under stress. Undetected, these patterns of behavior and response accumulate tensions which gradually result in immobility and sickness. "You translate everything," Alexander said, "whether physical or mental or spiritual, into muscle tension."[19]

The Alexander Technique educates people how to break with habitual patterns of posture and self-organization. Starting with the "Primary Control"— establishing the freedom of the neck and head—one uses this rudder to guide coordination down through the skeleton. Although underlying patterns often seem complex and permanently immobilized, Alexander believed that one could literally begin coordinating instead of unconsciously discoordinating oneself. He emphasized not merely the learning of techniques but their kinesthetic integration in new patterns of movement—the "means-whereby" leading to the end—rather than trying to skip the means and aim directly for the end ("end-gaining"). He felt that one had to stop habitual patterns from developing by constantly halting the preparation for an activity (his "inhibition").

The "end sought" (which is an unexamined priority in Western civilization) is not indispensable (or even desirable) if it mainly reinforces a strained and dysfunctional set of habits. Such an ostensible goal must be inhibited—in essence, sacrificed—for a freer, more efficient use of the body/mind. Getting results is gradually replaced by efficient means, relaxed coordination, and unencumbered movements regardless of ends sought. Then any desired goals—like speaking on stage or riding a bike—become more feasible.

To be about to do something is not the same as actually doing it. The Alexander Technique rests on this simple discrimination. Through gentle hands-on work and instruction in subtle movements the Alexander practitioner teaches a client how to halt an instinctive action at the moment of preparing to act prior to actually acting.

An Alexander Teacher will gently alter the pupil's position in order to release tension

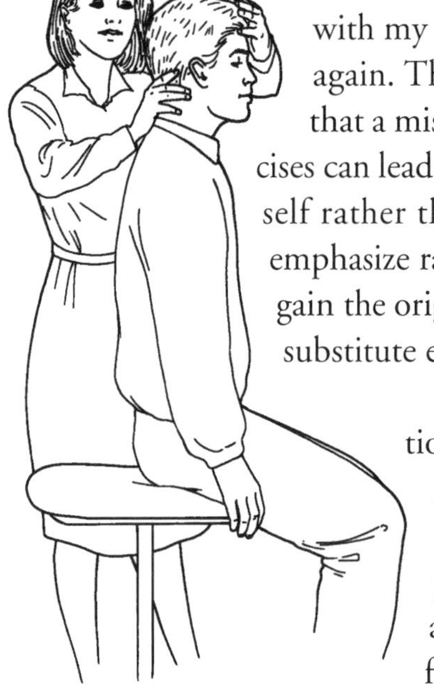

Reprinted from *The Alexander Technique Workbook* by Richard Brennan, Element Books, 1992.

Yet the compulsion toward normal proficiency and use is very strong. Alexander himself experienced automatic and devious resumptions of old speech habits even after, through great persistence, he had changed his fundamental coordinations and pathways. At critical moments his regimen would betray him, and he would revert to dysfunctions tied to accustomed routines (in his words, "misdirections associated with my old wrong habitual use"); he lost control of his voice again. There is also the possibility, given the power of habit, that a misapplication of any one of these "dehabituating" exercises can lead to *increased* miscoordination and deepened misuse of self rather than improvement. That is why Alexander came to emphasize radically new habits, along with an absolute refusal to gain the original end, in place of any mindless repetition of mere substitute exercises.

Alexander took it for granted that a client's conception of a movement was invariably misguided, resulting in unnecessary tension and interference with healthy functioning. He developed a variety of ways for people to "inhibit" their unnecessary preparation for an activity (even as he had learned how to inhibit himself from becoming hoarse). After inhibiting or stopping, they were naturally able to make better use of the primary control in their activities.

In a certain sense the basis of Alexander Technique is learning to trick oneself out of repeating a habitual pattern. First, one inhibits the programming of the primary control (plus any trackable secondary and tertiary controls); then one projects new intentions in direct response to familiar stimuli. It is a matter of rehearsing a new habit while snuffing out an old one. For instance, while intending to speak, a person goes through the process of being about to speak, then remains silent and instead raises a hand. The act of suddenly refusing to gain a sought-after end provides the opportunity for derailing a poor use of self. Inhibiting a desire to move in a familiar way creates the space for a new way of being, an existentially different experience of one's own identity.

An Alexander session begins with the teacher's observation of the student's pattern of sitting down and rising from a chair. Sitting is reconceived not simply as an act of getting oneself into a chair. The student gains an ability to become conscious of movement patterns that previously have been wholly habitual. The act of sitting becomes a means for exploring not just free movement but mental preconceptions as well. Next the teacher begins to guide the student with his hands, focusing on various parts of the body, though always returning to the primary relationship: head-neck-back. As with other kindred systems, the emphasis is on receptivity—the therapist's touch must not push or bully a person into new patterns. It must communicate a rational and experiential mode of being which the patient can gradually make his own.

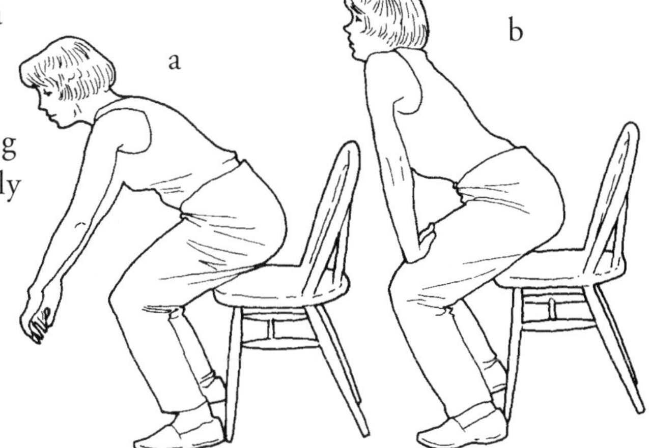

Even when standing up we can put enormous strain upon our entire structure. Beware of swinging up (fig. a) or pushing (fig. b).

Reprinted from *The Alexander Technique Workbook* by Richard Brennan, Element Books, 1992.

An Alexander Teacher helps the pupil to move in new ways, putting less strain on the body. The teacher encourages the pupil to go "up" when sitting, and to keep length when bending.

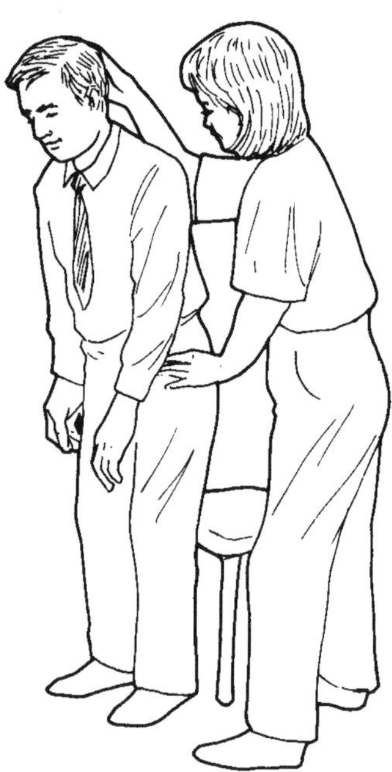

Reprinted from *The Alexander Technique Workbook* by Richard Brennan, Element Books, 1992.

An Alexander session may consist of any of the following general modalities: the maintenance of the vertical orientation of the head and body while in a sitting posture, how to lengthen the arms by extending them parallel to the ground outward from the chest and then raising them above the head and lowering them onto the thighs, the floating upward of the head away from the body while walking, the synchronization of an uncompensated raising of a leg to the point where its thigh is parallel to the ground simultaneous with the floating of the head, the lifting of the toes with the heels on the floor, the raising of the heels with the toes on the floor, the bending of the knees with the hips and ankles held straight and the body perpendicular to the ground, and the efficient transfer of weight to the feet when rising. All of these processes are carried out in combinatorial series with an attention to widening the back while lengthening the limbs, torso, and distal parts

of the body, all the time relaxing and releasing tension.[20] However, Alexander practitioner Jerry Sontag objects to the above repertoire on the basis that it "implies a postural focus, or a series of exercises, neither of which are relevant to the Technique."[21] While I would agree that a static list trivializes the system, it does give a simple Alexander vocabulary.

More dynamically, the Technique emphasizes breath control, the origination of muscular movement in thought preceding the intention to move, the recognition that habits define as "right" actions that may be damaging, the understanding that patterns are not always instinctual and reflexive but learned, and the explicit inhibition of habitual movement. During lessons, the student is taught to "direct." The mental directions are a means for exercising conscious control over the use of the head-neck-back relationship.

Alexander demonstrated that one could change muscular patterns, as well as mental patterns, by first stopping the old habits, and then "projecting messages from the brain to the body's mechanisms and conducting the energy necessary for the use of these mechanisms." He taught that one could "think" new shapes into the torso by imaging them and directing them through attention. "You come to learn to inhibit and direct your activity. You learn, first, to inhibit the habitual response to certain classes of stimuli, and second, to direct yourself consciously in such a way as to affect certain muscular pulls, which processes bring about a new reaction to these stimuli."[22]

Inhibition is the key to the Alexander Technique. Other educational somatic systems (Feldenkrais Method, for instance) are more involved with teaching new and different patterns to replace nonfunctional or self-destructive ones. Alexander decided merely to unpeel the onion. His Technique is about "not doing." If one avoids initiating the discoordinating gesture, then the body will naturally regain its prior harmonic functioning. So if one can learn *not* to tighten the neck, that inhibition alone will free the head and spine and ultimately the organs.

Getting into and coming out of the semi-supine position

Figure a. Find a suitable area to lie down. Take the correct amount of books in your hand.

Figure b. Maintaining a vertical torso put one leg forward and go down on one knee.

Figure c. Place the books to your right or left, roughly where your head will be when you are lying down.

Figure d. Place your hands on the ground so that you are on all fours.

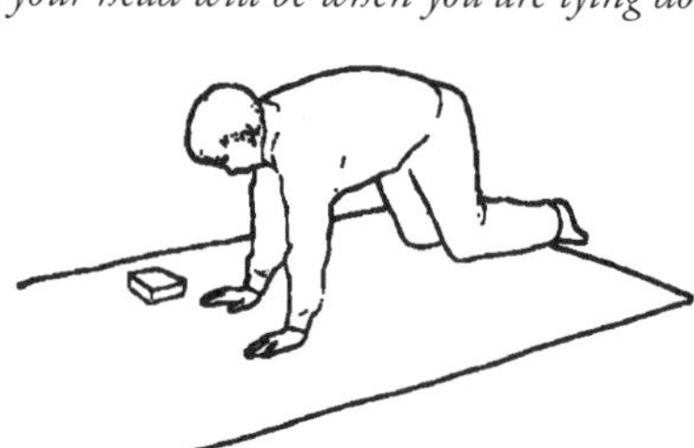

Figure e. Lift yourself up so that you are balanced on your hands and toes.

Figure f. Lower your legs to the ground with your knees pointing to the opposite direction to the books.

Figure g. Gently roll over onto your back, adjusting the position of the books so that they are comfortably under the back of your head.

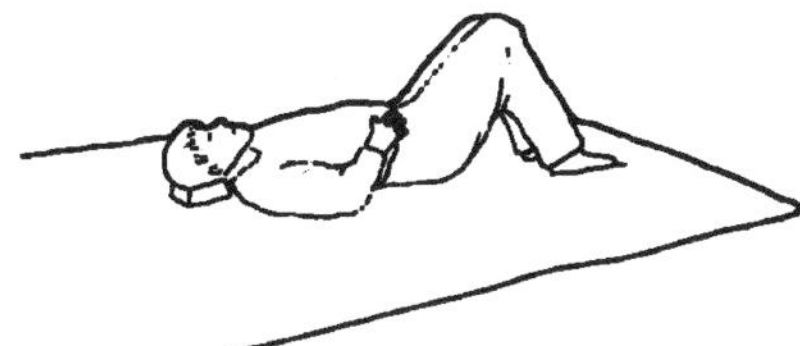

Figure h. Bring your knees upwards positioning your feet so that they are as near as possible to your torso while still remaining comfortable.

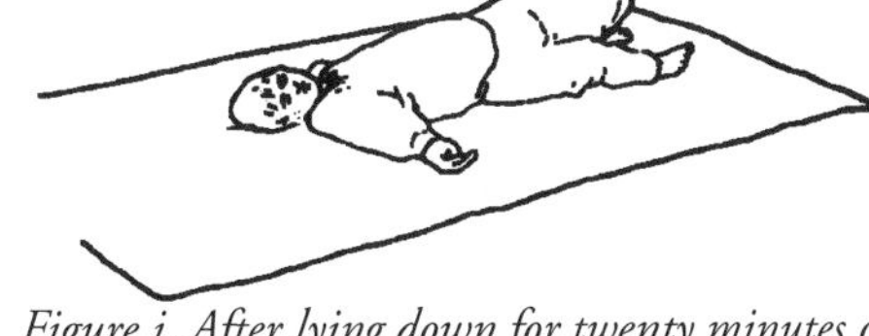

Figure i. After lying down for twenty minutes or so, take a few moments to think about how you can get up while still maintaining the length in your spine.

Figure j. Decide which way you wish to get up. Look in that direction and then let your knees roll in that direction. Let your whole body roll off the books.

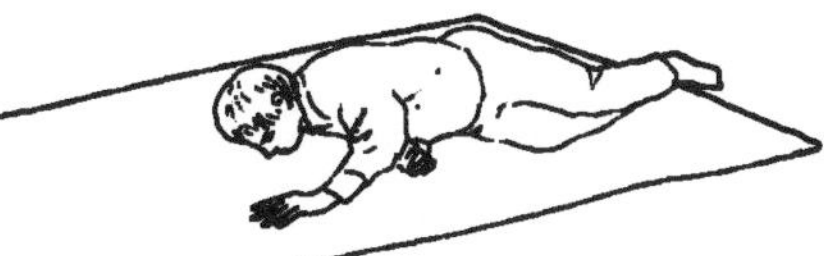

Figure k. Roll over onto your front with the support of a hand and a leg.

Figure l. Raise yourself until you are on all fours once again.

Figure m. Pick up the books and then place one leg in front of the other.

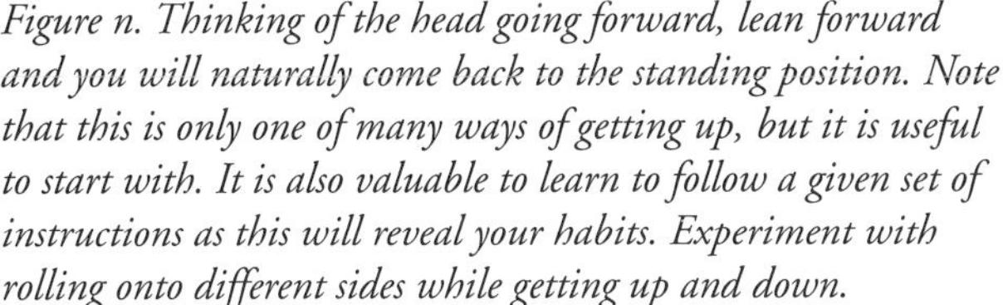

Figure n. Thinking of the head going forward, lean forward and you will naturally come back to the standing position. Note that this is only one of many ways of getting up, but it is useful to start with. It is also valuable to learn to follow a given set of instructions as this will reveal your habits. Experiment with rolling onto different sides while getting up and down.

Reprinted from *The Alexander Technique Workbook* by Richard Brennan, Element Books, 1992.

Reprinted from *The Alexander Technique Workbook* by Richard Brennan, Element Books, 1992.

Alexander lessons can be applied to practically any activity.

An Alexander practitioner often communicates this by asking his client *not* to do an act. When he says, "I want you not to sit down," he actually means, "I want you to sit down without any of the stressful prerequisites you bring to the act of sitting." But this new version of sitting is not recognized by the nervous system as sitting, so the therapist has to say instead, "I want you not to sit down" in order to communicate the action he is requesting. The first few times he may guide his client into the chair, holding his head and neck in such a way that they float free while the spine and pelvis are sinking. Next he may take the client slightly off his balance while in the chair. In fact, he may do this a number of times, pushing him gently backwards while supporting him. The client must find his balance again each time. The goal, over several sessions, is to build a new inner sense of what sitting, standing, and being in balance are, so that habitual versions of these acts don't always reimpose themselves. Standing, sitting, and balance are chosen not because of any inherent significance but because they are easily demonstrated and performed in a practitioner's office and because they are customarily repeated with tension many times daily in Western civilization.

Regardless of the exercise or lesson, the Alexander training process always begins with inhibition. Not doing an act leaves space for a new and simpler act. Not doing an act also allows a person to locate the component of the act which is dysfunctional, neurotic, or stressful. Sontag describes recommending to a phone stutterer not to answer the phone. That meant he was to let it ring three or four times, trusting that the party would not hang up, and then, even when he lifted the receiver, he was not to answer the phone—that is, not to repeat kinesthetically the act his system recognized as "answering the phone."

In summary, the Alexander Technique comprises the following principles and goals:

- "Without awareness, we cannot change."[23]
- "In performing an action, the minute you 'think,' the muscles begin to move."[24]
- Our kinesthetic sense, our ability to tell how we are functioning, is faulty, which causes myriad psychophysical problems.
- The faulty sense occurs because the relationships of the head, neck, and back are not working properly. This limits choice in both movement and thought. "Think about the neck moving in space. Then 'allow' it to move back.... Let the torso lengthen and widen."[25]
- To change our kinesthetic sense to become more reliable, we must consciously stop the old patterns of tension—Alexander's inhibition.
- When these old patterns are stopped, new mental directions can be sent from the brain to encourage movement patterns that are freer and more consciously chosen.
- The benefits of the Technique are an improved kinesthetic sense, a better overall functioning, including breathing and movement, a better ability to maintain one's own health, and an increased consciousness of one's relationship to the immediate environment.

On the surface, Alexander Technique might seem an enlarged version of a subset of Feldenkrais exercises. But that is because Feldenkrais is more widely practiced today. Alexander was historically prior and actually provided a part of the template from which Feldenkrais built his method (see below). Inhibition is certainly one of the keys to many Feldenkrais lessons. When I mentioned my superficial impression that Alexander was subsidiary to Feldenkrais, a bodyworker familiar with a range of systems objected that they were each entirely self-sufficient, holistic systems with quite unique orientations. She thought of Feldenkrais as being more earthy, involved with the basic animal, neuromotor processes, bringing people into the thick core of their bodies, while Alexander was light and puffy, expanding people's movement outward and giving them a celestial kind of airiness. The singlemost Alexander gesture is floating out while expanding across. Feldenkrais never denied the value of Alexander's lessons, and he was well aware of the importance of inhibition (which played a role in his development of his own method), but he created a much vaster system with a complex array of techniques and applications. Alexander felt that his own basic repertoire of inhibitions and recoordinations was sufficient.

Alexander and Feldenkrais not only met but Feldenkrais received a number of early lessons from Alexander that influenced his own development. When Feldenkrais showed Alexander a draft of the book he was writing, Alexander decided to end the tutorial. According to Israeli therapist Mia Segal, "… while living in England and writing *Body and Mature Behavior*, Moshe met Alexander. Moshe used to say that Alexander had the best hands he had ever felt. If I remember correctly, Moshe showed him *Body and Mature Behavior*, and Alexander said, 'Actually you copied it from my book!' This, I suppose, ended the relationship."[26]

Alexander practitioner Walter Carrington, who also worked on Feldenkrais, remarked years later, as diplomatically as he could, that Alexander's main objection to Feldenkrais was not so much that Feldenkrais used Alexander as a source for *Body and Mature Behavior*, but that he published his book without written citations or acknowledgments to Alexander, Reich, or others he drew on, giving the impression that he developed his system whole cloth from his own mind. However, during his workshops Feldenkrais was quite forthcoming concerning the many influences on him and, as is obvious in Segal's quote, generous in his praise of Alexander. He considered Alexander a genius for originating and developing the concept of the "use of self." Perhaps the paucity of written citation comes from the fact that right from the beginning Feldenkrais intended such a different application of the "use of self" that to fuse his work to Alexander's would have created false expectations and confusion.

In retrospect now, it is clear that Feldenkrais' medicine is vast and complete in a whole other way, so it makes more sense to think of it substantially independent of Alexander's influence. Yet Alexander continued to feel, justifiably or not, that Feldenkrais stole his technique out of *his* own teaching.[27]

Alexander Technique has been historically popular with artists, musicians, dancers, architects, psychotherapists and intellectuals. The founder taught his method directly to John Dewey, George Bernard Shaw, Sir Charles Sherrington, and Aldous Huxley, the latter of whom extolled the technique in his novels *Eyeless in Gaza* and *Ends and Means.* Dewey lauded Alexander by saying that his Technique "bears the same relationship to education that education itself bears to all other human activities."[28] It was also acclaimed by Nikolaas Tinbergen in his acceptance speech in 1973 for the Nobel Prize in Medicine. Tinbergen wrote that "every session clearly demonstrates that the innumerable muscles of the body are continuously operating as an intricately linked web."[29]

In his famous poem "Maximus, to Gloucester" the American poet Charles Olson reinvents his experience of being taught Alexander Technique as a young actor in Worcester, Massachusetts. Spinning a transformational metaphor from his Alexander lessons to a Mediaeval vision of man back through the exercises to the sensation after orgasm to the

origin of the human shape in an Ice Age anthropoid, he infuses a contemporary landscape in its prehistoric origin while never losing its immediacy in the inflation and decorousness of myth. Although not the best description of the Technique, "Maximus, to Gloucester" does cast Alexander—and somatics in general—in an epic context:

"to tend to move
as though drawn,"

Or might it read
'compare
the ripe sun-flower'?

The old charts
are not so wrong
which added Adam
to the world's directions

which showed any of us
the center of a circle
our fingers
and our toes describe

(one taught us
how to stand in crowds
there we were, three actors,
in a loft above Tarr's Railway
in shorts, in front of her,
doing,
her bidding: "Buttocks
in & under, buttocks"

seeking,
like Euclid,
the ape's line, the stance
fit for crowds, to watch
parades, never
to tire

It was in our minds
what she put there,
to get the posture
to pass from the neck of,
to get it down,
to get the knees bent

not as he was shown, arms out, legs out, leaping

another Adam, a nether
man

It does stem. And the joker
that the sense is
of a sash-weight,
after the head is clear,
after the burst

a sash-weight does hang
from between the legs

if you are drawn

if you do unite

If you do be

pithecanthropus[30]

Bates Method[31]

Eyeglasses have become such a staple of modern civilization that we barely notice the ubiquity of these odd facial props. Goggles to enhance seeing are considered as commonplace as clothes to keep warm. We take it as axiomatic that visual clarity (and lack of clarity) are hereditary and fixed and that artificial lenses are the only recourse for blurs and other nonpathological deficiencies of sight. The entire optometric profession exists to counteract poor eyesight by fitting mechanical aids onto the face. In the late twentieth century this partial prosthesis has

been made so unobtrusive and socially acceptable it is no longer a major encumbrance or a stigma. In some circumstances, eyeglasses are even a source of pride and an opportunity to style attitudes and personalities. Many healers and holistic practitioners wear glasses without considering that poor vision might be a significant aspect of their general mind/body state. They presume that the capacity of the eyes to focus is somehow separate from well-being as a whole. Thus, clarity of vision has become the most conservative bastion of allopathy, the last to yield to somatic holism.

Yet what if visual clarity and blurs are no more hereditary or immutable than the habits of tension and stress explored by Alexander? What if relearning the natural patterns of movement underlying sight could dramatically improve just about everyone's ability to see clearly?

This hardly seems likely given the universal acceptance of optometry and the large number of educated and medically trained men and women who themselves wear glasses or contact lenses. Surely they are not all victims of delusion or fraud. After all, how could somatic education alter something as fundamental as the focal length of an inborn lens or the shape of an eyeball?

THE GENERALLY ACCEPTED theory of sight holds that clarity of vision is regulated by the lenses of the eyes and the ciliary muscles around those lenses. In response to the changing distances of landscapes and objects, these muscles recoordinate the shape of the lenses in a manner loosely akin to that of the focusing knob of a camera. A healthy eye, one capable mechanically of being broadly refocused (its muscles adjusting properly), renders sharp images across a range of distances.

By this theory the basic errors of visual accommodation (i.e., responding to objects near and far) are the results of either unfortunate eyeball lengths or a deterioration of the lens from an injury or aging. Distortions attributed to inherited structure and function include nearsightedness, farsightedness, astigmatism, amblyopia ("lazy eye"), and crosseyedness. Presbyopia, the increasing difficulty people have around the age of forty in focusing objects near at hand, is considered an effect of the gradual hardening of the lens such that it loses its pliability to accommodate for near vision and can focus only in the distance.

Alternate scientific theories base poor vision in part on flaws in the cornea, the retina, and the vitreous chamber, almost all of which are likewise inherited.

BORN IN 1860, William H. Bates became a prominent New York opthalmologist and eye surgeon. In the course of examining more than 30,000 patients while adhering to familiar theories of eyesight, Bates began to suspect that the famous "lens model" was not supported by experience. He noticed that sight fluctuated markedly from day to day and even hour to hour. People with poor accommodation sometimes improved for short periods of time. How could this happen if the proposed explanation for poor eyesight were accurate?

In truth, the existing orthodoxy made neither physical nor logical sense, nor was it experimentally testable or consistent. For instance, why should presbyopia, as a general hardening of the eyeball, cause only farsightedness? What about people in their eighties who have rigid lenses but still see up close perfectly? How does one explain the plight of those who become farsighted before the age of forty, likewise those who suffer nearsightedness (but not farsightedness) after the age of forty? Why, when there is no physical connection between the two eyes, do most people suffer the same distortion in both eyes at the same time? Why, if one plays a game of constructing a pinhole with a fist and stares through it at a previously blurry object, does the object come into sharp focus? Why should a movie on the screen be blurry and sharp at different cinematic distances when these actually are all at the same distance from the viewer? These events, considered collectively, indicate that deficiencies of eyesight may originate not in the eyes themselves but in subtle and profound links among the eyes, the rest of the body, and the mind.

Challenging what he called "theories, often stated as facts,"[32] Bates set out to discover the actual causes of clear vision. From the turn of the century he performed an elaborate course of experimentation, eventually summarizing his findings in 1920 in the landmark book *Perfect Sight Without Glasses.* The opthalmological profession was outraged, and he was dismissed from his position at the New York Postgraduate Medical School. Predicting that an "incalculable amount of human misery"[33] would result from the rejection of his theories and the continuation of opthalmological delusion, he spent the rest of his life continuing to study eyesight and teaching his method.

Even today, eyeglasses set at one focal length (or bi- and multi-focal lenses) remain virtual requirements for correcting poor eyesight and are universally recommended, while Bates' techniques are considered fallacies or quackery. Yet through these "fallacies" many people who were once legally blind have improved their vision to the level where they are no longer required to wear corrective lenses to drive a motor vehicle. Bates teacher Tom Quackenbush's myopia and astigmatism, which resulted in a 20/100 diagnosis at age ten and deteriorated to 20/500 by the time he was thirty, improved by 90 percent after he began practicing the Bates Method.

In place of traditional explanations for the errors of visual accommodation, Bates established to his satisfaction that blurs and similar distortions were caused almost solely by strain and tension in the extrinsic muscles of the eye (as opposed, for instance, to inherited eyeball shape or the pliancy of the lens or intrinsic ciliary muscles). In proper visioning, the six muscles around each eyeball automatically change its shape to effect clarity. These cords literally squeeze the delicate, watery organs to appropriate focal lengths. Their compression is not particularly deep. A deformation of millimeters has a dramatic effect on the clarity of images passing through the soft eye. (Bates' mechanism of focus can be approximated by squeezing and stretching a rubber model of an eye between one's fingers.)

In the case of near vision, the two oblique muscles above and below the eye wrap around it from left to right and cause it to go long (they squeeze the eye long so that the cornea has a higher curvature and the image falls further back in its chamber and is larger). For far vision, the four recti muscles originating way in back of the eyeball near the brain extend forward and wrap, respectively, around the top, bottom, left, and right of the eyeball. In these positions they can pull the front of the eyeball back against the fatty tissue filling the hollow bony orbit cushioning the eye, causing it to go short. The curvature of the cornea is reduced, and a smaller image lands closer to the front of the eye. For middle vision all six extrinsic muscles combine to round the eye into a sphere. The image lands midway and is of medium size.

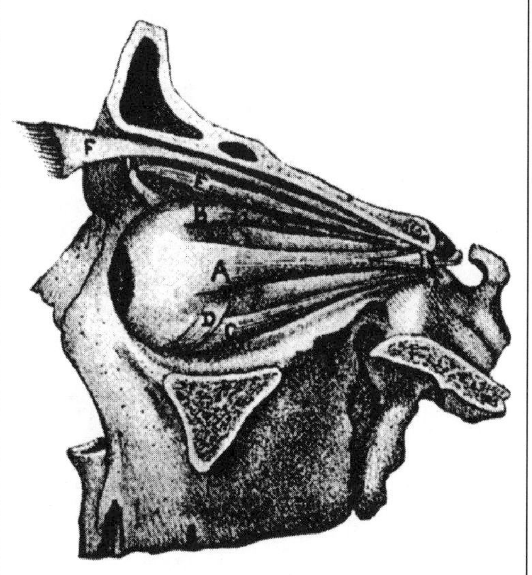

Extrinsic Muscles of the Eye

A. External rectus muscle B. Superior rectus muscle
C. Inferior rectus muscle D. Inferior oblique muscle
E. Superior oblique muscle F. Levator of upper lid

If the two oblique muscles remain chronically contracted, the recti muscles cannot squeeze the eye short to focus far objects more clearly. The result is nearsightedness (myopia). Excellent near sight is permanently fixed. Likewise, if the recti muscles are chronically contracted, the two oblique muscles cannot stretch the eye to see near objects more clearly. This leads to farsightedness (hyperopia). The eye becomes a rigid telescope.

This proposed mechanism of accommodation was not just another abstract opthalmological theory. Bates observed the actual changing shape of the eyeball in response to proximate movements of nerves and muscles in the spinal column. He determined that the extrinsic muscles altering the shape of the eyeball were the sole direct cause of successful or unsuccessful accommodation. Blurs of nearsightedness, farsightedness, and astigmatism, and other symptoms of poor vision

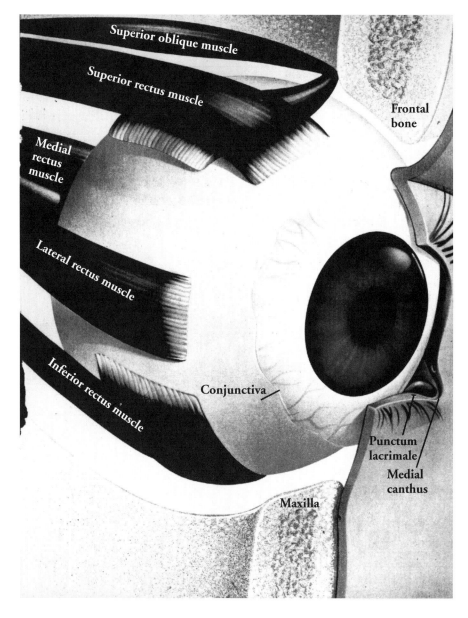

were caused by these muscles gripping too tightly in one way or another. Crosseyedness was caused by their being twisted out of position. Thus, natal eyeball shape and lens pliancy are secondary to the movements of extrinsic muscles in determining clarity of vision.

His own discoveries convinced Bates that, since eye habits were not fixed at birth, they were quite mutable. If the muscles could become chronically tense, they also could be relaxed. Once relaxed, they would adjust the eye properly and naturally clear vision should result.

We must not mistake either the simplicity or the radical nature of Bates' proposition. He argued uniquely that improving vision had nothing to do with opthalmological or optometric attention to the eyes themselves. On the contrary, it had everything to do with the extrinsic muscles around the eyeball and the contingent neuromusculature of the neck. Since all of the dynamics connecting these tissues were at least partially disorganized by stress and other psychosomaticized habits, Bates looked solely to non-opthalmological techniques for improvement of vision. He did not want to do anything to the eye, either by surgery or optometry. He sought only to get the extrinsic muscles working again autonomically.

To restore natural movement to the neck and muscles is much more efficient for the larger somatic equation than to stabilize poor vision at selected focal lengths of corrective lenses. Additionally, tension in the extrinsic muscles is often made worse by the wearer's unconscious attempts to see through eyeglasses at distances different from those for which they were prescribed. Thus, eyeglasses and contact lenses can become a self-fulfilling prophecy, making vision worse by freezing dysfunctional patterns (and thus requiring ever new, stronger prescriptions). Chronically tense muscles also squeeze the retina and ultimately damage the eyeballs.

Bates improved accommodation by teaching new neuromuscular habits through educational paradigms not unlike those of Matthias Alexander and Moshe Feldenkrais. All of Bates' techniques in one or another way introduce movement into the eye-neck relationship and challenge kinesthetic stagnation. His central practice is called "shifting," which is little more than the collective motions of natural relaxed vision. Shifting means keeping the eyes moving and centralizing, focusing one

point at a time. The eyes graze freely about a landscape. They "see" as they focus single objects sequentially. They do not stare, and they do not diffuse. They do not glaze over into seeing "nothing," and they do not try to see too much at once. In fact, Bates argued, too many people try to see more than one point at a time with the result that everything is out of focus. That is because in fact only the cones, located in an extremely small pit (the fovea centralis) at the back center of the retina, focus sharply. The more abundant rods, distributed in membranous layers throughout the retinal periphery, enhance night vision and detect movement. They do not register sharpness of detail. Chickens, with only cones, pick grains from dust in the daytime but are sightless after dusk. Owls and bats, with only photosensitive rods, rouse at dusk but otherwise shun bright light and cannot see detail without a blur.

Its indented morphology exposing cones to photons of light, the fovea centralis occupies less than one percent of the total area of the eyeball. The exposed cones are not only limited (for all practical purposes) to this tiny pit, but they are even more concentrated in its minute center. Thus, sharp vision comes solely from moving the fovea centralis to each object of interest. Super-sharp vision comes from moving the center of the fovea centralis. Objects may be as distant from one another as a ship on the horizon and a watch on one's own hand, or as close to one another as indentations on a grain of rice in which a Tibetan monk is carving a Buddha or contours on the inside of a chestnut shell in which a Greek scribe is transcribing the *Iliad.* The human eye is capable of remarkable feats of clarity and microscopy, but only if the cones properly move, centralize, and track.

In summary of the above, the human retina comprises photosensitive, achromatic night receptors (the rods) and a highly sensitive plate with focal color capacity (the cones). Trying to see too much means attempting to focus with rods, which are incapable of accommodation, hence a blur. Centralizing means always bringing the cones of the eye to the object ones wishes to see. People with excellent vision merely

centralize and shift rapidly, seeing things in sequence. They do not have a larger visual field even though it might seem to them as if they do.

Inhibition of both staring and diffusing is central to the Bates Method. Inhibition means putting an end to attempting to focus with the periphery. Shifting and centralizing are simply *not* staring and diffusing. They are "seeing." Bates insisted that staring always strains the muscles and reduces vision. It is the end result of a series of dysfunctional attitudes. People stare and diffuse because they want to escape. They want not to be present in uncomfortable situations. Diffusing is the consequence of attempting to hold too large a visual field in focus. It literally "spaces" a person out of seeing. It is also a form of escaping and "not seeing." Blurry vision is automatic when one tries to see lots of different things at once or strains to focus one's peripheral vision. This fact seems obvious, but the present epidemic of poor vision proves it is not.

The principles of the Bates Method can be learned in less than an hour, but it takes many classes and much practice and reinforcement for most people to unroot their subtle habits of staring. This is because stares come in many forms, both blatant and subtle. For a person truly to achieve clarity means to eliminate (or reenergize) all stares—first, obvious fixed stares, then minute "micro-stares" camouflaged in habit, attitude, and shallow breathing, and finally stares of the mind itself which can occur with virtually no neuromuscular affect.

Eyes are pure brain tissue honed into landscape-replication by the effects of sunlight. It should be no surprise that they express character, attitude, and interest. Symptoms of stress, anxiety, and depression often manifest directly through the neuromusculature of vision.

Acts of staring are fixity, compulsion, rigidity. They are mini-phobias. To stare is to attempt to hold reality in place, to be unmoved and invulnerable, to be locked in anxiety or fright. To stare is to be drawn magnetically and obsessively toward single things away from one's own center and mobility. The stares that lead to poor vision habits are ubiquitous symptoms of modern life. They represent alienation, fear, boredom, and dependence on electronic representations of images. They

are the opposite of relaxed vision in open sunlight (practiced by all tribal societies). Glasses are their validation and prop.

When a person loses interest in the environment, she begins to stare rather than sketch. The natural quick movements of alert, clear vision are replaced by degrees of resistance to events, people, and tension. The environment literally is not exciting or safe enough to encourage active vision. (Phobias and anxiety patterns are equivalent "stares.")

Transitions from centralizing to diffusing are so gradual and subliminal that one is not even aware of the process. It seems as though the eyes themselves are losing acuity.

Staring and diffusing are ultimately universal states of being (as are moving and centralizing). Vision is merely their most apparent metaphor. When a person tries to ease tension by first doing an internal inventory of her body and then relaxing any "held" muscles one by one, she is, in a sense, releasing her neuromuscular "stares." Such a process of alternately tracking and letting go can be remarkably effective in moving someone from stress and anxiety to a sense of calm and personal freedom. No bodyworker is necessary; the mind carries out the necessary acts.

Effect of superior oblique muscles on eye movement

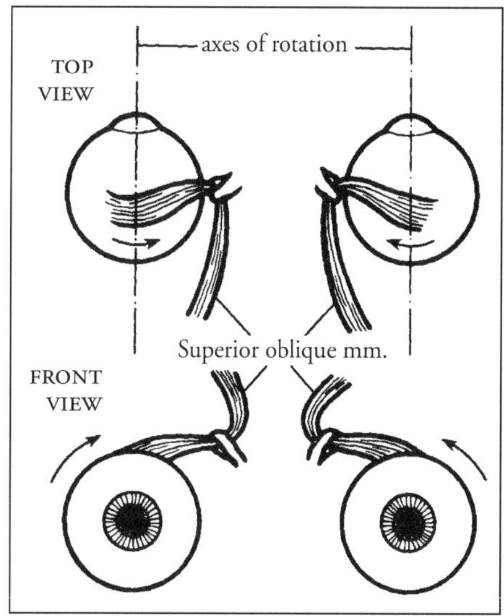

Reprinted from *Craniosacral Therapy II: Beyond the Dura* by John E. Upledger with permission of the publisher, Eastland Press, Inc., P.O. Box 12689, Seattle, WA 98111.

The first hurdle is in overcoming one's own internal numbings that lead to glossing over tight shoulders, belly, jaw, etc. The second hurdle is in feeling ever more minute degrees of tension in underlying tissues. These tiny "holds" are keys to unlocking major rigidities of mind/body. Merely finding them is an act of liberation. Perceptible breath rushes to their release.

The most imposing hurdle, however, is the fixation of mind itself. Often a well trained person is able gradually to relax every palpable point of tension, both gross and subtle, and yet still experiences a knot of underlying tension without a seeming neuromuscular locus. This

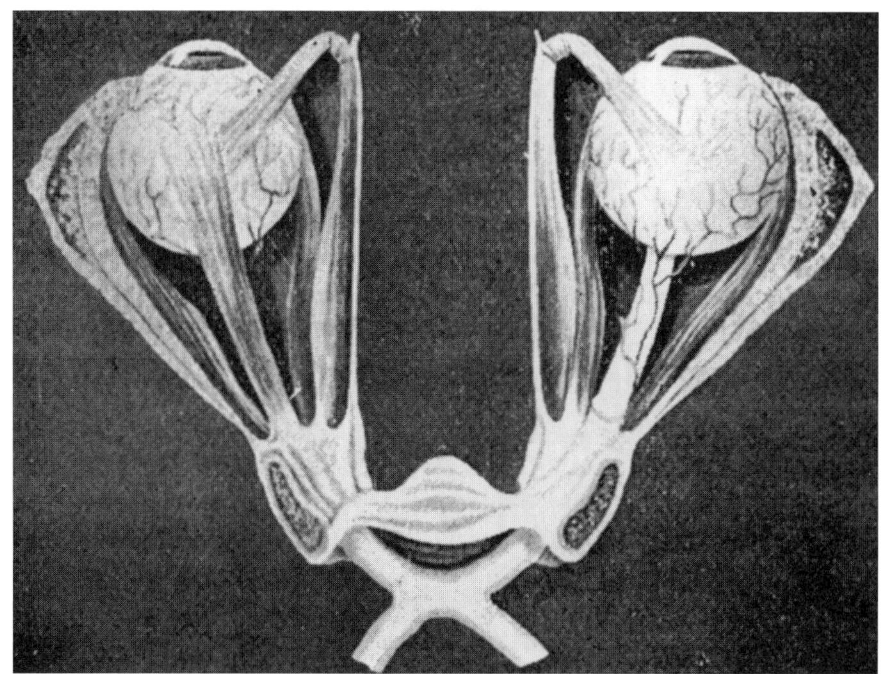

The relative positions of the eyeballs, muscles, and nerves

tension clearly has a profound hold on the body and seems to pour out of the center of "mind" like a black, diffusing light. It marks the point where mind and body meet and are indistinguishable.

By the Bates Method a skilled practitioner similarly can release all her micro-stares and sketch freely yet may still experience a fixation of mind patrolling through superficially darting eyes. Blurry vision is the result. Exercises rarely dislodge such a fixation. The most intractable stare may not park the eyes at all but pours out of them anyway—a dead, black gleam. It is pure boredom and alienation. It also marks the threshold at which eyes are portals of the soul.

Bates did not live long enough to confront the global fruition of an optometric scam, but he understood its early implications. People are encouraged to think that their worsening vision is the effect of age, hence that they need glasses. As both vanity and worry over aging influence their attitudes, they strain harder to see, to convince themselves

they are not losing clarity. Straining to see immediately makes their vision deteriorate. After glasses are prescribed and they begin to see more clearly, they are convinced they are on the right path and have a good doctor. However, the glasses themselves lock in poor vision. This scenario has now become a boondoggle of major proportions.

Contemporary Bates practitioners teach a form of shifting called "sketching" or "brushing" in which a student imagines, for instance, that she has a short pencil or feather attached to the end of her nose—not a soft pink plume but a sleek pointed feather. She then sketches or brushes objects with it, touching them imaginarily as she selects them for seeing: her own fingers, a friend's face, a stranger's hat, a fence in the distance, a tree at the horizon, clouds, even the Moon. Brushing *is* seeing. Instead of needlessly straining the eyes to focus better, brushing consciously uses the nose as a compass and the muscles of the neck as a clarifying rod.

Brushing places the fovea centralis right on the object being viewed. The precision of this act can be illustrated by a reverse mechanism. On a dark, preferably moonless night, try brushing single stars. Effective brushing should make each star disappear at the moment the nose-feather touches it. As acutely as the cones register detail in daylight, they are fully blind at night. Thus, if one can accurately impose the viewing field of the cones on a night object without the assistance of the rods, that object should disappear. The fact that each brushed star vanishes demonstrates that the effective area of visual clarity is as fine as the arc of a single star.

For this reason, brushing cannot be an exercise. It must become a subliminal habit. It would be far too difficult to brush intentionally every object one wished to see.

If one is brushing, then they can't be staring. The two together are impossible. Thus brushing is effective first in tricking the mind into not trying so hard to use the eyes to see and second in allowing the mind to exert another, more relaxing fulcrum to achieve clarity. The object attached at the end of the nose indirectly loosens the contraction in the ocular region. It also centralizes.

The Bates Method is a course in relearning neurological patterns. It is an attempt to educate people to regain the natural habits of good vision most of them had at birth (or in the sightless realm of the womb). The fact that the animation of stares and "micro-stares" enhances metabolism, immunity, and emotional states makes the Bates Method more than just vision improvement. It is a form of holistic healing grounded in the mechanism of the eyes, the internalization of vision, and ocular habits. It is based on locating and healing the mental patterns that give rise symptomatically to misuse of the visual apparatus and to a vicious circle in which poor vision habits lead to rigid, phobic thinking, and vice versa.

The Bates Method differs from other somatic learning techniques insofar as it is the invention of an opthalmologist, is based exclusively on the role of vision in systemic health and organization, and thus deals specifically with improving eyesight. It is based on the physiology and function of the extrinsic muscles of the eye, the retina, the fovea centralis, the muscles of the neck, and the mind. Its goal is not so much to teach the body new overall patterns of organization as it is to restore the single act of seeing to a subliminal level. The rest should naturally follow.

Bates practitioners use any method they can to get an individual to relax and make vision unstrained again. Some are tricks, some are visualizations, some are puzzles or games, and some are mnemonic devices for forming new habits (a red tag on the little finger, for instance). But Bates techniques can never be mere isolated mechanical remedies. Since the eyes regulate so many interpersonal functions and aspects of personal identity, the regaining of natural movement in their extrinsic muscles generally means an improvement in overall mental and physical health. Likewise, neurotic patterns must precede poor eyesight. The eyesight becomes weaker when a person doesn't want to relate or see, perhaps

because his job or environment imposes stress, perhaps because there is nothing joyful to see. Relearning to see is relearning sensuality.

Insofar as Bates practitioners acknowledge the holistic aspects of eyesight and its kinesthesis, they respect Alexander and Feldenkrais work. However, they deny that these can have any lasting effect on vision because they do not address the muscle patterns in the eyes pragmatically and thus can deal with vision only secondarily as an aspect of somatic organization. These systems miss the single point of relaxing the six extrinsic ocular muscles, so they improve eyesight only by chance or because they train a general harmony and the eyesight follows.

Today the Bates Method is used in collaboration with many other somatic therapies, often to treat serious injuries affecting eyesight. An osteopath may correct an underlying spinal lesion while a Bates practitioner teaches ocular relaxation. This combination has worked well in instances of near blindness after car accidents and muggings.

Many of Bates' other techniques are obvious to the point of syllogistic, and all of them involve relaxation. The simple process of "palming" was something Bates came upon quite accidentally when, one day, he removed his own glasses and cradled his head in his hands, cupping his eyes. The resulting darkness was so restorative and calming that he kept his eyes covered for about fifteen minutes. Upon removing his hands he noticed a new vibrancy of color throughout the office. Later he formalized "palming" as a soothing placement of one's own cupped palms over the eyes with fingers crossed on the forehead to avoid touching the eyes themselves. In Bates' time the hands were usually rubbed together first to generate heat. Nowadays forming an initial *"chi"* field between separated rounded palms is more popular. The palmer can later summon up internal landscapes and play his eyes over these, focusing alternately on imaginary objects near and far. This is closed-eye "sketching."

Another elegant therapeutic method Bates called "sunning." This involves closing the eyes and rotating the head slowly from side to side

so that the sun lightly massages the outer surface of the eyelids. Sunning rebuilds light tolerance and color intensity and restores some diurnal/nocturnal vision resilience. Natural light passing through the eyes is a nutrient for the whole body (see "Healing by Color" in Chapter Eight).

Bates also recommended self-massage, fuller breathing, and conscious blinking. In fact, he urged blinking softly (like a butterfly's wings) every two or three seconds until it becomes a habit. This naturally lubricates the eyeball and antidotes the scourge of visual accommodation: staring. Bates considered soft blinking (all by itself) to be the best natural remedy for a whole range of eye disorders, including "dry eye syndrome" and blurry vision itself.

Although Bates eschewed pure exercises, some techniques taught by contemporary Bates practitioners are in fact relaxation exercises. "Swinging" is initiated by setting the feet approximately a foot apart and then turning the body to the right while lifting the left heel. The head and eyes remain stationary, and the apparent movement of motionless objects is ignored. As the left heel returns to the floor, the body turns to the left, and the right heel is raised. This sequence of alternately raising right and left heels and turning is carried out for about five minutes in order to recoordinate movement and vision.

Such exercises should not confuse the basic issue. Relearning natural eyesight is training a habit which ultimately must become second nature. As Tom Quackenbush enjoys commenting, "I don't teach exercises. The Bates Method is not about exercises. It's about relaxation. It's about relearning how to see and move naturally. You only have to practice twenty-four hours a day."[34]

What makes relearning vision habits by the Bates Method so formidable (as to require an entire course) is that, ultimately, natural seeing can occur only at a subliminal level. Conscious sketching, breathing, and blinking will never in themselves restore clarity. They are rough approximations of an extremely subtle mechanism that must be activated unconsciously. Thus, a person in the process of learning the Bates Method may find himself at the theater unable to see the characters on stage clearly. Having already improved his vision over seven weeks of classes, he may struggle hopefully to sketch, breathe, and blink, and be disappointed when the figures remain blurred. At such a point it would be better for him to accept his blur and stop straining because the thing that ultimately restores clarity is not sketching, breathing, and blinking as he knows it. It is a deeper and subtler version of these acts. Furthermore, when the so-called exercises of clear vision are carried out in crisis mode in a goal-oriented situation they cannot work. In fact, it is precisely such straining that undermined good vision in the first place.

At its core, the Bates Method teaches relaxation and movement. Any of its "exercises" can be either helpful or harmful depending on whether they are practiced in a context of ease or one of tension.

Seeing happens at the speed of light and thought; thus any actions meant to enhance seeing must sink to such an autonomous level. Only when these acts become natural again does clarity slowly return. The key to the Bates Method is not in learning techniques of focus. It is in retracking the system to the point where natural, primordial coordination takes over. At the end of his life Bates summarized his training in precisely these terms:

> The importance of practicing certain parts of the routine activities at all times, such as blinking, centralizing, and imagining stationary objects to be moving opposite to the movement of the head, is emphasized. The normal vision does these things unconsciously, and the imperfect vision must first practice them consciously until they become unconscious habits.[35]

Eutony

Overview and Ground Systems

As much a forerunner of modern somatics as Alexander Technique, Eutony was developed by Gerda Alexander (no relation to Matthias)

in the context of Eurhythmics and Music Education in Germany during the 1920s and thereafter became a popular and influential system of movement awareness. Starting with a goal of pure relaxation and the means to accomplish it, Alexander gradually went on to explore bodily sensation, personal expression, artistic improvisation, and the somatic basis of dance, music, and theater. Eutony (literally "good tonus") means learning how consciously to alter involuntary bodily patterns, "to be open and receptive to others without diminishing one's individuality."[36] It is social behavior reconceived as bodywork. It is also bodywork fashioned as arts and crafts.

Using slow, complex movements, Alexander built a repertoire of reliable exercises to expand "presence" and release tension. These were based not on conscious breathing or formal imitation but recovering inherent biorhythms. They were lyrical, even operatic, in scope. In other sets of lessons, she had clients 1) model human bodies out of clay with their eyes closed, 2) draw what they felt in their own bodies, and 3) draw human skeletons. Pupils molded and sketched such body images both before and after their Eutony courses. Some initially projected their own harmonious unity; others portrayed cavities, asymmetries, atrophied areas, and gaps.

Over the years most patients came to Alexander for psychosomatic or neurotic ailments (in her words), but she also treated insomnia, circulatory troubles, disc degeneration, lumbago, tics, phantom pains, the after-effects of polio, asthma, and many other conditions. She believed that insofar as Eutony was an open-ended method of dynamic equilibrium finding mind and body in each other, its potential for liberating energy and healing was limitless.

Her somatic principles emphasized "optimal freedom of all joint movements, based on the normal length of muscles at rest . . . , the importance of conscious release of tension . . . , the capacity to use the right amount of energy based on the postural reflex, the bone structure, on tonus adaptation and on optimal circulation and autonomous involuntary breathing, giving maximum strength without strain . . . ,

and the importance of clear directions and elongations in space for the equalization of the tonus level."[37] The client practices letting go and finding in herself her own parameters of relaxation. If she is not initially successful, the Eutonist, instead of interfering, deepens her sense of her own body and presence. This awareness can carry to the client without direct touch. It is a longstanding principle of holism that the healer transmits the cure through intention.

Alexander recognized that most people engage the world from superficial to profound sensation, from epiderm to connective tissues and reflexes, so she focused first on the precise contact of the surface of the body with the environment, catalyzing through the great organ of the skin "the dispersion and harmonization of the tensions of the organism."[38] One method was having clients lie on the floor, feel its resistance, and then roll into different positions bringing heels, calves, thighs, lumbar muscles, etc., into contact with the ground. Tapping the autonomic nervous system by improvisational, latent motions (micro-stretches, seated cross-legged bends, and bone vibrations), she guided clients from enhanced surface sensations to methods of shifting and rebalancing striated and smooth muscles that had become rigidified. Then she directed them to their innermost bodily spaces—the outer sheaths of bones and the substance of tissues and organs. From this interior sensation and skeletal security they could project outward back into the world. She also developed exercises in which clients contacted the ground using bamboo sticks and elastic balls, or even the hands of the therapist. By artifactually enlarging the body's domain, she achieved dramatic releases of tension and coordination of proprioceptive reflexes.

In 1933, as Hitler came into power, Alexander moved her center to Copenhagen. Then, through her travels and those of her students, Eutony rapidly spread throughout the world. By the time Feldenkrais developed his own method, Eutony was the most well-known and popular system of movement awareness in Europe, especially among performers and dancers and those in academic educational circles. Given that

the theater was also Matthias Alexander's first love, we cannot ignore the origin of a substantial wing of somatics as training and self-improvement developed *by* performers *for* performers. Among those initially most receptive to the new "Alexander" disciplines were opera singers, actors, and dancers. Eutony, for instance, teaches musicians how to harmonize their musculature with their instruments and actors how to "create a real and 'tangible' contact with the audience and other actors."[39]

Alexander further reveals her theatrical bent by quoting Constantin Stanislavski, peerless stage-master, in relation to her system:

> . . . [T]he muscular tension impedes the inner life in unfolding naturally. As long as our muscles stay tense, we cannot even imagine the subtle nuances of our sentiments, nor penetrate into the spiritual life of our person.[40]

Thus, Eutony is an improvisational performance of emotions with a priority of dynamic contact in space. The inner sense of self generates a feeling of "psychosomatic and spiritual unity of the total person."[41] The expanding sensation of others around one leads to a genuine experience of community. The community becomes a dance company, a mime troupe, a circus, and an orchestra. The art of therapy migrates from the stage into the secular world and makes the embodied psyche a performer in her own play.

Feldenkrais Method

Moshe Feldenkrais is one of the founders of twentieth-century somatics. Born in Poland in 1904, he immigrated to Palestine as a teenager and lived there for ten years before moving to Paris to study physics at the Sorbonne. He fled to Britain just ahead of the Germans during World War II. There he worked for the Admiralty on the science of submarine detection and anti-sub warfare.

> He was required to be on a ship every day. Ships at sea pitch to and fro and the constant jostling was wreaking havoc with his knee injured

years earlier in a soccer accident. His wife, a pediatrician, introduced him to one of the best surgeons in England. The surgeon concluded that an operation would probably prove successful. Feldenkrais asked what he meant by "probably successful." The surgeon gave Feldenkrais 50–50 odds that he would walk normally and 50–50 odds that he would have to spend the rest of his life walking with the help of a cane. Feldenkrais replied that 50–50 odds were no better than mere chance and that in designing experiments he would look for something like a 98–2 probability; otherwise it was a waste of time.[42]

He told the astonished surgeon he would repair his own knees. The surgeon promised that he would be back within six months begging for an operation. From such a gauntlet a whole system of Functional Integration emerged.

First, Feldenkrais began his own study of existing kinesiological literature and texts of developmental anatomy. Nothing suited his needs. Anyway, from what he gleaned he began to make subtle manipulations of his knee. He kept careful records of his attempts. He would note the effect during the manipulation, then thirty seconds, a minute, five minutes, an hour, a day after each one. He gradually found the right combination of manipulations to restore his knee to functioning. Or so he thought.

> Walking on a sidewalk in London, Feldenkrais hailed a cab. Stepping off the curb into what he assumed would be the street, he in fact stepped into a storm drain. The added distance jarred his knee and reinjured it. Feldenkrais realized, in his words, "I was like every other idiot who fixed a part and didn't look at the whole system...." He began an inquiry into the activities of daily life. This inquiry led to his greatest realization: that whether one walks "poorly" or "gracefully," unless one knows the "how," both are equally mechanical.... As Feldenkrais began again the project of restoring functioning to his knee he now knew that he had to proceed very differently.[43]

Gradually, by slow trial and error, he rehabilitated himself and at the same time developed a teachable "method." He returned to Israel

to practice and soon after established a training center (the Feldenkrais Institute) in Tel Aviv. After his work became known internationally, he traveled widely to lecture and give demonstrations, including a legendary stint at Esalen Institute in 1972. Feldenkrais died in 1984.

LIKE MANY OTHER somatic innovators, Feldenkrais did not invent every element of his system; he grafted many of them from other traditions. Yet his system stands totally on its own, transforming its component elements so that they take on new identities and function uniquely in terms of the logic in which he rearranged them. Among the somatic areas he studied were auto-suggestion, hypnosis, neuroanatomy, yoga, Alexander Technique, the martial arts, and the teachings of G. I. Gurdjieff. He was familiar with the prevailing European movement traditions, including Eutony and the work of Elsa Gindler (which led directly to the practices of Marion Rosen and Charlotte Selver in the United States). Gindler taught a system of sensory awakening which, in defiance of Hitler's demand, she refused to name. Her radical experiments in sensing included hours of sitting, standing, or jumping, all trying to develop pure attention to function and recover an immediacy of experience. Selver later called her own work "Sensory Awareness." We see this same mode of inquiry in Feldenkrais' development of what he called Awareness Through Movement.

While also clearly influenced by Gerda Alexander, Feldenkrais contended that Eutony relied on random nonspecific explorations as opposed to a logical scientific framework. This may be true to a relative degree. However, Alexander's practices were surprisingly specific given the context of their development at such an early stage in the history of movement awareness. In fact, for some people today, they function precisely in place of Feldenkrais exercises for some of the same learning experiences.

Disciple Jack Heggie has proposed, perhaps whimsically, that Feldenkrais took the essence of

Shaolin martial arts and Taoist energy practices and translated them into an entirely different format for the West.[44] This may be more legend than history, though Taoist practitioner Kumar Frantzis has noted, "In the West, it has been the author's observation that the Feldenkrais Method is the only method which has principles in common with Chi Gung therapy in terms of re-educating the body's physical tissue and central nervous systems." However, Frantzis adds, "The Feldenkrais system does not have a *chi* component in its diagnostic or treatment methods. . . . The Chi Gung therapy methods are not derived from only the genius of one man but from thousands of years of refining consistent research and development."[45] That such a dedicated promoter of *Chi Gung* would even consider Feldenkrais in the same league as the entire lineage of Taoist masters is high praise indeed!

Feldenkrais work does not particularly resemble *Chi Gung* except in cultivating awareness of minute components of movements. Yes, it is an empirical, kinesthetic tracking system written in the language of awareness exercises, but it concerns habit and psychosomatic restriction not intrinsic energy. We will discuss this issue further at the end of this section and in the section on *Chi Gung* in the next chapter.

The Method does not resemble American Indian shamanism either; yet after Brooke Medicine Eagle trained in Feldenkrais work, she went back to the Northern Cheyenne reservation and observed the activities of the medicine men anew. "Now," she declared, "I saw what they were doing."[46] Even though the Feldenkrais technique does not specifically interpret cross-cultural rituals, Medicine Eagle had learned the effectual subtle components of *movement itself* and thus could understand shamanic gestures on this basis. As Feldenkrais himself said at the outset of his North American training in 1975: "I am going to be your last teacher. Not because I'll be the greatest teacher you ever encounter, but because from me you will learn how to learn."[47]

More to the point historically, Feldenkrais came from a family of rabbis, a direct descendant of Pincas of Koretz, elder of the innermost circle of Hassidic Judaism. In fact, Feldenkrais' gravestone in Israel identifies him solely by this genealogical fact, ignoring his international renown as a master of somatic innovation. Although this was hardly the intention of the omission, unavoidable is the insinuation that Feldenkrais performed first as a Hebrew mystic, second as physical educator. His entire Method becomes one more subset of a vast qabbalistic legacy, springing yet another legend: that his exercises tap a tradition of secret Hassidic dances paralleling extant Taoist techniques. At the very least, his work embraces "Russian, German, French, English, Yiddish and Hebrew ways of being embodied."[48]

One should also not underestimate the role of Feldenkrais' expertise in physics. Like Still, he attained a thorough comprehension of engineering principles. Then he worked in the Paris laboratory of Nobel laureate Frederic Joliot-Curie and "had a very contemporary systems and field theoretical approach to the physical world"[49] that flouted the mechanistic and Newtonian view of nature and the body. Thus, his somatic methods were always based on mechanical as well as relativistic and psychological understanding of structure and movement. Additionally, whether he found the age-old secrets of the Shaolin Temple or not, Feldenkrais became an adept enough judo practitioner to write books on the subject. In fact, he earned one of the first European black belts:

> In judo one's posture must permit without prior readjustments movement in any of six cardinal directions—up/down, forward/backward, left/right. Most attackers or defenders move in one plane, e.g., forward or back, left or right, up or down. They become predictable targets.... Counting time, the martial artist moves in four dimensions or rather becomes four-dimensional. The personal self, which is time/space bound in a cultural matrix of lower dimensionality, disappears. Intentional multidimensionality, closely linked with what Feldenkrais called awareness, is one by-product of changing our way

> of moving.... By educating, differentiating and integrating the movements of the lower torso and upper legs—the so-called "center"—one apportions strength to the strongest muscles, freeing the limbs for expression and sensitive contact. With action organized from the center the skeleton becomes a means for transferring force from the lower torso outward to the extremities. Additionally, one learns how to utilize and turn the strength of another against him, how to transform the fear of falling into rolling, how to "re-educate" the opponent rather than destroy him or her.[50]

Elizabeth Beringer, a contemporary practitioner and teacher, told me that she conceives of the Method primarily as the dynamism of judo fused with the rigor of physics, not exclusive of other influences but as their core.[51]

The Feldenkrais Method of neural reeducation is comprehensive, with myriad elements operating at different intellectual and somatic levels. Its repertoire includes a highly structured but flexible sequence of lessons taught to individuals as Functional Integration and to groups under the name Awareness Through Movement. The emphasis is on sensory-motor experience: reintegrating functions and becoming aware of previously unknown areas of the self and connecting them one to another. The techniques range from methods of gentle manipulation—often to relieve pressure from a particular zone and allow a client to move in a more efficient way—to games of practical anatomy so direct and playful they could be taught in primary schools.

What stands out about the Method is the degree to which it is involved in cognition as well as manipulation—that is, conscious learning and not just unconscious directives to the nervous system from the hands of a practitioner.

Teacher more than hands-on healer, Feldenkrais devised lessons to show people on simultaneously kinesthetic and cognitive levels why they moved in the ways they did, where the restrictions they felt were located, and how to evolve new patterns of movement and activities from the ground up. Yet he had no ambitions to train "improved" behavior the way one might drill athletes. Freedom rather than performance was at issue—how people build modes of being out of the rudiments of their own sensations. There are no formally sequential protocols. In fact, current Feldenkrais teachers express amazement at how vast and unending the system is. Using the basic model, therapists conceive new methods of treatment and ingenious variations on familiar exercises almost daily. During his life Feldenkrais was hardly concerned whether he applied his Method conventionally to bodily rigidity or to relanguaging, bed-wetting, and obesity. He instructed one very overweight woman at a seminar always to leave one bite on her plate, one spoonful in her bowl. Since no previous diet had worked, he was instructing her to change her habits of eating instead.

After years of doing this work, Dennis Leri finally concluded:

> Throughout the many hundreds of ATM (Awareness Through Movement) lessons, with all their varied themes, there are two general injunctions: 1) Move only in one's comfort zone. Work smarter rather than harder . . . 2) Carry out the instructions only as long as one is able to attend to what one is doing. If the mind begins to wander, if the movement becomes mechanical, stop.[52]

FELDENKRAIS TURNED AROUND the traditional paradigm of physical therapy. Instead of asking, "What can I touch to change this person?" (as most therapists do), he wondered, "How can I initiate the transformative effect of awareness itself?" The Feldenkrais Method is first and foremost a learning model. The therapist is trying to create a situation in which a client can learn—literally learn—a new way of doing things.

For instance, like Matthias Alexander, Feldenkrais found that interrupting preexisting patterns was extremely useful both in diagnosing

impediments and in developing new possibilities of movement. It didn't matter whether these patterns were "successful" or not. New behavior always emerged from their dissolution.

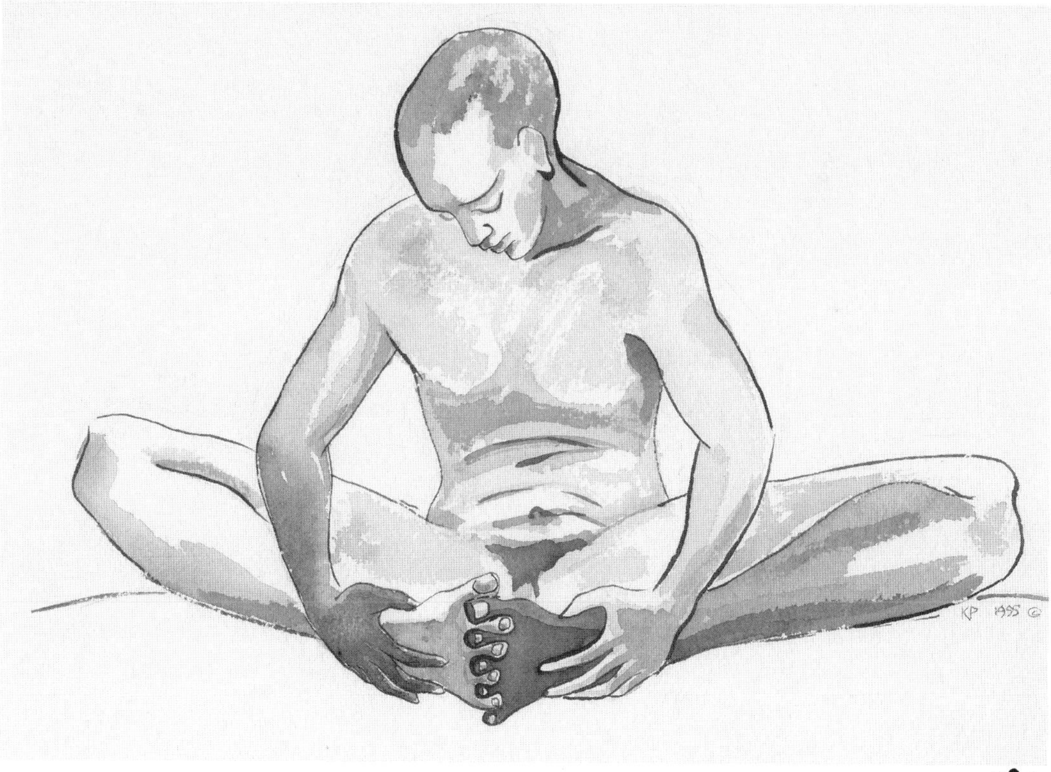

So he taught nonhabitual movements to trick people into giving up their habitual patterns. These were as indirect as osteopathic adjustments. Simply interlacing one's fingers with the right thumb on the outside (if the left thumb is habitual in that position) is enough to challenge basic kinesthesia throughout the body. Interlacing one's toes is even more exotically nonhabitual. If the eyes are closed and the muscles moving them are held to one side (the extreme left or right or directly up or down), then the head may moved independently of the eyes. After one direction is completed to satisfaction (a few circuits are usually sufficient), the other side may be attempted. After all four directions are completed, they may be combined in several orbits of a circle. For the

more advanced student, the eyes and the head may be tracked in opposite circuits, clockwise and counterclockwise, or vice versa. That is, each attempt rotates these components simultaneously and smoothly in opposite directions. A parallel set of exercises may be carried out holding the head in place and moving the eyes. In subsequent rounds the shoulders may be integrated in a series in which any two of the three (eyes, head, and shoulders) progress in one direction while the third is tracked in the other direction. This constellation of techniques is startlingly effective in extending range of movement, relieving head, eye, and neck pain,

and reducing the frequency of headaches. What is equally astonishing (although not so much so if one remembers reciprocality throughout the body) is that the exercises may also increase the range of motion of the arms or pelvis. Conversely, restriction in the head area can be relieved by pelvic and leg exercises.

Another method Feldenkrais favored was the creation of double binds and paradoxes in order to have students abandon habitual patterns and improvise new ones. He liked to pose purposely ambiguous instructions in order to see how class members would interpret them and put their bodies to different uses. In this manner, he was able to expose the often rigid relationship between languaging patterns and somatic activities. During one breathing exercise, he instructed:

> Don't breathe.... Don't hold your breath either.... Just don't breathe. Don't breathe in any way that you know to be breathing.... Don't hold your breath.... Don't make efforts.... Don't breathe with your chest.... Don't breathe with your abdomen.... Don't do any of the things that you know.... Just don't breathe, that's all.[53]

Clearly getting people to differentiate between languaging mannerisms and actions was one of Feldenkrais' gateways to affecting core behavior. You could not reeducate function unless you persuaded people to sever their unexamined bond between clichés of thought and clichés of action:

> Linguistic articulations, verbal and non-verbal codings, make mute the protean somatic articulation from which they emerge. Our body broken by language is reassembled with conjunctions. We say the hand *and* the wrist *and* the arm *and* so on, creating a body of thought apart from our organismic body. To make language a part of our biology we need to be able to read, access, and utilize the organismic body's "alphabet," "grammar," and "vocabulary".... Any learned behavior [including speech, reading, and writing] obscures the learning processes used to construct it. Feldenkrais lessons access and recombine the patterns of somatic learning used to construct any meaningful behavior.[54]

For Feldenkrais, differentiation was crucial—differentiation of a part of the body from its contiguous parts and differentiation of one axis of movement from another. Without differentiation, there is no alphabet of behavior. Differentiation was the embryogenic and historical way in which the primitive tissues of our bodies located themselves in space and in relation to other tissues and thus knew how to shape fascia, bones, and viscera. How the embryo forms in layers of tissues becomes how the infant learns primary motor skills, always distinguishing similar motions and aptitudes until they are fully distinct from one another. Thus, rolling one's head and pelvis on the floor in opposite directions breaks an integrated pattern; this movement can then be used to invent more complex, less rigid patterns.

FELDENKRAIS' INITIAL CHALLENGE is to lie on the floor. People in a group feeling the contact of the ground with their bodies will each perceive points of solid connection—floor against self—and points where the connection is broken, intermittent. Simply becoming aware of each of these sensations and what they represent teaches a person which muscles are overworking to hold irrelevant parts of the body up from the floor. If these are released, even partially, one's overall use of the skeleton is improved.

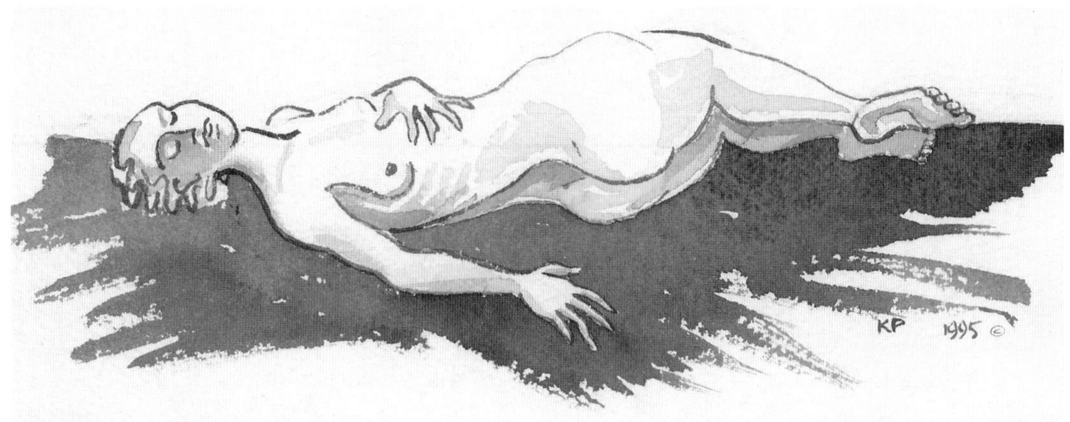

Sitting in chairs is a great deadener of the proprioception of the hip joints. Feldenkrais explains:

> The awareness of the location and function in these joints is nonexistent compared with that of people who sit on the ground and not on chairs. The chair sitter is almost without exception completely out of place when locating the hip joints. Moreover, he uses his legs as if they were articulated at the points where he has them articulated in his body image and not where they are.[55]

We become robots, forcing our actual living bodies to carry out the imaginary functions of nonexistent abstract bodies. These are our character states, often ridiculously stylized masks or caricatures of our ambivalences. Where imaginary functions depart from actual anatomy, we become ineffective and must compensate both physiologically and emotionally. Styles of presence in modern life are often based on the tensions between our idealized images of self and what is anatomically elegant. In order to be more present, we must become more aware of the ways in which we embody these strained characters, at the expense of our natural, motile selves.

FELDENKRAIS' GUIDING TENET was that people are born with a large repertoire of movement, much of which they inhibit. Like Freud and Reich, he presumed a crisis underlying this situation, but unlike Freud and Reich, he did not idealize the primacy of trauma in the formation of armor. He believed that many blocks were the incidental result of habituated mislearning, and that others were deep-seated not from the force and static content of a traumatic moment but because of an ultimately unnecessary repetition of a dysfunctional or restricted pattern of movement, or of an essential kinesthetic ambivalence that continually furnished opposed sets of behavior. They were ruts—pure and simple—without deep-seated charge.

That is, whereas Freud presumed that people had complicated emotional reasons for their neuroses, Feldenkrais believed that while

resistances were legitimately retreats into positions of imagined security, the neural energy binding them was no more cathected and trenchant than, for instance, the unwillingness to speak a new language (like French) before one knows enough of it to express oneself.[56]

I cannot emphasize enough how important this point is. Whereas Freud said, "We need a trauma to get neurotic or dysfunctional," Feldenkrais said, "A bad habit is enough to do it." If we "practice" a dysfunctional movement again and again, even without a trauma (perhaps simply from a neurological confusion or dyslexia-like displacement), the mere repetition of that movement will gradually cut deeper and deeper into the organization of the whole organism, often leading to physical disease from the blocking or distorting of natural visceral and neuromuscular functions. Yet there may be nothing more behind it than an innocent mistake.

Most people, when asked to enact a simple motion like raising their eyebrows, will move many other unrelated parts of their body at the same time: the jaw may open in the other direction, the forearms tighten slightly, the rib cage contract, the toes may even curl—all seemingly to aid the raising of the eyebrows. These other movements are "parasitic" and contribute nothing; in fact, they detract from the intended movement. The arrays of parasitic movements throughout our bodies at all times accumulate in multiple levels of pain, uncoordination, numbness, lack of differentiation, and, ultimately, counterproductive behavior. Feldenkrais writes in *The Potent Self:*

> Many people fail to recognize the true cause of their inability or failure. The cause is very often not lack of ability, but improper use of self—there must not be too little an urge to do, a desire to act, nor too much. Now, we may not be able to influence our inheritance [i.e., our genetic anatomy], but we have a large measure of control over our urges and over the means of freeing them from inhibiting agents of which we are rarely aware. We can learn to adjust our body tensions and the state of the nervous system, so that self-assertive and recuperative functions alternately dominate our frame. In this

state of unstable balance, we find ourselves able to enact what we want more expediently.[57]

That is, by learning to carry out sets of empirically tested exercises, we can rewire our neural and psychological patterns. The goal is—note—not some imaginary perfection, but an "unstable balance" free always to change into something else. Feldenkrais continues:

> We may be in a state of inability to enact any projected idea, from writing a letter to loving. Impotent rage and impotent love have a great deal in common. In both, the *desire* to do is excessive, and prevented from expression by extraneous and contradictory motives of equal intensity.... [Yet] that which is formed through personal experience is essentially alterable and, *a priori*, capable of being influenced by a new personal experience.[58]

Elsewhere in the same book he writes:

> The apparent ability of all of us is far below our latent ability, as contradictory motivation diminishes and tempers most of our actions....
>
> My considered opinion is that in general we only use a fraction of our latent capacity in most walks of life. The rest is buried in habitual contradictory motivation, to which we have become so accustomed as to be unable to feel what is happening.[59]

When asked sarcastically by a frustrated student how to become "a genius like you," Feldenkrais answered with the resonance of an Hassidic wizard:

> Most people spend their whole lives using their strengths to cover up and hide their weaknesses. They expend tremendous energy in keeping themselves a house divided. But if you surrender to your weakness therein lies your pathway to genius. A person who knows and utilizes his true weakness and uses his strength to include it is a whole person. He may seem rough around the edges, but there are so few people like that that they lead their generation.[60]

ALTHOUGH THE DESIRE to change is important, contradictory motivation doesn't just melt under will. If double binds were that mutable, they would not become rigidified simultaneously in the brain, the neuromusculature, and the personality. "Each and every person, via the agency of their nervous system, makes the best choices possible given their perception of choices.... Granting intelligence to someone's personal history validates it. The practitioner's task is to create conditions for more choices. It is not to correct errors, right wrongs or straighten people out."[61]

The genius of the system developed by Feldenkrais is that, without invalidating or indicting present behavior, it provides schematic body-movement instructions for differentiating one's motivations and activities and unlocking the behavioral grid in which they are trapped.

WITH A NOD to osteopathy, Feldenkrais developed an explicit method of going with distortions until they released on their

own. Working with a person with scoliosis, he might instruct him to lie down and then take the shorter leg on the thicker side and stretch it toward the head. While this makes the leg all the shorter, it also prevents the psoas muscle (that has been pulling the leg) from continuing to strain. Because the student is making the leg shorter than the

muscle can pull, the muscle relaxes. Then the counter muscle can be stretched even longer. Both muscles now have new information, are in balance and communication with each other, and at the same time stimulated by fresh blood.[62]

> In another situation, Feldenkrais worked with a small boy with cerebral palsy whose knees pressed spastically together as he walked. He worked on the boy with his hands until his knees were "slightly separated, no longer locked in place." Then:
>
> Feldenkrais makes a fist, places it in the new space between the knees. "Now Ephraim," he says. "Please, can you press your knees against my fist." Then: "Come on, you can do better than that! Close your knees on my fist as hard as you can." He keeps it up, and Ephraim, no longer relaxed, is now straining mightily with the weak muscles on the inside of his thighs, an unaccustomed workout. Soon, "listening" carefully with his fist, Feldenkrais is satisfied that the time is right.
>
> "All right, Ephraim," he says, "you don't have to close your knees anymore. You can open them now." With clear relief, Ephraim relaxes, and opens his knees—all the way.
>
> "See how much easier it is to have your knees open? To close them requires work. To keep them open, you don't have to do anything at all." The boy moves his legs in and out, in apparent disbelief, then bursts into a peal of delighted laughter....
>
> In this session, Feldenkrais did not "contradict the nervous system" by trying to stretch the knees apart but utilized instead the boy's spastic pattern of holding his knees together. By exaggerating his "symptom," Ephraim was able to learn to make an involuntary movement voluntary.[63]

This feature of "not contradicting the nervous system" sets Feldenkrais work apart from many other forms of adjustment and manipulation in which practitioners try to antidote dysfunctional patterns by imposing new ones. It was not that Feldenkrais lacked a sense of concrete goals; it was that he chose to teach them to each organism in a series of proprioceptive puzzles. For instance, in describing Functional Integration in Copenhagen Feldenkrais explained:

> I never deal with the affected member or articulation before an improvement in the head-neck relationship and the breathing has been brought about. This, in turn, cannot be achieved without a betterment of the spine and thorax configuration. Again the pelvis and abdomen must be corrected. In practice the procedure is a successive series of approximations, each one allowing a further improvement in the segment just dealt with....
>
> The head movements must have no predilection for particular directions. The "normal" head should have easy access to all directions of the anatomically possible range. The limiting factor should be the skeletal structure and not the muscular impediments....
>
> The healthy coordinated movements of the body as a whole obey the mechanical principle of least action, while the muscles work in step and perform their task with the least expenditure of metabolic energy.[64]

Function (and health) are marked by unrestricted and graceful movement within the limitations of the skeleton. Smoothness and elegance are important reference points in the training. "Correct coordinated action," to paraphrase Feldenkrais, is elegant action. To the outside observer and from the inside, such movement seems effortless, though there may be a great deal of actual work involved in sustaining it. Activity becomes more graceful the more it is felt. What is not felt, axiomatically cannot be changed.

Even victims of severe diseases, such as Parkinson's and multiple sclerosis, or paralyzing strokes and accidents can learn alternate neuromuscular pathways to seemingly lost behavior (walking, speaking, cognizing colors and faces). But the pathways must be forged step by step. Forced uncoordinated bursts at the impossible only habituate overefforting and a sense of defeat. New coordination is invented by the body learning all over again how to move and enact functional behavior and record it in nervous tissue, much as it did in partnership with the mind in the first place.

The medical "meaning" of Feldenkrais' work is clearly established by his success in re-laying neural templates. For a stroke victim to be

able to talk and write again is not dismissable as mere "pop psychology." Of one patient he treated successfully, Feldenkrais wrote:

> Nora, like every one of us, was not aware that the functions she had lost [by her stroke] were originally learned and not inherited as was her digestion or temperature regulation. Were these latter lost, then life would come to an end, but she had lost learned organization and like everybody else saw no difference between the *Homo sapiens* part of her and the animal part. She could not help herself and neither could anybody who was not aware of the difference. Many of the evils from which we suffer are rooted in our conception of human education as the training of a complete being to do this or that, as though we were making a computer perform a desired activity.[65]

Feldenkrais based his entire hope for the future of *Homo sapiens* on the belief that human beings had just begun to learn the range of things they were free to do. What he discovered in the treatment of those who had severely damaged nervous systems was tantamount to a realization that all of us operate as if we were victims of neurological disorders. What he sought was a compassionate and scientific way for us to extricate ourselves from the dilemma of our own trap.

On the one hand, one might agree with Frantzis' assessment of the Feldenkrais Method as the work of a single man and thus a mere shadow of a millennial system like *Chi Gung*. On the other hand, the Feldenkrais Method is also a millennial system, for it encompasses the entire history of Western civilization, from the first anatomical experiments of Hippocrates and Apollonius of Cyprus and the philosophical ontology of Aristotle to the early research of neurology and phenomenological psychology.

Western science is not a single stream (like Taoist science); it is a diverging and anastomosing river. Feldenkrais picked up the branch of empirical inquiry into physiology and self-knowledge and carried it through to its natural conclusion. Under his care it bore unimagined fruits—methods of reeducating movement and breaking habitual patterns that no prior scientists had considered, at least in part because

they were in such trances they were not even aware of the habitual patterns in which they proclaimed their freedoms and the freedom of science. As Dewey said in praise of Matthias Alexander, education at this level bears the same relationship to education as a field of study that education as a field of study bears to all other human activities.

In the language and methodology of the freedom of science, Feldenkrais liberated human behavior. He formulated this in a method particularly suited to assimilation by Western consciousness. In his own words, he taught people how to learn. Thus, in principle he taught them how to learn *Chi Gung* as well as to stop overeating and regain mental function after a stroke. By contrast, a *Chi Gung* teacher transmits "something"; whether his student locates her own *chi* or doesn't, he has no way of relating success or failure to particular sensory-motor habits. He can define *chi* only by its own existence and its existence by his spontaneous discovery and subsequent utilization of it. Thus, it may be argued that, while a hypothetical student might never find *chi* by mere Feldenkrais lessons, the lessons could teach her states of being that would make her receptive to *Chi Gung* lessons. Without the prior Feldenkrais work, she might always organize away from *chi.*

The Feldenkrais Method is thus much more than just the method of Moshe Feldenkrais. It is the primary method of Western (and possibly human) sensory-motor education. As such, it is at the beginning of its historical development, and its possible uses and ramifications are limitless. Its ultimate success would be a planet-wide reorientation to the fact that we all need to learn new habits in order to make a more functional society. Then, long after people knew the name "Feldenkrais," each generation could set about inventing its own appropriate lessons.

Rolfing

Overview and Ground Systems

Like Moshe Feldenkrais, Ida Rolf developed her method of bodywork later in life only after engagement in a number of other spheres. In Rolf's case a Ph.D. in organic chemistry from Columbia University

was followed by extensive instruction in yoga, osteopathy (including Sutherland's cranial work), and homeopathy. While in London learning the Alexander Technique, she participated in a Gurdjieffian group at which she met fellow members Greta Garbo and Georgia O'Keefe, both of whom were to become patients of hers years later. She also studied Alfred Korzybski's General Semantics. However, the osteopathic influence was by far the most extensive and fundamental. According to historian of somatics Don Hanlon Johnson:

> Ida spent nearly fifty years of her professional life within the community of osteopaths and chiropractors. Her first encounter with that work occurred when she was a young adult on a camping trip to the Rockies in 1916 after graduating from Barnard College. While she was tying up her gear one afternoon, her horse kicked her. The next day she developed pneumonia. Within a very short time her breathing became so impaired and her fever so severe that she had to be taken to a small Montana town for help. To her surprise, the doctor prescribed a treatment from the local osteopath. After a . . . manipulation of her spine, her fever was immediately reduced and her breathing became normal. . . .
>
> The Montana osteopath's simple act of adjusting her spine was to have a lifelong impact on her conceptions of healing. It dramatically convinced her of the truth of the basic osteopathic principle enunciated by Andrew Still that structure determines function.[66]

The system devised by Rolf is a direct manipulative method of improving health and changing behavior by altering structure. It could have been osteopathic, but it was not for a variety of reasons. First of all, Rolf devised her method of manipulation out of physical therapy and yoga; she was a biochemist not an osteopath. Secondly, she practiced at a time of far more rigid boundaries between fields than prevail today; she kept her own method distinct from osteopathy, Feldenkrais Method, and other techniques she respected and studied because she did not want to infringe on the professional territory and she wanted her own trademarked territory (critics would say, her own empire).

Thirdly, she was never actually permitted by the osteopathic establishment to study osteopathy as an affiliated outsider. Yet so curious was she about the training and techniques that she volunteered as a secretary and went under cover to meetings in order to learn what was being taught.[67] Thus, it is impossible for there not to be a major complement of osteopathy in Rolfing, but Rolfing is also a separate invention and the entrepreneurial undertaking of an ambitious and independent-minded physical therapist.

Whereas Feldenkrais emphasized gradual reeducation, Rolf developed an actual regimen for reorienting the parts of the body in relationship to one another so that they would function efficiently in the universal field of gravity in which we all exist. This meant establishing a central vertical axis—the collective centers of gravity of all the centers of gravity in the body. This "Line" of gravity would be straight if all its centers were properly organized in relationship to one another. To Rolf, the healthy body described by medical kinesiologists and even most osteopaths was actually poorly organized and functionally compromised. Eyeballing how the Line might look if a patient were integrated—and then carrying out the manipulative procedures necessary to approximate if not achieve this—was her method.

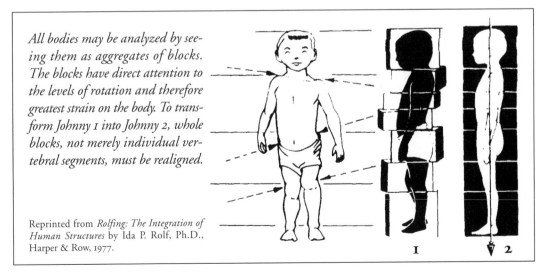

All bodies may be analyzed by seeing them as aggregates of blocks. The blocks have direct attention to the levels of rotation and therefore greatest strain on the body. To transform Johnny 1 into Johnny 2, whole blocks, not merely individual vertebral segments, must be realigned.

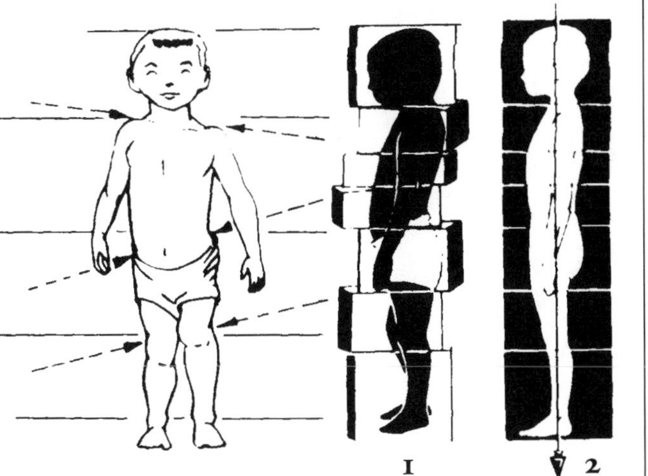

Reprinted from *Rolfing: The Integration of Human Structures* by Ida P. Rolf, Ph.D., Harper & Row, 1977.

> If man weren't a standing, two-footed animal, he would have fewer problems. But he is standing, he is walking as best he can. He's been doing this since he was a kid—climbing up the side of his playpen and somehow getting his legs under him. Possibly he got his legs under him very badly, but he wasn't paying attention to that. He had one goal: he wanted to be like big brother, and big brother was able to walk. . . . .[H]e didn't care how he did it, he only cared that he did it . . . any old way. . . . Any old way disorganized his pelvis, disorganized his ribs, disorganized his head, disorganized the whole overlying structure.[68]

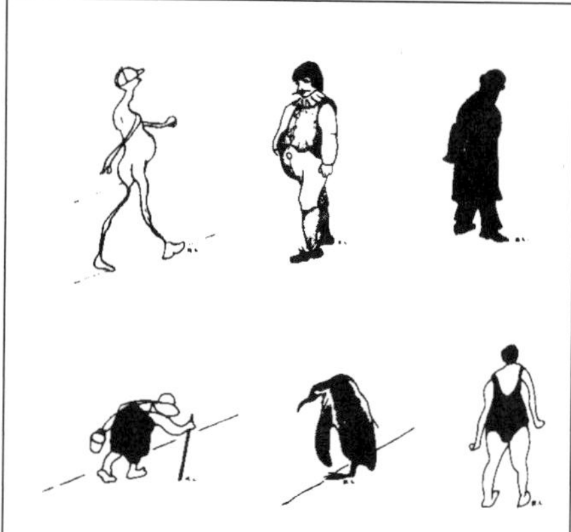

Many of our fellow citizens might be cartoons rather than patterned human energy fields. Their body language betrays their misuse of gravitational energy.

Reprinted from *Rolfing: The Integration of Human Structures* by Ida P. Rolf, Ph.D., Harper & Row, 1977.

From this point of view it was not possible to achieve a structurally integrated and functional organism without the practitioner introducing major changes directly into tissue. Massage, light adjustments, and exercises alone were inadequate. Thus, conventional osteopathy needed to be supplemented by a direct and explicit structural technique to address disorganization of the skeleton under the vertical force of gravity.

The present rationale behind deep tissue work is that if the organism knew how to break its dysfunctional patterns of behavior, it would. It doesn't, so a therapist must support—and even carry out—the feat. Rolf believed that verbal instruction and light, energetic touch (as was common in cranial osteopathy) could not penetrate the full depths of the somaticization of armor. The trained Rolfer molds tissue to whatever degree of depth is tolerable to and integratable by the patient (and a little beyond, some might aver). The goal over a number of such sessions is to accomplish a thorough and dynamic reintegration—a change in structure sustained at a skeletal level.

Rolfing uses the elastic qualities of the fascial connective tissues found everywhere in the body—they are the substructure of muscle fibers themselves bundled in fascia and surrounded by fascia, and the tendons, cartilage, and bone that grow from muscles as the body shapes itself in three dimensions. Made up of collagen fibers, fascia respond to injury, emotional trauma, and other pathology by shortening and becoming static. They lose their basic fluidity. The fascia invariably hold the strain patterns in the body as they struggle to find their most comfortable alignment in the gravitational and social field. But fascia can change as well as maintain form, so they become collectively the vehicle for redesigning and recovering the architectural integrity of the body. Correctly applied tactile pressure can restore the initial state of fascial mobility, alter the fascia, and literally resculpt the body in them. Writes Rolfer Jeffrey Maitland:

> An organized body will ... exhibit an orthogonal order observable as horizontal and vertical lines/planes throughout the body's tissue. Fascial strain patterns are observable as twisting and/or oblique patterns or lines in the tissue. As these lines of fascial strain are eased through Rolfing manipulation, you will actually begin to see horizontals and verticals [lines and planes] in the tissue.[69]

Despite its reputation, Rolfing is not simply a vehicle of force. As much as Feldenkrais work it is a mode of education. Feldenkrais stated

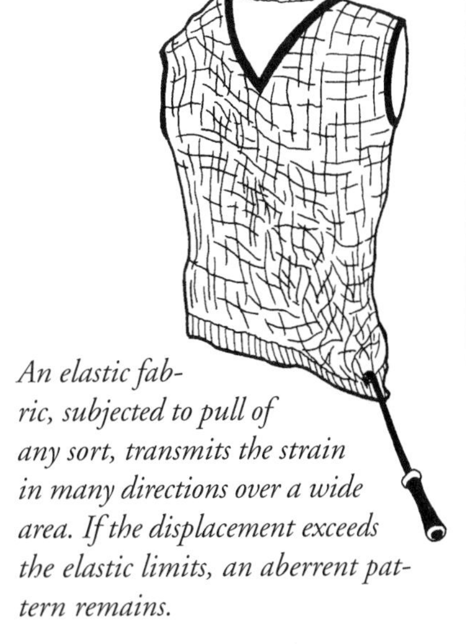

An elastic fabric, subjected to pull of any sort, transmits the strain in many directions over a wide area. If the displacement exceeds the elastic limits, an aberrent pattern remains.

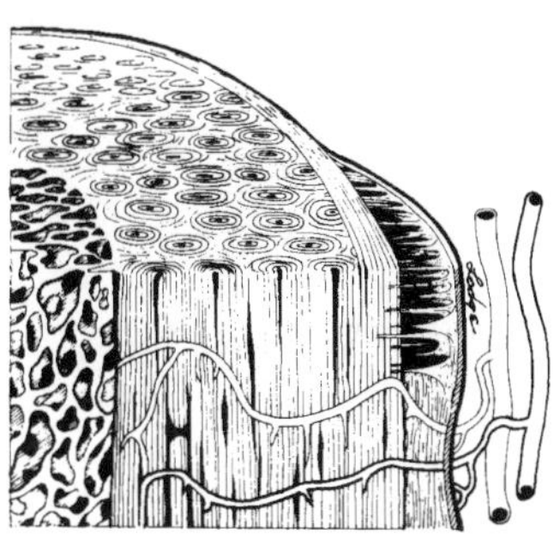

Bone structure seems unitary although it is a patterned aggregate whose elements are unified only by their collective derivation from connective tissue. This is impregnated with deposits of calcareous salts that qualitatively and quantitatively vary according to age, mobility, exercise, etc.

Reprinted from *Rolfing: The Integration of Human Structures* by Ida P. Rolf, Ph.D., Harper & Row, 1977.

The Pelvis Has Many Facets

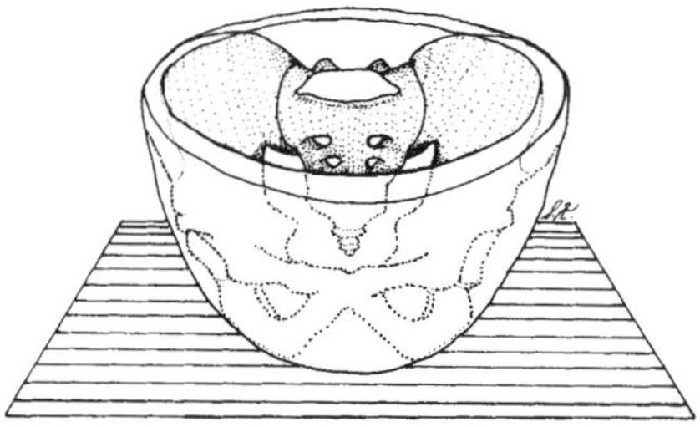

The pelvis is a bony basin.

LUMBAR VERTEBRAE
SACRUM
COCCYX
ILIUM
PUBES
ISCHIUM

Components of the pelvis. *While the function of the bony pelvis can be summarized as that of a bony basin, it should be remembered that the development is from several smaller bones. Lateral views show the fashion in which these bones coalesce to form the pelvis and how the relative size of the individual segments alter and shift to form the pelvis from child to adult.*

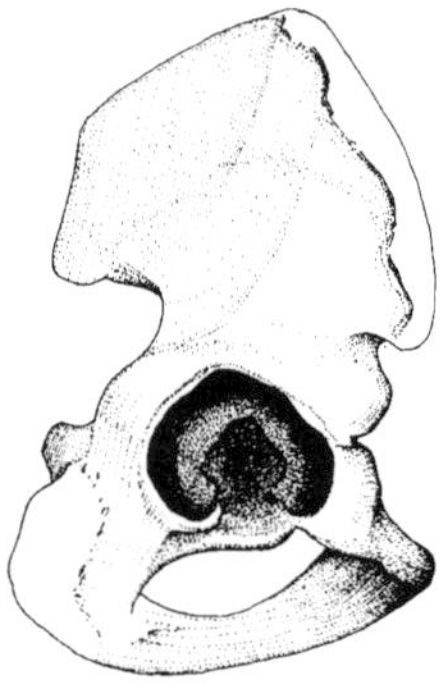

Child Lateral view

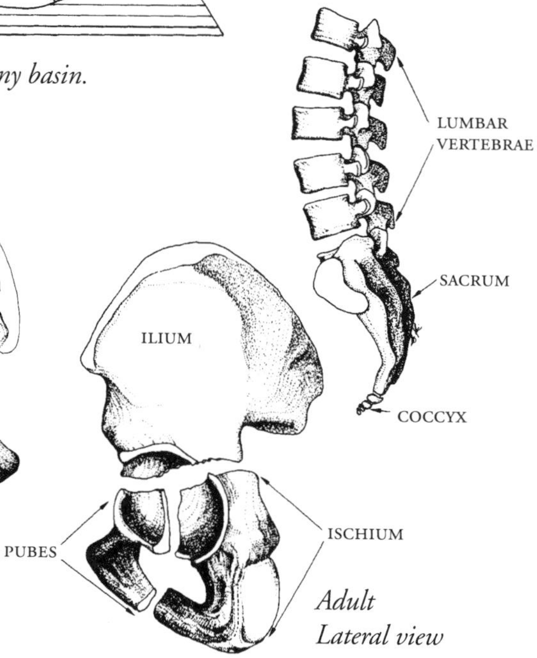

Adult Lateral view

Reprinted from *Rolfing: The Integration of Human Structures* by Ida P. Rolf, Ph.D., Harper & Row, 1977.

this unambiguously when he wrote to Rolf on the occasion of her eightieth birthday:

> Structural Integration and Functional Integration have much more in common than the word that connects them. Indeed, in the case of humans, structure and function are meaningless, one without the other.... [W]hen you integrate structure ..., you improve functioning.[70]

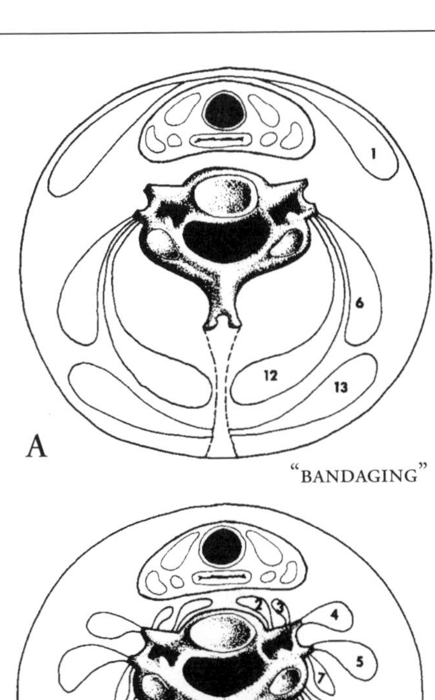

"BANDAGING"

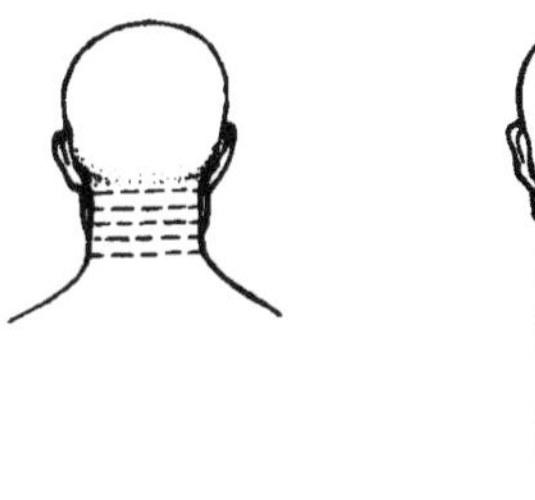

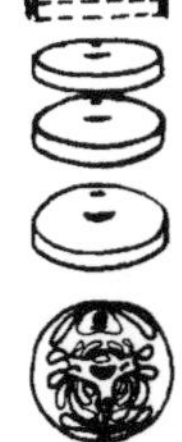

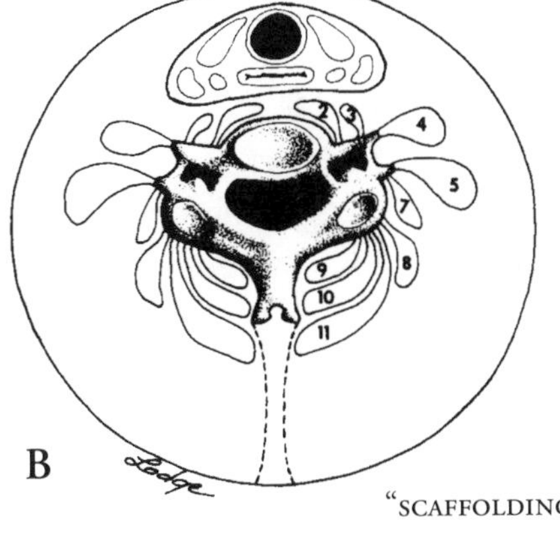

"SCAFFOLDING"

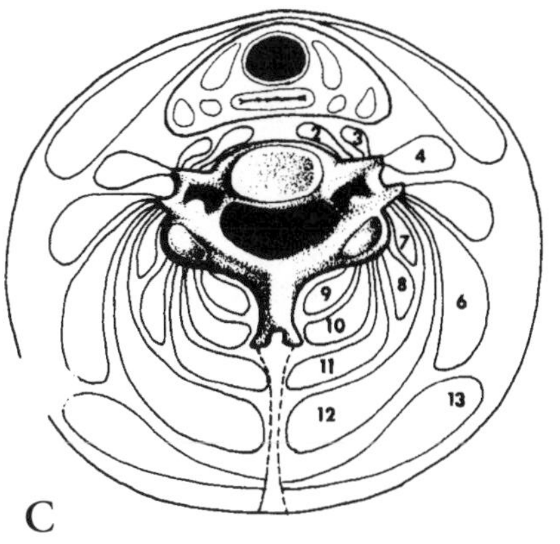

All three of these schemata are cross sections through the same upper cervical vertebra. A pictures muscles of the superficial level (in our terms, the extrinsic level), which act as bandaging and protection. B is the deeper level (in our terms, intrinsic), which as scaffolding maintains the position and spacing of vital cervical structures—autonomic nervous plexi, glandular units (thyroid, parathyroid), etc. And C is a combining of A and B. These muscles, attached horizontally to the bony vertebral structure at one end only, are directionally oriented by planes of fascia. Like all fascial planes, they are plastic and by slight elongation or shortening can change the tone of the related muscle. In so doing, they lessen or exaggerate pressure on vital structures. This changing pressure is the clue to migraine headaches—in fact to all headaches. Key: 1. Sternocleidomastoid. 2. Cervicis longus. 3. Longus capitus. 4. Scalenus anterior. 5. Scalenus medius. 6. Levator scapulae. 7. Costocervicalis. 8. Cervicis longissumus. 9. Multifidus. 10. Semispinalis cervicis. 12. Semispinalis capitus. 12. Splenius. 13. Trapezius.

Reprinted from *Rolfing: The Integration of Human Structures* by Ida P. Rolf, Ph.D., Harper & Row, 1977.

Maitland adds:

> The struggle with gravity and form is the human struggle. Our fondest theories about freedom and the transformation of consciousness are empty fantasies unless we realize that freedom at every level is always a matter of liberating our bodies. And liberating our bodies is a matter of creatively appropriating gravity. We cannot change gravity, but Dr. Rolf discovered and created a system of manipulation and movement education that can transform the way our bodies move and balance by transforming our relation to gravity....
>
> Beginning with the insight that the human body is a unified structural and functional whole that stands in a unique relation to the uncompromising presence of gravity, [she] asked this fundamental question: "What conditions must be fulfilled in order for the human body-structure to be organized and integrated in gravity so that it can function in the most economical way?"[71]

THE NOTION OF full integration within the gravitational field marks the development of Rolfing as a mature system. However, in the

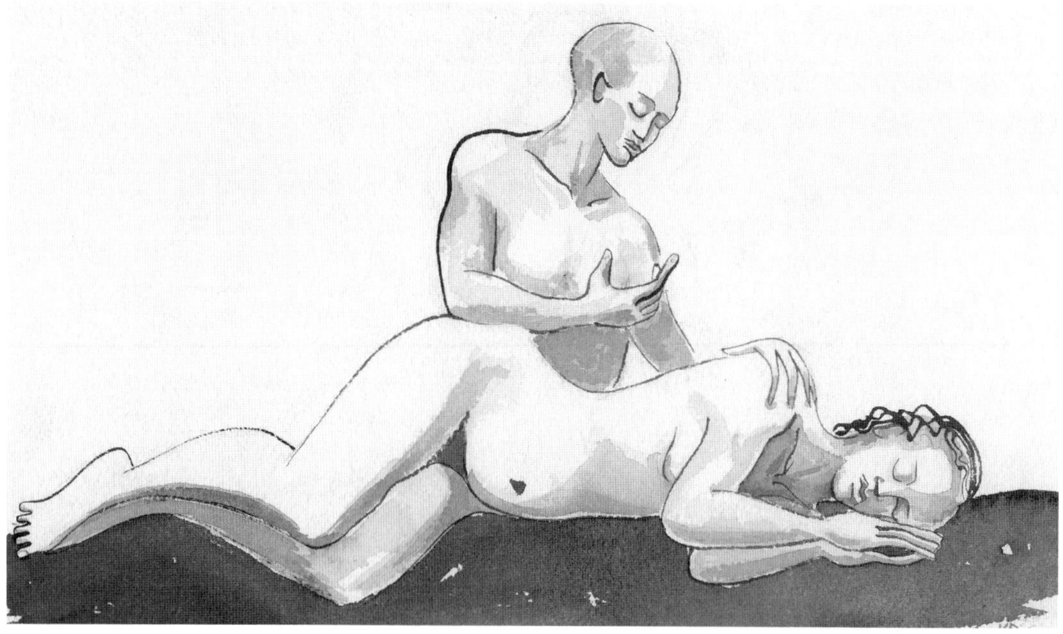

early days, in 1942, after years of osteopathic study, Rolf began her new method of working with a far more modest first principle: "moving the soft tissue toward the place where it really belongs."[72] To accomplish that she used whatever part of the body presented the most effective tool—fingers, fists, and elbows—massaging not to relax and soothe but to adjust flesh even if the pressure was painful. "The manipulation is slow and often extremely deep, the fingers going all the way through the abdomen, for example, to touch the psoas muscle which lies directly in front of the spinal column. Or behind the hard into the soft palate of the mouth, even up into the nasal passages."[73] Slowly, day by day shifting the tissue of a forty-five-year-old friend who had been crippled from age eight as the result of an accident, Rolf got her on her feet and walking.

Years later, Rolf developed the skill of intuiting in a snapshot the alignment of a body and likewise its misalignment through fascial strain. As she grasped what was needed, she developed a strategy for treatment. The process of reintegration might begin with the practitioner

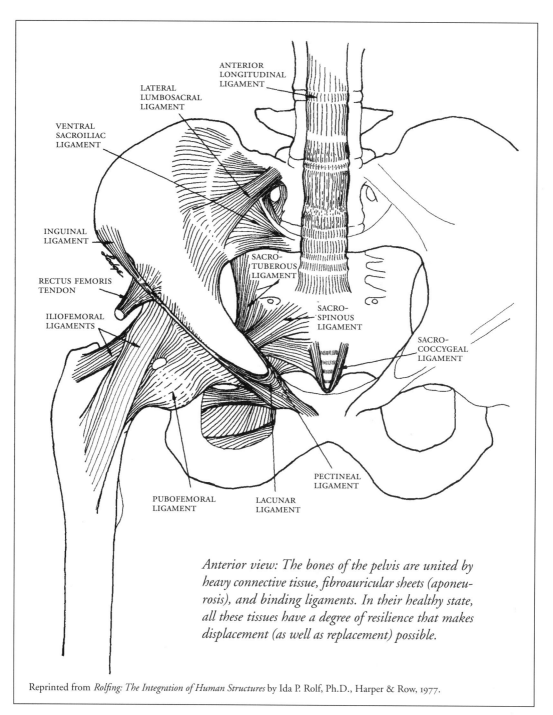

Anterior view: The bones of the pelvis are united by heavy connective tissue, fibroauricular sheets (aponeurosis), and binding ligaments. In their healthy state, all these tissues have a degree of resilience that makes displacement (as well as replacement) possible.

Reprinted from *Rolfing: The Integration of Human Structures* by Ida P. Rolf, Ph.D., Harper & Row, 1977.

freeing the patient's rib cage to enhance general breathing. The legs then become discriminated from the pelvis by deep-tissue massage around the hips, hip joints, and thighs. Later the fascia of the back are loosened, leading to release around the neck and also the crest of the ilium. In subsequent sessions the legs, ankles, feet, shoulders, and back are extended and molded into relationship with one another. The therapist might stretch out the legs by starting from the buttocks and working slowly down their dorsal musculature, at times instructing the client to resist her movements (which refines the sculpting and also provides instructional counterpoints). The goal here is to open and give length to the entire body much like elongating a coiled worm. In a still later session she might work the fingers and palms in along the forearms (right side, then left side), uncurling and freeing tissue around an imaginary bowl into the chest and ribs. Each week a different region is molded or a prior sequence is repeated depending upon how much of the new architecture endures. The direction is always expansion, relieving pressure while spreading radially from the core.

Sometimes poisons are dislodged in the process and flush out through bodily fluids, leaving a bitter taste and stench. On that level Rolfing is a deep cleansing of the whole stream of blood and breath.[74] As in Zen, the pain serves as a reference point for remembering, a way to learn how to inhabit new postures. It also provides a margin of safety between the therapist and the client. The process must not go so fast that nothing is learned. Thus, the most skillful Rolfer works right at the edge.

The pain of being Rolfed is its most fabled aspect. Rolfing *does* hurt but as an effect of pulling open blocks, restoring feeling, and working back through old pains according to the Hippocratic law of cure. It makes the body feel like crumbling clay coming to life as resilient granulation. It is an electric rubbery sensation that cleans one's whole neural wiring and leaves one full of breath, empty of thoughts, entranced and embodied both. At spots (for instance, around the pelvis and at the sacrum) the Rolfer's deep penetration may be like the shock of a lightning bolt

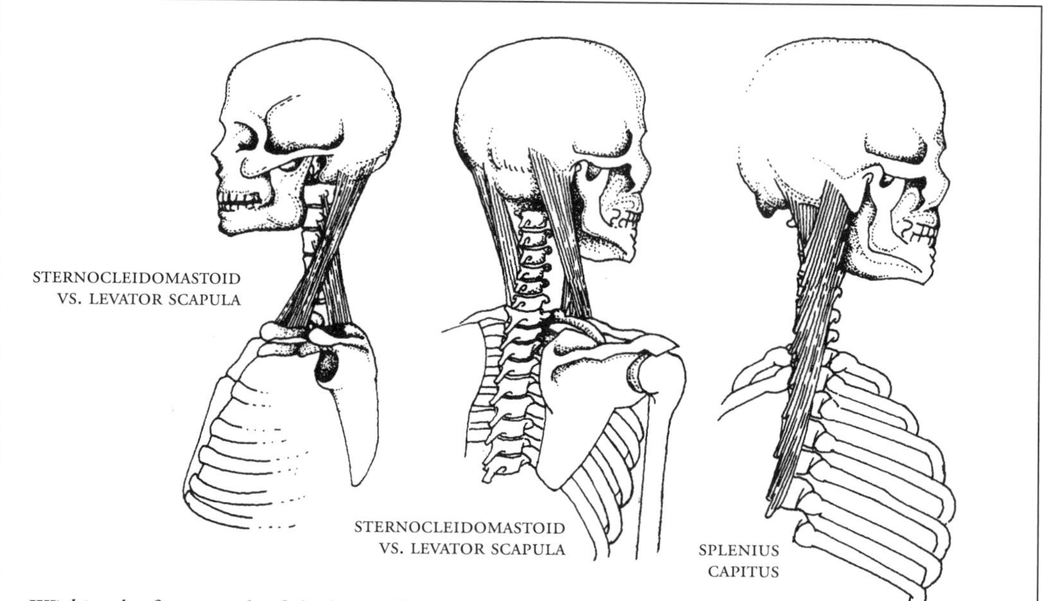

Within the framework of the larger flexor-extensor reciprocity in neck and shoulders, there are many smaller balances. Though dealing with smaller elements, they are nevertheless vitally important to the whole. The relation among sternocleidomastoid, splenius, and levator scapulae is such a reciprocal. If the balance between true flexors and extensors is destroyed, secondary relations also collapse and verticality in the cervicals deteriorates.

Reprinted from *Rolfing: The Integration of Human Structures* by Ida P. Rolf, Ph.D., Harper & Row, 1977.

which (ideally) dissolves into sensual tingles. Thus, it is a pleasurable pain, though that doesn't necessarily make it endurable at the time. Many tell Rolfing "war stories," but it is usually with the pride of someone who has been through a shamanic battle zone.

In the decades that followed her development of a template, Rolf continued to expand her system, developing her own training program and educating generations of practitioners. Ultimately she proposed a four-part protocol:

1. Consider the body as an aggregate of larger segments of weight (head, thorax, abdomen, pelvis, legs, feet) moving in the field of gravity.

2. The relationships among the segments (a person's unique body structure) are a function of balance and tension in the connective tissues that bind the segments into a unity.

3. Those tissues—fascia, tendons, ligaments and muscle groups—are plastic, capable of radical change.

4. The direction of this change can be either in the direction of entropy due to aging and trauma, or, through sensitive manipulation and educated self-awareness, in the direction of balance and harmony with the vertical field of gravity.[75]

In the early years the inner circle of practitioners of Structural Integration was small. Rolfing was viewed as an offshoot of osteopathy, bone-setting, and physical therapy, and Rolf got her recognition as a specialist ranging across disciplines. People today often ignore this actual origin of Rolfing and approach it as an exotic system in a vacuum. Prior to the introduction of Rolfing into the counterculture, Rolf spent some forty years teaching osteopaths, physiotherapists, adventurous orthopedic physicians, and others in seminars and developing her reputation from work with autistic children and within the general rehabilitative and physical-therapy community. Gradually she lost some of her standing within this guild because of her psychologically existential notions of personal freedom and her avoidance of a medical model as too rigid. But she also became legendary in her own milieu. Soon what she practiced became trademarked. It wasn't osteopathy or massage; it was Rolfing—a mythic feat carried out by a charismatic woman.

Through the Human Potential Movement of the mid-1960s Rolf's work flowered and became known to the general public. The success of one of her early pupils in treating the serious heart condition of Fritz Perls, the founder of Gestalt, led to Perls bringing Rolf to Esalen Institute. There she found an eager group of trainees, many of them already advanced in radical psychiatry, genres of manipulation, meditation, and holistic modes of healing. Among these students Rolf became an elder statesperson—at once seer, medicine woman, grandmother, and relentless critic. Although she graduated to the level of a "Human Potential" guru, she was never comfortable with the blending of her work into Gestalt therapy, Reichian analysis, and avant-garde bodywork. She considered herself a Structural Integrationalist, and she did not favor the egalitarian energetics of the counterculture. Toward the end of her life, she viewed Rolfing as a means of sculpting a new humanity according to a perfect Line—hardly a way to pass muster in today's "politically correct" environment.

The depth and humanity of her teaching resonate in her emphasis on "harmonious spiritual consciousness" and attempts to keep her students from trying merely to effect functional cures. The rigidity and provinciality of Rolfing are reflected in its culture-bound notions of movement, body shape, and wholeness, and her failure to accommodate the wide variety of body types and movement styles practiced by non-Western peoples across the planet.

Ida Rolf was trapped in many levels of paradox and contradiction. She suffered the dilemma of teaching a doggedly physical system in the context of holistic conceptions of mind, body, and spirit; yet she had old-fashioned ideas about authority, discipline, and transmission. At times, though, she stepped aside from orthodoxy and flouted her own pure mystery:

> One morning ... Ida Rolf clumped into her living room at Big Sur where about twenty of us were assembled. "Word's going around Esalen that Ida Rolf thinks the body is all there is. Well, I want it known that I think there's more than the body, but the body is all you can get your hands on."[76]

Notes

1. Ilse Middendorf, *The Perceptible Breath: A Breathing Science* (Paderborn, Germany: Junferman-Verlag, 1990), pp. 189–90.

2. Stanley Keleman, *Somatic Reality* (Berkeley, California: Center Press, 1979), pp. 90–91.

3. Don Hanlon Johnson, "The Way of the Flesh: A Brief History of the

Somatics Movement," *Noetic Sciences Review,* No. 29 (Spring 1994), p. 27.

4. Ibid., p. 28.

5. Gerda Alexander, *Eutony: The Holistic Discovery of the Total Person* (Great Neck, New York: Felix Morrow, 1985), p. 26.

6. Bonnie Bainbridge Cohen, letter mailed to members of the somatics community concerning results of a two-day conference entitled "Research in the Field of Somatics," California Institute of Integral Studies, San Francisco, November 1992.

7. Ibid., p. 1.

8. Ibid., pp. 1–2.

9. Ibid., p. 2.

10. Don Hanlon Johnson, quoted in Bainbridge Cohen letter (see note 6 above), p. 4.

11. Stanley Keleman, "Professional Colloquium, October 29, 1977" in Grossinger (ed.), *Ecology and Consciousness: Traditional Wisdom on the Environment* (Berkeley, California: North Atlantic Books, 1992), p. 25.

12. Randy Cherner, remarks during a class, Corte Madera, California, 1990.

13. Nevill Drury, *The Healing Power: A Handbook of Alternative Medicines and Natural Health* (London: Frederick Muller Ltd., 1981), p. 16.

14. Don Hanlon Johnson, *Body, Spirit, and Democracy* (Berkeley, California: North Atlantic Books, 1993), p. 65.

15. Richard Brennan, *The Alexander Technique Workbook* (Rockport, Massachusetts: Element Books, Ltd., 1992), pp. 2–3, 9–11.

16. In these descriptions I received help from Alexander practitioner Jerry Sontag, whom I gratefully acknowledge.

17. Brennan, *The Alexander Technique Workbook,* pp. 3–4.

18. Johnson, *Body, Spirit, and Democracy,* pp. 65–66.

19. F. Matthias Alexander, quoted in Brennan, *The Alexander Technique Workbook,* p. 12.

20. Drury, *The Healing Power,* pp. 16–17.

21. Jerry Sontag, notes on *Planet Medicine,* 1994.

22. Brennan, *The Alexander Technique Workbook,* p. 67.

23. Ilana Rubenfeld, "Alexander: The Use of the Self," in Leslie J. Kaslof (editor), *Wholistic Dimensions in Healing: A Resource Guide* (New York: Doubleday & Company, Inc., 1978), p. 223.

24. Ibid.

25. Ibid.

26. Mia Segal, interview in *Somatics* (Autumn/Winter 1985–86), p. 10.

27. Jerry Sontag, personal communication, 1994.

28. Quote supplied by Jerry Sontag.

29. Quoted in Rubenfeld, "Alexander: The Use of the Self," p. 224.

30. Charles Olson, *The Maximus Poems* (originally 1950) (Berkeley: University of California Press, 1979), pp. 64–65.

31. The section on the Bates Method has been developed through discussions with Thomas R. Quackenbush, founder and director of the Natural Vision Center of San Francisco.

32. William H. Bates, quoted by Thomas R. Quackenbush, personal communication, Berkeley, California, 1995.

33. Ibid.

34. Quackenbush, personal communication, Berkeley, California, 1995.

35. William Bates, quoted by Quackenbush.

36. Gerda Alexander, *Eutony,* p. 8.

37. Ibid., p. 168.

38. Ibid., p. 54.

39. Ibid., p. 148.

40. Quoted in Gerda Alexander, *Eutony,* p. 149.

41. Gerda Alexander, *Eutony,* p. 169.

42. Dennis Leri, "Learning How to Learn," unpublished draft used as the basis for a variety of published articles.

43. Ibid.

44. Jack Heggie, personal communication, 1994.

45. Bruce Kumar Frantzis, *The Tao in Action: The Personal Practice of the I Ching and Taoism in Daily Life,* unpublished manuscript (tentatively North Atlantic Books, 1996).

46. Robert Spencer, personal communication, 1994.

47. Quoted in Leri, "Learning How to Learn."

48. Leri, "Learning How to Learn."

49. Ibid.

50. Ibid.

51. Elizabeth Beringer assisted me by writing notes on this section and a critique of my earlier version which I have drawn upon for the current version.

52. Leri, "Learning How to Learn."

53. Moshe Feldenkrais, quoted in Mark Reese, "Moshe Feldenkrais' Verbal Approach to Somatic Education: Parallels to Milton Erickson's Use of Language," in *Somatics* (Autumn/Winter 1985–86), p. 27.

54. Leri, "Learning How to Learn."

55. Moshe Feldenkrais, quoted in William S. Leigh, *Bodytherapy* (Coquitlam, British Columbia: Water Margin Press, 1989), p. 56.

56. Moshe Feldenkrais, *The Potent Self: A Guide to Spontaneity* (New York: Harper and Row, 1985), p. 130.

57. Ibid., pp. 3–4.

58. Ibid., p. 4.

59. Ibid., p. 28.

60. Quoted in Leri, "Learning How to Learn."

61. Leri, "Learning How to Learn."

62. Leigh, *Bodytherapy,* p. 56.

63. Moshe Feldenkrais, quoted in Reese, "Moshe Feldenkrais' Verbal Approach to Somatic Education," p. 28.

64. Moshe Feldenkrais, quoted in Leigh, *Bodytherapy,* pp. 54–55.

65. Moshe Feldenkrais, *The Case of Nora: Body Awareness as Healing Therapy* (originally 1977) (Berkeley, California: Frog, Ltd., 1993), p. 64.

66. Johnson, *Body, Spirit, and Democracy,* pp. 81–82.

67. Michael Salveson, personal communication, Berkeley, California, 1974.

68. Ida Rolf, *Ida Rolf Talks About Rolfing and Physical Reality* (New York: Harper & Row, 1978), p. 70.

69. Jeffrey Maitland, *Spacious Body: Explorations in Somatic Ontology,* unpublished manuscript at time of publication (Berkeley, California: North Atlantic Books, 1995).

70. Moshe Feldenkrais, quoted in Leigh, *Bodytherapy,* p. 23.

71. Maitland, *Spacious Body.*

72. Ida Rolf, quoted in Johnson, *Body, Spirit, and Democracy,* p. 84.

73. Johnson, *Body, Spirit, and Democracy,* p. 85.

74. Leigh, *Bodytherapy,* pp. 9–10.

75. Johnson, *Body, Spirit, and Democracy,* p. 87.

76. Don Hanlon Johnson, *The Protean Body* (New York: Harper and Row, 1977), p. 140.

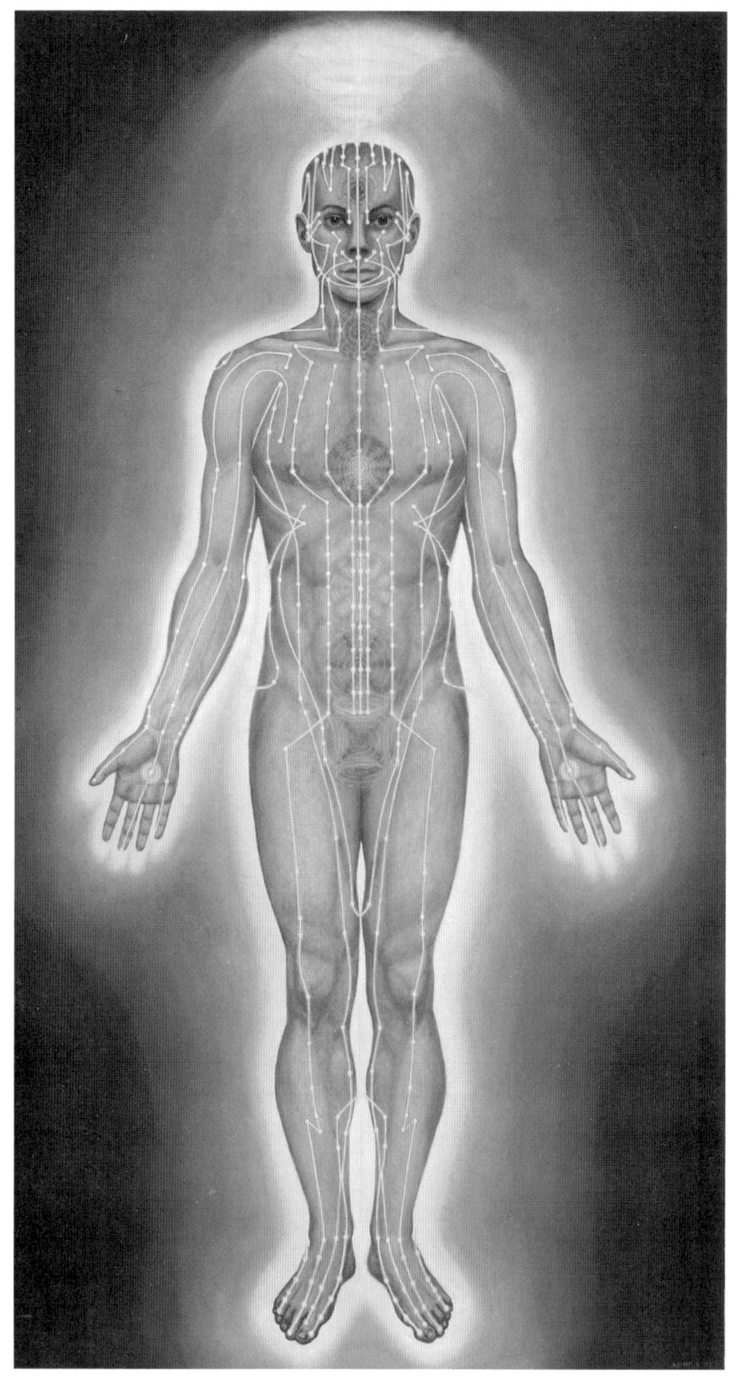

CHAPTER FIVE

Elemental and Eurasian Systems

Somatics from Outside the Euroamerican Orbit

The majority of somatic systems on the Earth are lay manipulative and energetic crafts and did not develop in a scientific framework or the professional context of osteopathy, Eutony, Feldenkrais, Rolfing, etc. We have discussed a number of these throughout both volumes of this book, so the goal of the present chapter is not to repeat this chronicle but to examine in depth a few particular non-Western systems that have been integrated into the Euroamerican bodywork nexus. However, initially I will provide a map for locating these geographically and ontologically diverse practices in the context of one another and of the general paradigms offered thus far in this book.

The first group of Eurasian systems is a generally nonsystematic complex of hands-on techniques practiced historically in peasant and tribal communities. These include the stamping, trampling, and natural mechanical methods described in the two sections on "Mechanical Ethnomedicine" in Volume One, Chapter Five and in the section on "Osteopathy" in Chapter Three. In the present chapter I include a portrait of one such tradition which has made it into the West in a refined and altered form—Breema. Although Breema also has components of yoga and energetic touch, its basis is a mechanical application of the fundamental aspects of human anatomy and movement.

The second group of Eurasian systems is composed of energetic medicines arising from either Taoism or Ayurveda. The somatic component of these medicines is based on accessing *chi* or *prana* and using it for healing. The *chi* is generated internally in the practitioner and transmitted in a disciplined manner to the recipient (this rigor makes such systems quite different from spirit and faith healing). People can also learn to self-heal through cultivating and applying energy internally to their own bodies and emotional fields. Energetic medicines in this category all train the mind as the source emanating healing power and directing it into the body.

Chi Gung, described in Volume One, Chapter Nine, is the primary such system I will cover here. All the Taoist martial arts (plus likely *aikido* as well) arose either directly or indirectly from *Nei Gung*. These forms are covered in detail in the sections on "Internal Martial Arts" in Volume One, Chapter Nine, and "Martial Medicines" in Chapter Two. They provide crucial features of the contemporary somatic landscape. Even a system as divergent from basic martial arts themes as the Feldenkrais Method arose in part from their influence.

All the bodywork systems depicted in this chapter share some features of energetic medicine. However, I have selected only *Chi Gung Tui Na* as an example of pure empirical energetic somatics.

The third set of traditions originates in the elemental aspects of Indian, Tibetan, East Asian, and Southeast Asian sciences. It includes the somatic components of Ayurveda and Tibetan medicine, as well as the explicitly elemental levels of Chinese somatics, particularly acupuncture, all described in Volume One, Chapter Nine. It also comprises the Oriental massage and "pressure point" techniques described in the section on "Bodywork" in Volume One, Chapter Twelve. In this chapter I am presenting Polarity Therapy as the most pure contemporary application of elemental medicine. However, we should not forget that Polarity is also a spiritual medicine with modalities of deep-tissue work resembling bioenergetic methods of touch.

The fourth non-Western modality is that of pure mind-body-spirit exercises. The epitome of this group is meditation which, though seem-

ingly an event occurring in the mind, is actually a form of the strictest bodywork and the most sublime transmission of somatic impulses internally (see "Buddhism" in Volume One, Chapter Twelve, and "Meditation" in Chapter Eight). The bowing aspects of meditation alone make up a quite complex system of somatic practice resembling *Chi Gung*. The Tibetan exercise system *Kum Nye* is a similar mixture of aerobic exercises and prayers.

Yoga is another system of exercise cultivated simultaneously for health and spiritual development. Its postures clearly involve not only stretching of muscles but focused intention. Like *Chi Gung*, yoga works from the outside into the viscera and bones.

I have not explored bowing, yoga, and *Kum Nye* in depth in this book insofar as I have emphasized medical dyads and energy systems over exercises for health. However, basic nonsectarian aspects of all three of these modalities are utilized in both Breema and *Chi Gung* and provide a template of training for many other therapeutic methods as well.

Ultimately, strict divisions are not useful because of the large amount of overlap among somatic systems in terms of both techniques arrived at independently in different traditions and the contemporary integration of all of these modalities and their separate epistemologies. The main point of this map is to clarify that specific principles and techniques arose in discrete cultural and historical circumstances and took on particular meanings from those circumstances. Those meanings continue to be applied as subtexts within the somatic framework.

Polarity Therapy

POLARITY THERAPY IS classified under somatic systems, but its originator, osteopath and chiropractor Randolph Stone, intended it as a union of holistic health, diet, exercise, massage, and spiritual practice. Healing and health, he proposed, are the outcome of energy flowing unrestrictedly—while disease is solely a reflection of energy impeded. The cells of the body are viewed as a sentient microcosm of

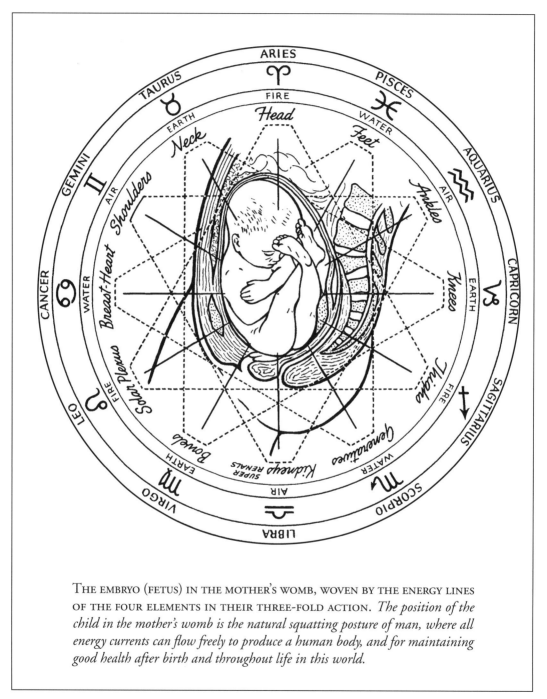

The embryo (fetus) in the mother's womb, woven by the energy lines of the four elements in their three-fold action. *The position of the child in the mother's womb is the natural squatting posture of man, where all energy currents can flow freely to produce a human body, and for maintaining good health after birth and throughout life in this world.*

Illustration from Polarity Therapy *by Dr. Randolph Stone, CRCS Publications, Sebastopol, California, 1987*

the unfathomably deep spirit that permeates the universe. This spirit is present everywhere. We do not need to alter anything about ourselves in order to be expressions of it. Our very awareness—our extensions of tenderness, the sheer delicacy of our sentience, the longing and exquisite beauty in all our acts—is spirit flowing into matter, emanating anew among the polar fields of incarnation.

When our cells are free to resonate with their cosmic source, they express their intrinsic nature and heal automatically. When tension, resistance, and fear impede their vibrations, they lose a degree of their attunement with the Oversoul and fall under the influence of negative and unconscious forces. These influences germinate as diseases of body, mind, and emotions. Yet spirit is ever present, rushing along the cutting edge of our beings (which is also the cutting edge of the universe itself). Pathologies are little more than fixations of past threats, which melt immediately upon one's opening to a cosmic destiny.

Not only can the universe get stuck, apparently we are the very nodes where this happens. When we cease to be present with our cosmic body, when consciousness threatens us, creative evolution around us is interrupted.

Polarity Therapy, in its simplest definition, is the intention of a skilled practitioner to provide a safe, sacred space in which the cells and intelligence of a sick person can regain their natural attunement with spirit and the universe at large. When balanced (polar), they are capable of healing everything at the deepest level. The techniques of Polarity are intended solely to release energy blocks and attract consciousness back to the growth of the individual. They are prayers as much as they are palpations. Their real agenda is to effect a realignment (through the individual) of the harmonic fields of cosmic evolution itself.

Since Polarity has so many separate branches, it is often confused with Ayurveda, Reiki, Zero Balancing, *shiatsu,* Breema, and even macrobiotics—systems which differ significantly from one another. What distinguishes Polarity is not so much its individual remedies and techniques as the implementation of these according to Stone's cosmology. He saw

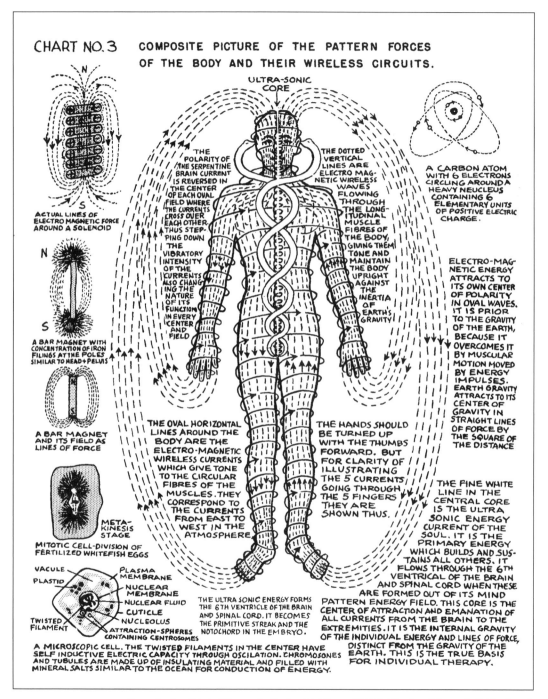

CHART NO. 3 COMPOSITE PICTURE OF THE PATTERN FORCES OF THE BODY AND THEIR WIRELESS CIRCUITS.

N

S

ACTUAL LINES OF ELECTRO MAGNETIC FORCE AROUND A SOLENOID

N

S

A BAR MAGNET WITH CONCENTRATION OF IRON FILINGS AT THE POLES SIMILAR TO HEAD + PELVIS

A BAR MAGNET AND ITS FIELD AS LINES OF FORCE

META-KINESIS STAGE

MITOTIC CELL-DIVISION OF FERTILIZED WHITEFISH EGGS

VACULE

PLASTID

PLASMA MEMBRANE

NUCLEAR MEMBRANE

NUCLEAR FLUID

CUTICLE

NUCLEOLUS

TWISTED FILAMENT

ATTRACTION-SPHERES CONTAINING CENTROSOMES

A MICROSCOPIC CELL. THE TWISTED FILAMENTS IN THE CENTER HAVE SELF INDUCTIVE ELECTRIC CAPACITY THROUGH OSCILATION. CHROMOSONES AND TUBULES ARE MADE UP OF INSULATING MATERIAL AND FILLED WITH MINERAL SALTS SIMILAR TO THE OCEAN FOR CONDUCTION OF ENERGY.

ULTRA-SONIC CORE

THE POLARITY OF THE SERPENTINE BRAIN CURRENT IS REVERSED IN THE CENTER OF EACH OVAL FIELD WHERE THE CURRENTS CROSS OVER EACH OTHER. THUS STEPPING DOWN THE VIBRATORY INTENSITY OF THE CURRENTS ALSO CHANGING THE NATURE OF ITS FUNCTION IN EVERY CENTER AND FIELD

THE DOTTED VERTICAL LINES ARE ELECTRO MAGNETIC WIRELESS WAVES FLOWING THROUGH THE LONGITUDINAL MUSCLE FIBRES OF THE BODY, GIVING THEM TONE AND MAINTAIN THE BODY UPRIGHT AGAINST THE INERTIA OF EARTH'S GRAVITY

A CARBON ATOM WITH 6 ELECTRONS CIRCLING AROUND A HEAVY NEUCLEUS CONTAINING 6 ELEMENTARY UNITS OF POSITIVE ELECTRIC CHARGE.

ELECTRO-MAGNETIC ENERGY ATTRACTS TO ITS OWN CENTER OF POLARITY IN OVAL WAVES. IT IS PRIOR TO THE GRAVITY OF THE EARTH, BECAUSE IT OVERCOMES IT BY MUSCULAR MOTION MOVED BY ENERGY IMPULSES. EARTH GRAVITY ATTRACTS TO ITS CENTER OF GRAVITY IN STRAIGHT LINES OF FORCE BY THE SQUARE OF THE DISTANCE

THE OVAL HORIZONTAL LINES AROUND THE BODY ARE THE ELECTRO-MAGNETIC WIRELESS CURRENTS WHICH GIVE TONE TO THE CIRCULAR FIBRES OF THE MUSCLES. THEY CORRESPOND TO THE CURRENTS FROM EAST TO WEST IN THE ATMOSPHERE

THE HANDS SHOULD BE TURNED UP WITH THE THUMBS FORWARD. BUT FOR CLARITY OF ILLUSTRATING THE 5 CURRENTS GOING THROUGH THE 5 FINGERS THEY ARE SHOWN THUS.

THE FINE WHITE LINE IN THE CENTRAL CORE IS THE ULTRA SONIC ENERGY CURRENT OF THE SOUL. IT IS THE PRIMARY ENERGY WHICH BUILDS AND SUSTAINS ALL OTHERS. IT FLOWS THROUGH THE 6TH VENTRICAL OF THE BRAIN AND SPINAL CORD WHEN THESE ARE FORMED OUT OF ITS MIND PATTERN ENERGY FIELD. THIS CORE IS THE CENTER OF ATTRACTION AND EMANATION OF ALL CURRENTS FROM THE BRAIN TO THE EXTREMITIES. IT IS THE INTERNAL GRAVITY OF THE INDIVIDUAL ENERGY AND LINES OF FORCE, DISTINCT FROM THE GRAVITY OF THE EARTH. THIS IS THE TRUE BASIS FOR INDIVIDUAL THERAPY.

THE ULTRA SONIC ENERGY FORMS THE 6TH VENTRICLE OF THE BRAIN AND SPINAL CORD. IT BECOMES THE PRIMITIVE STREAK AND THE NOTOCHORD IN THE EMBRYO.

Illustration from Polarity Therapy *by Dr. Randolph Stone, CRCS Publications, Sebastopol, California, 1987*

human beings as the embodiment of an ocean of Eternal Spirit. All wounds are cosmic wounds to be healed through spiritual activity and compassion. All injuries and diseases are challenges to an expanding, evolving universe which requires gaps and resistances in order to grow. All healing is healing of the spirit, and the methods used to attain it are merely diverse reifications of cosmic polar fields.

The Polarity bodyworker regards the organism always from a karmic and energetic point of view—as an expression of evolutionary forces manifesting through organ systems. In the form of a cosmic rotating field (like that described in Volume One, Chapter Nine, under "Esoteric Anatomy"), these forces incarnate simultaneously in creature bodies and the planets of the solar system. Their activity has as its goal bringing the materializing universe into harmony with the transdimensional *Sattvic* universe.

A three-part creationary force differentiates as five elements (Ether, Air, Fire, Water, and Earth) which fuse in the physical realm to incubate each human being. Their electromagnetic spirals thread together equally in the yarn of molecules and at the pitch of waves as well as in all medial domains. The two poles (matter and energy) yield a creature at once dense and airy, wired and wireless. In more technical language, each of us is an "etheric energy body . . . created by wave circuits [and describing] a spatially oriented triaxial set of polarity relationships."[1] From this eddy of primordial particles and secondary geometric currents emerge *chakras,* personality states, "and lifestyle habits as well as the fluids and tissues of the coarse metabolic body."[2]

The Polarity therapist is literally a physician of the sacred anatomy (i.e., polarity grid) of the body. Insofar as all Stone's remedies and methods are based on this cosmology, they share more with Reiki and astrology than with osteopathy. Their goal is not so much to adjust or treat the body/mind as to awaken the inner being by balancing its confused (or cross-circuited) polar energies—awaken us, that is, to the psychospiritual journey on which we have embarked by being born.

Like Paracelsus, Stone traveled widely, especially in Asia, collecting useful pieces of a variety of indigenous systems. He synthesized aspects of *chakra* and *tridosha* theory, Ayurvedic dietary practices, palpation with reference to acupuncture points, cranial osteopathy, native American herbal remedies, shamanic rituals, alchemical medicine, *shiatsu,* Reichian bodywork, massage, chiropractic, and other not so familiar therapeutic methods. While the "polarity model" was developed for *pranic,* spiritual work, Stone was eminently secular and pragmatic. He prescribed herbal tea blends, sprouted seeds as miracle foods, heavy dry chewing and insalivation, liver flushes, a light breakfast following the repair of mucous linings during sleep, then a large lunch.

Polarity massage techniques are anatomically rigorous and function not as pure faith healing but deep *shiatsu*-like touch in the context of breathing lessons and visualization. Stone's exercise regimens included a variety of squats, hunkering-downs, and hanging off edges, all gently and gradually enacted.[3] In this respect Polarity far more resembles Rolfing than it does any form of spiritual healing. Highly specified grids of release points and organ cleansing channels have in effect translated Stone's curriculum into a nondenominational grammar for the spiritual practice of *all* systems of transpersonal and somatic psychology. That is, by using Polar energetic theory and his or her own palpation or counselling modality, a therapist adjusts and cleanses the body/mind along physical and mental parameters within a cosmic Etheric context.

During the mid 1970s the founders of a very physically based bodywork system at Lomi School were so inspired by Stone's practice they brought him to California to teach his techniques, many of which were later integrated into the Lomi repertoire. In the 1990s the Polarity model is becoming newly merged with osteopathy, Breema, and other methods to produce "a middle-range theory and effective empirical technique . . . linking body, mind, and spirit."[4]

Polarity may be summarized more simply as a formal method for balancing organs and freeing energy channels. Calibers of balance

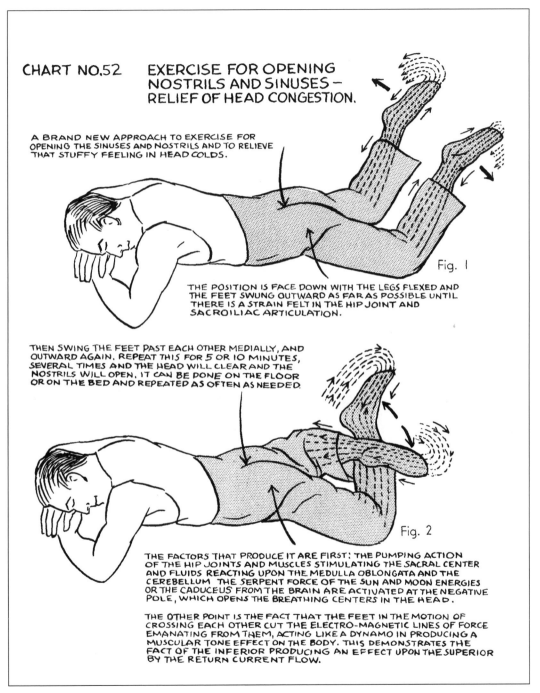

CHART NO.52 EXERCISE FOR OPENING NOSTRILS AND SINUSES – RELIEF OF HEAD CONGESTION.

A BRAND NEW APPROACH TO EXERCISE FOR OPENING THE SINUSES AND NOSTRILS AND TO RELIEVE THAT STUFFY FEELING IN HEAD COLDS.

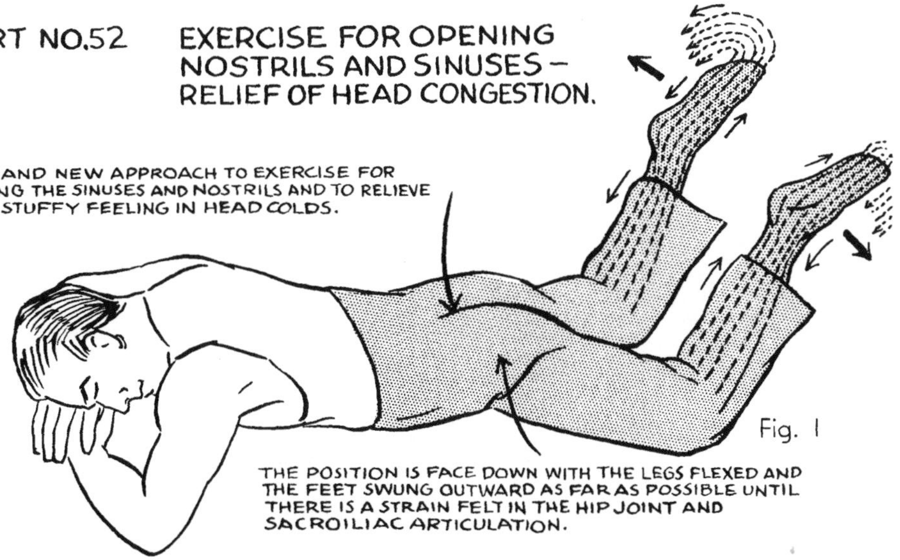

Fig. 1

THE POSITION IS FACE DOWN WITH THE LEGS FLEXED AND THE FEET SWUNG OUTWARD AS FAR AS POSSIBLE UNTIL THERE IS A STRAIN FELT IN THE HIP JOINT AND SACROILIAC ARTICULATION.

THEN SWING THE FEET PAST EACH OTHER MEDIALLY, AND OUTWARD AGAIN. REPEAT THIS FOR 5 OR 10 MINUTES, SEVERAL TIMES AND THE HEAD WILL CLEAR AND THE NOSTRILS WILL OPEN. IT CAN BE DONE ON THE FLOOR OR ON THE BED AND REPEATED AS OFTEN AS NEEDED.

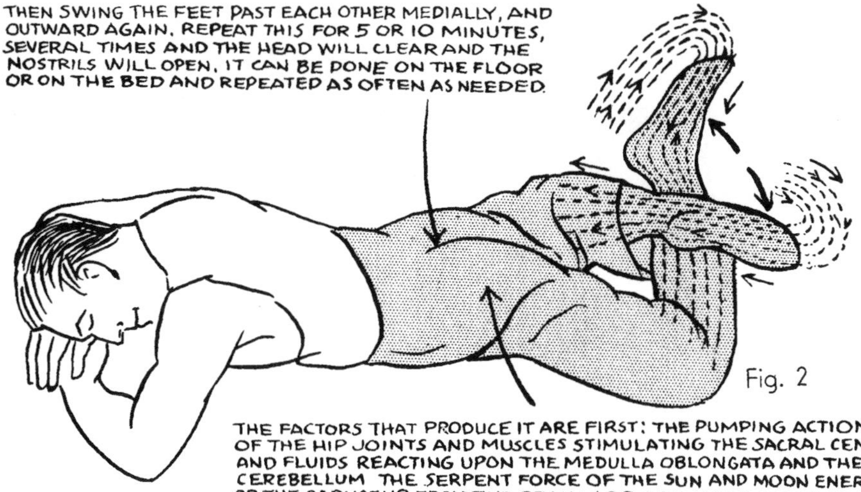

Fig. 2

THE FACTORS THAT PRODUCE IT ARE FIRST: THE PUMPING ACTION OF THE HIP JOINTS AND MUSCLES STIMULATING THE SACRAL CENTER AND FLUIDS REACTING UPON THE MEDULLA OBLONGATA AND THE CEREBELLUM THE SERPENT FORCE OF THE SUN AND MOON ENERGIES OR THE CADUCEUS FROM THE BRAIN ARE ACTIVATED AT THE NEGATIVE POLE, WHICH OPENS THE BREATHING CENTERS IN THE HEAD.

THE OTHER POINT IS THE FACT THAT THE FEET IN THE MOTION OF CROSSING EACH OTHER CUT THE ELECTRO-MAGNETIC LINES OF FORCE EMANATING FROM THEM, ACTING LIKE A DYNAMO IN PRODUCING A MUSCULAR TONE EFFECT ON THE BODY. THIS DEMONSTRATES THE FACT OF THE INFERIOR PRODUCING AN EFFECT UPON THE SUPERIOR BY THE RETURN CURRENT FLOW.

Illustration from Polarity Therapy *by Dr. Randolph Stone, CRCS Publications, Sebastopol, California, 1987*

EVOLUTIONARY ENERGY SERIES

EVOLUTIONARY MIND ENERGY FLOWS FROM THE MIND PRINCIPLE OVER THE BRAIN AND THE NERVOUS SYSTEM AS PRIMARY ENERGY WAVES. SECOND, AS CONDUCTED IMPULSES OVER INSULATED NERVES LIKE WIRES FOR ALL SPECIFIC PHYSIOLOGICAL FUNCTION. THIS SERIES OF EVOLUTIONARY ENERGY CHARTS SHOW MIND AND LIFE IMPULSES FLOWING OVER THE BODY LIKE WAVES. THEY LOOK LIKE A WHEEL WITHIN A WHEEL ALMOST AS THE PROPHET EZEKIEL SAW THEM WITH LIFE ENTHRONED IN THE CENTER. THE FIERY LIFE CENTER IN THE UMBILICUS LINKS THE ENERGIES INTO PHYSICAL LIFE THROUGH THE UMBILICAL CORD FROM THE MOTHER INTO THE EMBRYO. IT IS THIS CYCLE OF NOURISHMENT AND ENERGY WHICH BUILT THE EMBRYO IN A PERFECT NEUTRAL POSITION IN THE WOMB. WHEN THE CORD IS CUT, THE BABY IS AN INDIVIDUAL AND FUNCTIONS ON THE PERPETUATION OF THIS ENERGY CYCLE BY TAKING NOURISHMENT DIRECT. THIS PRIMARY VITAL IMPULSE IS THE MOST IMPORTANT FIERY ELEMENT IN OUR LIFE FOR DIGESTION OF FOOD, ASSIMILATION, ELIMINATION AND OXIDATION. THESE ARE THE HEALING REPAIRING AND BUILDING FACULTIES IN OUR BODIES. THEY ARE UTILIZED AS A THERAPY TO KEEP THIS VITAL ENERGY FLOWING WHEN OBSTRUCTED IN ILLNESS AND BY DISEASE. IT IS TRULY A VITAL APPROACH TO RELEASE VITAL FORCES PRIOR TO CHEMISTRY AND MECHANICS.

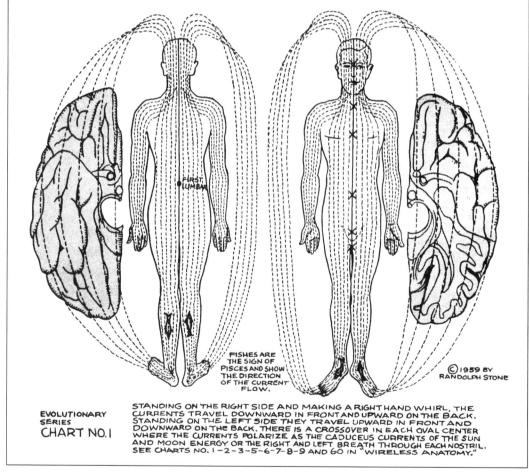

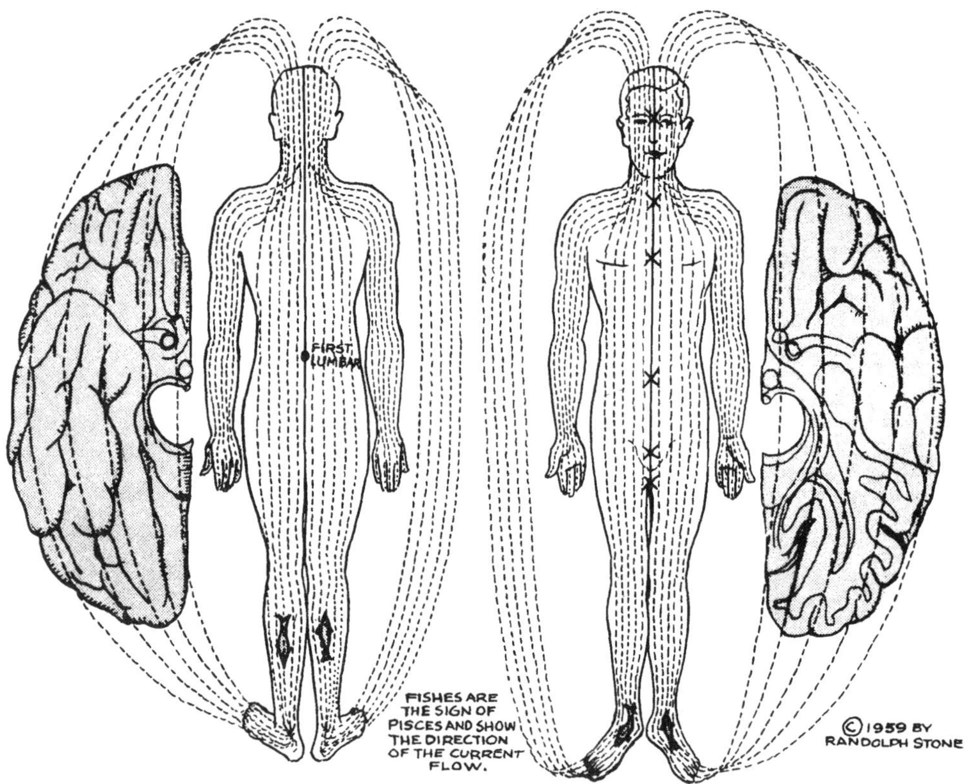
FIRST LUMBAR
FISHES ARE THE SIGN OF PISCES AND SHOW THE DIRECTION OF THE CURRENT FLOW.
©1959 BY RANDOLPH STONE

EVOLUTIONARY SERIES
CHART NO. 1

STANDING ON THE RIGHT SIDE AND MAKING A RIGHT HAND WHIRL, THE CURRENTS TRAVEL DOWNWARD IN FRONT AND UPWARD ON THE BACK. STANDING ON THE LEFT SIDE THEY TRAVEL UPWARD IN FRONT AND DOWNWARD ON THE BACK. THERE IS A CROSSOVER IN EACH OVAL CENTER WHERE THE CURRENTS POLARIZE AS THE CADUCEUS CURRENTS OF THE SUN AND MOON ENERGY OR THE RIGHT AND LEFT BREATH THROUGH EACH NOSTRIL. SEE CHARTS NO. 1-2-3-5-6-7-8-9 AND 60 IN "WIRELESS ANATOMY."

Illustration from Polarity Therapy *by Dr. Randolph Stone, CRCS Publications, Sebastopol, California, 1987*

and measures of energy come from models of the expression of five elements in an electromagnetic field. Within this lodestar, positive (expansive) and negative (contracting) vibrations interact without ever quite achieving neutral (balanced) being. While the therapist may massage and adjust individual tissues and test anatomical relationships for asymmetry, axes of pivot, and "gravity of the ultrasonic core," the organizing principle of his work is to balance phases of energy. He conducts currents and emotions from an unchanging neutral source into a positive field of manifestation and then back to the source in a negative eliminating cycle.

Insofar as the body's electromagnetic dissonances must be equalized, the hands of the therapist function not only as direct modulators of energy but living polar nodes with a phase dynamic between them. Their paramagnetic field is applied to knots of tension, blockages, and misalignments—all to facilitate the flow of energy.

As the locus of neutral being, Mind is a natural transmitter of healing energy throughout the body. It is never permanently stuck in the dilemmas and repetitive problems of existence but has the capacity to see through the great Elemental play and go to the heart of the matter. Thus, the Polarity therapist appeals to the Mind of his client at all times. Stone repeats this formula in slightly different versions throughout his writings:

> Mind Energy is the finest form of matter.... In the human body Mind Energy flows over the brain and the nervous system and becomes animated Intelligence, Feeling, Perception, Consciousness; the root of all senses and the awareness of all sensations in and through the form of matter.... Soul is Consciousness; "Prana" is Life; Mind Energy is a neuter meeting ground between soul and matter.[5]

> The mental body as the neuter pole of action can affect the whole from any standpoint because it is the center core of all neuter fields and forces in the body and in nature. Even as the mental body blends with the physical in every cell of being, function and structure, so does the mental body, as the finest essence and phase of matter, penetrate

> every tissue cell of the entire body, in normal health.... Every tissue cell has a mind, as a diffused particle of the central mind.[6]

> All conditions and limitations are produced by mind essence and substance.... [P]leasure and pain, health and sickness, etc., are formed by *our own thought patterns* of harmony, limitations or discord.[7] [original italics]

Stone drew heavily on Oriental medicines for his attribution of seasonal and diurnal cycles to the phases of disease and health, stress and relaxation, despair and elation, ego death and spiritual rebirth. Polarity Therapy, in that context, is not meant to "cure" anything but to bolster the organism in its passage through inevitable manifestations. Disease is primarily a stage in which one rests and gathers energies for the next transformation the universe requires.

Each organ system propagates its idiosyncratic mode of "thought pattern" ailments. These are specified not by happenstance germs or misfortunes but by susceptibility based on that organ's cosmic relationship to an individual's journey along the karmic path. Even a sprain or wound occurs in tissue which needs work; otherwise, it would be supple enough to avoid injury. Accidents are viewed symbolically as ways to protect the core being from evolutionary demands for which the ego is not yet ready. When a particular set of needs confronts an individual (such as diminished capacity to feel, incomplete autonomy, frustrated self-expression, etc.), illnesses develop in areas of the body or organ resonant with each need's corresponding aspect of cosmic energy. Thus, body posture, fluidity, sickness, and health are the direct results of openness or resistance to a transcendental process which, in the end, is evolutionary and growth oriented.

In an echo of other classic somatic systems, Polarity views dysfunction as the result of "a myriad of confused, contradictory, and ineffectual impulses to the musculature."[8] Like deep-tissue work, it intercedes directly in the fascial network. Like cranial osteopathy, it energizes and releases traumas which have become encysted in the body.

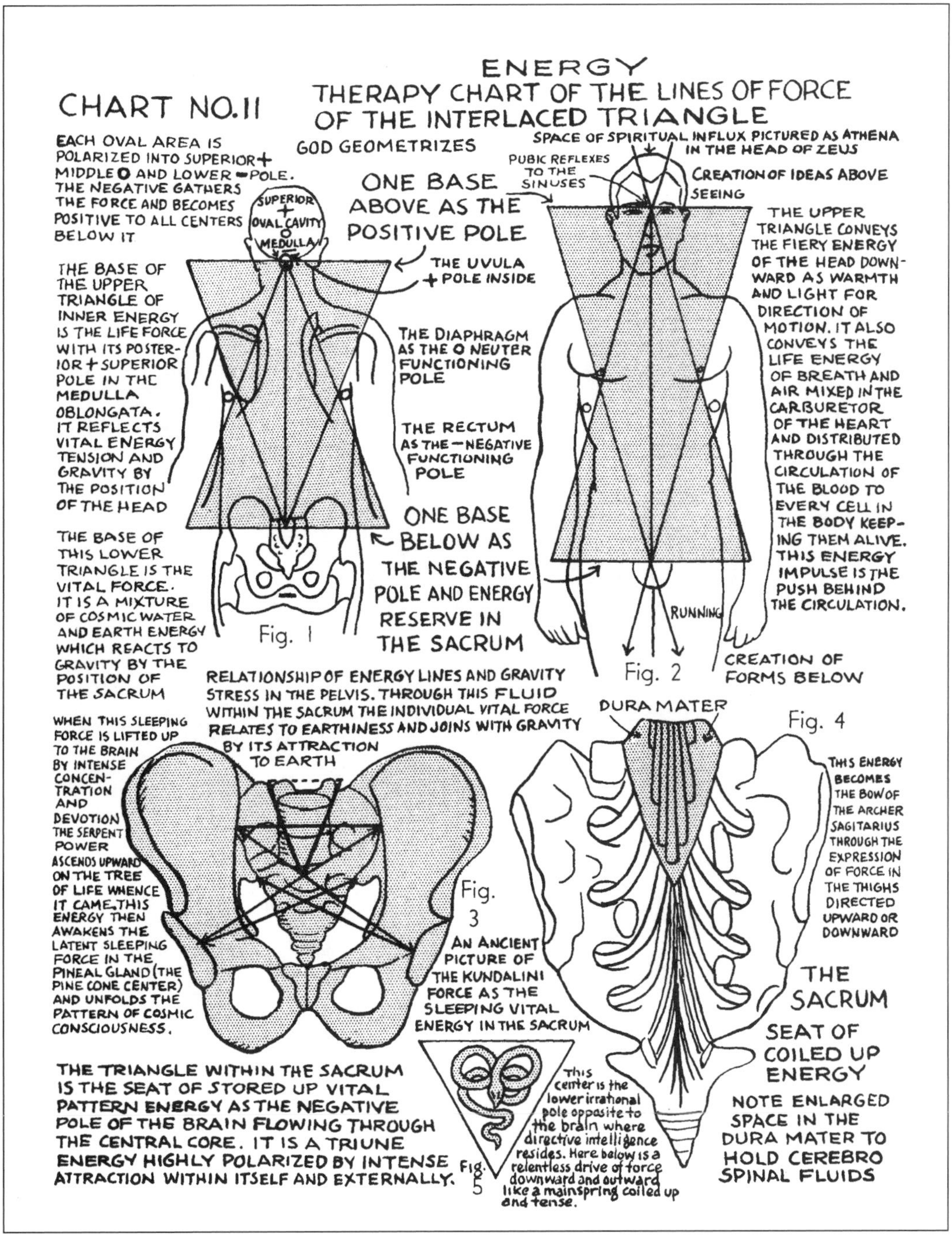

ENERGY
THERAPY CHART OF THE LINES OF FORCE
OF THE INTERLACED TRIANGLE
CHART NO. II
EACH OVAL AREA IS POLARIZED INTO SUPERIOR + MIDDLE O AND LOWER − POLE. THE NEGATIVE GATHERS THE FORCE AND BECOMES POSITIVE TO ALL CENTERS BELOW IT
GOD GEOMETRIZES
SUPERIOR + OVAL CAVITY O MEDULLA −
ONE BASE ABOVE AS THE POSITIVE POLE
THE UVULA + POLE INSIDE
THE BASE OF THE UPPER TRIANGLE OF INNER ENERGY IS THE LIFE FORCE WITH ITS POSTERIOR + SUPERIOR POLE IN THE MEDULLA OBLONGATA. IT REFLECTS VITAL ENERGY TENSION AND GRAVITY BY THE POSITION OF THE HEAD
THE DIAPHRAGM AS THE O NEUTER FUNCTIONING POLE
THE RECTUM AS THE − NEGATIVE FUNCTIONING POLE
ONE BASE BELOW AS THE NEGATIVE POLE AND ENERGY RESERVE IN THE SACRUM
THE BASE OF THIS LOWER TRIANGLE IS THE VITAL FORCE. IT IS A MIXTURE OF COSMIC WATER AND EARTH ENERGY WHICH REACTS TO GRAVITY BY THE POSITION OF THE SACRUM
Fig. 1
SPACE OF SPIRITUAL INFLUX PICTURED AS ATHENA IN THE HEAD OF ZEUS
PUBIC REFLEXES TO THE SINUSES
CREATION OF IDEAS ABOVE SEEING
THE UPPER TRIANGLE CONVEYS THE FIERY ENERGY OF THE HEAD DOWNWARD AS WARMTH AND LIGHT FOR DIRECTION OF MOTION. IT ALSO CONVEYS THE LIFE ENERGY OF BREATH AND AIR MIXED IN THE CARBURETOR OF THE HEART AND DISTRIBUTED THROUGH THE CIRCULATION OF THE BLOOD TO EVERY CELL IN THE BODY KEEPING THEM ALIVE. THIS ENERGY IMPULSE IS THE PUSH BEHIND THE CIRCULATION.
RUNNING
Fig. 2
CREATION OF FORMS BELOW
RELATIONSHIP OF ENERGY LINES AND GRAVITY STRESS IN THE PELVIS. THROUGH THIS FLUID WITHIN THE SACRUM THE INDIVIDUAL VITAL FORCE RELATES TO EARTHINESS AND JOINS WITH GRAVITY BY ITS ATTRACTION TO EARTH
WHEN THIS SLEEPING FORCE IS LIFTED UP TO THE BRAIN BY INTENSE CONCENTRATION AND DEVOTION THE SERPENT POWER ASCENDS UPWARD ON THE TREE OF LIFE WHENCE IT CAME. THIS ENERGY THEN AWAKENS THE LATENT SLEEPING FORCE IN THE PINEAL GLAND (THE PINE CONE CENTER) AND UNFOLDS THE PATTERN OF COSMIC CONSCIOUSNESS.
Fig. 3
AN ANCIENT PICTURE OF THE KUNDALINI FORCE AS THE SLEEPING VITAL ENERGY IN THE SACRUM
DURA MATER
Fig. 4
THIS ENERGY BECOMES THE BOW OF THE ARCHER SAGITARIUS THROUGH THE EXPRESSION OF FORCE IN THE THIGHS DIRECTED UPWARD OR DOWNWARD
THE SACRUM
SEAT OF COILED UP ENERGY
NOTE ENLARGED SPACE IN THE DURA MATER TO HOLD CEREBRO SPINAL FLUIDS
THE TRIANGLE WITHIN THE SACRUM IS THE SEAT OF STORED UP VITAL PATTERN ENERGY AS THE NEGATIVE POLE OF THE BRAIN FLOWING THROUGH THE CENTRAL CORE. IT IS A TRIUNE ENERGY HIGHLY POLARIZED BY INTENSE ATTRACTION WITHIN ITSELF AND EXTERNALLY.
Fig. 5
This center is the lower irrational pole opposite to the brain where directive intelligence resides. Here below is a relentless drive of force downward and outward like a mainspring coiled up and tense.

Illustration from Polarity Therapy *by Dr. Randolph Stone, CRCS Publications, Sebastopol, California, 1987*

CHART NO. 13. FIG. 1. RELEASE OF PATTERN ENERGY BLOCKS IN THE CEREBRO-SPINAL FLUID.
FIG. 2. STRUCTURAL BIPOLAR RELEASE OF RESPIRATORY MUSCLES.

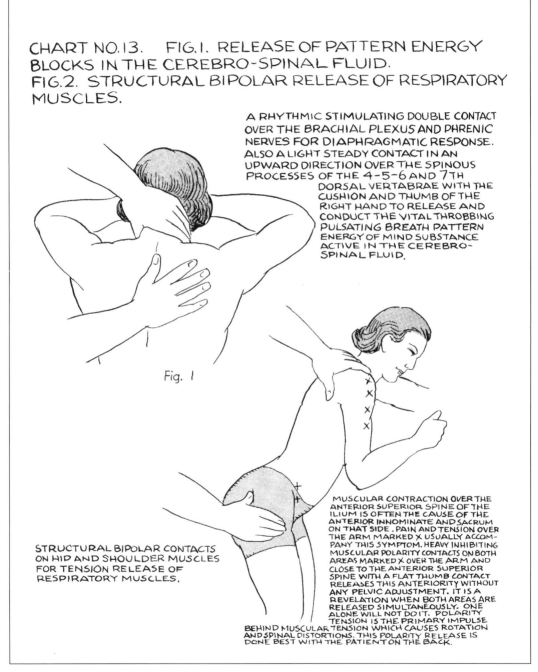

A RHYTHMIC STIMULATING DOUBLE CONTACT OVER THE BRACHIAL PLEXUS AND PHRENIC NERVES FOR DIAPHRAGMATIC RESPONSE. ALSO A LIGHT STEADY CONTACT IN AN UPWARD DIRECTION OVER THE SPINOUS PROCESSES OF THE 4-5-6 AND 7TH DORSAL VERTABRAE WITH THE CUSHION AND THUMB OF THE RIGHT HAND TO RELEASE AND CONDUCT THE VITAL THROBBING PULSATING BREATH PATTERN ENERGY OF MIND SUBSTANCE ACTIVE IN THE CEREBRO-SPINAL FLUID.

Fig. 1

STRUCTURAL BIPOLAR CONTACTS ON HIP AND SHOULDER MUSCLES FOR TENSION RELEASE OF RESPIRATORY MUSCLES.

MUSCULAR CONTRACTION OVER THE ANTERIOR SUPERIOR SPINE OF THE ILIUM IS OFTEN THE CAUSE OF THE ANTERIOR INNOMINATE AND SACRUM ON THAT SIDE. PAIN AND TENSION OVER THE ARM MARKED X USUALLY ACCOMPANY THIS SYMPTOM. HEAVY INHIBITING MUSCULAR POLARITY CONTACTS ON BOTH AREAS MARKED X OVER THE ARM AND CLOSE TO THE ANTERIOR SUPERIOR SPINE WITH A FLAT THUMB CONTACT RELEASES THIS ANTERIORITY WITHOUT ANY PELVIC ADJUSTMENT. IT IS A REVELATION WHEN BOTH AREAS ARE RELEASED SIMULTANEOUSLY. ONE ALONE WILL NOT DO IT. POLARITY TENSION IS THE PRIMARY IMPULSE BEHIND MUSCULAR TENSION WHICH CAUSES ROTATION AND SPINAL DISTORTIONS. THIS POLARITY RELEASE IS DONE BEST WITH THE PATIENT ON THE BACK.

Illustration from Polarity Therapy *by Dr. Randolph Stone, CRCS Publications, Sebastopol, California, 1987*

Not surprisingly, craniosacral work is currently being integrated into Polarity Therapy by the board members of the profession. A version of the Upledger protocol has been claimed by Polarity therapists as an offshoot of the esoteric branch of their legacy. In truth, one-time osteopath Stone declared the primacy of the craniosacral system as early as 1940:

> The cerebrospinal fluid seems to act as a storage field and conveyor for the ultrasonic and light energies. It bathes the spinal cord and is a reservoir for these finer essences, conducted by this fluidic media through all the fine nerve fibers as the first airy mind and life principle in the human body.... Where this primary and essential life force is present, there is life and healing with normal function. Where this primary and essential life force is not acting in the body, there is obstruction, spasm, or stagnation and pain, like gears which clash instead of meshing in their operation.[9]

In particular, following the craniosacral pulse and holding stillpoints have been revived in a Polarity context.

Polarity balancing can be similar to Reichian therapy in (often painfully) invoking old traumas, but in a more spiritual modality, the pain is treated as emotional and libidinal only in one of its manifestations. Over and over the therapist reinvokes the template of a vision quest or psychospiritual initiation in which he is literally accompanying the client and interposing his own body/spirit as an electromagnetic pole to guide this passage. After all, Polarity is proposed as a systemization of the transmission of curative love and compassion through the electromagnetizing field of the hands.

Polarity is also a breathing system, similar to rebirthing, and likely with historic roots in the same lineages of yoga. Cycles of breath are the very mechanism of healing during Polarity bodywork. The therapist instructs the client to use each in-breath to put himself in touch with the radiant cosmic field, each out-breath to collapse that field and allow the dispersal and elimination of negative forces—unreleased emotional energy and rigid mental constructs. Thus, traumas and resistance are located by breath and, without being stigmatized, flushed from the system. What is healed is not the fact of disease as much as its cellular retention. Once this compulsive bond is snapped, armor is dissolved, and the person suddenly feels attunement with higher Intelligence. Life takes on a sudden lucidity and purpose, viewed not in its often meaningless terrestrial context but from the perspective of a higher being.

Polarity differs from rebirthing in its physical intercession to assist the breathing process. The therapist presides as a combination Rolfer-yogi-shaman, alternately pressing into the perineum to release physical blocks and toxins; testing the reflex on the client's third toe; calling his attention to his higher self and to the combination of masculine and feminine characteristics within him (and the universe at large); inhibiting his psoas muscle; releasing his scapula by rocking his neck; urging him to image his moment of birth or a difficult time during childhood; *shiatsu*-draining his lymphatics, neck, and nasal mucosa;

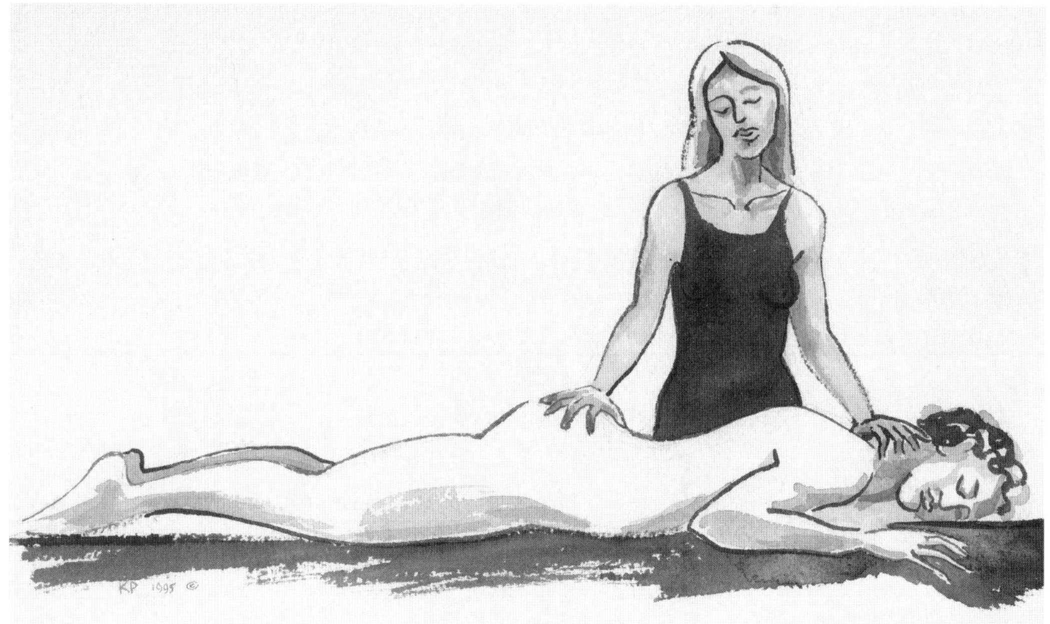

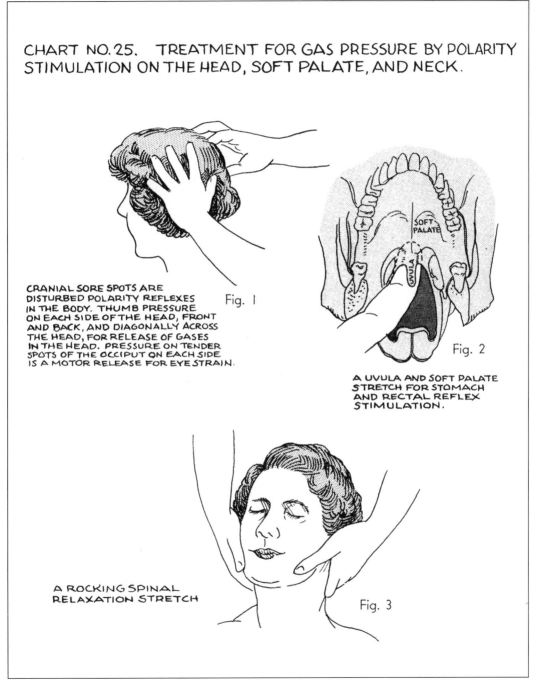

CHART NO. 25. TREATMENT FOR GAS PRESSURE BY POLARITY STIMULATION ON THE HEAD, SOFT PALATE, AND NECK.

CRANIAL SORE SPOTS ARE DISTURBED POLARITY REFLEXES IN THE BODY. THUMB PRESSURE ON EACH SIDE OF THE HEAD, FRONT AND BACK, AND DIAGONALLY ACROSS THE HEAD, FOR RELEASE OF GASES IN THE HEAD. PRESSURE ON TENDER SPOTS OF THE OCCIPUT ON EACH SIDE IS A MOTOR RELEASE FOR EYE STRAIN.

Fig. 1

SOFT PALATE

UVULA

Fig. 2

A UVULA AND SOFT PALATE STRETCH FOR STOMACH AND RECTAL REFLEX STIMULATION.

A ROCKING SPINAL RELAXATION STRETCH

Fig. 3

Illustration from Polarity Therapy *by Dr. Randolph Stone, CRCS Publications, Sebastopol, California, 1987*

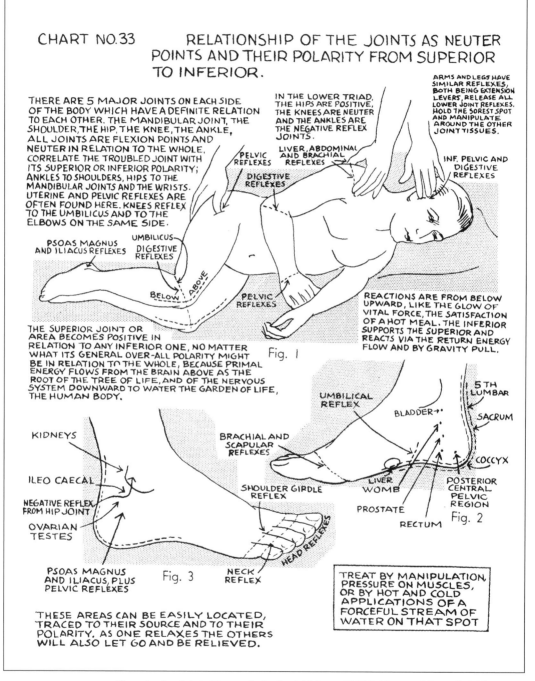

CHART NO.33 RELATIONSHIP OF THE JOINTS AS NEUTER POINTS AND THEIR POLARITY FROM SUPERIOR TO INFERIOR.

THERE ARE 5 MAJOR JOINTS ON EACH SIDE OF THE BODY WHICH HAVE A DEFINITE RELATION TO EACH OTHER. THE MANDIBULAR JOINT, THE SHOULDER, THE HIP, THE KNEE, THE ANKLE, ALL JOINTS ARE FLEXION POINTS AND NEUTER IN RELATION TO THE WHOLE. CORRELATE THE TROUBLED JOINT WITH ITS SUPERIOR OR INFERIOR POLARITY; ANKLES TO SHOULDERS, HIPS TO THE MANDIBULAR JOINTS AND THE WRISTS. UTERINE AND PELVIC REFLEXES ARE OFTEN FOUND HERE. KNEES REFLEX TO THE UMBILICUS AND TO THE ELBOWS ON THE SAME SIDE.

IN THE LOWER TRIAD, THE HIPS ARE POSITIVE, THE KNEES ARE NEUTER AND THE ANKLES ARE THE NEGATIVE REFLEX JOINTS.

ARMS AND LEGS HAVE SIMILAR REFLEXES, BOTH BEING EXTENSION LEVERS, RELEASE ALL LOWER JOINT REFLEXES. HOLD THE SOREST SPOT AND MANIPULATE AROUND THE OTHER JOINT TISSUES.

PELVIC REFLEXES

LIVER, ABDOMINAL AND BRACHIAL REFLEXES

DIGESTIVE REFLEXES

INF. PELVIC AND DIGESTIVE REFLEXES

PSOAS MAGNUS AND ILIACUS REFLEXES

UMBILICUS

DIGESTIVE REFLEXES

BELOW

ABOVE

PELVIC REFLEXES

REACTIONS ARE FROM BELOW UPWARD, LIKE THE GLOW OF VITAL FORCE, THE SATISFACTION OF A HOT MEAL. THE INFERIOR SUPPORTS THE SUPERIOR AND REACTS VIA THE RETURN ENERGY FLOW AND BY GRAVITY PULL.

THE SUPERIOR JOINT OR AREA BECOMES POSITIVE IN RELATION TO ANY INFERIOR ONE, NO MATTER WHAT ITS GENERAL OVER-ALL POLARITY MIGHT BE IN RELATION TO THE WHOLE, BECAUSE PRIMAL ENERGY FLOWS FROM THE BRAIN ABOVE AS THE ROOT OF THE TREE OF LIFE, AND OF THE NERVOUS SYSTEM DOWNWARD TO WATER THE GARDEN OF LIFE, THE HUMAN BODY.

Fig. 1

UMBILICAL REFLEX

BLADDER

5TH LUMBAR

SACRUM

BRACHIAL AND SCAPULAR REFLEXES

COCCYX

LIVER

WOMB

POSTERIOR CENTRAL PELVIC REGION

PROSTATE

RECTUM

Fig. 2

KIDNEYS

ILEO CAECAL

NEGATIVE REFLEX FROM HIP JOINT

OVARIAN TESTES

SHOULDER GIRDLE REFLEX

HEAD REFLEXES

PSOAS MAGNUS AND ILIACUS, PLUS PELVIC REFLEXES

NECK REFLEX

Fig. 3

TREAT BY MANIPULATION, PRESSURE ON MUSCLES, OR BY HOT AND COLD APPLICATIONS OF A FORCEFUL STREAM OF WATER ON THAT SPOT

THESE AREAS CAN BE EASILY LOCATED, TRACED TO THEIR SOURCE AND TO THEIR POLARITY. AS ONE RELAXES THE OTHERS WILL ALSO LET GO AND BE RELIEVED.

Illustration from Polarity Therapy *by Dr. Randolph Stone, CRCS Publications, Sebastopol, California, 1987*

balancing his sphenoid bone from the orbits of his eyes; making gentle rotary contact with the units of his upper spine and neck while evoking images of guardian angels; using the craniosacral rhythm to balance the pelvic and pubic regions of his body with bones in his skull, i.e., the pubic arch with the mandible; leading him in chanting mantras while releasing gas from his colon with a rocking embrace, a lift, and an expansion-stretch across his chest; stimulating the umbilical region and its myriad energy contacts; lifting and rocking opposing zones of the anatomy; intoning sound directly into the treatment in order to deepen the breathing; stretch-releasing the hip-shoulder connections and the hands finger by finger; rhythmically squeezing the heart *chakra* with the thumb; draining the prostate through ankle palpation; and embracing the client at moments of pain or important passages and encouraging him to trust in the brotherhood (and sisterhood) of sentient beings and to allow their spirit to move through him.

This choreography represents not an actual Polarity treatment but a hypothetical itinerary through stages of body, mind, and spirit. Individual therapists develop their sequences depending on the nature of their own practice and the requirements of the patient.

Chi Gung and Chi Gung Tui Na

Chi Gung Tui Na (literally, "energy-power-push-pull") is a distinctly Oriental bodywork science. It is a system of great antiquity and, over generations, has come to include a rigorous set of exercises and treatments for carrying out its procedures. Its frame of reference lies not in a Western view of anatomy but Chinese cosmology (see the latter part of the section on "Martial Medicines" in Chapter Two). Kumar Frantzis, as one of the few practitioners with an experiential knowledge of both Eastern and Western systems, not unexpectedly comes down heavily in favor of Taoist bodywork as a complete system in relationship to which Western bodywork is just beginning to develop the rudimentary fields. For instance, Frantzis proposes that Western craniosacral therapy recognizes the attributes of only one of the three cerebrospinal rhythms familiar to the Chinese traditional practitioner. He recommends that Chinese approaches can "save the West hundreds of years by simply not reinventing the wheel in terms of somatic bodywork."[10]

He adds:

> Readjusting a vertebra that is out of alignment is a relatively straightforward procedure. The difficulty lies in how quickly the vertebra goes out again. Sometimes simply stretching the tissue around the misaligned vertebra is sufficient, but often in chronic cases this is not enough. The Chi Gung Tui Na therapist will trace the Chi from the offending one or more vertebrae to everywhere else in the body that is either being imbalanced or disconnected by the problem in the vertebrae, or is generating energy that is causing the Chi in the vertebrae to go awry and become physically misaligned. The bodyworker will then do appropriate corrections to relieve the stress on the vertebrae from both directions. This will relieve the negative cause-and-effect relationships throughout the whole body.

[In the case of a broken ankle,]

> . . . the Chi Gung bodyworker will want to go into more detail [than a Western therapist] using twisting techniques, acupressure, and anti-inflammatory medicine to reduce swelling. He/she will want to check energetically if the damage has extended up the client's Chi lines to their hip, spine, internal organs, neck and arms. The therapist will then use both physical and energetic techniques to correct the broken Chi connections, to prevent the client from in time developing problems in the hip, spine, liver, kidney, shoulder, neck, etc. By doing work at the level of Chi, the Chi Gung bodyworker ensures that a cascading effect does not issue from a minor ailment and become a severe problem later on. . . .[11]

As noted in the previous chapter, all bodywork has an energetic component. However, *"chi"* bodywork is carried out on either an energetic plane or the imaginal replica of an energetic plane; thus, its physical, neuromuscular components are either secondary or artifactual.

On the surface, *Chi Gung* exercises look distinctly non-Western and non-medical. They resemble exotic dances or martial arts sets. The arms move up and down and in circles; the fingers float and flick; the bottom of the foot kicks in swift tiny arcs; the torso twists and rotates. The person looks like a combination warrior and necromancer. (In one class Frantzis demonstrated the "actual" sound of a movement that looked like a mere outward fling of his arm and hand. But he let out such a roar that his arm suddenly became a fire hose releasing an invisible gas.)

> The Chi Gung Tui Na therapist at work will sometimes look very strange. While the left hand is working on the physical tissue of a client's damaged shoulder, simultaneously, the right hand can be on his/her belly, knee, foot or head, correcting a Chi imbalance. The right hand may stay on one spot, or in the course of a few minutes move ten or twenty times to different body points, to make Chi balancing adjustments. The hands may even leave the patient's body to clear out connected Chi imbalances in the person's external etheric body aura. The therapist will move back and forth between physical tissue manipulations, acupressure points and other Chi balancing interventions. His/her hands will move over the client's body like a piano player's over a keyboard.[12]

Traditionally Oriental bodywork systems have been distinguished as a class from European ones. Practitioners, training programs, and professional somatic organizations tend to represent exclusively one sphere (Eastern or Western) and to validate the contingent and competing modalities within their own lineage while maintaining at least a passing knowledge of their frames of reference. At the same time they usually have an ignorance about the methods and strategies of the other hemisphere.

This split between Eastern and Western somatics reflects both a real divergence of etiology and orientation and a superficial isolation for present lack of a Rosetta Stone to link the two. For instance, whereas *Chi Gung* is considered an energy system based on *chi* flow, Occidental body medicines are often defined as manipulative or, at best, neuroelectric.

Even those Western systems which are explicitly energetic do not situate or attempt to move energy in the same manner. So, is *chi* the same substance or Etheric fluid as that released by chiropractic bone adjustment or Polarity breathing? Or is it a unique discovery of *Nei Gung?*

There is, of course, ultimately no *real* barrier between Oriental and Western "bodies"; any "field theory" of somatics requires that they trade in the same currency. That is, there is no distinct realm of bodily experience in the East or the West that does not meet a corresponding realm of the other in the bones, blood, fascia, auras, and organs of actual bodies.

The complexity we intuit is real, even if it cannot be anatomically mapped. By approaching the composite energy body from different angles, at varying layers of depth, and with their own idiosyncratic emphases, particular somatic systems activate discrete properties and currents which manifest in the physical body in unique ways.

In the context of its own culture the *chi* body is a complete body, an esoteric body, made of finer and more seminal stuff than the visceral body. It is the energetic template for the elemental body and its discrete organ systems. In the healing sense, it is a superior body. When harmonizing adjustments are made in the *chi* body, these translate exponentially to the organs. Likewise, when the integrity of protective *chi* is violated, the organs are more susceptible to diseases. The various different forms of medical *Chi Gung* are precisely different patterns of *chi* generation and transmission based on an actual geography of *chi* in the body. If *chi* were not real and empirically confirmable, this geography would be ridiculous.

Frantzis attributes the discrimination of *chi* to different etiologies of education:

> The first year or two of Chi Gung Tui Na are spent learning how to make the hands sensitive to the flesh and Chi they are feeling in the body. Without "the hands" no form of bodywork will be totally effective. Often people spend months or years learning various somatic bodywork techniques to no avail. Although they have the intellectual knowledge of anatomy or acupressure/trigger points, they are

> not accurately able to feel the body's reaction to their touch. Many techniques in Chi Gung Tui Na are devoted in the first two years of training to simply learning to accurately feel the body. For example, when touching the surface of the belly one can accurately discern how flesh is moving all the way down to the spine. This becomes critical in knowing how to vary pressure and when one is forcing the body (which can cause resistance or damage) or when the body is giving its permission for the safe bodywork procedure to continue. It also allows the therapist to gather critical information which a pair of dead hands cannot. The training also shows the therapist how to project energy accurately and with precision over long distances in the body—so that, for example, by working on a client's foot the therapist can tell how the Chi is changing in the patient's head, hands, spine, or even closer, their ankles or knees. Without this sensitivity it becomes impossible to track the Chi in a patient's body and to change one's technique appropriately and instantaneously based on the most effective possible therapeutic intervention.[13]

Chi Gung Tui Na is based on feeling energy, and Frantzis believes that the relative absence of this sensitivity severely limits Western bodyworkers, though he adds that he is encouraged by recent developments in craniosacral therapy, visceral manipulation, Rolfing, and myofascial work because of their emphasis on hand sensitivity. Of course, this is the view from within the *chi* model, and Western practitioners usually assume that they have arrived at similar or equivalent modes by more scientific techniques. Certainly there are many quite sensitive practitioners of palpation and other modes of touch in the West. What Frantzis may be noting is that the particular form of self-deceit that allows one to practice bodywork mechanically with dead hands in the West is much less common in China.

(In Taoist and Buddhist cultures and in Ayurvedic cultures in other ways, boys and girls are trained young to recognize their own *chi* and to cultivate it. They cup balls of *chi* energy in their hands and carry them in their versions of calisthenics. *Chi* is considered a real substance from one's day of birth and is established experientially, not philosophically

or mythologically—for instance, by the practice of *t'ai chi ch'uan.* So, an inner referential image of the *chi* body matures with the individual. By contrast, Western youth are rarely trained in the experience of *chi* or *prana,* so they must develop their apperception of these realms later in life and in the contexts of other modes of knowing. When I was in high school in the 1960s and a very precocious friend attempted a version of *prana* practice during basketball warm-ups, the coach called him a fag and dismissed him to the locker room!)

INSOFAR AS THE *chi* body exists beyond a metaphor of vital energy, Western healers must also have historically interacted with it under different names. Not only must it have been inherited in a protean version from a Eurasian base culture, but it must have been rediscovered empirically many times over the last two millennia.

In fact, there seems little question that systems like osteopathy, Rolfing, and Eutony each affect a *chi* body in their own ways. It is merely that none of them are defined in terms of direct *chi* experience or *chi* channeling; thus, they have effects upon *chi* not necessarily accounted for in traditional Oriental systems. But they *do* influence elemental energetic flow, and if it were not for such flow (i.e., if we were only mechanical and electrical), these Western systems would not have the extraordinary power they do. In truth, they do not have to reify *chi* in order to locate a general energy field in the body. That energy field likely contains dozens, if not hundreds or thousands, of distinguishable energetic layers and phases, which collectively provide the justification for a heterogeneity of therapeutic modalities.

Cultural context plays a critical role in rendering systems both practicable and meaningful. It is never a case of which system is more sophisticated or traditional but which system brings the practitioner to a functional therapeutic level. In the end, cure is nondenominational (as we have repeatedly averred), but accurate practice of any technique must account for its idiosyncratic cultural metaphors and definitions. Once this is done, Rolfing, *Chi Gung,* Feldenkrais, Eurhythmy, and all

sorts of other systems may be used independently or interdependently with great success and yet with no conventional map as to whether they overlap or even what is actually happening.

To this degree, *Chi Gung* is a somatic system in the same way that various Western systems are. It is based on internal discriminations that make extraordinarily fine distinctions between degrees of visceral sensation. The *Chi Gung* practitioner must *feel* where nodes and energy gates are located in order to move energy and must then track that energy through grids that become recognizable only by his paying attention to hair's-breadth sensations cultivated through practice.

Feldenkrais Method, by contrast, as a relatively new system, is based more on scientifically defined neuromuscular discriminations and chronic losses of function originating from the habits of technological civilization. It defines function in a manner that is logical to Western anatomy, and, as noted in the last chapter, the discriminations it makes are usually far more accessible to Western practitioners for awakening to all bodily energies, including *chi,* because they arise from familiar modes of perception and build from those by gradual heuristic procedures. However, there should be no illusion that Feldenkrais (or any other European technique) can be anything more than a first step (by Taoist standards) toward fully functional techniques for medically generating and utilizing *chi.* They may be necessary first steps for some, to bring them even to the point of experiencing enough sensation to be able to search for *chi,* but finding *chi* involves a particular mode of differentiation within that sensation. This is true whether *chi* exists as a concrete substance or not. Quite apart from the reality of *"chi"* is the *"chi"* experience—the sense of the arms suddenly elevating and of energy rising and sinking within the body—this exists as an existential fact. The issue is then how to cultivate and enhance the experience, not how to categorize it in Eastern or Western nomenclature.

The thousands of distinct *Chi Gung* sets are not unlike, superficially, the letters of Eurhythmy. What these represent, however, are highly practical maneuvers for gathering and clearing *chi*—nothing

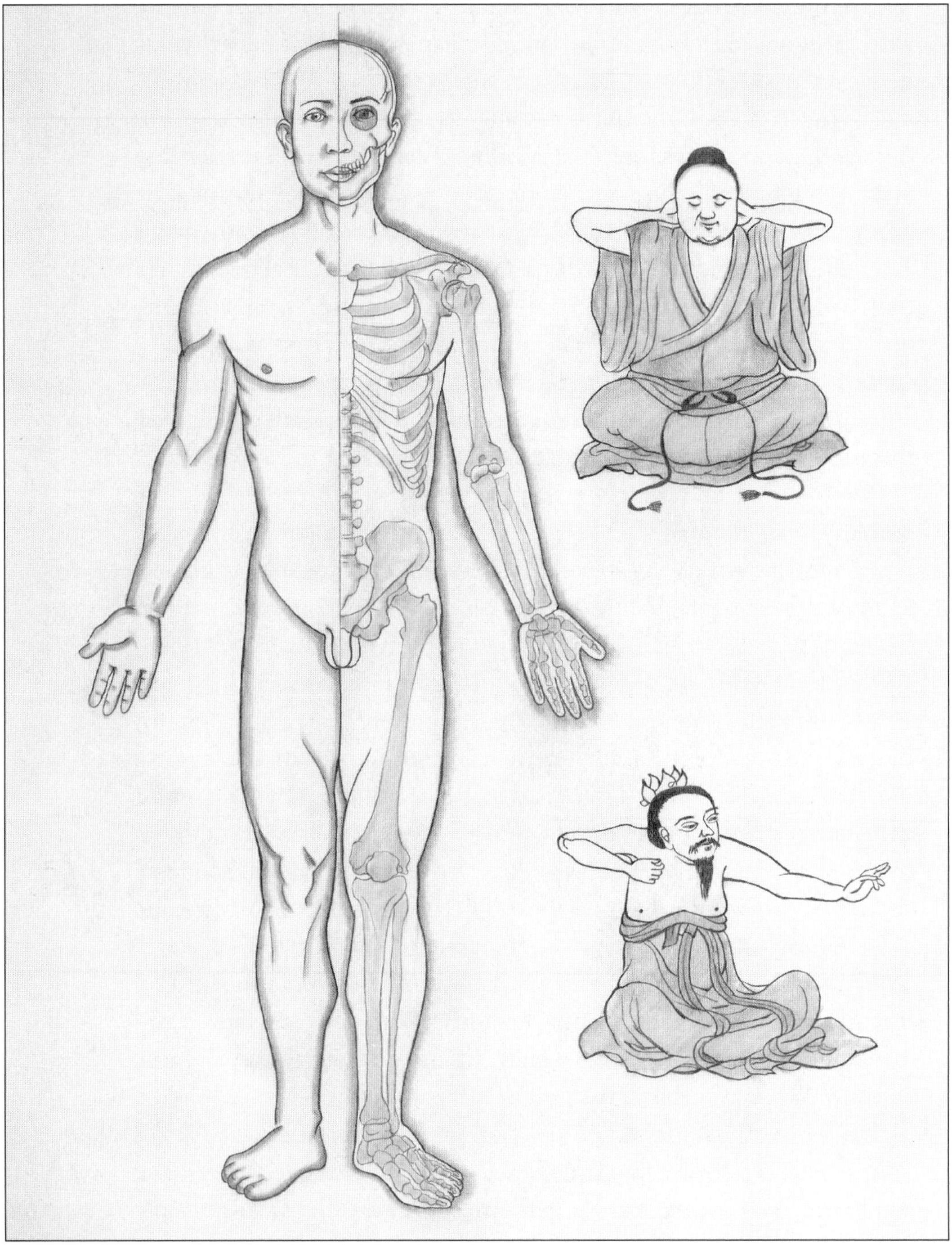

more (no decorative add-ons) and nothing less. In application, *Chi Gung* movements are repeated again and again and again. The seemingly external motions replicate and reinforce an internal process of contacting and moving *chi* and at the same time literally palpate the *chi* field, which is larger and more charged than the physical body. The practitioner sweeps and gathers up his own *chi,* disperses stagnant energy, pushes energy into the ground, and, by the principle of Yin and Yang, circulates fresh energy up into the organs (*chi* fluctuates like water, swelling up to balance any dispersal downward). The movements pass through exactly those zones around the body where *chi* is thickest and at orientations to the body which most efficiently gather *chi* and instigate its flow. The variety of *Chi Gung* sets may be itself an empirical reflection of the abundance of patterning through which *chi* can be activated.

THERE IS A distinction between Buddhist medical *Chi Gung,* which pretty much matches the series of exercises described above, and Taoist *Chi Gung* based in *Nei Gung,* which has its own repertoire of external forms but prioritizes a purely interior method of visioning and dissolving blocks. In one of its many techniques, the practitioner closes his eyes and starts perceiving inwardly, beginning at the energy field above his head. Working his way slowly down his body on the outside and inside, he tracks sensations. He passes through the crown of the cranium, the temples, the third eye, the eyeballs, the neck, the shoulder girdle, the shoulder blades, armpits, vertebrae, sternum, solar plexus, belly, liver, kidneys, genitals, anal passage, perineum, pelvic bone, thighs, ankles, feet, bottoms of the feet, right through the energy field in the earth beneath his feet. Of course, there are many other locations possible to visit. Any tissue or organ is a candidate for penetration and dissolution. It is simply a matter of sensitivity, patience, and capacity. A beginner tracks the body close to its surface (because that is what he is capable of). It may not be possible at first for him to get through his eyeballs to their interface with the brain, so the surface of the eyes is

felt and energized. By degrees he goes deeper. Merely to locate the pelvis internally is difficult for most people. Later the goal is to send attention right through the bone. Likewise, as a cancer preventative, one learns to work his or her mind gradually up the anal canal. The overall process is one of continually gathering and sweeping all excess energy downward, paying particular attention to contractions, areas of tension and strength, and any other sensations, "especially," Frantzis emphasizes, "if you do not know what they are." During these sweeps, one softens and releases blockages, turning "ice to water, water to gas."[14] The mutation from ice to water is a relatively straightforward one of sensing and relaxing. From water to gas is a sophisticated alchemy that follows the true introduction of *chi.*

Standing erect in a balanced, open posture, a trained practitioner can complete a cycle of the body in ten minutes, an hour, or many hours, depending on the speed and depth of awareness. One can move a millimeter at a time or an inch at a time. Subsequent passes over the years can go deeper until one is cleansing not only the surface meridians, but the blood, the marrow of the bones, and the inside of the brain.

As should be clear from prior discussions of internal methods (primarily in the section on *Chi Gung* in Volume One, Chapter Nine), this is not a visualization technique. It is a process of actually tracing proprioception from the dense physiography of the body into its *chi* field and thereby activating it. The question of whether honoring every subtle sensation leads to the *chi* field is irrelevant because *there is no other way to find it.* A practitioner cannot guide a person into his own *chi* field road sign by road sign; he can only give him a set of clues through which he can ultimately intuitively arrive at it himself. If he picks up other sensations along the way, these can be sorted out as the awareness of the *chi* field is confirmed by repeated sweeps over periods of time. Eventually the movement of *chi* becomes clear and the other sensations also become clear as what they are.

Initially the *chi* feeling may be so subtle as to seem like nothing,

but it is this minute sensation that attention must follow until something more is apprehended. Many people feel *chi* most readily in the field formed by opposing the rounded palms of both hands to each other. This "ball" of energy is also the *t'ai chi* ball that is rolled through the postures of the martial arts set. A more subtle trace of *chi* can be picked up in the equivalent "bubbling well" points at the base of the feet. Both of these areas are critical gates in the medical movement of *chi.* A next stage of development might be sequential forays pulling *chi* from the inner surface of the arms into the palms of each hand and then pushing it back in. Later, *chi* is sent along one arm into the body, through the heart, and out the other arm without the aid of the palm.

Once again, this is not a mere exercise technique. The purpose of Taoist *Chi Gung* is to heal tumors, chronic tension, and broken bones, and to repair the damage of strokes, radiation exposure, and viral infection—major medical ambitions. None of this would happen if there were not a *chi* body to contact and if such a template body were not accessible in a manner that alters fascia and viscera in the physical body. Frantzis himself used Taoist *Chi Gung* after his back was broken in a car accident in New Mexico. Told he would never walk again, he summoned up his strength and began working his way down from the top of his head, encountering and dissolving immense resistance, especially at the damaged points.[15] Because he already knew *Chi Gung,* he was adept in internal tracking and was able to attain the level of depth required for such a drastic treatment. Not only did he walk, but he regained his prowess as a highly mobile and effective martial artist.

Breema

TAUGHT AS A combination of massage and spiritual exercise, Breema was introduced to the West by Manocher Movlai, a Kurdish rug merchant in Oakland, California. It is unclear how much of his system is native Kurdish and how much was adapted and improvised by Movlai. He cites his great-grandfather as his original teacher:

Dancing on the Grapes

> He would do a lot to make us view the body not as an anatomic object. This alive, dynamic phenomenon is in constant change. This energy system is connected to the totality of existence on all levels.... He would say, to touch a human being, another body of [a] human being, is as mystical as touching the stars.[16]

Breema can be performed as a one-person cycle of movements and breathing exercises which, from the outside, appear combinations of ceremonies and exercises. Their names are directly evocative: "Grinding the Wheat," "Chasing the Arrow," and "Dropping the Load." Self-Breema includes breathing cycles, hops, stretches, foot and head rubs, and facial and bodily brushes ("Erasing the Page") plus combinations of these (such as holding one's hands on the kidneys and hopping in such a way as to pull and twist the torso and points of contact in "Dancing on the Grapes"). The emphasis is on letting natural movements and weight shifts stretch and massage parts of the body as the simple effect of posture and gravity.

More commonly Breema is practiced by two people as a bodywork session. The same use is made of natural movements and weight shifts,

but posture and gravity are now the effects not just of one body moving in space but two bodies acting on each other as fulcra, ballasts, pulleys, wedges, gears, etc., in complex sequences of shifting positions. Movlai emphasizes that during such treatments, both participants are equally the givers and the receivers. The exchange is based solely on their mutual and simultaneous presence and permission, their breathing in unison, and the reciprocal weights of their bodies. He explains this in his inimitable English (somewhat sanitized with my bracketed inserts):

> My mind receives [an] impression of [your] body, [your] body receives [an] impression of [my] mind. While [my] mind [is] receiving [an] impression, [my] body is active. While [your] body receives [an] impression, my mind is active. If this active/receptive principle is understood within myself, then this gentleman who is lying down here becomes . . .who is body, who is mind? He is body while I am mind. I am the body while he is the mind.
>
> [The] division—I am me and you are you—which is falsity and [which] I created all of my life, disappears. . . . In the principle of active/receptive, there is only me or there is only you. . . . In that non-verbal understanding, that which you do is in harmony with yourself, with the person you're working with, with the whole universe.[17]

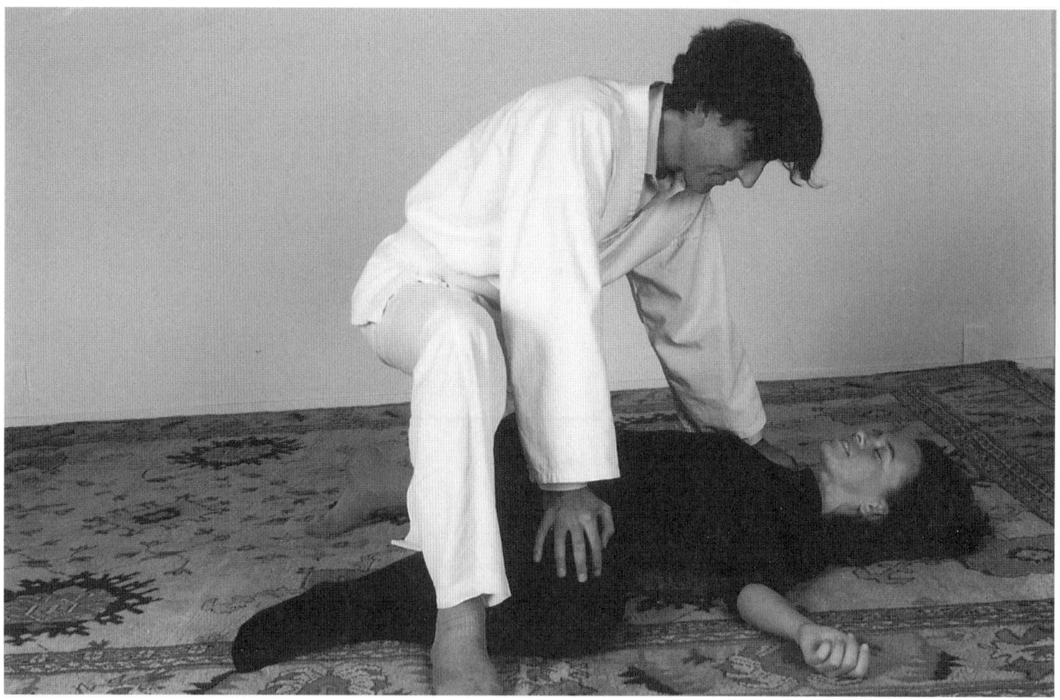

The two people doing Breema are engaged in a process, partly choreographed, partly improvisational, of mutual aid and support, of recognition of each other's bodily presence, each other's gravity and breath. Breema is a kind of two-person yoga involving a subtle energetic and emotional transfer between the bodies that enlarges and heals both of them without diagnosis.

The Breema practitioner makes contact with the other person's body by first taking into account the location and relative ease of her own body. After settling into a comfortable position and internally acknowledging her own breath and weight, she puts a hand or foot on her partner. Although there are standardized sets, the placement may be anywhere, and in some cases the knees, elbows, or belly become the massaging "limb." Simply stepping on the insoles of the feet of a prone partner and then slowly transferring one's own weight to them is a common

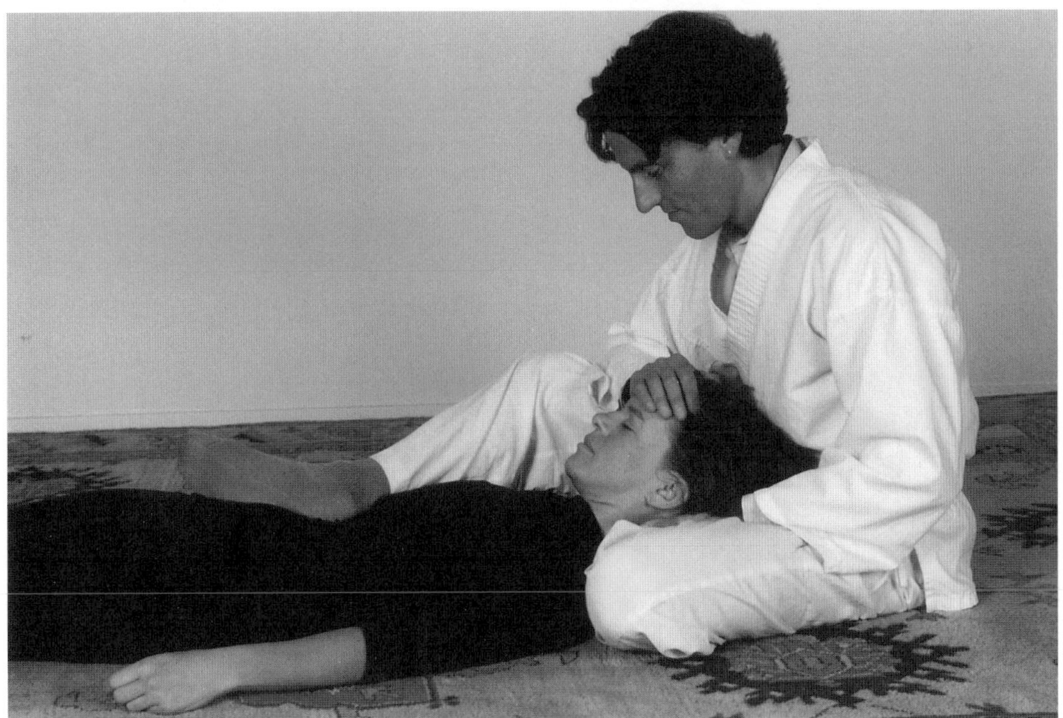

and effective starting point. Many moves involve taking a strategic position contiguous to one's partner and then leaning in such a way that one's weight is transferred to the other person's body. Sometimes the weight transfer is direct and linear. Sometimes it curls along an edge of the body, giving a deep-tissue massage. Sometimes it turns into a lift or displacement so that the two bodies acrobatically support each other in a stretching position.

In the most linear sequences, each of these leaning transfers bears the relationship of a dot in a dotted line to a complete continuum, with an arm or leg or path along the torso of the partner representing the vector. The shift and its cessation follow a pattern of "press, hold, release": the press is merely the weight transfer, the hold is the duration of the breath, and the release is the transfer back.

> A lean involves a gentle but firm transfer of weight from the practitioner's body to the recipient's. Equal time is given to the lean toward the recipient, to the "hold" at the deepest point of the lean, and to the release of the hold, as the practitioner's weight shifts away from the recipient and back toward her own body. Leans often take on a rhythmic quality of their own and can have a deeply soothing effect.[18]

The dotted line can go anywhere. One of the simplest such sequences involves a single hand on a partner's leg, then pressing, holding, and releasing consecutive points, traveling the length of the thigh, down the calf, along the ankle, foot, toes, and aura beyond the toes. After a parallel track down the other side, the practitioner closes the sequence with three light brushes back over both paths simultaneously.

> ... Gentle nurturing brushes which strengthen and deepen the effects of the treatment ... can be done with the feet, but more commonly the hands are used. Brushes are done with a relaxed hand; again, the movement comes not from the arm and hand but from the body's center....
>
> After a particular series of leans, the practitioner might change the recipient's position by, for example, standing up and carrying the recipient's leg up and along with her, then gently placing it on

the other side of the recipient's body, causing a twisting action in the spine.[19]

One such succession of moves involves stretches in which one transfers weight to a partner by holding onto one or both of their limbs like a vine and then extending the person by gradually leaning backward oneself, supporting the other body all the way.

In a compressive sequence, one places a partner's feet on one's own belly and then very slowly, with long pauses at each degree of arc, raises and folds his legs and brings one's own weight to bear down through the partner's feet, rolling his knees toward his head a fraction of an inch at a time.

Other moves involve rocking and cradling the partner in postures ranging from hands cupped on his ears to a full therapeutic embrace, rapping or drumming on his forehead or chest, and raising his limbs

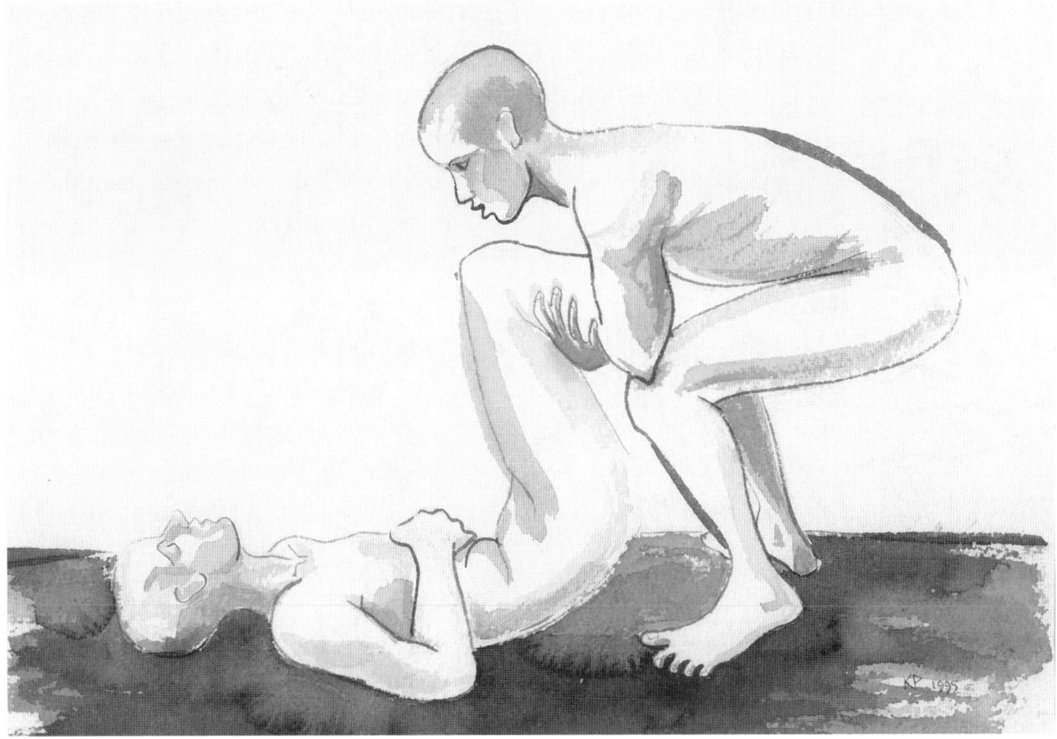

and dropping them suddenly in a sequence of tosses around his prone body.

All of these activities are consensual and collaborative. Movlai repeatedly emphasizes that the parties are equal healers, supplying complementary weight and breath, which has a mutual stretching and expanding quality for both.

> In Breema, we don't have lift.... I want to do that, I lift. The word "lift" mind understands [as] one thing: order the body to LIFT. But, I lean and I lean. I lean and I lean.
>
> Also, in Breema we don't have the word "pull." Pull, pull. Mind understands pull as force. Pull. Breema is no force. No force ever is used in Breema. The weight of the body is used as a carrier of energy, that's all. So, instead of having pull and push, we have lean forward, lean backward. Lean forward, lean backward.[20]

The effect is of a person exercising alone and seemingly by accident drawing along a partner. At the same time, this indirect attention is transposed into the recipient's body as if it is the practitioner's own. An elbow on the partner's shoulder blade is another favored position or, most exotically, a belly resting on the belly of a partner (Movlai uses the Japanese designation—the *hara* on the *hara*—in place of the more obscure Kurdish *delegen* on *delegen*). Transferred between bodies is a subtle energy, a sense of presence, plus the continual element of surprise. This "startle" is crucial to keeping the mind of the receiver open and in a state of wonderment: 'What will she do next?' is an endless silent question until there is no question and everything that happens is instantaneously received. Each range of unlikely juxtapositions projects its own new reality.

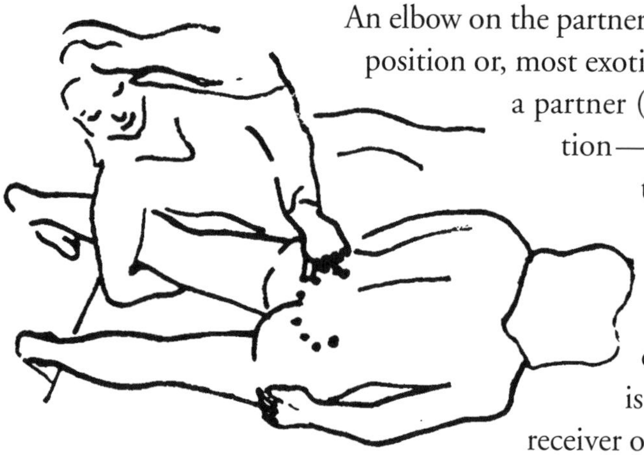

Because of the regular interchange of the practitioner's feet and hands as primary treating agents, the person being touched loses his

basic orientation vis-à-vis a simple hands-on massage. The sense is instead of being touched by more than one person or by one person so nimble as to be in many places at once. Movlai points out that as a result of their location so close to the brain, the hands are far more detrimentally judgmental than the feet or *hara.* When the feet are used instead, on a very deep level the partner experiences the absence of probing. The treatment feels more like spiritual and animal company—the innocent curiosity and comfort of another creature. Movlai says:

> Everything we do in Breema, we do it with all of the whole body. So, we don't have "brush with the hand." We have body, body. Body, body. And then something magnificent happens.
>
> That which is the total emanation of this entity [the practitioner] and that which is the total emanation of this entity [the other person], they create a new emanation of this entity [makes a gesture encircling both people]. This new emanation has the power to bring everything into harmony.[21]

The first time I received a treatment I slid into a trance and experienced a closed-eye movie of luminous, rapid-fire archetypal images that seemed right out of a Jungian opticon—temples, mandalas, sphinxes, buddhas, tapestries of the Flower of Life, spinning geometric forms, replacing one another in drumbeats. It was as though my mind had nothing to do with the procession. As the demonstration flipped by in routine fashion, I felt obscure emotions and a sensation of wholeness. But was this medicine?

Movlai remarks:

> Breema is the only method I know of [that] has nothing to do whatsoever with diagnosis, does not diagnose, does not even look, does not even study, doesn't have anything to do with the client or patient or whatever you wish to call it.
>
> In order to have this non-judgmental activity, the mind, which by nature is judgmental and classifies, has to be occupied in such a way that it does not have any energy left

to go through the root of the habit of judgmentality.

Therefore, this mind has to be constantly like a recording machine. Always, [its] job is to record body having a weight, body breathes. As soon as I want to look to see how she [the client] is, my mind is incapable [of recording] these two things together: weight of the body and breathing of the body....

Then why is it Breema doesn't want to diagnose? [It] is really [a] magnificent thing why this is so. Because, you see, Breema does not believe there is such a thing as an illness or sickness. Now you may say, half of this planet or ninety percent of this planet, people are ill and sick. How come Breema can say such a thing; it's absurd. I agree with you.

But ...Breema does not believe in sickness, although we experience it. But, we experience it in the absence of vitality. [It is] the same way Breema doesn't believe in darkness. But we experience it in the absence of light. Light carries the substance, darkness does not. Vitality carries substance, sickness does not!

So, where do you put emphasis? Where there is substance? Or where there is not? You go to the dark room and fight with the darkness. In a few minutes, all your energy drains because you have to hit [an] imaginary, non-existent something.[22]

This is a hallmark of energetic medicine: forget disease, which is a mere pock, an obstruction in the flood of universal life force drawn from the cosmos. If you merely go toward disease with the intention of diagnosing it or fixing something, your mind and intention will become imbued with the contagious limitation of disease. You will be a moth irreparably compelled to a flame. You will always be sick. If you go toward pure energy, you will become energy. By that definition, all our systems of medicine derive and provide the diseases we then bring to our medicine women and men to treat. Meanwhile, Breema-like systems will provide cures for some of these diseases without either a diagnosis or a name.

We cannot fix each other, Movlai is saying. Only the "architect" within the body has true knowledge of what is happening; only it can

heal. But "you can support and give guidance and help one another." You can lead another person to "his own essential nature."[23]

Psychospiritual Transformation versus Psychotherapy in Somatics

FROM A PSYCHOANALYTIC standpoint, all somatic systems—Western and non-Western—face limitations of their literalism, misplaced concreteness, and charismatic inflations. Substituting concepts of energies, energy fields, healing touch, and "sacred" anatomy for the dynamics of transference, they make admirable attempts to contact "core" and, through their respective definitions of "core," to heal and transform fundamental strata of body, self, and soul. Their trap is not that they are not profound; they are profound and meticulous. Their trap is that, in contexts where they do not also confer insights or conscious understanding upon ancient and primary conflicts, their literalisms and inflations provide raw material for trenchant neurosis. While deepening personality on energetic, spiritual, and visceral levels—literally creating space and texture for the self to grow—somatic therapies emotionally rigidify too.

For a person sitting *zazen* or practicing *karate*, functional insight comes unconsciously and transforms the heart. This is also professional somatics' purest form of healing. It inculcates spiritual and bodily change but not necessarily psychological change. Somatic psychotherapy still awaits a contour map of the projections, shadows, and aborted transferences cast by over-enthusiastic bodywork and the energetic metaphors it purveys.

Notes

1. Bruce Burger, from his journal notes on professional Polarity documents, 1994.

2. Ibid.

3. Alexander Binik, "The Polarity System," in Edward Bauman, Armand Ian Brint, Lorin Piper, and Pamela Amelia Wright (editors), *The Holistic Health Handbook* (Berkeley, California: And/Or Press, 1978), pp. 99–107.

4. Bruce Burger, personal communication, 1994.

5. Randolph Stone, *Polarity Therapy,* Vol. I, Book 1 (Sebastopol, California: CRCS Publications, 1986), pp. 18–20. This and the succeeding two quotes were adapted by Bruce Burger for this edition of *Planet Medicine.*

6. Ibid., pp. 55, 8.

7. Ibid., p. 5.

8. Bruce Burger, *Esoteric Anatomy,* unpublished manuscript, tentatively North Atlantic Books, 1995.

9. Randolph Stone, *Polarity Therapy,* Vol. I, Book 3. (See note 5 above.) This quote was also adapted by Bruce Burger.

10. Bruce Kumar Frantzis, *The Tao in Action: The Personal Practice of the I Ching and Taoism in Daily Life,* unpublished manuscript (tentatively North Atlantic Books, 1996).

11. Ibid.

12. Ibid.

13. Ibid.

14. Bruce Kumar Frantzis, verbal instructions during a class, November 1993.

15. Bruce Kumar Frantzis, *Opening the Energy Gates of Your Body* (Berkeley, California: North Atlantic Books, 1993), pp. xxviii–xxix.

16. Manocher Movlai, transcribed from a class at the Breema Institute, Oakland, California, November 30, 1992.

17. Manocher Movlai, transcribed from a class at the Breema Institute, May 18, 1992.

18. Cybèle Tomlinson, "Breema Bodywork," *Yoga Journal* (November/December, 1994), p. 97.

19. Ibid., pp. 97–98.

20. Manocher Movlai, transcribed from a class at the Breema Institute, June 2, 1988.

21. Ibid.

22. Ibid.

23. Manocher Movlai, transcribed from a recorded talk at the Breema Institute, no date given.

CHAPTER SIX

Contemporary Systems

Somatic Philosophy

In mapping the evolution of somatic systems during the last century, we might consider as baseline disciplines: bone-setting, therapeutic adjustment, martial arts, movement rituals, traditional massage, *Chi Gung,* Ayurvedic exercises, yoga, and a variety of shamanic and spiritual practices (such as Gurdjieffian work and Native American vision quest). Freudian psychotherapy and Reichian characterological bodywork contributed a new dimension to the practice of all somatics by reifying a symbolic relationship between memories and life events, on the one hand, and physiological structures and movement patterns, on the other. All of the other systems discussed in this and the previous chapter may be characterized as second-generation syntheses, built up from the raw material of the above baseline practices in some combination or other. For instance, Rolfing has roots in therapeutic adjustment, Gurdjieffian work, and yoga. Feldenkrais has roots in yoga, movement rituals, and martial arts as well as Western science. Polarity has roots in Ayurveda, bone-setting, and shamanism.

I do not mean to declare a fixed historical hierarchy, but rather I am trying to sort the complex influences of somatic systems on one another. These influences may often be time-bound and practitioner-bound, but they reflect a general developmental process. For instance, the sets of relationships among the elements of first- and second-

generation systems can be as complex as a new Rolfer picking up traditional aspects of therapeutic adjustment and bone-setting indirectly through Rolfing, or learning them in their more pure osteopathic form from either an Upledger training or a cranial osteopath and then reapplying them to Rolfing at another level. Thus, it is not unusual for osteopathy or Reichian therapy to appear at more than one level of Rolfing (or of Feldenkrais work, Alexander Technique, etc.). Of course, any Rolfer inherits indirect techniques specifically from Ida Rolf's use of them, but then, for instance, well-known Rolfer Michael Salveson reads the craniosacral pulse during his structural integrations in a manner learned from John Upledger, at the same time applying such energetic techniques as V-spread and *Chi Gung Tui Na* to stubborn areas. His practice of Rolfing becomes a dialect of Rolf's original system. At Esalen, Rolfing was combined by "consciousness" practitioners with Gestalt psychology and a Reichian etiology to form a broader-spectrum Human Potential therapy which is not pure Rolfing. (See also Hellerwork below.)

Lomi Work is grounded in the Esalen hybrid of Rolfing and Gestalt. Polarity Therapy was subsequently integrated within Lomi as a derivation of a set of exercises taught to founders Richard Heckler and Robert Hall by Randolph Stone. Later, elements of Reichian therapy, *aikido,* and Vipassana Meditation were added by practitioners, and Lomi officially adopted and recognized its new layers and took on a more improvisational form in their context. Currently, Lomi emphasizes relationships among conscious touch, creative movement, mindful living, community, and ecological awareness. It is still a somatic discipline, but it is also an emerging philosophy of social activism grounded in self-knowledge and spiritual practice.

Meanwhile, Polarity Therapy is practiced entirely differently at Northern California's Heartwood Institute, where it is combined with alchemical hypnotherapy, Taoist dietary practices, and psychotherapeutic massage. Additionally, Heartwood founder Bruce Burger has developed a specific shamanic version of Polarity, merging aspects of

Stone's methods with spiritual modalities from his own Hindu and Plains Indian teachers.

Applied kinesiology has been adapted to the protocols of the Yellow Emperor, while Tibetan medicine is occasionally practiced in a Goodheart-derived template. Chiropractic has been redefined in a softened mode by Feldenkrais "Awareness Through Movement" practitioners. There is no limit to the hierarchies of accretion and no requirement of purism except for a practitioner to keep his treatments cohesive and therapeutic. Integration is critical insofar as the addition of new procedures inevitably means the deemphasizing of former ones and a change in the meaning of the system as applied.

Rolfing can also be integrated with Feldenkrais (much as the founders of each envisioned) in a sequence in which Rolfing initiates new structure and Feldenkrais teaches how to inhabit the structure. In one such syncretic system Judith Aston, a one-time student of Ida Rolf, has put together elements of Alexander Technique, Feldenkrais Method, and osteopathy but in such a distinctive and subtly idiosyncratic amalgam that Aston-Patterning is considered a modality of its own. Aston employs three very different kinds of hands-on manipulation, one similar to Feldenkrais' mode of light touch with verbal instructions, a second using manipulation to make the joints more mobile, and the third a subtle palpation of the connective tissues of the body. These may represent a spectrum of intuitive touch rather than three distinct modes. In still other therapeutic circumstances, she teaches her own version of "Awareness Through Movement" exercises as well as some contrasting, very discrete movements that seem as though they might have originated with F. Matthias Alexander.

Aston diverged from Rolf particularly on the issue of the symmetrical line:

> Unlike more traditional body mechanics of symmetry and alignment of the body perpendicular to the ground, I found that all movement is naturally asymmetrical and that everybody develops slight asymmetries through the intrinsic structure of having one heart, one

> liver, etc., as well as through adaptation to all the kinds of injuries, sports, and daily habit patterns....
>
> Around 1975–77, I made two discoveries that were critical to the development of Aston-Patterning: (1) That movement came from asymmetry and (2) That I was seeing a very different model for body mechanics than the one based on accepted medical and human factors that designers model.[1]

Aston took her inquiries in an unusual (though ingenious) somatic direction—directly into the artifacts of a ubiquitous technology. After all, the health implications of a mechanical world-view are not limited to the explicit practice of medicine; they extend to all patterns imposed by structures arising from that world-view. What Matthias Alexander began by having his clients practice sitting in a chair and then standing, Judith Aston continued by examining and then remaking a variety of furniture, clothing, vehicle interiors, and tools:

> My paradigm participates in [the] general realization that linear causality doesn't properly explain the way things work.... Since 1975 I have been working with a very specific aspect of a paradigm shift. This unique aspect has to do with the understanding of assumptions about the body's best posture and mechanics for motion and the body in relationship to any object that it touches such as utensils, a chair, a keyboard, golf club, steering wheel, and so on.[2]

After all, a golfer or basketball player, as well as a truck driver or plumber, is regularly adjusting his or her body by engagement with the movements and artifacts of a trade. These unintentional manipulations, reminiscent of the "lifting cure" of Norway, the "probing" exercises of Eutony, and the original mechanics of chiropractic, have far-reaching consequences. Aston proposed to introduce a new understanding of artifact kinesthetics into daily life:

> The idea of ergonomics was the final piece in this body-sense puzzle. For once you have changed, you may need assistance to use these changes in your normal everyday environment. I found that no mat-

> ter how long I worked with people and no matter how great the changes seemed, if they climbed right back into the same car seat or old shoes, for example, old patterns would be immediately reinforced. I started using duct tape, foam and towels to modify people's car seats, office furniture, kayaks, etc. I then saw the immense possibility for change beyond the few things I had been working on. Most products people habitually use were in need of redesign. I realized that people needed ergonomic education for their cars, homes, and office places to assist their bodies so that they can be in more natural, comfortable and effortless alignment....
>
> About five years ago I went to a patent attorney to see if I could patent my biomechanical mathematics theory. He looked into it and called me back with the good news/bad news message. "The good news," he said, "is that you may have discovered a new law of nature. The bad news is that, like the Theory of Relativity, a law of nature cannot be patented. You will have to patent each of your 300 designs."[3]

Joseph Heller was an aerospace engineer at the Jet Propulsion Laboratory in Pasadena when he became interested in human development, bioenergetics, and Gestalt psychology. Like A. T. Still and Moshe Feldenkrais, he applied insights from physics to physiology, particularly in an interpretation of structural mechanism and stress. After studying with Ida Rolf for six years, he became the first president of the Rolf Institute. However, he was not satisfied with "ten session" structural reintegration. From an insight that altering the fascia did not ingrain long-term or permanent psychological and emotional changes, he enlarged the Rolfing model to include prominent elements of Reichian and bioenergetic bodywork, Feldenkrais Method, and Aston-Patterning. Under the name Hellerwork, he developed a system that combined deep tissue integration with movement awareness and expression of emotion. In classic bioenergetic fashion, while carrying out the basic Rolfing protocol, he elicited a fuller verbal exploration of the feelings that inevitably arose from fascial engagement, seeking their developmental sources while teaching the client new avenues for their expression. At the same time, he reeducated their sensory-motor activities directly. In his own words:

> As Hellerwork highlights psychological issues and patterns embodied by physical structure, it also explores energy, starting with gravity and including the sense of connection people can discover between themselves and the universe beyond them. . . .
>
> Release of the rigidified musculature is, itself, a teaching aid through which the practitioner enables the client to see what her body has done in the past, what effect its doing so has had in the present, and what choice she has about realigning her relationship with her own mechanical, psychological, and energetic components, as well as with those of other people.[4]

MANY SOMATIC INTEGERS have been discovered more than once in different contexts. After all, each time a person goes inside his own body/mind experience, he derives some fundamental truth. While working out on the beach in the 1920s, Milton Trager, a teenager from a Chicago slum, independently glimpsed some of the same units of habitual movement and techniques of retraining as Matthias Alexander and Feldenkrais had. The young Trager was not only a dancer and acrobat at the time but also a body-builder and boxer. He made his most radical discovery when, reversing roles after a round in the ring, he decided to massage his manager and sparring partner instead of being massaged.

Trager discovered that true body-building lay in softening and loosening hard, rigid muscles, rather than in making them tougher and tighter. He went on to cure his father's sciatica, and then he began to help polio victims learn to walk again.[5] Later, he enlarged and refined his techniques into a full somatic system, became a doctor, and combined the practice of medicine with bodywork while working in Hawaii and, later, Northern California.

He originated a system of Psychophysical Integration, including a mode of gentle, penetrating manipulation (with a distinctive shaking of limbs) that has become known as the Trager Approach. "Trager had

discovered that he could release tension from the joints by shaking, rocking, or gently moving each part of the body in a rhythmic way that sent ripples through the flesh like a soft sonar wave. Wherever the undulating rhythm stopped or changed, Trager identified some rigidity blocking the natural path of this movement, as if a solid island had stopped a wave in water. He could then shake or manipulate the tension free from the point of the block."[6]

ALTHOUGH IT IS not in all cases chronologically accurate to speak of their development in this way, I prefer to categorize those systems which combine baseline methods with second-generation practices as third-generation somatic syntheses. For instance, Randy Cherner's work recombines Lomi therapy with Feldenkrais and craniosacral work to produce a unique modality of palpation. Amini Peller, a practitioner in Oakland, well trained in Breema, Zero Balancing, craniosacral work, psychic healing, vision quest, and Cherner's method of touch, has reintegrated elements from all of these in one practice. She is able to work on the aura and neuromuscular components simultaneously, and she is never without a hawk feather, mandala, or piece of energized quartz. There is no name for what she does, but everyone who has worked with her knows exactly, at an experiential level, what she is doing and how it is unique.

The most important feature of any somatic modality is to follow an experience where it leads rather than to use each client anew to express an allegiance to rigid rules. As much as Buddhism or *kung fu,* somatic work is continuously reexperienced in terms of what is immediate and functional (rather than what is asserted) and it is reinvented every day spontaneously.

Categories of treatment alternately complexify, i.e., go down into more profound layers of a method (as craniosacral work complexifies cranial osteopathy), and simplify, as Cherner's practice discards historical and ontological questions and hierarchies of exercises in the attempt to establish an elegant, functional mode of palpation. When

I studied with him, I became quite disoriented in the early weeks of the training. I kept trying to establish for myself the difference between our Feldenkrais work, our craniosacral work, and our Lomi work. Then I asked him for the appropriate circumstances in which to use "following" touch and in which to use grosser muscular palpations, cognitive exercises, or direct movements of parts of the body. He argued that there was no dividing line, only a spectrum in which one was always "following" even when lifting a whole leg or flexing the body into knees and elbows touching, and one was also always discriminating movements and habitual rigidities. Feldenkrais lessons and Lomi breathwork maintained continuously in respect to craniosacral rhythms make a refined and subtle mode of treatment.

Innovations within somatics are now more common than orthodoxies. In fact, I would propose, with some misgivings, that just about every system coming into existence recently under a new name (or emerging subsequent to the publication of this book) will be a third-generation somatic system rather than an entirely new method. It will also be a new method insofar as its "molecules" will be arranged in a novel way. Though nickel and neon reduce to the same molecular building blocks, on our level of manifestation they function as the most radically different entities.

WHAT STANDS OUT about the overall somatic "profession" is that syncretism is now assumed and each genre emerges naturally from others, much as systems of philosophy emerge from one another. In such a manner, modalities of "somatic philosophy" might be conceived as differentiating in the way existentialism, phenomenology, Whitehead's "process and reality," neo-Marxism, the Frankfurt School, deconstructionism, etc., did, and continue to, not by proposing new systems but by deriving modes of inquiry directly out of the syntax of prior modes (as well as generically out of the epistemology of inquiry itself). By comparison to mind-based philosophy, though, somatic philosophy and movement aesthetics are in their infancy. They are

potentially large enough to have their Platos, Kants, and Heideggers. In fact, Moshe Feldenkrais, Ida Rolf, F. Matthias Alexander, John Upledger, and Bonnie Bainbridge Cohen may be regarded as somatological philosophers inquiring into the substance of multiple ontologies of meaning. They are also grand system-makers in a classical sense. Many of the more recent somaticists tend to be opposed to system-making with its implicit hierarchicalization and thus do not formalize their techniques.

To the pure somaticizers we may also add innovative martial artists like Bruce Lee, Derek Jones, and Peter Ralston and a whole range of improvisational choreographers and multimedia artists all involved with redefining the uses of the body and the relation of mind and intention to action. These are constellations in the larger somatic universe.

There is one obvious major difference between systems of somatics and the more traditional ones of philosophy. Philosophy is for the most part "noisy," i.e., generative of text; somatics by comparison is silent and text is hard to come by. This is not because philosophy is not also somatic in its origin and somatics is not language-based but because the professions are carried out, one in words, the other in palpation. Philosophy is concerned with the continuously changing face of existence, the nature of time and space in the context of language, and the articulate obliteration of language. Somatics is concerned with precisely these same things but insofar as they are expressed mutely in the movement patterns and inner life rhythms of living organisms.

Zero Balancing

ZERO BALANCING IS a system of somatics developed by Fritz Smith over many years.[7] The son of a prominent chiropractor, Smith trained as an M.D. and osteopath in the 1950s, and subsequently became a certified acupuncturist and also a student of Shakti Yoga as taught by Swami Muktananda. He studied with Ida Rolf and on one occasion was her model for seven hours. Out of these various experiences, he formulated his own distinctive set of ideas and techniques, though he did not initially give them their own title of Zero Balancing (a student would later do that).

Smith defines Zero Balancing as a hands-on body balancing and integrating methodology which aligns energy fields with structure. Zero

Balancing has one of its taproots in osteopathy but is distinct in that it is a nonmedical approach to health and wholeness, which uses "energy" as its guiding metaphor. Alignment through Zero Balancing atomizes stress in a vibration flowing through the person, releasing at the same time any compensatory reactions within the nervous system and body/mind. Thus, Zero Balancing tends to be a complementary health system to craniosacral therapy, Polarity, acupressure, acupuncture, and Body-Mind Centering.

Although Bonnie Bainbridge Cohen, the founder of Body-Mind Centering, had no prior contact with Zero Balancing, she did experience its work at the source when she arrived at Esalen a few days early for a 1989 seminar and found Fritz Smith teaching. Joining the class, she discovered a strong affinity to her own system and a range of techniques that she felt were quite successful.[8] Later she wrote: "Dr. Fritz Smith, osteopath, acupuncturist, and the founder of Zero Balancing, transmitted to me the dynamic and mutable life of bone."[9]

Zero Balancing is at once a practical, empirically developed technique and the reflection of a philosophy. Smith conceived the relationship between energy and matter much as Rudolf Steiner did in his development of anthroposophical medicine. Insofar as bone is the densest modality of incarnating tissue, Smith describes himself as working not on soft tissue but the fulcra of a physical and vibrational body as represented by the bones and their junctures. He emphasizes bone

because the deepest and strongest currents of energy in the body flow through it.

The Zero Balancer assesses skeletal energy by sensing and evaluating currents within bones. He feels each bone, working his way down the body from the neck and spine to the hips, legs, and metatarsals, paying specific attention to the skeleton. He tests every rib, vertebra, and each of a specific class of joints known as foundation and semi-foundation joints. The sacroiliac joint, the intervertebral, costovertebral, and costosternal joints, and the tarsal and carpal joints of the feet and hands have more to do with the transmission of energetic and mechanical forces than they do with providing locomotion for the body. The Zero Balancer weighs the end range of motion and the supporting ligament tension of these joints as a gauge of their energetic integrity. That is, he holds the bones and joints in stillness and, lifting slightly with his fingertips into an area of tension or void, waits there for a few seconds or so. Creating a fulcrum (or balance point), he pauses until the client's energy releases or fills the area.

The hands and fingers alter the geometric equation forming each skeletal nexus and thus provide them in turn with an energetic as well as a mechanical basis for reorganization. Zero Balancing involves learning positions of holding which transmit "balance" to the organism—not those positions which are precisely symmetrical but which mean "balance" in organismic terms. "A fulcrum," Smith says, "is a balance point or lever around which movement occurs and by means of which energy and forces are brought to bear."[10] He has described these as three-dimensional grids of pressure around which systems within the body start to move and reorient themselves. The power of such grids is in the transmission of their shapes inward and outward, large and small ripples which give off hundreds of replicas of themselves, both larger and smaller, with each replica then casting out countless more. Very complicated geometric forms enter the body/mind at different levels. By repeated use of fulcra, a skilled practitioner can balance the body's entire field of energy.

Smith explains:

> Of fundamental importance is the fact that if the foundation and semi-foundation joints become imbalanced, the body tends to compensate around the imbalance rather than to resolve it directly. This results in the formation of subclinical patterns of stress and imbalance which not only limit a person's full function but can eventually lead to gross and symptomatic pathology.
>
> For instance, the small tarsal bones of the feet are designed to absorb the impact of walking and the tremendous pounding they receive every time a step is taken. If they become energetically out of balance, then every time a person walks, the stress of impact goes deeper into their body because it is not being absorbed by the first line of defense located in the feet. Zero Balancing helps to recalibrate these joints to absorb stress and thereby lessen stress patterns elsewhere in the body.[11]

Smith came to define his cosmology by a familiar metaphor from contemporary physics: that light exists as both a particle and a wave, and that, in a sense, we represent "entrapped light." Physical or structural bodywork attends to our particle nature, and vibrational or meridian flow contacts our wave. Zero Balancing addresses both of these aspects of creation—structure and energy. The hand holding the bone feels the body simultaneously as wave and as particle. By creating a balance point, a fulcrum, and holding this in stillness, the therapist guides the particle and wave to the point of zero where they vibrate equally, wave as particle, particle as wave.

Smith adds,

> Another analogy I make is to a sailboat: we have the sail as the structure and the wind as the energy. Somewhere the wind hits the sail; somewhere in the body energy and structure meet. They have an interrelationship. Zero Balancing looks at that relationship, the interface of energy and structure. The pure energy systems, like acupuncture and homeopathy, or *Chi Gung* and Reiki, work with one side of the equation; the pure body handling systems, like osteopathy,

chiropractic or Rolfing, work on the other side of the equation. Zero Balancing does both by bringing energy and structure into one working piece.[12]

After defining his system, Smith reflected that Ida Rolf was probably working with both energy and structure while teaching from the perspective that she was reshaping things only structurally:

> When I was studying Rolfing I was fortunate to be Ida's model for seven sessions.... In those days "energy" had not yet been "discovered" by the West, and there was no "energy vocabulary" by which Ida could describe or teach exactly what she was doing. It was only years later, after I knew that vocabulary and had learned to control energy through touch, that I surmised that Ida was actually working with energy as well as structure and thereby didn't create hurtful pain. As she'd go through my fascia, a bolus of energy developed in front of her thumb or elbow which opened up my field, so that when she got there with her own structure, my physical body was already in motion.[13]

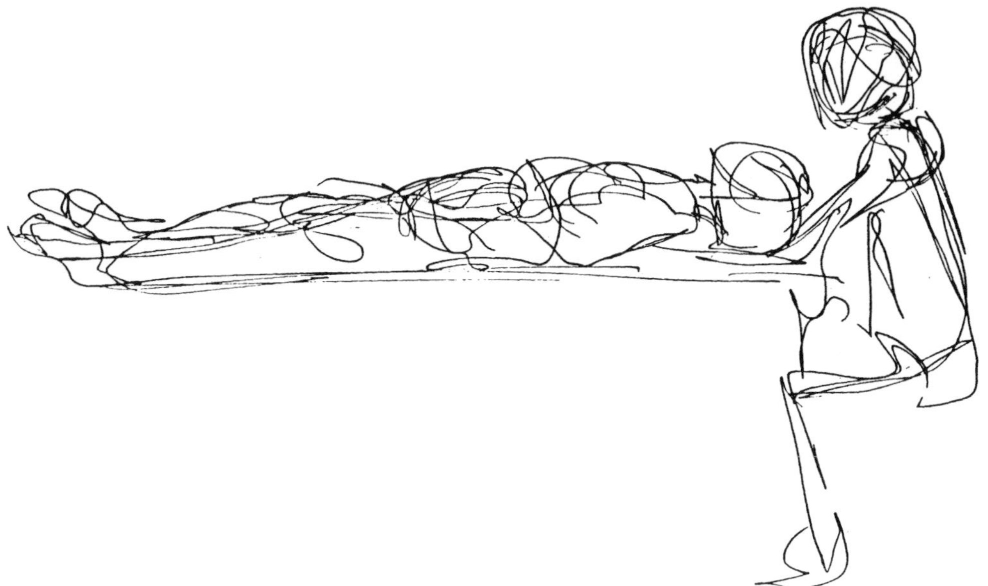

Zero Balancing may be *chi*-based, though in ways different from *Chi Gung.* It resembles Reiki in its "holding in relationship to energy." But Smith distinguishes it from pure spirit healing as "structure-holding energy" that is directly osteopathic.

Zero Balancing and craniosacral work are both influenced by osteopathy and both rely on palpation of the body. Practitioners of these two approaches try to delineate key differences in their work. The Zero Balancer works directly with the vibration of the bone itself, and from the interface of touch, which keeps separate the energy fields. He does not read the craniosacral rhythm or blend energy with that of the client. He tracks precisely where his energy ends and another field begins, and then he maintains that separation consciously. Although there is no extensive somatoemotional release, Zero Balancing offers a profound unwinding of its own, quite physical and with a direct grounding impact. As one Zero Balancer told me, "Craniosacral work can feel like a trance. In fact, many people have the sense that nothing is happening and discount it for that reason. In Zero Balancing, there is a very clear sense of boundary and that something is happening. There is a profound way in which the simple holding of the bones touches a person at the core, often relieving intense chronic conditions in just a session or two."[14]

Each Zero Balancing treatment takes about a half hour. The patient lies on his back. The holding is done through clothing. The entire body is touched during a session, though the arms, for being off the central axis, are usually paid less attention.

The impact of adding Zero Balancing to his repertoire for any somatic practitioner will depend on prior training. For the clinician with little or no experience in hands-on bodywork, it presents an integrated body-handling approach. For an acupuncturist or skilled energy worker it shows the body side of the body/energy equation and offers new ways of opening structural blocks which may impede the energy therapy. For the bodyworker it supplies the energy side of the body/

energy equation and opens a new dimension of hands-on touch. For the psychologically oriented therapist it shows how directly to engage and work with expanded states of consciousness induced through touch. For the field theory of somatics Zero Balancing represents one more highly individualized approach which, although paralleling other methods, offers a distinct vocabulary and set of techniques.

Body-Mind Centering

Bonnie Bainbridge Cohen has been a participant not only in some but in virtually every major somatic system thus far described, as well as in many dance, movement-related, and neuro-developmental systems not described. She is a modernist in the sense that her work defies systemization and crosses traditional boundaries—between, on the one hand, dance, performance, voice, and sports, and, on the other, occupational therapy and classical bodywork; likewise, she shifts from ceremonies to treatments, from improv sessions to classes, etc. Bainbridge Cohen is evocative and seminal, but she is not (nor does she intend to be) systematic in a conventional or academic fashion. Thus, her training opens up areas that would not ordinarily be accessible or even definable. Like Gerda Alexander, she developed a complex system within an artistic and aesthetic framework and then enlarged it in a therapeutic context (or perhaps vice versa, for she was always a therapist as well as a dancer). Coming out of dance notation, for instance, she proposes describing the exact vectors and presence of each organic gesture, be it the strike of a polar bear's paw or a baby struggling to walk. She carries out these definitions only at the deepest levels of the origins of these movements and in order to capture the spirit at their core.

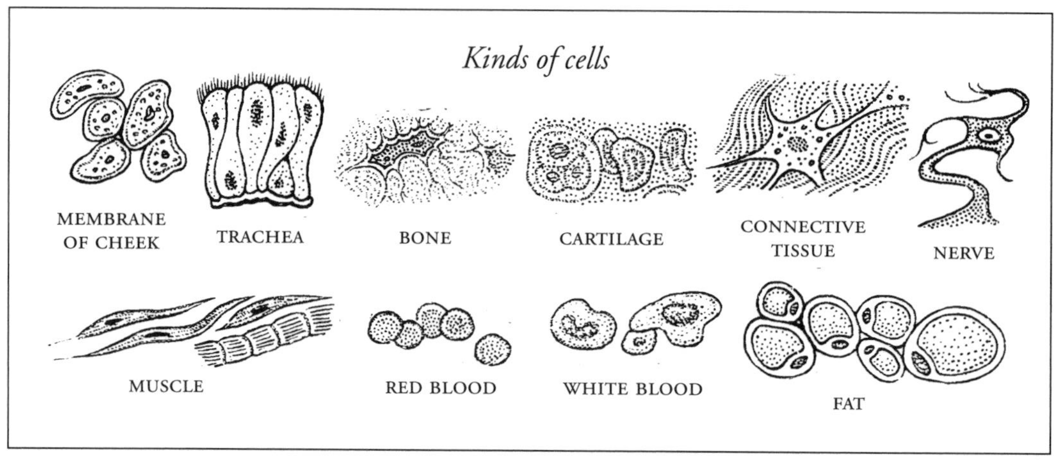

A student of hers, a former classical ballet dancer who became a Rolfer, gives an appreciation of her range and depth:

> Bonnie's work allows you to go, through attention, from your body as an organism, to a particular organ, to the actual cells that make up the organ. Once you get to that depth, you can decide what tissues you'd like to access. Then you allow those cells to initiate the movement.[15]

This means "cells" as units of mind, "cells" as cultural categories, and, at the same time, the billions of actual independent entities making up our bodies. One is reminded of the Sun which took a whole novel (Frank Herbert's *Whipping Star*) to slow down its perception and find a narrow enough wave-band on which to send a critical message to the tiny human beings on one of the worlds that circled it.[16] Choreographer Phoebe Neville notes:

> Instead of learning about the colon from a book, we learned what it feels like to mobilize it, to move from it. It can be very intense because the innervation of the organs goes up to the limbic system in the brain, the center of emotion and memory. When one starts exploring different organs, memories and emotions come up—old accidents, eating disorders.[These connections recall] the Chinese medical model, where organs are associated with different emotions."[17]

Bainbridge Cohen explains:

> Though we use the Western anatomical terminology and mapping, we are adding meaning to these terms through our experience. When we are talking about blood or lymph or any physical substances, we are not only talking about substances but about states of consciousness and processes inherent within them. . . .
>
> The study of [Body-Mind Centering] includes both the cognitive and experiential learning of the body systems—skeleton, ligaments, muscles, fascia, fat, skin, organs, endocrine glands, nerves, fluids; breathing and vocalization; the senses and the dynamics of perception; developmental movement (both human infant development and the evolutionary progression through the animal kingdom); and the art of touch and repatterning.[18]

Skilled at imparting pathways to proprioception, Bainbridge Cohen has students color in parts of skeletons, or guides them as they take their minds into certain zones of the body, such as the thoracic cavity, and feel the distinctive oddities there. Each area discovered expands a deepening awareness of other areas. She instructs students on moving in ingenious ways that awaken dormant senses of organ presence. She is always working toward more interiorized apperceptions and away from mere skeletoneuromuscular perceptions (though these are part of the overall awareness). She invokes down to a cellular level from the standpoint that the cells are the layer most primitively responsive to intention. But she has not even given up on atoms, molecules, and, for that matter, quarks, or whatever else exists underneath those. If these are there, they contribute in some way to the overall kinesthesia of mind and existence. Put differently, if they were not there, how would we feel? Don Johnson writes:

> She once worked with me lying on my back, while she sat behind me, hands cradling the occipital region of my head. She said, "Now I am in my bones moving your bones." I experienced unusually clear feelings of my cranial bones and the articulations of my skull and the vertebrae of my neck. I told her of my arid spinal sense. She con-

> tinued, "I will go into my fluids. Now I am in my fluids." As she gently cradled my head and rocked it, I felt the gushing of fluids contained in my head and neck, followed by vibrant pulsings inside my spinal column. It felt like oil flowing deeply through my bones, so unfamiliar that my mind went blank for a moment, and I felt an ecstatic pleasure.[19]

If her practices sound fantastic, her childhood prepared her for them. She was born in 1942 into "the Ringling Brothers and Barnum & Bailey Circus, where her father sold tickets and her mother was a trapeze and high-balance artist and Roman racer; who rode two horses with one foot on each."[20]

"Ordinary reality consisted of acrobats risking their lives on the highwire, the bearded lady and the snake lady. The structure of her everyday experience reflected the polymorphous quality of three rings filled with horses, elephants, clowns, acrobats and fire-eaters, all performing simultaneously."[21]

"I grew up," she says, "with the extraordinary being natural, and therefore things other people considered miraculous or impossible never were impossible for me.... It took me two years to figure out how to get into my blood, to differentiate it from lymph. That's where the circus influence came in—it gave me the sense of possibility."[22]

At a young age Bainbridge Cohen became an occupational therapist, gradually enlarging her repertoire by learning various forms of dance therapy and neuro-muscular reeducation. In 1968 she "went to Europe, where she taught movement and bodywork at the Psychiatric Research Clinic of the University of Amsterdam and worked with injured dancers at the Pauline de Groot dance studio ... During her year abroad, she also trained in England with Karl and Berta Bobath, originators of neurodevelopmental therapy, a method of restoring developmental movement patterns in children with brain injuries."[23] After she married Leonard P. Cohen in New York, she moved to Japan at the end of the 1960s so that he could continue his studies of aikido. While there she began teaching at the Tokyo government's new rehabilitation

school for the training of occupational and physical therapists and at another established training program under the auspices of the Japanese national government. This required her (with a smattering of Japanese language) to treat and educate physically disabled Japanese students, who had perhaps better but still limited ability to converse in English. During this time, unknowingly she was laying the groundwork for Body-Mind Centering. Soon thereafter, like William Sutherland and Matthias Alexander, she began to conduct experiments on herself and to recognize the separate states of consciousness within the different zones and organs of the body. She did this by literally projecting her attention into bones, tissues, mind, and cells. She not only put her focus on the major bones and organs but worked her way down into the tiny bones and boundaries between organs, dwelling in each place in order to experience its intrinsic feeling of itself. She traveled through, if not the Underworld the Intraworld, with the faith of the *Chi Gung* master, to feel what is there to feel, nurture it, and follow it further inward.

After reading the above description, Bainbridge Cohen elaborated:

> Exploring movement and consciousness has always been at the root of my being. It is my inherent language—my primary perception and mode of existence. My mother always said that I began dancing in the womb. The challenge of translating movement consciousness into the exact science of Western anatomy, however, began in 1973, but I did not realize that it would entail all tissues until 1976, when I had the insight into the organ and endocrine systems. It then took me until 1982 to "break the code" and embody all of my systems.[24]

Bainbridge Cohen emphasizes that BMC *is* a highly systematic approach to transmitting embodiment of all of one's body tissues within the context of one's history and developmental process, but the transmission occurs improvisationally according to the moment, the relationship of the people, and the environment.[25] Body-Mind Centering does not rely on a programmatic way to attain either postures or functions or even a sustained set of educational techniques. It is a process of going deeper and deeper into the natural, intrinsic possibilities of movement and somatic expression.

A series of unwindings strives to express itself through the varied poses and styles of daily life but usually is suppressed by requirements (or imagined requirements) of etiquette and by limited views of the self. That is why new modes of organ expression need to be developed and liberated, and also why the aesthetics of radical movement attract people so loyally and persistently. A great dance is not only appreciated by the minds of those watching but their livers, hearts, lungs, and kidneys. The body cries out for the motions it needs.

The natural expressions of emotions forever manifest the underlying reality and hidden life of the organs. The hoisting of partners in modern dance, our everyday chattering in consonants and vowels, the turning of a double-play in baseball, a girl's flirting at a party—all of these are direct expressions of lungs, heart, spleen, gonads, lymph, blood, and ultimately cells. The precise feeling of each of them provides a way back into more discrete and subtle levels of tissue. Bainbridge Cohen, after all, is a performance artist who developed some of her concepts while collaborating with Contact Improvisation master Nancy Stark Smith, so her lessons are more like organ and tissue dances than exercises.

In her book *Sensing, Feeling, and Action* Bainbridge Cohen explores the organs and circulatory flows of the interior body through photographs of individual human "street" poses ranging from spleen and gonad intensity to liver exaltation and relaxation, pancreas-and-gallbladder sweetness, and pure open-heartedness. These snapshots come from different milieus and cultures and each represents the unconscious abandonment of a man or woman to a desire or will originating in an organ substratum. Bainbridge Cohen tells us: "Notice the outward radiating of this woman's heart and the drawing in of her gonads ... reflected in the crossing of her legs, the holding in her ankles, and the expression of modesty.... Notice the woodcutter's active, assertive intent through the energy emanating outward from his liver.

LIVER: *In the man on the left, notice the release of his liver as he relaxes in his chair. Visual clues are the soft expansion through his liver area and the relaxed widening through his elbows.* GONADS: *In the woman, notice her energy drawing in through her heart and gonads, creating a seductive posturing.* GONADS: *In the man on the right, notice his energy emanating outward through his gonads, contained in his liver, neutral in his heart, and emanating outward through the lower lobes and inward through the upper lobes of his lungs.*

Captions by Bonnie Bainbridge Cohen. Photos by Bill Arnold.

Visual clues are the expandedness of his liver area and outward widening of his elbows."[26]

We are always acting out the desires and fears of our organs. "They" experiment with and reembody each of the stances, activities, and "artifacts" of our everyday life. So do our regular motions and gestures yield autonomic medicines. How much more powerful these become when they don't have to cut wood or act coy but are permitted unrestrained range in a dance or ritual designed just for them!

Bainbridge Cohen seeks the same depth of expression from clients in sessions:

> As important as knowing the name of the reaction/response, and as important as doing the patterns, is to understand what the reflexes, righting reactions and equilibrium patterns have to do with expression. For example, in this little girl I'm working with, on her right

> side which is fine, she's really bloodful and she waves her hand up and down. Yet she never waves the other hand up and down. She might *reach* for something, she'll use it *mechanically,* but it's like it doesn't *belong* to her, it doesn't have the bloodfulness. She's stuck in her nerves. I feel that it's the reflexes that carry it to the blood level.
>
> Without the reflex, there isn't expression and without the expression there isn't the reflex. So one of the things I'm trying to do is help get emotion into the movement of her arm....
>
> Anything, anything. Stroking her mother's hair, grabbing her daddy's beard, slapping her hand on the table to make rhythm, playing, flailing her arm in anger.[27]

Bainbridge Cohen's transmissions to her trainees are stubbornly subtle. Their art comes from her privileging her own (and their own) internal excursions and the capacity of these to provide their own creative modes of action through experience. She will not give up complexity and potential in order to bottom out in a simplified version of a discovery, though she will lead a student from one fully experienced domain to another to get eventually to the one she originally targeted. For instance in an ocular exercise, she tells students, "When you go to look, don't *try* to move your muscle or your bones, but let the eye respond to the light that's being reflected. Once you become receptive to that phenomenon, let *go* of the reception as your purpose and let that become the *support* for seeing."[28]

Another exercise is to embody each specific muscle of the eye and to perceive how the activation of each muscle alone and in various combinations affects one's vision, consciousness, and movement.[29]

> "The CSF (cerebrospinal fluid) is a rarefied fluid," Bainbridge Cohen tells a class; "it gives the feeling of being suspended between heaven and earth. Find the internal fluid and let it travel; it goes into lightness—not because I push up but because I rarefy through the CSF." As she says this, she rolls over on the floor, then rises on her toes with arms floating upward. For those less able to experience the CSF quality kinesthetically, she suggests, "Play with images, like a leaf

falling." Around the room the students resemble an introductory modern dance class—waving, dipping, rolling....

"There's something so luscious about fat, and so powerful," she remarks. "But in our culture, this soft power has been repressed."[30]

The healing effect of this work resembles the transmission of nonlinguistic messages. It arises from a combination of touch, intrinsic movement, and the therapist responding naturally to her clients and providing them with new matrices of behavior.

"All natural phenomena fall into patterns," Bainbridge Cohen says. "The nervous system has the potential for innumerable patterns, but the patterns are not accessible to us until they are actually stimulated into existence, until we actually do them."[31]

Bainbridge Cohen specializes in applying BMC in the treatment of infants and young children who have mild to severe developmental difficulties (the younger the better), at least in part because they put her at the gateway to the whole psychosomatic domain and also because children are moldable and receptive to techniques in unexpected ways. Bainbridge Cohen continues, "The children have been my mentors. They teach me constancy of presence, immediacy of response, direct perception and love."[32]

Homolateral movement

Spinal movement

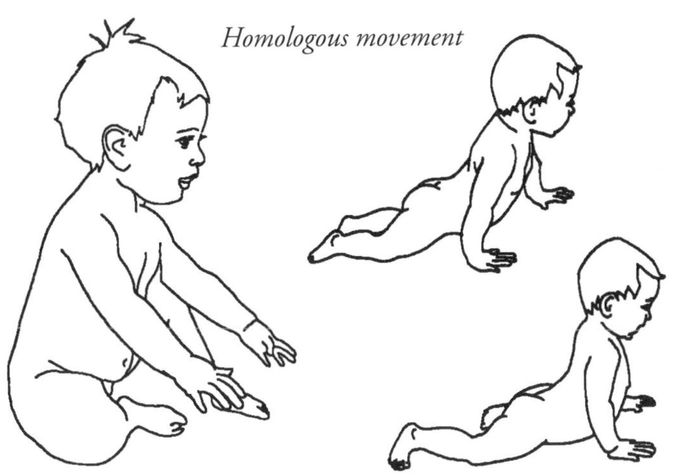

Homologous movement

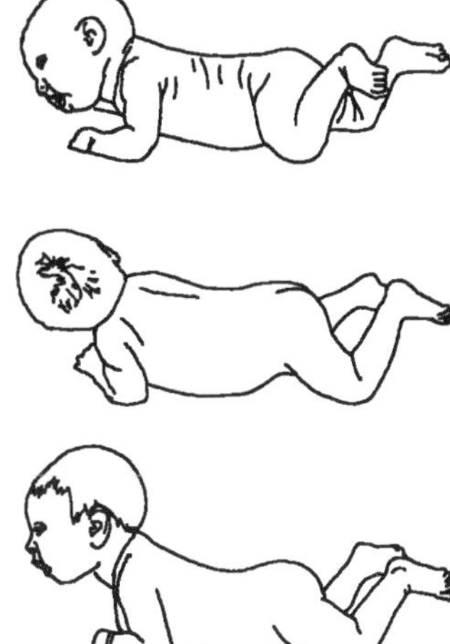

After reading an earlier version of this section, Bonnie Bainbridge Cohen wrote me that the text constituted for her "a challenge to draw into words. Therefore you will receive many shadow words."[33]

Looking at the broad sweep of the book and then the somatics chapters as a subset, she offered a central point about her own development:

> I am a daughter of the matriarchal lineage and not a synthesis of the male heritage you have so carefully scribed....
>
> The following are excerpts from a journal I kept for an individualized science research class while a senior in high school (age 16 years). There were 12 students in this class, each exploring a research project of our own for the year.
>
> (dated October 6, 1958)
>
> I have chosen to study the muscular and skeletal systems of the cat.... Besides knowing the names of the muscles and bones, I want to know what they do, how they work, and if possible, if something happens to them if they can be cured, and if so, how.[34]

Subsequent journal notes record her after-school visit to a Cerebral Palsy Home concurrent with a wish to study dance therapy (though her high school counselors had no knowledge of such a field) plus a description of coloring in the parts of a cat on a drawing. A "Prospectus for Possible Research," written at the age of twenty-one while an occupational therapist at Bird S. Coler hospital in New York, shows how early the substantial roots of Body-Mind Centering were in place.

Bainbridge Cohen then adds that many of the somatic modalities I put in her lineage are incidental to the formulation of Body-Mind Centering, the curriculum for which was substantially in place by 1982. She recalled having three or four early Feldenkrais sessions and "observed one or two classes of Moshe ... and him working with a client the last year he taught (about 1983?)." She also received some Alexander sessions in the mid-1970s, "the first three Rolfing sessions in 1980 and the other seven in 1989.... While I am very grateful for the help these practitioners and approaches provided me, they are not the roots of BMC.

However, I am extremely indebted to them for the environment they have created in the culture, so that the development of BMC has flourished."[35]

She continues:

> I describe the following of movement in terms of the cerebrospinal fluid because it is the basis of effortless movement, which I have been exploring with consciousness since 1965 and teaching as a distinct fluid since 1982. What John Upledger and Dick McDonald gave to me was the awareness of the rhythmic flow of the CSF when the body isn't moving and the knowledge of its flexion/extension pendular rhythm.[36]

In place of the above, Bainbridge Cohen lists dozens of teachers, all of whom have provided her with some essential link in her chain. Among these just from the 1960s:

> Dr. Adolf Haas, my professor of psychiatry, showed me the existential nature of being, the blessing of suffering, and the limitless range of compassion. He taught me about "the shadow," I and Thou, and the reality of the imagination.... He also taught me never to introduce a person into a world in which he or she cannot live.[37]

Would that mainstream psychiatry still had such integrity of wisdom and compassion!

> Erick Hawkins, one of the giants of modern dance, gave me a technique that allowed me to embody my philosophy of life and to extend it into moment by moment awareness. He showed me effortless movement and the art of doing without doing.[38]

He also offered her the position of taking over his dance company.

> Yogi Ramira, an Indian yogi and physical therapist from Madras, introduced me to the techniques of yoga, its power in the healing of organic imbalances, and the effect it has upon one's state of mind.
>
> Berta Bobath, a physical therapist, and Dr. Karl Bobath, world leaders in the treatment of persons who have brain dysfunction,

taught me that if a person doesn't change directly under my hands each moment, then I should do something else. They showed me how the developmental process underlies all movement and how to repattern the nervous system based on that process, regardless of the manifested problems.[39]

Then from the 1970s:

Professor Cheng Man-ch'ing, a master of t'ai chi, Chinese medicine, poetry, and art, gave me a glimpse of the enormous power of effortless strength, in the guise of a laughing old man....

Haruchika Noguchi ... showed me the reality and power of magnetic energy as experienced through off-the-body touching....

Irmgard Bartenieff, dancer, physical therapist, and student of Rudolf Laban (founder of the Labanonotation and Laban Movement Analysis), stimulated in me unfathomable questions of how the body moves. These questions led me to an expanded view of how muscles move, the dynamics of flow and quality within movement, and the phenomenon of spatial tension and harmony....

Eido Roshi, Zen teacher, showed me how to sit. He along with Chögyam Trungpa, Rinpoche, Dr. Yeshe Donden, and other Buddhist teachers show me that presence both transmits and is transitory....

From aikido, the martial art, I learned how following, harmonizing, and blending with the ki of others forms the basis of repatterning.[40]

She concludes:

Being a nonlinear processor, Richard, I feel I can now say what I mean. The development of Body-Mind Centering has many roots and yet it has always existed inside of me. It has been transmitted through my blood—through the experience of all my mothers. Its blueprint is contained homeopathically in my bodily fluids. All others have helped me to clarify, elaborate and articulate it.[41]

I would extend Bainbridge Cohen's version of her own lineage to all somatic systems. Dancers, wizards, guardians, and angels play hide-

and-seek with us our whole lives. Their origins are not only vast and diverse but mysterious and transcendental. We are flooded with microdoses from within and without, from archetypal as well as cultural (and perhaps also cosmic and astrological) templates, messages that travel as long and far as meteor-seeds through an empty universe and then demand us for their expression at last. New forms burst into bloom everywhere from the same background which, though invisible, is as ripe as the arras of pomegranates behind the High Priestess in the second trump of the tarot. As we see the falling fruits, we imagine them on linear vines, the stems of which we trace to the ground into which they disappear. But there is also a nonlinear process that draws on so many other branches, on dimensions that go way beyond branches. In that sense, there is no history; there is only fire.

The extraordinary range of somatic systems can leave one with the sense that almost anything is possible, that any combination of techniques has some key functional effect. This is not an irrelevant perception. It is likely that the whole of somatics is beginning to open up a larger vocabulary of attention, movement, and touch through which we are all capable of becoming our own doctors, experiencing our own innards, and treating one another as peer healers. Nothing could be more useful in the present health crisis, which is characterized by a rapidly aging population and a ridiculously narrow protocol of approved methods for treating disease. In this sense, somatics is—as I proposed at the outset—not just a branch of alternative medicine but a new paradigm for medicine itself.

The multitude of systems suggests an uninvented cosmology of health. Not knowing its central truth, we arrive at its almost endless manifestations in the world, each of them represented by a different core of techniques—in *karate* dojos and dance studios, occupational therapy labs and zendos—as well as in holistic clinics. These techniques reveal the different subtle layers of our somatic existence and the interpolations of these layers with one another. The systems literally replicate our own complexity. Thus, there will be no end to new forms until,

imaginarily, we have tapped our full human complexity. In that sense, Body-Mind Centering is a benchmark of the innovative forms now emerging, systems which phenomenologically, improvisationally, regain the present moment, and at the same time pay their historical dues to the myriad techniques and tools developed by their forebears.

The Return to Autonomous Movement

Emilie Conrad-Da'oud grew up in New York in the 1930s and '40s, training from her youth to become a professional dancer. Her specialties were classical ballet and primitive dance. In 1955, longing to experience the primal rhythm at the roots of so many dance forms, she traveled to the West Indies. Entranced by the music and the culture, she ended up staying five years, immersed in Haitian dance and religion and organizing her own dance troupe. She became "half Haitian."[42]

After her return to her birth culture she found it impossible to escape the beat of the Indies. "Once she was back in New York ... the dissonance between the liquid, organic rhythms of Haiti and the frantic, manufactured pace of Manhattan grew to such a pitch that Conrad-Da'oud thought she would go mad.... In the midst of her inner chaos [she] began to realize that what we call our body is, to a large extent, a cultural construction. The disparity between how New Yorkers and people in the West Indies move and view their bodies convinced her that each culture 'imposes on its members a definition of the human form.' Beneath this construct, Conrad-Da'oud sensed only movement."[43]

It was that original movement, preceding culture, preceding any form of cognitive knowledge, to which Conrad-Da'oud would address all her future inquiries.

During the initial formative years of being caught between cultures, she modeled, taught primitive dance, and organized a dance troupe. "On occasion, she and her troupe did performances in nightclubs based on voodoo rituals. She has recounted ... the night during an ecstatic

solo fire dance, when she suddenly felt she had 'crossed over, beyond the possibility of ever coming back.' That 'crossing over' meant for her the breakdown of her culture, with all of the categories of meaning and bodily experience."[44]

In 1967, after a move to Los Angeles and a serious automobile accident—in a state she experienced as a "black hole," constantly dizzy and blandished by voices and visions from ancient cultures—she decided to give in entirely and let what was happening guide her. After all, those voices and visions intimated what she had been seeking ever since she had embarked on her study of dance almost thirty years earlier—an inherent form of movement.

> I had to give up everything I believed.... I saw that what I called "my body"—how I moved, talked, even how I thought—was a cultural imprint. With all my training, I had been teaching "my body" to dance. But deep inside there was already a dance going on, if I would perceive it—a dance of myriad movement forms beyond anything I could think of. I had to feel it....[45]

This boundless reservoir of fluid energy Da'oud likened to pure love. It was as automatic as breathing and imbued every cell and molecule of her organism. From an intuition of this state she began to explore what she later called "micromovements," initially while lying in bed at night. She understood these felt sensations as glimmerings of movement trickling out of her absolute nature. She distinguished them from the externally visible and culturally recognized movements of most choreography and somatic work. "The result [was] Continuum, an approach to the body based on intrinsic felt movement rather than imposed patterned movement."[46]

Later, as she took up working with people suffering from severe neuromuscular afflictions, she saw that such intrinsic glimmerings manifested even in paralyzed persons.

In the case of one twenty-three-year-old woman partially paralyzed by polio since age one, "Emilie simply stayed present with her hands

on the young woman's body. She sat like this for hours at a stretch, giving no instructions, not even guiding her in visualizations. At first, Susan felt only heat. Then one of her legs began to shudder and move in strange ways that were similar to the ways that Emilie had found herself moving in her bed. Over a four-year period of weekly four-hour sessions, many of which were observed and subjected to electromyographical analysis in the UCLA kinesiology laboratory, Susan manifested a range of subtle and finely articulated movements. . . . 'Paralyzed people,' she writes, 'can feel movement inside their bodies, but because our culture does not value this kind of movement, they think they cannot move. Helping Susan get in touch with the movement within her atrophied leg allowed the inner movement to surface and ripple across the skin and eventually enabled Susan to lift her leg.' "[47]

The movements of Continuum are unlike any other somatic form. The body undulates as if an anemone in water. Its solid parts ripple. Ribs become waves. The spine reverts to a soft notochord. As pulses of energy flow radially outward, front and back are indistinguishable. The lower back looks like a belly; shoulders resemble breasts. Such plasticity reminds one of a body-builder flexing muscles. However, Da'oud emphasizes unconscious, unpredictable, nonserial motility. Her patterns arise as certainly in paraplegics as in athletes. She refers to them as "liquid smoke" or "singing the body electric."

Over the years Da'oud built a practice based on these discoveries, teaching workshops in micromovements and treating a diversity of ailments by eliciting people's natural forms of motility. This mode of treatment is reminiscent in different ways of *Chi Gung, katsugen-undo,* Eurhythmy, and Body-Mind Centering.

> "I want you to move," Da'oud tells people, "but not with your space probes, not with your arms and legs. I want you to feel the movement in your body. Start anywhere, with your ribs or with your ass." She begins to demonstrate. Her buttocks move, almost imperceptibly at first. The movement spreads to her back. "Suddenly aliveness

happens," she continues, now in a droning voice. Her eyes are slits. Her right shoulder begins to twitch. "Pay attention to how the movement wants to go. It takes strange pathways." Her left leg is lifting off the floor, her right arm twisting forward. Her elbow bends, her fingers curl and twist, her torso undulates in slow waves. "I am an unpredictable thing."[48]

Of course, not all creative and avant-garde dance or performance styles are healing or healthy, no matter how "new age" their movements seem or how eliciting they are of healing mandalas. Change either happens or doesn't. Spontaneous cures are precisely that: unexpected, inexplicable events. We are not supposed to prime them like gamblers waiting on a jackpot (or performers waiting for our organs to applaud). Just being an artist or living a creative or radical life guarantees nothing. It don't work like that! The profundity of sustained practice, the silent truth of a movement or gesture, an innate grace spreading medicinally—these are ineffable events and cannot be subordinated to a flash of insight or *tour de force,* no matter how brilliant, no matter how acclaimed the performance and how extreme the genre.

At one Continuum workshop a woman with the intestinal disorder known as Crohn's disease (who had just been diagnosed as having only a few months left to live) began moving in an utterly innovative fluid manner. The next day her doctor could find no evidence of the illness. In several instances of people with major spinal cord damage, Da'oud has been able to track alternative pathways to their central nervous systems. She encourages crippled people to crawl on their hands and knees across the floor and then follow their own unexpected micromovements. Some clients she instructs to intone "wo," "sth," or other unfamiliar sounds from far back in their throats or by vibrating their tongues against their palates. Other exercises involve moving one part of the body, like the ring finger, slowly for fifteen minutes. Each instruction consists of eliciting intrinsic motion and letting it expand into multidimensional space.

Here the underlying units of dance and Haitian voodoo merge into a primordial form of medicine. This is an archetypal not a post-modern event. When shamanic healing occurs in our own culture, it likely replicates thousands—if not millions—of such instances prehistorically and among ahistorical cultures. Micromovements presided at the birth of speech, magic, and ritual courtship, and inform even the decoys and guiles of hunting strategy. It is no wonder they emerge again from

music and dance and in the sensory expression of each person's core being.

AMIDST THE DIVERSITY of somatic strategies and disciplines, one rather simple theme stands out—freeing movement. The majority among the human species have lost their inheritance—basic and autonomous function. If unstifled, true hearts and minds perform ideas and actions sympathetically and do not require our abstract homilies for them. From the silence of their sheer depth, they inform behavior and realize inherent substantiality. They energize the stale shadows of disease.

In our striving for intentional performance we have forgotten that we embody natural movements and automatic motions, not only at a neuromuscular level but at the differential of cells and molecules. Thus, while creating a science-fiction superculture, we have ignored that our survival and well-being rest on a substratum of tissue and fascia that are sustained by a realm of water, oxygen, and chlorophyll. We squander this milieu by not inhabiting it fully. "'We do not move. We are movement,' Emilie Conrad-Da'oud tells her students over and over again."[48]

We are heartless when we cannot feel our hearts, and we are mindless when we do not experience mind in all our tissues. In their place, we derive pretentious and egoistic substitutes for physical existence. Yet we are homeostatic fields right from our seed.

Embryonic embodiment occurs as global and regional waves responding to the topological exigencies of prior waves, all moving forth from a microscopic template of two cells to billions of separate currents and zones of tissues making up a functional life-form. This process expresses exquisite mathematical and musical properties: rhythm, octaves, chords, seriality, counterpoint, melody, and commutability. Notes and integers appear in entirely logical but unpredictable places. It is because we *are* music that we respond to its vibration so profoundly.

The mind also has natural movements and patterns. Aspects of these jell as insights, emotions, complex modes of proprioception, and ecstasy.

Birth and maturation are naturally unfolding mind-forms; death is also a natural mind-form "embodying" dissolution. Yet we have embraced our more mechanical aspect and the personae that support it.

Animals nearly always move and think autonomously. Aboriginal men and women were likely more "flowing" than their socialized descendants have become. It is a reasonable presumption that powers of self-healing and healing—and perhaps even telekinesis and telepathy—occurred immediately and uncritically among Cro-Magnons and their kin. That is, they didn't even know that there was such a thing as *chi* or psychic energy; yet they experienced them as absolutely as wind, prairie, and self.

Whether these abilities were once generally accessible or always elite, it is clear that we have a great deal of difficulty inculcating them today. In fact, we are not sure they even exist. This leaves us in a global state of schizophrenia. Seeking to generate power extrinsically while denying it intrinsically, we become in fact powerless.

"If Martians were looking at us through some interstellar resonating device," says Emilie Conrad-Da'oud, "I am sure they would marvel at how our planet has arranged us.

"'Look, look,' they would say. 'Their bodies are mostly water and yet they move about the earth in this apparently solid way.'

"'Just look at how each organ is maintaining its link with all of its undulating strands.'

"'They are like fish out of water, but they carry it with them.'

"'How amazing these humans are!'"[50]

FOR ALL ITS other avocations, somatics is on the cutting edge of our urgency to confront the crisis of faith in ourselves and restore autonomous function. It would be an oversimplification to state that somatic systems seek only to break down millennial habits of cortical overfunction and resistance and to restore natural movement and homeostasis to the human body and psyche, but to overlook this component would be to miss one of the few universal somatic themes.

The craniosacral rhythm is apparently a reliable intrinsic compass of well-being. When the flow of cerebrospinal fluid is uniform and unimpeded, a person is more at peace and healthier, more capable of compassion and creativity. Thus, cranial osteopathy and craniosacral therapy seek to restore a primordial condition of fluidity and cohesion.

Systems like the Feldenkrais Method, Alexander Technique, Eutony, and various forms of dance and movement therapy all provide the organism with means of getting around conscious overdrive, past the cerebral cortex into autonomous movements. Their lessons are intended to trick or guide the body into more basic, less artificial functioning. In that sense they are the precise opposite of most educational practices, which seek to compound cognitive structures and gain full control over emotions and spontaneity. All of these somatic, sensory-motor modalities tell us that the habits of repression whereby we have subjugated our animal selves lead also to poor health—neurosis, dysfunction, and skeletal and neuromuscular blocks in which tissue pathologies breed. So their scripts prompt the bones and tissues to their own mysterious dances.

The Taoist arts have as their centerpiece the inherent flow of *chi.* As noted, Stone Age people were likely aware of *chi* and knew how to stimulate it from the feedback of daily experience. They were probably also aware of the rhythm of the pulse and the cerebrospinal fluid. They recognized their own capacity to direct energy outward; hence, were masters of voodoo and the "evil eye." We have transferred all of these functions, in whole or in part, to intellectual categories and machines.

Western science has no discrete definition of *chi. Chi* is not blood, lymph, cerebrospinal fluid, or even electricity and magnetism. At times it is proposed as a concurrence of these things or as a proportion including mind. But is *chi* not also simply a fusion of autonomous movements, all working together as one movement with the virtues of all of them combined in a single elixir-like sensation of a healing current? Although *"chi"* training is a lesson in feeling a specific thing called "*chi*

energy," that may simply be a custom of historical Chinese nomenclature. *Chi* may also be the ground state of autonomous movement itself, and its therapeutic and shamanic virtues may be the sum benefaction of natural body/mind flow. The practitioner claims to be raising *chi,* but there may never be a concrete substance to raise like water in a well. There may only be the full coherence of living tissue and its creative capacity—and this may represent all modes of cosmic as well as psychic energy.

"What we call 'body'," says Conrad-Da'oud, "is not 'matter' but movement. The body is a profound orchestration of many qualities and textures of movement, interpenetrating tones of fertile play, waiting to be incubated. What I see as body is the urging of creative flux, waves of fertility. The cosmic play that we enter this atmosphere with still goes on at an intrinsic level—we are mostly not aware of the world we carry.

"It is *there* in this cosmic soup disguised as organs and cartilage and tissue that the universe is moving in its creative flux like a giant egg waiting to be fertilized. The amniotic matrix moves with the same undulations that started the cosmic swirl that we call earth in the first place.

"Our intrinsic world *is* our cosmic connection, it is our legacy of love and wonder—it is where God plays at midnight, it is the big bang, the splitting of atoms, and the message of Jesus."[51]

The goal of this discussion is not to reduce all somatic systems to one denominator or to suggest that a return to the stars or to the wild is the goal of somatic epistemology. Animals, though in a state of freedom, are in a prison so diabolical we should be glad to entertain our own self-made demons. The fact is that men and women live in society and in bodies conditioned by society and minds shaped by cultural concepts. Natural man became tribal man, and tribal man became a farmer, an artisan, a merchant, and a politician. If natural man had been in a state of perfect grace, none of these overlays would have

encompassed him. In fact, "he" would have happily remained a lizard and a tiger for the duration.

The complications and responsibilities of a phenomenological and spiritual world portend the subtleties of psychological, philosophical, and somatic practices. Even as some sort of accreting force is driving us toward global society and a purely metaphysical realm of experience, an original dissipative force is attempting to restore to us (and restore us to) our birthright as living organisms. We are not ideas, and we will never be machines. We are creatures. All our joys, grievings, and resolutions must be based in the density, limitations, boundaries, and kinetic charge of tissue. We cannot transcend this condition cybernetically or prosthetically. We cannot become cyborgs or inhabit virtual reality. Despite certain New Age fantasies, the flesh is not merely a vehicle to deliver the spirit seed to a higher dimension. The flesh and biosphere are extremely powerful manifestations of spirit seeking identity and experience in waves and holograms of matter. The goal is not to blast out of bodies but to transform bodies into temples of learning and vehicles of compassion. Bodies are the ultimate test (in this realm anyway) for spirits on a vision quest. They are spirit's choice. They are the grail. They are what it needs (and has always needed) in order to become whole.

Somatics is thus literally a healing art and at the same time the primary metaphor for a healing imperative we have yet to develop. On a planet beleaguered by physical destruction, denial, duplicity, and the ceaseless false hope of symbols, magic formulas, and gurus, bodywork systems represent one of the few positive signs of renewal. We do not know why we are unreliable and unfaithful. But these systems do not judge us. They assume the good will of every man and woman. They teach us how to be who we are at our best. In that sense, Reich was on target: no revolution is possible until its requirements of mental and physical hygiene have been met. Somatic systems invariably train us to act on behalf of the planet because this is what we do naturally when we don't interfere or are not bought off by superficial and substitute pleasures. When we honor the flesh, we honor the biosphere.

If bodies are the spirits of the universe in crisis, somatic systems address their spiritual nature directly and with dignity. Body-oriented therapy is spiritual therapy because, as Ida Rolf proposed, there is no other way to go to the house of the spirit. The body is the only part of the spirit we feel from within. Thus, unless we learn to live in bodies in a physical realm, we cannot contact our spirits. They told us precisely this by becoming bodies and by making that brazen act the sheer density of the world and ourselves. This time we chose not to be able to escape. We vowed to see this one through.

We are cosmic beings having a human experience.

We certainly cannot contact spirits as religious abstractions or pieties at the end of rituals. For all the translucent specters and high radiant forms presented by world religions and the New Age for worship and transmutation, there are startlingly few usable replicas of spirit invested in body. We are still pretending through our elaborate ceremonies to be somewhere else.

Animals do not encounter the riddles and existential dilemmas that men and women do. Men and women require the realm of symbols and artifacts to mediate the exigencies of this exquisite condition. But men and women also need their animal roots, their animal powers. They must become animals to become humans. That was the collective perception of shamans and medicine teachers worldwide at the dawn of history. That is now our injunction—to become animals while remaining capable of self-awareness and reverie.

Thus, the singularity of somatic systems speaks to a uniform need to throw off the neurotic habits and pathologies that have come with civilization. The diversity of somatic systems and definitions arises from a melding of diverse and subtly evolving forms of exercise and palpation with recognitions of the varying degrees of separation we have from our autonomous natures. The different systems seek to restore us to those natures, but never by a miracle from on high. They each lead us to encounter some essential aspect of freedom and well-being which is blocked by a once necessary but now extraneous habit or affectation

of cultural process. Thus, somatic modalities are as kaleidoscopic and embattled as we are.

Notes

1. Judith Aston, "Three Perceptions and One Compulsion," draft of an essay for Don Hanlon Johnson (editor), *Bone, Breath and Gesture: Practices of Embodiment* (Berkeley, California: North Atlantic Books, 1995).

2. Ibid.

3. Ibid.

4. Joseph Heller and William A. Henkin, *Bodywise: Introduction to Hellerwork* (Oakland, California: Wingbow Press, 1986), pp. 84–85.

5. Ibid., p. 71.

6. Ibid., p. 72.

7. I am grateful to Fritz Smith, M.D., for his help in completing this section.

8. Don Hanlon Johnson, personal communication, 1994.

9. Bonnie Bainbridge Cohen, *Sensing, Feeling, and Action: The Experiential Anatomy of Body-Mind Centering* (Northampton, Massachusetts: Contact Editions, 1993), p. 159.

10. Fritz Smith, note on the text of *Planet Medicine*, 1994.

11. Ibid.

12. Ibid.

13. Ibid.

14. Wazir Peller, personal communication, San Carlos, California, 1994.

15. Stephanie Golden, "Body-Mind Centering," *Yoga Journal* (September/October 1993), p. 126 (quote from Don Van Vleet).

16. Frank Herbert, *Whipping Star* (New York: Berkley, 1977).

17. Golden, "Body-Mind Centering," pp. 90, 126.

18. Bainbridge Cohen, *Sensing, Feeling, and Action*, p. 2.

19. Don Hanlon Johnson, *Body, Spirit and Democracy* (Berkeley, California: North Atlantic Books, 1993), pp. 212–13.

20. Golden, "Body-Mind Centering," p. 89.

21. Johnson, *Body, Spirit and Democracy*, p. 209.

22. Bainbridge Cohen quoted in Golden, "Body-Mind Centering," p. 89.

23. Golden, "Body-Mind Centering," p. 89.

24. Bonnie Bainbridge Cohen, notes on the text of *Planet Medicine*, 1994.

25. Ibid.

26. Bainbridge Cohen, *Sensing, Feeling, and Action,* pp. 46–51.

27. Ibid., p. 148.

28. Ibid., p. 20.

29. Bainbridge Cohen, notes on the text of *Planet Medicine,* 1994.

30. Golden, "Body-Mind Centering," p. 87.

31. Ibid., p. 99.

32. Bainbridge Cohen, notes on the text of *Planet Medicine,* 1994.

33. Ibid.

34. Ibid.

35. Ibid.

36. Ibid.

37. Bainbridge Cohen, *Sensing, Feeling, and Action,* p. 158.

38. Ibid.

39. Ibid., p. 159.

40. Ibid.

41. Bainbridge Cohen, notes on the text of *Planet Medicine,* 1994.

42. Johnson, *Body, Spirit and Democracy,* p. 115.

43. Carolyn Schaffer, "An Interview with Emilie Conrad-Da'oud," *Yoga Journal,* no. 77 (November/December 1987), p. 52.

44. Johnson, *Body, Spirit and Democracy,* p. 115.

45. Johnson, *Body, Spirit and Democracy,* p. 116.

46. Schaffer, "An Interview with Emilie Conrad Da'oud," pp. 52–53.

47. Johnson, *Body, Spirit and Democracy,* p. 117.

48. Schaffer, "An Interview with Emilie Conrad Da'oud," p. 54.

49. Ibid., p. 52.

50. Emilie Conrad-Da'oud, "Life on Land," in Don Hanlon Johnson (ed.), *Bone, Breath and Gesture.*

51. Ibid.

PART III

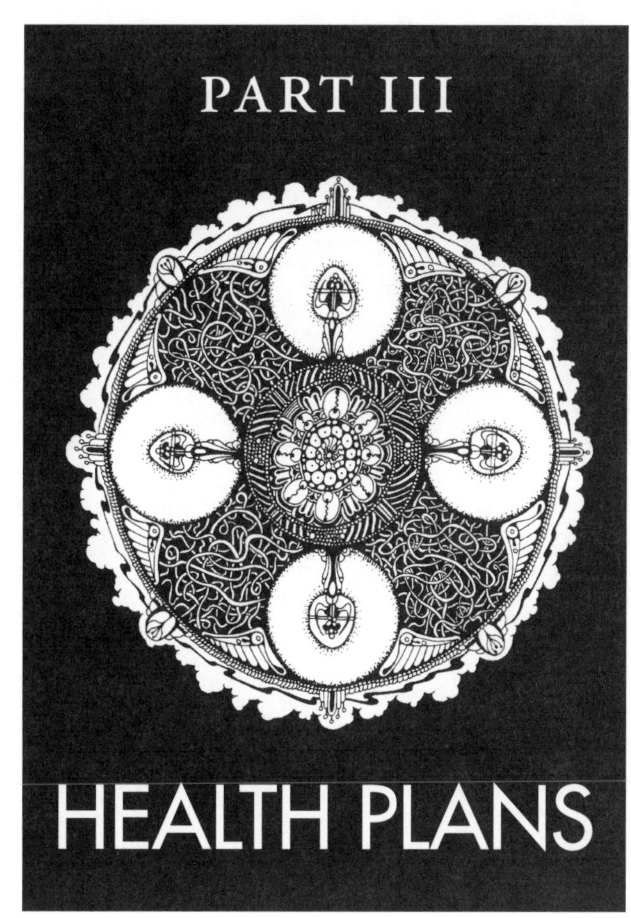

HEALTH PLANS

CHAPTER SEVEN

Beyond Ideology

Levels of Healing

THE INFORMATION IN this book—or in any book of medicinal theory or self-help—exists disguised on a number of levels in relation to any reader, including the author. One theory tells us that medicine must be vital and energy-oriented, as disease is; another, that insofar as incarnation is physical, only herbs and bodywork (drugs and surgery) operate on the carnal plane. The global pharmacy now offers us a choice of potions, distillations, syntheses, potentizations, images, and archetypes of the same basic substances. Of a given plant, does one ingest the seeds, soak the petals in water, succuss the pulp into a "minimum" non-physical dose, combine in complex formulas with artificial substances, or meditate on its signature? Should the bones or the meridians be palpated to affect the organs, or is surgery the only real manipulative medicine?

It seems there is always another system of medicine claiming that the real disease lies deeper or that the cure of symptoms by a rival modality is pure placebo or merely displaces the pathologizing force. Virtually every holistic practitioner has some blind spot, is closed to some other method. An acupuncturist may attribute poor eyesight to *chi* stagnation with age and deem the Bates Method quackery. Yet a Bates practitioner may improve her visual accommodation without ever *directly* activating her meridians. A Rolfer may laugh at the notion of potentized microdoses as effective somatic agents. A Feldenkrais practitioner may denigrate Breema or Reiki as unscientific "hippie" bodywork. A Reiki healer or Polarity Therapist may then propound that diseases are solely impediments of spirit and *all* physical methods are merely vehicles to awaken cosmic energy.

When the renowned Greek homeopath George Vithoulkas spoke a few years ago in San Francisco, I overheard a cluster of Reichians outside the auditorium discussing how deeply armored he was—this present paragon of a homeopathic physician. From a different part of the room a local homeopath pointed to the circle of Reichians and told his colleagues: "There you see the pure sycotic miasm* on the hoof."

Such a lack of generosity is also a failure of holism, for on some deeper level these dichotomies must merge. True systems all heal, even if they begin at different points and work through different levels. How can we be sure that the active elements of homeopathy, acupuncture, chiropractic, or even allopathy are not simply psychokinesis guided by a therapeutic mythology?

Can a homeopathic remedy remove layers of "Reichian" armor from the forehead and belly? In direct answer to this question, I would say no. I think that somaticized trauma is structured deeply and rigidly in the mind/body and can be dissolved only by a process of breathing, exercise, and imagining akin to the pathways by which it was incorporated. However, a homeopathic dose could alleviate a digestive ailment associated with belly armor and thereby participate in its bioenergetic dissipation. A potency might also release the miasmatic and dermatological aspect of a "mask" and so energize the dissolution of facial armor.

*"Sycosis" (literally "figlike pathology") is the homeopathic name for gonorrhea; a miasm, homeopathically, is a deep-seated, often-inherited disease complex.

Health Plans

An alternate answer would be: each system elicits its own categories of reality and devises processes relevant to these. A pure homeopath wouldn't think of asking a patient to breathe more deeply or begin massaging his belly. These are not part of his universe. It would be just as inconceivable for a Reichian to prescribe a microdose. As long as we stay totally in either system, the other domain does not even exist. Thus, the question of interchangeability, arising as it does at a purely semantic level, is meaningless. Treatments are totally distinct and cannot be substituted on a literal basis; yet the therapeutic grammar behind each of them overrides the separate ideologies. Cases of mutually interactive or reciprocal healing, embracing conventional allopathic treatments, are probably more prevalent than people realize, because our reflexes are profoundly unconscious and create their own pre-semantic symbols and constructs.

Many a system of radical cancer therapy sets as its absolute one-to-one requirement a specific drug (apricot pits, shark cartilage), a dietary change (macrobiotic, vegetarian), a lifestyle modification, the elimination of a particular microorganism or proto-cellular substratum, the replacement of metallic dental work, a bioenergetic or primal-scream therapy, or some other distinct modality. Each claim uniquely to have discovered the sought-after cure, and each present themselves as a victim of orthodox medical prejudice against unsanctioned methods. Likely, some cancer patients will be successfully treated by each of these methods, leading its supporters to claim universality. Yet I doubt that any of these authoritative systems is, by itself, the answer, though each may represent a vector to the core where the answer lies.

Cancer may be a complicated set of interacting forms, catalyzing physical, emotional, and psychospiritual layers. It may not be a unique disease. It may not have a singular cure.

Beyond Ideology

Misplaced concreteness is as much a hazard of alternative systems as it is of mainstream ones. It may finally be the case that an authentic

cure for any condition is the one that confronts and releases a patient along her particular line of resistance—diet for some, herbs for others, bodywork for others, prayer for still others, etc.

ONE CANNOT DO everything, so it is hard to know where to begin. All around us are various orthodoxies proclaiming: eat macrobiotic food ... take out mercury fillings ... primal therapy (or rebirthing) to clear early trauma ... yet only a homeopath can dissolve inherited miasms ... vaccinate to prevent disease ... antidote your vaccinations to prevent even worse disease ... filter fluoridated water to protect your immune system ... replace milk with whey to avoid heart disease.

It becomes crazy-making because healing cannot be *instead* of living. An ocean of creature experience and biological process, by definition unexamined and beyond remediation, underlies any medical directive. Thus, attention and refinement are far more critical than attempting to cover all bases. If one tracks one's own process, he or she may be drawn from allergy shots to psychotherapy to diet to meditation, or, in other instances, in the reverse cycle. As a condition changes, so must one's attention and the direction of treatment. "Listening" is the key to both life and healing—staying with the pattern a particular event (or act of attempted cure) initiates and following its effect to the next level of diagnosis or insight.

A successful herbal treatment—or pill or operation—does not eliminate disease; it merely shifts it to another, ideally less debilitating level. For example, a homeopathic remedy sometimes requires concurrent psychological work for its completion; otherwise the condition it was treating may lapse into dormancy, re-energize there, and return either in its previous guise or as some other ailment. Despite the literal implication of the word "holism," the human organism is, as we have seen, a fragmented entity and must be addressed level by level, persona by persona (some levels and personae will not even appear in a lifetime, and cannot be treated). Surgery and drugs may effectively penetrate one level; Gestalt therapy, another; Bach flower remedies,

another; chiropractic, another; and so on. Some levels may be touched only by magic, love, or a song.

Because these levels must be interpenetrating fields, medicines and meanings introduced into one will be transmitted to all. Such is the optimism and legitimate promise of holism. However, a medicine will be directly curative only on the level at which it is introduced. What it translates to other levels may or may not be functional; it depends on the cohesiveness and receptivity of the organism and the timing and synchronicity of the cure. A remedy may also subliminally whisper, "Seek a different level of cure." For example, one hopes that a homeopathic or chiropractic treatment will also clear the mind and inspire the individual to pursue psychoanalytic or spiritual modalities to continue her healing process, or vice versa.

It is possible too, as we have seen at various points throughout this text, that an effective treatment, even a vitalistic one, may have secondary pathological consequences if it introduces energy into a persona that cannot contain and integrate it. Perhaps this is why Edward Whitmont prefers not to use homeopathy separate of psychoanalysis. He is concerned about setting in motion forces that the personality will then either cathect neurotically or suppress.[1]

There is a certain level at which no one ever has a real idea of what medicine or event cures an illness, nor is an identification of the modality relevant to the ultimate health or well-being of the patient. A sick person may try dozens of different modalities on either a chronic or serious condition without results and then find that the ailment dramatically improves, perhaps because of the treatment most immediately proximate to the improvement, perhaps because of the collective momentum of treatments, or perhaps because the complex of factors underlying the illness changed over time or changed over time in catalysis with the treatments. The best doctors simply shrug and say, "Whatever works!" and then go on their way without needing kudos. Less confident doctors need to demonstrate with surety the cure's trajectory.

The mystery and complexity of curative cause and effect are not

just a limitation of alternative modalities. They are as much a factor in standard medicine. However, the custom in allopathy is for the patient to attribute cure in an absolute and linear fashion to the category proposed by the doctor. Very often this is more religious catechism than scientific verity. It can also be dangerous insofar as it implants false beliefs in the patient regarding future health and curability.

In truth, symbol systems operating at the level of language, pure soma, genetics, and perhaps even molecules and atoms determine the fate of the organism. It is foolhardy to think that anyone can see or track such discrete, deep-seated, and fast-moving originations through the camouflage of much more explicit physical events. Thus, one of the ironies of most alternative medicines is that they propose cures only nonspecifically. They identify each healing event more or less with a protocol of treatment, but they usually add some impalpable or ineffable factor such as vital energy, synergy, an activitation of the life force, a reinforcing belief system, or the magical effect of holism itself.

Alternative medicines generally (and usually unintentionally) encourage the total demedicalization of healing. Their practitioners know that certain regimens or remedies tend to lead to cures, so they prescribe them with confidence within a broad holistic context. On the other hand, conventional allopathic medicines are always trying to capture the precise quantum of cure within medical liturgy. Either way, though, the match between putative cure and actual cure is pure uncertainty theory.

A naturopath may conclude a session by handing her client a note page full of prescriptions—herbs, dietary changes, modes of exercise, a homeopathic constitutional, a biweekly bathing ritual, and points on the body on which to do self-acupressure. The sincere patient may well undertake all of these things but forget about pressing two Intestine points at the creases of his elbows. Ten years later another healer from a different tradition may emphasize *only* those points—and this time the person remembers, and the result is a more sustained overall cure. That does not mean healing was not taking place all along: the wave

merely changed frequency and amplitude, which it does anyway throughout life.

A different person with a similar diagnosis might never remember to press those two points but then unknowingly (and efficaciously) incorporate their meridians in a sequence of *Chi Gung* exercises, intoning "kaaa!" or "ssss" within a cycle of "animal form" motions, breath-awareness, and light massage of the heart meridian. If one moves with spirit and fills holes as they appear, then many of the big questions are answered without having to be asked. A physician merely isolates and objectifies a natural cure when the body/mind has lost its way.

Perhaps a person visits both a homeopath and a psychotherapist and experiences a subsequent sense of empowerment along with gradual relief of chronic indigestion and flatulence. Years later the same person may replace twice-a-week red meat in her diet with biweekly chicken, then drop meat altogether and substitute a dish combining brown rice, miso, seaweed, and carrots. Along the way she may undergo periods of susceptibility to colds, irregular menstrual cycles, and a range of unfamiliar emotions, but then, with the more vegetarian diet, she experiences a new feeling of lightness, freedom from colds, and general well-being. This phase doesn't simply emerge like a new image popped into a slide projector. The homeopathic and psychological cures began a process of change on the vital and emotional planes that led to a shift in attitude, that led to a change in awareness and even food taste. Her entire metabolism responded to her new identity. The psychological work roused something *pre-psychic* in her organism. Quite likely, dietary attention alone (initially) would not have sparked a character change and might not have even had the same healthful and profound physical effect. On the other hand, another person might begin with diet and then move to therapy. Someone else might never alter their diet and experience a similar change from a craniosacral treatment. Someone else might actually be healthier eating meat. There are infinite variations and idiosyncrasies.

Beyond Ideology

Cures are not always dispensed in linear time and space. There is

a mistaken tendency to expect doctors of all persuasions to diagnose a condition and offer its remedy in the form of a pill, regimen, physical adjustment, prayer, or some even more esoteric currency; the petitioner assumes that he or she "gets" it then.

This is often the case. Yet on another level medicines may contact such deep-seated conditions that some of their effects will not be felt for years, or even decades (this is axiomatically true for autogenic "medicines" like dreams, life experiences, and sudden insights that change orientation to one's own character and to the world). Thus, any medicine is simultaneously short-term and long-term, exoteric and esoteric, activating and internalizing. While a dose of comfrey instantly energizes an intestinal condition, a concurrent use of barley grass or microflora may begin flushing the liver of deeper-seated toxins. The person may experience some degree of immediate relief from the comfrey (more ease digesting, less frequent constipation), but also a painful intensification of other symptoms (chronic pain, emotional distress, burning tears, diarrhea) that betray longer-term cleansing.

It is a subtle, even evasive point at which the true healer works both toward curing the disease and giving the patient the lesson *from* the disease. Native healing, as we have seen, cultivated this well. We have lost and are forced to regain that meaning in our own medicine complexes because, as we have become mechanical and nihilistic, there is no universal repertoire of meaning as such which sustains the corrective tilt of any one disease in its cure.

Recently an acquaintance with a severe lung malady sought both explanation and (of course) relief by visiting a succession of renowned allopaths with different specialties. She elicited diagnoses ranging from exotic respiratory parasites to lupus, but none of the treatments for these brought any change in her painful symptoms and mood of despair. Then with no cure in sight and her pain so searing she was at the point of suicide, she scheduled an appointment with a homeopath as a last resort, got diagnosed according to different parameters (as having the disorder currently euphemized as Chronic Fatigue Syndrome), was

given potentiated microdoses, and experienced a marked improvement. Her pain and despair both became less deeply rooted. But she was still quite weak until a form of Korean finger acupuncture relieved a whole cluster of symptoms. Later, a different doctor offered a series of *dō-in* exercises and dietary transitions (eliminating all sugars and meats). This ameliorated most remaining symptoms. She was also a different person by then. The disease seemed almost to be the condition of a more passive, less mature self. Her next stage might be a term of Jungian therapy to transform the layer of self that accepted the disease initially on an archetypal level. Or she might just live her new life until another challenge. In her own mind the original pathology had been reconceived as a harbinger of growth, a deathlike blow dislodging an even more profound systemic morbidity.

Admittedly, I have presented an optimistic outcome. However, for not only this actual case but in general in this book, I am trying to propose what is possible when things *work,* not to recount the all-too-well-known ravages of progressive pathology. This succession of treatments—or even anything resembling it—would also probably have no dynamism for another person diagnosed with the so-called "same" Chronic Fatigue Syndrome but having a different constitution, individuation process, or etiology of disease. (Plus, as we saw in the chapters on faith healing and linguistic codes, symbolic cures may penetrate the disease core, even without modality or linear cause-and-effect. When we most seem to know the path of a cure is often when we least know it.)

Alternative treatments need not rely on vague holistic diagnoses and purely lifestyle issues. They can also be categorical and concrete. Recently someone close to me was stricken for two years with a seemingly undiagnosable and untreatable ailment. In retrospect, he was probably sick for at least another year and a half before that, but it took that long before he recognized something unusual was wrong with him.

The year and a half began with a case of pneumonia and continued with increasingly severe ankle pains and muscular stiffness. After he dropped out of graduate school and came home, he was seen by a series of physicians, starting with a family doctor for an exam and eventually including, over the two years, two podiatrists, an endocrinologist, a rheumatologist, a famous "sports medicine" surgeon, two separate doctors at a pain clinic, and a foot surgeon. He underwent extensive lab tests plus a variety of exotic X-rays, bone scans, and MRIs. Although the doctors speculated on a number of conditions throughout this process, the end result was an inability of all of these people (including the radiologists) to find anything wrong with him. It should be noted that at different points in the examination process, at least three of the doctors and radiologists did think they detected deterioration in the ligaments around the ankles (one said, "as though he had jumped out of a six-story building and landed on his feet")—a diagnosis that was routinely refuted by the next physician to whom he was then referred. Additionally, none of their symptomatic treatments (orthotics, anti-inflammatories) seemed to alleviate his pain.

During the same period of time he had appointments with two homeopaths and series of sessions with a chiropractor, a Rolfer, a Feldenkrais practitioner, a Lomi therapist, and two doctors of Chinese medicine. Except for the homeopaths, each of these practitioners had a significant positive effect on him. His posture and digestion improved, his breathing deepened, and he got stronger and generally healthier. Yet none of them could alter the basic condition—identical pain in both ankles making it impossible to walk more than a short distance, plus other severe neck and shoulder stiffness making it difficult to read and write. In fact, the Rolfer, while stating clearly that the condition was outside the range of his practice, expressed doubt as to whether the pain actually originated in the ankles since he could not affect it either positively or negatively at the ostensible source.

Near the end of the second year the patient took to getting around in a wheelchair most of the time. The last doctor he saw was a prominent

foot surgeon who literally threw up his arms and then suggested casts on both feet as a last resort.

At the beginning of the third year the patient was seen informally by John Upledger at the end of a workshop. Within minutes of beginning his palpation, Upledger felt severe restriction in the dural tube. After all the hedging and bafflement of the other doctors, to Upledger the pathology was immediately obvious and unambiguous. It was located not at the ankles but in the meninges of the spine. The pain at the ankles as well as the other symptoms were probably, Upledger thought, areas of prior weakness. They expressed chronic structural and developmental problems that had begun to be successfully treated by the Rolfer and chiropractor but could not be improved any further without getting at the core illness. The source of the pain was clearly in the spine. The failure of the dural tube to transmit cranial motion had congestive and restrictive ramifications throughout the body, more severe in some areas than others but clearly both pathologizing and symptomatic. "I have no idea why the pain ended up in the ankles," Upledger said. "Probably it was already a weakened area. But if we succeed at the core, it is likely that the periphery will follow."

He began his regimen two days later during another workshop session. This consisted of himself and an assistant mutually stretching out the restricted tissue, restoring its elasticity from the top of the spine and the sacrum, respectively. Of course, completing this was not as quick and direct as pulling off a rubber glove. The process had to be accomplished by minute degrees from different angles over half a year, with intervening periods for relaxation and integration.

Upledger's method was enacted by two bodyworkers (one trained by Randy Cherner, the other a chiropractor). Within a month the patient was out of the wheelchair. After six months the condition had improved to the point where he was functioning at perhaps 75 percent of his former strength and mobility and beginning to deal with peripheral physical and emotional issues. The crisis itself had passed.

Although no precise cause was ever given for the disease, Upledger thought it likely that a series of unusual vaccinations (followed by a fever) three and a half years earlier (just before the pneumonia) had provoked the acute condition (a meningitis-like reaction). The patient had received these vaccinations during a summer job so as to be qualified to handle raw sewage safely while building alternative waste-treatment plants. It was possible too that a toxin from the sludge had gotten into his system. The disease itself (whatever it was), Upledger emphasized, had long since passed; that was why so many doctors reported the patient was healthy. The after-effects of the disease were the ongoing stiffness and pain from the constricted tissue and fluid flow.

The power of simple educated touch—of being able to set hands on a body and feel its visceral and neuromuscular restrictions—is becoming a lost art in the face of ever more complex microchemical and cybernetic techniques of diagnosis (often missing the forest for the trees). The former respects the vital energy of the individual; the latter consigns each body to statistical purgatory.

Remember: the last treatment recommended by the foot surgeon was immobilization in a cast for six months. He had no particular rationale for making that suggestion, merely that he could find no cause for the pain. He boasted dryly that he was well qualified to diagnose absence of pathology because he had written the textbook on surgery of the particular ligaments involved. "The buck stops here. You've either got *me,*" he said, "or you've got someone who's been trained by my textbook." Undoubtedly this was true. Yet at the end of the quest stood a prominent foot surgeon with a waiting room full of patients concluding, "Pain of unknown origin. Deer hold up their wounded limbs. Maybe immobilizing both feet will help."

This was precisely the opposite of the treatment employed by Upledger in curing the condition. It is quite possible that immobilization was contraindicated and would have made the condition worse by further restricting the rhythms of the skeleton. While the surgeon did not have a surgical resolution, Upledger, in a sense, recommended a kind of surgery, a gradual holistic surgery with plenty of opportuni-

ties to make subtle adjustments along the way. Each step of the treatment was followed by a week or so of ordinary life; then the "surgery" continued.

Regardless of the actual cause of this condition, one is led to ask, "What would have happened if the person had not been lucky enough to see a John Upledger and had continued his search among allopathic physicians?" After all, this is the plight of most people in the Western world (and many in the developing countries as well). It is presently the plight of thousands of Gulf War veterans "complaining of persistent headaches, rashes, nausea, chronic fatigue and body aches. Military doctors at first said their symptoms had nothing to do with the war. One man was told that his rash was age spots, his low red blood cell count a dietary deficiency, and his hacking cough a function of pollution. Others were told they were suffering from stress."[2] Add to these disabilities an invisible domain of genetic damage resulting in a plethora of birth defects.

There is, finally, a gut sense of wellness whose "symptoms" are a lucidity and the freedom to act, an ability to move without internal resistance. We may never be totally cured, but we can have intimations of what it would be like to be healthy in a healthy world, and we can set ourselves on that path by the guideposts that are intuitively most true. If this book has a practical purpose it is to sharpen people's senses of how to recognize those guideposts and how to keep their options open when medical or holistic rhetoric clouds the issue.

Holistic Caricatures

Many people involved in holistic health look to it for answers it cannot provide. They assume something has become wrong in them or was always wrong and that a radical treatment will correct it. Soon they become the representative of their idealized correction instead of who they were. And they remain sick.

NOW!
coming to the pages of
CROOKED KOMICKS...

MAN
and the

UNIVERSE
to be reprinted, in serial form, word for word, in its entirety, from the original best seller by...
A.K.S. SWAMIMUNI PARAMSHNUKRISHNA PHD.
without a doubt, the smartest man alive!
FINALLY, AN ANSWER – to all those plaguing questions about the "so-called" meaning of life!
COMPLETELY PRESENTED – in concrete form:
* the entire collected wisdom of the HUMAN RACE!
* the "once-and-for-all" cosmology. Complete with 40 pages of diagrams!
* the TRUTH about levels of consciousness, mind and matter, the will, the unconscious, eternity!
BEHOLD – your atman merging with the clear light of the void!

God revealed!
We made it!
cosmic truths!
absolute answers!
the search is over!
at last!

Health Plans

There are health and therapy junkies who go from treatment to treatment, looking for the one that has the insight to recognize them or the power to intercede in their behalf. Their overly earnest search for a cure becomes another symptom, and the longer the quest goes on, the less chance there is that they will regain their own priority. In flaunting their holism, they become solipsistic and righteous. They begin acting like the caricature of a medicine, which is really like a disease.

One bioenergetic therapist tells of leading a group on the floor in a simple breathing exercise when a man unexpectedly crawled onto an adjacent young woman who had recently given birth and tried to suckle her. When she pushed him off, he shouted "Bitch!" as if *she* had violated the spirit of the exercise. Then he added, to the group, as if in explanation, "I'm expressing myself."

The therapist said, "I found myself wondering, 'What are we teaching these people? What kind of a world are we telling them this is?' "[3]

The most abiding holistic illusion is the dream that there is no planet, no history, no context, no undeserved pain or injustice, only empowerment workshops, friendly shamans and spirits, and the elusive search by individuals for their inner psychic power, forgotten victimizations, and lost lives. If this planet is wasted, another higher dimensional domain will replace it. Among the masses it becomes the unabated (and unabatable) appetite for spiritual experiences and goods that will somehow confirm their own flimsy existence. One does not have to accept the whole pessimistic message of political refugees and homeless mendicants to realize that they are telling the truth when they report: "There is a world out there, and it's got teeth." The karmic situation in which we find ourselves is real and cannot be replaced by an imaginary asylum. There is not only no one to blame but nothing that blame can expiate.

The same therapist concluded at the end of another fable: "Having a sixty-year-old man run around in diapers crying may have therapeutic value, but as a statement on the human condition, it's fucked."[4]

Beyond Ideology

It is not a matter of simply lying on the floor pounding and breathing more fully or escaping on a science-fiction journey through exotic

herbs and needles of the Yellow Emperor. Each episode comes to an end, and the same issues in the world prevail. Despite these bizarre artificial villages we live in, we are still wild animals in tribes howling at a totem moon. From the beginning of the Ice Age till now, nothing has been solved, nothing at all. So holism is hardly a ticket to the big carnival or ultimate New Age expo.

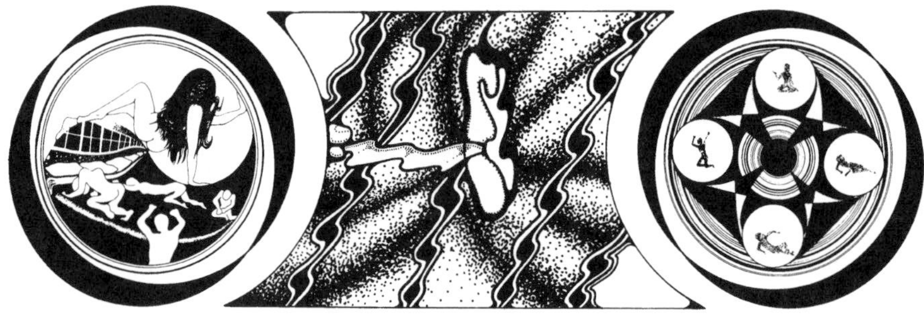

In the late 1970s there was a plague of naive, "enlightened" M.D.s and psychologists who adapted versions of acupuncture, chiropractic, homeopathy, and macrobiotics into their general standard practices. Some attended holistic meetings as authorities and gave papers on "wellness," biofeedback, shadow pain, biodynamic nutrition, and cosmic healing energy. They preached a mixture of religion, lifestyle, health, exercise, and charisma. Yet they had no more training in these fields than an average educated person would have in surgery from reading a few books.

The 1977 edition of *Planet Medicine* presented a caricature of such a doctor that by now reads as a caricature of itself: suntan, leather pants, (astrological or Tibetan) medallion hanging in his chest hair, and a classic holistic smile; jogs, does *aikido;* acts as though ancient wisdom has come through all of history to anoint him. If challenged, he will quickly cite his training in physiology and the "hard" sciences. Another version was the cosmically receptive shaman-lady with her Ph.D. My villains may still exist but they are hardly as blatant. Instead we have new holistic clowns.

For instance, one chiropractor claims to have been "kidnapped by a tribe of sixty-two aboriginal [Australian] natives and forced to go on a walkabout. For four months, she walked barefoot through the desert. She was subjected to various privations and indignities. She was required to listen to muddy spiritual chitchat from people who chose to speak in capital letters. Finally the purpose of her journey is revealed. The earth is in such terrible shape that the aborigines have chosen to have no more children. There is war and killing and pollution, and the aborigines are fed up. Before they die out, they have chosen one person, one 'mutant' to carry their warning back to civilization. They have chosen a chiropractor from Lee's Summit, Missouri...."[5]

This is the present sort of cosmic prophecy people associate with spiritual healing—self-glorifying myths on one side and, on the other, self-proclaimed homeopaths claiming to represent the Knights Templar and the Order of the Solar Temple while leading fifty-three people in suicide, murder, or both. In the guise of channeled salvation, it's a "Whole Earth" plague of messianic cults and apocalypticists piling up personal fortunes and arsenals from decommissioned Cold War troops.

Journalist Jon Carroll refers to the supposed walkabout as "another example of white people using brown people as mantel ornaments or game tokens. It's cultural imperialism masquerading as harmless New Age spiritualism. Its racism is no more lovely for being unwitting." In fact, the author was paid $1.7 million for the rights to her self-published account and, though promising that a portion of the proceeds would go to the Doonooch Self-Healing Centre run by Aborigines in Mowra, New South Wales, had sent not a penny as of September 8, 1994.

Carroll concludes:

The real message of the aboriginal peoples is: Give us back our land. It's a nasty, greedy, materialistic message; it's one that requires us to do something other than think good thoughts. So much better to make aborigines passive children of God, praying for the misguided white people while committing cultural suicide. How touching, to see them and their claims to our social services disappear into the gloaming.

Mutant Message Down Under is fiction; it's also a disgrace.[6]

Something new *has* been emerging, from within our individual and collective souls—but it is different from the entire holistic health and New Age movement. It is both more and less—potentially more but presently less. There are in fact two movements—the true political medicinal revolution and the one in flight from it which borrows its symbols and tries to masquerade as the same thing. The true one comes from within our historic process and *is* our historical realization. The other seeks to enlist every passing fad, in hopes of postponing any real change. So close together are these two that for a moment now they seem to merge.

The trouble with our revolutionary insights and belief in the holistic cure is that these are too good to be true. They have nothing to do with the lives most people lead. Pursuing exogenous images of enlight-

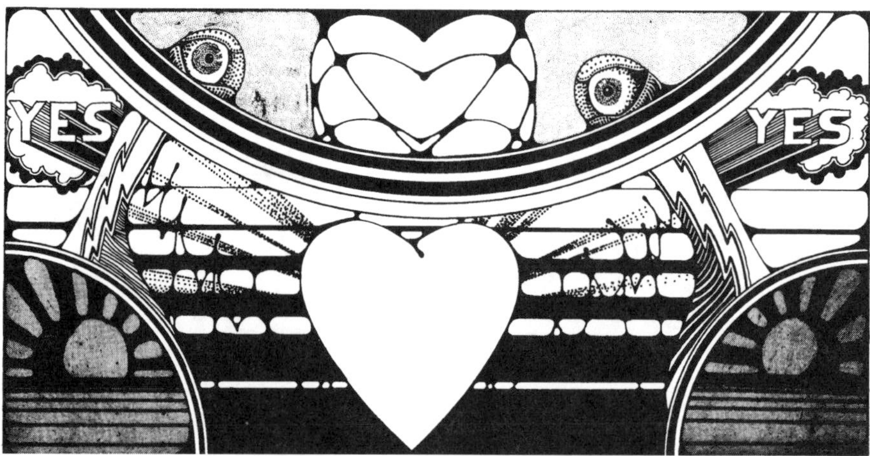

enment, men and women lose the sense of what it is to experience *themselves.* They attach themselves religiously to their craniosacral unwindings, muscle-testing results, or regimens of homeopathic doses; they see environmental illness and New Age allergies everywhere and guard their diets zealously; they become workshop junkies, worshipping Angeles Arrien or Stanislav Grof and taking the same classes over and over again. Doing nothing and entertaining their own shadow would often be more efficacious than even the most energizing therapy.

Carl Jung diagnosed the holistic disease as long ago as 1929:

> One cannot be too cautious in these matters, for what with the imitative urge and a positively morbid avidity to possess themselves of outlandish feathers and deck themselves out in this exotic plumage, far too many people are misled into snatching at such "magical" ideas and applying them externally, like an ointment. People will do anything, no matter how absurd, in order to avoid facing their own souls. They will practice Indian yoga and all its exercises, observe strict regimen of diet, learn theosophy by heart, or mechanically repeat mystic texts from the literature of the whole world—all because they cannot get on with themselves and have not the slightest faith that anything useful could ever come out of *their* souls. Thus the soul has been gradually turned into a Nazareth from which nothing

good can come. Therefore let us fetch it from the four corners of the earth—the more far-fetched and bizarre it is the better! . . . Were it so, then God had made a sorry job of creation, and it were high time for us to go over to Marcion the gnostic and depose the incompetent demiurge. . . . But man is worth the pains he takes with himself, and he has something in his own soul that can grow.[7]

Blaming the Sick Person

One of the flaws of holistic and positive thinking is that often the victim of disease is blamed for something that is out of his or her control. Nowadays cancer is spoken of in some circles as retribution, as the disease of an archetype, the cells themselves ostensibly picking up the nihilism of the person, punishing the failure of faith or belief with disease. We have all heard preachers blaming the gay "lifestyle" for the AIDS infection.

Whereas archetypally disease is destiny and is not arbitrary or meaningless in terms of the life of the organism, it is also true that most of this happens in such a deeply unconscious dimension that no one but the most enlightened saint or yogi could possibly control his absolute health and destiny, and these can only for a period of time before they too submit to natural law and decay. Those born into African epidemics are surely not responsible for their diseases. At most, one interacts creatively with present conditions in a struggle for health.

Whitmont points out that,

> [W]hile relatively valid as one particular view of the illness dynamic, the exclusive [dependence upon the ego] as the sole focus tends to place too much emphasis upon the ego's deliberateness, power and freedom. Our historical patriarchal and heroic religions, myths and cultural viewpoint have tended either to burden us with full responsibility and guilt for becoming ill, or conversely, in the nineteenth-century positivistic-mechanistic backlash version, to present us as hapless victims of random "accidental" events or malfunctions.[8]

Illness originates from below without regard for belief systems either way. The worst curmudgeon, even an assassin or hit-man, may thrive, while a compassionate "Florence Nightingale" or "Mother Teresa" may struggle with lifelong disease. Sickness is not itself a judgment.

Carton-a-day smokers, bearers of transplanted organs, and workers in carcinogenic factories outlive faith healers and lamas who die of stomach cancer or leukemia at relatively young ages. Genetic and karmic factors are imponderable, and pure longevity is not the major criterion anyway for depth of life experience. Because a particular monk fasted and meditated regularly and then died at forty does not mean that we should not practice yoga or manage our diets according to therapeutic principles. We do not know all the factors in his case or ours. Because a *t'ai chi* master succumbed suddenly in middle age does not mean that *t'ai chi* is not curative. Whatever keeps people alive and well does so for unique and individual reasons, and for different reasons in different people. If George Burns, after smoking all those cigars, survives to sing at eighty: "I wish I were eighteen again, going where I've never been," then something keeps him alive, perhaps an original vaudeville elixir. Something else keeps Bob Hope and Ronald Reagan alive in this same parable.

Whitmont spells out this drama in a dialect quite different from mine:

> There should be no need to emphasize that, even in the case of secondary gains, it is not necessarily the conscious ego personality that "wants" to be ill. Neither, as a rule, is one able to produce illness by conscious volition, nor is one necessarily aware of the underlying dynamic that leads to illness.
>
> Illness is the "invasion" of a dynamic that arises out of the Self field and leads to a dramatic conflict which encodes itself psychosomatically. The form impulses that motivate our life's dynamic in terms of need for love and emotional closeness, power and assertion, and meaning and self-expression (the domains of Freud, Adler, and Jung respectively) imprint themselves in the codes of our vital, behavioral,

> emotional, and mental fields without necessarily reaching conscious awareness. (Even thoughts can be unconscious; we may, for instance, feel and act on the basis of convictions which we take for granted as "obvious" facts.) . . . We may suffer stomach cramps without being conscious of the fact that we are afraid of something, or rheumatic stiffness without realizing our existential stiffness. The formal patterns simply "become" innervation, ways of moving, of behavior, emotion, or thoughts, depending upon the code form of their incarnation. Our wills, thoughts, and emotions, hence, are not necessarily the originating causes of our psychosomatic ailments. Rather, like their bodily counterparts, they are forms of enactment of archetypal impulses.[9]

He emphasizes the importance of observing this mystery and not drifting into unexamined holistic ideology:

> To challenge the sufferer with questions like "Why did you want to get ill?" or "What are you doing wrong to make yourself sick?" has become a not infrequent implication by "New Age" practitioners. Such challenges are cruel and burden the ego with a responsibility for unconscious incursions which are not in its power to stop or prevent. By adding guilt to the already existing suffering, they may, in fact, increase ego defensiveness and thereby delay the receptivity to helpful insights into the possible meaning of the suffering. . . .
>
> We must beware, therefore, of apportioning guilt, shame, and blame to ourselves or others for not "individuating adequately" or not being able to heal ourselves, whether psychologically, by "right living," or through "sufficient faith." The very assumption that we can always do the "right" thing amounts to hubris of assuming that god-like powers can be available to us always and just for the asking. For anyone at any time, even for the "strongest" or "most conscious" and responsible person, the invading claim of the new can be too much. Therefore, while in principle at least, every illness can be healed through the "appropriate sacrifice," not every ill person may always be curable. While we are alive, illness as a potential or actualized fact is our constant companion.[10]

The Addiction to Therapy

One of the strangest outcomes of psychoanalysis is the current decision of so many individuals to replace their own existential memories and sense of self with induced memories, often under hypnosis or from some more "holistic" trance. People are so unsure of who they are they no longer know if they were abused sexually by their fathers, kidnapped and probed by aliens, or reigned as kings and queens in Atlantis and served with Alexander the Great. Their own existence seems incomplete, so they ask a doctor to lead them inside themselves, invariably to a "memory" they then adopt as their guiding star. Just ask anyone who has been "anointed" with rape, alien abduction, or execution during the Cathar massacre. They serve these images as faithfully as if they were present experiences. They give up the priority of the moment as lived. Yet the bardo is everywhere, now as well as then. It is never a matter of where one has been. It is where one is now, which is always "bardo." If memory were crucial to being, we would never forget.

In the most recent fad of "recovering repressed memory of sexual abuse," so-called victims are defined by eager therapists as anyone who suspects or comes to believe that such abuse must have taken place or even anyone who "feels different from other people."[11] Sexual promiscuity and lack of interest in sex are taken equally as confirmatory symptoms. Patients are encouraged to stifle all doubts about whether such abuse ever took place.

> The recovery movement, it must be plainly understood, is not primarily addressed to people who always knew about their sexual victimization. Its main intended audience is women who aren't at all sure that they were molested, and its purpose is to convince them of that fact and embolden them to act upon it.[12]

"Acting upon" has taken the form of women accusing their fathers of rape, Satanism, necrophilia, and murder of other children with consequent lawsuits and even criminal trials. The so-called process of healing is "not about surmounting one's tragic girlhood but about keeping the psychic wounds open, refusing forgiveness or reconciliation, and joining the permanently embittered corps of 'survivors.'"[13]

This has developed into an unexamined ritual in which therapists come to prefer the recovery of molestation fantasies to the often substantial difficulties of facing the realities of present life. Of course, there are real victims, but this ceremony has little to do with them, except insofar as it requires their confirmation for its own survival.

On the other hand, I don't accept the "pre-psychotherapeutic" trashing of therapy. If one has little sense of an internal life or of the cause-and-effect cycles of their emotions, then they can be changed in remarkably healthful ways by working with someone who is artful beyond the diagnostic manual. As long as both parties are clear about the limitations of the exercise and neither has heroic goals, then transference can be healthy.

Once one has a sense of an inner life and an intuition of personal symbols, yet still feels depressed, anxious, or otherwise hampered, it may seem that only more therapy will sponsor true change. However, this is when contemporary psychotherapy too often provides a person with a new story or pseudo-memory to replace a so-called wounded or fragmented one. That fiction can be based upon the Freudian notion of an "original trauma," or it can be highly visioned, as many neo-Jungian and shamanic versions are, with gods and goddess functions, Amazons and heroes, reenactments of ancient myths and socially constructed images of masculinity and femininity. (Jung himself would likely be appalled by the present worship of the archetypes.)

The goal of therapy is always adaptation to a therapeutic story. And by whose authority is one tale truer than another? The lives of Christ and other great teachers have been scandalously abused by various denominations of preachers as well as by Church hierarchies themselves for centuries, i.e., have been used to steal people's own mysterious lives and replace them with blind allegiance to a literalized account

that can be managed and exploited. Even the most benignly expansive healers and gurus run the risk of habituating their disciples to the utopian cure and themselves to their own authoritarian system.[14]

The person seeking clarity in the marketplace of therapy is reduced finally to choosing among models of co-dependency, primal violation, archetypal quest, and low self-esteem. But what about the actual and immediate life he or she is also leading? Does it just become a shadow of therapeutic reality and imagined or real victimization? Can it be made one's own without first shattering therapeutic authority and its act of clan initiation?

It would seem that our soul-doctors have blundered into just the confusion of psychological and spiritual authority our Constitution sought to guard against by separating Church and State. Tithing to a therapist for personal growth and vision is perhaps only superficially removed from tithing to a priesthood. And who is to say that the psychiatric profession is not the priesthood reinvented?

But I emphasize—this is not a hardhat anti-therapy position; it is a "post-psychotherapeutic" anti-authoritarian position well worth expounding in a book likely to be read by people favoring depth analysis.

It may be that therapy without a therapist is more liberating. That is, one casts his or her voice into the void and takes the answer that returns, no matter who is speaking or if the void is inhabited or not. Oftentimes traditional divinatory methods (like Navaho myth-chanting and sand painting) or oracular therapies (like reading the *I Ching*) can have profound and creative impacts by supplying totally novel images in circumstances where an imposition of archetypes or Westernized shamanism would represent only a continued assault of an authoritarian consciousness. And this is because the unconscious answer is always liberating, always a process-oriented response to the mysteries of psyche ... as long as one doesn't literalize or become superstitious about its meanings.

Beyond Ideology

The casting of astrological charts, for instance, has the possibility of revealing cycles which are beyond consciousness and unconsciousness

both (and are routinely ascribed to stars and planets for lack of any other metaphor). "Uranus and Venus in opposition" or "three planets in the twelfth house" are potentially radicalizing challenges, not programmatic myths. At worst, they can be made into programmatic myths, and then the astrologer or diviner (or even the planets themselves) are elevated to the level of authorities.

In place of psychoanalysis I would recommend Polarity Therapy, *Chi Gung*, craniosacral work, and, in some instances, Gestalt and other vision quests as substitute "psychologies"—in other words, therapies that energize one to make a new life rather than tell a new version of an old story. In the end life itself is what the gods of Egypt (or any nome) put on the scales; they make no dispensation for sanity or insanity, no extraneous distinction between myth and reality. They say simply: "Live!"

Wanting to Get Well

MEDICINE HAS NO MEANING. That is, medicine cannot supply the missing meaning or direction to a life. After the healing, deep-sea divers return to the sea; musicians return to their music; philosophers go back to language and reality. As Werner Erhard, L. Ron Hubbard, and other "human potential" business people have proven, money-makers continue to make money—more money. Those who looked out for number one continue to look out for *Numero Uno*, etc. A medicine can be proposed around any process and play into a variety of possible meanings. The same skeletal adjustment can lead to quiescence in one person and aggression in another.

In our emphasis in this book on hidden process and the unconscious mind, we have forgotten consciousness, where our lives and selves (as we know them) occur. It is mostly in the conscious mind that systems of medicine form and the doctors do their diagnoses. It is in terms of the ego that will is aroused and a decision to get better is initiated. The discipline required by the most powerful societies of ritual

magic and healing reminds us that the conscious mind has a necessary role in this affair.

Health Plans

The modern student of *t'ai chi ch'uan* tries to hold himself up with a habitually stiff torso; what is sinking is the *chi,* which is supposed to sink; but against a history of damming, the pain is unbearable—for the disciples of Ida Rolf and Matthias Alexander, too. Gravity is a dread opponent.

The exercises must be repeated thousands of times, tens of thousands of times, day after day, for years, and finally for a lifetime. The student is told, in effect, to practice. The teacher cannot do *t'ai chi* for him any more than he can eat or sleep for him. All he can do is demonstrate and correct, demonstrate and correct. At some quite early point, the student runs into insoluble difficulties; he finds it painful to move through the positions in the prescribed manner, so he adjusts to take strain off his weaker areas. The teacher corrects this, and ultimately the student is asked to correct it himself, to learn to observe when one part of his body tightens to allow another part to carry out a difficult movement. The corrections are painful, but the goal is to move as a whole, according to principle, despite the pain.

There is a relationship between conscious will and internal intelligence. In order to grow and heal, one must suffer, either in redirecting attention under hardship or in having life itself shift painfully after being healed passively. Systems which involve direct suffering allow a person to participate consciously in changes rather than become a straw in their wind. Such bringing to consciousness is one of the things life *is.* In his spiritual school in France, Gurdjieff hung educational aphorisms on the walls of the Study House, including:

> The worse the conditions of life, the more productive the work—always provided you remember the work.[15]
>
> Only conscious suffering has any sense.[16]

Beyond Ideology

We are reminded of the culminative moment of Jean Cocteau's *Orphée,* where Death and her helper Heurtebise struggle to force Time

backward in order to undo their damage. Heurtebise screams that it is impossible. An invisible wind ripples his hair; his every muscle strains. But they lean back against the flow of events and force the film to unravel to its beginning. All the while Death continues to shout at him, Death as the woman, the actress he loves, urging him to use his will, reminding him, "Without our wills, we are cripples." Even "Death" is.

Medicine has long known that the organism must want to get well in order to get well; it must want to live in order to live. We have seen through this book that the wanting comes from the core of one's being and has little to do with surficial greed for life. It does not mean that all diseases are finally curable if the patient wants to live. It means that the medicine itself is not the final court; the individual is. The medicine sets into action the healing force and reminds the body of its implicit desire to be well (the same desire that originally led it to *be* at all). Remember—this must be a single message and not a mixed message; it must be a specific unignorable shot. The body knows how to resist mixed messages.

An irritation is more compassionate than a salve when it is more definite and communicative. It is brief, swift, and precise, like a homeopathic remedy. Acupuncture uses a fine needle. The bioenergetic therapist seizes the pinpoint of the patient's compulsion and fear and exacerbates it. Nurturing is curative too. After all, an organism can be irritated into exhaustion or terror unless there is something in the irritation to which it can respond positively.

A shift in bodily attention is then communicated back to the will, to express itself in the life of the person. It may not be recognized as coming from the medicine, but the mind—sweeping back and forth across its accustomed territory—seems always to come up with new ideas.

Discussions about whether a person wants to get well are doomed to go around in circles, for wanting and not wanting can be indistinguishable ploys of the self. Not wanting to get well is itself part of the disease, but it also can be the irritant catalyzing the cure.

The arguments in our culture about what constitutes actual death and when we can legally stop trying to save someone who does not want to live are telling indications of our dilemma. When we don't know why we are alive and have bodies, nor how to inhabit them happily, we put the issue to every desperate test. At the same time, we stand stupefied before legalistic and problematic definitions of things we must ultimately know from the inside if we are to know them at all.

It is as though people try only partially to be healed, only partially to be alive. The dichotomy becomes: now I do this/now I am me. When they are being cured of something, they withhold their more sophisticated part, making the experience as if a cure of someone else to whom they are allotted special access.

During a seminar in Vermont in 1977, the poet and homeopath Theodore Enslin was being questioned along these lines when someone raised the issue of the relative importance of symptoms in homeopathy, implying that the wish to get well *must* be a more significant symptom than calluses on an elbow. Enslin objected:

> If you're really trying to get into homeopathic thinking, you have to erase those artificial boundaries—that thought is different from a hangnail. It's not. It's a manifestation of you. I've always loved that story about the guy who went to [Charles Godlove] Raue, who was one of the Philadelphia school, a really very eminent homeopath. And he was an old man. He had many many things wrong with him. He had gout. He had prostatitis. And he had loose teeth. And he had all these things. So Raue gave him a pill. He said, "Well, now, is this for my gout? Or is it for my loose teeth?" and so on. And Raue finally said, "Your name is Miller, isn't it?"
>
> "If you were really going to be a good homeopathic patient, there wouldn't have to be any more discussion. You simply realize *it's all one thing.* You cannot consider one ailment or another. You have a burn on your arm which doesn't heal. The aim of usual medicine is to clear that one spot. Cure it. Fight it. Homeopathically, we don't think that way; we think about the whole organism. Because there is that one disease manifestation, there is an indication that the entire

organism is diseased and you've got to treat it that way."

"But still," the questioner persisted, "isn't not really wanting to get better such a basic and serious symptom that one won't even seek out a doctor in the first place? How do you overcome that?"

"Well, that is a personal decision," Enslin replied. "There are certain medicines that can bring you to the place where you *do* want to. But sometimes not. Some so-called failures of treatment can simply be traced to a personal resistance."

"But then isn't a personal resistance just another symptom?"

"Yes it is. Yes it is. Of course we're always looking for the miracle that will cure us of everything. I don't think that homeopathy or very much of anything else will ever do that for us. And when people weren't talking about psychosomatic disease, Hahnemann himself was the first one, by saying, yes, the mental symptoms are equally important. But they are sometimes hard to deal with. You get to the point of [James Tyler] Kent and the mental symptoms are more important than anything else. I think he got to the place where perhaps he *over*emphasized them. He did because there was absolutely no support for them anywhere. I mean there *is* a balance. The thing that we really need to do, the thing that more than anything else can get over that kind of resistance, is simply the admission that there is no difference between any kind of symptom and any other. The old division of mind and body—with all our philosophizing about it—means we still think we are superior to the animals, we still think that somehow our thinking brain is going to bail us out."

He paused for a moment and then continued:

"You asked in our earlier talk: 'Would you say we are, as a race, diseased?' I would say, 'Yes we certainly are.' Because we place an emphasis on something which has nothing to do with what makes us move. We think that—we *think!*—that is the problem."

The questioner still proceeded: "Whose chances of cure are greater: the person who wants to get better but doesn't take a homeopathic medicine or the person who doesn't want to get better but has the right medicine prescribed for him?"

"Well, the chances of cure without a homeopathic medicine are far greater than without a feeling that one wants to be cured. I mean

> there are many instances of the whole placebo thing. A person is convinced that this *will* do it, and he *really* wants to be cured: therefore he *is* cured! That, in a sense, is a homeopathic high potency. It is a strong enough wish in the person to outrage the system to the point where it will cure itself, which is the principle behind all of this."
>
> "But where does the resistance to being well come from in the first place? How do we get to the bottom of it?"
>
> "There is a direction to your repeated question. You're hammering at this one particular thing. But you see, in doing that, you're actually doing what we all do when we depend upon our thinking processes. It's a very difficult thing, because somehow we're going to have to do it in reverse if we're ever going to get to the place where all of these things are in balance. But there are places where probably this is the wrong direction to take—if you really want to know. If you really want to know, don't want to know! I mean, enlightenment never comes if someone wants to be enlightened."[17]

This is a paradox in the history of medicine and philosophy. The wish to be cured *does* locate in the will, but it is not the conscious self-expressed will we understand in language; it is the real inner will of the body, the It. The conscious will must, at some point, work counter to literal intention, to itself, in order to incorporate the "meaning" of the deeper will. The way a person expresses to himself that he wants to get well may in fact be the way to stay sick. One thing is clear: the ambition itself is not the desire; the ambition is the disease. So the person must suddenly discover how *not* to want to be well (which is certainly not the same as wanting not to be well).

Enslin continued:

> "I think the only real problem and the only real resistance to this whole way of thinking is this refusal to admit that there are no divisions. You can sit and talk philosophically about it, and it's very popular to do that. You can talk about a holistic universe and so forth and so on, but we don't *think* that way. If we started to do that, probably there would be far less disease. And homeopathy or any other

specialty would fade away. You wouldn't need this particular way of looking at things because everything was looked at in the same way."

"What would our lives be like if we did think in that way?"

"I have no idea. It would seem to me, from every indication that I've had personally, simply looking at animals, trees, or anything else, that it would be far easier to do things that we really want to do, or say we want to do. We have simply forgotten. We think. We think we are the masters. We forget that we aren't any more important than a raccoon. We think of *our* lives, the preciousness of *our* life. Even a man like Schweitzer: he is a humanitarian, but he is not a totalitarian—the reverence for life; there is always the feeling, 'human life—this is more important.' If we could just drop this, maybe we wouldn't have to go through this backward trip through the labyrinth to get to where we could really function."

"Well, we can say we're going to do that. We can theorize it—"

"Don't theorize it. Do it! Of course it's impossible: therefore do it!"[18]

Notes

1. Edward Whitmont, personal communication, New York, 1975.

2. Anna Quindlen, "Gulf War's Killing Legacy," *San Francisco Chronicle* (October 10, 1994), from *The New York Times* wire service.

3. Ian Grand, personal communication, Berkeley, California, 1979.

4. Ibid.

5. Jon Carroll, "The Odd Saga of Marlo Morgan," *San Francisco Chronicle* (September 7, 1994), p. E8.

6. Carroll, "The Odd Saga of Marlo Morgan," *San Francisco Chronicle* (September 8, 1994), p. E10.

7. Carl Jung, *Psychology and Alchemy,* translated from the German by R.F.C. Hull (London: Routledge and Kegan Paul, 1953), pp. 95–98.

8. Edward C. Whitmont, *The Alchemy of Healing: Psyche and Soma* (Berkeley, California: North Atlantic Books, 1993), p. 15.

9. Ibid., p. 129.

10. Ibid., pp. 130, 168.

11. Frederick Crews, "The Revenge of the Repressed, Part II," *The New York Review of Books,* Vol. XLI, Number 20 (December 1, 1994), p. 50.

12. Ibid., p. 49.

13. Ibid.

14. See Charles Poncé, *The Archetype of the Unconscious and the Transfiguration of Therapy: Reflections on Jungian Psychology* (Berkeley, California: North Atlantic Books, 1990), for a full discussion of this issue.

15. G. I. Gurdjieff, *Views From the Real World: Early Talks* (New York: Dutton, 1975), p. 273.

16. Ibid., p. 274.

17. Theodore Enslin, at a seminar at Goddard College, Plainfield, Vermont, recorded in May, 1977.

18. Ibid.

CHAPTER EIGHT

The Spectrum of Healing

Internalizing and Externalizing Medicines

All medicines can be viewed in relation to one another on a spectrum from Internalizing/Active to Externalizing/Passive. Most holistic and non-Western medicines are based to some degree on the internalization (internal transformation) of events and substances. The images placed by the medicine man in his sand painting; the darts, sigils, and swords of the shaman in his *mesa;* the letters fed to the patient in the Eurhythmic alphabet; the breaths during meditation; and, on another level, the subtle and molecular qualities of food and herbs—all are meant to be taken into the whole being—absorbed and assimilated. Their true power is long-term and secondary. They require an active response from the recipient—and likely stimulate one—and because they work according to laws of cure, from the inside out, their seeds give rise to levels of healing often quite removed from their initial effect. On the other hand, as we have seen, conventional medicines are generally external and work *on* the recipient, usually at once. They do not stimulate a secondary curative response, or if they do, it is random.

Just as medicines of internalization progress from external substances, so the medicines of externalization internalize, though usually the remedy has a different internal meaning from its proposed external intent—and even from its external biophysical effect. The long-range consequence of an antibiotic in the latency and potentiality of the body/mind is often more profound and "medicinal" (even if pathologically so) than its effect on the original disease or than the disease itself (despite the fact that the medicine's external activity may be successful in reversing the external form of the disease). Iatrogenic disease is a major health problem in the West; liver damage, change in blood chemistry, kidney dysfunction, neurosis, slurred speech, and fungal infestation are all regular by-products of popular antibiotics. However, the real problem is since these medicines are not chosen according to any laws of cure (Hahnemannian, Ayurvedic, shamanic), they can be internalized ultimately only pathologically. After surgery removing his spleen a patient may have no further physical symptoms, but the field of his meridians, his emotional balance and kinesthesia may be so altered as to incubate a psychosis or tumor over time.

In a complex world there is no easy solution to this dilemma, but in general, a person should choose the most internalizing medicine of which he or she is capable and which the immediacy of the disease allows. At the same time, he should be developing other more internalizing methods as an aspect of overall personal development. That way healing will reach most safely to the deepest level. However, this does *not* mean risking one's health or life trying to operate at a more internal, active level than one is presently capable of. The chart on the opposite page offers a hypothetical spectrum.

The lower the number, the more active the person treated has to be—the more he or she has to cure himself or herself. Cures represented by the higher numbers are, by degree, relatively quicker and more mechanical. A pathology in the seventh category is dealt with in a matter of months or even minutes. The first level requires years (though spontaneous cures of faith are possible). As one moves up the scale and the treatments allow more leeway of passivity by the patient, the physician substitutes techniques for internal power.

The chart should be viewed flexibly, as an intuitive guide, not a taxonomy. Although the medicines of the first and seventh levels are

	Internalizing/Active Pole
First Level:	Meditation, Prayer, Self-Reflection (Taoist *Chi Gung,* Reiki)
Second Level:	Activity (*Dō-in, T'ai Chi Ch'uan,* Chanting, medical *Chi Gung,* some Feldenkrais exercises)
Third Level:	Healing by the Senses (touch, vision, hearing, dreams), Craniosacral Therapy, Zero Balancing
Fourth Level:	Diet and Herbs, Polarity Therapy
Fifth Level:	Bodywork (Massage, Adjustment, Rolfing), Sensory Stimulants
Sixth Level:	Acupuncture, Psychotherapy
Seventh Level:	Surgery, Radiation, Drugs
	Externalizing/Passive Pole

extremes, those in between differ by only minute degrees and can overlap even across five or six levels depending on how they are practiced.

The examples are rough approximations. Most medicines are multilayered and combinatorial, and include elements of self-reflection, activity, diet, and healing by the senses within their primary modality. For instance, craniosacral massage can be done subtly at the level of chanting. Acupuncture can soften to *dō-in.* Taoist *Chi Gung* resembles meditation; Buddhist medical *Chi Gung,* exercise. Even coarse factory drugs have some curative herbal properties in them, for they are based on herbs historically and pharmaceutically. Although in this discussion I take a highly critical view of passive externalizing medicine, the hierarchy is not ideological; it represents a range of potential. One starts where he or she is and works toward (ideally) a more internal cure.

The pure vitalist medicines are left off the chart because they could be considered at any level depending on interpretation. They are herbs if one chooses a metaphor with pills and infusions, and they are prayers if one thinks of them by analogy with the "currents" of faith healing. Drugs, radiation, and surgery are clearly not outside of the spectrum but at the opposite pole from meditation. "There are no wrong medicines," said Paul Pitchford, the acupuncturist and Chinese herbalist, when he arranged the original chart on which this one is based. "People choose the medicine they need."[1]

HEALERS AT THE seventh level work on a physical/mechanical plane. It would be useless for them to try acupuncture or praying over patients. In fact, as noted, it is dangerous when healers at this level are attracted by the holistic fad. Unless they transform their whole experiential base, they simply turn other methods into metaphors of mechanical medicine.

Yet we cannot usefully rate doctors for purity and holism just as we cannot rate them according to the technologies to which they have access. There is no "healing authority" that declares which treatments are health-bearing and which ones are iatrogenic or secondarily pathological. The outcome rests in the mystery of individual process.

Some paths usefully include radiation and allopathic drugs. The image of all mainstream doctors as money-hungry hacks is no more than a New Age cartoon. Most of them are well-trained, able to heal, and use good judgment on the plane on which they work. Almost any of them are capable of extending lives and relieving painful and debilitating ailments. Mechanistic medicine may be linear and algorithmic, but that is the same linearity and algorithm that gave us the combustion engine and the computer chip, without which we would live quite different lives anyway.

For most people in the West today, medicine practiced at the seventh level is perfectly acceptable; even its failings are acceptable. People demand gross, immediate change at any cost, and this is what they tend to get. They are like "advertisers" laying out hundreds of thousands of dollars for the seconds of prime-time, which happen to be their lives.

Those who prefer the seventh level are the same people who reach nervously for a cigarette, a cup of coffee, or the symptomatic relief of their jobs or social lives. Heart surgery is another high for the home-improvement, standard-of-living junkie in all of us. We go on amassing artifacts of externalization. And yet we live this way, some of us for a long time.

Holistic medicine may be understood as an attempt to practice our life and health crises as transformational; it is also an attempt to get us well without complications. It is not a guarantee of freedom from disease or of longevity.

The Most Internalizing Medicines: Prayer, Meditation, Self-Reflection, and Activity

Meditation is a conscious method for entering unconscious being and transforming it through concentration. For the practitioner his thoughts are a slipstream of breath, organs and mind, a thoughtless mind that penetrates the whole body, directing breath to organs in need of healing. The breath more "reinvents" organs than operates as a bellows flooding prior apperceived sites. In *Chi Gung* the activated and internalized mind operates within the subtle medium of the *chi* itself. This is totally different from even the most contemplative sort of cognitive mind. If the *chi* is not immediately perceptible—as it is not for most people—then the mind tracks what *is* perceptible until that reveals what it is, then the next most barely perceptible thing, and so on through the layers. One Sri Lankan master writes: "[The] method of allowing the simple facts of observation to speak and make their impact on the mind will be more wholesome and efficacious than a method of introspection that enters into inner arguments of self-justifications and self-accusations, or into an elaborate search for 'hidden motives.'"[2] To work on an illness, meditation must cut deeper than the illness and avoid being trapped in the intrinsic arguments of that illness at any level of body/mind. That is, to cure even the most deep-seated physical illness would require only *thinking* the cure and conducting those thoughts to the seat of the pathology.

Of course, we have trouble clearing our minds enough to think *cures* rather than *about* cures, and we are not comfortable enough with our sensations or cognizant enough of their exquisitely minute impulses to direct them along a path to a disease. Yet, as we have seen throughout this book, the pain of disease is its mindfulness and, if at all possible, it should not be routinely anesthetized. It is the most direct connection (i.e., path) to not only the ailing organ but the principle of holism. It leads through sensation to the source.

Meditation also allows one to penetrate neurosis—first, by perceiving it as only a thought-form; second, by detaching oneself from subservience to its patterning; third, by getting beneath the character structure of one's invention of a personal reality; and finally, by discovering the emptiness beneath the roots of all thought-forms and dissolving them in a burst of lucidity. People who spend a year living in a cave meditating do not suffer this privation because of the imagined piety of suffering. They intend to cure, in one intense dose of practice, conditions which deepen and spread over a lifetime and become most difficult to root out piecemeal among the distractions of the world.

Most diseases for most people fall beyond the realm where the meditation of which they are capable can heal. Yet the commitment to meditation, even in the first halting try to listen to a thought, is a step onto a path that leads ultimately to the point where mind and disease meet.

PRAYER IS A different sort of medicine from meditation, though the two combine in mantras. Whereas meditation arises from knowing and being, prayer emanates from faith and ritual. When Jesus says, "Your faith has healed you," he means not an obedient act of thought but a spontaneous meditation that changes one's nature in the universe.

For prayer to heal, one must have faith in the gods inside oneself and in the forces of the cosmos to which they correspond. Submission is an instantaneous act, but developing the capacity to submit takes most of a lifetime.

Prayer often works best in a community context, as with Navaho sand-painting rituals and Christian faith healings. A group of people collaborate on a common mind in which individuals among them can be touched. The "mind" includes supernatural beings and mythological events, so it penetrates into the cultural identity of the group, where many illnesses originate. The following invocation, part of the Navaho Beautyway Ceremony, retains its primal power even in translation:

Prayer to Big Snake Man at Dropped-out Mountain

Young man this day I gave you my tobacco, at Dropped-out
   Mountain, Young Man Big Snake Man, Head Man!
Today I have given you my tobacco, today you must make my feet
   and legs well, my body, my mind, my sound, the evil power
   you have put it into me, you must take it out of me, away, far
   away from me!
Today you must make me well, all the things that have harmed
   me will leave me
I will walk with a cool body after they have left me.
Inside of me today will be well, all fever will have come out of me,
   and go away from me, and leave my head cool!
I will hear today, I will see today, I will be in my right mind today!
Today I will walk out, today everything evil will leave me, I will be
   as I was before, I will have a cool breeze over my body,
   I will walk with a light body.
   I will be happy forever, nothing will hinder me!
I walk in front of me beautiful, I walk behind me beautiful, under
   me beautiful, on top of me beautiful, around me beautiful, my
   words will be beautiful!
I will be everlasting one, everything is beautiful![3]

In the right context, prayer can change exactly what it proposes to change. Otherwise, it is decorative and of little efficacy.

SELF-REFLECTION MIGHT be defined as the continuous act of noting and internalizing events—not narcissistically but as a token of one's objective presence in the world. Every interaction—a purchase at a market, a stray image of a building on a side street—is reexperienced silently for its unstated assumptions, its physiological background, its passage into body/mind. Dreams, feelings, play, even washing the dishes become careful exercises.

Self-reflection changes one's frame of knowing and being and thus changes the matrix within which health and disease occur. The potential of this process will differ from person to person, and some will no doubt substitute clever habitual thinking for true self-reflection. For instance, Gurdjieff claimed that, despite the strong desires of individuals, it was impossible to cultivate a true will without a specific shock or tension to break with the abstract polarity imposed on life. Only such a jolt could separate a "third force" and release us from our dualism and existential mirage. His exercises were to prepare and cultivate this.

ACTIVITY IS THE somatic counterpart of self-reflection, or in the unity of the mind/body, it is reflection moving through the organism. This definition includes regular activities such as walking, standing, breathing, talking, tensing, relaxing, eating—"lifestyle," as they are contemporarily affiliated. Are we grounded in ourselves or do we lean like magnets toward every charismatic influence? Do we act from roots? Or do we graze from the surface, feeding ourselves symptomatically, moving anxiously, and adrenalizing our emotions?

The issue of lifestyle in disease was emphasized in the 1980s fad of studies linking inactive and stress-based styles to heart disease and cancer. A growing awareness of the importance of aerobics and exercise spawned new activities from ritual jogging to gym workouts, fitness parlors, and "jazzercise" classes. These may represent increased degrees of recreational self-reflection; but our actual pathology is more than just a lack of action, and when a flush of compulsive activity is added without internalization, the imbalance is merely displaced. It is preferable to move slowly and consciously through small awkward spaces than to labor mightily in an attempt to break through.

In an exercise based on Feldenkrais principles, one is instructed to move a part of his or her body in a circle like the hand of a clock. The part of the body may be the chin (lower jaw), eye, whole head, foot, a single toe, shoulder, pelvis, etc. Where the circle gets cut off, e.g., from the hours between 2 and 4 or between 8 and 11 (or any other arc) being skipped, then there is the possibility for learning how to scan through that missing zone and regain its awareness and depth of mobility. This is not accomplished through force, skill, or speed. Ballet dancers and gymnasts who can twist in remarkable ways tend to lack this skill. In fact, they are often quite paralyzed by the "clock." The only way to fill in arcs is to execute a gradually widening circle and "experientialize" the components that are missing. Likely they were known once and lost through fear, rigidity, and postures based on lack of self-esteem and reinforced repetitively through the years. In rounding out the circle, one restores an aborted series in oneself. Jaw and foot circles may be small, but they transfuse their circularity throughout the body/mind. Toe and eye circles are incredibly powerful, for they require the mind to inhabit minute sections of arc. Every abandoned section represents a loss of something for the whole being. All of life experience, in one way or another, is an opportunity to restore degrees of arc. Our ineffable desires ultimately seek such wholes rather than isolated "hits" of feeling or explosions of movement. This mobility and cohesiveness separate real health from mere endurance or agility.

D*ō-in* is an ancient Oriental form of self-massage and daily exercise. A practitioner regularly familiarizes himself with his body/mind by interacting with surfaces, bones, and organs, draining waste, removing calluses and surface deposits, breathing, praying, intoning. The entire physiology is included: the spiral of the ear, every joint of every finger and toe and the space between them, every orifice and wart. The connections of all the organs and meridians at the ears, at the eyes, on the feet, and at numerous other points can be used for diagnosis, stimulation, and sedation.[4]

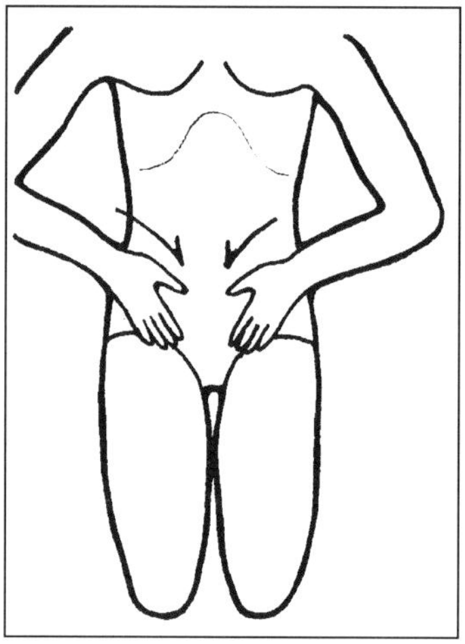

Some of the separate exercises are like mantras; others are primal calisthenics and adjustments. In one set of movements, eyes look into the infinite distance while the person kneels with hands clasped at the level of the heart. Sounds are heard, but no particular sound is listened to. The hands are clapped clearly and sharply. Then the body is twisted around. The teeth are beaten together.

In a related sequence, the tongue is used to collect and taste saliva from the upper region of the palate. In another, each finger is rotated at the point where it connects to the hand. The fists are drummed on the back with the spine held straight: this is to relieve not only sciatic nerve pains but throat congestion and hemorrhoids.[5] We should remember that the point of each exercise is not to strengthen any particular muscle or capacity but to redistribute attention and vital energy. *Dō-in* is physical movement directed toward spiritual movement—to clear the mind and to move fear and anger while wastes are drained from the body.

Healing by the Senses and by Dreams

A CERTAIN PORTION OF any cure is mediated by the complex nonalgorithmic feedback between the senses and the organism. A pure intrinsic medicine is assimilated from this process, no matter the external modality or originating mechanism. An untold number of people develop illnesses, even potentially fatal ones, then heal them endogenously without ever knowing they had such a disease. The choices people make in their daily activities, seemingly based on other issues, turn out to be, synchronistically, the correct medical decisions. In this manner the caduceus is passed from the outer to the inner physician.

The five senses also play direct roles. They are orifices into and out of the viscera, active channels that contact all parts of us through the part of us that is sentient. In healing through the senses, we are altering the epiderm not only of consciousness and memory but of the elemental process and the polar field of the body.

Imagery is an activating element in many techniques. Chanting transmits vibrations. Taste and smell are distinct catalysts in healing by food, flower essences, and herbs. Touch is a component in virtually every cure. It marks the continuous seam of tangency between any herb and the body—on visceral, cellular, molecular, and atomic levels. Touch also generates an array of primary and secondary effects in massage, bodywork, *marma* therapy, and chiropractic, including sensations of kinesthesia, body balance, and polarity.

Memory is another collective sense: even an amnesiac remembers that he or she exists. Through our recall we are surrounded by ancient layers of sensations, senses, and cognitive fields that interfuse new impulses as they occur. Psychoanalysis, from that perspective, is a sensual medicine of the memory, for it changes people by changing their histories.

The senses also provide points and fields of focus and surprise in healing. Surprise within the organism initiates new organic and psychosomatic processes. Gurdjieffians seek the octave of transformation and separate the "third force"; a faith healer "jolts" the mind/body set of lameness (or deafness); the healing shaman presents the visible form of the disease; an emetic "vomits," leading to spontaneous cleansing. Eduardo Calderón, the Peruvian shaman, shoots a startling spray of holy water from his mouth into the moonlight. The psychotherapist manifests the moment of trauma. These are bolts of energy, allopathic or homeopathic shocks. Surgery and drugs offer such "shocks" too, but (as in the ironic case of shock treatment) they usually work to deaden the senses, away from pain; they *remove* a symptom by shock without kinesthetic and elemental activation. In a material age, an age of anesthesia and painkillers, the doctor who does not arouse the senses is often a hero!

A healing process begun by a jolt or an evocative image or an essential aroma must be integrated over time. The more intensely the initial surprise is able to penetrate the overall systemic stasis and get into the viscera, usually the deeper its impact and the more primal the healing processes it activates (see also "The Healing Dialogue" and "Holism and Coherence" in Chapter Two).

DREAMS ARE A complex form of spontaneous healing through the senses and the memory. Physiologists now restate an esoteric truth: nightly dreaming maintains psychosomatic equilibrium. It little matters whether the images of sleep inspire our auto-medicines or the medicines autonomically require dreams to bear them; images and chemistry are linked in a synchronous cycle. In our discussion of Freud's dream dynamics, we explored the curative basis of dream in terms of passive sublimation, transformation of negatively cathected elements, and the requirement of wish fulfillment. Here we will examine dreams in terms of phenomenological events that spontaneously energize cures.

Curative dreamwork can be made active, whether through focusing on the dream's images and events after waking or by actually trying to wake within the dream (as yogis and shamans do from the metaphor that life is another dream in which we must learn to awake). In either case, we assume that dream images are a symbolic and archetypal counterpart to the underlying elixir of sleep. They provide a semantic and narrative stage for our "inner physician," who lies beneath language and does not recognize temporality. Whether the "physician" could heal in isolation without a wake of images we will never know, but dreams appear to generate a deeper rejuvenation and transition than any study of hormonal chemistry substantiates.

Dream beings do not respond to direct commands like: "Pay attention to this problem!" or "Heal this!" Core resistance is stronger than the mere cognitive suggestion of change—ever the dilemma of the superficial hypnotherapist. False responses, either of compliance or resistance, or (more likely) both, replace authentic links. Insofar as the Freudian laws of the unconscious describe a gravitational field, more intricately whorled than Jupiter's or that of any other "simple" physical body, suggestions must be mediated always through a distortion or reversal that mirrors the precise strain lines of projection and distortion in the dreamwork. If psychosomatic transformation is to occur, it must correspond to the hidden transformations already potentially occurring on another level in a dream, or on a series of ever more obscure and unconscious levels that may take decades to rise even to the level of dream formation (if they earn the currency to get out of the Underworld). The desired healing may sometimes get stuck in its own syntax of transformation in such a way that it will repeat and reinforce a pathology or alter only its surface features.

Can the dream imagery (beyond our idealization of the process) actually jolt the "physician" into a new RNA code sequence? Is that in fact its evolutionary function? Or does the often ornate and Gothic imagery provide a mere leaching bed, an overflow valve, for an imageless electron-like jump of *"chi"* at the nucleus? Is the process even more complex and beyond any negotiations of taxonomy and structure?

A MAN IS WORKING with a dream teacher in waking life (perhaps a therapist), but for many months this teacher's advice has no impact on the man's dreams. Then suddenly the teacher appears *in* a dream as a guide. His directive there is one of which neither teacher nor dreamer is consciously aware. He is conducting a dream class on swimming in a strangely heavy medium from which one propels oneself into the air; it also takes place in an ordinary swimming pool at an old Y. Students from all over the country have come to this archetypal pool for a lesson. The dreamer is suddenly standing by the ocean trying to track something very complex happening in the waves. The guide-therapist appears, makes a banal comment, and the dreamer dismisses him with, "You will no longer do." The guide stands there looking forlornly at the sea. His presence now leads the dreamer's attention to a complexity previously unnoticed in the waves. Now that the teacher is gone, something is beginning to manifest. That is the end of this episode, but the guide is replaced in successive dreams by a master of martial arts, a naive female social worker, and an authoritarian baseball manager. He has no fixed identity except by interpretation of a cumulative disjunction of characters. The lesson is that change can only occur by being experienced, and can be experienced only gradually through a rebus—can be experienced, in a sense, only as some other thing.

The dream guide teaches that all elements of the dream express aspects of the dreamer—the lost children in him or her, the undeveloped creatures, the disenfranchised physicians, the hostile shadow-beasts, the vast fields and blue skies of other worlds, the genetic forces of the Yin-Yang fields of one's incarnation, the remote systems of one's uncompleted self. Attention to each integer of this material compels the dream to deepen, for although dreaming (to occur) must allow some of the unconscious to become conscious (and thus potentially curative), it can never allow unconsciousness itself to become conscious.

A woman in a dream may not be a woman at all, she may be a medicine. But she is so alluring at that moment, the dreamer's desire for her is so strong, she transcends her personification and suggests a

new experience. She may be felt again among the stings during an acupuncture treatment. She is also the unintegrated female element of the dreamer, intuited as he thumps lightly on his ear doing *dō-in,* setting up a vibration in his jawbone.

There is a unity within, and the different medicines and therapies express their variant harmonies of it. In a dream an herb may be personified as a magician, a magician becomes a chiropractor, the chiropractor moves a rock that represents the sick organ, but the rock later turns into the archetype of a homeopathic remedy—and all this is still a shadow play for a deeper procedure of mind, matter, and energy that may be concretized in waking life by visits to actual practitioners.

A REPULSIVE MAN—bald, misshapen, and covered with a sickly oil—is chasing children from his house with a shotgun. Before the dream is over, the dreamer must embrace him and hold him tight. In another dream during a bout of diarrhea and a rash for which the dreamer, while awake, has been seeking herbal aid, a possible inner holistic doctor has been supplanted by a huckster at a fair handing out gross antibiotic tablets in gaudy plastic wrappings with the dreamer's name on them. The dreamer asks his therapist-guide for advice; the teacher recommends ingesting the tablets because the dreamer can remedy any side effects later with vitamins. So he does. They make him immediately nauseous, but a dramatic improvement occurs in waking life. The rash and diarrhea clear up in a day.

In dream language these tablets are herbal remedies, homeopathic potencies, expressly by *not* being them; they are the thing one would not consider in waking, which makes them the actual medicine within dreaming. This is a statement of syntax necessary to break the lethargy of the system. An act of reconciliation is carried out on an unconscious level with depreciated substances of the very pharmacy one is trying to avoid (conceived of as symbolic poisons), i.e., depreciated aspects of oneself. Dreams heal by representing the medicine as exactly what it is not so they then can transform it through the distortion into elixir.

In one dream during a flu I was "successfully" prescribed the contents of a can of Red Flag ant poison. The poison when dreamed (as when potentized homeopathically) potentiated its own image, through my resistance, to become something uncontacted and unknown.

Dream "vitamins" usually do not appear as actual pills, but, for instance, as a flood of icy water over a previously parched and sterile yard. The dirt responds with exotic flowers of all colors. The yard has also moved closer to the sea so that bright-colored fish are now mating in it. Trees drop purple and pink maché blossoms into the water. Whether these are the symbolic "Bach waters" or the dreamer's own auto-medicine, or both, they now carry out an actual healing through the dreaming process. A few nights later the dreamer finds himself in an egg, which he recognizes as an egg because huge fields of yolk-like matter are separating around him. He has the sense of his entire self shifting in relation to unconscious elements. In a subsequent dream he uses the swimming technique taught months ago at a seedy pool in a dream YMCA to swim toward the stars. The stars become Easter eggs in a meadow. Now the entire cosmic field is shifting; a curative relationship is evolving between the rudiments of individuation and the archetypal unconscious realms of the self behind the dreamer. This may be as close as he will ever come to experiencing the embryogenic meridians as forms.

The dreamer decides in waking life that he no longer needs a guide; he is tired of working on a symbolic level. He replaces the therapist with herbs, Thai massage, and acupuncture, all of which induce dream-like sensations. His nocturnal dreams become lucid. He is led almost by the hand through a demonstration of the whole dwindling "dis-ease." The symptoms are so graphic and didactic that no glossary is necessary. The ailing organs are rooms and streets but no particular room or street is an identifiable organ. The decision to drain and cleanse on a physical level has relieved the goal of fancy symbolism, freeing the dream to complete its own deeper process of transformation. A new healing cycle begins in the unconscious depths. A new disease is brewing far out over the ocean. This process does not end. An experience of god realms is inevitably followed by a new round of hungry ghosts.

Dreams propose the method by which multiple healing systems work together. As one progresses through layers of confusion, non-clarity and disease, one requires and accepts different levels of work at different times, different types of therapists and different therapies. Long-term practices like meditation, *t'ai chi ch'uan,* and dietary change may be maintained throughout but continually change their relationships to specific remedies. A dream reflects bodywork, as bodywork reinvokes a dream. A homeopathic dose blends with dream analysis so that the remedy is at least partially expressed and activated through a series of archetypal images in sleep. The *t'ai chi* student goes to a Rolfer to open a sacral block of which he had no awareness before the second year of *t'ai chi* and which is preventing further progress in the form. Then the *chi* generated thereby improves the whole spine. As an adjunct to a particular acupuncture treatment, a client is given a prescription of cleansing and sedating herbs. A rebirther learns to emphasize her in-breath for accumulating *prana;* then she joins a Zen meditation group and follows her out-breath for dissipation. Both are real; each has discrete results relative to the other it would not have alone. A woman who has changed enormously in relation to childhood traumas through two years of Reichian bodywork suddenly feels overwhelmed by the confrontative aspect of her personality and herself in the world; life has lost some of its texture in becoming richer. A breathing exercise leads her to meditation; a whole new apperception emerges, far sparer and exploring a different interior.

Somewhere within, surgery, flower potency, breath, and dream meet and converge. Despite the medium, all healing is finally improvised. That's *how* it works and *why* it works. (Many so-called holistic and spiritual treatments merely enact a metaphor of this fact in their attempts to maintain ideological exclusivity.) Sometimes apparently everything else about a treatment fails, except an inner transformation.

Metaphysical and Karmic Healing

Paranormal and unconscious "senses" such as telepathy, intuition of distant events, instincts, and archetypes may also be medicinal. After all, we are not completely conscious organisms; we are beings immersed in a world of unknown phenomena experiencing cognitively only the outer layer of existence.

For instance, Western science conceives of a primordial sequence of instincts inherited biologically from our ancestors much the way birds inherit capacities of navigation and spiders the ability to find food immediately after birth. Jungian and metaphysical systems postulate a collective unconscious of presymbolic matrices. The Jungian doctor attempts to put the sick person in touch with archetypal imagery, which literally becomes medicine even as the compounds fashioned by alchemists were medicinal, first in the act of mixing raw substances and observing their fiery and frothy interaction and second by the production of real pharmaceuticals (see "Jungian Psychology" in Volume One, Chapter Twelve).

Other systems claim deep pathogenic effects from specific ranges of unconscious phenomena. Scientologists may or may not believe in an available cosmic memory going back billions of years to events in other galaxies, but they attempt to use the pretense of such a memory curatively. Buddhists and Hindu physicians routinely accept past lives, not only as the causative substratum of this life but as a level of karmic existence contactable only through meditation. To regain an intimation of this memory is to heal this life by putting it in its actual frame. Diseases then literally become guides between incarnations. In indigenous tribal systems, awareness of a collective lineage of ancestors and mythological beings is cultivated through an interchange with replicas of these beings in rituals and vision quests. Healing then becomes a mediation between conscious forces of individuation and unconscious forces of nature—personal, collective, and cosmic.

The active domain of disease and healing is often a mystery, and it little matters where an ailment seems to be located—in ethnic memory, childhood trauma, or past lives. What we cannot resolve we must simply treat. John Upledger tells this story:

> In January, 1980, Jean-Pierre Barral was visiting us in Michigan. He examined me "off the body" as he does. He told me that there was an abnormal heat pattern over my upper left abdominal quadrant and over the left inferior costal region. He uses heat or energy patterns to determine how old the person was when the injury or illness occurred. He only needs to know the subject's age. Jean-Pierre moved his hands about for a few minutes. His face developed an expression of disbelief. His voice developed a tone of marked astonishment. He finally said, "John, this is an injury from 140 years ago." This would be the year 1840.
>
> As he spoke I remembered an experience from prior to our move to Michigan in 1975. A friend and I were playing around with hypnoregression. As the subject I had seen myself as a black slave in Charleston, South Carolina. I decided to run away. I ran for a day and hid the first night in an unknown farmer's barn. He found me asleep in the barn the next morning. I came awake suddenly with him standing over me about to plunge a pitchfork into my body. I died of fright before he stabbed me in the upper abdomen and lower left thorax. As I died I flew up above and watched the anger of this farmer plunging the pitchfork into my vacated body. I laughed at him derisively.
>
> In retrospect, I reconsider my behavior at the time of this death. My attitude of derision was deplorable. I see again this angry farmer so controlled and driven by his emotions, prejudices and hatred acting so inhumanely against another human being. I recalled this incident as Jean-Pierre worked with me non-verbally. Suddenly I felt total compassion for this farmer. I hope that some time I can see him and help him as I may be able. He needs to shed himself of this negative emotion. Perhaps we have met again since 1840.
>
> Since Jean-Pierre's evaluation and my resolution of this "experience" I have had no further recurrence of my shingles....
>
> Could it be that we carry trauma from one life to another?[6]

A REINCARNATIONAL LEVEL MIGHT be intentionally aroused through a particular ceremony or hallucinogen. There are many selective modes of entering unconscious frames without having to become conscious of any of them. "The shaman, himself, is important, primordial," says Eduardo Calderón, "and without substitution in the field of curing. He uses the San Pedro which affects special points of a person, and gives him a 'sixth sense' in accord with the topic with which he is dealing. Taking San Pedro makes him leap into a special dimension."[7]

A parallel process likely occurs in Hopi healing ceremonies, African myth-enactments, *ayahuasca* shamanism, and Australian Aborigine Emu dances—initially through bright feathers, pigmentation on the dancers, chanting to open the interior field of sound, incense, herbal visions, rhythmic dancing, and secondarily through the collective invocation of mythological "memory."

"The *mesa,*" says Eduardo, "is nothing more than a control panel by which one is able to calibrate the infinity of accesses into each person."[8] He speaks of the bioelectromagnetic power *(poder bioelectromagnético)* which gives potentiality to his staffs of power in the healing *mesa (potencialidad a la vara).* The staffs then vibrate precisely according to the account, the reason for the sickness *(la cuenta, a la razón de la enfermedad).*[9] At the elemental level, the bioelectromagnetic field, the work of massage and herbs, and the chanting combine.

Individual Sensory Modalities (Healing by Sound, Scent, and Color)

EARLIER I MADE a distinction between autogenic sensory healing (of which daily activity and dreams are obvious instances) and sensory medicine (including color therapy, music therapy, biofeedback, and aromatherapy). Autogenically, the senses are catalysts of *any* healing process. Active at all times, they may also be cultivated through meditation, the sensory modes of Ayurveda, or innumerable other practices. Conversely, a particular external substance or mechanism may be *directed* into the organism through the senses. Either modality can be effective, but autogenic sensory healing and mechanical sensory treatments fall at diametrically opposite phases of the spectrum. Healing by the use of music and electronically generated sound or in a biofeedback machine is at least as passive and externalizing as deep-tissue bodywork, whereas natural sounds, scents, and dreams are often extensions of self-reflection and awareness.

On the chart of healing modalities, it is not only true that certain modalities are more or less internalizing, but also substances and dosages within modalities are more or less subtle; thus scents, images, and sounds can replicate prayer or, at their most mechanical and artificial extreme, surgery. There is no question the latter can also be therapeutic, but the former are potentized, thus affect the body primarily on a cellular, perhaps even an atomic level (as well as the equivalents of those levels in the energy body and the mind). Frantzis compares the grosser external movements of medical *Chi Gung* to upping the wattage in a light bulb from maybe 40 to 100 but the internal movements of Taoist *Chi Gung* to changing to a whole new order of light.[10]

Sound is fundamental. Some healers believe it is the primary ontological sense, the auditory crease emerging first among sensory orifices during gestation. Providing a channel for the configurations of cosmic vibration, sound delivers the literal earmark of reality; it is the sense by which people ground themselves in this realm. A variety of practitioners over the years have experimented with direct sound as a medicine—chanting mantras, intoning vibrations, generating vibratory waves in electronic oscillators, or composing music to have a curative effect, often broadcasting melodies to particular *chakras.*

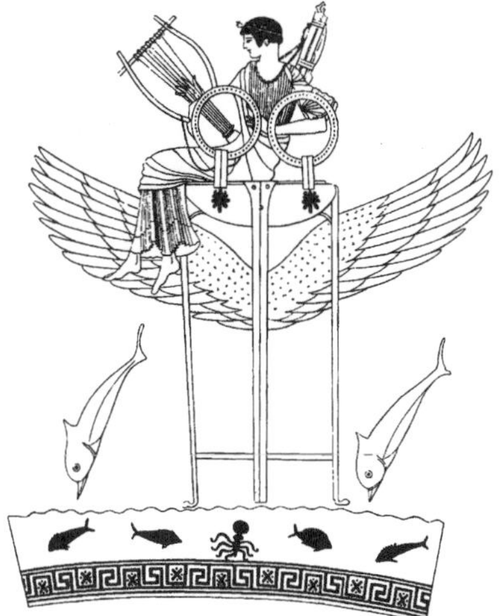

The most refined technique from among these is the one developed by French ear, nose, and throat specialist Alfred Tomatis, who began his career by training singers to increase their vocal range. Later he experimented with projecting electronically filtered music into his clients' inner ears. Different patterns and angles turned out to have curative impact on a broad range of diseases not ordinarily associated with hearing, especially psychopathologies.

> Tomatis took Mozart, Gregorian chant, and, where possible, the voice of the client's mother and electronically filtered out all the low-frequency sounds (below 8,000 hertz). Through special headphones, the client attentively listens to many hours of this filtered music—sixty hours is typical—over three to four months. The idea is to return the client to the sonic atmosphere in the womb, then retrain his or her entire listening function from its formative stages. Gradually, two tiny but important ear muscles are reconditioned to respond to a broader frequency spectrum.[11]

This is an auditory version of "awareness enhancement" from the standpoint that increasing the range of sensation makes the organism healthier and provides more channels for emotional expression. Sound is also used therapeutically by those caring for the terminally ill:

> In the Chalice of Repose, music is delivered solely through voice and harp, usually nonrhythmic selections (free of pulse or count) with regular alternations between silence and music. The music helps alleviate pain, dissolve fear, liberate the spirit from the body, and enable people to let go.[12]

Therese Schroeder-Sheker, a composer who trains people in this method in Missoula, Montana, places the origin of musical healing in the eleventh-century Cluniac monasteries of France. She describes her initial experience, singing Gregorian chant, at the urging of a priest, into the left ear of an irritable, dying man in his eighties:

> He rested in my arms and began to breathe much more regularly, and we, as a team, breathed together. It was as if the way in which sound anointed him now made up for the ways in which he had never been touched or returned touch while living the life of a man.

> These chants are the power of love. They carry the flaming power of hundreds of years and thousands of chanters who have sung these prayers before.[13]

Music serves as a window, an "'audible glimpse' into the immediate future ... in the sacred role of mediation between dimensions."[14] In many traditions, we incarnate by measures of tone—sacred chants and drumming by our ancestors delivering the *"wakan"* into flesh. Panpipes convey a haunting sense of the "beyond," which becomes medicine as their notes radiate through body and mind. Choirs of voices heal the spirit by summoning remote landscapes into being. Because sound is not limited to the parameters of sight, these magic realms appear everywhere at once, including within:

> In the darkness something was happening at last. A voice had begun to sing....
>
> Then two wonders happened at the same moment. One was that the voice was suddenly joined by other voices; more voices than you could possibly count. They were in harmony with it, but far higher up the scale: cold, tingling, silvery voices. The second wonder was that the blackness overhead, all at once, was blazing with stars. They didn't come out gently one by one, as they do on a summer evening. One moment there had been nothing but darkness; next moment a thousand, thousand points of light leaped out—single stars, constellations, and planets, brighter and bigger than any in our world.[15]

Because it speaks directly to a spirit body, sound is most powerful at the moment of death. During much of life, it grazes over us or is tuned and fiddled for worldly pleasures; at the end of life, it regains its sacred role and rings at the nucleus of the dissolving organism.

A WIDE RANGE OF techniques has been developed to inspire or heal people through their senses of smell. Leading into primitive lobes of the brain, the nose activates hormonal chains and instinctual actions of which we are but dimly aware. We intuit their power by the effects even random scents have on our whole being. Aromas are profoundly

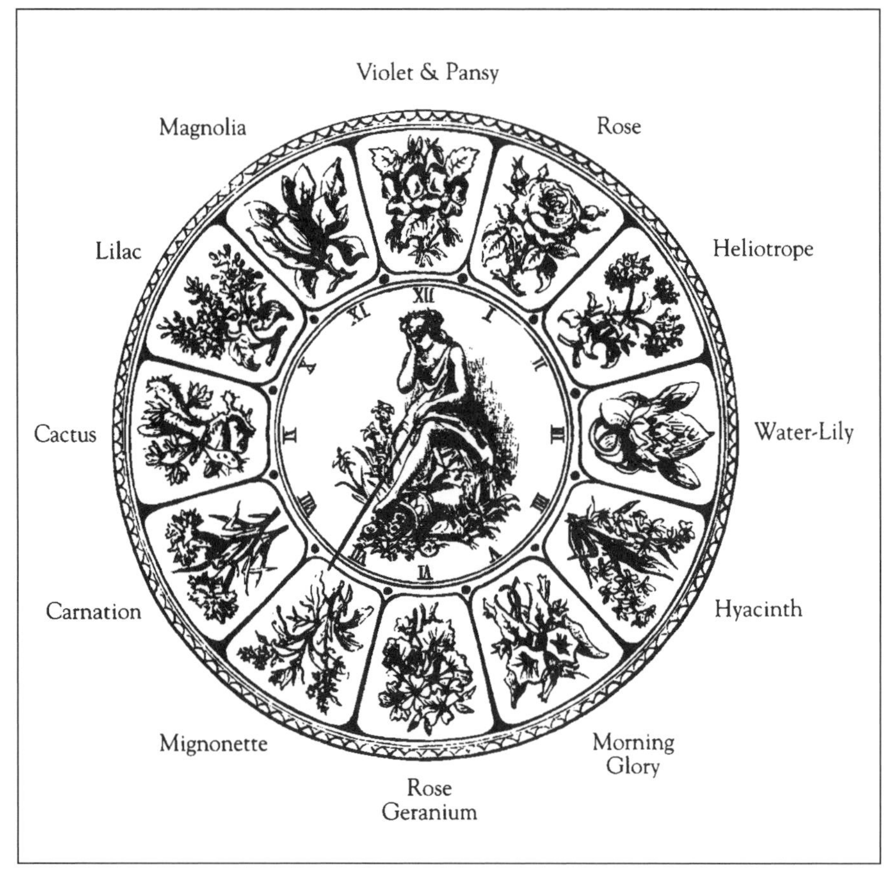

aphrodisiac and also alert animals instantaneously with a primal nip of danger. The olfactory canal is also the first testing mechanism of food.

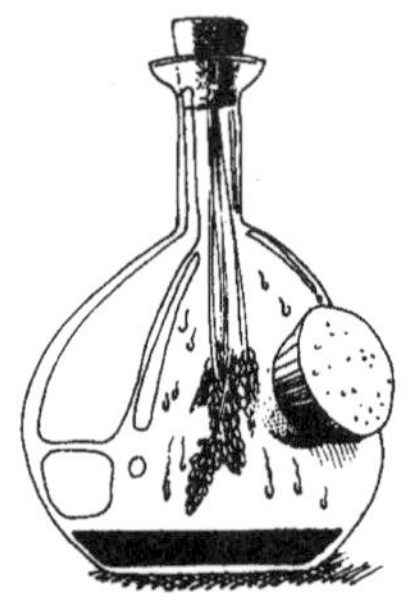

Some of the flavors and elixirs sought traditionally by alchemists and herbalists reside innately in scent-bearing nimbi and invisible dust percolating within simple landscapes. Even without a formal aromatherapy we pass along streets and trails (in sun and in rain) and are transformed in mood by elusive fumes and fragrances—why not in metabolism and health too? Gardens, glens, ponds, shifts in wind, nearness to a beach, even stale office buildings carry both pathogens and medicines. This subtle, ever-shifting play of scent won't necessarily cure an existing disease, but it continuously juggles the matrix from which either vitality or degeneration later develops.

The incense of a fir forest after a rain or a magnolia tree at night in spring is more than just luxury or nostalgia. In some inexplicable way these molecules go to the roots of our soul. It is no wonder then that scents bear medicinal vitality. In fact, medical aromatherapy has full institutional standing in France, the nation of its professionalization.

Perhaps one reason the essences of oil that the French use in their aromatherapy are curative is that scents such as lavender, orange, and rose treat replicas of tissue that once experienced the anonymous reptile healer directly, molecularly. This primordial language of smell cannot be abstracted in primate philosophy because it emerges prior to our ocular and three-dimensional reconstruction of the environment. Yet magicians have always known the transformation that is available in a poof!

More than sights or touch, and even more than vibrations of sound, smells enter the body as substance. They are herbs directly processed through our lungs, heart, and bloodstream. They are vaporized medicines. Jeanne Rose explains:

> Aromatherapy is a way of treating mental and physical illnesses through inhalation and through the external application of essential oils with pressure-point therapy or simple massage....
>
> The direct inhalation of the odors generally affects the mind psychologically, although inhalation can also have ... physiological effect via the limbic system in the brain and the blood circulation. For example, rubbing oil of Jasmine on the temples, pressing firmly ... in a circular motion will definitely ease away a headache. The Jasmine enters into the body both through the skin as well as the nasal mucosa.[16]

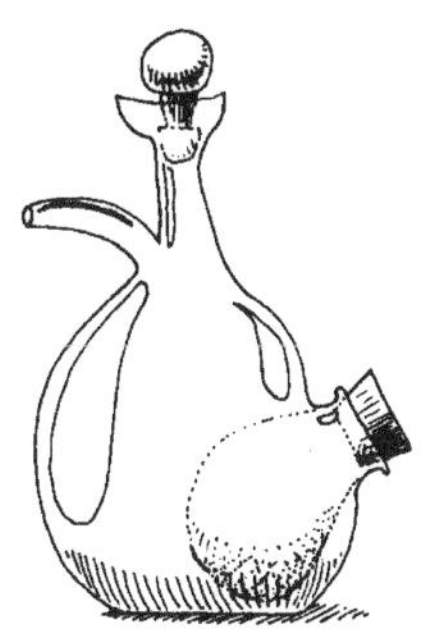

Though millions of diffuse scents roam wild in the world at large, the therapeutic specificity of essential oils comes from the concentration of their substance (for instance, 80 pounds of roses to produce one and a half drachms of Rose oil). These essences are triturated and evaporated from leaves such as Lemon Verbena, Fir needle, and Eucalyptus; flowers such as Lavender, Orange blossom, Vanilla, and Ylang Ylang; and fruits, bulbs, rhizomes, roots, and barks such as Almond, Fennel, Onion, Ginger, Cinnamon, and Cedar. They are extracted by distillation and condensation using steam and water or just steam. This craft is at least as old as the solar-powered stills of the Egyptians. In fact, aroma healing is one of the few medicines we know the Egyptians practiced.

Although there is no one-to-one linear chart of aromas to the ailments they cure, among some of the more commonly used treatments are Turpentine oil for worms and infections of the urinary tract; Tea Tree oil for acne and athlete's foot; Rosemary oil for rheumatism and to speed the healing of wounds; Lavender oil as a sedative, for convulsions, and for burns; Garlic oil for sinusitis, to remove warts, and to strengthen the immune system; Bulgarian Rose oil for herpes; Melissa oil for heart palpitations; Lemon oil for infections of the eyelids and loss of voice; and Peppermint and Eucalyptus oils for bronchitis.[17]

Health Plans

When aromatherapist John Steele was asked to address a conference of corporate perfumers in early 1990, he knew it was a radical departure of corporate policy for them to even invite him. He shared the podium with marketing experts and executives from Fabergé, Calvin Klein, and Revlon, but whereas the speeches they delivered concerned only the promotion of scents as business, he put forth a theory of layers of consciousness activated by smell. "Most of them hadn't the slightest idea of what I was talking about," he told me, "but a few were really excited—like this was something they had always suspected but had no idea how to talk about."[18]

"What did they think aromas were if not consciousness?" I asked him.

"The usual things—sexual attractiveness, power, commerciality, the manufacture of desire. They are totally cynical in that sense. They presume that it's all a seduction and that the goal is to market scents in such clever disguises that people will be attracted to them but also basically fooled because they are really—well, nothing—you know, wisps of flavored air, immaterial gas." He pressed his fingertips together and sprang them apart. "It was as though perfumes couldn't be real, so they continually repackage them to keep everyone fooled."

"Do they think desire is only artificial and manipulable?"

"I, like you, forget that anyone still thinks that way," he laughed, "but of course, they do. Notions like 'the earth is alive' or 'the reptilian brain is what responds to scents' would strike them as the most outrageous sort of California nonsense."

The Spectrum of Healing

Color is also utilized as a therapeutic modality. If sound octaves penetrate the body, even subtler vibrations enter it as light, microdoses which have profound and often unknowable effects on tissues and energy fields. At least one modern rationale for the healing effects of colors is based on a discovery that 80 percent of the nerves and receptors of the body are connected directly or indirectly to the optic nerves. The presumption is that through direct or habitual use, certain colors then work their way into the viscera and peripheral nerves.

Throughout history and in all parts of the world people have imbued themselves with and meditated on hues. Such rituals are based on a belief in the curative power of colors on specific conditions. Direct therapeutic colors can be administered in a variety of ways. The spectrum ranges from the colors of foods eaten to the colors of sheets and blankets slept in and of clothes worn (for instance, beets, radishes, and red night-shirts to improve blood circulation and relieve paralysis; bananas, curry, and millet, and a yellow hat to increase digestive capacity, relieve constipation, stimulate lymph, reduce the effects of diabetes, and disinfect the throat and eyes).[19]

Contemporary color therapists proceed by first consulting with a patient on the various aspects of his or her life and then recommending colors to encourage in the future. This might include hanging paintings with those colors dominant, listening to music associated with those colors, eating foods of those colors, or even bringing the elements of the astrological sign and planet of a particular color into one's life.[20] Color therapist Fai Lloyd describes a favorite breathing exercise of his:

> Holding the visualization of the color, see it as a radiant color breath travelling rapidly upward beneath the outer skin, rising in a spiral about the body and ending above the head in a brilliant swirl of cleansing, transmuting color. At the same time raise the arms above the head in a relaxing gesture. Then exhale, gently feeling the color breath pass out through the pores of the skin carrying all impurities with it.[21]

In this manner one not only envokes a desired red, blue, or green but purges its complement which, physically, *is* its substance (as opposed to the mere illumination we see).

MODERN COLOR THERAPY has a longstanding esoteric lineage, from the Healing Temples of Light and Color at Heliopolis in Egypt, to Buddhist and Hindu curative mandalas, to the mystical color interpretations of Rudolf Steiner and C. W. Leadbetter that take into account scientific discoveries about the nature of photons and radiation and the mechanical principles of the spectrum.[22] In Tibetan *tangka* paintings, colors are a vehicle of passage between bardos. Meditating on particular brilliances lights a path through psychic realms which manifest those hues. Thus, when color changes from the background to the foreground it has not only therapeutic but cosmological implications.

"Gradually, contemporary science has quantified the old folk wisdom that expresses the intimate connection between color, human health, and subtle anatomy in clichés like seeing red, feeling blue, in the pink, green with jealousy, black with rage."[23] The implication is that emotional fluctuations lead to changes in the colors of our own electromagnetic fields. Likewise, illnesses drape themselves in invisible colors and are dispersed by complementary waves.

In formal healing, the yellow-red (solar) end of the scale tends to be stimulating—sympathetic to the rapid circulation of fluids in the body—while the green-blue-indigo (interstellar) edge of the scale extends neurological and spiritual relaxation. Among traditional applications of color are: orange hue to stimulate the pulse and to increase the manufacture of milk in the new mother, also to dissolve kidney- and gall-stones and heal hernias and appendicitis, and as a burst of anti-depressant glow; emerald green to soothe nervous disorders, hay fever, ulcers, influenza, syphilis, malaria, and colds; blue to calm emotions, lower blood pressure (reduce bleeding), treat breathing problems, rheumatism, colic, skin disorders, and burns, and in general to relax the whole body in a luminous sea; indigo for conditions involving the pituitary gland, also to heal cataracts, migraines, skin aberrations, and deafness, and in general to soothe and sedate the nervous system, particularly the eyes and ears; violet for conditions involving the pineal gland and to increase spiritual power, also for psychological and emotional disturbances, arthritis, and to assist in childbirth; and magenta for pathologies of the heart and a range of otherwise-untreatable psychopathologies. Colors are also used in combination, for instance, green, yellow, and violet to treat skin cancer at an early stage.[24]

Post-scientific color medicine began to evolve in the United States during the 1870s. General August Pleasanton, author of *Blue and Sun-Lights,* "reported that blue light, either from the sun or from artificial sources, effectively stimulated the glands, nervous system, and secretory organs of animals and people. In 1877 a prominent physician named Seth Pancoast discovered that sunlight filtered through panes of blue or red glass relaxed or accelerated the human nervous system. In the next year Dr. Edwin Babbitt, in *Principles of Light and Color,* described his 'chromo disk,' a device that projected light through filtered discs onto the body, and his 'chromo lens,' a method of passing solar-potentized water through color filters to produce 'solar color tinctures.' "[25]

In the early years of the twentieth century, various screens (forerunners of Kirlian science) were set up around objects and creatures to make their auras visible photographically. Rainbow patterns shone from within living fields, reflecting an outer pale blue haze with warmer hues at the interior. In the 1920s M.D. Dinshah Ghadiali, author of *The Spectro-Chromometry Encyclopedia,* applied color similarly, by shining light through differently tinted glass, either directly on his patients or on water that was then drunk by them.

> Ghadiali correlated the primary color emission from each element with its known physiological function in the human body, contending that chemical elements were linked with specific color waves and that colors represented chemical potencies of subtler vibrations.... In Ghadiali's model color's radiant energy restored balance at the body's energetic, not physiological, level. In the tonation process, Ghadiali used a set of twelve precisely adjusted color filters enclosed in a projector that shone light directly onto body regions mapped according to chemical element, physiology, and color band.
>
> Harry Riley Spitler, an M.D. and optometrist, hypothesized that colored light projected through the eyes was the key to balance. Spitler, who introduced his new ocular light therapy, called syntonics, in 1927, discovered that alterations in light received through the eyes was the "master key" to the brain's major control centers and, through these centers, to body function, behavior, and physiology.

Spitler's syntonics system used thirty-one different color filter combinations, adjusted to each individual's nature, to balance and integrate the nervous system. The College of Syntonic Optometry, which he founded in 1933, is still operating.[26]

In a neo-Atlantean obsession with occult anatomy, current color therapies generally emphasize the medicinal applications of pure colors on *chakras* and energy fields. Bioenergetic therapist John C. Pierrakos has measured "cloudlike auric envelopes and their precise chromatic pulsations relative to body metabolism, breathing rates, emotional states, humidity, and air ionization. Pierrakos, like [Walter] Kilner, postulated that the aura springs from a 'longitudinal core of energy' in the physical body, possibly connected with the central nervous system, that radiates outward through the skin to activate the immediate atmosphere and form the triple aura."[27]

According to William Croft, contemporary biologists "have discovered that a weak (quantum) form of coherent light is being used as a communications medium both within cells and between cells of our body. In this respect the light appears to be an organizing field which facilitates communication within whole organisms. Through a technology recently developed, it becomes possible to discover and release blockages that occur in the light/*chi* communications paths within our bodies. Such blockages can cause imbalance, or dysfunction, or simply keep us from functioning at the full and vibrant potential of our beings. The technology involves shining very pure colors of variable frequency light onto the energy centers of your body. The light produces a resonance phenomenon, not unlike striking a tuning fork next to a harp or piano. The string that resonates with the tuning fork will begin to sound its own note in harmony with the tuning fork."[28]

The Downing Technique, developed by an optometrist in Northern California, uses a machine called the Lumatron to "feed" the body the colors it needs to balance itself. The functional part of the Lumatron is housed in a hood which fits over a person's head. Once within the machine, the healee receives directly illuminated fields of color—

red, orange, yellow, blue-green, blue, indigo, or violet—through a lens at different rates of flicker (the particular color or sequence of colors is selected by the therapist during a prior field test). The intensity of a single color is expected to wash gently over the eyes and be transmitted through the optic nerves to the whole body.

The interpretation behind this method is that the organism has come to block out certain colors because of stress or traumatic events associated with them, so even someone working all day in full sunlight is selectively assimilating bands of the spectrum. The Lumatron provides stimulation by the lacking hues. It also affords an opportunity for the organism to reprocess events associated with color blockages. These past experiences may take the form of limited vision, blind spots, and startles. Ellen Eatough, a Colored Light therapist, told me that most people see things or experience visual and sensual effects in the Lumatron that aren't physically there. In the center of red or blue, they will see a different color or a series of shapes. She uses a form of light hypnotherapy to guide clients to recall the life events underlying these projections.

THE GOAL OF all color therapies is not merely an external impression of a medicine but a sense of its hue arising from within and bathing us in pure light. After direct or indirect treatment, one should have autonomous experiences of that color penetrating the whole being, including sudden visions of the color, scents of it, and even after-tastes of it on the tongue and lips.

While working on this section of the book, I had two such spontaneous experiences. During a bodywork session with Amini Peller, I felt myself slide into a very deep place, like a waking dream. She suggested that I might be able to "see" the *chakras* in this state. As I tried to gauge where I was with my eyes closed, I suddenly noticed a glow of intense orange light. This orangeness was actually present in me and could not be diluted by imagining other colors. Scanning up and down my body, I saw (or felt) the glow blending smoothly in a spectrum to red, yellow, green, and blue at my throat. Then a few weeks after taking a *Chi Gung* workshop from Kumar Frantzis, I dreamed of standing in a kind of planetarium and him conducting our class there. The planets of the Solar System came by above us, and as each one (Mercury, Venus, Mars, Jupiter) passed in procession, with a wave of the hand Frantzis turned its body into a spiralling orb which unravelled toward us in yarns of color and vibration.

Food

THE VECTORS AND primordial substances that make us up proliferate in the environment. Air is a food. Rain is a tea even when absorbed from the atmosphere without drinking. Heat and cold pass through pores into the body, too. Everything in the environment is potentially drawn and assimilated into our organisms—sounds, images, tastes, impressions. How we take substances, coarse and fine, into mind, stomach, and lungs (and how we keep them out) determines to a large degree who we are.

On a mass cultural level, though, Americans end up choosing Colonel Sanders and the chefs at McDonald's as their teachers, along with Coors beer barons and the corporate heads of canned-food conglomerates—not ancient forests, Ayurvedic chefs, or the raw vegetables and mineral waters of the Earth. The mistake of the West is to reify only the mechanical, molecular aspects of food—and then to reify them only in terms of the grossest effects of their ingredients, ignoring trace amounts, pesticides and herbicides, preservatives, synthetic flavors, and nutritionless artificial substances as mere neutral additives, having no statistically measurable effect on health. This is hardly a homeopathic perspective.

Pharmaceuticals, vital substances, and modes of touch can all catalyze marvelous cures, but eventually one must make an attempt to consume whole foods and unpolluted water and minerals; to stop eating meat, fatty foods and rancid oils, sugar and artificial sweeteners, and pesticided food. Few things are as basic to health as diet, whether one considers food on a physical plane as supplying the actual material of life or on an elemental level as potentiated forces necessary to balance the energy in the body. Despite the possibility of biological transmutation of elements propounded by some, we can hardly count on alchemy for survival.

Unquestionably some people override this one, just burn right through the modern cyberworld on a steed of virtual reality, keeping the economy going at the expense of their bodies. But most people are going to get weaker from the modern civilized diet and stronger even just from the conscious attempt to treat food as a matter of practice rather than a neutral body-and-emotion fuel. That is, unexamined stuffing of material in one's system is a kind of phenomenological poisoning that may intensify the toxic molecular effects of the food itself. To cut off sensation is to give disease its first foothold, is the beginning of not wanting to live.

Eating and digesting are intricate processes, modes of psychic as well as physical integration. Thus, it is medicinal to recognize and acknowledge at some level the suffering of animals that become meats, not only as compassion for fellow sentient beings, but as a decision not to dull ourselves to the reality of our situation. One must assume that Buddha and Jesus were not merely spouting pieties on this issue. Buddha in fact skips over all the subtler and psychological issues of modern existential Buddhism and says simply, "Don't eat meat." We don't have to assume that all discussion of the matter stops there, but a reasonable interpretation of his teaching sets diet prior to philosophy in matters of enlightenment.

If we numb our systems to the nature of our food, we cut ourselves off from our own true nature, too. Our foods become heavy and deadening, producing wastes on all planes. Eating is not just a matter of gulping down or savoring unknown and unnamed substances in response to hunger—the classic American posture of well-being, even in gourmet circles.

A constant readiness to eat (to take in food as pleasure)—an "I consume" mentality ranging from snacks and coffee breaks to gourmet meals—suffuses existence with dolor and inertia. We become the victims of our hungers, thus never satiate them. It is not just a matter any longer of avoiding gluttony; our collective malady is one of addictively flooding taste cells and tissue with dense superficial medicines in order to relieve an existential disease of the soul. It is a pathology most difficult and unpleasant to face. Those in the West certainly mean to protect their consumption empire from the face of Kali which stares into it from every Third World portal and the homeless lying in doorways (not to mention the eternal famine of unconscious mind and its representation in the night).

A person might consider walking *past* those bagel and donut shops and steak barbecues he usually frequents. Instead of stopping to consume, he simply breathes the aromas and imagines what it is he craves. Microdose replaces compulsive overdose. Suddenly his senses become alert to the many different textures and layers of existence. Hunger turns out to be subtler than a desire for food. It is satisfied by scent, by image, eventually by fasting. Yogis who famously breathe the air for *prana* and "drink" from the sun through their skin not only prophesy a planet with a healthier ecosphere, they likely taste intrinsic qualities (sour, bitter, salty, sweet) that Western civilization gets only symptomatically from its roast ribs and chocolate fudge cake.

Fasts (even short ones) can be surprisingly strong medicines. The effect on the body is obvious: the organs have more time to assimilate and cleanse; digestion goes deeper into the static layers of tissue, reaching older congestion. Da Free John writes: "The stress of fasting favors healthy or growing cells. Defective cells do not function well under stress; they die shortly and are eliminated. Thus the body literally 'eats' its own wastes and diseased or dying cells, and it fully eliminates whatever it cannot consume."[29] Fasting is a form of silence, and silence is the beginning of listening. From listening, the mind, tissues, and organs discover one another and find their intrinsic unity.

But if we feed the body predominantly meaty protein and processed meals, we substitute in advance, passively, what it must do for itself in manufacturing and sustaining tissue, and so we rob it of its vitality. Drugs and alcohol are disease agents because they liberate unbalanced forces at the expense of systemic equilibrium. Wastes from foods and medicines that are shunted off to the cells must eventually return as at least minor restrictions, more likely as diseases. Just because they are hidden and because the body invariably compensates does not mean that the organism is functioning well. As we get older we should move away from what spiritual teacher Da Free John calls the "celebrants" of our twenties—meat, alcohol, sugar and coffee—to the finer elemental strands on which life is strung.[30] As one eats more consciously, substances are assimilated more fully and chewing approaches prayer. At this level, eating and digesting are internal yoga. Chewing is especially important, first to mix the food with saliva and change it chemically, and second for the internal experience of that food. The abstract roles of the allergist and nutritionist are absurd in the ancient sense: we are supposed to be able to *feel* which foods harm us and which foods nurture our growth.

IN THE FIRST edition of this book I completely overlooked the role of diet. By ignoring the topic I betrayed my own illusion at the time that disease and health operated on either an antiseptic or vital level entirely separate of food and other gross consumption. Right away, a reviewer set me on the right track:

> In one respect . . . *Planet Medicine* is lacking. It fails to draw the essential connection between the quality of a people's diet and the quality of their health. The issue of proper medical care cannot be spoken of apart from the quality of a person's food, for the quality of diet reflects also the attitude of a society towards the soil which nourishes it. Writers such as Wendell Berry have argued eloquently the connection between people's relationship to the soil, the food they grow upon it, and the quality of their physical and spiritual lives. To

avoid the issue of agriculture and diet is to view preserving public health, ancient or modern, as remedial therapy after an inherent well-being has already been lost. A true planet medicine would place no distinctions between civic health and daily life, and the most healing of all therapies may take place in our own kitchens.[31]

Soon afterwards, Paul Pitchford gave me my first lessons on the importance of diet, and a few years later I encouraged him to write a book on "Food as Medicine." It took him seven years to put together an encyclopedic compendium called *Healing with Whole Foods.* This volume places in perspective the full range and depth of the topic. Pitchford shows how our rhythm of eating, drinking, and consuming is a primary aspect of health and disease complexes that arise and heal or deteriorate slowly throughout a lifetime. Every food, drink, and mixture in and of itself and in the context of its degree of freshness and pollution, manner of preparation, heat when served, time of day when ingested, etc., has a role in the primary elemental cycles regulating the energy and health of the organs and meridians.[32]

Pitchford points out that much of the medicinal practice of diet takes place on the level where all foods are herbal. In fact, most Oriental healing systems consider foods (grains, vegetables, spices, fruits, meats, etc.) as the equivalents of herbs.

The simplicity of most herbs makes them concrete and precise. If one eats iris or black cohosh or quercitrin tree bark, they are supplying their organs with raw building blocks that contributed to the genesis of these plants. Of course, the organs of the body will not make plants out of them, but they will use them in ways that would be impossible if the molecules did not originate herbally.

Grains, fruits, and vegetables should be chosen just like any other herbs and medicines, individually according to individual constitutions and metabolisms, for their direct effects on the organs. Diet must be seasonally attuned, balanced elementally, and grounded in an intuitive realization of the effects of each food.

Figs moisten the lungs and clean the intestines. Apricots aid in anemia. Bananas with their skin lubricate the intestines and help with constipation, ulcers, and drug addiction. Tomatoes purify the blood. Potatoes strengthen the kidneys and lower blood pressure. Carrots augment the connective tissues and rid the body of parasites. Celery renews joints and arteries and lowers blood pressure. Cabbage heals skin eruptions and warms cold feet. Beets rejuvenate the heart. Radishes clear sinuses. Turnips ameliorate asthma, more effectively when raw. Coconut tonifies the heart. Of course, not all of these foods do this all of the time in all people, and they each have other attributes and side effects. The point here is not merely to list the myriad natural medicines but to provide a medicinal context for viewing foods in general. All fruits and vegetables are medicines—perhaps dense, slow, dilute medicines, but medicines all the same. Even meats are medicines. They are used selectively to strengthen blood, calm the nervous system, reduce coughs and bleeding, etc. They may also induce toxic effects even in small doses, but all foods have some toxic side effects, and the ideal goal should be to consume everything at appropriate times in balanced proportions.[33]

I violate the relativity of my text to make this one suggestion: if you are sick, change your diet—of impressions as well as of food and drink. At least practice a consciousness of consumption. Challenge unexamined, undifferentiated omnivorousness.

Herbs

ALTHOUGH ALL FOODS are medicinal, herbs are specifically "medicinal foods." Foods (most herbs included) start with substance which becomes energy only through its relationship to organs. Herbs are foods which enter the system not so much to provide molecules to digest and incorporate but as catalysts for the natural functions of the organs. They are prescribed to reactivate lethargic processes or slow down overactive ones. Insofar as they transfer power, herbs are rarely iatrogenically pathological. Some are given according to homeopathic principles (fever-causing herbs for fever), and others are prescribed by the law of opposites (cooling herbs for fever). Either way, their action is discrete.

Most herbs are to some degree foods, but there exceptions: microdoses and many vitamins provide no substance for the organs and tissues to digest. Microdoses start as pure energy. Normal doses of herbs still have relatively more energy and less substance than most other foods. What is subtle is also basic. "Proven" region by region over millennia for their healing precision, herbs are the cream of empirical medicine.

Herbs apparently contain fundamental "messages," prehieroglyphic signatures. We can discern and taste these. A blend for calming the liver based on peony root has a unique orange-clay flavor; dandelion root is earthy too, but sweeter. The spotted colors and tangled horns of foxglove suggest heart arrhythmia. The sparkle of phosphorous evokes the fragile hypersensitivity of its remedy. Reality is sometimes so basic it is a wonder we lose it in background abstractions.

FLOWERS ARE AMONG the most visible herbal physicians: blossoms of elk clover for bronchitis, dandelion and yarrow for purifying blood, saffron to stimulate liver *chi.* Herbal berries include rose hips for soothing nerves, quisqualis and may apples for tumors; among medicinal seeds are poppy, wild carrot, pumpkin, and oat straw (providing minerals for bones and connective tissue). Fenugreek, flax, and fennel combine with comfrey root and dandelion root to make a strong intestinal mixture for absorbing liquids and eliminating wastes. The leaves of horsetails are prescribed for teeth and prostate, raspberry for checking menstrual flow, and parsley to dry mucus; the leaves of mugwort are medicinally burned into the meridian points in moxibustion. Apple bark is used to lower blood pressure, cherry bark as an astringent, bayberry bark for ailments of the gall bladder.[34]

Echinacea and golden seal cleanse the blood and remove infections. Lobelia oil reduces congestion. It is combined with drops of citrus seed extract to form a substitute "antibiotic" in some contexts.

Garlic is a mythical cure-all, providing heat for circulation, removing stagnation, and inhibiting viruses. A clove of garlic wrapped in cotton and soaked in olive oil may be placed gently in the ear sometimes to treat infections. The garlic gradually seeps into the nasal and oral cavities. No root is a more honored physician than ginseng. Apparently wild ginseng is such a deeply rejuvenating medicine that the Asian variety was stalked to extinction, and all we have left are the semidomesticated varieties. Stephen Fulder describes ginseng as true stimulant, a medicine that restores energy and harmony and confers long life and *yang* rather than draining these as pills and coffee do. He quotes from a Russian writer's description of finding one of the last wild roots in 1934:

> I sat with the Chinese and we were all staring, when to my great amazement I noticed that the root had a human form: here was a separation between the feet, there were hands, and there, a neck, and on it the head and even a little plait. The fibres of the hands and feet were like long fingers.
>
> I was ... overwhelmed by these seven people wrapped in contemplation of the root of life ... I could hardly bear their faith. The

> lives . . . of millions of people seemed to me to be in relation to the enduring faith like the waves are to the sea. The waves began rushing towards me, the living, as to a beach, begging me to grasp the power of the root. Not with my flesh, because that will soon go, but with the wisdom of the stars and the constellations and maybe something beyond that.[35]

Can one doubt the living figurine of the planet shaman in this signature?

Cross-culturally, herbs include such varied ingredients as olive oil; wheat germ oil; walnut husk tincture; bamboo sap as an expectorant; honey to neutralize toxins; crystal; bear gall*; fungi of all varieties; kelp, kombu, and other sea vegetables for diseases of the nervous system; haliotis and oyster shells; pearls for headache and insomnia; animal excrement; rhinoceros horn* and toad secretions to cool and detoxify the blood; the scorpion as a nerve tonic; and the fossilized bones of dinosaurs as tranquilizers and antispasmodics. In China a variety of substances is used to cure different fevers: the whole earthworm, the exuviae of the cicada, the rhizome of the cnidium, and the tortoise shell.[36] The Chinese also use human hair calcined and powdered as an astringent and dried human placenta for impotence, infertility, and ailments that do not improve with other treatments.

Cinnabar, sulphur, fluorite, and other minerals are used medicinally. Ayurvedic physicians form very pure and fine wires of metals like gold, silver, copper, and tin, and after dousing them in plant juices, make them into a powder which is then mixed with other herbs. Supposedly metal can be given in this fashion without aggravation.

*Endangered species are no longer considered acceptable to hunt and kill for medicinal uses.

Herbal iron enters the blood faster than in an allopath's intravenous injections and without gastric side effects.[37]

Salt is a great herb with "clarifying, alkalizing, purifying, and centering qualities." It cools the body; counteracts toxins; aids the kidneys in moistening; helps move the bowels; reduces hardness in glands, muscles, and lymph nodes; and balances beans, peas, grains, and other acidic foods. However, salt is most medicinal in a now rare form of gray seasalt which contains the complete complement of trace minerals. This true herbal salt cannot be sold in the United States for internal consumption. First it must be "purified" so that it is toxic. Then it contributes to high blood pressure, kidney damage, reduced absorption, cancer of the stomach, and weakened bones, nerves, muscles, and heart. French bathing salt is one of the few guises in which medicinal seasalt can presently be legally imported.[38]

Recently Paul Pitchford directed me to a traditional pharmacy in Oakland Chinatown. From the moment I stepped into the shop I was charmed to see how raw and unadorned its products were: parts of animals hanging from the ceiling and walls—horns, antlers, fur, cuttlebones; micaceous earth; grasshoppers and cicadas; animal galls; dried earthworms and smaller worms; huge chunks of fungus, rind, and bark; roots of all sizes and topologies; whole fish; and other unidentifiable items that looked disconcertingly like the exports of cannibals. (One might wish we had access downtown to Australian Aborigine and African pharmacies, too.)

When I asked for my prescription of abalone shell the clerk couldn't find it, and I had to wait for her to fetch the proprietor to consult his chart to the many drawers that lined the wall behind the counter. This series of exchanges was carried out uncertainly and in painstaking English with the help of other customers. Any fear I had that the language barrier might lead to my getting the wrong "herb" was quickly dispelled when he opened a seemingly random drawer and pulled out a handful of distinctive whole shells glistening iridescently. He slid them into a sack, weighed them quickly in midair on a delicate scale, then said, "Fifty cents."

I wasn't ready for such a literal response, so I tried to explain that I needed to make a tea. He agreeably unwrapped them and dumped them in a metal mortar; then he beat and crushed them with a pestle until they were chips and powder. Every tenth stroke he hit against the side of the mortar, setting it ringing. This demonstration of the transposition of raw shells into "medicine" was quite dramatic. Any abstraction was certainly demolished, so that when I poured hot water over the midden I knew what I was drinking. I even imagined the mineral shimmer asking interesting questions of my cells as they encountered it—questions they likely had not heard for many years.

Drugs

REFINED PHARMACY CHANGES the characteristics of its "herbs" into more immediately activating substances that are less subtle and probably less creative, hence more toxic (for their lack of adaptability). The classic medicinal smell of the hospital is really the odor of the industrial laboratory. It is also the liquor of embalming fluid, the new bitter elixir of life. We all live today by virtue of its endowments.

I have placed medicinal herbs with food at the fourth level; these begin a treatment, but the patient must complete the cure by responding. However, both food and herbs can appear anywhere on the chart depending on how they are used. Drugs are antibiotic or anesthetizing "herbs" that are meant to "replace" the organs in carrying out a process in relation to a particular pathology. They operate at the seventh level. Their after-effects are intrinsic to their nature: the body/mind can respond to them only as outsiders, initially as brilliant physicians from out of town, but secondarily as thieves who have left the organs with only relative powers to carry out their own functions.

There are certainly strong herbs that resemble drugs, in fact are the forerunners of specific modern drugs, but they do not work as indiscriminately. Correct diagnosis is crucial to their use as are precise preparation, dosage, frequency, and assimilation. When enthusiasts hear that an herb is cleansing they often rush to the "word" with the same obsessiveness and unconsciousness with which they have accumulated disease. Too collapsed or lethargic to respond to treatment, their systems simply become weaker.

Commercial pharmaceuticals are both gross and abstract—gross in their chemistry but abstract in their relation to the body-mind's actual dynamics of survival. These highly synthesized medicines are more semantic than substantial. They originate in and then generate clichés and presumptions that unconsciously alter so-called objective biochemical research and prescribing. A gap, usually completely unacknowledged, exists between the semantics of drugs and the reality of mind/body after their ingestion. It is not as though drugs and diseases speak the same language, and neither of them have anything to do with the propaganda that appeals on pharmaceutical packaging. One often ingests someone else's fantasy, a cumulative guess as to what a standard condition and its range of potentiation are. This is vintage seventh-level medicine, and it works extraordinarily well in heading off or postponing major crises. People do not realize that the drug "action" they experience is often a combination of autogenic process, placebo effect, and cultural conditioning. They accept the marketing at face value. After all, it is written in the language of desire.

At a party I once watched a traditional Chinese doctor informally take the case of a middle-class American woman who had never consulted such a practitioner (and wouldn't have considered it outside the fortuity of the social event). She had major digestive problems, and the doctor was trying to be of service. He took down her complete diet. Many times he asked her not to leave anything out. Then he prescribed an herb.

Several days later he made a special trip to her house to find out the results. After listening to her carefully, he said, "Are you sure you didn't eat anything else?"

She thoughtfully went back over her actions and meals of the last few days. "No," she replied with certainty.

"Think. Is there anything else at all?"

"Well, I took Gelusil. But you don't mean that?"

"Of course, I mean that. How much?"

It turned out to be a full package a day!

"This is the most important part of your diet."

"But it's just Gelusil. It's not even a drug."

"It is a drug. It's supplying you with calcium which you should be getting from elsewhere."

Talk of cultural categories masquerading as medicines!

What sticks in my mind is the fact that in this society the packaging is so soporific and disarming we often have no idea what we are consuming or that it is even real.

ANTIBIOTICS KILL GERMS, but they do so at the expense of the immune system and the overall vitality of body/mind. While the tundras and rain forests breed healthy organisms, antibiotics (and pesticides) breed more and more virulent germs (and "pests"). Our mindless attack upon an imagined world of germs and parasites has left us weaker than our supposed enemies, for we not they are the ultimate victims of relentless mutations. They in fact are the beneficiaries. There is a growing belief that the host of newer immunity-related diseases is at least partially the side effect of antibiotic residues in people's systems. Cattle feedlots and hospitals in particular have become rich breeding grounds for exotic viruses and bacteria.

Directly toxic medicines may sometimes be necessary (even as guns may be necessary in the face of a direct adversary), but they are *never* a strengthener of overall health or immunity and should not be sought as cure-alls. In a community context, they lessen the ability of our species to fend off germs arising even naturally in the environment. They numb the biological responsiveness of the planet as a whole (or perhaps they transpose it to the realm of microscopic bugs).

Vaccinations (especially the routine childhood DPT shots) may be even more hazardous than antibiotics. Who knows how the body reacts at the deepest level to being fed disease products to induce an immune response? Although no links to serious ailments have been proven beyond doubt, a number of researchers believe that isopathy may have far more significant consequences than simply to immunize against specific diseases. It may transpose aspects of pathology into overall systemic activity and thereby set in motion more intractable and exotic neurological disorders, including the compulsion to commit murder and other crimes. One would be advised to consult the references available on this topic and carefully weigh the pros and cons before taking any "shot."

Sedatives, anti-depressants, anti-anxiety drugs, psychotropics, and the like are stopgap measures that numb one's organism to pain, hence to the real crisis. They are police measures in a security- and property-conscious state.

The other "drugs"—crack, heroin, ice, etc.—are hardly the toys of a kick-happy society. They are last-resort medicines for people who cannot handle the input of a materialized, external-value, bottom-line-only lifestyle in which family and community are already nostalgias. Environmentally we may have some margin left, but psychically and in our inner life we have reached *Blade Runner* and *Mona Lisa Overdrive.* Recreational drugs are medicines of despair, not fun. "Just say, 'No!'" is the most ironical of jokes when everyone who takes these medicines addictively has already said a far deeper "No!" than Nancy Reagan or George Bush could fathom.

Notes

1. Paul Pitchford, from a lecture at the Pacific College of Naturopathic Medicine, San Rafael, California, 1982.

2. Nyanaponika Thera, *The Heart of Buddhist Meditation* (New York: Samuel Weiser, Inc., 1969), p. 71.

3. Father Berard Haile, recorder and translator; in Leland C. Wyman

(ed.), *Beautyway: A Navaho Ceremonial* (New York: Bollingen Foundation, Pantheon Books, 1957), pp. 141–42.

4. Michio Kushi, *The Book of Dō-In: Exercise for Physical and Spiritual Development* (Tokyo: Japan Publications, 1979).

5. Jacques de Langre, *Dō-In 2: The Ancient Art of Rejuvenation Through Self-Massage* (Magalia, California: Happiness Press, 1978).

6. John E. Upledger, *SomatoEmotional Release and Beyond* (Palm Beach Gardens, Florida: UI Publishing, 1990), p. 217.

7. Eduardo Calderón, Richard Cowan, Douglas Sharon, and F. Kaye Sharon, *Eduardo el Curandero: The Words of a Peruvian Healer* (Richmond, California: North Atlantic Books, 1982), p. 42.

8. Ibid., p. 45.

9. Ibid., p. 42.

10. Bruce Kumar Frantzis, personal communication, 1994.

11. Richard Leviton, "Healing Vibrations," *Yoga Journal* (January/February 1994), p. 63.

12. Ibid., p. 124.

13. Ibid., p. 125.

14. Ibid., p. 124.

15. C. S. Lewis, *The Magician's Nephew* (New York: Collier Books, 1970), pp. 98–99 (originally published in 1951).

16. Jeanne Rose, *The Aromatherapy Book: Applications & Inhalations* (Berkeley, California: North Atlantic Books, 1992), p. xiv.

17. Ibid.

18. John Steele, personal communication, 1991.

19. Nevill Drury, *The Healing Power: A Handbook of Alternative Medicines and Natural Health* (London: Frederick Muller Ltd., 1981), p. 53.

20. Richard Leviton, "The Healing Energies of Color," *Yoga Journal* (January/February 1992).

21. Quoted in Drury, *The Healing Power,* p. 53.

22. Leviton, "The Healing Energies of Color," p. 47.

23. Ibid., p. 48.

24. Drury, *The Healing Power,* p. 53.

25. Leviton, "The Healing Energies of Color," p. 47.

26. Ibid., pp. 47–48.

27. Ibid., p. 47.

28. William Croft, C. S. T., "Light Energy Practices (Yoga/Qigong/Aikido) and *Working with Light*—a Synergy," flyer, 1993.

29. Bubba Free John (Da Free John), *The Eating Gorilla Comes in Peace: The Transcendental Principle of Life Applied to Diet and the Regenerative Discipline of True Health* (Middletown, California: The Dawn Horse Press, 1979), p. 178

30. Ibid.

31. Otto Max, review of *Planet Medicine, East West Journal* (August 1981), p. 80.

32. Paul Pitchford, *Healing with Whole Foods: Oriental Traditions and Modern Nutrition* (Berkeley, California: North Atlantic Books, 1992).

33. Ibid.

34. Pitchford, *Healing with Whole Foods,* plus a variety of other sources.

35. Stephen Fulder, *The Root of Being: Ginseng and the Pharmacology of Harmony* (London: Hutchison Publishing Group, 1980), p. 86.

36. Rechung Rinpoche, *Tibetan Medicine* (Berkeley, California: University of California Press, 1973); Hong-Yen Hsu, *How to Heal Yourself with Chinese Herbs* (Los Angeles: Oriental Healing Arts Institute, 1980), and a variety of other sources.

37. A. Lade and R. Svoboda, *Tao & Dharma—A Comparison of Ayurveda and Chinese Medicine,* unpublished manuscript at the time of publication.

38. Pitchford, *Healing with Whole Foods,* pp. 156–64.

CHAPTER NINE

The Politics and Spirituality of Medicine

Medicine and Society

THIS BOOK BEGAN with the proposition that the new healing paradigm was more a cultural than a medical statement. I would reinforce that prejudice now in different words: healing modalities arise from ecological and cultural imperatives and address diseases of the social body. This generally indiscernible process can be represented at two levels:

First, diseases originate as totemic categories (even in Western civilization) and categories of cure match them symbolically in kind. Despite much seeming evidence to the contrary, there are no purely natural diseases—although parasites and toxins approach lightning and snow in their guilelessness. But even germs and poisons must make their way through various differential layers of voodoo, spirit protection, immunity, protective *chi,* etc. Their passages through these and subsequent manifestations are always funnelled into taxonomies and delegated to cultural classifications. Likewise, there are no medicines not mediated at some level by social constructs.

Secondly, the large-scale ecological and cultural diseases of the Earth give rise spontaneously to drastic modalities of cure. The relationship between disease, cure, and society is even more basic than that: the present plague of pathologies (cultural, physical, psychological, and spiritual) is precisely its own first stage of cure. If we want to know what is wrong with us, we must look to our wars, crimes, diseases, and injustices (especially those that cross lines of nation, class, and species). If we want to discover what the treatment should be, we may observe its first homeopathic prescription in the disease manifestations themselves. Look to our planetary plague and you will see, albeit drawn in executioner's robes, the first ugly stages of our arousal to self-cure. The functional remedy may be a hundred years away.

Alternative medicines represent actual traditions, legacies, and innovations of cure in respect to specific states of disease and dysfunction, but they also comprise a metaphor for an extraordinary and radical response to a universal disease crisis. Collectively they are more than a metaphor; they are the second tier of treatment of planetary disease. At the level of subtext, their modalities invariably address what is awry with the Earth as well as what is ailing in any one client.

The metaphor is this: social, political, ecological, and economic change must occur first in the body/mind of man and woman; second in the forest of symbols that make up global culture; and third in the physical forests, seas, and atmosphere of the planet. We can posture all we want toward social and corporate change through direct action, changes of governments, laws, and constabularies to enforce them. However, the opposition to these changes will always operate by brute force through and against the bodies of actual men and women. Companies will bull their way around regulations and deposit toxins where they want; they will harvest whatever life-forms they care to. Terrorist armies will do likewise. There are too many of them, and they have access to much more direct and Machiavellian techniques for carrying out their will. We can scream "Scoundrel!" and "Thief!" all we want, but we are paper tigers. Laws and ethics are flimsy superstructures compared to the direct power of the body. The Thirty Years War in seventeenth-century Germany, with its Halloween cast of armies sweeping over the populace, is a better indication of what we are up against than the antiseptic meltdown of the Gulf War. Cocaine is a perfect modern

weapon (disease), operating as it does simultaneously on the body/minds of men and women and the economies of nations. It is a virtual reality weapon; there is no way to stop it by conventional means.

Yet we are not merely paper tigers; we pretend to be because, frankly, we fear if we showed our teeth we would simply become one of them—Tutsi and Hutu, Palestinian and Israeli interchangeable. If we are going to show our teeth, we must learn how to become the alchemical Lion, not just another predator in regal guise. That is why somatics (without its pretentious name) is ultimately the equal of cocaine. Guns and prisons are not.

Despite the growing fad of nihilism and despair in our present arena, hope lies in the reciprocity of diseases and their cures. All of these pestilences, environmental disasters, and bombings are medicines—medicines in their raw and unrefined state, alchemical Lions unborn. The "planet medicine" paradigm, which I will discuss at length in the Epilogue, is an early clue to a new direction. Whether it is too little too late we will not know for a long time, probably long past when we have concluded the opposite.

I would offer that the promise of radical medicines is that they address the body directly and then are assimilated in tissues and cells and translate into new mind-sets. They change the meaning of life and death, transform our ethics, and give us new goals and responsibilities as creatures on a planet. More than ecological imperatives or grass-roots action, they get inside people and make them different. The medical paradigm is really the social paradigm translated into medical language because social and economic disruption is now so widespread and trenchant it is unamenable to other reifications. Likewise, social change must become "radical medicine" if it is to affect anything more than what people say.

I do not mean to argue against ecological and political modes of activism and transformation. These are aspects of a therapeutic process and inevitably mutate into medicines as they sink to their own roots. I mean to suggest that in our present constellation of ideologies, "planet

medicine" is the one that bears the most urgent message, for, like disease, it proposes to change the body/mind and to carry out the work of destiny or karma in the living fabric of the Earth. It provides rhetoric and then a lesson which begins: "Our behavior is so despicable and destructive because our hearts are closed. We wander from media image to media image, zombies detached from our spirits." Alternative medicine does not represent ultimately as much a repertoire of exciting new cures as a means of opening our hearts and putting us back in touch with our spirits.

Until a second or third tier of cure is infused directly into the body of the species, medicinal language, i.e., the language of this book, is directed more at the corporate devastation of the world and of meaning than to the presumed matter of clinical alternatives for medical orthodoxies. "Planet medicine" means an injunction to "planet healing," but only in the largest sense.

The Present Status of Medicine and Disease

We have come to see medicine as a flux of practical techniques, remedy provings, scientific experiments, acts of transference, and mutative symbols. It is a *cul de sac* but also an infinitude, for there is nothing in the cosmos that is not an aspect of a disease, that is not potentially a medicine too.

Watch the players on the field in a sporting event. Despite all else that is happening (the millions of dollars, the heavy equipment, the attention of masses of people), they too are involved in a struggle to rectify some condition, the same condition that makes their exercise possible. When they are done, it will end. They are not doing it for themselves, and what they are drawing out and shaping may not become visible in their lifetimes. (Most warfare puts its disciples up against opponents far more lethal than they have developed the power to handle—today far more lethal than they could develop the neutralizing move for in a thousand lifetimes.)

Peasant ailments run banshee from the village doctor into the hills; they return armed as revolutionaries. If they were deeply sick, their illness has been transformed by a new possession; but it is not cured, for history merely deals a succession of diseases. They sit behind corporate desks, granting lives and deaths more mundanely than any surgeon. Their medicines abound on any city street—autos, currency, tank tops, vibrations, billboards, cigarettes, microwaves, reflections in glass, unknown substances that are part of every impression and breath.

Poisonous urban sprawls and military machines mark interior devitalization. Like the capacity to kill without compassion, these are symptoms of powers suppressed and distorted, not powers achieved. Gangs of juveniles preying on the old and homeless are site-specific eruptions of profound collective diseases. They shudder with the dance of raw life. They want to live. But within the planet's homeostasis they are statements of relative health, for as long as there is a vital force left, we will not see the disease, we will see only our desperate stands against its ravages. This is what punk-ritualized decadence, crack cocaine, brutal carjackings, and the "epidemic of guns" must also reflect: our natural resistance (so close is the malady now to the heart). To become the disease is, esoterically, to attack the disease. This remedy may well not cure the single junkie or heal gang members and corporate raiders, but its vibration will slowly fan out to the society at large. The process may take generations, but it is inevitable if our planet is to survive.

To writer Andrew Harvey, the Indian teacher Mother Meera gave a vision:

"'*Now I will show you the twentieth century.*

"'Gaze with all your courage into its darkness.'

"I saw writhing bodies, burned, flayed, spattered with blood, I saw bombs flowering, the faces of mad dictators as they cut open the eyes of living children, torturers masturbating over the women they had just electrocuted. I saw all these nightmares arising out of the darkness and returning to it.

"Then, just as I thought I would faint because I could not bear the sight and smell of so much horror, I realized, with a clarity and certainty beyond my power to express, that this terrible, unparalleled filth and depravity, this unspeakable desolation spread out over every continent and enacted in every culture, was feeding the New Light.

"'*The spiral of light rises out of the darkness.*'

"She had come because the cries of the tortured and mutilated had called her; She was here because a million tears and screams had pulled her to her torn and battered creation. The horror that humankind had revealed to itself had driven it to call for a new hope, a new world. The depth of that cry was answered, I saw, by a force, a passion, a height of Divine Light that sprang directly out of the heart of the horror, that flamed out, invincible, from its center."[1] He asks her:

"'Has the evil of this century happened to make humanity aware of the madness of living without God?'

"'Yes.'

"'So humans can turn to God now and take the leap into another Being that God is preparing for them?'

"'Yes. This leap is certain. It will happen. It is happening now.'"[2]

ON THE ONE hand, all is lost and the world is submerged in millennial miasm; on the other, we are drenched with a universal medicine, and upon the slightest impulse in the right direction our beings are capable of curing themselves of anything. At each moment we see both sides of the polarity. An incalculable darkness is there at the best moments, rejoicing in our freedom and joy, warning us in our high. For being one of us, it requires integration too.

Our dilemma is that all of these healing and denigrating processes are latent, interwoven, interdependent. Meanwhile other forces that do not share our consciousness—or at least are not integrated—weave about us. Given the violence we carry out routinely toward one another and with "mere" external tools, and given our unadmitted psychokinetic power, is it any wonder, asks parapsychologist Jule Eisenbud (see Volume One, Chapter Five), that our unguarded death wishes and curses may be collectively more pathogenic than all the bacteria and viruses on the Earth combined? Our responsibility for this ongoing murder spree, erupting from the large to the small, in wars, plane

crashes, and sudden heart attacks, may be the primal guilt which Freud displaced onto a mythological Oedipal event because he would not acknowledge the full and present impact of mind on matter. Our whole technological civilization might then be one vast denial of both our voodoo and our healing powers. We may still doubt the evidence and the interpretation, but Eisenbud is speaking from fifty years of research and against his own likings ("... a vital part of me rejects the whole as pure nonsense"[3]).

There is clearly something at hand—dangerous and unfathomable—whether it be this factor or another. Eisenbud's paradigm at least alerts us that there is an intruder in the house. The creative energies assigned to *chakras,* auras, meridians, and thought-waves throughout history have their negative counterparts in curses, vampires, malevolent aliens, and "evil eyes." The modern therapist cannot begin to diagnose a plague that so-called primitive shamans were thousands of times closer to than we, and it is a joke to think we can cure such disease. We cannot even tell when our own headaches begin: at the moment the first symptoms (of anything) are perceptible the condition is already irreversible. When the poisons start to eke out, the mother serum has also already been prepared. To "banish" our troubles with palliatives is to waste our time and delude ourselves. Imagine—those who cited "a clear and present danger" thought that by arming ourselves with nuclear weapons (or canisters of germs) we could become safer! Not when the elemental forces of voodoo still rule this world.

"It may be one of the most tragic paradoxes of history," writes Eisenbud, "that throughout the tortuous course of what is somewhat charitably referred to as 'the ascent of man,' the repudiation of such an aim (the 'destruction of the enemy,' to use the utterly emotionless military abstraction) in the ordinary transactions of everyday life has led to a never-ending assault on an omnipresent and protean enemy-by-proxy on a scale that would have been unimaginable to the primitive."[4]

No wonder the Tlingit shaman chanting sounds positively demonic, even to his followers around him. "One creates devils when one acts

badly," says Eduardo Calderón, the Peruvian *curandero.* " . . . We should not confuse ourselves that the spirit, that the evil shadows, frighten us, kill us. One frightens oneself; it is not the shadow that frightens one."[5]

HEALING IS PAINFUL because so much has become unconscious in us; only a millennial journey to the Underworld could reclaim our birthright. We are working against time to save what is left and transform what is active—as are the crews assembling apartment buildings and power lines in the transient cities. We worry now about whether there are resources just in the sense of minerals and fuels and fish in the sea for another century of this, let alone an eternity. But even as the disease is not visible, the true energy is not within our present frame, either. So we pretend, with our cities and automated clinics, to conserve mere time and restore quantifiable matter.

We can't begin to address the plague, but at least we know that no one is innocent, no one is immune, no one is safe, and no one gets off with a plea of insanity. We must now climb to the level of the giant and meet his eye with ours.

The whole of Western technology was an attempt to make life safer and easier by progressive externalization of the gross properties of matter and refinement of that externalization to produce and control energy. Such an attempt had to be made, and we are now the millage and the overseers of its experiment. Passing through this monstrous externalization is crucial to all, from the Yellow Emperor proposing harmony in a shattered world to the Eskimo shaman cursing the cold he cannot cure while the children die around him. He prayed through a glass darkly in an olden time for the sanctuary of machines in which we and he now dwell. The present milieu is our only answer to the deep and dark voodoo of nature. It is this relief we requested collectively and perhaps even psychokinetically, and it is this disease we must now heal.

Doctors like yogis must begin to treat the nuclear weapons and environmental pollution within all of us, the internalized war from which the external armaments come. It does not mean abandoning science; it does not portend a return to the abuses of traditional magic. It might be no more or less than an enlargement of science to include all its faces, inward and out. The mindfulness and bare attention of the Buddhist monk are not irrelevant to the medical effort necessary to gather the tremendous energy now on the loose, to return it to its causes which alone can detoxify it. This cannot be done without also including auto workers in Detroit and Hokkaido, prostitutes in Bangkok, neo-Nazis in Bavaria, war lords in Somalia, shipbuilders in Gdansk, and the descendants of aboriginal Africans, Australians, and Americans.

In one of our ideal medicines of the future, doctors will treat how the nation is ruled as well as its rulers, and how goods are transferred as well as the buyers and sellers, but they will not be called doctors, and there will also be no politicians or police in the present sense. "Polis" will stand as a synthesis of justice, production, and healing. What doctors practice will not be called medicine. Senators and corporate directors will also be philosopher-scientists.

Some may insist that such a "polis" has already been, in Atlantis or Old China, and we have destroyed it, and continue to obliterate its fragments today; but this must not be true, or we would not be in such disharmony; we would not have inherited millennia of war. Or maybe it is true, and we have lost all memory in a cataclysm. In any case, we have only the present Earth to work from. We begin again today.

How we behave and how we treat the other entities on this world affect relative disease and health. Until all living things are healthy, no living thing can be healthy. But that truth is going to take a long time to get our unflinching admiration.

Even though there is every reason to be pessimistic in the midst of so much pathology, there is equal reason to be optimistic because we are alive in an unbroken flow of breath and insight. As we struggle against this decay of culture and contamination of nature, we are individuating and externalizing. The very process of life that brings us into being and sets our uniqueness against the vastness of nature is medicinal. We

have phenomenal untapped powers (if we cultivate and earn them), and some of the changes we might effect would heal not only ourselves but the world (and the invisible planes that attend it). Harvey laments to Mother Meera:

"'But the power and force of evil are terrifying.'

"'Stop being afraid.' She has raised her voice slightly. 'Root yourself in the Light.' She pointed to the plants in the windowsill. 'Live on the Light like those plants live in their earth. Make the Light your earth, your food, your strength, and nothing can destroy you.'"[6]

The Problem of Authoritarian Evangelism

THE YEAR I wrote the first version of this book, I reported on Ruth Carter Stapleton's visit to the Berkeley Holistic Health Center to perform Christian healing ceremonies on a calendar with a Celestial Rainbow Healing Evening and a *t'ai chi* class. This was a hopeful glimpse of the emerging "planet medicine." In the same month her brother Jimmy Carter, President of the United States, appealed to the Black African continent in America's behalf as against the state atheism of the Soviet Union. These loosely paired events evoked a mythic allusion to a legendary time. One could imagine a global-political fusion of spiritualism, voodoo, and evangelism—United Churches of Africa and the Mississippi in alliance with the Rosicrucian Temples of Bohemia and California. That moment has since passed, its potential degraded into religious fascism and ethnic cleansing.

Occult medicine, faith healing, and the invocation of spontaneous cures unfortunately tend to spawn corrupt gurus and authoritarian institutions. The mysterious and often hierarchical nature of healing requires unquestioning faith and invariably a charismatic leader not under the social constraints present in indigenous tribal situations. The healer is literally one who makes contact with spirits, gods, death, or unknown forces abroad. He is the hope of all who view him and put their fate in his magic; thus, he (or she) can control the lives of clients

and disciples, or even whole communities. All charismatic healers are susceptible to fraud and betrayal—sometimes intentionally perpetrated, more often the result of their own unconscious ego inflation. It turns out to be difficult even for the most enlightened and carefully trained masters to care for their compliant disciples. "Healing" has thus become the tool of hierarchical, nonhumanist, and nonprogressive movements throughout history.

At the moment the physician loses interest in and compassion for his patients, they serve merely as objects to aggrandize him and increase his power. This process is not limited to the politics of esoteric cures. Conventional allopathic doctors, non-Western spiritual gurus, and charismatic revolutionary leaders equally run the risk of ego inflation. All cures are to some degree esoteric and power-transferring. All healers exchange treatments for power: their second, silent task is to return that power to the patient.

Chairman Mao Zedong was considered the beneficent modern father of the Chinese people; in the West, he was a shining Left Wing hero. Yet, it appears that he abused his power right from the beginning. For decades, while he was honored as a Marxist philosopher king, egalitarian general, and founder of a new epoch of reform and class justice, he was actually replicating the lives of the most debauched feudal emperors of China. Alienated from his comrades and isolated from most human contact, he held nightly orgies with proscripted concubines, in part to gain longevity according to the Taoist theory of taking on *chi* during intercourse. His personal physician for more than twenty years, Dr. Li Zhisui, describes how Mao ordered women brought to him from peasant homes and from official acting and dancing troupes.[7] This same Mao, the author of brilliant texts about the plight of the poor and hungry, once rose to power as a savior of the disenfranchised masses.

While partying and indulging himself with consorts, he was presiding emotionlessly over the slaughter of millions, unleashing saturnalian waves of Red Guards murdering, disembowelling, and cannibalizing

those unfortunate enough to be fingered as class enemies. When Dr. Li told Mao he was spreading genital herpes to his sexual partners, the Chairman seemed puzzled at his concern. "If it's not hurting me," he said, "then it doesn't matter." In the same spirit, he refused to take a bath. "I bathe myself in the bodies of my women," Mao boasted. He meant also that he was bathing in their *chi* for the good of the nation. "The Chairman is such an interesting person," one liaison told Dr. Li. "But he cannot tell the difference between one's love of him as the leader and one's love of him as a man."[8]

It is a small step from mass evangelical healing to mob lynchings, genocides, etc. In fact, the organized militias and spontaneous gang violence and torture that distinguish the twentieth century draw on the same ecstatic and intrinsic energies that serve occult physicians. The lineage of medicine must always bear the caution of these abuses; it provides the healer with an array of magics, so it must also provide him with their ritual antidotes. Spirit forces that heal are not merely pliable allies in the service of good: they are also agents of disease and madness that occupy the border-zone between epiphany and apocalypse. The collective spirit of a Navaho sand-painting ceremony is under strict sanction and ruled by lineage and ritual. All its mythological references, symbols, and internal legends conspire to keep disjunctive forces at bay. The fact that no one may remember their exact relationships and applications is an advantage because everyone is subject to their unconscious meanings and egalitarian order and no one can appropriate snakes or vultures or lightning for personal use.

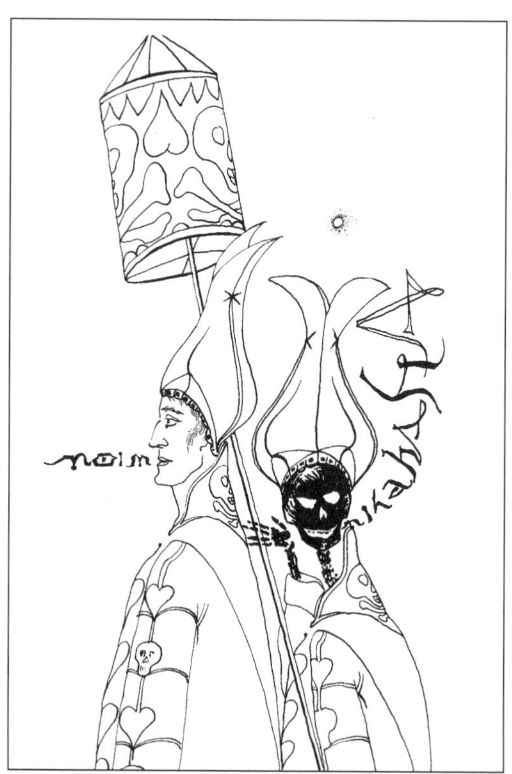

On the other hand, the collective spirit of a populace in economic and social turmoil is under no sanction and potentially ruled by psychopathology and pandemonium. The faith healer, in different guises, becomes the charismatic politician, the hooded inquisitor, and the prophet demanding collective suicide unto a golden world. All too often healers and gurus want the lives of their devotees as gratitude for their spectacular deeds of prayer and energy mediation. The transition from healing to maiming is subtle and often imperceptible. Within an emotional context it is the transition from respect to contempt.

As the disease present and undiagnosed in society is turned against both the corrupted evangelist and his victims, the parapsychological becomes the paramilitary, and fascist generals discard their preacher masks. The Haitian voodoo priest is suddenly the colleague of the junta, and Mao turns out to be a *Chi Gung* pornographer overseeing Potemkin villages.

In a mob no one is sick (or cares if they are sick) because their attention has been directed against an exterior evil, usually in the form of objectified human beings. The esoteric danger of diseases of the spirit is that once they have numbed individuals, their victims turn the pathology blindly against the innocent. Zombies kill the living, or order the living to kill each other. Was anything more clear, Rwanda 1994?

A spirit doctor directs a tremendous and authentic force toward his other. Sometimes what cannot be saved he curses and wounds (out of frustration or as ransom against future healings), what cannot be healed he feeds to demons that inhabit the zone between grace and malignancy (because they must be fed, too). All it takes for a condition to be considered incurable is for it not to be "us"; hence a whole people can be sacrificed for the health and affluence of another people, as though *they* were the disease.

Healing in the theater of apocalyptic religion awakens the mute masses and calls out what is deep and silent (and unwilling to be cured) in them. It is medicinal shamanism on a mass scale at the same time that it is diabolic sorcery and voodoo—again, different faces of the same

mystery. The so-called dark forces—precisely along the same tracks and with a different attention and relationship to the *chakras*—shadow those of light. Adolf Hitler practiced his street politics and theater in the time-honored tradition of charismatic healing. He converted "tingling" into its shadow-half: gas chambers and machines of death. Since his downfall, humans have merely institutionalized such medicine, creating more ingenious and antiseptic machineries in the name of therapy as well as in the name of God. Guns and bombs are now also weapons in a battle of angelic and demonic powers that underlie health.

The charismatic physician must transcend duality in himself or herself before practicing on others. He must be able to tell the difference between himself as a healer and himself as a man. He must not bathe in the bodies—or spirits—of his subjects. In that context, egalitarian political influences on healing are crucial. This is in fact the major accomplishment of institutional allopathy (despite widespread individual abuses).

The Samurai Doctor

HOLISTIC MEDICINE IS made both powerful and socially responsible by the divergences of its separate tributary streams. It provides a common path on which political activists and faith healers can meet, for health is a nonideological event. It provides a vehicle for post-cyberpunk *chakra*-chargers even as it culls the echoes of shamans and medicine men and women of dying cultures. Everyone wants to feel good and to act sanely: revolutionaries and post-Marxians as well as Buddhist practitioners, farmers, millenary Bible-reading Christians, athletes turned therapists, psychics turned athletes, etc. The shaman, reggae singer, and voodoo master are phases archetypally of the surgeon and the war chief.

Aikidoist Richard Heckler can actually be hired by the U.S. Army (1985) to teach meditation, spiritual discipline, and Oriental martial arts to the Special Forces because these skills might lead to better per-

formances. Despite his misgivings about his new students and their goals, he finds that, compared to narcissistic therapy junkies in the counterculture, the Green Berets are quite willing to make the sacrifices necessary to become healers. They are frustrated shamans—seeking the painful and perilous vision quests of shamans but offered only the technology of war. Before Heckler arrived, they were willing to jump out of airplanes and perfect submarine sabotage as their skills of initiation. Afterwards they had intimations that a Green Beret was first a samurai and a samurai was once a medicine man—and this is the kind of medicine soldier needed by the planet, one who must not be co-opted by its separate warring nationalities.[9]

Is this the America that Jimmy Carter unknowingly wooed Africa with ten years earlier? Is this the diaspora of the Snake Dance and the Tibetan lama? Can we yet train healers to reach to the dying heart of a humanity caught up in corporate denial and global disease and drifting toward the Bosniazation of a whole world?

If not, then the forces of disease and genocide may overcome those of life.

The radical Left and the sciences have both failed us, as has the People's Revolution. Once those were our cutting edge, the paths to new worlds. But they became arrogant and inflexible; they did not change our lives, and then they denied that anything could change our lives.

If the new samurai-doctors achieve their destiny, they will practice more than medicine. They will challenge the principles of government and those of science too, and they will bear the seeds of new values that might not be mere hierarchical values in new clothing, nor merely other tyrants bankrolling the overthrow of the present regime.

Ecological Update

TO A DEGREE that had not been so explicit at the time of my original writing, planetary disease threatens the continuation of our species and all other species on this world. We cannot exist indefinitely

in an escalating carbon-dioxide climate with a fraying ozone layer, spreading deserts, radioactive lakes, and an increasingly devitalized biosphere—even assuming legendary *Chi Gung* and *feng shui* masters and homeopathic potencies adapted to oceans and rivers. After all, faith healers and shamans cannot turn Mars or Venus into habitable planets on the physical-incarnate sphere. Even leaving aside matters of intra- and interspecies slaughter (in the names of science and civilization), even conceding nuclear winter and atomic waste as politically addressable issues, there remains a foolhardy and mindless squandering of farmland, rain forest, and atmosphere; an offhand poisoning of the layers of life; and an arrogant extinction of species (and with them, their unique ecospheres, genes, medicines, and spirits). Some have observed that the planet itself now has AIDS, its immune system weakened to a degree even Gaia cannot reconstitute it without hard yoga from its inhabitants.

If this is the case, as sooner or later it will be, then the big medicinal task of the coming decades is to understand that issues of individual health and planetary health are inextricably linked in increasingly shorter and simpler cycles. It is probably not too late for people to heal themselves and then begin healing the environment (or vice versa for those of more activist bent), but both are necessary. Just like the body, the world is incarnate; it responds to realities not laws, to molecules of carbon and oxygen, photons radiating from the sun, and whatever vital and psychic energies obtain. The ecological crisis has no agenda; in fact, it is no more a crisis than chlorophyll or fog are. Thus, it cannot ultimately be solved in an arena of discourse. With drug addiction, car-jacking, child pornography, and gang wars on the mere surface of American life, there are hardly "50 simple ways."

One of the most striking symptoms of our civilization is that it is almost impossible (especially in the capitalist countries of the First World and those that imitate them) to find ordinary food. Try driving down the streets of any city or town in North America and look at what the supermarkets and restaurants advertise and offer as normal—synthesized by-products with overdoses of preservatives, hormones, and artificial flavors to create the illusion of prosperity and satisfaction. It is consumption addiction, not nutritional or medicinal eating. Or perhaps it is one more face of the petroleum rush that locates us in our shallow and desolate materialism—a materialism that does not even deign to examine the internalization of the images it floods us with, let alone the substances we ingest through those images.

Our political and elite establishment would prefer to face petty crises of economics and military adventurism than to change the real patterns of our existence. The reality that is served with the morning newspaper and chatters twenty-four hours a day on radio and television runs a meaningless gamut from left-wing to right-wing, from greed to humanitarianism, from nihilism to ecstasy, but it is all a clever mirage in place of real activity. In terms of overall impressions and mental patterns, the Hollywood/Madison Avenue complex is as deadly as the Military/Industrial one. We are fed images that destroy our sense of well-being, our mental health, our uniquenesses, and our ability to act from the heart.

A civilization of drugged junk-food addicts working at psycho-spiritually vacuous jobs will not respond to the crisis in time—no matter how many aluminum cans they recycle, contributions they make to Greenpeace, recovery groups they join. When the patient has AIDS you don't simply berate the manufacturers of fluorocarbons. You speak to the hollow at the heart of the modern world.

As one East German skinhead put it, "Radical ain't bringing your aluminum cans to the recycling center. 'Radical' is holding a gun to the butcher's head and saying, 'Give me that steak!'" We have ignored this voice so long now, it is speaking as directly as it must—with Uzis, car bombs, street gangs, and oil wells on fire.

Home

THE PRESENT DEMOGRAPHY of homelessness is more than a growing cadre of people who have either the courage or desperation to bottom out on the streets. We are all blown by a careless wind. This planet is stirred up like a hornet's nest, and none of us any longer know our true ancestral homes. The streets are at least real. They keep no illusions of meaningless repetitive labor for tawdry wages or fake possession of fortress-spaces that must then be paid for again and again with toy money. They offer only the reduction of time and breath and landscape to what it is, what only it is—that we are here in a mystery and "bound away" to a mystery, even as the "wide Missouri" was to an earlier ragtag people.

The sense of forced migration, which has famously displaced the native peoples of North and South America and much of Asia, Africa, and Oceania, we now understand is displacing everyone, if not geographically, then economically—or both—sometimes with poverty, sometimes with guns, sometimes with heavier artillery. The wind is strong enough they are blown to sea in paper boats and driven shoeless across snowy mountain passes. Even those who remain in the lands of their ancestors suffer global-mafia intrusion and displacement of the meaning and crops of their lives. The stratosphere is filled indiscriminately with images, MTV, and triple-X-rated gossip, pure scat and static.

Those Indians and Aborigines who continue to conduct ancient ceremonies on the landscapes of the Dreamtime are one by one being enticed and corrupted by the corporate New Age packaging of their so-called epochal truths. The dominant culture is desperate to be loved by everyone, even those who carry the last embers of another reality. It is in the interest of the cocaine/virtual-reality megastructure to seduce every lama, shaman, artisan, and Divine Feminine, if not with power, material goods, and sex, then with dreams of flying the cargo-cult airplanes and saving the soul of Mother Earth. Such is the commodization

of sacred life and homelands. The money that is paid in greater and greater decimals to blackmail even Cassandra to stop crying out to us to see who we are means less and less as we are more and more spun each year in the cyclone World Market. No wonder some choose to stop living this hollow cinema and sit begging on the streets. The shadow of our decimation must be cast somewhere. Cassandra must eventually occupy her given throne.

Rockets aimed at hospitals and suicide bombers dominate one media image, with diasporas stretching from Apache lands, Maori villages, Palestine, Cambodia, Tibet, et al.; yet the exile of jungles, tree spirits, fish, amphibians, reptiles, birds, and mammals fills the akashic records of this planet. The righteous scourge of *interawahme* in Rwanda is the karmic equivalent of the nuclearization of Tibet and the despoliation and depopulation of its forests and monasteries. Even algae and microbes have been set adrift in poisoned waters and air. A sense of being disoriented in oneself infects the dwellers of urban ghettos and lavish suburbs, as endemic to lords in their British castles suffering sexual decadence as it is to Mexican Indians displaced by agricultural and timber barons and the radioactive propaganda of a bankrupt state apparatus. No wonder the "aliens" come to abduct and abuse, in all their guises, from the denizens of unearthly biology to the most intimate members of our own families. Yeats' rough beast does indeed slouch closer and closer toward Bethlehem to be—is the word ... "born"?

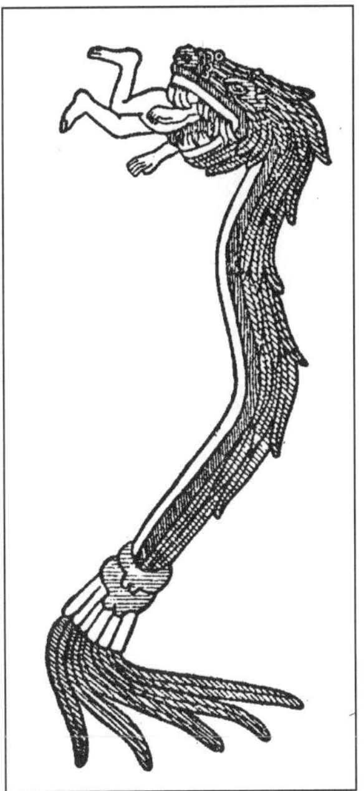

Our personal intuitions of displacement are a harbinger of millennial planetary dislocation. All of us are already in continual bardo, wandering in life as the teachings tell us we will between lives. Home must now be found inside us, in our hearts, from where the embers of compassion might be rekindled, from where alone our feeling of isolation might end. This does not mean the sentimental heart, the fantasy of "home sweet home." It means the actual bloody heart, the esoteric

body represented—in fact manifested in—the physical body, in its manifold fields and sheaths of energy and layers of nerves and flesh. Here we might begin to be the kind of creatures who can live for five minutes in a place without depleting it with cynicism or greed masking terror. When we can look out again into the vast field of stars (we now know contain homelands of billions upon billions of creatures beyond imagination), when we can acknowledge our nativity without diminishment but with a sense of the universal affinity and eternal domain of spirit, then we will find, even now in the midst of degradation and polluted city slags, the intimation of coming home.

Art

Between the fourth and fifth editions of this book (in January 1990) I participated in a Native American ceremony conducted by a Western woman who had trained with a Cheyenne medicine man. Well into the rite she took up a small hoop-shaped drum I hadn't noticed and began beating it in rhythmic sequences punctuated by distinct pauses. We had already burned cedar and chanted. She had shaken a rattle and held a hawk feather over me.

The drum could not be evaded. The seriality of its beat and texture of its thumps resonated at different levels of my being.

"I could see your mind being chased by my drum," the medicine lady told me later. "So slippery it is, so tricky; you have so many ways and places to hide, so many ways to pretend to my drum you are there when you are not."

"Right," I thought. "All through *Planet Medicine* as well, I run."

"Your mind does you no good at this point. You must turn, embrace its unruly form, and carry it to your heart."[10]

When the right hand of *t'ai chi* forming a needle has been placed and taken from sea-bottom, then one's arms are shot out like a fan from the roots, and one *is* briefly an herb: intrinsic energy patterns change. But it is difficult to keep this in mind, in heart—or to remember, as the old musical avowed (though not necessarily about needles at sea-bottom), "The moon belongs ... to everyone."

One tries to get down under, to beneath the rapt but insensible qualities of their own tendencies to move and consume. In our suicidal civilization there is some question of how many of us want to transform the poison and go on living. Most people it seems would rather manufacture more and more poison so that they can die more quickly and anonymously, with the least pain. But cure is change; it always involves suffering: separation before new unity. It is far easier to live and die grimly and accept that existence comes from the oblivion of catabolic dissociation. No doubt part of the attraction of modern science is that it disdains a universe of karma (with all its necessary growth and struggle) and replaces it with a sterile panoply of atoms and molecules. At least those atoms and molecules are under interdict to obey *our* mechanical laws. So the bad news of medical science is always that we are obliterated in the end, but the good news is that at least we get to have "the big sleep," the ultimate disease. We do not have to "get out of here alive."

Once we drop the idea of medicine and think instead of wanting to live, it becomes clear again how everything is a medicine.

People remark offhandedly: "That woman is my medicine." "My work is my medicine." "Dancing is a medicine." "Rock and roll is a medicine."

Interviewed on TV, the rock singer Bruce Springsteen recalled: "When I was a kid, rock and roll was the only thing that always came through. It was the only thing that never let me down. Now I can't let those kids out there down. I let them down and I let myself down."

It is the same for the Cherokee chanter. He grew up hearing the voices and the rumbling tune. They were his medicine. They delivered him into life. Now he is *their* voice.

Not a medicine? Watch how the audience responds rhythmically,

expressing a collective pulse and resonant feeling. Not a doctor? Watch how the wave emanates from him and how he leads them through the exegesis, the riff.

When people live for something, that thing becomes engaged with their psychic and physical process. The will to live may not be expressed as that directly, but it is expressed through love or life as an art form. When disease is encountered, it is transmuted through desire. The more complex and true to the heart a dance or painting or religious ceremony, the more access it gives the artist to the depths of his or her own being. But we must not have the illusion that these visions are imposed on people, like visitors from the beyond. Rock and roll and the twist arise from the very fact of human life in the biosphere. They express the direction and the yearning of that life, the immense satisfaction of its biological and spiritual core. That is why they are so effective in melting and transforming the difficulties people bring to them. That is why we are still dancing.

The artist, whether she knows it or not, works side by side with her health. The development of a style and work, initially in youth, becomes part of her maintenance system. It unfolds on a level prior to division, hence prior to remediation. The inspirational moments in an artist's work, as well as the plunges into the depths, are entanglements with the roots and seeds of being.

Sometimes these adventures stir up material that the artist cannot deal with; after all, many have lost their health in their work, too—Vincent Van Gogh and William Faulkner are famous examples. But if we can learn to transform the seeds in their raw primary form, we can enact a cure prior to a disease. The language of poetry is so valuable exactly because it is the language of the self. A dance, if done authentically, is the dance of the self.

Moby Dick was Melville's cure, given how sick he was writing it and the calm that came upon his life afterward. *Pierre,* his next novel, reads as the sweating off of a profound ague in its last vestiges. Laura Dean's choreography of spirals, performed in 1978 in New York, shares features

with the colors and positional codes of a Navaho sand painting ritual; they are both psychosomatic objectifications. Why shouldn't they contain the same sort of incipient healing possibility? Cecil Taylor's music is an old African medicine, a lineage Pharaoh Saunders made explicit by naming his *Healing Song.* Art and politics are as old as medicine, as the bison on the cave walls at Lascaux and the X-ray turtles and serpents on rocks in the Australian desert—why not as primary? Why not as overseers and handmaidens of our initiation?

Existence is primal and pagan, and Coleridge's "negative capability" is probably still a more accurate gauge of our potential for growth and change (and cure) than even the most healthy regimen of Whole Earth Medicine. That is why we have to be careful not to be too "good" and why we should remember how "bad" the natives were when they put on their costumes and practiced for real. The Osage Rite of Vigil (with its vapor baths, Sun Turtles, sacred moccasins, war clubs, and House of Mystery)—and the Navaho Beautyway Ceremony (with its Mountain Gods, Magic Tobacco, Big Snake with No End, and Monster-Slayers)—remain the micro-encoded infrastructures for a true BIG "planet medicine" yet to be born.

Stan Brakhage, an experimental film maker, spoke of his early works as medicines for his asthma because of the way in which the splicing and montage taught him to breathe in visual rhythms and put his lungs and heart into a visualized landscape.[11] Poets like Charles Olson and Diane di Prima long considered the breathing in poetic syntax a declaration of how to get right, how to be well. They—and the whole school of Beat and radical artists—were self-declared geomancers and shamans. They were also an anarchist political party. Dr. William Carlos Williams wrote:

My heart rouses
thinking to bring you news
of something
that concerns you
and concerns many men. Look at
what passes for the new.
You will not find it there but in
despised poems.
It is difficult
to get the news from poems
yet men die miserably every day
for lack
of what is found there.[12]

It is, literally, "my *heart* rouses," not the mind and not the voice, which later give it shape.

In that sense, song and glyph are natural folk medicines. They need not be literate; in fact, they rarely are. Rap and break-dancing liberate inner-city kids. Their hearts may not stay open, but at least they know themselves profoundly for a moment in time. Young graffiti artists cultivate highly personal traditions and styles. They are medicine men too. *Saturday Night Fever* is both the medicine and the disease for which it is the cure. Nothing but disco can carry these dancers into a sense of their desires, unshaped personalities, and potential for absolute freedom. In the dance, they are alive. Without it, they are inert, trapped.

We see anew that medicine is real not because it alone heals or because it can finger the agent or the cure, but because it alone contains the metaphor for change. Despite their failings, the new medicines fill us with joy and hope and give us something to do during the long hours. When the clouds descend to ground zero and we cannot find a surface or a direction, these sacred practices provide the skin with which to inhabit and shape the fog. All other materials and events fall back into the relativism of the world and mystery of not knowing who we are and how we got here.

Notes

1. Andrew Harvey, *Hidden Journey: A Spiritual Awakening* (New York: Henry Holt & Company, Inc., 1991), p. 191.

2. Ibid., p. 186.

3. Jule Eisenbud, *Paranormal Foreknowledge: Problems and Perplexities* (New York: Human Sciences Press, 1982), p. 231.

4. Ibid., p. 229.

5. Eduardo Calderón et al., *Eduardo el Curandero: The Words of a Peruvian Healer* (Berkeley, California: North Atlantic Books, 1982), p. 38.

6. Harvey, *Hidden Journey*, p. 186.

7. Tai Hung-chao (trans.), *The Private Life of Chairman Mao: The Memories of Mao's Personal Physician, Dr. Li Zhisui* (New York: Random House, 1994).

8. Ibid.

9. Richard Strozzi Heckler, *In Search of the Warrior Spirit: Teaching Awareness Disciplines to the Green Berets* (Berkeley, California: North Atlantic Books, 1989).

10. Michelle Haviar, personal communication, Garberville, California, 1990.

11. Stan Brakhage, personal communication, Rollinsville, Colorado, 1964.

12. William Carlos Williams, "Asphodel, That Greeny Flower," from *Pictures from Brueghel and Other Poems* (New York: New Directions, 1962).

Planet Medicine

Training

When I entered Randy Cherner's seminar in the fall of 1990, I was the least experienced "practitioner" in a group of approximately thirty, and one of only three who were not professionally engaged in some form of somatic or psychotherapeutic practice. Most of the other enrollees had seen clients for periods ranging from five to twenty-five years. I was also farther than anyone else toward the intellectual end of an "intellectual to sensory-motor aptitude" scale. In functional terms this meant that I lagged behind the group in my comprehension of specific "Awareness Through Movement" exercises and my ability to carry them out. It also meant that, in many of the lessons, I tended to pick up different things than others.

I came into the class expecting to learn a range of techniques and methods. However, the main "technique" I encountered was the complex nature of "palpation" itself, which is less a set of physiological skills than an intuitive exploration of direct touch and sensation. The skills arise from nondiscursive levels of touch rather than vice versa. Coming to trust one's touch and learning to think and move in terms of it involves a monumental shift, especially for one who started out viewing his hands and fingers as mere tools for acts of dexterity. All the fields of somatics require this degree of sensitivity. I soon found out that no repertoire of skills could compensate for an invasive and overly mechanical touch. Yet a subjective awareness of how to touch and how not to impose rigid patterns could overcome almost any lack of technique. In one sense, the effect of my three years of study was to bring me to a starting point where my training in somatics could begin.

The most frustrating aspect of intuitive "expression through touch" was learning to sustain and replicate success and to recognize when a particular piece of work was completed and so to make smooth transitions to the next. Conversely, the most exhilarating aspect was achieving therapeutic results before having mastered the full choreography of particular techniques.

I experienced these same dichotomies in the work of classmates as well. Some were more mechanically proficient than others with often negligible or even countertherapeutic results; others always got good results and, more importantly, led their training partner into new ground. From this experience I am convinced that receptivity of connection is the heart of somatic healing, and the techniques, while critical to any sophisticated and discriminating practice, mean nothing alone.

Two-thirds of the way through the training, Cherner asked us to write down the things we either had learned or were wanting to learn during the remainder of the course. I include my own list here as a kind of gloss, after the fact, not so much on medicine *per se* but the text of this book and the impediments readers might run into in approaching the issues I raise. The following are informal journal notes and should be read more as aphorisms and rough koans than injunctions:

> ☙ I can't ever do any better work on someone else than I can on myself. If I treat myself impatiently and mechanically on a daily basis, I can't suddenly switch and magically treat someone else with care. If I demand unrealistic performance from myself, I will demand it from a client. Even if I try consciously to make the switch to being an impeccable practitioner, my attitude toward myself will translate into an impatience or distractedness in my touch.

> ☙ When I am unconscious, spaced out, or generally grumpy, the answer—meaning the dissolution of that state—is in-toward, not

abstracting myself further and thinking to be aloof from it, which merely tightens its grip. The mistake is to think that melting is an act of inattention. Melting can be an act of the sheerest attention and emotional authenticity.

ଓ Always do less. And then do less than that. Attention is critical here. It is only possible to do less if I am aware of what I am doing. Few techniques are more dangerous than the sense of urgency that "nothing is happening," thus trying to rush things ahead by doing more. The habit is to think, "This sure isn't working. Do I have any more tricks?" Or, in the worst scenario, one escalates from technique to technique, always up the invasive scale.

If nothing is happening, do less. If nothing is still happening, then do less than that.

Wait for something—anything—to begin on its own.

ଓ Right at the cusp of profundity I try to make things more profound—and that's where I lose it. I have to trust to let profundity develop by itself and emerge, not to overwhelm it by "amping" in impatience for a big experience. Amping diminishes. It turns an authentic experience emerging in its own time into melodrama or theater. Adding emotion does not enlarge or deepen experience. Quite the contrary.

ଓ Stand by what I do. It is already done anyway and, if it is "wrong," it cannot be negated. Don't be ready to give up a technique the moment someone questions me or I look around the room and see everyone is doing a different rendition. The game is not "Simon Sez." Don't judge my work only against someone else's proficiency.

ଓ There IS time.

ଓ I don't have to know what a technique is in order to be able to do it. Manocher Movlai has his students repeat: "I don't know what I am. I don't know what this is."

ଓ When Ron Sieh was teaching me *hsing-i,* he said rather unexpectedly one day, "I'm trying to teach you to be as good as you can, but you obviously have some other agenda."

ꕥ I can't underestimate the number of ways in which I am addicted to giving up. Anxiety to change technique or the compulsion to flee comes uncannily at the moment when something is about to happen. It is always a matter of waiting *a little bit longer,* as long as I don't count the seconds while waiting.

ꕥ I occupy more space than I think I do.

ꕥ My tendency is to assume that affectations and unconscious gestures, little "faults" in myself I apparently can't correct, are residual matters to the overall task of training. In fact, filling unlived spaces, however incidental each unlived space seems, is the path in. Often the more minor the habit, the more central it is as a means of access to one's center. The over-effort at improvement, imposed by having external goals, is simply a reaffirmation of not being able to fill in my own gaps. The same is true for the client one is working on.

ꕥ It is not important to be "correct," at least not at the expense of the above. Being correct—being liturgical—is often just another excuse for not doing it. Anyone can be right theoretically. But not everyone can do the right thing, especially when there are no "theoretics" to back it.

ꕥ The most damaging impediment we put in our own way is looking at a task and presuming it can't be done, thus flailing away in sorry imitation of it, demonstrating mostly our conviction of personal incapacity. Any technique, or new skill, is learned in pieces, piece by piece . . . piece by piece. Any task undertaken, no matter how monumental, is accomplished a step at a time. The cliché is correct.

If you stare at the wall across a room and plan to get there some other way than by taking a step at a time, you have found the sure way never to get there. Many people spend their whole lives not taking the first step because they have convinced themselves they could never reach the wall. They'd just as soon not undergo the tragedy of taking years worth of steps and falling short anyway. Or they fear embarrassment along the way.

People don't love because they assure themselves in advance that

their love isn't enough, that another person won't love them, or that they will never love enough to make a difference. The essence of somatics work is teaching oneself and others *how* to take "first steps."

ᘓ In a difficult technique, instead of trying to do everything right, how about first doing *one thing right.*

During a weekend intensive after the second year, our class as a whole spent a day participating in the Prison Integrated Health Program at the Federal Correctional Institute at Dublin, California. One of our group (Kathy Park) was co-director of the program (with two other Lomi-trained therapists, aikidoist Wendy Palmer and M.D. Tracy Thompson).

We met a self-selected group of about thirty women in a rec room set aside for the joint training. We were white with one Asian; the inmates were mostly African American and Hispanic. The structure of the workday was an extended version of our class. Cherner led the entire group through a "lesson," which was a series of "Awareness" exercises based on Feldenkrais work, designed to teach us to explore new modes of feeling and movement as well as to understand the basis of techniques he was about to teach. We lay on the floor in a mixed group and carried out his instructions for about forty-five minutes, differentiating movements of our arms from our torsos and neck, our legs from our pelvis. Afterwards, using "client" models from the prison group, Cherner demonstrated how the same techniques functioned as healing modalities. Then we shared lunch at the prison cafeteria. The bulk of the afternoon was set aside for each of us to treat an inmate.

Giving a session in that environment meant going into the teeth of every ambiguity and inequity present. It was difficult for me not to experience a profound disquiet relating through touch in a prison, and additionally with a woman who was cut off from any other intimate contact with a man. The fine line between, on the one hand, the therapeutic and kinesthetic aspects of touch and, on the other, its sensual components was further narrowed by the poignancy of the situation.

Richard –
For a lover of words, I have the hardest time finding the right ones. I will put aside some quiet time and space to write to you later.
A gillion thanks.
♡ Laura

Richard.
Tu eres una persona especial al obsequiarnos tu tiempo y sabiduría.
Gracias Gladys.

Dear Richard,
We need each other, we all need each other, as well as all forms of life in order to understand & grow. Our interconnections are invaluable & necessary to reach the truth of our beings. Thank you!
Lucy

Richard—
Thank you for your presence & for your enthusiasm for the program. We can bring about healing even in places as bleak as a women's prison. Thanks too for your help & contributions to the library. Many blessings.
Peg

Dear Richard:
I hope your cup of love was filled too!
Peace love & Forward!
Ida

Card sent to author by women in Federal Correctional Institute at Dublin, California, after day of lessons and treatments there.

After an awkward beginning and three false starts, I fell back on our teaching, which was to work in response to situations exactly as they arose, to blend appropriate techniques into each other, and to foresee what kinds of touch might be experienced as disturbing or invasive. It meant "being present" in a situation I would normally space out from; in fact, it trained "being present" because any lapse in attention left one excruciatingly exposed.

The goal of bodywork in general is a medicine which arises experientially, incorporates movement awareness and mutuality, and works to enhance health through feeling, visceral adjustment, and kinesthetic reorientation. The mere introduction of such a form into a prison—

no doubt without the full understanding of its implications by the authorities—augurs a society (not this one, 1994) in which there might actually be a way of guiding inmates (including so-called violent offenders) into new modes of being (Palmer and Park have also taught these practices in similar circumstances in men's prisons with dramatic results among even some of the more hardened inmate populations).

Stealing and killing arise from somatic substrata too; their "attitudes" take root in the same layers of flesh in which love and healing are nurtured, and they are cultivated and hardened likewise as habits and modes of practice. Being able to pull out a gun and shoot someone requires layers of deep neural support. It is not, despite seeming evidence to the contrary, a simple, mindless act. Once learned, it cannot easily be renounced or abandoned. Yet, without a somatic vocabulary in our culture, we rarely consider or teach how one energetic state leads to another; we fail to provide people with the means to rescue themselves from a habit of violence and crime. We expect them to carry out their own miracle in a vacuum. Some people can (and do) catalyze their emotions and change on a dime (unfortunately, this sometimes means toward destructive as well as creative acts). Others need to be supported and educated somatically in order to move from a new place. Yet rehabilitation rarely considers the somatic component.

At Dublin there is a secondary benefit to the Health Program, for at the same time that it provides healing for those desperately needing it, it trains these women in a potentially remunerative occupation which they were unlikely to discover on their own (especially given their cultural milieus) and for which they are (in some cases) particularly talented from the same energetic charge and charisma that may have led them to incarceration. So while they are encountering their shadows, they are practicing skills they can bring back to their communities when they leave prison. They might be able to earn a living from these; they might train others in them; and the techniques themselves might provide some answers for despair and addiction. The prison sentence can be an invitation to a vision quest.

TOWARD THE END of our visit to Dublin, Cherner held a question-and-answer session. It quickly became a raucous exchange of jokes, riffs, and teasing by the women, directed alternately at one another and us (as they ran back and forth across the room to deliver their acknowledgments and jibes). Bawdy sexual humor dominated, and no one was spared. The bodywork had so charged the room with energy, the potentially distancing innuendos of the occasion were tossed on stage and blasted away with laughter. Personal styles of those present and enmities among the inmates were caricatured and cleared.

The event closed near five o'clock with a singing circle. Popular folk songs were followed by the ballad "Harbor Me." Different parts of the circle were assigned sequential choruses at changing pitches: "Har-bor me. Oh, won't you harbor me. Har-bor me."

This was another world, *another country* (James Baldwin), another time.

But that was not the grand finale. After the conclusion of "Harbor Me," different women led us in the national anthems of their homelands: Chile, Colombia, Mexico, and Puerto Rico (three of them had been arrested as members of a Free Puerto Rico guerrilla group, and an untold number were South American nationals taken into custody because of husbands or boyfriends in the drug business). Most of us by then were in tears.

True medicine *is* finally a matter of communal solidarity and planetary survival. And though we should be able to achieve that without extreme rituals in extreme places, we do not seem to be. Our huge (and ever growing) prison population is itself testimony to our loss of the ability to touch one another. Somatics provides new rituals and tools that have the capacity to heal not only individuals but communities and perhaps one day nations. There is no present groundswell to use them, but then there is no present groundswell for anything that is rooted in our hearts.

Planetary Hygiene

One of the problems with *Planet Medicine* as a concept as well as a book has been keeping it to a manageable size. Recently when I told a longtime reader I was rewriting the book, she wondered how I could reconsider what was already so vast. She noted that even the first edition might well have been called "Planetary Hygiene" or "Planetary Existence" because, after all, isn't "medicine" merely "how to live"? Another reader said he hoped I would write a "book" this time because he found the first edition impossible to read:

"I couldn't make head or tails or it," he confided, "until I decided to treat it as a homeopathic medicine rather than a text."

I agree with these readers in that I hope what distinguishes *Planet Medicine* is not so much that its subject is medicine as that its context is our planet-wide search for a healing imperative and then a medical paradigm. The subject of the book is "medicine" insofar as disease itself is a text written on the body of man- and womankind. But disease, like medicine, when approached through mind, is both a polity in search of laws and a gap (or gash) in search of meaning. Disease doesn't think text; it just is, brilliant and profound. Any medicine which attempts to neutralize it must become textual (or nontextual) at the same depth and degree of subtlety.

In summary, I am addressing directly our global perception of a malaise, a sickness transcending the conventional notion of disease that has come to include environmental despoliation, genocide, poverty, greed, necrophilia, and other pathological mayhem. Certainly the nuclear and chemical arsenals and toxic industries of nations, the sheer number of land mines buried in the earth, are as much diseases as smallpox, schizophrenia, and the Black Plague. Any paradigm we invent must find a way of addressing them. Equally relevant to a text on medicine is an investigation of the role of the various so-defined medical professions in engendering or intensifying rather than ameliorating diseases.

Of course, this *is* the twentieth century, and some may argue that human beings are free to act as they wish—that "disease" is a purely subjective and pejorative judgment (especially when applied as a concept to something less concrete than chicken pox or malaria). I won't challenge this position. Instead I will point out that various alternative healing systems, by providing more functional and behavioral definitions of health, confront the problem of our global "health" crisis more effectively than morally absolutist domains of allopathic medicine or political critiques of the same. In this farflung crisis of values and resources, a new phenomenology would be far more useful than a new ideology.

Rewriting the American Health Plan

The Clinton Health Plan was not a health plan. It was a money plan. Nowhere did it say anything about health except as a legal and economic commodity. What the Clinton plan did minister to was the inequitable redistribution of costs and profits arising from a system of treating human bodies purely as commodities. It proposed legislatively to adjust relative balances within a regulated marketplace. As one cocaine addict on the street remarked about the heralded arrest of a Colombian cartel kingpin, "It don't mean nothin'. It's just a corporate thing, a change in middle management."

Thus, all the debate about the Health Plan and its relative distributions of expense was so much verbiage about who got the bucks and who paid the bills. There wasn't any change proposed in health care. Although the role of the insurance companies in pulling their greedy share of unearned profits out of the potential pool of health-care resources was directly challenged (especially in single-payer versions), the legislation in *every* version presupposed the continuing commodization of health care.

No national plan has yet questioned that commodization, and none gives the inkling that there is anything wrong with viewing disease and

medicine solely in market terms. Needless to say, the Clinton Health Plan did not even begin to address the underlying assumptions of the reigning medical paradigm or the explosion of iatrogenic disease.

I will grant this one thing, though, to Clinton himself: he recognized and then took a direct stand on the relationship between the availability of guns and the high cost of health care. This was a single giant step in the right direction. But there are a lot of other less obvious "guns" that need calling out. In fact, it may not be possible to improve health care without first confronting the pathologizing effects of the public education system, the food and meat industries, and the advertising cartel.

To give a monopoly to one company is a classic way to set costs skyrocketing. Yet even Republicans are mesmerized by the allopathic paradigm and have been willing to eliminate that most sacred tenet of capitalism: free markets and open competition. After all, competition brings prices down and encourages commerce. Lack of competition requires prices to rise and traps wealth. That is why no one tells auto manufacturers they have to design one kind of engine or use only one metal in the manufacture of cars. No one tells computer firms they may use only one kind of disk operating system. But politicians of all ilk are so buffaloed by the medical lobby and indoctrinated by the chimera of a proven model of disease and cure that they are willing to give the AMA the sole right to manufacture a health-care product. Why? To protect the public from quacks? To prove to themselves that they belong to an advanced civilization on the cutting edge of future technologies? In presumption that the ultimate medicine will be transmitted by a hand-held computer like the one wielded by Dr. Leonard McCoy in *Star Trek?* To avoid looking like anti-scientific fools? To reassure everyone that disease is under control and that the current economic hierarchy is the best of all possible worlds? To maintain the doctor as one of the bulwarks of social authority? To serve the gods of materialism and quantification? To suppress a potential revolution in values that could spread to other institutions? To avoid the consequences

of an admission that generations of service to a single template was wrong?

This much is true: the governmental protection of one kind of medicine has led to wildly inflated prices for services and goods. The monopoly of allopathic health care not only devours an increasing share of the GNP but threatens to suck up *all the surplus wealth in the society.* And this is the real problem, not how the bills are paid.

WHAT WOULD CONSTITUTE a radical change in health care in this country—and on the planet as a whole—would be a recognition of different actual modes of healing, a legitimization of each of them relative to one another, and a strategy for making them all available in appropriate circumstances. Allopathic medical treatment could be one of these, but sharing a venue with cranial osteopathy, *Chi Gung,* shamanism, homeopathy, Feldenkrais, etc., it would be less expensive, less rapacious, less universally preferred, and more acutely self-monitoring. Simply from the therapeutic paradigm expanding, the medical monopoly ending, the overall cost of health care would plummet. Suddenly people's lives would be less commodities to be mortgaged, bartered, and experimented upon and more existential mysteries to be lived. We would become responsible for ourselves. Doctors would no longer get to tell us who and what we are or pretend to write marginalia excusing us from destiny. We would have to become real. We would have to recognize our actual place in the universe.

As creatures who lived in the wilderness so long, we are afraid of going back out onto the open road, of having to define our own meaning again. We want to be protected by codes, sanctions, trade guilds, and the weapons of litigation. We want to play by our own rules rather than the rules of nature, so we have medicalized our incarnation even as we have suburbanized the wilderness. But we are not doing too well thus far living the lives deeded us by the "hospital," these protected lives (and deaths) of medical statistics.

Once health care was fundamentally redefined, then it would make

sense to offer "Universal Coverage" and to attempt to balance the cost of that coverage among the segments of society that could most afford it. To pretend to do this without first reformulating the entire meaning of health care is, as I said in Volume One of this book, to saddle our country—in fact, our whole civilization—with a ridiculous, unmaintainable algorithm in which actual health and well-being have no meaning except a quantitatively defined longevity and an illusion of protection from certain arbitrarily isolated categories of diseases (and in which the legal right to pseudo-health replaces any responsibility for real health). Such is the myth of "Universal Coverage."

Our vanity is that we think we can control time and space by quantifying them. Yet we don't understand what temporality and spatiality really are beyond grids of streets and orbits of clocks. By defining health and well-being likewise, we think to prioritize the ego's control of meaning and to reify each individual in the template of the average individual. In truth, we are abandoning people in the quicksand of a superficial personality cult. Men and women hardly know any longer whether they want their lives prolonged and their diseases abated, but they grab for a medicalized solution because it makes them at least as real as a car.

There is no bureaucratic limit set on how long bottomless resources can be poured into nonfunctional and even iatrogenic responses to the allopaths' favored disease modalities. In theory, the entire resources of the Earth could be put at the service of prolonging one person's life—and even that would not ultimately be enough. One might as well pave over the topsoil, use the oceans as formal dumps, attempt to raise the planet's food in greenhouses and fishponds, and jail the entire expanding population to put an end to crime. All of these are more expensive than we can afford, and they are ploys to evade the reality of our plight and to pretend that the universe is a place of business not of destiny.

We will lose. And we will lose big. Better to call it now and change the system before we tinker grandiosely with the method of payment.

Commodization and Loss of Power

As must be clear by now, a paradox lies at the core of this book. On the one hand, we are sick as a species, and getting sicker. On the other, we are beginning to realize that we can heal ourselves, even with the mind alone—perhaps not by a patter of simple thoughts but by a process akin to mentation and meditation. The most optimistic thing is that we are realizing it historically for the first time as a combination of industrial science and psychospiritual practice. This synthesis is not even half-born, so we have no idea how far we can go with it. To this point we are still trying to get machines to do all the work without realizing that machines are merely other projections of our mentation.

Parallel to our hopes and labors for a true science of the mind, the blatant commodization of health and the empowerment of medical conscription have vaulted far beyond any nineteenth-century fantasy of Mary Shelley or William Blake. The health constabulary has disenfranchised individuals in a systematic and profound manner. It has disempowered them on a cultural basis and, just to make sure, it has disempowered them on a skeletal-visceral basis. It has disenfranchised them through a collusion of industries, schools, media gossip, and churches impersonating spiritual institutions. It is no wonder that true compassion is in short supply, for mere sensationalism has replaced sensation.

Meanwhile we tend to incriminate a medley of criminals, soldiers of fortune, hunters of endangered animals, murderers, corrupt politicians, and even bureaucrats. We blame other people always for the heedless and selfish behavior of our species. We condemn a world in which everyone seems "out for themselves," as if we could individually hide behind the superficial and disingenuous screens of innocence we erect in our minds to separate ourselves from "them" who are doing the bad things.

The bomb in Oklahoma City (April 19, 1995) carved out precisely the negative space behind the temple of love we have not inhabited

and do not know how to inhabit. It was like an asteroid colliding with a moon — mute, sterile, antipathetic, millennial. It gave absolutely nothing. It took away everything. It didn't even have a reason. It was an act of destruction in place of the act of healing we deny in our hearts. Deny it long enough, and the centurions of its antipode will spring up like weeds. Where the cure is depreciated or renounced we can expect an explosion of exactly the opposite order, a cataclysm in place of *prana* or microdoses because something must occupy the void. In place of the shaman's transforming chant we hear the muffled shriek of an empty heart.

If we will not produce healers, then we must produce killers. If we refuse acts of faith, we will get wounds — terrible wounds — that drive us to the bottom where only faith and redemption remain.

But even the worst deeds of recreational killers exist only in a collective consciousness. They are the deeds of all of us. How can beings trapped in their minds begin to open their hearts? How can creatures feeding themselves on addictions and adrenalin rushes know their life desires? Until these questions are answered, it is pointless to ask whether our species as a whole, as it pillages and wastes sentient life everywhere, even has a conscience or a heart. Though we are behaving like hungry ghosts in the global marketplace, we have many other sides to us, unexperienced and untested. (Some Buddhist groups in Nepal claim that humans have slaughtered so many individual animals—in feedlots as well as in the wild—so swiftly while destroying so many of their genetic templates and habitats that the spirits of these animals have no choice but to come back *as people.* That is why there are too many people. That is why so many of them behave like beasts. They *are* beasts. Which is not to say that beasts act badly, merely that they may not be ready to participate in human society.)

The point is that we are substantially cut off from the qualities that make us human, and this dilemma is institutional as much as it is personal. In fact, our entire justice system is an attempt to make most crimes seem purely personal (i.e., to assign actionable blame for the

outcomes of class structure and other collective deeds). Conversely, our entire medical system is an attempt to make personal destiny institutional (i.e., to redefine diseases and immune responses as universal pathological categories). These twin instances of "misplaced concreteness" combine to crush hope and dehumanize daily life.

WHEN SCIENTISTS LOOK across the vastness of the physical universe, they see mindlessness, arbitrariness, and the utter insignificance of human beings. Against fields of starry matter we are surely zero. Jupiter alone is 1316 times the volume of the Earth. Any single star, perhaps trailing many Jupiters and Marses, is millions to billions of times the Earth's volume. The galaxies of the heavens contain untold numbers of such stars, stretching to eternity. The universe is not only beyond comprehension; even an attempt to comprehend it is beyond comprehension.

How science calculates this state of affairs is to declare the human condition trivial in advance. We are random, temporary motes of accidental molecular accretion in a hollow cavern filled with immense fires that go on forever.

Yet this gargantuan universe has no extrinsic meaning or intelligence. Its size is raw. We are not "out along" it. We are "in."

I understand the vastness and brilliance of the cosmos in precisely the opposite context to traditional science. I see a giant wheel fashioned of pure murk, a baby yawning, a god in the process of being born. Everywhere the wheel sets down its cutting edge amid Orions and Cassiopeias, mind trembles through dust and mud.

Where we are, the universe has never been. It is exploring the possibility of its own nature through us. It is using our experience to make itself alive. Thus, its profundity and scope are our profundity and scope. We are its rough margin struggling at the frontier of dreams, and what is becoming conscious as we are becoming conscious (we and all sentient beings everywhere) is the creation itself. The fires and luminous clouds of the night mark how vast and poignant we can become if we follow our destiny. They are raw intelligence. We are focused, incarnated

intelligence. As long as we stare into our diminishment, that long will we suffer not only an incredible sense of hopelessness and loss but the diseases and depravities of denial and suppressed spirituality.

MEDICINE, AS CONSTITUTED TODAY, has little to do with internal experience. It is the slave of objectification. From computer analyses of bodily fluids and radiation images, doctors purport to know everything about a person—her past, her future, her propensity to disease. Since everyone is contaminated in one way or another, there is always a bad omen somewhere. Now, with chromosome mapping and its offshoots, not only are people's present bodies turned into medical images but their entire destinies have become exotic quantifications, the implacable outcomes of myriad inevitable preordinations. All diseases are, at root, DNA mistakes. Even sexual orientation has been assigned to a genetic locus.

Though it was never the intent of the benign Hippocratic guilds to take over lives, their unequal alliance with technology has yielded the palpable whole of human existence as the spoils. The truth is that both capitalist and communist world-views of the twentieth century have sought ruthlessly to turn everything into products—animal, vegetable, and mineral alike—products to be exploited, consumed, and taxed, all in the name of greater collective welfare and prosperity, always in the guise of equity and justice. As the more obvious products become depleted, newer and more abstract ones are invented. This is the unstated agenda of cyberspace. This is why sensationalism has replaced sensation.

As I noted at several points in the opening chapter of Volume One of this book, the subtext of medicine has been to turn us into consumers (literally customers) of our own body/minds. We get to buy ourselves piece by piece—fertility, birth, immunity, beauty, life insurance, the license to hold organs and body-parts renewed annually. As the subliminal messages of Big Brother have it, we must purchase our health, our sexuality, our right to live from one company or another. We are not conceded these things by birth.

Certainly cosmetic accoutrements and tranquilizing drugs are insidious enough in their erosion of self into product. But the big pay-off is industrial medicine itself which, by a seeming trick of mirrors, has convinced a majority of the populace that they must petition it regularly for an okay body. We don't get to live autonomically and go into our own depths from there. Instead we are repeatedly called out from our depths to confront our existence as mere burlap and bricks. Life is no longer a mystery or an alchemy through which we arrive on this plane to test the karma of our spirit and destiny of our soul. It is hospital garbage. Existential existence has become the most marketable commodity of all, for without a life, a consumer can make little use of the other luxuries for sale. This is what medicine now offers first and foremost—not health but the ransom to buy back a life which was stolen.

I make no argument with the validity and usefulness of a great majority of medical procedures, but the way in which they have been institutionalized leads people to presume on a subtle level that their bodies are not their own. How can people whose bodies are not their own heal them through their minds? How can people whose bodies are not their own take responsibility for the hungers and the crimes of those bodies?

As long as the medical establishment claims not only the omnipotence of its procedures but the exclusive key to the province of healing, people will not even begin to seek intrinsic sources of healing or explore how much they can train themselves to do. They will constantly look outside themselves, for maintenance as for amusement.

Orthodox medicine may well retain its technology and millennial scientific quest—these are great works—but it must give back the essential right of people to their own bodies and the responsibility of their own lives.

A New System of Health Care

It is perhaps absurd for anyone to propose a practical alternative to the present medicine monopoly with the intention of it being adopted

and working, but it would be irresponsible to come this far without taking at least a shot in that direction. I don't expect my suggestions to be taken seriously at a level of policy, but they provide a critique of the bill of goods we are being sold. In fact, I challenge those who disagree to demonstrate why my fantasy is any less practical and economically feasible than the jumble of bureaucracy being offered by the Clinton administration or the Democratic and Republican alternatives.

What I propose is a six-part medical system. For clarity of illustration (alone) I will place each sphere within this system in a different region of North America. This region shall be its research center, its university, and its court of ethics. Satellite clinics and practitioners will also be spread throughout the other regions. Needless to say, all systems belong in every region.

In New York and the greater Northeast I will place the allopathic schools of surgery and pharmacy—in other words, the majority of what passes now for modern medicine, including most forms of psychoanalysis, nutrition, immunology, allergology, and laboratory research. They are the most scientifically advanced therapeutics, by far the most expensive, and the ones requiring the most refined technologies. The drug companies can continue to do research necessary to discover new vaccines, antibiotics, and other medicines, as well as methods of diagnosis for all manner of conditions, including cancer, AIDS, birth control, and genetic defects. The surgeons can apply their acuity to the victims of organ disease, severe injury, and war. Those who, for ethical or psychospiritual reasons, do not want this form of medicine can simply avoid the outreach from this center. Just by our making it not the only sanctioned "scientific" modality its actual value will become clearer and that shift in perspective will lessen the compulsion to attack every malady with heroic methods and to prolong life in its most minimal state by default.

In Toronto and the greater Midwest I will base a school of constitutional and dietary medicine. It will include at its heart Ayurvedic principles but will also prescribe foods and herbs from all over the

world, including from Chinese recipes, American Indian formularies, African, Pacific, and Australian ethnobotanies, etc. It will include culinary schools teaching practitioners how to prepare food, blending ingredients in manners simultaneously health-giving and tasteful. Everyone will be trained in food-balancing principles, the relationships of taste qualities to diseases, the roles of climate changes, modes of clothing and habitats—in other words, general environmental cycles in health. Ideally this school can develop a new ecological medicine out of ancient Oriental as well as Western principles and send its teachers to the agribusinesses and farms to teach healthy methods for raising food.

In Seattle and the greater Northwest (with reference to the Indians of the Pacific Basin and the John Bastyr College of Naturopathy already there) I will set a college of *chi*-based medicine. The doctors will teach their students methods of apprehending and moving *chi,* including those of Taoist martial arts and the different realms of *Nei Ching.* This school will also include yoga, acupuncture, moxibustion, Buddhist meditation, and will have its own branches of herbalism and bodywork.

In the San Francisco Bay Area (acknowledging the Hahnemann Clinic already in Berkeley) I will place energy medicine. This will include homeopathy, Bach flower remedies, radionics, Reiki, forms of psychic medicine, *chakra* and color therapies, massage and induction of the different sheaths of the energy body, and faith healing, and will be involved in research into all paraphysical modes of healing. Thus, the laboratory of Kirlian photography will be in the basement of the university of this branch. Any mediums who want to channel healers from other dimensions will be able to train here, too. Jacques Vallee will oversee UFO research from his base in San Francisco (and from the point of view not that "they" are aliens—friendly or malicious—but that they are here and we don't know what they are). Vallee's journal notes upon seeing his first UFO in 1958 could serve as an epigram for this school: "I am left with the single strong impression that we

must respond; that human dignity demanded an answer, even if it was only a symbolic acknowledgment of our lack of understanding. I realized then and there that I would forever be ashamed of the human race if we simply ignored 'their' presence."[1]

In Taos, New Mexico, and the greater Southwest (into Northern Mexico), I will set the shamanic school of medicine. Here students will learn ceremonial sand painting, visualization techniques, healing dances and chants, indigenous and Western art therapy, the dynamics of abreaction and methods of reinvoking trauma, vision questing, the uses of hallucinogens in diagnosis and treatment, and healing with feathers, drums, crystals, amulets, and stones. This branch will also house a school of world literature and mythology. Shamans—both Third World and industrial—from all over the planet will be invited to serve stints on the faculty. Thus, techniques will be pooled and preserved, and each of the traditions—Siberian, Fijian, pan-Australian, native American, African, East Indian, etc.—will have a faculty within the greater department of shamanic healing. I would think that many Freudian-trained psychoanalysts would prefer to study and practice here (or in Florida) than at the New York school.

In West Palm Beach, Florida, and the greater Southeast (honoring the Upledger Institute) I will place the school of neo-osteopathy, which will cover all modalities of manipulation and attendant methods of psychological investigation and clearing of psychosomatic blocks. This university will have independent departments representing the major somatic traditions such as Feldenkrais, Eutony, Body-Mind Centering, Rolfing, Zero Balancing, Visceral Manipulation, Aston Patterning, Chiropractic, Reichian, Acupressure, etc. There will also be a research sector studying the relationship among not only these somatic therapies but those practiced at the other regional centers (for instance, Polarity in Toronto and Contact Improvisation and shamanic "polarity" in New Mexico). Psychotherapists practicing here can learn techniques of nonverbal dialogue and contacting character resistance by touch and words together.

I do not mean to give osteopathy priority over the other somatic systems. I merely mean to invoke the underlying osteopathic model of a whole system of medicine fully equivalent—on the level of palpation, sensory-motor education, and manipulation—to the competing system of drugs and surgery.

A MEDICAL CULTURE SET up in this way would inspire a refreshing range of flexibility and choice. A person suffering from any form of mental disorder (depression, compulsion, panic attacks) could choose to see a conventional psychoanalyst in New York or a practitioner in any of the other centers. He could engage in a nonverbal, craniosacral dialogue and experience somatoemotional release in Florida. He could learn *chi* movements in Seattle. He could go on a guided vision quest in New Mexico. He could also obtain dietary aid in Toronto, potentiated pharmaceuticals in California, Chinese herbs in Seattle, or psychotropics in New York.

Not only is such a system more humane and profound in how it approaches medical diagnosis and treatment, it is bound to be more cost-effective. Most of the modalities other than allopathy are flat-out less expensive. If even a small percentage of the population elected to use them, the core technological medical glut would be eased dramatically. Additionally, these modalities tend to favor shorter treatments, the patient taking responsibility for his or her own health, and an acceptance of death in its proper time rather than the employment of Herculean methods to maintain life at all costs. That is, these centers as proposed have ethical and ontological sophistication and would tend to approach all crises as opportunities of meaning rather than as random attacks. Thus, their practitioners would be in a position (as enlisted traditional practitioners in China were after the Cultural Revolution) to ask the patient, for instance, to practice a *Chi Gung* exercise or meditation regularly and perhaps to prepare for the spiritual transformation of death when that is the "healing" modality needed—all this instead of just giving a pill, a placation, or a "curtains" prognosis.

Such a medical system would also leave open the possibility of dealing with a number of other extremely serious, trenchant societal problems not ordinarily associated with medical treatment. For instance, youth in gangs could be viewed as shamanic initiates rather than as criminals and could be sent to train as samurai, vision-quest leaders, or even bodyworkers and herbalists. This may sound ridiculous on the surface, but in fact few people would choose an outlaw existence if there were another option for a fierce, creative life. Many gang members, for instance, would prefer to play in the National Basketball Association if they had the skills and were given the chance. Why not enlarge the "National Basketball Association" to its full scope, i.e., make its "skills" the skills needed for healing society as well as—but with the same aplomb and "badness" as—shakin', bakin', and dunking. Gang roles require courage, ingenuity, and physical prowess—why not also the full enactment of an internal martial art and the assumption of a leadership role? Would it not be better to provide opportunities for warriors than to put twenty percent of the civilian population behind bars? Would it not make a healthier society to spread the megabucks among half a million "Michael Jordans" and "Bruce Springsteens" playing neighborhood ball as osteopaths, sound healers, and shamans?

Vision quests lead to magical healing skills. These are more likely to provide prosperity and, finally, life itself than gun-battles, drug wars, and extortion are, despite the quick-fix lure of the latter as a method for getting off the bottom of the caste system. Gangs are simply the shadows of the roving teams of barefoot doctors and "Guardian Angels" we desperately need. Holistic medicine means to give all people rainbow bodies, or an intuition that rainbow bodies are possible. Gang members at least understand how tough this world is, how hard it is to get and maintain any kind of "rainbow" in the battle with rival spirits in the anonymous void of the stars and streets. They probably have developed some of the prerequisites of the power necessary to stay with a *chakra,* skills that a civilian would not have. True healing has more kinship with wild Bear Doctors who maim and kill than it does with intellectual

philanthropists and academic technicians. And, in any case, many of the patients the gangs would treat at first have already been abandoned by the safety net and are far too cynical to accept medicalized palliatives. They might be willing to look the spirits of healing squarely in the face, for they dwell in the darkness from which they come.

We can see fragments of this process already activated in newly urbanized areas of New Zealand where Maori villages have been overwhelmed by suburban scourge. In a single generation tribal youth form motorcycle gangs, chant rap, sell drugs, and kill. Yet they also cover themselves and one another, face and body, with intricate traditional tattoos; they mix Maori songs into their rap; and they invoke Maori warrior rituals and their own ancestors in their pointless combat. They are not yet all hollow automatons like the stricken generations of many indigenous peoples throughout this planet, rootless and addicted to alcohol, speed, and materialism. As seen in the movie *Once Were Warriors* they are a spiritual fire trapped in a wasteland, burning and condensed at their core, ready to erupt in a pure *toiora* that will consume, destroy, and redeem the world around them. Even though they don't know how to use it, they hold the medicine bundle in their collective agon. They are the original purveyors of spirit and voodoo and the motility of bone.

It is the original tribal fervor and essence at a Gaian level—that direct line to Palaeolithic symbols of power and samurai training—that must arise in thousands of different contexts in every region of the Earth. It cannot be tribal warfare this time or ethnic cleansing. It must join to the deeper ritual at the core where all totems meet and release this planet's great and encumbered heart. The waves of compassion, the flow of *wairua* from there, will sweep over seas and jungles like an electromagnetic *prana* field. For now it is too soon and the sources too corrupted, but it still represents our best possibility.

Gangs and ragtag militias have potentially the same radical power warrior societies did in indigenous cultures. Practicing how to kill, facing their own death regularly from childhood, some gang members

know archetypally how to heal many diseases and states of madness medical professionals do not even begin to address. These members do not even realize that they have cultivated the prerequisites, if not the techniques, of charismatic healing. And that is their pure talent, without considering subsequent retraining in *Chi Gung Tui Na,* barefoot-doctoring, cranial osteopathy, etc. This is not to deny that other members are trenchantly addicted to violence, but I believe that these are as much the minority in the 'hood as they are in tribes and villages at large.

Maybe the various sports leagues (Major League Baseball, the National Basketball Association, and the National Football League) could donate a portion of the excess profits the players and owners are currently (1994) fighting each other for. They could settle their labor difficulties by contributing all disputed sums to programs training inner-city youth in various modes of healing. Thus, revenue arising from selective media glorification of certain athletic skills could go into developing other "athletic" skills society more desperately needs (and among just the people most needy). Charisma would spread from victories in games and championships to charismatic acts of life and death in gangs become healing guilds. And everyone would be a potential "Big League" participant, not only the stars. No doubt the rock industry and Hollywood could do likewise. All of these "entertainment" businesses that benefit from making *some people* into ikons could remedy this imbalance by using a portion of their profit to provide roles for *other people.* There would still be so much money left for all parties that few could spend it wisely and productively in their lifetimes.

We can imagine parallel programs for "criminals" already in jails and homeless people. After all, not everyone requires a formulaic medicine. Some people merely need jobs. Many even violent criminals are potential healers gone totally into the shadow, so deeply that they identify with it and do not even imagine a way out. At that level the shadow requires a complete puppet show, like a dance of zombies, on its behalf. This is what we oversee in growing epidemic numbers. But it is only the trance level of a profound energetic shift. Most of these people are not awake, so they don't have the slightest idea how close what they are carrying out, in decadence or predation, is to healing and restoration.

Viewed from an entirely different perspective, the drug addictions that lie at the source of so much urban misery and crime have their basis partially in the fact that people are so sick they assume they need some kind of medication, and the only drugs (or vision quests) being offered (by many legitimate pharmacies as well as street sellers) are ones making them sicker and more catatonic.

Many homeless people, by the very challenge of living on streets and in alleys, are on vision quests and have developed serious credentials from that. Others are just plain sick and require treatment more from a constitutional medicine center or an osteopathic center than from a psychotropically oriented counselor. But none of this potential for healing (either way) is cultivated. It is all wasted to the same degree and in the same way that raw materials are squandered in factories producing junk and farmlands are washed away in pesticide-based, monocrop agriculture.

We don't have the slightest idea either how many criminals, homeless people, gang members, or simply chronically sick individuals and sufferers of anxiety and depression would regenerate and become productive if they were given homeopathic medicines, Chinese herbs, cranial treatments, Feldenkrais lessons, Reiki, or taught Zen meditation or rebirthing.

The potential role of holistic and energy medicines in transforming the hygiene of civilization is virtually one hundred percent unexplored. Instead, political solutions and health plans are offered as tip-of-the-iceberg palliatives, more prisons are constructed, and stiffer sentences are handed down with blind righteousness (or the truly violent are set loose, in the sloppiness of bureaucratic arrogance, to kill again). It is almost as though, at the deepest level, we prefer retribution to rehabilitation. But it is ourselves we are punishing as deeply as those who bear the actual wounds.

Kumar Frantzis describes being invited through a priest by the pris-

oners at the New Mexico State Penitentiary in Albuquerque to teach them *t'ai chi* and *Chi Gung.* This was the site of one of the worst prison riots in United States history. Frantzis not only was well received but had dramatic success in improving both the health and the mood of inmates. "The prison is an extremely stressful environment," said Frantzis; "it's an incredibly violent place. Most of the people who have been in prison a very long time are sick people. I mean they are physically ill in every way that you could possibly imagine. And if you remember the story of Androcles and the lion, when the thorn was taken out of the lion's paw, the lion stopped eating people at random."

One man with extremely high blood pressure had been on medication for eleven years. When interviewed by a television reporter from KNME, he reported not only that his blood pressure was considerably reduced by *Chi Gung* but that he was about to have his medication reduced in half. "Everybody is much happier," he added, "much friendlier, jokes more. No one has threatened to kill anybody in six or seven months. So, that's pretty good. I just wish I had found this when I was like eighteen or twenty. I believe it would have made a difference between me going to prison or not."[2]

Realistically speaking, it would take a great optimist now to believe that we stood a better chance of healing ourselves than of ending up with a planet-wide Bosnia or a catastrophic environmental episode. However, men and women have no choice but to work toward solutions that have dignity, humanity, and compassion for other sentient beings. Anything less not only furthers and deepens the pathology but deepens the connection of that person in this lifetime to the pathology, a deepening which tends to vitiate any small rewards and pleasures gained in the process. Our lives themselves are statements of either the impossible or the very consciousness of the universe itself. Either way, true gestures we make will not be squandered. We have to understand that. Even if the Sun erupts in a supernova or a pole shift sheers the planet with thousand-mile-per-hour winds, nothing is wasted.

As Vallee put it, "... I would be forever ashamed of the human race if we simply ignored 'their' presence."

TO EFFECT ANYTHING resembling the restructuring of medicine suggested above would require a massive shifting of resources from not only military and industrial uses but the corporate superstructure in all the financial giants—the United States, Japan, and Germany—and the rest of the Common Market of Europe, successful Asia, and Brazil. It would require committed participation by Russia, Uzbekistan, China, the Balkans, Africa, Mitsubishi, Paramount, Kaiser, Wal-Mart, Georgia Pacific, the International Money Fund, a variety of nongovernmental organizations, militias, the National Institutes of Health and their equivalents in all nations, powerful scientists upholding a mechanical world-view as liturgy, megabucks rock stars and athletes, the Papal establishment, the mullas of Iran, Norwegian fishermen, the various mafias, the Swiss banks, and innumerable other governments, companies, individuals, and indigenous and Third World peoples. That is, it would require everyone, but first those with the most power and investment in the existing order. It would also require at least as much attention to the planet's oceans, forests, soil, and atmosphere, not in a righteous, ideological fashion, but as part of a general enthusiasm for a larger vision quest and opening of the heart.

It can't just be a bureaucratic reorganization or a righteously liberal proclamation of a requirement of goodness. That has never worked, and it tends to bring out not only the skinheads and white warriors but the skinhead and fascist elements in everyone. If it can't be raunchy, sassy, and blasphemous, and as multi-layered and many-mooded as humanity is, it won't work. It clearly won't work as any sort of religious fundamentalism or piety. It also won't work from the standpoint of one ethnic superiority or another. We are all equally the bad guys in this. We are all jews and niggers and nazis and honkies and hutus and japs in the way we treat the planet and one another. We are all likewise the only aryan and zulu warriors left that can be counted on to rescue us.

Of course, none of this will come easily. Many people will choose to go down fighting for the status quo, even as they are already. However, a commitment in the direction of hygiene will make a big difference just by its intention. After all, the dominant current commitment in the direction of planetary destruction, individualistic greed, and gross consumptionism is hardly a major conviction or uniform enthusiasm. It is a slight leaning in a particular direction which, because of the nature of the direction and the encouragement of xenophobic and self-aggrandizing politicians, resembles an intense allegiance, an avalanche. It is maybe an imbalance of 55 percent/45 percent, reinforced by economic imperatives and mass media and maintained mostly in fear. People are truly hypnotized, walking around in low-grade trances like the hum of fluorescent lighting. They think of their trances as mellow living and high times. They think they are awake and conscious and choosing the good life. A gentle push in another direction may give time for a deeper change to flower over generations. Each of us might contribute .00001 percent to that push.

But it won't begin as long as people are fooled into believing that technology and gerrymandering health plans are going to do it for them, or that it's anybody's responsibility except their own to get well.

THE MONEY NEEDED to pay for just my proposed transformation would be astronomical, but every day on this planet astronomical money pays for something; vast resources go somewhere. Trillions of gallons of sunlight and orgone and *chi* pass daily unused into interstellar space. Reiki and shamanic gestures flirt idly in the marketplace and evaporate into thin air. Human and psychic energy is trapped in plastics factories, sweatshops, stock exchanges, consumption, envy, greed, and various forms of addiction and prostitution. There is no lack of energy. It is all either stifled or in the wrong places.

It would not cause economic collapse to find ways to direct a little bit of money in other directions. Admittedly, by the measures stock markets use, any little bit is a painful little bit; 1 percent alone would be gargantuan, but enough to let the true depth at the heart of humanity have hope of expressing itself. Initially it will mean new activities, the beginning of hope, and the sense that we are not God's worst fuck-ups in the universe. It will mean doing activities which make sense in terms of a possible future for our species. Even one such sustained activity could turn around a paradigm in a few generations.

Later it will mean facing the truth instead of killing one another and everything else that breathes in hopes of numbing the heartbeat. It will mean responding to the sight of those on the streets and in jails instead of engaging in a habitual mechanism of blocking out. It will also mean that those who have been most committed to punishment, retribution, and palliation will have to weep and suffer the pain of awakening. But once they do, they will also experience how vast this life actually is and how long an eternity we face. They will receive a gift far greater than any concession they make.

When all the other systems fall into their appropriate perspective, allopathy will be able to join "planet medicine" as a necessary partner. The great surgeons with their elite equipment, the laboratory pharmacists and brilliant diagnostic anatomists can take their rightful place at the table of medicine, and all other practitioners, from shamans to homeopaths to Ayurvedic masters and breath-workers, will send them those patients who need their craft. Right now the technicians are being asked to do everything, and it is just plain impossible. The heart and spirit and energy fields and karma of every human being are vast, and disease is their foil and dervish, their playmate. We will finally need the doctors of anatomy for their scrupulous attention to what-is, which is the most powerful manifestation of this deed of incarnation.

* * *

"PLANET MEDICINE" is finally more than a metaphor or even an evolving set of paradigms. It is a statement of the diversity of systems of healing among sentient beings and the continuous generation of those systems from within the depths of unconsciousness. It is a transhistorical link between an elemental dance and the chariots of civilization.

Medicine represents each unique cultural, aesthetic, and intuitive response to the crisis of being alive in a magical (if fragile) situation on a planet of wonders. It is an attempt to reveal texture, express compassion and hope, and respond with dignity to the engines of destruction that epitomize the vast, anonymous nature of which we are clearly part. It is one of the oldest human guilds, with unbroken roots back into the Ice Age. The most educated surgeon carries in himself the aura, however faint, of a half-conscious beast brandishing the horns of another beast and conducting raw spiritual power.

Healing is one of the first bonds of maternity and sorority, hence of society. In every primary and subsequent form it addresses the blanks that separate man and woman from each other and from themselves. It nurtures longing bodies and guides lost spirits home, but it also unleashes deadly ghouls and smashes transient artifacts (including creatures of energy and flesh). It is first and foremost disease itself in another form. From the beginning, healing was hunting, killing, hexing, and making poisons. It was never as simple as mere fixing and tonifying. It cannot now be as facile and friendly as a *chi* workshop or a "quantum" clinic.

The present enthusiasm for alternative and holistic systems is a response to a primordial flood emerging from uncharted depths and changing the Earth and its life forms utterly. In the minds of those species who are awake, there is a need to know and name the nameless. Thus our new healing imperative is a struggle to shape a metaphor or paradigm out of forces that are expressing themselves simultaneously in cataclysms, wars, and diseases and in the remediations of these conditions. We call it "medicine" when we reify only the ideological and therapeutic aspect of an amorphous thing.

These are powerful times. It is no surprise that they initiate remarkable healers.

"Planet medicine" is never the intention to cure or save the Earth. It is not a stagnant lineage of successively more skillful or radical forms of healing. It is not a doctor in a hospital. It is not a therapist chanting symbols. It a not faith healer turning energy into matter. It is solely the impulse to transform what is stagnant.

The Earth doctor is a wild, rabid animal. She is change itself wearing the temporary, eroding mask of a wise Bear. She carries within herself the most devastating forces of destruction as surely as the most miraculous agencies of restoration. This is what makes her a true shaman and warrior.

IF THIS BOOK is timely, it is not because medicine has become such a hotly contested topic. It is because we are beginning to see where we fall on a planetary scale of healers and where the current epoch comes in world history. The text ends, rightly, at the moment when medicine returns us to our own inevitability.

Notes

1. Jacques Vallee, *Forbidden Science* (Berkeley, California: North Atlantic Books, 1992), p. 16.

2. Bruce Kumar Frantzis, personal communication and archival videotape, Fairfax, California, 1994.

RESOURCE GUIDE

THE GOAL OF this guide is to share with interested readers my sources for some of the practices that lie behind *Planet Medicine.* It is limited to the modalities and practitioners discussed in the text. It is also limited to institutions and people with whom I have had direct experience (though in a few cases I have listed people whose work I know reliably secondhand).

A complete resource guide would be an enormous undertaking of its own, well beyond the scope of this book. To be useful to the majority of readers, it would have to include major urban areas and rural communities in at least the English-speaking world. It would also have to be researched and corrected on a regular basis. Too many directories are simply copied from one source to another and are untested, out of date, or both.

Most readers will not be able to use this guide practically, but they may be able to find equivalent local options by reading practitioner directories (usually free at alternative bookstores and markets), querying natural-foods markets and health-food stores, checking community bulletin boards, asking friends for referrals, and contacting national organizations (in the case of some modalites) for listings in their area.

I will try to update this section from edition to edition. However, individual practitioners may move, may also elect not to take on new clients, and may be too busy to respond.

Acupuncture (See American College of Traditional Chinese Medicine, Chinese Medicine, Amini Peller, Paul Pitchford)

Aikido (See also Richard Heckler)

Aikido of Tamalpais
76 East Blythedale
Mill Valley, California 94941
415-383-9474
Richard Heckler, Wendy Palmer, and George Leonard teach here.

Alexander Technique

North American Society of Teachers of Alexander Technique
P. O. Box 517
Urbana, Illinois 61801
800-473-0620

Jerry Sontag
347 Dolores Street, Suite 212
San Francisco, California 94110
415-861-6830

American College of Traditional Chinese Medicine

455 Arkansas Street
San Francisco, California 94107
415-282-7600
415-282-9603 (clinic)
The American College of Traditional Chinese Medicine serves as a training institution for people wanting to practice acupuncture and moxibustion and to prepare and prescribe Chinese herbs. It also emphasizes methods of diagnosis and treatment, the study of classical texts, and Chinese approaches to nutrition and massage. For more advanced students, work in the clinic provides an opportunity to develop skills in differential diagnosis and observing the progressive manifestations of disease and cure. The four-year graduate degree providing a Master of Science in Traditional Chinese Medicine may be completed in three

years. A number of students from a variety of professions (mostly but not exclusively health-related) attend this and equivalent schools in order to make mid-life career changes.

Aromatherapy

John Steele
Lifetree Aromatix
3949 Longridge Avenue
Sherman Oaks, California 91423
818-986-0594

Jeanne Rose
219 Carl Street
San Francisco, California 94117
415-564-6785

Ayurveda (see Lotus Press)

Ba Gua (See Bruce Kumar Frantzis, Peter Ralston)

Bates Method

Thomas R. Quackenbush
Natural Vision Center of San Francisco
P. O. Box 16403
San Francisco, California 94116-0403
415-665-2010

Body-Mind Centering (Bonnie Bainbridge Cohen)

The School for Body-Mind Centering
189 Pondview Drive
Amherst, Massachusetts 01002-3230
413-256-8615

Breema

The Institute for Health Improvement
6076 Claremont Avenue
Oakland, California 94618
510-428-0937
IHI is the source of information for courses and intensives taught by Manocher Movlai and others, free-treatment evenings, and names of practitioners.

Additional Practitioners:

Jon Schreiber
6201 Florio Street
Oakland, California 94618
510-428-1234

Kathy Vahsen
c/o Institute for Health Improvement
or 510-527-5213

Cybèle Tomlinson
3367 Dwight Way
Berkeley, California 94704
510-848-3852

California Institute of Integral Studies Somatics Program

This is a M.A. program with a degree either in Somatics itself or in Psychology with a specialization in Body-Oriented Family Therapy. The course of study includes an integration of Western and non-Western approaches to the human body in relation to psychology, the healing arts, and spiritual practice. It is derived from methods created at the turn of the century by such people as Sigmund Freud, Elsa Gindler, F. Matthias Alexander, Wilhelm Reich, and Moshe Feldenkrais, who challenged the splitting of body, mind, and spirit into the rigid categories that have dominated Western theory and practice. Among contemporary modal-

ities studied in this program are Authentic Movement, Focusing, The Lomi School, Continuum, Body-Mind Centering, Process-Oriented Psychology, Aston Patterning, Gestalt Therapy, Sensory Awareness, Hakomi, Trager, Rolfing, and the various branches of Reichian psychotherapy. This program does not train students in the practice of these methods but provides a groundwork in the theories, strategies, and transformational attitudes that are required in any somatics training. Don Hanlon Johnson is the Program Director, and Ian Grand is one of the core faculty. John Conger is an adjunct faculty member, and Ilse Middendorf, Charlotte Selver, Robert Hall, Bonnie Bainbridge Cohen, and Emilie Conrad-Da'oud give regular presentations and training classes.

Randy Cherner

Deer Run House
15 Deer Run
Corte Madera, California 94925
415-924-2685
Michael Wagner, a practitioner trained by Randy Cherner, is also available at the same address and phone number.

Chi Gung (See Bruce Kumar Frantzis)

Chinese Medicine

Health Concerns

8001 Capwell Drive
Oakland, California 94621
510-639-0280
Contact Health Concerns for referral to a licensed practitioner using herbs, or herbal training for health practitioners and lay persons.

See also American College of Traditional Chinese Medicine for training programs and clinic and Paul Pitchford for diet and phone consultation.

Ching-Chun Ou
3901 Grand Avenue
Oakland, California 94610
510-547-6798

Chiropractic

Tom Hendrickson
406 Berkeley Park Boulevard
Kensington, California 94706
510-524-8256

Don Cohen
556 Ocean Avenue
Santa Cruz, California 95062
408-425-1422

Linda Mayo
1301 Solano Avenue
Albany, California 94706
510-524-5800

Bonnie Bainbridge Cohen (see Body-Mind Centering)

Craniosacral Therapy

Contact The Upledger Institute (see The Upledger Institute) for a list of practitioners. Craniosacral Therapy is also part of the work of Amini Peller, Marilyn Radojcich (Visceral Manipulation), and Randy Cherner, listed in this section.

Additional Practitioners:

Kathryn Waddell
1050 East South Temple
Salt Lake City, Utah 84102-1502
801-350-4111

Suzanne Scurlock-Durana
2230 Wakerobin Lane
Reston, Virgina 22091-4106

Judith Bradley
1496 Beddis Road
Salt Spring Island, British Columbia
V8K 2E3 Canada

Downing Technique (Colored Light Stimulus)

Ellen Eatough
Light Impact
205 Camino Alto, Suite 155
Mill Valley, California 94941
415-388-6766

Connie Martin
1317 Crestview Drive
San Carlos, California 94070
415-637-1292

Dream Work

Charles Poncé
586 19th Avenue
San Francisco, California 94121
415-668-5645

Eastland Press

1260 Activity Drive, Suite A
Vista, California 92083
800-453-3278
The best source for books on osteopathy and visceral manipulation, also titles on acupuncture, craniosacral therapy, and chiropractic.

Feldenkrais Method

Feldenkrais Resources Center
830 Bancroft Way
Berkeley, California 94710
510-540-7600
Feldenkrais Resources provides tools, literature, and lists of practitioners for the Feldenkrais Method.

Elizabeth Beringer
510-527-0302
Elizabeth Beringer may also be contacted directly through Feldenkrais Resources.

Food (See also Paul Pitchford at Heartwood Institute)

Microlight Nutritional Products
124 Rhodesia Beach Road
Bay Center, Washington 98527
800-338-2821
Source for high-quality blue-green algae and bee pollen.

HealthComm, Inc.
5800 Soundview Drive
Gig Harbor, Washington 98335
800-648-5883
HealthComm, Inc., is the source of a nutritional product (UltraClear Sustain) for digestive problems and immune difficulties based on changes in the thin lining that separates the intestinal tract from the rest of the body. This product requires physician supervision for purchase and use.

Bruce Kumar Frantzis

P. O. Box 99
Fairfax, California 94978-0099
415-454-5243

Frantzis teaches *Chi Gung* in a beginners' program (Dragon and Tiger *Chi Gung)* and an intermediate program (Spine *Chi Gung*—Bend the Bow). He also teaches Wu and Yang style *T'ai Chi Ch'uan, Ba Gua* Form Work and Self-Defense, *Hsing-I Ch'uan,* and Eight Drunken Immortals (a martial art composed of extremely flexible reeling, lurching, drunken movements and a playful fighting style). Although most of his training is done in Northern California, he runs workshops worldwide, including regular trips to New York City, Boston, Martha's Vineyard, and Munich.

Bob Frissell (Rebirthing)

300 Hazel Avenue
Mill Valley, California 94941
415-383-3828
Contact Bob Frissell for Rebirthing and for Flower of Life Workshops.

Heartwood Institute

220 Harmony Lane
Garberville, California 95542
707-923-2021
Located in rustic, isolated residential facilities 190 miles north of San Francisco, Heartwood Institute teaches courses in Polarity Therapy (Bruce Burger); alchemical hypnotherapy; general massage and bodywork (including Swedish/Esalen massage, deep-tissue massage, Trager Psychophysical Integration and Mentastics, lymphatic and visceral massage, Zero Balancing, and Zen *shiatsu*/acupressure); and food, Chinese herbs, acupuncture, and *T'ai Chi Ch'uan* (Paul Pitchford). Heartwood also offers periodic classes on astrology, male and female empowerment, American-Indian-taught shamanic practices, and clearing the trauma of sexual abuse.

The training and certifications provided by Heartwood meet licensing requirements in most parts of the United States. A 750-hour massage course has been approved by the American Massage Therapy

Association. For Transformational Therapist certification, there is an 870-hour course (combining body therapy, hypnotherapy, breathwork, and dream-body modalities with communication skills, stress management, and the development of intuition to stimulate deep inner change). Heartwood also offers an Addictions Therapist career program.

Richard Strozzi Heckler

4101 Middle Two Rock Road
Petaluma, California 94952
707-778-6505
Heckler works as a Lomi therapist, a martial arts teacher, an aikidoist, a consultant to the military and to corporations, and a psychotherapist.

Homeopathy

For information about homeopathic practitioners and materials for self-treatment, contact:

Homeopathic Educational Services
2036 Blake Street
Berkeley, California 94704
510-649-0294

or

National Center for Homeopathy
Suite 306
801 North Fairfax Street
Alexandria, Virginia 22314
703-548-7790

Additional Practitioners:

Ben Hole, M.D.
West 508 6th Avenue, Suite 704
Spokane, Washington 99204
509-455-6810

Randall Neustaedter
Classical Medicine Center
360 Bryant Street
Palo Alto, California 94301
415-324-8420

Hsing-I Ch'uan (See also Peter Ralston, Ron Sieh, and Bruce Kumar Frantzis)

David Tircuit
Evolving Body/Mind Kung Fu Academy
Epworth United Methodist Church
Fellowship Hall
1953 Hopkins Street
Berkeley, California 94704
510-549-9432
Tircuit and his associates offer *Hsing-I Ch'uan* (as taught by Master Zhou Rong Quintsai) and Northern Shaolin Kung Fu.

Lomi School

343 College Avenue
Santa Rosa, California 95401
707-579-0465
The Lomi Professional Training offers an intensive ten-day series of workshops for practicing therapists who want to incorporate a somatic approach in their work, use touch and hands-on work as a legitimate and ethical way of expanding the therapeutic relationship and uncovering hidden content, and deepen their understanding of the spiritual essence of our nature. The training emphasizes the role of body language, nonverbal cues, and conscious movement in the psychotherapeutic process and the emergence of transference/countertransference issues in the context of bodily sensation and psychoenergetic processes. In general, the Lomi approach combines psychotherapeutic and med-

itative techniques with Reichian and Polarity somatic modalities.

Lomi-Vipassana Meditation Retreats bring together Lomi practitioners and Buddhist meditation teachers, and combine aspects of both traditions.

Lotus Press

P. O. Box 325
Twin Lakes, Wisconsin 53181
414-889-8561
Source for books on Ayurvedic medicine.

The Middendorf Breath Institute

Jürg Roffler
198 Mississippi
San Francisco, California 94107
415-255-2174

More University

1507 Purson Lane
Lafayette, California 94549
510-930-9244

Amini Peller

2150 White Oak Way
San Carlos, California 94070
415-595-5660
Energy and Chakra Work, Craniosacral Work, Somatoemotional Release, Zero Balancing, Breema, Spiritual Counseling. Amini Peller also works with Wazir Peller, acupuncturist, Zero Balancer, craniosacral therapist, lymphatic masseuse, and Chinese herbalist.
415-592-9851

Paul Pitchford

Heartwood Institute
220 Harmony Lane
Garberville, California 95542
707-923-9290
Pitchford is available for phone consultations.

Polarity Therapy (see Bruce Burger at Heartwood Institute)

Prison Integrated Health Program

Wendy Palmer
809 Vendola Drive
San Rafael, California 94903
415-472-1619
The Prison Integrated Health Program is a sponsored project of the San Francisco Women's Centers. The program needs qualified volunteers and donations. The *Gateways Newsletter* is available.

Peter Ralston

The Cheng Hsin School of Internal Martial Arts and Ontology
6601 Telegraph Avenue
Oakland, California 94609
415-658-0802
After December 1, 1995:
P. O. Box 11483
Hilo, Hawaii 96721
As well as his own form and workshops in ontology, Ralston teaches *Hsing-I Ch'uan, T'ai Chi Ch'uan,* and *Ba Gua,* sword forms, boxing, and general self-defense.

Rebirthing (see Bob Frissell)

Rolfing

International Rolf Institute
P. O. Box 1868
Boulder, Colorado 80306
800-530-8875
The International Rolf Institute will provide a list of accredited practitioners in your area.

Michael Salveson
Structural Integration
1430 Leroy Avenue
Berkeley, California 94708
510-548-8270

Jeffrey Maitland
8300 North Hayden Road, Suite 104
Scottsdale, Arizona 85258
800-934-7189

Brant Secunda (see Vision Quest)

Sexuality (Man-Woman Relations) (See More University)

Ron Sieh (Internal Martial Arts)

7501 Potrero Avenue
El Cerrito, California 94530
510-215-9627
If unable to contact, phone for new address: 612-888-8259
Sieh is particularly skilled teaching children and young adults. He has been a "kung fu" babysitter and also works with ages from kindergarten through high school. He serves as a consultant to schools interested in replacing more competitive gym programs with classes in consciousness and martial arts.

T'ai Chi Ch'uan (See Peter Ralston, Ron Sieh, Paul Pitchford, and Bruce Kumar Frantzis)

The Upledger Institute

11211 Prosperity Farms Road
Palm Beach Gardens, Florida 33410-3487
Phone: 407-622-4334
For Course Information: 800-233-5880 (ext. 65)
The Upledger Institute conducts courses in craniosacral therapy, somatoemotional release, visceral manipulation, Aston Patterning, Zero Balancing, Strain/Counterstrain, muscle energy, spinal release, Process Acupressure, and a number of other modalities. These courses are held over weekends in a large number of cities in North America and abroad, including New York, Baltimore, Boulder, Boston, Brunswick (Maine), Santa Cruz, Dallas, Madison (Wisconsin), Lebanon (Ohio), Seattle, Toronto, San Diego, Tucson, Hartford, Minneapolis, Albuquerque, Atlanta, Philadelphia, San Francisco, Edmonton, Lexington (Kentucky), Detroit, Fort Lee (New Jersey), Missoula, Ottawa, Fort Lauderdale, Vancouver, Washington (D.C.), Cincinnati, Salt Lake, Gainesville, Saskatoon, Rochester, Reno, Little Rock, Fredericton (New Brunswick), Calgary, Anchorage, Maui, Amsterdam, Munich, etc. Please contact them for sites and dates. They do have requirements for enrollment, but one does not have to be an advanced practitioner or currently in practice.

Clinic: 407-622-4706 (for local treatments in Palm Beach Gardens)

Upledger Institute Europe

Postbus 86
6880 AB Velp
The Netherlands

Visceral Manipulation (See also Upledger Institute)

Marilyn Radojcich
4546 El Camino Real, Suite A 15
Los Altos, California 94022
415-327-6536

Vision Quest

Brant Secunda
Dance of the Deer Foundation
Center for Shamanic Studies
P. O. Box 699
Soquel, California 95073
408-475-9560

Zero Balancing (See Upledger Institute)

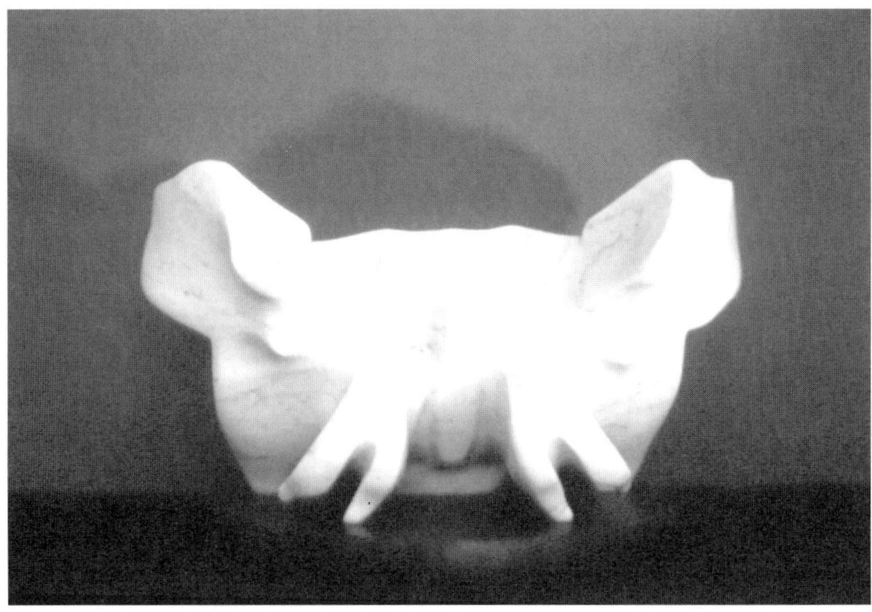

BIBLIOGRAPHY

The Academy of Traditional Chinese Medicine. *An Outline of Chinese Acupuncture.* Peking: Foreign Languages Press, 1975.

Ackerknecht, Erwin H. "Problems of Primitive Medicine," *Bulletin of the History of Medicine,* Volume XI, 1942.

Alexander, Gerda. *Eutony: The Holistic Discovery of the Total Person.* Great Neck, New York: Felix Morrow, 1985.

Alon, Ruthy. *Mindful Spontaneity: Lessons in the Feldenkrais Method.* Berkeley, California: North Atlantic Books, 1995.

Amaringo, Pablo, and Luis Eduardo Luna. *Ayahuasca Visions: The Religious Iconography of a Peruvian Shaman.* Berkeley, California: North Atlantic Books, 1991.

Aston, Judith. "Three Perceptions and One Compulsion," in *Bone, Breath, and Gesture: Practices of Embodiment.* Don Hanlon Johnson, ed. Berkeley, California: North Atlantic Books, 1995.

Bach, Edward. *Heal Thyself.* London: C. W. Daniel, 1931.

Baginski, Bodo J., and Shalila Sharamon. *Reiki: Universal Life Energy: A Holistic Method of Treatment for the Professional Practice/Absentee Healing and Self-Treatment of Mind, Body, and Soul.* Mendocino, California: Life Rhythm, 1988.

Baker, Courtney, Robert Dew, Michael Ganz, and Louisa Lance. "Wound Healing in Mice (Part I)," in *Annual of the Institute of Orgonomic Science,* Vol. 1, No. 1, September 1984.

Baker, Wyrth P., Allen C. Neiswander, and W. W. Young. *Introduction to Homeotherapeutics.* Washington, DC: American Institute of Homeopathy, 1974.

Barfield, Owen. *Unancestral Voice.* Middleton, Conneticut: Wesleyan University Press, 1965.

Barral, Jean-Pierre, and Pierre Mercier. *Visceral Manipulation.* Seattle, Washington: Eastland Press, 1988.

Barrett, S. A. *Pomo Bear Doctors,* University of California Publications in American Archaeology and Ethnology, Vol. 12, No. 11, July 11, 1917. Berkeley, California: University of California Press, 1917.

Bateson, Gregory. "Restructuring the Ecology of a Great City," *Io* #14, *Earth Geography Booklet No. 3, Imago Mundi,* Cape Elizabeth, Maine, 1972.

Bauman, Edward, Armand Ian Brint, Lorin Piper, and Pamela Amelia Wright, eds. *The Holistic Health Handbook.* Berkeley, California: And/Or Press, 1978.

Bennett, J. G. *Gurdjieff: Making a New World.* New York: Harper/Colophon, 1973.

Binik, Alexander. "The Polarity System," in *The Holistic Health Handbook.* Bauman, et al., eds. Berkeley, California: And/Or Press, 1978.

Boas, Franz. *The Religion of the Kwakiutl Indians, Part II: Translations.* New York: Columbia University Press, 1930.

Böhm, Karl. *The Life of Some Island People of New Guinea: A Missionary's Observations of the Volcanic Islands of Manam, Boesa, Biem, and Ubrub.* Berlin: Dietrich Reimer Verlag, 1983.

Bookchin, Murray. *The Ecology of Freedom: The Emergence and Dissolution of Hierarchy.* Palo Alto, California: Cheshire Books, 1982.

Bordeu, Théophile. *Oeuvres.* Paris: Caille & Ravier, 1818.

Brennan, Richard. *The Alexander Technique Workbook.* Rockport, Massachusetts: Element Books, Ltd., 1992.

Britton, Nathanial, Lord, and Hon. Addison Brown. *An Illustrated Flora of the Northern United States, Canada, and the British Possesions.* New York: Charles Scribner's Sons, 1913.

Buckley, Mary. "Feng Shui: The Art of Grace in Place," in *New Dimensions Journal,* Spring 1993.

Burger, Bruce. *Esoteric Anatomy.* Unpublished manuscript at the time

of publication. Berkeley, California: North Atlantic Books, 1996.

Calderón, Eduardo, Richard Cowan, Douglas Sharon, and F. Kaye Sharon. *Eduardo el Curandero: The Words of a Peruvian Healer.* Berkeley, California, North Atlantic Books, 1982.

Cannon, Walter B. "'Voodoo' Death," in *American Anthropologist,* XLIV, 1942.

Carroll, Jon. "The Odd Saga of Marlo Morgan," *San Francisco Chronicle,* September 7, 1994, p. E8 and September 8, 1994, p. E10.

Castaneda, Carlos. *The Teachings of Don Juan: A Yaqui Way of Knowledge.* Berkeley, California: University of California Press, 1969.

——. *A Separate Reality.* New York: Simon & Schuster, 1971.

——. *Journey to Ixtlan.* New York: Simon & Schuster, 1972.

——. *Tales of Power.* New York: Simon & Schuster, 1974.

Caufield, Charles R., with Billi Goldberg. *The Anarchist AIDS Medical Formulary: A Guide to Guerrilla Immunology.* Berkeley, California: North Atlantic Books, 1994.

Celsus, Aulus Cornelius. *De Medicina.* Three Volumes. Translated by W. G. Spencer. Cambridge, Massachusetts: Loeb Classical Library, Harvard University Press.

Chancellor, Philip M. *Handbook of the Bach Flower Remedies.* London: C. W. Daniel Co., 1971.

Chopra, Deepak. *Quantum Healing: Exploring the Frontiers of Mind/Body Medicine.* New York: Bantam Books, 1989.

Codere, Helen. *Fighting with Property: A Study of Kwakiutl Potlatching and Warfare, 1792–1930.* Monographs of the American Ethnological Society, Volume XVIII. New York: J. J. Augustin, 1950. Reprinted in *Indians of the Northwest Coast.* Tom McFeat, ed. Seattle, Washington: University of Washington Press, 1966.

Cohen, Bonnie Bainbridge. "Research in the Field of Somatics," California Institute of Integral Studies, San Francisco, November 1992.

——. *Sensing, Feeling, and Action: The Experiental Anatomy of Body-Mind Centering.* Northampton, Massachusetts: Contact Editions, 1993.

Cohen, Don. *An Introduction to Craniosacral Therapy.* Berkeley, California: North Atlantic Books, 1995.

Coles, William. "Adam in Eden, or The Paradise of Plants," republished in *Io #5, Doctrine of Signatures,* Ann Arbor, Michigan, 1968.

Collin, Rodney. *The Theory of Celestial Influence.* London: Stuart & Watkins, Ltd., 1954.

Conger, John P. *The Body in Recovery: Somatic Psychotherapy and the Self.* Berkeley, California: Frog, Ltd., 1994.

——. *Jung & Reich: The Body as Shadow.* Berkeley, California: North Atlantic Books, 1988.

Cook, James. *The Journals of James Cook: The Voyage 1776–1780.* London: Hakluyt Society, Vol. I, No. 36, extra series.

Corbin, Henry. *Creative Imagination in the Sufism of Ibn 'Arabi.* Translated from the French by Ralph Manheim. Princeton, New Jersey: Bollingen Foundation, Princeton University Press, 1969.

Coulter, Harris Livermore. *Divided Legacy, A History of the Schism in Medical Thought, Vol. I: The Patterns Emerge: Hippocrates to Paracelsus.* Washington, DC: Weehawken Book Company, 1975.

——. *Divided Legacy, Vol. II: The Origins of Modern Western Medicine: J. B. Van Helmont to Claude Bernard.* Berkeley, California: North Atlantic Books, 1977.

——. *Divided Legacy, Vol. III: The Conflict Between Homeopathy and the American Medical Association: Science and Ethics in American Medicine 1800–1914.* Berkeley, California: North Atlantic Books, 1982.

——. *Divided Legacy, Vol. IV: Twentieth Century Medicine, The Bacteriological Era.* Berkeley, California: North Atlantic Books, 1994.

——. *Homeopathic Science and Modern Medicine: The Physics of Healing with Microdoses.* Berkeley, California: North Atlantic Books, 1981.

Cousins, Norman. "The Mysterious Placebo," in *Saturday Review,* October 1977.

Covarrubias, Miguel. *Island of Bali.* New York: Alfred Knopf, 1938.

Cowan, Richard, and Douglas Sharon. *Eduardo the Healer.* Oakland, California: Serious Business Company, 1978.

Crews, Frederick. "The Revenge of the Repressed, Part II," in *The New York Review of Books,* Vol. XLI, No. 20, December 1, 1994.

Croft, William, C. S. T. "Light Energy Practices (Yoga/Qi-gong/Aikido) and *Working with Light*—A Synergy," flyer, 1993.

Crowley, Aleister. *The Confessions of Aleister Crowley.* John Symonds and Kenneth Grant, eds. New York: Hill & Wang, 1969.

——. *Magick in Theory and Practice.* New York: Castle Books, n.d.

Das, Baba Hari, and Dharma Sara Satang. "Ayurveda: The Yoga of Health," in *The Holistic Health Handbook.* Bauman, et al., eds. Berkeley, California: And/Or Press, 1978.

de Berval, Réné. *Kingdom of Laos.* Saigon, Vietnam: France-Asie, 1956.

de Langre, Jacques. *Dō-In 2: The Ancient Art of Rejuvenation Through Self-Massage.* Magalia, California: Happiness Press, 1978.

DeMeo, James, Richard Blasband, and Robert Morris. "Breaking the 1986 Drought in the Eastern United States," in *The Journal of Orgonomy,* Vol. 21.

Derrida, Jacques. "Freud and the Scene of Writing." Translated from the French by Jeffery Mehlman. *Yale French Studies.* New Haven, Connecticut: Yale University Press, n.d.

——. *Of Grammatology.* Translated from the French by Gayatri Chakravorty Spivak. Baltimore, Maryland: Johns Hopkins University Press, 1976.

Dhalla, Maneckji N. *Zoroastrian Civilization.* Cambridge, England: Oxford University Press, 1922.

Diderot, Denis. *Encyclopedié ou Dictionnaire Raisoneé des Sciences des Arts et des Métiers.* Paris: Edition Garniere Frères, 1765.

Dodé Kalpa Zangpo, quoted by Sogyal Rinpoche in *Dzogchen and Padmasambhava.* Berkeley, California: Rigpa Fellowship of California, 1990.

Dorn, Edward. *Recollections of Gran Apachería.* Berkeley, California: Turtle Island, 1974.

Dorn, Edward, and Gordon Brotherstone, "The Aztec Priest's Reply," in *New World Journal,* Berkeley, California, Vol. I, Nos. 2/3, 1977.

Drury, Neville. *The Healing Power: A Handbook of Alternative Medicines and Natural Health.* London: Frederick Muller Ltd., 1981.

Duesberg, Peter. *Infectious AIDS: Stretching the Germ Theory Beyond Its Limits.* Berkeley, California: North Atlantic Books, 1995.

Eisenbud, Jule. Interview conducted by Richard Grossinger, January 8, 1972, originally published in *Io* #14, *Earth Geography Booklet* #3, *Imago Mundi.* Republished in *Ecology and Consciousness: Traditional Wisdom on the Environment.* Richard Grossinger, ed. Berkeley, California, 1978. Revised second edition, 1992.

——. *Paranormal Foreknowledge: Problems and Perplexities.* New York: Human Sciences Press, 1982.

Elkin, A. P. *Aboriginal Men of High Degree.* Sydney: Australasian Publishing, 1944.

Emmons, George Thornton. *The Tlingit Indians.* Seattle, Washington: University of Washington Press, 1991.

Enslin, Theodore. "Journal Note," in *The Alchemical Tradition in the Late Twentieth Century.* Richard Grossinger, ed. Berkeley, California: North Atlantic Books, 1979.

Espanca, Jutta. "The Effect of Orgone on Plant Life (Part 7)," in *Offshoots of Orgonomy,* No. 12, Spring 1986.

Faraday, Michael. *The Chemical History of a Candle: A course of lectures delivered before a juvenile audience at the Royal Institution.* New York: Viking Press, 1960.

Feldenkrais, Moshe. *The Case of Nora: Body Awareness as Healing Therapy.* 1977. Berkeley, California: Frog, Ltd., 1993.

——. *The Potent Self: A Guide to Spontaneity.* New York: Harper & Row, 1985.

Ferenczi, Sandor. *Thalassa: A Theory of Genitality.* Translated from the German by Henry Alden Bunker. New York: Norton, 1968.

Fields, Rick. *How the Swans Came to the Lake: A Narrative History of Buddhism in America.* Boulder, Colorado: Shambhala Publications, 1981.

Fiore, Edith. *The Unquiet Dead.* New York: Ballantine Books, 1988.

Flammonde, Paris. *The Mystic Healers.* New York: Stein & Day, 1974.

Foucault, Michel. *The Birth of the Clinic.* Translated from the French by A. M. Sheridan Smith. New York: Pantheon Books, 1973.

Fox, R. B. "The Pinatubo Negritos: Their Useful Plants and Material Culture," in *The Philippine Journal of Science,* Vol. 81, Nos. 3-4, 1953.

Frantzis, Bruce Kumar. *Opening the Energy Gates of Your Body.* Berkeley, California: North Atlantic Books, 1993.

——. *The Tao in Action: The Personal Practice of the I Ching and Taoism in Daily Life.* Unpublished manuscript at the time of publication. Berkeley, California: North Atlantic Books, 1996.

Freud, Sigmund. *An Outline of Psychoanalysis.* Translated from the German by James Strachey. New York: Norton, 1949.

——. *The Interpretation of Dreams.* Translated from the German by James Strachey. New York: Basic Books, 1955.

Frissell, Bob. *Nothing in This Book Is True, But It's Exactly How Things Are.* Berkeley, California: Frog, Ltd., 1994.

From Bindu to Ojas. San Cristobal, New Mexico: Lama Foundation, 1970.

Fulder, Stephen. *The Root of Being: Ginseng and the Pharmacology of Harmony.* London: Hutchison Publishing Group, 1980.

Fuller, John G. *Arigo: Surgeon of the Rusty Knife.* New York: Crowell, 1974; Pocket Books, 1975.

Gelfand, Michael. *Medicine and Custom in Africa.* Edinburgh: Livingstone, 1964.

Gillispie, Charles Coulston. "Lamarck and Darwin in the History of Science," in *Forerunners of Darwin, 1745–1859.* Bentley Glass, Owsei Temkin, and William L. Straus, Jr., eds. Baltimore: The Johns Hopkins University Press, 1959.

Ginzberg, Jeremy. "Pharmaco-Hell Calling," in *East Bay Express,* Berkeley, California, January 21, 1994.

Golden, Stephanie. "Body-Mind Centering," in *Yoga Journal,* Berkeley, California, September/October 1993.

Goodwin, Kathleen. "Alternative Medicine: A Note of Caution," in *City Miner,* Berkeley, California, Vol. 3, No. 3, 1978.

Grey, Alex. *Sacred Mirrors.* Rochester, Vermont: Inner Traditions, 1990.

Groddeck, Georg. *The Book of the It.* Translated from the German by V. M. E. Collins. New York: Funk & Wagnalls, 1950.

——. "Psychic Conditioning and the Psychoanalytic Treatment of Organic Disorders," in *The Meaning of Illness.* M. Masud R. Khan, ed. London: The Hogarth Press, 1977.

Grossinger, Richard. "Alchemy: Pre-Egyptian Legacy, Millennial Promise," in *The Alchemical Tradition in the Late Twentieth Century.* Richard Grossinger, ed. Berkeley, California: North Atlantic Books, 1979.

——. "Cross-Cultural and Historical Models of Energy in Healing," paper delivered at the conference *Conceptualizing Energy Medicine: An Emerging Model of Healing,* University Extension and School of Public Health, University of California, Berkeley, California, March 28, 1981.

——. "The Dream Work," in *Dreams are Wiser Than Men.* Richard A. Russo, ed. Berkeley, California: North Atlantic Books, 1987.

——. *Homeopathy: An Introduction for Skeptics and Beginners.* Berkeley, California: North Atlantic Books, 1993.

——, ed. *An Olson-Melville Sourcebook, Vol. I: North America. Vol. II: The Mediterranean.* Plainfield, Vermont: North Atlantic Books, 1976.

——, ed. *Ecology and Consciousness: Traditional Wisdom on the Environment.* Berkeley, California: North Atlantic Books, 1978. Revised second edition, 1992.

——, ed. *Io,* 1964–79. Amherst, Massachusetts; Ann Arbor, Michigan; Cape Elizabeth, Maine; Mount Desert, Maine; Oakland, California; Plainfield, Vermont; and Richmond, California.

Gurdjieff, G. I. *Views from the Real World: Early Talks.* New York: Dutton, 1975.

Haehl, Richard. *Samuel Hahnemann: His Life and Work,* Vol. I. London: Homeopathic Publishing Co., 1922.

Hahnemann, Samuel. *The Chronic Diseases, Their Peculiar Nature and Their Homeopathic Cure.* Translated by Louis H. Tale from the second enlarged German edition, 1835. Philadelphia: Boericke and Tafel, 1904.

——. *The Lesser Writings of Samuel Hahnemann.* Collected and translated by R. E. Dudgeon. New York: Radde, 1952.

——. *The Organon of Medicine,* Sixth Edition. Translated by William Boericke, M.D. Calcutta, India: Roysingh, 1962.

Handy, E. S. Craighill, Mary Kawena Pukui, and Katherine Livermore. *Outline of Hawaiian Physical Therapeutics.* Honolulu, Hawaii: Bernice P. Bishop Museum, Bulletin 126, 1934.

Harley, George Way. *Native African Medicine.* Cambridge, Massachusetts: Harvard University Press, 1941.

Harman, Robert. "Current Research with SAPA Bions," in *The Journal of Orgonomy,* Vol. 21.

Harner, Michael J. *The Jívaro.* Garden City, New Jersey: Doubleday/Natural History Press, 1972.

Harvey, Andrew. *Hidden Journey: A Spiritual Awakening.* New York: Henry Holt & Co., Inc., 1991.

Hauschka, Rudolf. *The Nature of Substance.* Translated from the German by Mary T. Richards and Marjorie Spock. London: Stuart & Watkins, 1966.

——. *Nutrition.* Translated from the German by Marjorie Spock and Mary T. Richards. London: Stuart & Watkins, 1967.

Heckler, Richard Strozzi. *In Search of the Warrior Spirit: Teaching Awareness Disciplines to the Green Berets.* Berkeley, California, North Atlantic Books, 1989.

Heisenberg, Werner. "The Relationship Between Biology, Physics, and Chemistry," in *Physics and Beyond.* Translated from the German by Arnold J. Pomerans. New York: Harper & Row, 1971.

Heller, Joseph, and William Henkin. *Bodywise: Introduction to Hellerwork.* Oakland, California: Wingbow Press, 1986.

Herbert, Frank. *Dune.* New York: Berkley, 1965.

——. *Whipping Star.* New York: Berkley, 1977.

Herriot, Eva M. "Ayurvedic Sense Therapy," in *Yoga Journal,* Berkeley, California, January/February 1992.

Hickey, Gerald Cannon. *Village in Vietnam.* New Haven, Connecticut: Yale University Press, 1964.

Higgins, Mary, and Chester M. Raphael, eds. *Reich Speaks of Freud.* New York: Farrar, Straus and Giroux, 1967.

Hillman, James. *The Myth of Analysis.* Evanston, Illinois: Northwestern University Press, 1972.

Hippocrates. *Medical Works.* Four Volumes. Translated by W. H. S. Jones. Cambridge, Massachusetts: Loeb Classical Library, Harvard University Press.

Hoagland, Richard C. *The Monuments of Mars: A City on the Edge of Forever.* Berkeley, California: North Atlantic Books, 1986.

Hodosi, Oskar. *Tantra Partnerschaft: Neue Dimensionen der Liebe Durch Eine Jahrtausendealte Kultur.* Munich: Mosaik Verlag, 1992.

Holbrook, Bruce. *The Stone Monkey: An Alternative Chinese-Scientific Reality.* New York: Morrow, 1981.

Hsu, Hong-Yen. *How to Heal Yourself with Chinese Herbs.* Los Angeles: Oriental Healing Arts Institute, 1980.

Inglis, Brian. *A History of Medicine.* Cleveland: World Publishing Company, 1965.

——. *The Case for Unorthodox Medicine.* New York: Putnam, 1965.

Jarrell, David G. *Reiki Plus: Professional Practitioner's Manual for Second Degree.* Celina, Tennessee: Hibernia West, 1992.

Jenness, D. "The Carrier Indians of the Bulkley River," in *Bulletin No. 133.* Washington, DC: Bureau of American Ethnology, 1943.

John, Bubba Free (Da Free John). *The Eating Gorilla Comes in Peace: The Transcendental Principle of Life Applied to Diet and the Regenerative Discipline of True Health.* Middletown, California: The Dawn Horse Press, 1979.

Johnson, Don Hanlon. *Body, Spirit and Democracy.* Berkeley, California: North Atlantic Books, 1993.

———. *The Protean Body.* New York: Harper & Row, 1977.
———. "The Way of the Flesh: A Brief History of the Somatics Movement," in *Bone, Breath, and Gesture: Practices of Embodiment.* Don Hanlon Johnson, ed. Berkeley, California: North Atlantic Books, 1995.
———, ed. *Bone, Breath, and Gesture: Practices of Embodiment.* Berkeley, California: North Atlantic Books, 1995.
Jung, Carl. *Archetypes of the Collective Unconscious.* Translated by R. F. C. Hull. Bollingen Series XX. New York: Pantheon Books, 1959.
———. *Psychological Reflections.* Jolande Jacobi, ed. New York: Harper & Row, 1953.
———. *Psychology and Alchemy.* Translated from the German by R. F. C. Hull. London: Routledge & Kegan Paul, 1953.
Kahn, Morton C. *Djuka: The Bush Negroes of Dutch Guiana.* New York: Viking Press, 1931.
Katz, R. "Education for Transcendence: Lessons from the !Kung Zhu Twasi," in *Journal of Transpersonal Psychology,* November 2, 1973.
Keleman, Stanley. *Living Your Dying.* New York: Random House, 1974.
———. "Professional Colloquium," in *Ecology and Consciousness: Traditional Wisdom on the Environment.* Richard Grossinger, ed. Berkeley, California: North Atlantic Books, 1978. Revised second edition, 1992.
Kent, James Tyler. *Lectures on Homeopathic Philosophy.* 1900. Berkeley, California: North Atlantic Books, 1979.
Kerouac, Jack. *The Dharma Bums.* New York: Viking Press, 1958.
Khan, M. Masud R., ed. *The Meaning of Illness.* London: The Hogarth Press, 1977.
Kroeber, A. L. *Ethnology of the Gros Ventre.* Anthropological Papers of the American Museum of Natural History, Vol. I, Part IV, New York, 1908.
Kushi, Michio. *The Book of Dō-In: Exercise for Physical and Spiritual Development.* Tokyo: Japan Publications, 1979.
Lade, A., and R. Svoboda. *Tao & Dharma—A Comparison of Ayurveda*

and Chinese Medicine. Unpublished manuscript at the time of publication.

Lamb, F. Bruce. *Rio Tigre and Beyond: The Amazon Jungle Medicine of Manuel Córdova-Rios.* Berkeley, California: North Atlantic Books, 1985.

Lansing, Gerrit. "Fundamentals of Indian Medical Theory," from *Notes on Structure and Sign in Ayurveda.* Unpublished manuscript, 1981.

Lawlor, Robert. *Voices of the First Day: Awakening in the Aboriginal Dreamtime.* Rochester, Vermont: Inner Traditions, 1991.

Le Guin, Ursula K. *A Wizard of Earthsea.* New York: Bantam Books, 1975.

Leigh, William S. *Bodytherapy.* Coquitlam, British Columbia: Water Margin Press, 1989.

Leri, Dennis. "Learning How to Learn," unpublished manuscript.

Lessa, William A., and Evon Z. Vogt. *Reader in Comparative Religion.* New York: Harper & Row, 1958.

Lévi-Strauss, Claude. *From Honey to Ashes.* Translated from the French by John and Doreen Weightman. New York: Harper & Row, 1973.

——. *The Raw and the Cooked.* Translated from the French by John and Doreen Weightman. New York: Harper & Row, 1969.

——. *The Savage Mind.* Chicago: University of Chicago Press, 1966.

——. "The Sorcerer and His Magic," in *Structural Anthropology.* Translated from the French by Claire Jacobson and Brooke Grundfest Schoepf. Garden City, New Jersey: Doubleday/Anchor, 1967.

——. *Totemism.* Translated from the French by Rodney Needham. Boston: Beacon Press, 1963.

Leviton, Richard. "The Healing Energies of Color," in *Yoga Journal,* Berkeley, California, January/February 1992

——. "Healing Vibrations," in *Yoga Journal,* Berkeley, California, January/February 1994.

Lewis, C. S. *The Magician's Nephew.* 1951. New York: Collier Books, 1970.

Lindner, Robert. *The Fifty-Minute Hour.* New York: Bantam Books, 1956.

Liu, Qingshan. *Qi Gong: Der chinesische Weg für ein gesundes langes Leben.* Munich: Hugendubel, 1992.

Lo, Pang Jeng, Martin Inn, Susan Foe, and Robert Amacker. *The Essence of T'ai Chi Ch'uan: The Literary Tradition.* Berkeley, California: North Atlantic Books, 1979.

Maitland, Jeffrey. *Spacious Body: Explorations in Somatic Ontology.* Berkeley, California: North Atlantic Books, 1995.

Makavejev, Dussan. *WR: Mysteries of the Organism.* New York: Avon Books, 1972.

Mann, Felix. *Acupuncture: The Ancient Chinese Art of Healing and How It Works Scientifically.* New York: Random House, 1973.

Mann, W. Edward. *Orgone, Reich and Eros: Wilhelm Reich's Theory of Life Energy.* New York: Simon & Schuster, 1973.

Mars, Louis. *The Crisis of Possession in Voodoo.* Translated from the French by Kathleen Collins. Berkeley, California: Reed, Cannon & Johnson Co., 1977.

Marshack, Alexander. *The Roots of Civilization.* New York: McGraw-Hill, 1972.

Max, Otto. Review of *Planet Medicine,* in *East West Journal,* Boston, Massachusetts, August 1981.

McKenna, Terence. *The Archaic Revival: Speculations on Psychedelic Mushrooms, the Amazon, Virtual Reality, Evolution, Shamanism, the Rebellion of the Goddess, and the End of History.* San Francisco: HarperCollins, 1993.

Meek, George W. *Healers and the Healing Process.* Wheaton, Illinois: Theosophical Publishing House, 1977.

Melchizedek, Drunvalo. "Flower of Life Workshop," Dallas, February 14–17, 1992. Video recording.

Melville, Herman. *Moby Dick; or the Whale.* 1851. Berkeley, California: University of California Press, 1979.

Middendorf, Ilse. *The Perceptible Breath: A Breathing Science.* Paderborn, Germany: Junferman-Verlag, 1990.

Milne, Hugh. *The Heart of Listening: A Visionary Approach to Cranio-*

sacral Work. Unpublished manuscript at the time of publication. Berkeley, California: North Atlantic Books, 1995.

Mitchell, Faith. *Hoodoo Medicine: Sea Island Herbal Remedies.* Berkeley, California: Reed, Cannon & Johnson, 1978.

Moore, Omar Khayyam. "Divination—A New Perspective," in *American Anthropologist,* LIX, 1957.

Moss, Thelma. "Kirlian Photograph and the Aura," interview with Roy L. Walford, in *Io* #19, *Mind Memory Psyche,* Plainfield, Vermont, 1974.

Muldoon, Sylvan, and Hereward Carrington. *The Projection of the Astral Body.* New York: Samuel Weiser, Inc., 1970.

Müller, Brigitte, and Horst Günther. *A Complete Book of Reiki Healing.* Mendocino, California: Life Rhythm, 1995.

Murdock, George Peter. "Tenino Shamanism," in *Culture and Society: Twenty-Four Essays.* George Peter Murdock, ed. Pittsburgh, Pennsylvania: University of Pittsburgh Press, 1965.

Nicoll, Maurice. *Psychological Commentaries on the Teaching of Gurdjieff & Ouspensky.* London: Robinson & Watkins, 1952.

Olschak, Blanche Christine. *Mystic Art of Ancient Tibet.* Translated by George Allen. New York: McGraw-Hill, 1973.

Olsen, Stanley J. *Mammal Remains from Archaeological Sites, Part I: Southeastern and Southwestern United States.* Cambridge, Massachusetts: The Peabody Museum, 1964.

Olson, Charles. *The Maximus Poems.* 1950. Berkeley, California: University of California Press, 1979.

——. *Muthologos,* Vol. I. Bolinas, California: Four Seasons Foundation, 1978.

Oracion, Timoteo S. "The Bais Forest Preserve Negritos: Some Notes on Their Rituals and Ceremonies," in *Studies in Philippine Anthropology.* Mario D. Zamora, ed. Quezon City, Philippines: Alemar-Phoenix, 1967.

Orr, Leonard. *Bhartriji: Immortal Yogi of 2000 Years.* Chico, California: Inspiration University, 1992.

——. *Physical Immortality: The Science of Everlasting Life.* Sierraville, California: Inspiration University, 1980.

Ouspensky, P. D. *In Search of the Miraculous: Fragments of an Unknown Teaching.* New York: Harcourt, Brace, & World, 1949.

Oyle, Irving. *The New American Medicine Show.* Santa Cruz, California: Unity Press, 1979.

Palmer, Wendy. *The Intuitive Body: Aikido as a Clairsentient Practice.* Berkeley, California: North Atlantic Books, 1994.

Paracelsus. *The Hermetic and Alchemical Writings of Paracelsus the Great.* Translated by A. E. Waite. London: James Elliott, 1894.

Perlman, David. "Controversial AIDS Theories Debated at Forum in S.F.," *San Francisco Chronicle,* June 22, 1994.

Phillips, Wendell. *Unknown Oman.* New York: David McKay Company, Inc., 1966.

Pitchford, Paul. *Healing with Whole Foods: Oriental Traditions and Modern Nutrition.* Berkeley, California: North Atlantic Books, 1993.

Poncé, Charles. *The Archetype of the Unconscious and the Transfiguration of Therapy: Reflections on Jungian Psychology.* Berkeley, California: North Atlantic Books, 1990.

The Private Life of Chairman Mao: The Memories of Mao's Personal Physician, Dr. Li Zhisui. Translated by Tai Hung-chao. New York: Random House, 1994.

Ptashek, Alan. "The Moving Body: An Integrated Movement Course," in *Contact Quarterly,* Northampton, Massachusetts, Winter 1992.

Pujols, Lee, and Gary Richman. *Miracles & Other Realities.* San Francisco: Omega Press, 1990.

Quindlen, Anna. "Gulf War's Killing Legacy," *San Francisco Chronicle,* October 10, 1994.

Radcliffe-Brown, A. R. *The Andaman Islanders.* Glencoe, Illinois: Free Press, 1948.

Rappaport, Roy A. "Sanctity and Adaptation," in *Io #7, Oecology Issue,* 1970; reprinted in *Ecology and Consciousness: Traditional Wisdom on the Environment.* Richard Grossinger, ed. Berkeley, California: North

Atlantic Books, 1978. Revised second edition, 1992.

Rasmussen, Knud. *Intellectual Culture of the Iglulik Eskimos: Report of the Fifth Thule Expedition to Arctic North America.* Copenhagen, Denmark: Gyldendalske Boghandel, Nordisk Forlag, 1929.

Rechung, Ven. Rinpoche Jampal Kunzang. *Tibetan Medicine.* Berkeley, California: University of California Press, 1973.

Reese, Mark. "Moshe Feldenkrais' Verbal Approach to Somatic Education: Parallels to Milton Erickson's Use of Language," in *Somatics,* Novato, California, Autumn/Winter 1985–86.

Regardie, Israel. *The Eye in the Triangle.* Llewellyn Publications, St. Paul, Minnesota, 1970.

Reich, Peter. *A Book of Dreams.* New York: Harper & Row, 1973.

Reich, Wilhelm. *Character Analysis.* Third Edition. Translated from the German by Vincent R. Carfagno. New York: Farrar, Straus and Giroux, 1972.

——. *Cosmic Superimposition.* Translated from the German by Therese Pol. New York: Farrar, Straus and Giroux, 1973.

——. *The Emotional Plague of Mankind: Volume 1, The Murder of Christ.* Rangeley, Maine: Orgone Institute Press, 1953.

——. *Ether, God & Devil—Cosmic Superimposition.* Translated from the German by Therese Pol. New York: Farrar, Straus and Giroux, 1973.

——. *The Function of the Orgasm.* Translated from the German by Vincent R. Carfagno. New York: Farrar, Straus and Giroux, 1973.

Reichard, Gladys A. *Navaho Religion.* New York, Bollingen Foundation, Pantheon Books, 1950.

Reif, A. Veronica "Eurhythmy and Curative Eurhythmy," essay accompanying lecture at the Berkeley Anthroposophical Society, 1978.

Ros, Frank. *The Lost Secrets of Ayurvedic Acupuncture: An Ayurvedic Guide to Acupuncture.* Twin Lakes, Wisconsin: Lotus Press, 1994.

Roberts, Jane. *The Seth Material.* Englewood Cliffs, New Jersey: Prentice-Hall, 1970.

Rolf, Ida. *Ida Rolf Talks About Rolfing and Physical Reality.* New York: Harper & Row, 1978.

——. *Rolfing: The Integration of Human Structures.* New York: Harper & Row, 1977.

Rose, Jeanne. *The Aromatherapy Book: Applications & Inhalations.* Berkeley, California: North Atlantic Books, 1992.

Rubenfeld, Ilana. "Alexander: The Use of the Self," in *Wholistic Dimensions in Healing: A Resource Guide.* Leslie J. Kaslof, ed. New York: Doubleday & Company, Inc., 1978.

Rush, Benjamin. *Medical Inquiries and Observations.* Philadelphia: Pritchard and Hall, 1789.

Rutkow, Ira M. *Surgery: An Illustrated History.* St. Louis: Mosby-Year Book, 1993.

Sahlins, Marshall. *Stone Age Economics.* Chicago: Aldine-Atherton, 1972.

Sannella, Lee. *Kundalini—Psychosis or Transcendence?* San Francisco: Dakin, 1976.

Schaffer, Carolyn. "An Interview with Emilie Conrad-Da'oud," in *Yoga Journal,* Berkeley, California, No. 77, November/December 1987.

Schiotz, Eiler H., and James Cyriax. *Manipulation Past and Present.* London: William Heinemann Medical Books, Ltd., 1975.

Schreiber, Jon. *Touching the Mountain: The Self-Breema Handbook—Ancient Exercises for the Modern World.* Oakland, California: California Health Publications, 1989.

Schultz, Barbara L. "New Age Shiatsu," in *The Holistic Health Handbook.* Bauman, et al., eds. Berkeley, California: And/Or Press, 1978.

Schwartz, Jesse. "Some Experiments with Seed Sprouts and Energetic Fields," in *Living Tree Journal,* Bolinas, California, 1986.

——. "Science vs. Scientism," in *Brain Mind,* Vol. 18, No. 5.

Segal, Mia. Interview in *Somatics,* Novato, California, Autumn/Winter 1985–86.

"Sex Between Therapist and Patient," transcript of the June 21, 1976, meeting of the American Psychiatric Association, in *Psychiatry,* Vol. 5, No. 12.

Sharaf, Myron. *Fury on Earth: A Biography of Wilhelm Reich.* New York: St. Martin's Press, 1983.

Shklovskii, I. S., and Carl Sagan. *Intelligent Life in the Universe.* Translated from the Russian by Paula Fern. New York: Delta Books, 1967.

Siegel, Bernie. "Letter to the Editor," in *Common Boundary,* Bethesda, Maryland, September-October, 1994.

Sieh, Ron. *T'ai Chi Ch'uan: The Internal Tradition.* Berkeley, California: North Atlantic Books, 1993.

Smith, Harvey H. *Area Handbook for Iran.* Washington, DC: United States Government Printing Office, Foreign Area Studies, American University, 1971.

Sogyal Rinpoche. *The Tibetan Book of Living and Dying.* San Francisco: HarperSanFrancisco, 1992.

Speck, Frank G. *A Study of the Delaware Indian Big House Ceremony,* Vol. II. Harrisburg, Pennsylvania: Publications of the Pennsylvania Historical Commission, 1931.

Spencer, Dorothy M. *Disease, Religion and Society in the Fiji Islands.* New York: Augustin, 1941.

Stewart, Daniel Blair. *Akhunaton: The Extraterrestrial King.* Berkeley, California: Frog, Ltd., 1995.

Still, A. T. *Osteopathy: Research & Practice.* 1910. Seattle, Washington: Eastland Press, 1992.

Stone, Randolph. *Polarity Therapy,* Vol. I. Sebastopol, California: CRCS Publications, 1986.

——. *Polarity Therapy,* Vol. II. Sebastopol, California: CRCS Publications, 1987.

Suzuki, Shunryu. *Zen Mind, Beginner's Mind.* New York: Weatherhill, 1970.

Swadesh, Morris. "Diffusional Cumulation and Archaic Residue as Historical Explanations," in *Language in Culture & Society: A Reader in Linguistics and Anthropology.* Dell Hymes, ed. New York: Harper & Row, 1964.

Swanton, John R. *Religious Beliefs and Medical Practices of the Creek Indians,* 42nd Annual Report to the Bureau of American Ethnology, 1924-25. Washington, DC: Smithsonian Institution, 1928.

Tait, David. "Konkomba Sorcery," in *Magic, Witchcraft, and Curing.* John Middleton, ed. New York: The Natural History Press, 1967.

Tantaquidgeon, Gladys. *Folk Medicine of the Delaware and Related Algonkian Indians.* Harrisburg, Pennsylvania: Pennsylvania Historical and Museum Commission, 1972.

Teilhard de Chardin, Pierre. *The Phenomenon of Man.* Translated from the French by Bernard Wall. New York: Harper & Row, 1959.

Temple, Robert K. G. *The Sirius Mystery.* New York: St. Martin's Press, 1976.

Tenen, Stan. *Hebrew—First Hand.* San Anselmo, California: Meru Foundation, 1994.

——. *The Matrix of Meaning for Sacred Alphabets.* San Anselmo, California: Meru Foundation, 1991. Video recording.

Thakkur, Chandrashekhar G. *Ayurveda: The Indian Art & Science of Medicine.* New York: ASI Publishers, Inc., 1974.

Thera, Nyanaponika. *The Heart of Buddhist Meditation.* New York: Samuel Weiser, Inc., 1969.

Tierra, Michael. *The Way of Herbs.* New York: Simon & Schuster, 1994.

Tomlinson, Cybèle. "Breema Bodywork," in *Yoga Journal,* Berkeley, California, November/December 1994.

Tompkins, Peter, and Christopher Bird. *The Secret Life of Plants.* New York: Harper & Row, 1973.

Trungpa, Chögyam. *Cutting Through Spiritual Materialism.* Berkeley, California: Shambhala Publications, 1973.

Turner, Victor W. *Lunda Medicine and the Treatment of Disease.* Occasional Papers of the Rhodes-Livingstone Museum, No. 15. Northern Rhodesia, Zambia: Livingstone, 1964.

Tyler, M. L. *Homeopathic Drug Pictures.* Holsworthy, Devon, England: Health Science Press, 1942.

Upledger, John E. *CranioSacral Therapy II: Beyond the Dura.* Seattle, Washington: Eastland Press, 1987.

——. *SomatoEmotional Release and Beyond.* Palm Beach Gardens, Florida: UI Publishing, 1990.

Upledger, John E., and Jon D. Vredevoogd. *CranioSacral Therapy.* Seattle, Washington: Eastland Press, 1983.

Urquhart, David. *Manual of the Turkish Bath.* Sir John Fife, M.D., ed. London: Churchill, 1865.

Vallee, Jacques. *Forbidden Science.* Berkeley, California: North Atlantic Books, 1992.

Van Helmont, Jan Baptista. *Oriatrike, or Physick Refined.* London, 1662.

Vithoulkas, George. *The Science of Homeopathy: A Modern Textbook,* Vol. I. Athens, Greece: A.S.O.H.M., 1978.

Vlamis, Gregory. "Interview with Pierre Pannetier," in *Well-Being Magazine,* No. 28, 1978.

Waite, A. E. *See* Paracelsus, above.

Watson, James. *The Double Helix.* New York: Atheneum, 1968.

Westlake, Aubrey T. *The Pattern of Health.* Berkeley, California: Shambhala Publications, 1973.

Wheelwright, Philip, ed. *The Presocratics.* Indianapolis, Indiana: Odyssey Press, 1966.

Whicher, Olive. *Projective Geometry: Creative Polarities in Space and Time.* London: Rudolph Steiner Press, 1971.

Whitehead, Alfred North. *Process and Reality.* Toronto: Macmillan, 1929.

Whiting, Alfred F. *Ethnobotany of the Hopi.* Northern Arizona Society of Science and Art, Bulletin 15. Flagstaff, Arizona: Museum of Northern Arizona, 1939.

Whitmont, Edward. *The Alchemy of Healing: Psyche and Soma.* Berkeley, California: North Atlantic Books, 1993.

——. *Psyche and Substance: Essays on Homeopathy in the Light of Jungian Psychology.* Berkeley, California: North Atlantic Books, 1979.

Wildschut, William. *Crow Indian Medicine Bundles.* John C. Ewers, ed. New York: Museum of the American Indian, Heye Foundation, 1975.

Williams, William Carlos. *Pictures from Brueghel and Other Poems.* New York: New Directions, 1962.

Wilson, Robert Anton. *Cosmic Trigger.* Berkeley, California: And/Or Press, 1977.

Wisdom, Charles. *The Chorti Indians of Guatemala.* Chicago: University of Chicago Press, 1940.

Wyman, Leland C. *Beautyway: A Navaho Ceremonial.* Recorded and translated by Father Berard Haile. New York: Bollingen Foundation, Pantheon Books, 1957.

Wyvell, Lois. "Orgone and You," in *Living Tree Journal,* Bolinas, California, 1986.

Yates, Frances. *Giordano Bruno and the Hermetic Tradition.* Chicago: University of Chicago Press, 1964.

——. *The Rosicrucian Enlightenment.* London: Routledge & Kegan Paul, 1972.

The Yellow Emperor's Classic of Internal Medicine (Huang Ti Nei Ching Su Wên). Translated from the Chinese by Ilza Veith. Berkeley, California: University of California Press, 1966.

Yoe, Shway. *The Burman.* London: Macmillan, 1910.

Yogananda, Paramahansa. *Autobiography of a Yogi.* Los Angeles: Self-Realization Fellowship, 1946.

INDEX

This is a cumulative index for *Planet Medicine: Origins* and *Planet Medicine: Modalities* or Volume 1 and Volume 2, respectively. Accordingly, the page references for each volume are identified as follows: Vol. 1 *(Origins)* page references are listed first in each entry, with a 1 preceding that list. Page references for Vol. 2 *(Modalities)* are listed second in each entry, with a 2 preceding that list. Where both Vol. 1 and Vol. 2 references appear, the lists are separated by a semicolon (;). For example:

planet medicine
  changes necessary for, 1.527–30; 2.8–10, 11, 450–53

entry Vol. 1 *(Origins)* Vol. 2 *(Modalities)*

Page references in **bold** refer to illustrations or photographs. The term *passim* refers to a discontinuous discussion of a topic over several pages. The terms *above* and *below* refer to subentries within the main category. The letter "n" attached to a page reference refers to a note on that page.